The Columbia Guide to
Hiroshima and the Bomb

COLUMBIA GUIDES TO AMERICAN HISTORY AND CULTURES

The Columbia Guide to
Hiroshima and the Bomb

Michael Kort

COLUMBIA UNIVERSITY PRESS

NEW YORK

Columbia University Press

Publishers Since 1893

New York   Chichester, West Sussex

Copyright © 2007 Columbia University Press

All rights reserved

Library of Congress Cataloging-in-Publication Data

Kort, Michael, 1944–

The Columbia guide to Hiroshima and the bomb / Michael Kort.

p. cm. — (Columbia guides to American history and cultures)

Includes bibliographical references and index.

ISBN 13: 978-0-231-13016-5 (alk. paper)

ISBN 10: 0-231-13016-3 (alk. paper)

1. Hiroshima-shi (Japan)—History—Bombardment, 1945. 2. Hiroshima-shi
(Japan)—History—Bombardment, 1945—Sources. 3. Atomic bomb—United
States—History—20th century. 4. Atomic bomb—United States—History—20th
century—Sources. 5. Atomic bomb—Japan—History—20th century. 6. Atomic
bomb—Japan—History—20th century—Sources. 8. Title. II. Series.

D767.25.H6K68 2007

940.54′2521954—dc22

2006029177

∞

Columbia University Press gratefully acknowledges permission to reprint from the following:

Robert J. C. Butow, *Japan's Decision to Surrender* (Stanford University Press, 1954), Emperor Hirohito's
Surrender Decision, August 10, 1945, pages 175–6; Emperor Hirohito's Statement to the Imperial Conference, August 14, 1945, pages 207–8.

Excerpts from "To Die as a Samurai: 1 June–15 August 1945" from *Fading Victory: The Diary of Admiral
Matome Ugaki, 1941–1945*, translated by Masataka Chihaya, edited by Donald M. Goldstein and
Katherine V. Dillon. © 1991. Reprinted by permission of the University of Pittsburgh Press.

Emperor Hirohito's Soliloquy, 1946. Reprinted with permission of The Free Press, a division of Simon &
Schuster Adult Publishing Group, from *The Age of Hirohito: In Search of Modern Japan* by Daikichi
Irokawa, pp. 31–33. Translated by Mikiso Hane and John L. Urda. English translation: copyright ©
1995 by The Free Press. Copyright © 1995 by Daikichi Irokawa.

The Konoye Memorial, 14 February 1945. from John Dower, *Empire and Aftermath: Yoshida Shigeru and
the Japanese Experience, 1875–1954*. Cambridge, MA: Council on East Asian Studies, Harvard University Press, 1977, 260–264. Courtesy of Harvard University Press.

Henry L. Stimson Diaries: entries from May 15, May 31, June 6, June 19, June 26–30, July 2, July 3, July 19,
August 9, August 10 (all from 1945). Courtesy of Yale University Library.

Henry L. Stimson Papers:

Memorandum of talk with the President, June 6, 1945

Notes for the Diary, July 22, 1945

Memorandum for the President, 11 September 1945

Henry Lewis Stimson Papers. Manuscripts and Archives. Courtesy of Yale University Library.

For

Eleza and Tamara,

my wonderful and adorable daughters,

whose grandpa Jack fought in Europe

but did not have to invade Japan

CONTENTS

Acknowledgments ix

Introduction xiii

PART I

Historical Narrative 1

1. The Debate Over Hiroshima 3

2. Building the Atomic Bomb 14

3. The Pacific War 28

4. The Decision to Drop the Bomb 46

5. The Japanese Government, Ketsu-Go, and Potsdam 58

6. Hiroshima, Nagasaki, and Japan's Surrender 67

7. Hiroshima and American Power 75

PART II

Key Questions and Interpretations 79

PART III

Resources   117

Chronology   119

Glossary of Military Terms and Abbreviations   127

Glossary of Names   131

Selected Bibliography   135

Archival Collections   135
Government Publications   135
Microfilm Document Collections   136
Published Document Collections   136
Interviews and Personal Communications   137
Books, Articles, and Transcripts   137
Web Sites   145

PART IV

Documents   147

Guide to the Documents   149

A. American Civilian Documents   171
B. American Military Documents   240
C. MAGIC Diplomatic Summaries   277
D. Japanese Government Documents,
Military Documents, and Diary Entries   291
E. Japanese Surrender Documents   323
F. United States Strategic Bombing Survey:
Summary Report and Interrogations of Japanese Officials   337
G. Statements of Japanese Officials on World War II,
Military Intelligence Section, Historical Division, U.S. Army   369

Notes   395

Index   421

ACKNOWLEDGMENTS

I am indebted to several distinguished scholars and experts on the subject of the bombing of Hiroshima for their help in completing this book, but most of all to Richard B. Frank, who generously shared with me translations of more than a dozen important Japanese documents he had commissioned for his own work, provided an extraordinarily comprehensive and helpful critique of my manuscript, and responded with extremely detailed and insightful answers to queries on a variety of subjects; and to Dennis Giangreco, who provided constant encouragement, immediate assistance in locating a variety of resources and documents, and invaluable expertise and insight in his detailed critique of the manuscript. Robert P. Newman and Sadao Asada also read the entire manuscript and provided valuable suggestions that significantly improved it. Robert James Maddox, Robert H. Ferrell, and Larry Bland likewise kindly shared their vast expertise with me at various points during my work on this book.

In the course of gathering documents, I received vital assistance from archivists Larry McDonald and Will Mahoney at the National Archives; their help turned a relatively short visit to that daunting facility into a remarkably fruitful one. The staff of Boston University's Mugar Memorial Library was enormously patient and efficient in helping me track down documents and other resources, especially the interlibrary loan specialists, who refused to accept defeat when a particular item proved to be difficult to find. I also am grateful for the help I received from librarians during visits to the Boston Public Library and Harvard University's Lamont Library. Archivists and librarians at the Harry S. Truman Library, the George C. Marshall Historical Foundation, the Naval Historical Center, the General Douglas MacArthur Foundation, the U.S. Army Military Historical Institute, the U.S. Army Combined Arms Research Library, and the Wisconsin Historical Society all responded kindly and quickly to e-mail requests to track down and duplicate important documents, thereby saving me the considerable time and expense that would have been involved had it been necessary to visit those repositories personally.

At Columbia University Press, I was fortunate to work with two excellent editors. James Warren, an endless source of wonderful book ideas with whom I had worked on two previous volumes, including one for Columbia, conceived the idea of this project and encouraged me to undertake it. When circumstances directed his attention elsewhere, Anne Routon inherited this project, as it were, in midstream, with its author feeling a bit at sea; she immediately and reassuringly took the helm, treated the project as if she had been on board and invested in it from the start, and skillfully guided it around and past the many shoals and hazards that lie between completion of a manuscript and its publication. For the second time in as many books with Columbia, Gregory McNamee was a superb copyeditor and source of many valuable suggestions that improved the manuscript. Ronald Harris, Assistant Managing Editor at Columbia, ably and with extraordinary care oversaw the editing and proofreading of this book.

I consulted with Robert Wexelblatt and William Tilchin, my colleagues at Boston University's College of General Studies, on almost every aspect of this project, and their patience, good humor, and sage advice were crucial in helping me overcome numerous obstacles. I also benefited from discussing some of my ideas with colleagues at Boston University's International History Institute and, in June 2003, with specialists in American history from several countries at the annual Colloque International sponsored by the Observatoire de la Politique Etrangère Américaine (OPEA) at the Sorbonne Nouvelle in Paris.

My thanks to Boston University for providing me with a sabbatical leave during the spring 2003 semester to work full-time on this project, and to Jay Corrin, my departmental chairman, and Linda Wells, Dean of the College of General Studies, for their help whenever I needed funding for travel or reproducing materials. Barbara Storella, our departmental secretary, graciously volunteered to retype a large number of photocopied documents that quite literally were almost impossible to read, while continuously radiating a wealth of good sense and good cheer.

Special thanks to Roy L. Chvat, my brother-in-law, for vigorously debating various aspects of the events of August 1945 with me over many months from half a world away. We often disagreed, but our spirited email discussions helped me clarify many of the issues of contention and disagreements among historians I present to the readers of this book.

Finally, my profoundest gratitude, as with all my books and in everything I do, is to my daughters, Eleza and Tamara, and my wife, Carol, for their unconditional love and support and for making sure I did not allow this project or anything else to obscure what really matters in life.

INTRODUCTION

The purpose of this new contribution to the Columbia Guides to American History and Cultures series is to make available to a wide audience the primary source materials necessary for making a reasoned judgment about the American decision to use nuclear weapons against Japan during World War II. The use of the atomic bombs against the Japanese cities of Hiroshima and Nagasaki in August 1945 is arguably the most controversial single act in the history of American warfare. Each bomb destroyed an entire city and killed tens of thousands of people in an instant, something that was shocking and terrifying even against the horrific, genocidal background of World War II. Hiroshima and Nagasaki marked the use of weapons whose destructive power quite literally was a quantum jump beyond anything that had existed before in human history, weapons that for the first time had the potential to destroy all civilized life. In the decades that followed, those weapons became hundreds of times more powerful, and the capability of producing them did not remain an American monopoly: the Soviet Union became a nuclear power in 1949, and within fifteen years Great Britain, France, and the People's Republic of China joined the nuclear club. After the Soviet Union successfully tested its first atomic bomb, the ensuing Cold War arms race between Washington and Moscow resulted in the manufacture of thousands of nuclear weapons, leaving the world's two superpowers and, indeed, the rest of the world, under an atomic Sword of Damocles. The destruction of

Hiroshima and Nagasaki may have been the last military actions of World War II, but weapons used to destroy those cities made their fates an integral part of the postwar world as well.

It is important to note that in 1945 the war-weary American people and the citizens of other Allied countries overwhelmingly supported the decision to attack Hiroshima and Nagasaki with atomic bombs. To them, ending World War II as quickly as possible was an objective sufficiently urgent to justify the use of almost any weapon. Nonetheless, America's use of the atomic bomb inevitably became a source of controversy. One reason some people dissented from the prevailing consensus was the terrifying nature of those weapons. The dreadful mushroom cloud over Hiroshima had barely dissipated, and the bomb that would destroy Nagasaki had not yet been dropped, before the warning was heard that America's use of an atomic bomb against Japan had opened the door to a future nuclear war that could destroy civilization. Other early critiques, likewise voiced before the war itself was over, were based solely on principle, mainly religious and pacifist moral precepts. In addition, it was not long before some observers began arguing that, from a strictly practical military point of view, by the summer of 1945 Japan was on the verge of surrender and the atomic bombs had not been necessary to end the war. The atomic attacks of August 1945 also were profoundly troubling in certain circles because it was not one of the totalitarian or dictatorial regimes involved in World War II that had used them—the reason for that being that they did not have them to use—but the world's leading democracy, the United States of America, a country whose own citizens often argued that its conduct should be judged according to a higher standard than that used for other nations.

The use of atomic weapons therefore almost immediately put the men who took that step and the country they led into the dock of the court of history. At issue were two broad and multifaceted sets of questions. First, were atomic bombs necessary—or, alternatively, did American leaders at the time believe they were necessary—to end the Pacific War at a cost in lives, within a time frame, and on terms acceptable to the United States and its allies? Second, were American motives for using these weapons limited to forcing a Japanese surrender on terms consistent with fundamental Allied war aims, which included occupying Japan for the purpose of demilitarizing and democratizing Japanese society, or did they extend in part or even primarily to postwar concerns, in particular to the emerging international rivalry between the United States and the Soviet Union? The debate that emerged from these questions in effect turned into an informal but long and hotly contested trial, with testimony from several generations of prosecutors and defenders, that has yet to end. Over time, as American foreign policy as a whole became a matter of increasing public controversy, the forum within which the Hiroshima debate was conducted expanded from a coterie of specialists whose primary interest was history to a large circle of ordinary citizens who took time out from other pressing concerns to inform themselves about and comment on an issue that took on new life even as the events in question became part of an increasingly distant past.

This book is both an overview of the Hiroshima testimony and a repository of some of the key evidence upon which it is based. It is divided into four parts. Part one, a seven-chapter narrative overview, provides background information vital to understanding the conditions in which President Harry Truman and his advisors made their decision. The first chapter is an introduction to the debate over Hiroshima as it has evolved since the 1940s, including the controversy over the Smithsonian Institution's ill-fated proposal to mark the fiftieth anniversary of the bombing in 1995. The second chapter surveys the events surrounding the decision to build the atomic bomb and how, once a full-scale commitment was made, that remarkable effort was successfully completed in the incredibly short period of less than three years. This chapter also provides a historical perspective regarding the atomic bomb that includes the menace Nazi Germany posed to the civilized world, which is the reason the United States developed and built the bomb in the first place, and World War II as a whole. That struggle, long before Hiroshima and Nagasaki, became a total war on a scale and to a degree never seen before, in which technological advances repeatedly were employed as weapons of war as soon as they became available. In that regard, it is worth pointing out that there was nothing unusual about the speed with which the atomic bomb was rushed into combat. It is also important to keep in mind that the atomic bomb represented a revolutionary new technology and that when it was first used as a weapon of war, the full impact of its destructive power, especially the extent to which radiation would kill long after the explosion, was not fully understood. The third chapter is an overview of the Pacific War. Simply stated, the readiness of American leaders to resort to atomic weapons in August 1945 can only be understood in terms of what this country experienced in four years of bitter fighting during which Japanese soldiers consistently fought to the last man rather than surrender, taking tens of thousands of American soldiers with them to their graves. That requires, at a minimum, revisiting certain key land, air, and sea battlefields in the Pacific from Midway Island northwest of Hawaii to Guadalcanal east of Australia and to Okinawa at the doorstep of Japan. The fourth chapter covers American decision making in the spring and summer of 1945, the fifth Japanese decision making during the same time frame, and the sixth the bombing of Hiroshima and Nagasaki and the subsequent sequence of events that culminated in Japan's surrender. The final chapter places the debates over Hiroshima within the context of the discussion surrounding American foreign policy during the Cold War and the post–Cold War era.

The second part of the book, "Key Questions and Interpretations," surveys ten issues that essentially are subsidiary debates of the overall discussion of

Hiroshima. It refers readers both to documents that have been collected in this volume and to relevant scholarly books and articles.

Following a section of reference materials—a chronology, a glossary of military terms and abbreviations, a glossary of names, and an extensive bibliography—the fourth and largest part of this book consists of the documents themselves. These are introduced by a guide and organized into seven categories: American Civilian; American Military; Magic Diplomatic Summaries; Japanese Government Documents, Military Documents, and Diary Entries; Japanese Surrender Documents; the United States Strategic Bombing Survey Summary Report and Interrogations of Japanese Officials; and Statements of Japanese Officials on World War II compiled by the Military Intelligence Section of the United States Army.

PART I

Historical Narrative

CHAPTER 1

The Debate Over Hiroshima

At 8:15 in the morning on August 6, 1945, a specially modified American B-29, *Enola Gay*, flying at 31,600 feet, dropped an atomic bomb on Hiroshima, Japan. The weapon, nicknamed Little Boy, the product of cutting-edge nuclear physics and an enormously expensive top-secret government project, was an incredibly complex 8,900-pound device fueled by the fission of Uranium 235. It had been finished only weeks before after three years of intensive scientific research and development conducted at breakneck speed. Hiroshima was Japan's seventh-largest city, an important military center, and a major port on Honshu, the largest of Japan's four main home islands. The massive bomb fell for forty-three seconds before detonating 1,870 feet above a hospital near the center of the city, only 550 feet from the bridge that was *Enola Gay*'s actual aiming point. It was the most cataclysmic event in the long and horrific history of human warfare. Little Boy exploded with the power of 12,500 tons of TNT, a colossal force that at the time would have required about 1,500 B-29s carrying conventional bombs to deliver. There was a blinding light, immediately followed by strong shock waves that shook the plane violently and drove it upward as pilot Col. Paul Tibbets, his shuddering, groaning aircraft less than twelve miles from the epicenter of the blast, urgently executed a sharp 150-degree right turn to get as far away from the awesome destructive power of his high-tech cargo as possible.

Below was a scene from hell. The temperature at the burst point instantaneously reached several million degrees. Then a fireball formed with a surface temperature hotter than the surface of the sun. Searing heat rays and radiation shot out in all directions, followed by devastating shock waves. Within ten seconds the fireball was gone, but smoking, flaming black clouds, which *Enola Gay*'s navigator compared to a pot of boiling black oil, completely hid the city as they coalesced into a monstrous mushroom that billowed upward toward the stratosphere. After a moment of stunned silence, everyone on *Enola Gay* began talking at once. Co-pilot Robert Lewis was pounding Tibbets's shoulder and shouting, "Look at that! Look at that! Look at that!" Tibbets announced to his crew, "Fellows, you have just dropped the first atomic bomb in history," and shortly thereafter ordnance expert Captain William S. Parsons, the man who had armed the bomb en route to Hiroshima, sent a message back to *Enola Gay*'s base, more than a thousand miles away on a Pacific island called Tinian, that the mission had "succeeded in all respects." It had, but the "huge cloud" Parsons saw blanketing Hiroshima in some ways has not dissipated to this day. As a somber Lewis wrote in his log of the mission, "My God, what have we done?"[1]

In an instant, Little Boy had destroyed an entire city. Five square miles were completely leveled. About 70,000 of Hiroshima's 76,000 buildings were totally destroyed or damaged. We will never know how many people died from the bombing, in part because the exact population of Hiroshima, swelled by an influx of soldiers, wartime workers, and their dependents and then reduced by the evacuation of thousands of people during 1945, is not known, and in part because the bomb itself obliterated so much. A reasonable guess is that 350,000 people were in Hiroshima on August 6, 1945, that almost 80,000 died that day, and that the death toll from burns and radiation reached 140,000 by the end of the year, including thousands of Korean forced laborers brought there by Japanese authorities.[2]

Three days later, at 11:00 in the morning of August 9, another B-29, *Bock's Car*, hampered by cloud cover that limited visibility and dangerously low on fuel, dropped a second nuclear bomb on Japan, this one on Nagasaki, an important manufacturing city and major port on Kyushu, Japan's southernmost home island. The Nagasaki bomb, nicknamed Fat Man and about two thousand pounds heavier than Little Boy, was a plutonium-fueled device even more complex than its uranium cousin. It exploded 1,650 feet above the city with the force of 22,000 tons of TNT. Although it was released about a mile from the target and its blast was partially contained by nearby ridges that protected the city, Fat Man destroyed 40 percent of Nagasaki and killed more than 25,000 people on August 9, with at least 20,000 more dying from its effects by the end of the year.[3]

The next day, a stunned and bewildered Japanese government offered to surrender unconditionally, provided only that the Allies imposed no condition "which prejudices the prerogatives of His Majesty as a Sovereign Ruler"[4] (see Document E2), a qualification whose ambiguity and potential to permit the continuation of the current Japanese political regime threatened to derail an agreement. After several tense days of back-and-forth messages, punctuated by large-scale American conventional bombing raids on August 10 and 14, Japan officially announced its surrender on August 14. The formal ceremony took place on the battleship *Missouri* in Tokyo Bay on September 2, 1945.

A day after the bombing of Hiroshima, Hansen Baldwin, the country's leading commentator on military affairs among American journalists, wrote in the *New York Times*, "Yesterday we clinched the Pacific, but we sowed the whirlwind." In Baldwin's mind, that whirlwind consisted of "seeds of hate" that some day might provoke a catastrophic nuclear war, after which "we shall become—beneath the bombs and rockets—a world of troglodytes."[5] However, a second, albeit merely verbal whirlwind was sown on August 6, 1945: the debate over whether the United States was justified in using nuclear weapons to end the Pacific War with Japan. Most Americans strongly supported President Harry S Truman's decision to use atomic weapons against Japan. However, the first critics quickly made their voices heard, often but not exclusively arguing on the basis of pacifist or religious principles[6] (see Document A56). In 1946, the first relatively lengthy analysis of the issue appeared that went beyond moral editorializing, accusing the United States of wrongly and without sufficient military justification resorting to atomic warfare against Japan. Countercritics who argued the opposite responded, the first comprehensive defense of the president coming in early 1947. The debate continued at a relatively low level into the 1950s but gathered strength in the mid-1960s and 1970s against the background of the divisive Vietnam War. But the whirlwind its heated words generated blew powerfully enough only to overturn support for Truman's decision in some parts of a relatively limited though hardly unimportant sector of American life: the cloistered world of academia. In effect, although the debate over Hiroshima grew considerably in intensity, it remained largely confined to the ivory towers and ivied walls of academia and therefore was something of a tempest in a teapot.

That changed decisively in the early 1990s, by which time public opinion as a whole had shifted. That shift had less to do with what academics were saying than with broader changes in American society. By the early 1990s, the genuinely heroic memories of World War II were far less vivid. In their place, at least for the postwar generations, were lingering Cold War fears of nuclear annihilation and a legacy of mistrust of the government dating from the domestic turmoil that accompanied the unsuccessful Vietnam War. The public was increasingly skeptical of government claims, past as well as present. One result was that whereas in August 1945 about 85 percent of Americans had supported the atomic bombings, with only 4.5 percent opposed, by the 1990s one poll showed only 55 percent support for the bombings and 39 percent opposed.[7]

THE SMITHSONIAN INSTITUTION
AND THE *ENOLA GAY*

As the half-century anniversaries of the most dramatic final events of World War II approached—from D-Day in Europe to the atomic attack on Hiroshima in Asia to the respective surrenders of Germany and Japan—the debate over the American use of nuclear weapons against Japan burst the bounds of academia and became a regular feature of the mass media, generating a nationwide blizzard of articles, op-ed pieces, and letters to the editor. The immediate cause of the furor was a highly publicized proposed exhibit by the Smithsonian Institution's National Air and Space Museum (NASM) in Washington, D.C. The exhibit would include *Enola Gay's* forward fuselage (there was not enough room for the huge fully assembled plane), artifacts related to the plane and the crew that had flown the Hiroshima mission, and a "final major section" that would "treat the bombing of Hiroshima and Nagasaki themselves and the ensuing surrender of Japan."[8] This last part of the proposed exhibit, where NASM plunged into the debate over the justification of the bombings, caused a storm of controversy. The *New York Times, Los Angeles Times,* and *Washington Post* carried letters debating the tone and contents of the exhibit; so did, among others, the *Arizona Republic, Atlanta Journal and Constitution, Rocky Mountain News, Phoenix Gazette, St. Petersburg Times, Pittsburgh Post-Gazette, Orlando Sentinel, Sacramento Bee,* and *Baltimore Sun.*[9]

The NASM exhibit was so controversial because its message was widely viewed as presenting both the decision to use atomic weapons against Japan and the consequences of their use in an unfair and therefore unfavorable light. In September 1994, the U.S. Senate unanimously adopted a resolution critical of the exhibit. Supporters of the exhibit—there were prominent academic scholars on both sides of the debate—viewed the criticism as politically motivated censorship of serious, albeit uncomfortable, historical inquiry.[10] Still, as historian Robert P. Newman's meticulous tracing of the paper trail demonstrates, the script drew most heavily on scholarship that was critical of the bombing of Hiroshima and Nagasaki. Experts on the Pacific War, the functioning of the Japanese government during the last months of the war, the Truman administration, and other key subjects whose scholarship did not support a critical view of the bombings were not consulted, notwithstanding their outstanding credentials. To many people excluded from the process, the script was guilty of misrepresenting the circumstances that led to the use of the atomic bomb. Furthermore, it emphasized Japanese suffering to the point where a visitor would have left the exhibit believing Japan was more a victim than an aggressor that had caused enormous suffering across East Asia during the war. There also were complaints that the script wrongly implied that the atomic attacks on Japan had caused the postwar nuclear arms race, thereby also implying that the United States was to blame for that most dangerous development.[11]

The NASM curators and their allies in the academic community who vigorously defended the planned exhibit as historically accurate—its script went through five different versions during 1994—could never quite overcome the damage caused by several controversial parts of the first script, two of which attracted particular ire from critics. The first was a statement slated for the introductory section ("Unit 1") of the exhibit regarding the fundamental nature of the war. According to the script, "For most Americans, this war was fundamentally different than the one waged against Germany and Italy—it was a war of vengeance. For most Japanese, it was a war to defend their unique culture against Western imperialism."[12] The second lightning rod for critics was "Unit 4," which a NASM planning document noted was to be the "emotional center" of the exhibit. In that part of the exhibit, said the planning document, "Photos of victims, enlarged to life-size, stare out at the visitor."[13] The problem with the NASM approach, critics responded, was not so much that the exhibit showed the horrific results of the bombings; that was to be expected. Rather, what was seriously wrong was that the exhibit as a whole emphasized Japanese suffering at the expense of the vital context: the brutality and destruction of Japan's war of aggression in East Asia. According to an analysis by the Air Force Association (AFA), a group that vigorously supported the use of the atomic bomb to end the war, this bias could be seen in the exhibit's visual displays, which would have the greatest impact on ordinary visitors. By the AFA's count, the thirty-eight photos and artifacts in Unit 4 depicting Japanese suffering, especially of women and children at Hiroshima and Nagasaki, stood in stark contrast to only three photos of American casualties during the war on display elsewhere in the exhibit. Critics pointed to similar imbalances in the written text. For example, more than sixteen times as many pages were devoted to "ground zero" at Hiroshima and Nagasaki than to Japanese atrocities committed throughout East Asia, which claimed millions of victims. The script also contained ten aggressive anti-Japanese statements by Americans versus only one anti-American statement by a Japanese.[14] When NASM director Harwit sought an internal evaluation of the script from six museum employees dubbed the Tiger Team, its assessment likewise contained numerous criticisms. One member of the team, Colonel Donald Lopez, a retired Air Force officer and also a former NASM deputy director, told Harwit, "A visitor, expecting something honoring [the] 50th anniversary of WWII, either veteran, or with some connection to a veteran, will be appalled. . . . I would leave the exhibit with the strong feeling that Americans are bloodthirsty, racist killers who after beer parties and softball go out and kill as many women and children as possible."[15]

After more than a year of turmoil, the exhibition was cancelled. In its place the NASM displayed only the forward fuselage of the actual *Enola Gay*, accompanied by a few other items and a small plaque. That truncated exhibit quickly became the most popular special exhibit in the history of the NASM, drawing more than a million visitors its first year and almost four million before it closed in May 1998. In December 2003, the entire, fully restored *Enola Gay* reappeared, along with a vast array of aircraft of all types, in a gleaming new National Air and Space Museum building as part of a permanent exhibit dedicated to the history of aviation. The fourteen-line plaque describing the airplane, similar in length to the others in the exhibit, simply informed visitors that *Enola Gay* was the B-29—"the most sophisticated propeller-driven bomber of World War II"— that had dropped the atomic bomb on Hiroshima.[16] Visitors were left to draw their own conclusions about that act.

That denouement must have satisfied Paul Tibbets. At a 1994 news conference where he called the proposed NASM exhibit a "package of insults," the retired Air Force general had suggested that *Enola Gay* be displayed at the National Air and Space Museum with a one-line statement: "This airplane was the first one to drop an atomic bomb." The man who piloted *Enola Gay* on its famous mission to Hiroshima added, "You don't need any other explanation. And I think it should be displayed alone."[17]

THE HISTORIOGRAPHY OF HIROSHIMA

Notwithstanding some early critical voices, the historiography of the bombing of Hiroshima originally was dominated by commentators who argued that the bomb's use was militarily and morally justified, a viewpoint that over time has become known as the "orthodox" position on this issue. Henry L. Stimson, the secretary of war from 1940 to 1945, provided the most thorough and persuasive early defense in his article "The Decision to Use the Atomic Bomb," which appeared in the February 1947 edition of *Harper's Magazine*. In 1948 Stimson and coauthor McGeorge Bundy reinforced the argument for using the bomb in Stimson's autobiography, *On Active Service in Peace and War*.[18] Prominent historians Louis Morton and Samuel Eliot Morison did the same, respectively, in "The Decision to Use the Atomic Bomb" (*Foreign Affairs*, January 1957) and "Why Japan Surrendered" (*Atlantic Monthly*, October 1960). Pulitzer Prize–winning historian Herbert Feis endorsed Stimson's case in *Japan Subdued: The Atomic Bomb and the End of the War in the Pacific* (1961). To be sure, Feis accepted the 1946 conclusion of the U.S. Strategic Bombing Survey (USSBS), reached hastily and resting on problematic methodology, that blockade and bombing could have ended the war by November 1945. More fundamentally, he stressed that the decision to use the bomb was "governed by one reason . . . that by using the bomb, the agony of the war might be ended most quickly and many lives be saved." Feis added that American leaders before August 6, 1945, worried that "if it proved necessary to carry out plans for an invasion, the [American] losses might amount to hundreds of thousands." Further, the decision to develop the bomb had been military, "and the impelling reason for the decision to use it was military—to end the war victoriously as soon as possible."[19] Meanwhile, Robert Butow's *Japan's Decision to Surrender* (1954), the era's landmark study of Japanese decision making during the last year of the war and an invaluable resource to this day, stressed the crucial importance of Hiroshima and Nagasaki in breaking the political logjam in Japan and bringing about a surrender.[20]

The umbrella term usually applied to the wide range of historical writing critical of the American decision to use atomic weapons against Japan is "revisionism," that is, a revision of the "orthodox" view that the bomb's use was militarily and morally justified. The term also refers more broadly to historical writing critical of postwar American foreign policy. Revisionism as it relates to the atomic bombing of Japan first emerged in 1946 when Norman Cousins and Thomas K. Finletter, in the pages of the *Saturday Review of Literature*, accused the United States of using atomic weapons against Japan as a diplomatic tool to limit Soviet influence in East Asia, not as a military weapon to end the war. In 1948 the British physicist and Nobel Prize laureate P. M. S. Blackett, a Marxist strongly sympathetic to the Soviet Union, repeated this argument in far greater detail in a book called *Military and Political Consequences of Atomic Energy*; the book, cleansed of some of its original anti-American statements, was published in the United States in 1949 under the title *Fear, War and the Bomb: Military and Political Consequences of Atomic Energy*. Two years later it made its appearance in translation in Japan. Blackett relied heavily on the conclusions in the USSBS's *Summary Report (Pacific War)*, published in July 1946.[21] Four decades later, in the wake of closer examination of the body of evidence including key testimony from Japanese officials it collected, the USSBS would come under withering and justifiable criticism from professional academic historians for reaching a conclusion regarding when Japan would have surrendered that was contradicted by its own evidence. (See "Key Questions and Interpretations: Key Question #1," for an overview of that criticism.)

The early revisionists, in part because they lacked convincing documentary evidence, did not have a significant impact on public or scholarly opinion. During the late 1950s and early 1960s, prominent left-of-center historians William Appleman Williams and D. F. Fleming echoed the revisionist arguments in their respective books on American foreign policy, but theirs remained the distinctly minority position, despite Williams's growing celebrity status in certain academic circles. That situation changed in the mid-1960s and 1970s, not coincidentally against the background of the Vietnam War. The decision to use atomic weapons came under close, and often unsympathetic, scrutiny from many scholars. The book that made by far the largest impact, and which also took what may be called the hard-line revisionist position, was Gar Alperovitz's *Atomic Diplomacy: Hiroshima and Potsdam* (1965). Alperovitz argued that the Japanese had been prepared to surrender if granted terms permitting them to keep their emperor, that the United States knew it, and that Washington withheld those terms and instead bombed Hiroshima and Nagasaki to intimidate the Soviet Union and gain the upper hand in its postwar dealings with Moscow in Eastern Europe and to keep the Soviets out of the war in the Far East. This, he maintained, in turn precipitated the Cold War. Notwithstanding three versions of his book—the latest, *The Decision to Use the Bomb and the Architecture of an American Myth* (1995), numbering almost nine hundred pages and crammed with hundreds of footnotes—it is fair to say that Alperovitz's overall "atomic diplomacy" thesis, which debuted to considerable fanfare, retains only marginal support. From the start it was sharply criticized by numerous orthodox historians, some of whom, most notably Robert James Maddox, demonstrated Alperovitz's misleading use of sources. Even many staunchly revisionist historians shied away from Alperovitz's conspiratorial thesis regarding the use of the atomic bomb against Japan. Still, they borrowed some of his ideas to construct their own critiques of American policy during World War II and the early postwar era. Martin Sherwin provided the most notable example of that approach in *A World Destroyed: The Atomic Bomb and the Grand Alliance* (1975), a book that, like Alperovitz's, has appeared in three versions, the latest in 2003. Disagreeing with Alperovitz, Sherwin grudgingly granted that the primary motive for dropping the bomb was to end the war quickly, but he also found anti-Soviet diplomatic motives deeply entwined in the decision.[22]

By the mid-1970s the revisionist enterprise, albeit a more moderate version than that presented by Alperovitz, was flourishing. Numerous academics, while rejecting the Alperovitz thesis as a whole, wove bits and pieces of it into their own critiques of the bombing of Hiroshima, or of Truman's and Stimson's subsequent defense of it. The revisionist case became an expansive tapestry embroidered with a myriad of shapes and forms. Some of the better-received books that modified or extended the revisionist case in one direction or another include Gregg Herken's *The Winning Weapon: The Atomic Bomb in the Cold War, 1945–1950* (1982); Robert L. Messer's *The End of an Alliance: James F. Byrnes, Roosevelt, Truman and the Origins of the Cold War* (1982); Michael Sherry's *The Rise of American Air Power: The Creation of Armageddon* (1987); and Leon V. Sigal's *Fighting to a Finish: The Politics of War Termination in the United States and Japan* (1988). Whatever their differences or different emphases, by the 1980s revisionists agreed that the atomic bomb had not been necessary to force a Japanese surrender in 1945 and that there was no evidence to support Truman's claims for casualty estimates in the many hundreds of thousands had the United States been required to invade Japan in order to end the war. Beyond that, their scenarios varied. In *Dubious Victory: The United States and the End of World War II* (1973), Lisle A. Rose vigorously rejected the atomic diplomacy thesis but maintained that Japan would have surrendered without an invasion and denounced the use of atomic bombs against Hiroshima and Nagasaki. Barton J. Bernstein argued that Truman had used the bomb primarily to force a Japanese surrender, thereby essentially accepting a key point of the orthodox analysis, but he agreed with the revisionists that after the war Truman and Stimson exaggerated the number of casualties they expected from an invasion of Japan in order to justify its use.[23]

Revisionism's heyday lasted through the 1980s and into the 1990s. Then the historiographical ground began to shift. During the early 1990s a new body of scholarly work emerged, often based on hitherto unavailable documents, that countered many revisionist arguments about the bomb as a diplomatic weapon in 1945, the likelihood that Japan would have surrendered before the planned U.S. invasion had the bomb not been used, and the allegations that projected casualty figures for the projected invasion of Japan were lower than those cited by supporters of the decision to use the bomb. These scholars provided powerful support, based on military considerations, for Truman's decision to use atomic bombs against Japan. They also pointed to solid documentary evidence for Truman's postwar statements about high casualty estimates. Their new books and articles in effect refocused the discussion back to the issue of how the bomb was used to end the war as soon as possible, with the least cost in American lives. These works included Richard B. Frank's *Downfall: The End of the Japanese Empire* (1999), which received increasing recognition as the standard work on the end of the Pacific war. Two other important monographs were Robert P. Newman's *Truman and the Hiroshima Cult* (1995) and Robert James Maddox's *Weapons for Victory: The Hiroshima Decision Fifty Years Later* (1995). These books in turn benefited from Edward Drea's *MacArthur's Ultra: Codebreaking and the War Against Japan* (1992), a groundbreaking study whose many revelations include a summary of how U.S. intelligence tracked the Japanese military buildup on the home island of Kyushu in the months before the bombing of Hiroshima.[24] Military historians Thomas B. Allen and Norman Polmar marshaled evidence supporting Truman's decision to bomb Hiroshima in *Code Name Downfall: The Secret Plan to Invade Japan—and Why Truman Dropped the Bomb* (1995). Several scholarly articles also stood out in undermining revisionist assumptions, among them Sadao Asada's "The Shock of the Atomic Bomb and Japan's Decision to Surrender—A Reconsideration" (*Pacific Historical Review*, November 1998); D. M. Giangreco's "Casualty Projections for the U.S. Invasions of Japan, 1945–1946: Planning and Policy Implications" (*Journal of Military*

History, July 1997); Herbert Bix's "Japan's Delayed Surrender: A Reinterpretation" (*Diplomatic History*, Spring 1995); and Gian Gentile's "Advocacy or Assessment? The United States Strategic Bombing Survey of Germany and Japan" (*Pacific Historical Review*, February 1997). Meanwhile, several authors of the major new biographies of Truman published during the 1990s rejected the revisionist perspective and supported his decision as necessary to end the war without a prohibitively costly invasion of Japan's home islands. They included Robert H. Ferrell, widely recognized as the leading academic expert on Truman (*Harry S. Truman: A Life*, 1994); Alonzo L. Hamby, another prominent academic Truman scholar (*Man of the People: A Life of Harry S. Truman*, 1995); and David McCullough, whose *Truman* (1992) became a national bestseller and won the Pulitzer Prize.

Not surprisingly, these additions to the scholarly literature did not end the debate. John Ray Skates, in *The Invasion of Japan: Alternative to the Bomb* (1994), argued for low-end casualties in the projected invasion of Japan and said that American insistence on unconditional surrender prolonged the war. John D. Chappell, whose *Before the Bomb: How America Approached the End of the Pacific War* (1997) chronicled the growing war weariness and concern about rising casualties at home, agreed that insistence on unconditional surrender prolonged the war. J. Samuel Walker's concise articulation of a moderate version of the revisionist case in *Prompt and Utter Destruction: Truman and the Use of Atomic Bombs Against Japan* (1997) suggested that a combination of B-29 air raids, blockade, "and perhaps a moderation of the unconditional surrender policy might have ended the war without an invasion and without the use of atomic bombs." However, Walker did not speculate how long that would have taken. Walker also defended the NASM exhibit script against its critics and said casualties in an invasion of Japan would have been "relatively small but far from inconsequential."[25] Yet, in his 1999 review of Frank's *Downfall*, Walker wrote that Frank's analysis "drives a stake into the heart of the most cherished revisionist contention—that Japan was seeking peace and the United States prolonged the war by refusing to soften its demand for unconditional surrender."[26] Frank also pointedly rejected the thesis that modifying the demand for unconditional surrender to include maintenance of the imperial institution (that is, allowing the emperor to remain on the throne) would have shortened the war. In addition, his comprehensive overview of casualty estimates prior to the planned invasion of Japan likewise supported historians who had argued for high-end figures.[27]

As a new century began, Gian Gentile expanded his critique of the USSBS and its conclusions in *How Effective Is Strategic Bombing? Lessons Learned from World War II to Kosovo* (2001). Robert P. Newman did the same in *The Enola Gay and the Court of History* (2004), although the book's main focus was a critique of the NASM's ill-fated *Enola Gay* exhibit. The book that gained the most attention was Tsuyoshi Hasegawa's *Racing the Enemy: Stalin, Truman, and the Surrender of Japan* (2005). Hasegawa agreed with Frank that Japan was not prepared to surrender before the events of August 6–9. At the same time, he agreed with Alperovitz that the United States used the atomic bomb in order to force a Japanese surrender before the Soviet entry into the Pacific War. Hasegawa also maintained that the Japanese surrendered not because of the atomic bombings of Hiroshima and Nagasaki but because of the Soviets' declaration of war against them. Neither of the latter two contentions went unchallenged. Some critics responded that there is no evidence that Truman was "racing" to use the atomic bomb before the Soviet Union entered the war; rather, Washington's problem was that Moscow was asking too high a price for its entry into the Pacific War. Others, focusing on Japanese language sources cited by Hasegawa, maintained that the overwhelming weight of the evidence pointed to the atomic bombs, or atomic bombs combined with the Soviet entry, as the reason Japan finally surrendered.[28] Meanwhile, in a study with a somewhat broader focus, Wilson Miscamble maintained in *From Roosevelt to Truman: Potsdam, Hiroshima, and the Cold War* (2006) that Truman's decision to use the atomic bombs was motivated primarily by the desire to force Japan's defeat before paying the high cost in American blood of an invasion of the Japanese home islands. Miscamble explicitly rejected the notions that the bomb was used either to prevent Soviet participation in the war against Japan or to intimidate the Soviets by a demonstration of American power. The documents that make up the bulk of this volume have been selected to help the reader evaluate the competing claims with regard to these and similarly hotly debated questions.

CHAPTER 2

Building the Atomic Bomb

During the fall of 1938, the world of physics and the world of politics, two utterly different spheres of human endeavor, were about to collide and become locked in a historic embrace. Both worlds were in turmoil, the former because of new discoveries about the atom and their ominous implications, the latter because of aggressive actions of Nazi Germany and Imperial Japan and the threat they posed to the international order and world peace. The collision, actually a shadowy event that few people knew had even taken place, set colossal forces in motion. In less than a decade they produced not only weapons of mass destruction with heretofore unimaginable power but also what scientists called a new world: the atomic age.

In the 1938 world of politics, the country most feared by the United States and the world's other leading democratic powers was Nazi Germany. Adolf Hitler, Germany's fanatical dictator, had pushed Europe to the brink of war. Having annexed Austria the previous March, in September of that year he demanded that neighboring Czechoslovakia cede to Germany a mountainous border region called the Sudetenland, the majority of whose population was German-speaking. The Czechoslovak government was prepared to resist Hitler's demands, inasmuch as they violated all international norms and, if met, would leave the country defenseless against its powerful and aggressive neighbor. Czechoslovakia expected backing from other European nations, many of which were deeply worried that German aggressiveness would plunge Europe into catastrophic war for the second time in a generation. Above all, the Czechs were counting on the support of Britain and France, Europe's leading democracies. Instead, their erstwhile friends, whose leaders craved peace at any price as long as their countries did not have to pay it, deserted the Czechoslovakian cause. At a hastily organized conference in the German city of Munich in September, Britain and France caved in to German demands: in return for Hitler's promise to make no more territorial demands against Germany's neighbors, Czechoslovakia, which had been excluded from the conference that would decide its fate, would have to cede the Sudetenland to the Reich. Hitler had been appeased, but not for long. Within a year, Nazi Germany attacked Poland and plunged Britain, France, and most of Europe into the most destructive war of all time.

Meanwhile, by 1938 rapid progress was being made in the world of physics in uncovering the secrets of the atom. In 1911, Ernest Rutherford had theorized that each atom had a core, or nucleus, that was a storehouse of enormous energy. Barely two decades later, James Chadwick discovered the neutron, a subatomic particle without a charge and therefore in theory capable of penetrating the nucleus. That discovery quickly gave rise to numerous experiments in various European institutes, including a series in the fall of 1938 involving uranium conducted by two German chemists: Otto Hahn, the world's leading radiochemist, and his young associate, Fritz Strassmann. Earlier in the decade, the two men had worked with a third colleague, the distinguished physicist Lise Meitner, but as a Jew she had been forced into exile in Sweden to escape Nazi Germany's increasingly vicious anti-Semitic policies. When their experiments produced unexpected, and indeed baffling, results, Hahn and Strassmann wrote to Meitner in Stockholm for her opinion. She discussed the matter with her nephew, Otto Frisch, like her an outstanding physicist. In January 1939, they concluded that Hahn and Strassmann had achieved something truly momentous: the two German chemists had split the atom, a process that soon would be referred to as nuclear fission. If that process could be made to continue beyond a certain point, it would become self-perpetuating, a chain reaction, and release energy on a scale that exponentially exceeded anything humans had managed before.

The news of fission swept the world of physics like a firestorm. There was great excitement about the vast new realm of knowledge finally open to science, but also great concern. Leo Szilard, like Meitner a prominent physicist and Jewish refugee forced to flee the growing Nazi menace, expressed the reason for concern succinctly. Born in Hungary, Szilard had studied in Germany, but he left soon after the Nazis came to power and purged thousands of Jewish scholars and scientists from the country's universities and research institutes. He eventually found his way to the United States, where in January 1939 he wrote a letter to a friend (see Document A1) expressing his concerns:

I feel I ought to let you know of a very sensational new development in nuclear physics. In a paper . . . Hahn reports that he finds when bombarding uranium with neutrons the uranium is breaking up. . . . This is entirely unexpected and exciting news. . . .

This in itself might make it possible to produce power by means of nuclear energy, but I do not think that this possibility is very exciting, for . . . the cost of investment would probably be too high to make the process worthwhile. . . .

I see . . . possibilities in another direction. These might lead to a large-scale production of energy and radioactive elements, unfortunately also perhaps to atomic bombs.[1]

ENTER EINSTEIN AND ROOSEVELT

Szilard's sense of dread about what atomic energy could do was not new. Advances in physics had led him to think about the possibility of nuclear bombs since the early 1930s, but now politics gave those speculative thoughts a dramatic new urgency and worldly reality. Hahn and Strassmann had not made their discovery in an ordinary country: they were living and working in Nazi Germany. When Hitler, violating the Munich agreement with France and Britain, annexed the rest of Czechoslovakia in March 1939, the Nazis came into possession of that country's large uranium deposits. Then the Germans barred the export of all uranium from their new territories. There was little doubt in Szilard's mind that the Germans would try to build an atomic bomb. Neither was there much doubt in the mind of anyone without intellectual blinders that Hitler's ambitions were insatiable and would lead to war. A Nazi Germany armed with atomic weapons would be a threat to all humanity. As Szilard saw it, the U.S. government had to be warned of the threat and, more than that, convinced to develop and build an atomic bomb before the Germans did so.

Szilard enlisted the help of several other prominent nuclear physicists to get the message to American leaders. Among the first was Enrico Fermi, the Italian-born 1938 Nobel Prize winner who had left Fascist Italy that same year and taken a position at Columbia University. Late in July, that effort took the Hungarian physicist to the summer home of the world's most famous scientist, theoretical physicist and 1921 Nobel Prize winner Albert Einstein. Like Szilard, Einstein was a Jewish refugee from Germany who had found safety in the United States. The two men drafted a two-page letter, dated August 2, 1939, and signed by Einstein, to President Franklin Roosevelt. It warned that advances in physics had made an atomic bomb possible and that Germany was likely to try to build such a bomb[2] (see Document A2). The letter, along with additional information, finally reached Roosevelt in mid-October via a businessman and political associate of the president whom Szilard had enlisted in his cause.

By then, Germany's attack on Poland had launched World War II in Europe. The president, who considered Germany an imminent threat to American security, authorized the formation of a committee headed by Dr. Lyman Briggs, director of the Bureau of Standards, to investigate the possibilities of building such a bomb. The Briggs Committee's report, delivered on November 1, recommended investigating two possibilities: whether a controlled chain reaction could be a source of power for submarines and whether a chain reaction could become explosive and power a superbomb. The committee also authorized six thousand dollars to help scientists build what would become the world's first nuclear reactor at the University of Chicago. These funds turned out to be the minuscule down payment for a project that ultimately would cost two billion dollars.

It was a start, but barely. Little of substance had been done by June 1940, when Roosevelt approved the creation of the National Defense Research Council (NDRC), which absorbed the Briggs Committee. Its head was Vannevar Bush, the holder of a doctorate in engineering jointly issued by Harvard and the Massachusetts Institute of Technology (MIT), who had served as vice president of MIT and currently was president of the Carnegie Institution. A year later, in a major reorganization, a presidential executive order created the Office of Scientific Research and Development (OSRD), which was charged with the task of mobilizing the country's scientific talent and resources for the national defense effort and military needs. Bush became its director, and now for the first time he reported directly to the president. Aside from its role in the development of the atomic bomb, during World War II the OSRD played a crucial role in developing technologies used in radar, proximity fuses for shells, and a wide assortment of advanced weapons.

Meanwhile, important calculations were being made in Britain regarding the crucial question of how much $U235$ would be needed to make an atomic bomb, and these calculations suggested that such a bomb was indeed possible to build. There are two main isotopes of uranium in nature. It was known that the more plentiful $U238$ does not fission, which means it could not be used to power a bomb. Far less plentiful, amounting to only about 1/140th of the $U238$ found in nature, is $U235$. One of the great obstacles facing the developers of an atomic bomb was to find a way to separate the two isotopes efficiently so that the $U235$ could be used to make a bomb. At best, it would be a slow, laborious, and enormously expensive project, meaning that if too much $U235$ were needed— hundreds or thousands of pounds, for example—the task would be impossible, at least in the foreseeable future. It therefore was big news when two physicists, Otto Frisch and a German-born colleague named Rudolf Peierls, calculated that it would take only about two pounds of $U235$ to build an atomic bomb. Their memorandum on the subject soon reached a committee of scientists the British government had appointed to consider the feasibility of building a bomb. Called the MAUD Committee, it came up with a higher estimate, but still within the range of possibility. Its report, approved in July 1941, concluded that twenty-five pounds of U235 were needed for a bomb. The report added that while separating U235 from U238 was "a matter of great difficulty," a plant could be built that would be able to produce enough material for a bomb by 1943, albeit at great expense.[3]

The British government forwarded the MAUD Report to Vannevar Bush in October, who in turn personally brought it to Roosevelt. At that point Roosevelt formed a committee of high-ranking officials to consider the key policy decisions related to atomic weapons, the aptly named Top Policy Group. Its members included Vice President Henry Wallace, Secretary of War Henry Stimson, Army Chief of Staff George C. Marshall, Vannevar Bush, and James Bryant Conant, a distinguished chemist and president of Harvard University. Bush's next task was to enlist Arthur H. Compton, a Nobel Prize–winning physicist (1927) at the University of Chicago, to conduct an American review of the available science to determine the feasibility of building an atomic bomb. Compton called on some of the greatest scientists in nuclear research available in the United States, among them Fermi; Eugene Wigner, a brilliant Hungarian-born physicist and close associate of Fermi; Harold Urey, the 1934 Nobel Prize laureate in chemistry; Ernest Lawrence, the 1939 Nobel Prize winner in physics; Glenn Seaborg, a young chemist at the University of California at Berkeley and a pioneer in the development and identification of plutonium, a transuranic element; and another young Berkeley scientist, physicist Robert Oppenheimer, a brash and brilliant New Yorker destined to head the laboratory that eventually would build the atomic bomb. The conclusion of the six-page report that emerged, officially issued by the National Academy of Sciences and delivered by Bush to President Roosevelt in November, was positive, if not sufficiently precise: the mass of U235 needed to build a bomb "can hardly be less than 2 kg nor greater than 100 kg."[4]

On December 7, 1941, Japan bombed Pearl Harbor, and the next day the United States declared war. On December 11, Germany declared war on the United States. The United States now was at war not only with Japan, a country it was confident it could defeat, but also with Germany, the country whose scientific skills and ability to develop an atomic bomb it feared most. In January 1942, Roosevelt, in a short handwritten note, authorized Bush to speed up research on the atomic bomb. In effect, that meant going beyond just research to the development stage. The American effort to build a bomb was finally off the ground.

THE MANHATTAN PROJECT

For the first part of 1942, work on the atomic bomb took place under the auspices of Section 1 of the OSRD. The shorthand term for that office, S-1, provided the code name that officials would use to refer to the top-secret bomb until the first device was successfully tested three years later. In May, the S-1 leadership decided to pursue all of five possible methods that had been suggested to produce fissionable materials for an atomic bomb: three for separating U235 from U238 and two for creating the recently discovered transuranic element plutonium 239. The plutonium option was new, the result of work completed in 1941 by Seaborg and several colleagues that had produced the artificial transuranic element Pu-239 by bombarding U238 with neutrons. Having isolated plutonium, Seaborg and his colleagues then had determined that this artificial element, like U235, was fissionable. The decision to go forward with all the possible methods, a step that was certain to be staggeringly expensive, was dictated by the urgency of the perceived nuclear race with Nazi Germany.

In June 1942, Bush told Roosevelt that while the OSRD should continue to work on research and development, the time had come for the U.S. Army to take over the enormous task of building the factories and other facilities that would produce these fissionable materials. The army was the best candidate for the job because of its experience with large-scale building projects and because the huge costs of the top-secret project could be more easily hidden in its commodious budget. A colonel was put in charge of the army's part of the project, which operated as part of the Corps of Engineers and was given the name Manhattan Engineering District (MED). That soon was shortened in everyday references to the Manhattan Project.

Problems plagued the army's efforts from the start, including the unwieldy division of labor with the OSRD and the fact that the MED did not have the government's highest priority rating, which it needed to acquire massive amounts of critical materials needed to do its job. Then Colonel Leslie Groves was appointed in September 1942 to take over the project. Groves, the builder of the recently completed Pentagon, was a no-nonsense officer who did not let bureaucratic red tape, or anything else, for that matter, get in his way. That was not only his temperament, but also his job. As he put it after the war, "My mission as given to me by Secretary Stimson was to produce this at the earliest possible date so as to bring the war to a conclusion. That was further emphasized by his statement that any time that a single day could be saved I should save that day. The instructions to the project were that any individual in that project who felt that the ultimate completion, insofar as he understood it, was going to be delayed by as much as a day by something that was happening, it was his duty to report it directly by telephone, skipping all channels of every kind. So that urgency was on us right from the start."[5]

Groves was promoted to brigadier general upon receiving his new job and immediately started solving problems. Within a few days, he arranged to purchase 1,250 tons of high-quality uranium ore sitting in storage in New York and got the

Manhattan Project the government's first-priority AAA rating it needed for acquiring vital resources. Groves also arranged for the purchase of 52,000 acres of land in eastern Tennessee to build plants to separate U235 from U238 and a small pilot nuclear reactor to produce plutonium. These facilities gave birth to a new town, Oak Ridge. However, producing enough plutonium to make bombs demanded enormous quantities of space, water, and electricity, far more than was available at Oak Ridge. Therefore, in January 1943 the government bought 500,000 acres of land, the equivalent of 780 square miles, along the Columbia River near the small town of Hanford, Washington, to construct reactors and separation plants needed to produce plutonium. With regard to the OSRD, research begun under its auspices temporarily remained there for the sake of continuity, but by April 1943 General Groves had complete control over the entire effort to build an atomic bomb.

When General Groves took over the Manhattan Project and made these enormous commitments, there was no guarantee that an atomic bomb could be made. However, there were important advances on several fronts during the second part of 1942. Between July and September of that year a team in Berkeley under the leadership of Oppenheimer established the theoretical basis for the design of an atomic bomb. Early in October came a fateful encounter when Groves arrived in Berkeley and met Oppenheimer. The two men could not have been more different in terms of background, temperament, or appearance. Groves, the son of a Presbyterian minister, studied engineering at MIT and excelled at West Point before making a successful career as an army engineer. He was disciplined, conservative, devoted to the service, practical, down-to-earth, and often rude. Nor was he willing to take no for an answer. During the next three years he frequently gave building contractors, engineers, or scientists deadlines that seemed impossible and then drove them to make sure those deadlines were met.

Oppenheimer, suave and intellectual, was a man who when not immersed in the rarified world of theoretical physics learned Sanskrit for fun. He was born in New York City, the son of a Jewish immigrant from Germany who had prospered in the textile business and an artistic mother. Oppenheimer enjoyed a comfortable, cosmopolitan upbringing before excelling at Harvard and earning a doctorate in theoretical physics from Göttingen University in Germany. At six feet, the frail physicist was about an inch taller than the corpulent general and, at his maximum weight of 125 pounds, tipped the scales at less than half that of Groves at his leanest. Apolitical as a young man, Oppenheimer in the 1930s was drawn to the political left and eventually to the Communist Party; these political associations would cause serious problems for both himself and Groves. It is likely, but not proven to everyone's satisfaction, that Oppenheimer belonged to the Communist Party in the late 1930s and early 1940s.[6]

Despite these differences, and more, the two men, notwithstanding their share of conflicts, formed a successful partnership. In their initial meetings they agreed that a central, isolated laboratory was needed to deal with all theoretical and developmental aspects of building the bomb. A central lab would satisfy two conflicting but essential agendas. The government needed secrecy, and that imperative was one of Groves's responsibilities. It was essential that all information about the atomic bomb project be kept both from enemies such as Nazi Germany and allies such as the Soviet Union. That was why the Manhattan Project was organized so that most of the more than 125,000 people who eventually worked for it knew only about their specific assignments but nothing about what was going on elsewhere or the project as a whole, a system called compartmentalization, which Oppenheimer opposed. Scientific progress depended on the exchange of information and ideas, he argued. For him, a central lab was a good idea because it would bring together scientists working on different aspects of the bomb. Time would not have to be wasted traveling from place to place to hold meetings. In short, a central lab, properly located and administered, could meet the needs of both Oppenheimer and Groves. The scientists could have that exchange, but under conditions that permitted the necessary security, if they and their families were all in one place and subject to military surveillance. In mid-October 1942, Groves appointed Oppenheimer the head of the new laboratory that would take charge of research and design for the atomic bomb.

A month later, the MED bought a ranch in New Mexico about thirty-five miles from the town of Santa Fe. On April 1, 1943, it became the home for the Los Alamos laboratory. From an initial population of about a hundred scientists and their families, Los Alamos grew into a community of six thousand people by the end of the war. There they lived, all with the same post-office box address, under the strictest security: surrounded by soldiers and a barbed-wire fence, their mail checked and censored, their trips to Santa Fe supervised by army intelligence agents. Oppenheimer, who, like several other top scientists, had a personal armed bodyguard, was monitored especially carefully both because of security imperatives and to guarantee his personal safety. Similar security procedures prevailed at Oak Ridge and Hanford. Several top scientists had aliases, although not ones likely to foil trained intelligence agents: Arthur Compton was A. H. Comas, Enrico Fermi became Henry Farmer, and Niels Bohr was called Nicholas Baker.[7] Still, work at Los Alamos, as Oppenheimer had hoped, was characterized by close personal contacts that avoided bureaucratic entanglements. Morris Kolodney, an electrochemist-metallurgist who did pioneering work producing both pure plutonium and uranium, recalled many years later that one important reason for the rapid progress made at Los Alamos was that "there were no memos."[8]

Another major step forward during 1942 occurred at the Metallurgical Laboratory (Met Lab), which had been set up at the University of Chicago early in the year under the leadership of Arthur Compton. Its primary task was to build a nuclear "pile"—today the term used is nuclear reactor—that would create a controlled chain reaction to produce plutonium. Planning under Enrico Fermi began in May, and construction finally began on a round-the-clock basis in November under the stands of the university's football stadium. Aside from U238, the key ingredients in the pile were graphite, the material for the "moderator" in which the uranium was embedded, and cadmium, which absorbs large amounts of neutrons and therefore was the key ingredient in the control rods designed to regulate the chain reaction. On December 2, 1942, Fermi's team was ready. The experiment was successful: at 3:49 p.m., the chain reaction began as Fermi raised his hand and announced, "The pile has gone critical." He allowed it to continue for about four and a half minutes as his audience of scientists watched nervously before ordering it stopped. By generating less power than it takes to run a light bulb, the scientists had brought the world into the atomic age. As Compton put it in coded phone message to a colleague, "the Italian navigator has just landed in the new world." To everyone's relief, the dangerous experiment had gone off without a hitch and, as Compton put it, "Everyone landed safe and happy."[9]

SCIENCE AND ENGINEERING
IN THE NEW WORLD

On December 28, 1942, President Roosevelt, on his own and without consulting Congress, approved the huge construction projects necessary to build the atomic bomb and the expenditures, which were already spiraling upward at an uncontrollable rate, needed to fund them. During 1943, those buildings, factories, and support facilities, which dwarfed anything the government had done before, went up, although some of the facilities did not come fully on line until well into 1945 and others until after the war was over. One Oak Ridge structure, the K-25 gaseous diffusion plant for producing U235, was the largest building in the world. Four stories high and almost half a mile long, it covered two million square feet. Although fully automated—the first such plant in history—it still required three thousand workers at any given time. (Nine thousand people worked there in three shifts.) Another Oak Ridge complex called Y-12 consisted of 268 buildings and covered an area equal to twenty football fields. The reactors and separation plants at Hanford covered an area of 192 square miles, and the reactors alone required as much water as a city of one million people.[10]

In the incredibly short time span between 1943 and the successful test of the world's first atomic bomb in mid-1945, the scientists and engineers of the Manhattan Project faced and solved problems of unprecedented scale and complexity. Scientists at Los Alamos, sometimes working in laboratories that themselves were not finished, had to design weapons for which the nuclear fuel that would power them did not exist. Because of time restraints, the normal development sequence of research, design engineering, and production engineering had to be abandoned and all the work done concurrently. Various options for solving problems could not be followed according to which was the most promising; all had to be explored simultaneously. Perhaps the most important of the decisions to pursue different options at the same time, made by early 1944, was to work on both uranium and plutonium-type bombs. Industrial companies supplying the Manhattan Project scientists and engineers had to design and manufacture equipment far more sensitive and sophisticated than anything they had produced before. Many of those machines and parts required entirely new technologies or materials. Among the newly developed machines were pumps used to move the highly corrosive uranium hexafluoride gas through Oak Ridge's gas diffusion plant, which required a new material so that critical seals would not fail. A recently developed slippery compound was rushed into service; after the war, under the brand name Teflon, it found its way into nearly every American kitchen to do rather more mundane tasks.

Difficulties as monumental as the new high-tech facilities themselves threatened to derail the project, among them problems at both the K-25 and Y-12 complexes during the spring and summer of 1944.[11] Even worse, at first it had been assumed that a relatively simple mechanism called a gun assembly—in which a noncritical amount of fissionable material is fired into a noncritical target, thereby beginning a chain reaction—could be used for both $U235$ and plutonium bombs. The assumption turned out to be true for $U235$, but not for plutonium because of its high rate of spontaneous fission. This was not fully recognized until the summer of 1944. It meant that for a plutonium bomb the Los Alamos team would have to turn to a far more complex system called implosion, under which a mass of plutonium was compressed into a critical state by a symmetrical shock wave caused by intricate arrangement of explosives called lenses, because they focused the explosions in a way comparable to how optical lenses focus light.[12] Creating such lenses was a problem staggering in its difficulty, even for the cadre of geniuses assembled at Los Alamos. As for $U235$, the problems at the Oak Ridge separation plants meant that significant amounts of that isotope were not being produced. (Actually, what was produced was not pure $U235$ but what is called enriched uranium, material that has a much higher percentage of $U235$ than that normally found in nature.) In fact, while the problems of producing $U235$ eventually were solved, there was not enough enriched uranium delivered to Los Alamos for a bomb—it turned out that *Little Boy* required 50 kg of 50 percent $U235$ and 14 kg of 89 percent $U235$—until July 1945. Even then, production was so slow that it would take several months before there was enough enriched uranium for a second bomb. If the United States was going to have an arsenal of atomic bombs ready for use in 1945, those weapons would have to be made of plutonium.

That was not going to be easy because of the obstacles posed by implosion. In fact, the challenges of making implosion work were so formidable that Oppenheimer, just a year from his deadline of delivering a working bomb, despaired and actually thought of resigning. During the winter of 1943, Hungarian-born mathematician John von Neumann had designed an explosive arrangement for implosion that would work in theory, but the leap from theory to practice was enormous. It was achieved largely by Russian-born chemist George Kistiakowsky. A quarter of a century earlier, Kistiakowsky had fought against Soviet totalitarianism as a soldier in the Russian civil war; he now fought, with greater success, against fascist totalitarianism as a scientist. By March 1945, Oppenheimer was satisfied that Kistiakowsky had built and tested an implosion lens system that would work. Nonetheless, the complicated plutonium implosion system would have to be tested. In contrast, confidence in the gun assembly system meant that no test was deemed necessary once a uranium bomb was produced.[13]

TRINITY

By early 1945, the uranium separation plants at Oak Ridge were coming on line and beginning to deliver meaningful quantities of sufficiently enriched uranium, enough for a single bomb, to Los Alamos. The so-called Dragon experiment in April, an extremely dangerous investigation conducted by Otto Frisch that could easily have led to a runaway chain reaction, had shown that the gun assembly concept would work. At Hanford, full production of plutonium had started, and that element likewise was being delivered to Los Alamos. A site for testing a plutonium bomb, nicknamed "gadget," was being prepared at the Alamogordo Bombing Range in the New Mexico desert about two hundred miles from Los Alamos. The code name for the test and the site where it would take place was Trinity, a name chosen by Oppenheimer for reasons he never made clear. Aside from not knowing whether implosion would work, the scientists who had built it had no idea how powerful it would be. Estimates, according to the betting pool of the project's top scientists, ranged from a high of 45,000 tons of TNT to a low of 300, the number chosen by Oppenheimer. One pessimistic participant chose zero.

On July 14, 1945, the test bomb was placed on top of a specially constructed one-hundred-foot tower. The bomb was detonated before dawn at 5:29 on the morning of July 16, exploding with a force of more than 18,000 tons of TNT and leaving everyone who saw the event, scientists and soldiers alike, in a state of shock and awe[14] (see Documents A37 and A39). Physicist Philip Morrison remembered how, in the predawn darkness, "Suddenly, not only was there a bright light but where we were, 10 miles away, there was the heat of the sun on our faces. . . . Then, only ten minutes later, the real sun rose and again you felt the same heat to the face from the sunrise. So we saw two sunrises."[15] Oppenheimer turned to his Sanskrit readings for his imagery: "We waited until the blast had passed, walked out of the shelter and then it was extremely solemn. We knew the world would not be the same. A few people laughed, a few people cried. Most people were silent. I remembered a line from the Hindu scripture, the *Bhagavad Gita*: Vishnu is trying to persuade the Prince that he should do his duty and to impress him takes on his multi-armed form and says, 'Now I become death, destroyer of worlds.' I suppose we all thought that in one way or another. There was a great deal of solemn talk that this was the end of the great wars of the century."[16]

A short while later, as the witnesses gathered at their base camp after returning from their various observation posts, one of the generals present said to Groves, "The war is over." Groves answered, "Yes, after we drop two bombs on Japan." Groves then turned to Oppenheimer and said quietly, "I'm proud of you." Oppenheimer's simple reply was "Thank you."[17]

POSTSCRIPT I: THE GERMAN AND JAPANESE ATOMIC BOMB PROGRAMS

The American effort to build an atomic bomb was the direct result of the fear that Germany had the intent and the ability to do the same. In fact, by the fall of 1939 the Germans had begun investigating the possibility of building a bomb. The effort was led by physicist Werner Heisenberg, winner of the Nobel Prize in 1926 for his work on quantum theory and nuclear physics. It turned out that the Germans were only in the race for a few years, in part because of calculation errors made by its scientists, including Heisenberg, during 1939 and 1940, and the military setbacks in 1941 and 1942 that made it impossible for Germany, with its limited resources, to mount a major effort such as the Manhattan Project. In Heisenberg's case, he made erroneous calculations in both 1939 and 1940 that led him to believe it would take tons of U235 to build an atomic bomb, an error that in turn led to the conclusion it would be impossible to build a bomb during the current war.[18] Heisenberg also failed in his attempt to build a nuclear pile and create a controlled chain reaction. Military defeats in 1942 on the eastern front against the Soviet Union further sealed the fate of the faltering German atomic bomb project, although Heisenberg and other scientists continued their work until the end of the war. These setbacks did not influence work in the

United States because the Americans did not know about Germany's scientific failures or the impact of military defeats on its bomb program. The United States mounted an intelligence operation to find out about German progress, code name Alsos, a Greek word meaning "grove," a play on the name of the Manhattan Project's boss. However, not until the end of 1944, by which time the Allies had successfully invaded Europe and reached Germany's western borders, did Alsos conclude that Germany had failed to make significant progress in building an atomic bomb.

The United States never considered Japan a serious candidate for building an atomic bomb, which turned out to be an accurate assessment. Still, Japan actually did set up two programs to work on an atomic bomb, one under the army called the NI Project and headed by Yoshio Nishina, the country's outstanding nuclear physicist, and the other, the F Project, sponsored by the Imperial Navy. Neither project, given Japan's limited resources, constituted a serious effort compared to the Manhattan Project or made significant progress in essential research. Nishina's nuclear research laboratory in Tokyo was destroyed in an American air raid in April 1945, while the navy effort, headquartered in Kyoto, did not even reach the experimental stage.[19] Four months later, as he circled a devastated Hiroshima in an airplane and became the first Japanese expert on nuclear physics to assess the damage, Nishina confirmed what the United States had publicly claimed but some Japanese military leaders still were trying to deny: that "nothing but an atomic bomb could have done such damage."[20]

POSTSCRIPT II: SOVIET SPYING

As to the development of atomic weapons, a far more serious threat came from an ally, the Soviet Union. The Soviets had concluded by 1942 that the United States was working on an atomic bomb and had a small project of their own in place by 1943. But when it came to atomic bombs, their most successful wartime program by far was in the field of espionage. The most important proven Soviet spy was physicist Klaus Fuchs, who had fled Nazi Germany because of his left-wing political beliefs, found refuge in Great Britain, and eventually ended up working at Los Alamos, one of nineteen scientists from Britain who worked there during World War II. He was one of the witnesses to the successful Trinity test. Fuchs provided the Soviets with crucial information about the plutonium bomb, including critical data on the implosion process. Further valuable information on the implosion process came from Theodore Hall, a young American physicist who volunteered his services to the Soviets because of his political beliefs. Hall also provided information on the process for separating $U235$ from $U238$. Information provided by Fuchs, Hall, and other Soviet spies, perhaps most notably the ring led by Julius Rosenberg, enabled the Soviets to develop an atomic bomb about two years earlier than they otherwise might have and at a considerable savings in resources. Although the United States was aware of Soviet spying on the Manhattan Project by 1943 and revelations from Soviet archives opened since 1991 have greatly enhanced our knowledge of wartime Soviet espionage, mystery still surrounds several important spies, whose identities remain unknown to this day. The first Soviet atomic bomb, tested successfully in August 1949, was essentially a Soviet copy of the first American plutonium bomb. In 1951, the Soviets successfully tested a U235 gun-assembly bomb of their own design.[21]

CHAPTER 3

The Pacific War

The Pacific War between the United States and Japan was not unexpected by either side. By the beginning of the 1940s, the two countries had been rivals in East Asia for close to half a century. The United States actually began planning for the possibility of a war against Japan in 1906 and over the next thirty-five years reviewed and revised that plan, known as War Plan Orange, many times. Ironically, given how the war began in December 1941 and Washington's failure to anticipate that scenario, American war plans dating from 1936 suggested that Japan might attempt a surprise air attack on Pearl Harbor. Japan's basic plan for a war against the United States, conceived in 1907, was revised in light of the new strategic reality after World War I, when Tokyo acquired former German-held islands in the central Pacific. It was given a powerful physical dimension by new warships and other modern weapons developed and built during the 1930s.

Yet neither the United States nor Japan was prepared for the great war they fought between December 7, 1941, and August 14, 1945. In some ways, it is hard to blame them. The Pacific War was contested on the largest battlefield of all time—an empty ocean vastness of millions of square miles dotted with tiny islands and, where the ocean finally ended, a string of larger islands extending from just off the northern tip of Australia to the Philippines to Japan's home islands off the northeast Asian mainland—that dwarfed even the gigantic Eastern Front in Europe, where at the same time Nazi Germany and the Soviet Union were locked in their titanic fight to the death. The struggle for control of the sea, often contested in battles spread over an area so large that the ships of the two opposing navies never saw each other, changed naval warfare, as the aircraft carrier and its complement of modern planes replaced the venerable battleship, which had ruled the waves for centuries, as the dominant oceangoing weapon. Meanwhile, on scattered, sweltering islands—some no bigger than large parks in American cities and others covered by impenetrable jungle—hundreds of thousands of young men, their respective opposing armies squeezed together cheek by jowl, fought close-quarter, desperate battles of unusual savagery as Japanese soldiers, driven by battle ethics that allowed only victory or death, fought to the last man rather than surrender. The ferocious and fanatical Japanese way of fighting stunned the Americans, but American soldiers and marines also shocked the Japanese, who had been led to believe Americans were too soft and pampered to make formidable opponents.

In both how it began and how it ended, with destruction raining down from the sky in once unimaginable displays of air power, the Pacific War was qualitatively new. And the way it finally was brought to a close was revolutionary in the most profound and ominous sense of that word. The Pacific War, which began with a humiliating example of American political and military incompetence at Pearl Harbor and with thousands of American soldiers sent into battle carrying rifles dating from World War I, ended with an awesome display of American scientific wizardry, engineering and organizational prowess, and industrial and military power when two ultramodern American B-29 bombers equipped with an array of high-tech equipment attacked Japan with bombs whose revolutionary technology marked the beginning of the nuclear age.[1]

THE ROAD TO WAR

It was Japan that made the decision to launch the Pacific War. The Japanese government opted for war for two main reasons, one based on perceived national needs and the other on a surprisingly fatalistic assessment of the empire's chances for victory. By the mid-1930s, ultranationalist military officers controlled Japan's government, convinced that only expansion overseas could solve Japan's problems and guarantee the empire the greatness and world power it deserved. To that end, they tripled the country's military budget in 1937; by 1938, this accounted for 75 percent of all public spending.[2] In particular, Japan needed guaranteed access to raw materials and markets in East Asia to continue to grow and become a manufacturing power capable of competing with the major European industrial powers and the United States. In their view, Japan, a resource-poor country, had to be able to exploit China without interference and get access to raw materials in what Tokyo called the "Southern region," an area that included French Indochina, Malaya, the Philippines, and the Dutch East Indies. This ultimately required that China be reduced to a Japanese dependency and the Europeans and Americans driven from East Asia. The result would be what after 1940 Tokyo called the "Greater East Asia Co-Prosperity Sphere," a region dominated militarily, economically, and politically by the Empire of Japan.

Japan took its first major step toward its goal in 1931 by invading the northern Chinese territory of Manchuria and, in 1932, detaching it and setting up a puppet state called Manchukuo. In 1937 Japan launched a full-scale invasion of China, but by 1941 it was bogged down in a war in which it won almost every battle but could not deliver a knockout blow. A major part of the problem was the United States, which was not only pressuring Tokyo to exit China but was also providing aid on an increasing scale to the Chinese government. Meanwhile, the "Southern region" was largely under the control of European colonial powers or, in the case of the Philippines, the United States. But conditions there were in flux. By 1940, in the wake of German victories on distant battlefields, the European colonial powers that had once blocked Japan's ambitions were severely weakened. The French and Dutch were defeated and occupied by Germany, and Britain, while still relatively formidable in the Far East, was reeling under the Nazi onslaught. Japan meanwhile was allied to Germany and Italy by terms of the Tripartite Pact it had signed with the two European fascist powers in September of that year. The Soviet Union, always a potential threat, as it demonstrated in August 1939 when its army thrashed Japanese forces along the Manchurian border, had agreed in April 1941 to a mutual nonaggression pact with Japan. Nazi Germany's invasion of the Soviet Union in June completed the job of ending the Soviet threat to Japanese control of Manchuria.

Therefore, by 1941 Japan—with good reason—considered the United States the main obstacle to its imperial ambitions. The Japanese leaders were under no illusions regarding American power. The United States was by far the world's leading economic and industrial giant, dwarfing Japan and Germany. Sophisticated analysts in Tokyo understood the danger of going to war with the United States. They included Isoroko Yamamoto, the commander in chief of the Japanese Combined Fleet and the man widely recognized as his country's outstanding naval strategist, who warned in 1940, "Japan cannot beat America. Therefore we should not fight America."[3] Still, most Japanese leaders believed that the United States had weaknesses and Japan had strengths that could negate America's economic power. If Japan made the optimum use of its resources and struck at precisely the right time, it had a chance to win a war with the United States. Japan, its leaders believed, had a martial spirit far superior to that of the Americans, who were pampered and soft. That faith in turn had racist roots in the idea that the Japanese—or, as they called themselves, the "Yamato race"—were superior to other nationalities and had a destiny to be the "leading race" not only in Asia but in the world.[4] That belief in the "Japanese spirit" was one reason Japanese strategists underestimated the toughness and resilience of American fighting men. For example, naval strategists belittled the American submarine force because, in their judgment, Americans could not stand the physical and mental strain of lengthy submarine duty.[5] Training methods and new weapons, the thinking went, added to Tokyo's advantage. Indeed, the Japanese navy in particular had developed an array of weapons that were the best of their kind in the world, including a long-range torpedo and the fast and maneuverable Zero carrier fighter. As early battles of the war would demonstrate, the Japanese warships also had better night-fighting capabilities than American vessels, due in part to intensive training and newly developed optical equipment.

Timing was everything, primarily because of America's enormous industrial strength and military potential. As Admiral Osami Nagano, the navy's chief of staff, pointed out in July to the Liaison Conference, Japan's top policymaking body at the time, as of mid-1941 Japan was better prepared for war than its giant rival across the Pacific. Matters became more urgent when on August 1 the United States declared a total oil and gasoline embargo on Japan. In September, Nagano told the Liaison Conference that in light of Japan's burdens and America's reserves, the passage of time could only work against Tokyo. He added, with what can at best be called strained optimism, "Although I am confident that at the present time, we have a chance to win the war, I fear that this opportunity will disappear with the passage of time."[6] That "opportunity" included the fact that the United States was focused on Europe. Washington increasingly was committed to aiding Britain and the Soviet Union in the war against Germany and, the calculation went, could not afford a major war with Japan.

That thinking, in fact, was the basis of Yamamoto's plan to attack Pearl Harbor. Before Yamamoto suggested his idea in early 1941, Japan's strategy for defeating the American navy called for weakening it by submarine warfare as it started to cross the Pacific, depleting it further with attacks from carrier-based planes and aircraft based on Japanese-held islands west of Hawaii, and then defeating it in a decisive battle east of the Philippines. But Yamamoto argued that the Japanese could not wait for the Americans to come to them. They would have to be more daring in order to achieve what their military doctrine said was essential to defeat a major Western power: a decisive victory in a single great battle.[7] According to Yamamoto, if Japan's ultramodern and highly trained navy could catch the United States unprepared and destroy its Pacific fleet, especially its aircraft carriers, at its home base in Hawaii and then seize a vast amount of territory, including a series of Pacific islands, the Americans might find themselves compelled to negotiate a peace rather than fight a long war in the Pacific. That in turn would give Japan the free hand it needed in East Asia. It would allow the army to carry out its plan to "go south" and attack the Philippines, Malaya, and the Dutch East Indies.

Japan closed its options in a series of decisions during the second half of 1941. In mid-October, Hideki Tojo, a militant advocate of war, succeeded the more moderate and cautious Prince Fumimaro Konoe, who opposed war with the United States, as prime minister. During the following six weeks, Emperor Hirohito ended his wavering and cast his lot for war. Negotiations continued with the United States, but Washington would not agree to Japanese terms that would have left Tokyo with permanent control of Manchuria and other northern Chinese territory and China itself as little more than a Japanese protectorate. Tokyo's deadline for winning the desired American concessions was November 25. The next day, the government issued its final orders for the task force Yamamoto had gathered to sail for Hawaii and attack Pearl Harbor.

PEARL HARBOR TO GUADALCANAL

On January 24, 1941, Rear Admiral Richmond Kelly Turner, who would become the leading American amphibious commander in the Pacific War, directing landings from Guadalcanal in August 1942 to Okinawa in April 1945, issued a warning to his superiors: "If war eventuates with Japan, it is believed easily possible that hostilities would be initiated by a surprise attack upon the Fleet or the Naval Base at Pearl Harbor."[8] Turner's warning was ignored, as were many other signs that precautions should be taken to protect that vital base. While a Japanese attack was widely expected, virtually the entire American military and political leadership was taken by surprise at where it took place. Indeed, both the president and his secretary of the navy thought the initial radio messages of the attack referred to the Philippines.

Aside from demonstrating American ineptitude, the Pearl Harbor attack owed its success to bold, improvisational Japanese planning (something American strategists had assumed they were incapable of), skilled execution, and a good measure of luck. However, not all the luck was on the Japanese side. The three American carriers normally based at Pearl Harbor—*Saratoga*, *Enterprise*, and *Lexington*—were elsewhere when the attack occurred. That was one of the disturbing facts noted by Yamamoto after the battle and certainly one of the reasons he wrote to a fellow admiral, "This war will give us much trouble in the future. The fact that we have had a small success at Pearl Harbor is nothing."[9] Still, Pearl Harbor was a most impressive display of Japanese military prowess and a devastating demonstration of how effective and decisive carrier-based aircraft could be.

Japan followed its victory at Pearl Harbor with a rapid advance toward the rich prizes of Southeast Asia and strategic islands in the Pacific. By mid-1942, its conquests included Guam, Wake Island, Hong Kong, Malaya and Singapore, and the Philippines. Once again Japanese air power was on display, especially on December 10, 1941, when warplanes sank the British battleships *Prince of Wales* and *Repulse*, the first time aircraft acting alone had accomplished such a feat. The worst American debacle was in the Philippines, where the fall of the Bataan Peninsula in April 1942 resulted in the capture of twelve thousand American soldiers and more than sixty thousand Filipino troops, who were brutally treated en route to prison camps in what is justifiably known as the Bataan Death March. The island of Corregidor, the last American stronghold, fell in May. General Douglas MacArthur, the American commander in the Philippines, was spared the ordeal of surrender when in early March President Roosevelt ordered him to leave his embattled troops and escape to Australia. Meanwhile, Japanese brutality toward prisoners and civilians, already amply demonstrated in China, simultaneously was on display in the Philippines, Singapore, and elsewhere in Asia.

The reversal of fortune in the Pacific began in May 1942. By then the United States had a new command structure in place. MacArthur was in charge of U.S. forces in the southwest Pacific. Admiral Chester Nimitz, who had been serving in Washington at the time of Pearl Harbor, was the new Commander in Chief of the Pacific Fleet and the Pacific Ocean Area. He sent two aircraft carriers and their supporting ships to stop the Japanese advance southward toward Port Moresby on the island of New Guinea, from which point the Japanese could threaten the flow of American troops and supplies to Australia and even Australia itself. Nimitz knew of the Japanese plans because Allied cryptographers had broken the Japanese naval code. The Americans met the Japanese fleet in the Coral Sea, north of Australia. The ensuing battle was the first in naval history fought entirely by aircraft. The opposing ships, again for the first time, never saw each other. Although considered a narrow Japanese tactical victory in terms of losses — the most important vessel lost was the U.S. carrier *Lexington* — the Battle of the Coral Sea was both strategic and psychological victory for the United States: the Japanese advance had been stopped, making the Battle of the Coral Sea Japan's first significant setback of World War II. That said, the initiative in the war still belonged to Tokyo.

A much more decisive battle between the two mighty navies took place in June near a speck of land in the mid-Pacific appropriately called Midway Island, where the United States had a small but strategically important naval base. The Japanese attacked Midway for two reasons. First, it would firm up their defensive line in the Pacific. Second, and of primary importance to Yamamoto, who planned the campaign, the assault would draw into battle the remaining American carriers in the Pacific and give him another desperately needed opportunity to destroy the American fleet and knock the United States out of the war. Otherwise, Yamamoto was convinced, a long war would follow that Japan could not possibly win. The Japanese had advantages in the experience of their skilled dive-bomber and torpedo-plane pilots and, it turned out, in carriers (four to the Americans' three). The key American advantage was that, as at the Coral Sea, Nimitz knew from his codebreakers about the Japanese plans. (MacArthur would derive a similar advantage when army special intelligence codebreakers, in a project called ULTRA, deciphered their first Japanese army transmission in September 1943 and began providing a steady flow of intelligence in early 1944.) Real Admiral Frank Fletcher, who had led American forces at the Battle of Coral Sea, commanded the naval strike force Nimitz sent to fight at Midway.

Seven aircraft carriers and their complement of hundreds of airplanes, supported by dozens of ships and, on the American side, land-based aircraft from Midway, began their mortal combat shortly after dawn on June 4, 1942. At first the battle went well for the Japanese and badly for the Americans. But the Japanese, who began the battle by bombing Midway itself, did not know when they launched their raid on Midway whether American carriers were in the area or, once they realized they were by being attacked by carrier-based torpedo aircraft, how many carriers the Americans had or where they were. It was America's great good fortune that at 10:24 a.m., thirty-seven dive-bombers from the carrier *Enterprise* found and surprised the four carriers of the Japanese fleet. Dive-bombers from *Yorktown* quickly joined them. In just five furious minutes, one of the most important battles of the Pacific War was decided. The American dive-bombers fatally damaged three of the carriers—*Kaga*, *Akagi*, and *Soryu*—all of which soon sank. That afternoon, planes from the remaining Japanese carrier, *Hiryu*, badly damaged *Yorktown* and knocked her out of the battle (a Japanese submarine later sank her), but several hours later American planes found and sank *Hiryu*.

Japan lost four of its best carriers and 322 planes at Midway. It also lost more than three thousand men, including many experienced aircraft carrier pilots. More than that, as Yamamoto knew too well, the Japanese navy lost its last chance to cripple the American navy and force the United States to agree to a negotiated peace. Japan still had formidable resources and had not lost the war. But the empire was no longer in a position to win it.

The short, fierce, air-sea Battle of Midway was followed by the long, bitter struggle for the jungle island of Guadalcanal, a battle that seesawed back and forth for months. Guadalcanal, one of the Solomon Islands, lies northeast of Australia and due east of New Guinea. The Japanese had landed there in May 1942 and begun building an airstrip from which they could have threatened American convoys to Australia and set the stage for further offensives. That made the island an American target, and in early August 1942 more than 11,000 U.S. marines landed on Guadalcanal, along with 4,500 more on three nearby islands. They quickly took the Guadalcanal airstrip, which they named Henderson Field in honor of a pilot who had died at Midway. The hard part proved to be holding

Henderson Field in the face of Japanese counterattacks, even when reinforced by more marines and army troops. The campaign that followed lasted more than six months and was fought viciously in numerous battles on land, sea, and air before the United States finally emerged victorious. The two navies fought seven major battles and about twenty lesser engagements and together lost nearly fifty warships. In one encounter, the Battle of Savo Island, the United States navy lost four cruisers within an hour and suffered the worst defeat, other than Pearl Harbor, in its history. Hundreds of planes went down in more than thirty air or air-sea battles around Guadalcanal. Almost 5,000 American sailors died along with more than 1,700 ground troops. The Japanese lost 3,500 sailors and more than 1,200 airmen. On land, their dead numbered close to 25,000, more than half lost to starvation and disease, by the time Tokyo decided in February 1943 to salvage what it could and evacuated its 11,000 remaining troops.[10]

Two months later the empire suffered another disastrous loss when American fighters—acting on information provided by navy codebreakers—intercepted and shot down Yamamoto's airplane while he was on an inspection tour, killing the indispensable admiral.

Each side learned hard lessons at Guadalcanal. The Japanese, in the words of one naval officer who fought there, learned the price of relying uncritically on the "unfounded assurances" given by the army and of the dangers inherent in "a general contempt for the capabilities of the enemy." He added, "Thus lay open the road to Tokyo."[11] The Americans learned two important things. First, they could beat the formidable Japanese on land, air, or sea. Second, those victories would come at a terribly high price. As historian Richard B. Frank has noted, "The first intimations that the Japanese would literally choose death over surrender—and not merely an elite warrior caste but the rank and file—came . . . at Guadalcanal."[12] Japanese troops were not only fierce and superb jungle fighters, but time after time they had also fought to the last man. As one exhausted and exasperated marine told journalist John Hersey, who in 1943 chronicled a single jungle skirmish, one of hundreds, in his gripping *Into the Valley*, the Japanese "take to the jungle as if they had been bred there, and like some beasts you never see them until they are dead."[13] Major General Alexander A. Vandegrift, who led one of the marine divisions on Guadalcanal from August to December 1942, grimly observed, "I have never heard or read of this kind of fighting. These people refuse to surrender. The wounded wait until men come up to examine them . . . and blow themselves and the other fellow to pieces with a hand grenade."[14]

American soldiers did not have to wait long for confirmation of their experience on Guadalcanal. It was duplicated on nearby New Guinea, where an Allied offensive under MacArthur to drive the Japanese from the island began in late 1942. Although his campaign was largely successful, MacArthur would be engaged on New Guinea until 1944, and the last Japanese soldiers on the huge island did not lay down their arms until mid-September 1945, almost a month after their government surrendered. In May 1943, on the frozen and desolate island of Attu, part of Alaska's Aleutian chain, a Japanese garrison of 2,350 men fought until only twenty-nine were left, a fatality rate of 98.8 percent. Beginning in November 1943, American and Australian soldiers killed thousands of Japanese fighting, often hand to hand, in the fetid jungles and swamps of Bougainville, the largest of the Solomon Islands. Thousands more Japanese, cut off from reinforcements and supplies, starved to death. Yet others continued to fight and did not surrender until after the war had ended. The bitter experience of Guadalcanal would be repeated on an even larger scale in a series of bloody island battles in the Pacific. As historian Stanley Weintraub has put it, "Japanese resistance as the home islands became threatened increased from fierce to fanatical to suicidal."[15] If the road to Tokyo "lay open," it nonetheless was going to be a long, hard road, one that tens of thousands of American fighting men would never finish.

TARAWA TO THE PHILIPPINES

Now permanently on the offensive, in late 1943 the United States began to close the ring on Japan. It invaded and took strategic Pacific islands progressively closer to Japan's home islands, which finally made it possible for long-range American bombers to attack manufacturing centers vital to Tokyo's war effort. Meanwhile, American submarines, later assisted by carrier-based aircraft, gradually but inexorably sank the ships and closed the sea-lanes that brought oil, food, rubber, iron ore, and other essential supplies to the home islands. From the start of the war, Japan had lacked the economic and industrial base to match the United States in producing the modern arms and machines of war. As the war continued, that imbalance became more pronounced. Nonetheless, the Japanese fought on. At first, as outlined in a policy document adopted in September 1943, the goal was to establish a defense line that still stretched as far south as northern New Guinea and eastward to the Gilbert Islands. Prime Minister Tojo spoke for his colleagues when he told the emperor that "we have to fight onto the end regardless of how the war situation may develop hereafter. Nothing has changed in our resolve to fight until we achieve our aims."[16] After American forces in the southwest Pacific under MacArthur and in the central Pacific under Nimitz pierced that perimeter, the military and the emperor turned to a new version of decisive victory: a battle that Japan would not only win, but that also would so bloody the Americans that they would agree to a negotiated peace on terms acceptable to Tokyo. Meanwhile, each island and piece of territory would be yielded to the Americans only after extracting the maximum possible price in blood.

The first major step in the American offensive was the November 1943 attack on Tarawa, an atoll in the Gilbert Islands whose main value was as an air base. Almost five thousand men defended the atoll's main island, a chunk of coral smaller than New York City's Central Park or the Pentagon and its parking lots. It was the first amphibious assault against fortified beaches on a Pacific island, and mistakes were made, including failing to bombard Japanese positions sufficiently, an error that cost the lives of many marines who assaulted the beaches. The battle for Tarawa lasted three murderous days. When it was over, a thousand marines were dead. Of the four marines awarded the Medal of Honor in the battle, three received their medals posthumously. The Japanese again fought to the bitter end: only a few wounded men were captured, putting their death rate at 99.7 percent. When Admiral Nimitz visited the island, the sight of rotting corpses and body parts literally made him sick. To prepare the public for what they now knew lay ahead, the marines released, for the first time, pictures of the carnage to the American press, causing a wave of shock, revulsion, and fear across the country.

After securing the Gilberts, American forces took the Marshall Islands to the northwest in a series of relatively minor but still bloody battles. Once again, the Japanese garrisons refused to surrender, suffering fatality rates of more than 98 percent.[17] The next major battle occurred in the Mariana Islands, one of which, Guam, had been an American possession until the Japanese seized it shortly after Pearl Harbor. The Marianas were a critically important asset because they put Japan's home islands within range of America's B-29 bombers: both of the B-29s that dropped atomic bombs on Japan in August 1945 would take off from Tinian, one of the three main islands of the Marianas group.

The largest of three major battles was fought for Saipan, an island fourteen miles long and between two to five miles wide, where the Japanese had more than thirty thousand troops. There also were more than twenty thousand Japanese civilians on Saipan. The American invasion force consisted of 71,000 marines and army troops. The fight for Saipan began on June 15 and lasted for three weeks. The last major battle occurred on July 7, when about three thousand Japanese troops charged American positions in a suicide frontal attack called a banzai charge, the largest, though not the first, such desperate attack of the war. It left almost all the attackers dead but also inflicted heavy casualties on the Americans. It was impossible, even for veteran troops, not to be demoralized by what they had experienced. In the words of Lieutenant General Holland Smith, the marine commander, "Saipan was war such as nobody had fought before: a campaign in which men crawled, clubbed, shot, burned, and bayoneted each other to death."[18]

But there were shocks in store for the Americans that went beyond even the fighting. On July 11, at a cliff called Marpi Point, about a thousand trapped soldiers and a like number of civilians—including women and children—shot, beheaded, or drowned each other or killed themselves, despite attempts by Japanese-speaking American troops using loudspeakers to get them to stop. While many civilians committed suicide on their own, in many cases soldiers made sure that they could not choose the option of surrendering. Not even the pleas of Japanese prisoners, who told their compatriots that the Americans were treating them well, could stop the slaughter. As the waters around Marpi Point literally turned red with blood, even battle-hardened marines were forced to turn their heads, sickened by what they had seen and gravely worried about what the fanaticism it represented meant for them in battles to come.

Saipan also produced what seems to be the first rough estimate of what losses Americans would suffer in defeating Japan. It was part of a report submitted on August 30 to the Joint Chiefs of Staff, the top military body for direction of the war effort. The paper estimated, based on the ratio of American to Japanese casualties on Saipan, that "it might cost us half a million American lives and many times that number" to destroy Japanese forces defending the home islands against an invasion[19] (see Document B1). This "Saipan ratio," which would be followed by other projections in the wake of later island battles closer to Japan, had disturbing implications for American war planners. It clearly worried U.S. Army Chief of Staff George C. Marshall because of the high casualties it suggested for the future operations closer to Japan and against the Japanese home islands themselves[20] (see Document B2).

In attempting to defend the Marianas, Japan mobilized much of its remaining naval strength. The objective was to deal the American fleet a decisive defeat and reverse the tide of battle in the Pacific. Instead, a lopsided battle took place in the Philippine Sea, the section of the Pacific Ocean between the Philippines and the Marianas. In what Americans called the "Marianas' Turkey Shoot," on June 19–20 seasoned and skilled American pilots flying a new and improved aircraft, the F6F Grumman Hellcat, overwhelmed the inexperienced Japanese flyers, their ranks depleted of experienced pilots by earlier battles. The Japanese navy lost about four hundred aircraft along with three carriers. While most of its ships managed to withdraw, leaving the Japanese navy with enough powerful battleships and cruisers to remain a dangerous force, the back of Tokyo's naval aviation was broken. The Battle of the Philippine Sea, the largest carrier battle of the war, was also the last.

It also was the last battle for Prime Minister Tojo and his government, which lost the support of Hirohito and had to resign on July 18. Tojo was succeeded by General Kuniaki Koiso, who inherited the unenviable task of trying to salvage something from the disastrous war. His government would serve for eight months, until April 1945.

RETURN TO THE PHILIPPINES

Before attacking the Philippines, marines and army troops were sent to seize Peleliu, one of the Palau Islands about five hundred miles east of the Philippines. Rugged and covered with jungle, Peleliu turned out to be the scene of yet another incredibly difficult battle. At Peleliu, American fighting men encountered the new Japanese strategy of not defending the beach. Rather than expose themselves to withering bombardment from offshore ships, the Japanese on Peleliu remained inland, then contested every inch of the way from hidden positions as the Americans tried to move inland. The battle for Peleliu lasted from mid-September to mid-October 1944, about four times longer than expected. The casualties were staggering: the First Marine Division, which bore the brunt of the battle during the first two weeks, suffered a casualty rate of 53.7 percent. Other army and marine units had rates almost as high. It was no wonder that Private E. B. Sledge, in his memoir of fighting in the Pacific, remembered Peleliu as an "assault into hell."[21] That assault, it turned out, was not necessary. After the battle, American military planners concluded that Peleliu could have been bypassed, as were other Japanese-held islands as part of the American strategy known as "island hopping," without harming future operations.

The campaign to retake the Philippines was a vast operation that began on October 20, 1944, when the first of 200,000 soldiers landed on the island of Leyte. General MacArthur dramatically waded ashore that day in a scene he made sure was copiously photographed and that included his famous announcement, "People of the Philippines, I have returned!" Whatever the people of the Philippines thought of MacArthur's famous photo op, it was not a scene that endeared the general to American critics of his performance as a commander or those who could not suffer his enormous ego. By March, the capital of Manila on the main island of Luzon was secured and a Philippine civil government had been restored. On June 30, MacArthur announced that most of the country was liberated, but fighting went on, even on Luzon, until the end of the war.

The struggle for the Philippines included the titanic Battle of Leyte Gulf. The greatest naval battle in history, it engaged almost three hundred ships. Actually a series of encounters fought during three days in late October 1944 that extended outward from Leyte Gulf over tens of thousands of square miles of empty ocean, the battle effectively destroyed the Japanese navy as a fighting force. It also saw the appearance of the first organized attacks by squads of kamikazes, Japanese pilots who deliberately crashed their planes into American ships, taking a large toll. On land, especially on Luzon, American soldiers faced a skillful defense, organized by General Tomoyuki Yamashita. It allowed the Americans to land unopposed; once they reached mountainous inland terrain, however, a dense web of obstacles and fortifications forced them to move slowly and made them pay dearly for every advance. The battle for Manila was ferocious, the destruction it caused made worse by a massive wave of Japanese atrocities against Filipino civilians. By the time it was over, 100,000 civilians were dead from the fighting and atrocities committed by the Japanese. The city itself lay in ruins. Although the Americans received valuable assistance from tens of thousands of Filipino guerrillas, they paid a heavy price for liberating the Philippines: almost 14,000 killed and more than 48,000 wounded. An estimated 250,000 Japanese, including civilians, died in the futile defense of the archipelago. General Yamashita retreated into the mountains of northern Luzon, where he held out with about 65,000 troops until August 15, 1945, the day after the emperor informed the United States that Japan would surrender.[22]

IWO JIMA AND OKINAWA

Japan saved the worst for last: the battles of Iwo Jima and Okinawa. Iwo Jima, 660 miles south of Tokyo, is a volcanic island of about eight square miles shaped like a pork chop. Its name means "sulfur island" in Japanese, and it is a desolate place, reeking from sulfur and other noxious gases that seep from its sands and rocks as a result of low-level volcanic activity below its barren surface. Iwo Jima's rugged topography and the softness of its volcanic rock, which allows for tunneling and building underground fortifications and shelters, made it an ideal place to defend and a dreadful place to attack. Regardless of which side one was on and even before the start of the battle, Iwo Jima was a repulsive place. To one Japanese officer, Iwo Jima was "an island of sulphur, no water, no sparrow, no swallow." To an American marine, the island looked "like hell with the fire out, but still smoking."[23]

Iwo Jima became one of the worst battlegrounds of World War II because it was a vital part of Japan's inner defense zone, the "doorkeeper to the Imperial capital," as one Japanese officer put it.[24] Indeed, in late 1944 and early 1945 it partially blocked sustained bombing of Japan's cities by American B-29s. Despite their advanced technology, the B-29s were having limited success in their strategic bombing campaign, which was designed to destroy Japan's industrial infrastructure and thereby its ability to continue the war. The bombers were at the very limit of their range when they had to fly round-trip missions over open ocean from the Marianas to Japan's home islands. Once over Japan, poor weather conditions, including cloud cover about 70 percent of the time and winds that varied in direction and intensity, made it almost impossible to bomb specific targets with any degree of accuracy. It was, in fact, the failure of strategic bombing in late 1944 and early 1945 that led Major General Curtis LeMay, commander of the XXI Bomber Command, which had the assignment to attack Japan from the air, to turn to area bombing employing incendiary bombs. Those raids began in February 1945, but the first major attack took place in March when 300 B-29s from the Marianas attacked Tokyo. The results were devastating: more than 80,000 people were killed and at least 250,000 buildings and twenty-two major industrial targets destroyed. An area of more than fifteen square miles was leveled.

Still, the B-29s were at risk, and Iwo Jima was a big part of the problem. On their way to Japan, they faced attacks from fighters based on the island. Avoiding those attacks used up precious fuel, which for many crews meant they would run out of fuel during the return trip and have to ditch at sea, where rescue was problematic at best. Even after American bombers destroyed Iwo Jima's airfields, the island's radar provided warning to the home of approaching B-29s. Finally, the island, once in American hands, was the ideal place for fuel-starved or damaged B-29s to land on their return fight, something that happened for the first time in early March, well before the battle for Iwo Jima was over. Iwo Jima also could provide bases for new American P-51 Mustang fighters, which could then accompany the B-29s on their missions and protect them against Japanese fighters.

On February 19, 1945, the first elements of a force of more than seventy thousand marines landed on Iwo Jima. The battle that followed was the largest amphibious marine assault ever, and the bloodiest. Every day for more than two months before the actual landing, American bombers had attacked Iwo Jima. The seventy-four-day assault from the air, the longest of the war, had been followed by four days of point-blank bombardment by battleships, the largest pounding from the sea of the war. It was not nearly enough. The Japanese had built a network of 1,500 fortified caves, hundreds of pillboxes, blockhouses, and covered trenches, and miles of interconnected tunnels. Most of these fortifications survived the American bombardment, and from them, skillfully led by Lieutenant General Tadamichi Kuribayashi, the Japanese garrison of 21,000 men fought a dogged, vicious war of attrition. Kuribayashi decided not to defend Iwo Jima's beaches. Instead, his gunners allowed the Americans to come ashore. When the beaches were crowded with troops, the Japanese opened up with heavy weapons, pounding the exposed Marines, who had nowhere to go but forward into enemy fire. By the end of the first day, with 30,000 marines ashore, more than 560 were dead and almost 2,000 wounded.

Nor did matters improve as the Marines moved inland. One marine correspondent described a tiny part of the deadly cat-and-mouse fight his comrades faced on Iwo Jima's craggy hills and ridges:

Despite their preponderance of weapons, the Marines found that there were too many holes. They would attack one only to be shot at from another one half a dozen feet away. Moreover, the ridge was not a straight wall but, in many places, curved like an S. Entranceways protected each other, so that Marines would be hit in the back from holes guarding the one they were assaulting. The interconnecting tunnels inside the ridge also allowed the Japs to play deadly tag with the Marines. They would shoot out of one hole. But by the time Marines got close enough to that hole, the Japs had left it and were shooting from another one twenty yards away and higher up in the wall. The Marines had to post guards at every hole they could see in order to attack any of them. The tunnel also curved and twisted inside the ridge. The Japs could escape the straight trajectory weapons and grenades thrown into the cave entrances, merely by running back into the interior.[25]

The battle for Iwo Jima lasted for five excruciating weeks, into the last week of March, much longer than American commanders had expected. The Japanese garrison again fought to the end. Only about two hundred enemy soldiers were taken prisoner, and most of those were wounded. The Americans were staggered by their losses: more than 6,800 dead and almost 20,000 wounded, far more than the 10,000 casualties that were expected. Those casualties included more than 2,600 navy losses, many from kamikaze attacks against ships offshore. For the first time in the war, the Japanese in defeat had inflicted more total casualties than they had suffered from the victorious Americans. Of the twenty-four marine battalion commanders who landed on Iwo Jima, five were killed and twelve others wounded. Some regiments had casualty rates of 75 percent. Not even the medical teams were spared: twenty-three surgeons died on Iwo Jima, along with 827 medical corpsmen. Four of those corpsmen were among the twenty-seven Americans who were awarded Medals of Honor, a record for any battle, thirteen of them posthumously. Iwo Jima gave the country what was the most famous battle picture of the Pacific War: the five marines and one navy corpsman raising the American flag on Mount Surabachi on the fourth day of the battle, a moment captured by Associated Press photographer Joe Rosenthal. Of the six, three were killed in the fighting that followed and two others were wounded. The marine cameraman who shot the moving picture of the flag raising was also killed on Iwo Jima. Admiral Nimitz summed up what happened there as well as anyone could when he wrote that on Iwo Jima, "uncommon valor was a common virtue."[26]

Between March 1945 and Japan's surrender in August of that year, 2,251 B-29s carrying more than 24,700 crewmen made emergency landings on Iwo Jima. Because a significant number of those crewmen would have been lost at sea, and because P-51 fighters reduced B-29 losses over Japan, Iwo Jima did save thousands of American lives in the months to come. That did not make the looming prospect of invading Japan any more palatable to American planners, both because of the huge overall losses the Marines had just suffered and because many of the regiments expected to play a key role in the assault on Japan proper had been battered, and some virtually decimated, on Iwo Jima.

Okinawa, 794 square miles in area, the largest island of the Ryukyu chain, lies less than four hundred miles south of Kyushu, the southernmost Japanese home island. Annexed by Tokyo in the 1870, the Ryukyus were considered a part of the home islands by 1945, which accounted for Okinawa's emotional importance. Its strategic importance stemmed from its location: close enough to Japan proper for escort fighters and bombers other than B-29s to make the trip and to serve as the main staging area for the invasion of Kyushu, where the assault on Japan proper was expected to begin before the end of the year. Tokyo assigned its defense to Lieutenant General Mitsuru Ushijima, who had about 76,000 Japanese troops and 24,000 impressed Okinawan militiamen for the job. Like Kuribayashi on Iwo Jima, Ushijima would win the grudging respect of the Americans for his wickedly effective defense of Okinawa. General Simon Bolivar Buckner Jr. commanded the American assault force of 183,000 soldiers and marines. Like Ushijima, Buckner would die on Okinawa. Transporting and backing up the assault force was a huge naval flotilla of carriers, battleships, and other craft—a total of more than twelve hundred ships and a thousand carrier planes—that one sailor described as stretching "to the horizon. . . . I couldn't have imagined that many ships existed in the world."[27]

The Japanese were outgunned, outnumbered, and cut off from reinforcements, but they fought with the same fury and fanaticism that their comrades had displayed in previous battles. To that was added the most extensive and lethal use of kamikazes yet seen against American naval forces. The resulting collision between the irresistible and the immovable produced the deadliest single battle of the Pacific War.

The first American troops landed on Okinawa on April 1, 1945. After meeting no resistance on the beaches, they soon ran into elaborate and well-planned Japanese defenses and soldiers who fought from them like those on Iwo Jima. The Americans who had hoped that bombardment from artillery ashore and ships at sea would rout the Japanese from their dug-in positions were to be disappointed. As one marine commander recalled, "It seemed nothing could possibly be living in that churning mass where the shells were falling and roaring but when we next advanced, Japs would still be there, even madder than they were before."[28] Some of the worst fighting took place at Japanese fortifications in the southern part of the island known as the Shuri Line, which took its name from a nearby castle. E. B. Sledge, a veteran of the horror of Peleliu, described his experiences there:

The stench of death was overpowering. The only way I could bear the monstrous horror of it all was to look upward away from the earthly reality surrounding us, watch the leaden gray clouds go skudding [*sic*] over, and repeat over and over to myself that the situation was unreal—just a nightmare—that I would soon awake and find myself somewhere else. But the ever-present smell of death saturated my nostrils. It was there with every breath I took.

I existed from moment to moment, sometimes thinking death would be preferable. We were in the depths of the abyss, the ultimate horror of war. During the fighting around Umurbrogol Pocket on Peleliu, I had been depressed by the wastage of human lives. But in the mud and driving rain before Shuri, we were surrounded by maggots and decay so degrading I believed we had been flung into hell's own cesspool.[29]

Offshore, the navy was under assault by thousands of planes, many of them kamikazes, which over the course of the battle sank thirty-six ships and damaged ten times that many. Kamikaze pilots accounted for all but two of the ships that were sunk. The aircraft they flew included the newly developed Okha, Japanese for "cherry blossom," a rocket-powered plane launched from a bomber. A witness described one of the most destructive kamikaze attacks, the third of the day on May 14 to hit the carrier *Enterprise*, the most decorated ship of its kind in the U.S. Navy. *Enterprise* survived the attack but sustained enough damage to knock her out of the war:

All the batteries were firing: the 5-inch guns, the 40 mm and 20 mm, even the rifles. The Japanese aircraft dived through the rain of steel. It had been hit in several places and seemed to be trailing a banner of flame and smoke but it came on, clearly visible, hardly moving, the line of its wings as straight as a sword.

The deck was deserted; every man, with the exception of the gunners, was lying flat on his face. Flaming and roaring, the fireball passed in front of the "island" superstructure and crashed with a terrible impact just behind the forward lift. The entire vessel was shaken, some forty yards of the flight deck folded up like a banana skin.[30]

Okinawa was declared secure on June 22 and the battle itself officially declared over on July 2. The army and marines suffered almost 40,000 dead and wounded. Non-battle casualties resulting from causes such as disease and combat fatigue—the latter mainly the result of the intensity of the fighting and constant artillery and mortar bombardment—ran the total casualties to more than 72,000. Offshore, the navy suffered its largest single-battle losses in its history: almost 10,000 dead and wounded.

Far afield from Okinawa, a lot changed as the fighting raged from April through June. In Japan, the Koiso government fell. On April 8 a new government took office, with seventy-eight-year-old Kantaro Suzuki, a retired admiral and hero of the Russo-Japanese war, as prime minister. In the United States, on April 12, President Franklin D. Roosevelt died of a massive stroke; his successor was the inexperienced Harry S. Truman. In Europe, on May 8, 1945, Germany surrendered unconditionally to the Allies, ending the war in Europe and depriving Japan of its main ally. Meanwhile, the impact of the battle for Okinawa was felt in Washington and Tokyo, although not necessarily as one might have expected. In Tokyo, some military men took heart. Their troops on Okinawa, under extremely disadvantageous conditions, had held out for almost three months and inflicted huge casualties on the Americans. They anticipated, in part by using suicide weapons (manned torpedoes, midget submarines, and human mines as well as thousands of piloted kamikaze aircraft) to attack troopships, that they could inflict such heavy casualties on the Americans in the battle for Kyushu that Washington would abandon its demand for unconditional surrender, which had been Allied policy since it was announced in January 1943, and agree to a negotiated peace, one that would leave Japan unoccupied and its present form of government intact. In Washington, the dread of that next battle mounted, even as President Truman, on June 18, authorized the invasion of Kyushu to go forward[31] (see Document A27). At the same time, the search for a less costly way to end the war on Allied terms continued. That search would have its historic impact not only on Japan and the end of World War II but also on the entire postwar world that emerged from that horrific struggle.

CHAPTER 4

The Decision to Drop the Bomb

The decision to drop the atomic bomb on Japan, unquestionably one of the most momentous made by Americans during World War II and probably the most controversial, ironically was in many ways a nondecision: that is, the use of the bomb was integral to the decision to build it, the assumption being that the atomic bomb would be employed when ready if it was necessary to win or end the war. Although some critics have charged that racism played an important role in the decision to use the bomb against Japan and that it would never have been used against white Europeans, there is overwhelming consensus among historians that it would have been used against Germany had it been necessary to defeat the Nazis and end the war in Europe.[1] After all, before developing the atomic bomb, the United States used massed waves of heavy bombers, the most destructive force in its arsenal, against Germany. It also used incendiary weapons against German cities, albeit on a smaller scale than against Japanese urban areas. More to the point, the Manhattan Project was undertaken as a response to the German threat. President Roosevelt had made it clear that he was prepared to employ the bomb against Germany, and the original orders for training airmen to drop the bomb applied to Germany as well as Japan. By the fall of 1944, Germany no longer was a likely target, since it was increasingly clear that the Nazis would be defeated before the Manhattan Project could produce any atomic bombs. Still, in his memoirs, General Groves recalled that as late as December 1944, President Roosevelt told him, in Stimson's presence, that if the war in Europe was not over before the first atomic bombs were ready, the military should be prepared to use them against Germany. Therefore, in August 1945, when the news of Hiroshima reached a defeated and occupied Germany and some Germans were heard to say, "Thank God this came after we had been defeated and not before," they were right to feel lucky, in terms of both American intent and the sequence of events that spared Germany from sharing Japan's fate.[2]

As regards Japan, between the end of 1944 and August 6, 1945, nothing of sufficient significance occurred to cause the American leadership—and the British, whose approval was required by agreement—to reevaluate the assumption in place from the start that the atomic bomb would be used if it was needed to end the war.[3] Instead, events by degrees reinforced that assumption and ultimately turned it into a final decision. In particular, American policy makers saw no sign they considered credible that Japan was prepared to surrender on terms acceptable to the Allies. To the contrary, what they saw was Japanese resistance intensifying as the battlefront approached the home islands. On the American side, morale among troops slated to invade Japan was low, and war weariness was spreading on the home front, especially as civilians learned of the staggering casualty figures from the battles of Iwo Jima and Okinawa.

It is worth noting that the atomic bomb was not the only weapon originally developed for use against Germany but employed only against Japan. Before Japan was hit by atomic weapons, it was attacked for months by another new high-tech weapon developed at about the same time and at a similar cost (although brought to completion more quickly) with the German threat in mind but never used against the Third Reich: the B-29 Superfortress bomber. The development of the B-29 resulted in large part from the anticipated need to defend the United States against Nazi Germany if the Germans succeeded in overrunning Europe. That objective and the ultimate goal of carrying the war to Germany required a new long-range bomber, which turned out to be the B-29. The B-29, the development and production of more than three thousand of which actually cost more than the Manhattan Project, entered combat in mid-1944 and started bombing Japan from bases in the Mariana Islands in November. The first incendiary raids against Japanese cities took place in late February 1945, and the devastating attack on Tokyo that killed an estimated eighty thousand people took place in early March. The only plane in the American arsenal capable of delivering a load as massive as an atomic bomb, the B-29 therefore became the delivery system that brought those bombs from the American base on the tiny island of Tinian in the Marianas to the cities of Hiroshima and Nagasaki in Japan.[4]

Two other considerations led to the use of the atomic bomb. First, the United States and its allies were committed to a policy of unconditional surrender. That policy officially dated from the Casablanca Conference in January 1943 between Roosevelt and British Prime Minister Winston Churchill but had roots reaching back to the early days of the war. It was based on the conviction that both Nazism and Japanese militarism had to be uprooted in order to provide for a permanent postwar peace.[5] That meant that Germany and Japan would have to be totally defeated so that the Allies could occupy both countries and implement in each a thorough program of reform. The memory of World War I loomed darkly over American policy makers as they looked to the end of the current war. As one State Department analyst put it well before Casablanca, "We are fighting this war because we did not have unconditional surrender at the end of the last one."[6] The policy of unconditional surrender was controversial, and to some extent remains so, because of the belief in some quarters that Japan might have been willing to accept surrender before August 1945 had it been offered less onerous terms, in particular a clearly stated commitment to allow the emperor to remain on his throne. Others argue in response that there is no evidence whatsoever that such a commitment prior to the use of the atomic bomb would have brought about a Japanese surrender because the gap between minimum Allied demands and conditions acceptable to the men who controlled Japan was far too wide to bridge with that simple formula.

Second, the bomb was never viewed as certain to bring about an immediate Japanese surrender by itself. Rather, it became part of the mix to increase pressure on the Japanese government to the breaking point. Before July 1945, that mix included continuing the policy of bombardment and blockade on one hand and planning for an invasion of the Japanese homeland on the other. There was disagreement within the American military about those options, in particular whether bombardment and blockade alone could end the war within a reasonable time frame and how great the cost in lives would be in an invasion of Japan. Some top-level Navy and Army Air Forces officers (an independent air force was not established until after the war) believed that the United States could end the war through bombardment and blockade. However, General Marshall and the Army were convinced that only an invasion would force Japan's surrender within an acceptable period, and on May 25, 1945, the Joint Chiefs of Staff endorsed the first stage of a proposed two-stage plan to invade Japan. That plan actually combined all the available options: blockade and bombardment would continue until the projected invasion date of November 1, 1945[7] (see Documents B6 and B7). Another important factor in the Joint Chiefs' considerations was the promise made by the Soviet Union at the Yalta conference of February 1945, which at the time still had a neutrality pact with Japan, to scrap that agreement and enter the war against Japan three months after Germany's defeat. Soviet participation was considered vital, inasmuch as it would tie up Japanese forces in Manchuria that otherwise might be deployed to defend against the American invasion of Kyushu.

The question before June 1945 was what President Truman would decide to do. He had to make his decision in the wake of dreadful casualty totals in the battles of Iwo Jima and Okinawa, falling morale in the military as soldiers contemplated what awaited them when they invaded Japan's home islands, and pressure on the home front to end the war as quickly as possible without further massive losses.[8] Truman endorsed Operation Olympic, the first stage of the planned invasion of Japan, at a meeting with top advisors on June 18. A month later, the successful test of the plutonium bomb took place, and hopes rose that its use, in tandem with the other pressures on Japan, could force surrender. Interestingly, when the atomic bombings of Hiroshima and Nagasaki did not bring about an immediate unconditional surrender, General Marshall began thinking of using atomic bombs tactically in support of the upcoming invasion to wipe out Japanese beach defenses.[9]

FROM ROOSEVELT TO TRUMAN

As already noted, by the fall of 1944 Germany no longer was a likely target of atomic bombs. That left Japan, and in September 1944 Roosevelt and Churchill secretly agreed that when a bomb became available, "it might perhaps, after mature consideration, be used against the Japanese, who should be warned that this bombardment will be repeated until they surrender"[10] (see Document A6). In December, a special Air Force unit called the 509th Composite Group, commanded by Colonel Paul W. Tibbets, began training at a base in Utah to drop what its men were told with deliberate vagueness was a special bomb. On April 16, 1945, four days after he was inaugurated as president following Roosevelt's death, Harry Truman confirmed the American commitment to unconditional surrender in his first speech to Congress as commander in chief. He restated that position in a press conference in early May. Significantly, Truman, even as vice president, had only a general idea regarding what the Manhattan Project was building. Within a day of assuming the presidency he was given additional sketchy information by James Byrnes, formerly the director of the Office of War Mobilization, and Secretary of War Henry L. Stimson before receiving a full briefing from Stimson and General Groves on April 25[11] (see Documents A10 and A11). On Stimson's recommendation, Truman approved the formation of what the secretary of war called a "select committee of particular qualifications" to make recommendations for both wartime and postwar atomic policy[12] (see Document A11). Called the Interim Committee, it included Stimson as chairman and Byrnes among its eight members. The committee added to its ranks an advisory scientific panel composed of Oppenheimer, Fermi, E. O. Lawrence, and Arthur Compton. Two days later, another committee charged with only immediate concerns, the Target Committee, met for the first time under the chairmanship of Brigadier General Thomas F. Farrell, Groves's deputy at the Manhattan Project. The Target Committee included two Air Force officers, General Farrell, and five scientists. Its job was to come up with four possible targets that could be attacked with atomic weapons between July and September.[13]

While matters relating to the bomb obviously were of crucial importance, Truman had plenty of other urgent concerns requiring his immediate attention. The battle for Okinawa had begun on April 1 and had turned into yet another bloody quagmire, with casualty reports growing worse by the day. Truman also had to deal with unresolved and urgent diplomatic issues such as tensions with the Soviet Union related to the approaching end of the war in Europe and the formation of the United Nations. Domestic concerns, including getting his administration organized and preparing a budget for the next fiscal year, also demanded presidential attention. Meanwhile, work continued on building the bomb and planning for its use.

THE INTERIM COMMITTEE

It was the Interim Committee, in meetings on May 31 and June 1, 1945, that undertook the next significant discussions about the atomic bomb. Marshall and Groves attended both meetings by invitation. Once again, the underlying assumption was that these weapons would be used when they became available. As Arthur Compton later recalled, "it seemed to be a foregone conclusion that the bomb would be used. It was regarding only the details of strategy and tactics that differing views were expressed."[14] The meeting on May 31 covered a variety of matters. The participants discussed future development of atomic weapons, including the certainty that a thermonuclear fusion bomb, far more powerful than any fission bomb, could be built. The discussion of the Soviet Union yielded an interesting willingness in some circles to trust Stalin when Oppenheimer opined that "we might open up this subject with them in a tentative fashion and in the most general terms" and Marshall suggested two Soviet scientists be invited to witness the first atomic test, ideas immediately rejected by Byrnes. An important conversation among those present that was not recorded in the minutes because it took place during lunch concerned a possible demonstration of the new weapon before using it to attack a Japanese city. The idea ran up against the fears that the test might be a dud, which would be a disaster; that the

Japanese, who obviously would have to be told of the site of the demonstration, might stop it by bringing American prisoners there; or that the Japanese might shoot down the American plane carrying the bomb. When the meeting resumed, Oppenheimer touched briefly on the psychological impact of the bomb, in particular, how aside from its destructive force, its visual effect—"a brilliant luminescence which would rise to a height of 10,000 to 20,000 feet"—might undermine Japan's will to fight. This emphasis on the "shock value" of the bomb as a means of bringing about a Japanese surrender would be central in the thinking of several American strategists, including Marshall and Stimson. After further discussion, Stimson summed up what he considered the committee's conclusions: Japan would not be warned; the United States would not "concentrate" on a civilian area but nonetheless try "to make a profound psychological impression on as many . . . inhabitants as possible"; and that the "most desirable target would be a vital war plant employing a large number of workers and closely surrounded by workers' houses"[15] (see Document A15).

The June 1 meeting again included Marshall and Groves, as well as four "invited industrialists," whose expertise was sought mainly on a number of postwar issues. The "use of the bomb" was not discussed until the afternoon, after the departure of the industrialists and Stimson, with Byrnes in the chair. Aside from affirming the discussion of the day before, the committee agreed that the final selection of a target was "essentially a military decision" and that the bomb "should be used against Japan as soon as possible"[16] (see Document A17). Byrnes then informed Truman of the committee's conclusions.

Not everyone involved in the Manhattan Project believed the bomb should be used, especially not without further investigating other possible options. Some prominent scientists working at the Metallurgical Laboratory (Met Lab), concerned that a postwar nuclear arms race could lead to a war that would destroy civilization and encouraged by Leo Szilard, formed a committee to urge that the bomb not be used against Japan. The committee of seven, chaired by physical chemist and Nobel Laureate James Franck, issued its appeal on June 11. Having warned of a potentially catastrophic arms race, the Franck Report called for a demonstration of the "new weapon" before representatives of the United Nations "on a desert or barren island." The bomb could then "perhaps" be used if necessary, with the approval of the United Nations and the American public, "perhaps after a preliminary ultimatum to Japan to surrender or at least to evacuate certain regions as an alternative to their total destruction." These sentiments were echoed a month later in a petition circulated by Szilard and signed by sixty-eight Met Lab scientists[17] (see Documents A23 and A38). The Franck Report in turn became a matter for discussion by the Interim Committee's Scientific Panel. On June 16, Robert Oppenheimer, speaking for the panel, reported its members did not believe a "technical demonstration" would have the necessary effect on Japan and that therefore "we see no acceptable alternative to direct military use"[18] (see Document A24).

MATTERS OF DIPLOMACY

By June, discussions on the use of the bomb increasingly were entangled with two other pressing issues: Truman's upcoming conference with Stalin and Churchill at Potsdam, which had a wide-ranging agenda, from postwar arrangements and problems in Europe to the proposed Soviet role in the war against Japan, and the final decision whether to go ahead with the invasion of Japan. The president's conversation with Stimson on June 6 dealt with the Potsdam Conference. Relations between the United States and Britain on one hand and the Soviet Union on the other had been deteriorating since the Yalta conference of February 1945, mainly because the Soviets were imposing Communist-dominated governments on Poland and other Eastern European countries occupied by their armies. In his first diplomatic venture as president, a meeting on April 23 with Soviet foreign minister Vyacheslav Molotov, Truman had been exceeding blunt about American concerns, with no noticeable results. The president quickly changed tactics. In May, after Germany's surrender, he sent Harry Hopkins, who had been one of Roosevelt's most trusted aides, to Moscow to smooth things over with Stalin. Hopkins's assignment included solidifying the Soviet promise to enter the war against Japan and to propose a "Big Three" (Truman, Churchill, Stalin) conference to deal with a variety of urgent issues.

By the time of his June 6 meeting with Stimson, Truman was satisfied that Hopkins had been successful. Still, the question of how and when to deal with the Soviets regarding the bomb remained a concern. Stimson told Truman that the Interim Committee had concluded "there should be no revelation to Russia or any one else of our work on S-1 until the first bomb had been successfully laid on Japan." Although he knew that the Soviets, through their spies, were aware of the Manhattan Project, Stimson did not want the subject of the bomb to come up and complicate the difficult negotiations expected at Potsdam. At the same time, progress at Los Alamos was relevant to the conference. Truman, in concert with the leaders of Britain and China, was planning to issue a surrender ultimatum to Japan; preparation of that ultimatum, led by Stimson, began in late June. (The Soviet Union would not participate in the proposed ultimatum because it was not at war with Japan.) Since it took at least three months to produce enough U235 to make a single bomb, the only way to have an arsenal of atomic weapons available during 1945 was to build plutonium bombs, which could be built at the rate of three a month because plutonium could be produced more quickly than U235. A plutonium bomb test before Potsdam would influence the content of the surrender ultimatum. Stimson therefore was pleased when Truman said that the conference would not begin until July 15 (it actually began on July 17), for there presumably would be time for a test. The test also was important because it would give Truman a gauge of the need for Soviet participation in the invasion of Japan, and therefore how much he would have to concede to the Soviets in return for their help. As it turned out, the plutonium bomb test did not take place until July 16, nine days after Truman departed the United States on his journey to Potsdam[19] (see Documents A20, A32, and A34).

DOWNFALL AND THE MEETING OF JUNE 18

On June 18, 1945, Truman met with the Joint Chiefs of Staff and his top civilian advisors to decide about Downfall, the overall American plan to invade Japan. Downfall actually was a two-stage plan: Olympic, the first stage, called for the seizure of the southern third of the island of Kyushu beginning in November 1945; it would be followed in March 1946 by Coronet, the assault against the Tokyo region. Downfall involved what Truman called his "hardest decision to date," one that would require "all the facts"[20] (see Document A25). Of course, one vital fact was unavailable: whether the United States would have atomic bombs to use against Japan. In any event, as the June 14 memo from Admiral Leahy calling the meeting made clear, Truman was concerned above all else with American casualties and intended to decide future policy "with the purpose of economizing to the maximum extent possible in the loss of American lives"[21] (see Document A26).

Truman had called the meeting in the first place because of a memo he had recently received from former president Herbert Hoover, which urged that the Allies offer terms to Japan that in effect amounted to a negotiated peace. Hoover's main reason for recommending lenient terms was that he feared it might cost between 500,000 and one million American lives to defeat Japan[22] (see Document A19). Marshall's staff dismissed the estimate as being far too high, but at the June 18 meeting Marshall was unwilling to give Truman a specific estimate in its place. The best the Army Chief of Staff was willing to do was to provide a chart of losses in previous battles and in the ongoing battle on Okinawa, adding that he believed that losses during the "first thirty days in Kyushu should not exceed the price we have paid for Luzon"—which added up to 31,000 dead, wounded and missing. However, even that number revealed less than met the eye. Each entry on Marshall's chart ended with a ratio of American casualties to Japanese "killed and prisoners." While these ratios fluctuated from battle to battle, the unavoidable conclusion for everyone present was that since considerably more troops on both sides would be fighting on Kyushu than on

Luzon, the upcoming battle was likely to be a bloodier affair for Americans and Japanese alike (see Document A27). Nor did Marshall indicate how far beyond thirty days he thought the Kyushu campaign would last. The main dissent from this low-end estimate came from Admiral Leahy, who opposed the invasion. He suggested that any casualty estimate for Kyushu be based on the casualty rate suffered by U.S. troops on Okinawa, which he placed at 35 percent. A few minutes later Marshall offered that the total assault force for Olympic would be 766,700 troops. Although no one present openly did the math, Leahy's casualty percentage for Okinawa and Marshall's assault force numbers for Olympic pointed to a huge casualty total for the invasion of Kyushu (268,000), far higher than anything suggested by Marshall's vague formulations. In any event, Truman approved Olympic, although the casualty issue clearly still concerned him, as graphically indicated by his later comment that he "hoped that there was a possibility of preventing an Okinawa from one end of Japan to the other." He pointedly withheld approval of Coronet, yet another indication of his concern about casualties. After covering several other topics, the minutes for the meeting cryptically record, "The President and the Chiefs of Staff discussed certain other matters," a reference to the atomic bomb.[23] Exactly what was said is uncertain, but if the conversation concerned how atomic weapons would affect the invasion plans, it can only have been speculative since none had yet been produced or tested.

THE POTSDAM CONFERENCE, MAGIC AND ULTRA, AND THE POTSDAM DECLARATION

Harry Truman's first major venture into international diplomacy was a contentious conference. In Stephen Ambrose's apt summation, "Sniping and jabbing were the hallmarks of Potsdam."[24] Before the sniping began, however, Truman received notice on the evening of July 16 of the successful Trinity test. The next day brought more good news when Stalin agreed to enter the war against Japan by August 15. Subsequent reports on the power of the plutonium bomb, including a report from General Groves, lifted Truman's spirits and may have sharpened his negotiating style with Stalin after a series of difficult meetings. Still, Truman was frustrated by the expanded Soviet demands on China. Therefore, shortly after receiving Groves's report he asked Stimson if Marshall believed that the projected Soviet attack on Japan's army in Manchuria was still needed to support the American invasion of Kyushu, a line of inquiry he quickly dropped[25] (see Documents A36 and A39).

Intelligence reports during late June and July that painted a grim picture of Japanese intentions highlighted the need for Soviet entry into the Pacific War.

Two of the most valuable sources of intelligence were top-secret American code-breaking operations. The United States had cracked the Japanese diplomatic code before the war began, and the White House was receiving daily summaries of radio communications to and from Tokyo called the Magic Diplomatic Summaries (MAGIC). Even more important, U.S. codebreakers had cracked the Japanese army's code in 1943 and by 1944 were able to provide a wealth of information from its decrypted radio messages. This operation was known as ULTRA. (The Japanese navy code was deciphered sufficiently to provide valuable information by 1942.) By mid-July the evidence from MAGIC and ULTRA paralleled and reinforced each other. The most significant MAGIC intercepts were of cables between Japan's Foreign Minister Shigenori Togo and Naotake Sato, Tokyo's capable ambassador to the Soviet Union. Throughout the exchanges, of which President Truman was kept informed, Togo urged Sato to seek Soviet mediation to achieve a negotiated peace. With regard to unconditional surrender, Togo stressed on July 17 that Tokyo would not consider "anything like an unconditional surrender." Four days later, in response to Sato's suggestion that Japan consider a modified form of unconditional surrender that would preserve Japan's "national structure," Togo cabled that "we are unable to consent to it [unconditional surrender] under any circumstances whatever"[26] (see Documents C8, C9, C10). Meanwhile ULTRA was tracking a massive military buildup and reinforcement effort on Kyushu that by the end of July had reached proportions far beyond what the top military planners had expected when Truman approved Olympic at the June 18 meeting. Among other things, that buildup rendered obsolete the casualty estimates Marshall had given Truman at that meeting. As in the case of MAGIC, Truman was kept informed regarding ULTRA intelligence revelations.[27]

The decision to use the atomic bomb now moved to its conclusion. On July 24, Truman received and approved a plan prepared for General Arnold "for initial attacks using special bombs." Hiroshima and Nagasaki topped the list of four cities, which also included Kokura and Niigata. The significant omission was Kyoto, spared at Stimson's insistence. Kyoto's status as Japan's most important cultural center, Stimson had argued, meant that its destruction would create enormous bitterness in Japan that would make reconciliation in the postwar era much more difficult. Shortly after 10:00 a.m. on July 25, Truman met with Marshall to review the overall military situation in the Far East. Finally, on July 25, 1945, an order went out to General Spaatz, commander of the U.S. Strategic Air Forces in the Pacific, authorizing the 509th Composite Group to "deliver its first special bomb as soon as weather will permit visual bombing after about 3 August 1945." The order was issued on Spaatz's insistence. He had understood that the bomb was going to be used but demanded a written order, what he called a "piece of paper," before he was willing to use the new weapon. His order, signed by General Thomas T. Handy, Marshall's deputy, noted that it was sent "with the approval of the Secretary of War and of the Chief of Staff, USA"[28] (see Documents B18 and B19).

That left Japan a matter of days—Hiroshima ultimately was attacked on August 6—and one last chance to avoid a nuclear catastrophe. On July 26, the United States, Britain (which had formally given its approval to use the atomic bomb on July 4), and China issued the Potsdam Declaration. That declaration was the product of long debate about how to craft an ultimatum most likely to produce surrender. Stimson and former ambassador to Tokyo and undersecretary of state Joseph Grew had been among those urging the Allies to provide for retention of the emperor, on the theory that this was of crucial importance to the Japanese and therefore would increase the chance that they would respond positively. Winston Churchill agreed. It is crucial, however, to keep in mind that this formulation, as Stimson and Grew understood it, still meant that Japan's system of government would be fundamentally changed from an authoritarian regime in which power was held by a tiny circle of people and the emperor was considered divine to a Western-style constitutional monarchy in which the emperor would be reduced to a figurehead. This was totally unacceptable not only to Hirohito and the military men who controlled the government but also to anyone with influence in Japan. In the opposing camp were former Secretary of State Cordell Hull, current Secretary of State James Byrnes, and other influential State Department officials. Hull believed that it was too early to modify unconditional surrender and risk Japanese rejection of the new terms. It was better to wait until Japan had been further weakened by continued Allied bombing and Soviet entry into the war.

The Potsdam Declaration, issued on July 26, reflected the views of Byrnes and Hull. It began by warning Japan that its armed forces had to surrender unconditionally or the country would face "prompt and utter destruction." It stated that Japan's government would be completely overhauled, the influence of those who had planned and carried out the war would be eliminated, and that Japan's ability to make war would be destroyed. At the same time, it provided certain guarantees, as part of what the document called "our terms," not given the Germans, who had surrendered without any conditions whatsoever. Among them were that Japan would not be destroyed as a nation, its economy would be allowed to recover, the occupation would be temporary, and Japan's future government, which would be democratic, would be established "in accordance with the freely expressed will of the Japanese people"[29] (see Document A45).

On July 28, Japan rejected the Potsdam Declaration. At a news conference, Prime Minister Kantaro Suzuki used the word *mokusatsu*, which is usually translated as "to kill with silence," to indicate how his government planned to respond to the proclamation. There are other possible translations, including "take no notice of," "treat with silent contempt," and, most benignly, "ignore," but Truman probably was not far from the truth when he observed, "They told me to go to hell, words to that effect."[30] Nothing now stood between Japan and the American atomic bombs except the technical problems of delivering them to their targets.

CHAPTER 5

The Japanese Government, *Ketsu-Go*, and Potsdam

On July 18, 1944, ten days after the last major battle on Saipan and six days after the horrible mass suicide on Marpi Point, Emperor Hirohito, ignoring assessments from his military advisors that the situation was irretrievable, ordered that the island be recaptured. In doing so, he was mirroring earlier commands dating back to 1942 and Guadalcanal that had imposed unattainable objectives on Japan's military forces. However, as on several other important occasions, after Saipan the emperor's wishes were not translated into military policy. Naval officers did spend the next week planning and debating an operation to retake Saipan, but on July 25 they informed Hirohito that it could not be done. Still, while the emperor had to accept that depressing but accurate tactical judgment, his basic strategic thinking remained unchanged: the Americans could be stopped in their tracks and Japan could extract itself from its crisis if its forces could win one major victory. As he told the parliament in an official statement called an Imperial Rescript on September 7, 1944, "Today our imperial state is indeed challenged to reach powerfully for a decisive victory. You who are the leaders of our people must now renew your tenacity and, uniting in your resolve, smash our enemies' evil purposes, thereby furthering forever our imperial destiny."[1]

Hirohito was not alone in his confidence in the strategy of winning a decisive victory. That belief was held by most of the small group of men who controlled

Japan, and it resonated deeply in Japanese history. In 1905, the victory over the Russian navy in the Battle of Tsushima Strait decided the Russo-Japanese War and lifted Japan to the status of a great power. It had been the basis of Tokyo's military strategy vis-à-vis the United States since before World War II began and of Admiral Yamamoto's great gamble at Pearl Harbor. Perhaps even more to the point in the desperate years of 1944 and 1945 was the great Battle of Tennozan, considered one of the most crucial battles in Japanese history. Fought in 1582 near a small mountain from which it takes its name, Tennozan was an all-or-nothing gamble by a military leader named Hideyoshi. Having defied the odds and staked everything on that one battle, Hideyoshi won a decisive victory, and in doing so made himself Japan's supreme ruler and one of its greatest heroes as he united the country for the first time.

Of course, during the Pacific War "decisive victory" did not mean the same thing in mid-1944, and even less so in 1945, as it did back in 1941. As Japan's military situation deteriorated, Hideyoshi's successors lowered their expectations of what their decisive victory might accomplish. In historian Edward Drea's apt summary, it inexorably declined from "victory, to negotiated peace, to bloody stalemate." As for what that meant for the empire, by 1944 the dreams of military superiority and control over much of the Pacific and Southeast Asia had faded. In its place was the far more modest goal of avoiding a humiliating surrender and thus preserving what the Japanese called *kokutai*, their imperial system of government in which the emperor was sacred and sovereign and the military enjoyed primacy of place in political life. This, in fact, was what Prime Minister Hideki Tojo told the army's vice chief of staff late in June 1944.[2]

Along with Hirohito's order to recapture Saipan, July 18, 1944, also saw Tojo's government fall, its prime minister fatally discredited by the Saipan disaster. The new government was headed by the relatively unknown and nondescript General Kuniaki Koiso, who for the preceding two years had been serving as governor general of Korea. Like the impossible order regarding Saipan, the choice of Koiso reflected the deep malaise and inability to come to grips with reality that afflicted the Japanese leadership. That paralysis in no small part was a function of the country's system of government. Despite its parliamentary facade, the Japanese wartime government in reality was a dictatorship, but a complex one composed of formal and informal institutions based on Japanese traditions whose method of operation is not always easy for outsiders to understand. A tiny elite, headed by the emperor, controlled the government. Within the government, the power of the military—and especially the army—was decisive. This was because the army minister had to be a serving general nominated by the army itself. If the army minister resigned, the government would fall, and if the army refused to name a new minister, a new government could not be formed. Because the navy had similar authority, the military had a double-barrel gun pointed at the government. In addition, there existed what in effect was an inner cabinet, since 1944 known as the Supreme Council for the Direction of the War (SCDW). Although it had no constitutional standing, the SCDW exercised crucial authority by virtue of its membership: the prime minister, foreign minister, the army and navy ministers, and the chiefs of staffs of the army and navy. Aside from amplifying the power of the military by its membership, the SCDW, or "Big Six," did so further by requiring unanimity to reach a decision, the same debilitating system that prevailed in the larger cabinet.

Grafted onto and often dominating this awkward structure was the convoluted and often subtle role of the emperor, the figure whom the constitution called "sacred and inviolable" and whose status transcended the constitution itself. In fact, at its promulgation in 1889 the constitution was declared a gift to the people of Japan from the emperor. His power theoretically was supreme. Among other prerogatives, the emperor could convoke and dismiss parliament, select the prime minister, and issue emergency laws when parliament was not in session; he also was the supreme commander of the army and navy. However, reality and practice did not conform to theory. The constitution specified that the emperor had to carry out his powers in accordance with its provisions, one of which stated that "all Laws, Imperial Ordinances, and Imperial rescripts" required the countersignature of a minister of state. The emperor was expected to delegate his powers to public servants he selected to carry out his will, and this in practice removed day-to-day decisions and operations from his control. Still, Emperor Hirohito, assisted by his closest advisors, was a real and powerful political force behind the scenes. Despite practical limits on his activities and actual power, he exercised crucial and often decisive influence on governmental policy decisions. During the Pacific War he was briefed frequently and thoroughly on the military situation, although generally the information he received was filtered and hence distorted so that he would support the positions of his top army and navy officers. Nonetheless, during the course of hundreds of military briefings Hirohito could and did ask questions that both helped him understand the situation under discussion and enabled him to express his opinion. The emperor traditionally did not speak at meetings with top government officials called imperial conferences, which included members of the SCDW and several other functionaries and were held in order to record final decisions in his presence. However, he could and did influence the decisions that came before him by the questions he posed at meetings that preceded those conferences.

All this made Hirohito's actions and views critical in the spring and summer of 1945, when Japan was forced toward its final surrender. Throughout that period, his closest advisor, and a man who often expressed his views to members of the government, was Koichi Kido, a nobleman who held the position Lord Keeper of the Privy Seal and, as such, was what historian Robert Butow has called "the eyes and ears of the Throne."[3]

A third important event occurred on July 18, 1944, carrying the discussion of the country's mounting troubles beyond the governing elite. Even in a country where a dictatorial regime controlled most of the information about the war, by mid-1944 it was impossible to hide from the people the fact that Japan was in serious trouble. The government admitted as much in a statement issued on July 18 by Imperial General Headquarters, the body through which the emperor exercised his official role as supreme commander. The statement provided a detailed and surprisingly (though not entirely) accurate summary of the Saipan battle, including the final apology of the commanding general for his failure to hold the island. That was followed in August by a translation of an article on the battle from the American weekly magazine *Time*, with commentary by a Japanese correspondent based in Europe, in Japan's largest newspaper, *Asahi Shimbun*. It chronicled the end of the battle, including the suicides at Marpi Point. While both the Imperial Headquarters statement and the *Asahi Shimbun* article stressed the heroism of the Japanese and the enormous losses they had inflicted on the Americans, they also graphically told the Japanese people that the war was going badly and that the country faced an extremely difficult future.[4] Nonetheless, even as the American bombing campaign from mid-1944 until the eve of the atomic bombings pounded their major cities, most ordinary Japanese continued to believe their leaders' promises of ultimate victory and maintained their support of the war effort.

THE KOISO GOVERNMENT

The Koiso government spent much of its short life backpedaling. In November 1944 the prime minister proclaimed Leyte the new Tennozan. When things went badly there, he shifted the Tennozan venue to Luzon in January 1945. In February, as the Americans troops inexorably pushed forward on Luzon and its warships and planes relentlessly bombarded Iwo Jima, the emperor consulted with seven of his top advisors, including six former prime ministers who together formed an advisory body called the *jushin*, about what to do next. Almost to a man, they vigorously supported continuing the war. Only one, former Prime Minister Fumimaro Konoe, stressed an urgent need for peace. His "Memorial to the Throne," presented to the emperor on February 14, warned that the war was undermining the social order in Japan and creating conditions for a Communist revolution instigated by the Soviet Union. Responding to a question from Hirohito, Konoe even used the term "unconditional surrender" to describe what Japan should do, although his projection of what that would involve—the United States would not "reform" the *kokutai* and Japan would retain many of its non-Japanese territories—was fundamentally incompatible with the terms the Allies intended to impose upon a defeated Japan under their rather different concept of unconditional surrender[5] (see Document D2). That mattered little, inasmuch as Hirohito had no intention of following Konoe's advice, even in the face of intelligence reports he received the next day that the Soviet Union was likely to end its neutrality pact with Tokyo in the next few months and eventually join in the war against Japan. Although Hirohito admitted that he was worried about discontent at home, along with army and navy leaders he now looked forward to a post-Philippines decisive battle that would provide Japan with an opportunity it needed to end the war on acceptable terms.[6]

THE SUZUKI GOVERNMENT AND THE "FUNDAMENTAL POLICY"

During March 1945, American troops secured the Philippine capital of Manila, B-29 bombers firebombed Tokyo and several other Japanese cities, and marines quashed the last Japanese resistance on Iwo Jima. On April 1, American forces landed on Okinawa. Four days later, Hirohito brought down Koiso's government. His new choice for prime minister was Admiral Kantaro Suzuki, an aging but respected hero of the Russo-Japanese war. Suzuki was seventy-eight, hard of hearing, and reluctant to take the job. But he enjoyed the confidence of the emperor, and upon being nominated by the *jushin* he allowed Kido to talk him into accepting the post and its unenviable burden of finding Japan a way out of the war without the humiliation of surrender and with its *kokutai* intact.

That said, the Suzuki government was not willing to even consider surrender or, for that matter, seek an immediate peace. This is clear both from Suzuki's expressed views from April through July 1945 and from the men he chose for the key cabinet posts with membership on the Supreme Council for the Direction of the War. A number of key officials, including Shigenori Togo, Suzuki's choice for foreign minister, agreed that in April 1945 Suzuki's immediate strategy for improving Japan's postwar prospects focused on vigorously prosecuting the war.[7] Togo, who later recalled that Suzuki was prepared to fight on for at least two more years, in fact was the only member of the new Big Six who argued for some kind of strong peace initiative. He received no support from Suzuki and was relentlessly opposed by the most powerful man in the government, General Korechika Anami, the army minister. A man cast like iron in the classic samurai mold, Anami argued in the spring of 1945 that Japan, which still had a formidable army and controlled vast territories outside the home islands, had not been defeated. Even after Hiroshima, he would argue for continuing the war; in the end, he committed suicide rather than witness his country's surrender. Anami in turn was staunchly supported by Admiral Soemu Toyoda, who became Navy Chief of Staff in May, and Army Chief of Staff Yoshijiro Umezu. The navy minister, Admiral Mitsumasa Yonai, who had been against going to war with the United States in the first place, was slightly more moderate than his fellow military officers but not to the point of openly dissenting from their views until after the bombing of Hiroshima.

Indeed, the main focus of the SCDW when Suzuki and his colleagues took office was on the anticipated American invasion of the home islands. A few months earlier, in January 1945, Imperial General Headquarters had issued and the emperor had approved a directive to prepare to defend against that invasion that became the basis for all future homeland defense planning (see Document D1). On April 8, just after the Suzuki government took office, that plan emerged from Imperial General Headquarters in the form of Army Order No. 1299, or *Ketsu-Go* (Decisive Operation), yet another scheme for a decisive battle with the United States that would save Japan (see Document D3). One of the key provisions of *Ketsu-Go* was an emergency military buildup on Kyushu, where the Japanese military planners correctly anticipated the Americans would attack. Another was to inflict as many casualties as possible on the Americans by attacking packed troop transports out at sea, before they could transfer their vulnerable human cargo to smaller landing craft. That job would fall largely to "special attack units," or suicide attackers, primarily kamikaze aircraft, which would have first priority in matters of supply. One-man suicide torpedoes (*kaitan*) and "crash boats" (*renraku-tei*) packed with explosives also would attack and ram the transports. Near the beaches, human mines (*fukuryu*), divers carrying explosive charges, would swim underwater up to landing craft and blow them up. Those Americans who made it ashore would face not only regular troops but also an armed population prepared to die for the emperor, often in suicide roles, under the policy the plan called "Every citizen a soldier."[8] This military planning was translated into official government policy by the "Fundamental Policy to Be Followed Henceforth in the Conduct of the War," which rejected the idea of surrender and called for prosecuting the war to the bitter end. Despite a grim assessment of the toll the war was taking on the home front in terms of both production and public morale provided by two reports, the SCDW adopted the "Fundamental Policy" at a marathon meeting held on June 6. At that meeting, only Togo argued that the army's plans did not take into account the country's waning strength; Suzuki, on the other hand, militantly supported the army's position. The full cabinet endorsed the "Fundamental Policy" the next day, and it received the emperor's sanction at an Imperial Conference on June 8.[9]

There was a weak countercurrent to the powerful, surging tide of determination to fight to the finish. In a diary entry on June 8, Marquis Kido outlined what became his "Draft Plan for Controlling the Crisis Situation," which he delivered to the emperor the next day. Kido believed the only way for Japan to avoid a complete collapse was to secure a negotiated peace and, crucially, that this would require direct action by the emperor. He hoped to use the Soviet Union to mediate Japan's negotiations with the British and Americans. Japan's "very generous terms" would include offering to withdraw from the territories it had occupied and agreeing to accept a level of disarmament Kido called "a minimum defense." Kido thereby hoped to avoid an occupation and preserve Japan's political system[10] (see Document D14).

Kido's presentation and further bad news about the state of Japan's military forces had an effect on the emperor's views. Previously, he had been a staunch advocate of a decisive battle. Now he was prepared to endorse diplomatic efforts directed at the Soviet Union as Kido suggested. The idea of making some kind of approach to the Soviet Union was not entirely new; in May the SCDW had agreed that the foreign ministry should initiate discussions designed to make sure the Soviets maintained their current state of neutrality and stayed out of the Pacific War. These discussions, conducted at a low level, yielded nothing. However, the efforts of Togo and Kido did have results, at least in terms of getting Anami and his supporters to agree at a SCDW meeting on June 18 to approach the Soviets about their willingness to mediate peace negotiations. It was, to say the least, an extremely modest concession; according to Togo, the SCDW did not agree to request mediation, but only "to sound out" Soviet willingness to play that role.[11] The goal remained a negotiated peace that had nothing in common with the Allied demand for unconditional surrender.

The delusional nature of what the SCDW was willing to consider was not lost on Japanese officials with more realistic outlooks but no power to influence events in the councils of power. They included Naotake Sato, Tokyo's astute ambassador to Moscow, whose cables home repeatedly stressed that Japan could expect nothing from the Soviets and that the only way to avoid catastrophe was to bite the bullet and surrender unconditionally to the Allies. Those cables, and Togo's intransigent responses, were being intercepted and decoded by the American MAGIC operation and forwarded to policy makers in Washington, including President Truman[12] (see Documents C1–C17).

In any event, the emperor followed up the June 18 SCDW meeting by calling an Imperial Conference on June 22. He told the gathering, "I desire that concrete plans to end the war, unhampered by existing policy, be speedily studied and that efforts be made to implement them." In the face of military determination not to compromise its fundamental agenda, the members of the SCDW reached only a vague agreement to try to begin peace negotiations by approaching the Soviet Union. There was no agreement whatever about what peace terms Japan might offer. Meanwhile, a rapid military buildup to meet and throw back the American invasion began on Kyushu in April and grew with each passing month into the summer. In the succinct and apt assessment of historian Richard B. Frank, "At this juncture, then, Japan had neared only negotiation, not peace."[13]

THE POTSDAM DECLARATION
AND "*MOKUSATSU*"

On July 26, 1945, the United States, Britain, and China issued the Potsdam Declaration. The document presented Japan with strict terms, warned that the Allies would "brook no delay," and promised a grim alternative—"prompt and
utter destruction"—if Tokyo did not accept them. Japan would have to surrender unconditionally, undergo disarmament and an occupation, accept a reduction in territory to little more than its four home islands, and undergo a radical
overhaul of its institutions that would "eliminate for all time" the influence of
the militarists who had provoked the war and as a result would be tried as war
criminals. In return, Japan would not be destroyed as a nation, would be allowed
to recover economically, and could expect the right to choose a government
"based on the freely expressed will of the Japanese people" (so long as that government was "peacefully inclined") and an end to the occupation[14] (see Document A45).

Rhetoric and the severity of the terms aside, these *were* terms, something Nazi
Germany had not been offered when it was forced to surrender without any
conditions or promises whatsoever. Togo and his colleagues in the foreign ministry recognized this. When the Supreme Council on the Direction of the War
began its discussions on how to react on July 27, the foreign minister warned
against rejecting the declaration. He tried to convince his colleagues to delay
their response until the Soviet Union had responded to Japan's proposal that
Moscow mediate peace negotiations. Togo did not succeed. Although Anami
and the other military men on the SCDW at first had agreed to wait, they reversed field and pressured Prime Minister Suzuki to reject the declaration
openly. By then the Japanese press had been allowed to publish a censored version of the document, with parts that might make it seem acceptable excised.
Suzuki's news conference on the afternoon of July 28 ended any speculation in
Allied capitals about how Tokyo had received their ultimatum. He said Japan
would "*mokusatsu*" it. However one translates the possible meanings of that
term—from "ignore" to "kill with silence" or "treat with silent contempt"—
Suzuki's other negative comments that afternoon, in concert with the chorus of
insulting terms in the press, slammed the door shut on the Potsdam Declaration.
Although Emperor Hirohito was silent, it is clear that he did not disagree with
what was being done. Neither current documents nor his postwar statement
made in 1946 give any hint that Hirohito favored a more conciliatory response to
the Allied ultimatum.

Nothing of substance emerged from Tokyo in terms of opening some channels to the Allies after the rejection of the Potsdam Declaration, despite repeated
pleas from a few Japanese officials, particularly Sato, who recognized that Japan

was on the brink of disaster. Hirohito's only action was to express concern for the safety of what collectively were called the imperial regalia, several sacred objects associated with the throne. Admiral Yonai, supposedly more flexible than other military men on the SCDW, believed that time was on Japan's side. On July 28 he told a subordinate, "Churchill has fallen. America is beginning to be isolated. There is no need to rush." Speaking at a cabinet meeting on August 3, Prime Minister Suzuki seemed to think that the Potsdam Declaration indicated American weakness and that "if we hold firm, then they will yield before we do."[15] On August 4, the sensible and increasingly desperate Sato sent Togo a cable in which he again stressed that Japan had a lot to gain, especially in comparison to what had happened to Germany, by accepting the Potsdam Declaration. Then he warned, "However, if the Government and the Military dilly-dally in bringing this resolution to fruition, then all Japan will be reduced to ashes and we will not be able [to avoid] following the road to ruin."[16] Two days later, Togo and the rest of Japan found out how terribly right Sato was.

CHAPTER 6

Hiroshima, Nagasaki, and Japan's Surrender

There are several points to keep in mind regarding the intricate nine-day chain of events from August 6 to 14, 1945, that culminated in the surrender of Japan. First, after the atomic attack on Hiroshima on August 6, the Japanese government essentially was stunned and immobilized and made no move to surrender. In fact, the SCDW did not hold its first post-Hiroshima meeting until the morning of August 9, and, a court official recalled, it took place in an atmosphere of "impatience, frenzy, and bewilderment."[1] Only after Nagasaki was bombed that same day did Japan's locked wheels of decision making become unstuck and slowly grind forward toward making peace based on the Potsdam Declaration. By then, the August 8 Soviet declaration of war against Japan had landed with a crash on the scales Tokyo was using to weigh its limited options. Second, it took extraordinary intervention by Emperor Hirohito in the political process, not once but twice, initially on the night of August 9–10 and again on August 14, finally to bring about surrender. That intervention in turn was followed by yet another unprecedented imperial act: Hirohito's broadcast to the nation at noon on August 15 announcing the surrender to the nation, an event that marked the first time his subjects outside court circles had heard his sacred voice. Third, between August 10 and August 14, there were fundamental differences in what the United States and Japan meant by unconditional surrender, especially with respect to the status of the emperor, differences that placed the negotiations in peril. Fourth, leaders in both in Washington and Tokyo, even at this late date, respectively were deeply divided about what constituted the minimum terms their country could accept. In Japan, where the range of opinion included powerful elements opposed to surrender prior to a final decisive battle, the desperate effort to prevent the unacceptable led to a military coup, which fizzled even as some commanders overseas threatened to continue the war.

THE JAPANESE REACTION TO HIROSHIMA

Hiroshima was bombed on August 6, 1945, at 8:15 a.m., Japanese time (August 5, 7:15 p.m., Washington time). The first news of the catastrophic attack reached Tokyo within about fifteen minutes. However, the Japanese did not fully realize what had caused such massive damage until August 7, by which time President Truman's announcement about the use of an atomic bomb, made in Washington on August 6, had been broadcast around the world. Emperor Hirohito, a trained marine biologist, understood better than almost all of his subjects the enormous destructive power that now threatened his country. He received a preliminary report on the afternoon of August 6 and a more comprehensive briefing from Kido on August 7 confirming that an atomic bomb had indeed exploded over Hiroshima and destroyed the city.

The reaction of the country's military leadership was a mixture of desperation, disbelief, and defiance. At dawn on August 7, the vice chief of the Army General Staff, Torashiro Kawabe, received a report that stated, "The whole city of Hiroshima was destroyed instantly by a single bomb."[2] Kawabe understood the Americans had achieved a historic scientific breakthrough, but that did not erode his determination to keep on fighting. As he wrote in his diary, "If we expend time crying, the war situation will deteriorate further and become more difficult. We must be tenacious and active"[3] (see Document D16). These sentiments were widely shared by his military colleagues in both the army and navy. Some high-ranking officers initially denied that the Americans could have developed an atomic bomb or, alternatively, transported such an inherently unstable device across the Pacific Ocean. Others grasped at the fantasy that countermeasures were possible, a hope that General Anami expressed as late as August 14. Far more sensible, although likewise unfounded, was the thesis of Admiral Toyoda that the United States could have enough nuclear material only for a small number of bombs, which meant that the atomic attacks would not continue. Toyoda also suggested that world opinion would not tolerate further attacks, a viewpoint that found expression in an official Japanese protest issued on August 10 and delivered to Washington the next day.[4]

On August 8, Yoshio Nishina, Japan's leading nuclear physicist, inspected Hiroshima and confirmed that it had been destroyed by an atomic bomb. Meanwhile, Foreign Minister Togo was briefing the emperor and, most importantly, stressing that Japan had to surrender on the basis of the Potsdam Declaration. The emperor seems to have indicated support for that position, although to what extent is not certain. In any event, before the day was over, the Soviet Union, at 11 p.m. Tokyo time, delivered its declaration of war to Ambassador Sato in Moscow. Within a few hours, Soviet troops had begun an offensive against Japanese forces in Manchuria.

EVENTS OF AUGUST 9–10

On August 9 at 10:30 a.m., a day later than originally planned, the Supreme Council for the Direction of the War finally held its first post-Hiroshima meeting. The atomic attack and the Soviet declaration of war notwithstanding, the Big Six deadlocked over whether Japan should accept the Potsdam Declaration. After several hours of debate, news arrived at 1:00 p.m. that Japan had suffered a second atomic bomb attack, this time against the city of Nagasaki. More debate followed, as the Big Six split into two opposing groups. Prime Minister Suzuki, Foreign Minister Togo, and, apparently after some hesitation, Navy Minister Yonai argued for accepting the Potsdam Declaration, with the proviso that the emperor's position be guaranteed. Army Minister Anami, Army Chief of Staff Umezu, and Navy Chief of Staff Toyoda argued for three additional conditions: that there be no Allied occupation of Japan, that Japan's armed forces be allowed to disarm themselves, and that the Japanese government prosecute the country's alleged war criminals. The Big Six stalemate—attaching one condition versus attaching four conditions to any acceptance of the Potsdam Declaration— carried over into a marathon cabinet meeting, which went through two sessions, with a break of an hour, before ending in the same stalemate. Two atomic bombs, each of which destroyed a city, and the Soviet Union's declaration of war were not enough to produce a consensus to surrender. The best the cabinet could manage was a plurality for the one-condition position, not enough in a system that demanded unanimity in order to call in the emperor to confirm a decision.

At this point the peace advocates bent the rules, which under the circumstances called for the cabinet's resignation. Instead of following that path, Suzuki reported to the emperor and requested he call an imperial conference, which Hirohito promptly did. That crucial meeting began in the emperor's air-raid shelter just before midnight and spilled over into the early hours of August 10. Both sides again presented their cases. Anami's comments included his belief, widely shared in the army, that his forces could so bloody the Americans when they invaded Japan that Washington would have to offer Tokyo better terms. Umezu added that in the event of a decisive battle "we are confident of victory." Baron Kiichiro Hiranuma, a well-respected former prime minister and currently president of the Privy Council, an important advisory body, made other key comments. His careful questioning of several members of the Big Six, combined with his own observations, grimly highlighted his country's hopeless predicament and in the process buttressed the one-condition position. At the same time, Hiranuma, while removing three conditions, reinforced the remaining one. He specifically defined the position of the emperor as embodied in that condition to mean the retention of the imperial system with the emperor's powers and sacred status intact. In other words, Japan's system of government would not change. It seems fair to say that in doing so Hiranuma was only overtly stating what his colleagues who had suggested one condition in the first place had assumed was understood and therefore not bothered to articulate[5] (see Documents G5 and G6).

That left matters up to Hirohito. At 2:30 a.m. he rendered what has since been called his "sacred decision" (*seidan*) (see Document E1). The emperor had harsh words for the army, which had failed to match its words with performance, a failure that extended to its current inadequate preparations for an American invasion. The country could not endure further suffering, especially in light of the destructive power of the atomic bomb. Even though the emperor found it intolerably difficult to allow his troops to be disarmed by the enemy and see "faithful subordinates" put on trial as war criminals, there was no alternative but to "bear the unbearable." He endorsed Togo's proposal to accept the Potsdam Declaration with only one condition, the preservation of the emperor's position.[6] The imperial conference was over.

It remained for the cabinet to put a legal stamp on the emperor's expressed will, which by itself did not carry the force of law. This was done at a meeting at the prime minister's official residence about an hour after the imperial conference ended. What is crucial here is that Hiranuma's wording prevailed. The cabinet voted to accept the Potsdam Declaration "with the understanding that the said declaration does not comprise any demand which prejudices the prerogatives of His Majesty as a Sovereign Ruler"[7] (see Document E2). As historian Herbert Bix has pointed out, the Japanese government was affirming its intent to preserve Japan's current political *system*, with the emperor's sacred status and powers fully intact: "It was certainly not constitutional monarchy that the Suzuki cabinet sought to have the Allies assure, but rather a Japanese monarchy based on the principle of oracular sovereignty, with continued subjecthood or *shinmin* status for the Japanese people, and some postsurrender role for the military. In their extreme moment of crisis, *kokutai* meant to them the orthodox Shinto-National Learning view of the state and the retention of real, substantial political power in the hands of the emperor, so that he and the 'moderates' might go on using it to control his majesty's 'subjects' after surrender."[8] This was not an interpretation likely to find favor in Washington.

Meanwhile, Anami on his own was making sure in Tokyo that Hiranuma's interpretation was chiseled in stone. He pointedly asked Suzuki if he would be prepared to continue the war "if Japan could not confirm that the sovereign power of the Emperor will be recognized." (The words are those of Anami's brother-in-law, Colonel Masahiko Takeshita, who recorded them in his diary.) Suzuki, "in a low voice," answered yes.[9]

WASHINGTON REACTS

On August 9, Henry Stimson confided to his diary that he expected that "the bomb" and the Soviet Union's entry into the war "certainly will have an effect on hastening the victory." What was less certain was how long that process would take. The next day, as he was preparing to go on vacation, Stimson was pleasantly surprised ("Today was momentous") to find out he had at least part of the answer much sooner than he expected. Early that morning the Japanese offer had arrived in Washington via the Swiss embassy, which was handling diplomatic communications between the two warring powers. The problem was the reference to the powers of the emperor, "the very single point that I feared would make trouble"[10] (see Documents A53 and A54).

The first trouble occurred in the White House, where Truman met with Leahy, Stimson, Byrnes, and Forrestal to figure out how to respond. Leahy and Stimson, who previously had argued for retaining the emperor, restated that case and urged acceptance of the Japanese offer. Byrnes vigorously dissented, defending the pure version of unconditional surrender on the grounds that the American public would be furious over any concessions at this point, especially since the United States now had an atomic bomb and Russia had entered the war. The solution came from Forrestal, who essentially proposed a compromise unencumbered by too many specifics. His suggestion emerged in the official American response from Byrnes on August 11, which for the time being left Hirohito on his throne but stated that as soon as Japan surrendered "the authority of the Emperor and the Japanese Government to rule the state shall be subject to the Supreme Commander of the Allied powers." As for the emperor's long-term prospects, the Byrnes note, referring to the Potsdam Declaration, repeated that future government remained the province of "the freely expressed will of the Japanese people"[11] (see Document E3).

That was not the totality of the American response. In part to facilitate the diplomatic process and in part, as recorded by Secretary of Commerce Henry Wallace, to avoid killing another 100,000 people, including "all those kids,"

Truman ordered the suspension of atomic bombing until such time as he directly ordered otherwise.[12] Strategic bombing by B-29s, after a large raid on the morning of August 10, also was suspended, at first because of bad weather—a decision made by General Spaatz in the Pacific that had nothing to do with events in Washington—and then because Truman worried that resumption of those attacks would be taken as a sign that the negotiations had failed. He was also worried that the Japanese would not surrender. That was one reason bombing by other air force and navy aircraft continued. When no Japanese response to the Byrnes note was forthcoming by August 13, and radio intelligence suggested Japan's determination to continue the war, more B-29 bombing was ordered. It resumed on August 14 in a massive operation on several targets by more than a thousand planes, 186 of which were fighter escorts whose job it was to protect the bombers. The air force also dropped five million leaflets urging surrender and informing the Japanese people of their government's offer on August 10 and the American reply the next day.

JAPAN SURRENDERS

In Tokyo, chaos, confusion, and deadlock reigned. On August 10, two statements had been released to the press, one officially from a body called the Information Board and the other by the Army Ministry, although General Anami, the head of that ministry, had never seen the statement but only approved the ideas it expressed in principle. They were broadcast that night and published in newspapers on August 11. The former, supposedly intended to prepare the people for the impending surrender, used language that left many Japanese believing precisely the opposite: that they should be prepared for a bitter fight to the finish. The latter, invoking the leader who had repulsed the Mongol invaders in the thirteenth century, reinforced that impression[13] (see Document D9).

By the early hours of August 12, Japanese officials had the American response. No one was pleased. The statement that the emperor would be subject to the Allied supreme commander was bad news. Even worse was the affirmation that the Japanese people ultimately would decide the country's form of government, a formulation that did not guarantee the emperor's status. It put the advocates of accepting the Potsdam Declaration on the defensive, infused Anami and other advocates of a final battle—a group that included most of the top- and middle-grade army and navy officers—with new energy, and in many ways pushed the situation in Tokyo back to what it had been on August 9, before Hirohito had made his "sacred decision." Finally, the attitude of fanatical military officers unalterably opposed to surrender and their determination, if necessary, to defy even the emperor if in their eyes he betrayed the country, was an open secret. Their activities meant that the political maneuvering to extricate Japan from its crisis was taking place, in the apt phrase of political scientist Leon Sigal, "in the context of impending insurrection."[14]

On the morning of August 12, before the cabinet was able to meet, Umezu and Toyoda met with the emperor to stress the opposition to the American terms by both the army and navy and warn him that accepting them "may lead to a situation that can not be controlled"[15] (see Document D12). When the cabinet met that afternoon, it found itself as divided as on August 9, with the supporters of Togo aligned against those of Anami. In fact, if anything, the rejectionist forces were considerably strengthened when Prime Minister Suzuki came out for rejecting the Byrnes note. After the meeting ended, a distraught and angry Togo and later a concerned but more self-controlled Kido worked on Suzuki; Kido pointed out that the emperor supported the Togo position and convinced Suzuki to rejoin the peace camp. But that camp still was in disarray and losing its grip on the situation. As for Anami, he not only was aware of the plotting by some of his junior officers but also had met with them, albeit without committing himself to their cause.

On August 13, first the Big Six and then the cabinet met, only to find themselves divided, the former split along its familiar three-to-three fault line and the latter with a majority—which again was not enough given the unanimity requirement—for accepting the Allied terms. It took more maneuvering and some additional meetings to set the stage, but at 11:00 a.m. on August 14 another imperial conference met in the palace air-raid shelter. Along with the Big Six, those present included the entire cabinet, Privy Council President Hiranuma, and half a dozen other leading officials. The by now familiar arguments were rehashed, and then the emperor spoke. His brief talk paralleled the one he had given five days before. Hirohito pronounced the Allied terms "acceptable," warned that continuing the war would leave Japan "reduced to ashes," and told all those present they he and they had to endure the "unendurable." He added that not only would an imperial rescript be prepared announcing acceptance of the Potsdam Declaration, but that he would also read it himself in a broadcast to the nation[16] (see Document E5).

After Emperor Hirohito ended the imperial conference, the cabinet met to prepare and sign the official decision to surrender on Allied terms. Another key development that day occurred in the evening, when first Umezu and then Anami made it clear to their army colleagues that they would not defy the emperor's will by participating in a coup. They and several other top officers then signed an agreement stating, "The Army will act in accordance with the Imperial Decision to the last."[17] The foreign ministry's communication accepting the terms of the Potsdam Declaration reached Washington at 6:00 p.m. in the evening of August 14 and was accepted in a public announcement by President Truman to assembled reporters an hour later (see Document E8). The president then greeted a crowd on the White House lawn with a "V" sign, and the people responded with a loud cheer.[18] Meanwhile, in Japan, shortly before midnight Tokyo time — Tokyo time was thirteen hours ahead of Washington time — Hirohito recorded his imperial rescript. It was a busy night at the palace. Soldiers swarmed around as the hastily planned coup led by mid-ranking army officers briefly flared and failed. Not far away at the army minister's official residence, General Anami, having that afternoon issued orders to the army commanding obedience to the emperor's will (the navy issued similar orders) and leaving two short poems as his epitaph, committed *seppuku*, the traditional Japanese form of ritual suicide.

At noon on August 15, the Emperor's rescript was broadcast to a shocked and demoralized nation. Its work done, the Suzuki cabinet resigned. On August 17 a new government headed by Prince Naruhiko Higashikuni, who had close ties through marriage to the imperial family, took office. That same day Hirohito issued another imperial rescript, this one specifically calling on Japanese soldiers throughout Asia and the Pacific to lay down their arms[19] (see Document E12). The official surrender took place on September 2 aboard the battleship *Missouri* in Tokyo Bay. In an awesome display of power, more than 250 ships, most of them American, floated nearby, while 450 aircraft flew overhead as the proceedings opened and almost 2,000 more, including 400 B-29s, filled the sky above after they closed. The war in the Pacific, and with it World War II, was finally over.

CHAPTER 7

Hiroshima and American Power

The debate over the bombing of Hiroshima might have subsided long ago had it not become part of the larger postwar debate over the use of American power. That often contentious discussion in turn is largely the product of the fundamental shift in American foreign policy that took place after 1945. Before World War II, the United States stood aside as much as possible from major international disputes outside the Western Hemisphere, in particular those involving the European great powers. It followed George Washington's farewell speech advice to avoid "entangling alliances," a policy known as isolationism. The great exception was American participation in World War I on the side of Britain, France, and their allies against Germany and its allies. But even then, the United States did not enter the war until more than two and a half years after it had begun and officially fought as an "associated" rather than an "allied" power. After the guns finally fell silent in 1918, the United States refused to join the League of Nations and for the most part retreated into its prewar policy of staying out of European affairs.

In addition, as it had done after every previous war, the United States allowed its military establishment to wither, so that by the time World War II loomed on the horizon it required a crash program to build up this country's armed forces to respectable levels. World War II meanwhile approached America's shores like twin tidal waves rising simultaneously in the Pacific and Atlantic oceans, at first visible as distant though ominous undulations of storm-driven waters posing a potential rather than a direct threat and then, increasingly and inexorably, as towering, moving mountains packing terrible power as they came ever nearer. The effort to build up the military was not complete when the Pacific wave, jolted into deadly motion by Asian political tremors emanating from Tokyo, raced in from the west: on December 7, 1941, in the form of Japanese bombs and torpedoes, it slammed into the ships of the American navy moored at Pearl Harbor. Meanwhile, the Atlantic wave, larger and ultimately far more dangerous, born in the political earthquake that had taken place in Berlin when the Nazis came to power, surged across the Atlantic ocean from the east: it made landfall in Washington, albeit initially only as words, on December 11 in the form of Hitler's declaration of war.

When World War II finally ended, the United States faced an unprecedented security situation. Modern technology had shrunk the world, and with it the oceans to the east and west that had protected this country for so long. The great geographic barriers that had permitted the United States the luxury of isolation and, at least in peacetime, military weakness were gone. Again, to be sure, there was a debate about foreign policy. And again, as after World War I, the United States quickly demobilized, beginning the postwar era with a skeleton military force capable of little more than occupation duty in Germany and Japan. Nonetheless, America's isolationists were fighting a rearguard action they soon lost. It was widely assumed by American leaders that this country's isolationism had contributed to the breakdown of the international order that had allowed aggression first to go unpunished and then to run amuck and plunge the world into the most destructive war in history. Isolationism gave way to internationalism as the dominant paradigm in American foreign policy. It was assumed that United States needed a proactive foreign policy to help create an international environment in which it could live in safety and peace. The commitment to establish and participate in the United Nations became a central part of American foreign policy; indeed, that organization was founded in San Francisco even before the war in the Pacific was over. The dangerous growth of Soviet power and Moscow's establishment of a satellite empire in Eastern and Central Europe and the consequent onset of the Cold War further reinforced internationalism. A national consensus developed based on the idea that freedom at home depended on America making commitments to maintaining freedom abroad. The inevitable corollary of that consensus, which emerged somewhat later, was that the United States had to be militarily strong and, at times, to use its military power to defend its vital interests.

It was not long, even in the aftermath of America's postwar demobilization, before that outlook was translated into practical policy. As early as 1947, having proclaimed what is known as the Truman Doctrine, the United States intervened for the first time in its history in the affairs of a European country during peacetime by sending military and economic aid to Greece and Turkey, the former receiving assistance to help its government defeat a Communist guerrilla movement and the latter to shore it up against Soviet pressure. That was followed in 1948 by the Marshall Plan, an aid program under which America's economic might was used to help rebuild not only its World War II allies in Europe but also Germany, its former enemy, albeit by necessity only that country's western part, comprising the American, British, and French occupation zones. By 1949 the United States had taken the lead in founding the North Atlantic Treaty Organization (NATO), its first-ever peacetime military alliance. In 1950, America went to war to protect non-Communist South Korea after Communist North Korea invaded it and fought a bitter and costly three-year struggle with North Korean and Communist Chinese forces as a result. It was during that frustrating conflict that the United States rebuilt its military into a large, battle-ready force, which it has remained to this day. By then this country was engaged in a nuclear arms race with the Soviet Union. It lasted until the late 1980s and resulted in the development of thermonuclear weapons hundreds of times more powerful than the bombs that had devastated Hiroshima and Nagasaki and the building of tens of thousands of these weapons, many of which were mounted on unstoppable guided missiles that could fly thousands of miles and hit targets with terrifying accuracy.

The post–World War II American foreign policy consensus remained largely intact through a series of crises until the Vietnam War, which for this country began in earnest when combat troops were committed to the struggle in 1965 and ended in 1973 when the last U.S. troops left South Vietnam. In the wake of that costly failure to contain Communism in Southeast Asia, other actions undertaken by the United States during the Cold War, both successes and failures, come under close investigation and, often, criticism. The question of how the United States should use its power was debated with reference to events that had taken place in many different countries and at different times during the Cold War. The issues included direct military intervention, covert action to promote regime change, and other tactics that policy makers had considered essential to the defense of the country in an anarchic arena where the rules and restraints pertaining to domestic politics did not apply. In the contentious atmosphere of that debate, it did not take long for some critics to build an intellectual bridge across the tiny strait in time separating the Cold War from World War II. Not only the atomic bombing of Hiroshima and Nagasaki, but also the incendiary bombing of German and Japanese cities and indeed the entire strategic bombing campaign against Germany and Japan were enveloped by a debate that increasingly knew fewer limits in geography or time.

Of course, every issue in the larger debate of the use of American power is discussed at least in part on its own terms, and there is no necessary link between believing the United States was or was not justified in using atomic weapons against Japan and one's point of view regarding this country's policies in any number of Cold War and post–Cold War crises. These include, but are not limited to, American containment of Soviet power and Communist expansion in Europe during the second half of the 1940s, Washington's reaction in 1950 when North Korea invaded South Korea, how Washington responded to the challenge of Communist expansion in Vietnam, or how it managed the nuclear arms race with the Soviet Union. More recently, what one thinks about Hiroshima and Nagasaki may or may not have a connection to one's judgment about what the United States should have done in Bosnia and Kosovo, how it should have responded to the 1990 Iraqi invasion of Kuwait and to the crisis that led to the war in Iraq in 2003, or how it should confront the post-9/11 terrorist threat posed by Islamic extremism or the menace posed by terrorist-sponsoring nations (most notably Iran and North Korea) acquiring nuclear weapons. But Hiroshima and Nagasaki are linked to all of these issues, and many others as well, because they are about the use of American power and the extent to which its use can be justified in defense of this country's vital interests without violating moral standards consistent with democratic values and traditions.

This should be kept in mind while considering the following section, "Key Questions and Interpretations," as it regards the use of atomic weapons against Japan, as well as the documents collected in this volume. Going over these materials constitutes much more than simply studying history and events that happened long ago. It is also a matter of walking a mile in Harry Truman's shoes and thereby gaining an understanding that national leaders do not make security decisions in a vacuum. It is likewise a matter of preparing for the trials and responsibilities of citizenship in a country that is at once the world's leading democracy and its strongest military power and as such the object of judgment by critics worldwide using exacting standards that rarely are applied to other nations. Finally, studying the debates and documents connected to the bombing of Hiroshima and Nagasaki is a matter of confronting the grim truth that in international affairs there often are no perfect or even satisfactory solutions to major crises, only responses that allow nations to survive them with the least possible damage so that they will be in a position to cope with the inevitable new crises that await them just down the road.

PART II

Key Questions and Interpretations

The debate over the atomic bombing of Japan, like any debate over a government act of historic significance, is really a composite of many narrower debates. In the context of this volume, ten of those debates are briefly summarized as key questions and interpretations. These discussions inevitably overlap, and, more often than not, opponents on one issue are likely to disagree in a predictable way on most or possibly even all of the other issues. For example, commentators who argue that Japan was prepared to surrender before the atomic bomb was used against Hiroshima (see Key Question 1) often also maintain that after the war Truman and other members of his administration exaggerated the number of casualties they expected from an invasion of Japan in order to justify the use of the bomb (see Key Question 5). But this congruence is far from universal. In the case of the two questions mentioned above, it is quite plausible to be convinced that during the spring and summer of 1945 Truman and his advisors did not expect a Japanese surrender but that there were postwar exaggerations of the number of casualties expected in the invasion of Japan. Indeed, some historians see things exactly that way. It is also possible to believe that the bombing of Hiroshima was morally justified but that the bombing of Nagasaki was not (see Key Question 9), or that unconditional surrender was a reasonable policy (see Key Question 3) but that the atomic bomb was not a justifiable way of bringing it about (see Key Question 9). Nor is there any necessary link between how one views the evidence regarding why Japan was not given a warning or demonstration prior to the attack on Hiroshima (see Key Question 4) and whether the Truman administration practiced atomic diplomacy vis-à-vis the Soviet Union (see Key Question 8).

The questions are these:

1. Was Japan ready to surrender before the use of the atomic bomb against Hiroshima? If not, would it have surrendered without the bombing of Nagasaki?
2. What did the United States know and conclude about Japanese intentions and plans?
3. Was the policy of unconditional surrender justified?
4. Why was Japan not given a demonstration or warning of the atomic bomb before it was used?
5. What were the U.S. casualty estimates for the invasion of Japan? How did they change during the summer and fall of 1945? Which did President Truman hear and believe?
6. What were the alternatives to invasion before the bombing of Hiroshima?
7. Which event contributed more to Japan's surrender: the use of atomic bombs or the Soviet declaration of war on Japan?
8. Did the United States use the atomic bomb against Japan in order to practice "atomic diplomacy" against the Soviet Union?
9. Was the use of atomic bombs against Hiroshima and Nagasaki morally justified?
10. Why, in the end, did the Truman administration decide to use the atomic bomb against Japan?

Each of these questions must be evaluated separately based on an individual examination of the available documentary evidence and consideration of how expert commentators, who often do not agree, have interpreted that evidence.

KEY QUESTION 1.
WAS JAPAN READY TO SURRENDER BEFORE THE ATOMIC BOMB WAS USED AGAINST HIROSHIMA?

When P. M. S. Blackett first argued in *Fear, War, and the Bomb* (1949) that Japan would have surrendered during the summer of 1945 even if it had not been attacked by atomic bombs, his main evidence was the conclusion of the United States Strategic Bombing Survey (USSBS) as presented in its *Summary Report (Pacific War)* in 1946. The key sentence ran as follows: "Based on a detailed investigation of all the facts, and supported by testimony of the surviving Japanese leaders involved, it is the Survey's opinion that certainly prior to 31 December 1945, and in all probability prior to 1 November 1945, Japan would have surrendered even if the atomic bomb had not been dropped, even if Russia had not entered the war, and even if no invasion had been planned or contemplated"[1] (see Document F1). The USSBS conclusion subsequently became one of the two key pillars supporting the Japan-was-ready-to-surrender thesis. Two of the earliest and most influential revisionist scholars, Gar Alperovitz (*Atomic Diplomacy: Hiroshima and Potsdam*, 1965) and Martin Sherwin (*A World Destroyed: The Atomic Bomb and the Grand Alliance*, 1975) in effect accepted Blackett's assertions while themselves focusing primarily on American activities and decision making and paying only cursory attention to events in Japan. However, both also leaned on what became the second pillar of the thesis that Japan was prepared to surrender: the diplomatic cables between Foreign Minister Shigenori Togo and his ambassador to the Soviet Union, Naotake Sato, especially the transmissions intercepted by American MAGIC intelligence operations in July 1945. Neither Alperovitz nor Sherwin devoted much space to an analysis of those cables.

Both the USSBS and MAGIC pillars subsequently were undermined by further scholarly examination. The first systematic critique of the USSBS assessment was by Robert P. Newman in *Truman and the Hiroshima Cult* (1995). Newman carefully compares the conclusions of the *Summary Report*—which were repeated in a companion USSBS publication, *Japan's Struggle to End the War* (1946)—with the actual testimony of the Japanese officials upon which those conclusions presumably were based. He finds that they did not coincide. Almost unanimously, Japanese military and civilian officers stressed that before the atomic bomb Tokyo was *not* prepared to surrender. The only exception was a single remark, made after badgering by American interviewers, by the Marquis Koichi Kido, the Lord Keeper of the Privy Seal, a remark that stood in contrast to the bulk of his testimony and that Kido subsequently contradicted in 1947 during the Tokyo War Crimes Trial. Newman's assessment was that the USSBS's conclusions contradicted its own evidence. Gian P. Gentile reinforced that assessment in his article "Advocacy or Assessment? The United States Strategic Bombing Survey of Germany and Japan" (1997). Gentile demonstrated that the USSBS's own evidence did not support its conclusion that conventional bombing against Japanese cities severely undermined public morale and therefore was decisive in forcing Japan's surrender. Rather, Gentile asserted, the USSBS's reports "implicitly suggested that the atom bomb and Soviet declaration transformed the realization of defeat into surrender."[2]

That assessment was echoed elsewhere, including Japan. In "The Shock of the Atomic Bomb and Japan's Decision to Surrender—A Reconsideration"

(1998), Japanese historian Sadao Asada writes that Japanese sources "assuredly" do not support the ex post facto early-surrender conclusions of the USSBS.[3] The same conclusion was even expressed by some revisionist scholars; for example, in a 1995 *Diplomatic History* article Barton J. Bernstein writes, "Put bluntly, the survey's conclusions were undercut by crucial evidence that the survey basically ignored."[4] Nor did Herbert Bix, author of what is generally regarded as the definitive biography of Hirohito, see evidence to support an early surrender thesis. Richard B. Frank and Tsuyoshi Hasegawa, who disagree on precisely why Japan surrendered, agree that the early-surrender thesis of the USSBS is contradicted by the survey's own evidence.[5]

The documents section of this volume includes seventeen edited selections from the USSBS: two from its reports (see Documents F1 and F2) and fifteen from actual interrogations (see Documents F3 to F17). The excerpts from the interrogations are, insofar as possible, representative of what the USSBS was told. The Kido interrogation (see Document F6) contains his crucial acknowledgment that the war would have ended before November 1, even if the atomic bomb had not been used, along with some subsequent statements that appear to support that assessment. At the same time, it also contains statements that appear to undermine that conclusion, one about the bomb's enormous psychological impact (greater than the March 9–10 incendiary raid on Tokyo) and another regarding the army's confidence in its ability to resist an invasion. Meanwhile, in his interrogation (see Document F5), Prince Konoe rejects the November 1 surrender scenario, bluntly telling his questioner that the army was determined to resist an invasion and that had the atomic bomb not been dropped the war "probably" would have lasted until the end of 1945, an assessment he in effect repeats when the interrogator mentions the November 1 date. Konoe's assessment is echoed by Baron K. Hiranuma (see Document F7), the influential president of the Privy Council. One document that should be read with reference to what Konoe told the USSBS in November 1945 is what is known as the Konoe Memorial (see Document D2), a statement the prince made to the emperor in February 1945. In a response to a question from the emperor, Konoe mentions "making peace" and adds that Japan might have to "surrender unconditionally." At the same time, his understanding of that eventuality, as expressed in the Memorial, clearly excluded even a "reform" of Japan's emperor system of government (*kokutai*) and Japan's retention of considerable territory beyond the confines of its home islands.[6] In other words, Konoe's concept of unconditional surrender was incompatible with anything under consideration in Allied capitals during 1945, including options that would have modified the Allied understanding of unconditional surrender.

Perhaps most significant is the testimony of Prime Minister Suzuki (see Document F12), who told the USSBS that the Supreme Council for the Direction of the War did not believe the United States could win the war by bombing alone; only after the atomic bomb was dropped and it became clear the United States would not have to invade Japan, Suzuki maintained, did the SCDW decide "that it would be best to sue for peace."[7]

The other interrogations tell a similar story, albeit from varying points of view and with different emphases. Of particular interest because of the insight it provides about attitudes among the army's top leaders is the testimony of Lieutenant General Torashiro Kawabe (see Document F3), the army deputy chief of staff during the last months of the war, who worked closely with Army Minister Anami and Army Chief of Staff Umezu. Kawabe told his interrogators that the army leaders had "made up our minds to fight to the last man and thought we still had a chance." He added, that if "the war had continued to a finish fight, I would have crashed my plane into the enemy and I feel that everyone in the Air Force feels the same way."[8] What is most compelling about Kawabe's testimony in November 1945 is that it is confirmed by what he said during the crucial period in question in his diary entries of August 7–11, 1945 (see Document D16). Indeed, Kawabe's diary expresses a fatalistic determination to fight on even after the bombing of Hiroshima, the Soviet entry into the war, and the bombing of Nagasaki. It makes chilling reading, even sixty years after it was written.[9]

The intentions expressed in the USSBS testimony were reiterated in additional statements made by many of the same officials, and others as well, to researchers from the U.S. Army's Military Intelligence Section during 1949 and 1950. Kawabe again was among those interviewed, as was Admiral Seimo Toyoda, the navy chief of staff in August 1945, who also had been interrogated by the USSBS (see Documents G8, G9, G15, G16). However, the documents in this series that probably shed the most light on Japan's readiness to surrender are two sets of notes taken during the Imperial Conference of August 9–10, 1945, when that decision was made. They were taken respectively by Zenshiro Hoshima, the chief of the Naval Affairs Bureau of the Navy Ministry in August 1945, and Sumihisa Ikeda, the chief of the Cabinet Planning Bureau[10] (see Documents G5 and G6). This decisive meeting took place only after both atomic bombs had been dropped on Japan. Both sets of notes record the military's insistence on four conditions before accepting the Potsdam Declaration, among them no occupation of Japan and the maintenance of the country's current system of government.[11]

The MAGIC intercepts of Japanese diplomatic cables, which contain the communications between Foreign Minister Togo and Ambassador Sato, likewise are problematic for the pre-Hiroshima surrender thesis. In The Last Great Victory (1995), a massive day-by-day overview of the last month of the war, Stanley Weintraub reviews these cables and concludes that a "fantasy world" based on avoiding surrender continued to exist in Tokyo despite Sato's warnings; Hirohito's ministers, Weintraub suggests, "were listening only to themselves." One of the most comprehensive overviews of what MAGIC reveals is provided by historian Richard B. Frank in *Downfall: The End of the Japanese Empire* (1999).[12] Throughout these exchanges, it is clear that Sato, who was convinced that Japan either had to surrender or face destruction, was frustrated with the atmosphere of unreality he detected in Tokyo. In particular, this was manifested in Togo's refusal to state specific terms for ending the war that Sato might transmit to Moscow. At one point the ambassador angrily dismissed the foreign minister's instructions as "nothing more than academic fine phrases" (see Document C5); in another message Sato complained, "If the Japanese Empire is really faced with the necessity of ending the war, we must first of all make up our minds to do so" (see Document C6).[13] Frank focuses particular attention on MAGIC intercepts No. 1212 of July 20 (see Document C9) and No. 1214 of July 22, 1945 (see Document C10), the first of which includes a summary of a message Sato sent on July 18 and the second of which includes Togo's response on July 21. Together they speak to the point about whether a modification of the demand of unconditional surrender to allow the emperor to continue on the throne would have convinced Japan to capitulate. Thus, on July 18 Sato's message stressed that "it goes without saying that in my earlier messages calling for unconditional surrender or closely equivalent terms, I made an exception of the question of preserving our national structure." Togo's emphatic retort stressed that "with regard to unconditional surrender (I have been informed of your 18 July message) we are unable to consent to it under any circumstances whatsoever."[14] The warning Sato issued on August 4 also merits consideration: "However, if the Government and the Military dilly-dally in bringing this resolution to fruition, then all Japan will be reduced to ashes and we will not be able [to avoid] following the road to ruin"[15] (see Document C16). Two days later, Little Boy destroyed Hiroshima.

Several other documents available in this volume speak to the attitudes of leading Japanese officials before the bombing of Hiroshima. On July 1, 1945, Imperial General Headquarters issued its "Estimate of the Situation for the Spring of 1946" (see Document D5). It focused on several perceived American weaknesses, including the potential demoralizing impact on the Americans of high casualties and difficulties their new president might have in managing the war effort.[16] The diary entries of Marquis Kido for January 1, 1944 (his peace plan that would have left Japan with its conquests intact), June 8, 1945 (in which Kido outlines a new plan that concedes Japan will have to give up its conquests and focuses on the "supreme object" of maintaining its system of government) (see Document D14), and August 9 and 10 (see Document D15) trace the changes in thinking of the man closest to the emperor. The statement of Army Minister Anami broadcast on August 10 (see Document D9), official army telegrams of August 10, August 11, and August 12 (see Documents D10, D11, and D13), and the diary entries of Lieutenant Colonel Masahiko Takeshita (known as the Secret

War Termination Diary) (see Document D17) all provide insights into the mood and thinking of the top military commanders during the last days of the war. The diary of Admiral Matone Ugaki (see Document D19) is a record of unshakable devotion to the cause and unbearable despair that ended in suicide, an escape route taken by hundreds of Japanese military officers as the specter and then the reality of defeat, like the dark mushroom clouds that rose over Hiroshima and Nagasaki, gradually enveloped Tokyo and the rest of the country.[17]

Japan's military activities during the spring and summer of 1945 constitute another indication of its intentions before August 6. During the spring and summer of 1945, Japan was engaged in a massive buildup of its forces on the southernmost home island of Kyushu, where Tokyo's military planners correctly expected the planned American invasion of Japan to begin. By August, about 900,000 troops of varying quality awaited the American invaders on Kyushu, a total that exceeded the size of the projected invasion force. This activity was monitored by the American ULTRA codebreakers, although ULTRA, notwithstanding its great success, seriously underestimated the size of the Japanese force on Kyushu. The most authoritative overview of the ULTRA operation is Edward J. Drea's *MacArthur's ULTRA: Codebreaking and the War Against Japan, 1942–1945* (1992). Drea sees this buildup as a demonstration of Japan's determination to fight on and resist an American invasion. He adds, "On the eve of atomic warfare, ULTRA painted a menacing picture of a Kyushu transformed into an island bastion."[18] A selection of ULTRA reports (some of them labeled "MAGIC" — Far East Summary) is included in the documents section of this volume (see Documents B28–B38).

A corollary of the debate over Hiroshima is the disagreement over whether the bombing of Nagasaki was necessary to compel surrender. Barton J. Bernstein, while tentative on the need for the Hiroshima bombing, argues in "The Atomic Bomb Reconsidered" (1995) that the Nagasaki bomb "was almost certainly unnecessary." Interestingly, in the same article he states that no official in Washington expected one or two bombs to do the job; rather, they "expected to use at least a third, and possibly more." McGeorge Bundy believes that the Hiroshima bomb was necessary. Yet in *Danger and Survival: Choices About the Bomb in the First Fifty Years* (1988), he suggests that the attack on Nagasaki could have been delayed "for some days" and that such a delay "would have been relatively easy, and I think right." At the same time, Bundy admits that the Nagasaki bomb "strengthened the peace party and further shook the diehards" and does not offer a conclusive statement on its necessity in bringing about surrender.[19]

Richard Frank, Robert P. Newman, and Robert Maddox all vigorously disagree. They make the point that the Japanese Army and its allies opposed surrender even after Nagasaki, as was demonstrated by the continued three-to-three deadlock in the Big Six after the news from Nagasaki reached Tokyo. After

Hiroshima, as Maddox notes, "Militants had argued that the Americans had no more atomic bombs or, if they had, would refrain from using them because of adverse world opinion." Nagasaki shattered those arguments. Although the military still wanted to fight on, the impact of Nagasaki, coming in the wake of Hiroshima and the Soviet entry into the war, finally put Emperor Hirohito in the position to intervene in the political process and end the war. And even then, he had to intervene twice, first on the night of August 9–10 and then once again, even more directly and at last decisively, on August 14.[20]

Japan's Longest Day (1968), written by historians affiliated with the Pacific War Research Society, is a detailed, hour-by-hour account of the events in Tokyo of August 14 to 15 based on Japanese sources. It includes an introductory chapter, "The Days Before," that covers the period between August 6 and August 14. Originally published in Japanese in 1965, the book is a composite of interviews conducted by fourteen historians who spoke with every person involved in the decision who survived the war, the notable exception being Hirohito. Its account of the military's opposition to surrender and the attempted coup by junior officers on the night of August 14–15 raises serious questions about whether the emperor could have imposed his will on the military leadership and brought about surrender absent the bombing of Nagasaki.[21]

Several documents in this volume, either directly or indirectly, address the impact of the Nagasaki bomb. In his diary entry for August 10, Marquis Kido notes that "atomic bombs were dropped at Nagasaki City" and that this "gave a great shock to the nation." He adds that, along with the Soviet entry into the war, this led to "moves and countermoves" by both the war and peace factions. Kido, of course, was for peace, and it is interesting to note that despite all that had already happened he still saw "various difficulties ahead"[22] (see Document D15). In his 1949 testimony to the U.S. Army's Military Intelligence Section, Admiral Toyoda refers to his belief after Hiroshima that the Americans were unlikely to continue their atomic bombing because of a lack of radioactive materials and international pressure (see Document G15). Meanwhile, numerous documents in sections D, F, and G testify to the military's continued determination to fight on after Nagasaki.

KEY QUESTION 2.
WHAT DID THE UNITED STATES KNOW AND CONCLUDE ABOUT JAPANESE INTENTIONS AND PLANS?

There is no disagreement among scholars that American leaders were well aware what certain Japanese officials confidentially were saying to each other and were informed regarding Japanese military preparations during the spring and summer of 1945. Gar Alperovitz, Robert Newman, and Richard P. Frank all point out that Truman was aware of the information in the MAGIC Diplomatic Summaries. Frank adds that summaries of ULTRA intercepts circulated with the MAGIC summaries. Edward Drea notes that Marshall and other key decision makers read ULTRA.[23]

The disagreement, which parallels the differences of opinion about Japanese intentions regarding surrender, is about what this intelligence led Truman and his advisors to conclude about Tokyo's attitude about ending the war. Alperovitz argues that some military planners, key civilian officials (such as Secretary of War Stimson, Secretary of the Navy Forrestal, Undersecretary of State Grew, and Assistant Secretary of War John J. McCloy), and Truman himself understood from this intelligence that Japan was on the verge of surrender prior to the bombing of Hiroshima. J. Samuel Walker, writing in 1990 and again in 1996, maintains that the "consensus" among scholars at the time he surveyed the literature was that in the months before Hiroshima the atomic bomb was not needed to force a Japanese surrender and that "Truman and his advisor knew it."[24] The Alperovitz thesis has suffered substantially in the wake of recent scholarship, while Walker's assessment applies mainly to revisionist authors and overlooks what some scholars, even certain revisionists, were saying. For example, Lisle Rose, who believes that Japan would have surrendered prior to the use of the atomic bomb, nonetheless asserts in *Dubious Victory* (1973) that there was nothing in the Sato/Togo exchanges to lead Washington to that conclusion.[25] Edward Drea writes in *MacArthur's ULTRA* (1992) that the "confidential messages revealed by ULTRA gave no hint of surrender. Quite the opposite, they foreshadowed another bloody battle." John Ray Skates seconds Drea's assessment in *The Invasion of Japan: Alternative to the Bomb* (1994), noting that there was "no evidence" from ULTRA that Japan's military leaders "had modified their plans for an apocalyptic defense."[26] In *Weapons for Victory* (1995), Robert Maddox provides compelling evidence that until Hiroshima none of Truman's top military advisors believed that Japan would surrender before the planned invasion of the home islands. Robert H. Ferrell's discussion of the issue in *Harry S. Truman: A Life* (1994) supports that conclusion, as does Richard Frank's in *Downfall* (1999).[27] In addition, John D. Chappell's survey of the American press in *Before the Bomb* (1997) reveals that throughout 1945 the American public, no less than the country's leaders, was reading and hearing that Japan had no intention of surrendering. Those assessments included reports of defiant broadcasts by Radio Tokyo. It repeatedly beamed texts of articles and speeches to the United States that, Chappell notes, "reiterated that an invasion of Japan would result in casualties so vast that the Allies would decide to stop the war." Prime Minister Suzuki was among the Japanese officials quoted in those broadcasts.[28]

,Thus, when Suzuki rejected the Potsdam Declaration with his notorious *mokusatsu* ("kill with silence") comment on July 28, he was simply repeating what both the American public and its leaders had heard many times before. There was little reason not to believe that he meant what he said.

Many kinds of documents in this volume speak to this issue, albeit with varying degrees of authority. Truman's diary gives a fragmentary insight into his thinking. The entries of July 17 and 18, especially the latter, suggest that he briefly was optimistic about a Japanese surrender either before the Soviet Union entered the war or as a consequence of that act. Yet there is nothing to indicate that he knew or was in any way convinced that Japan was prepared to surrender. Thus, while on July 17 he wrote, "Believe Japs will fold up before Russia comes in," his next sentence stated that he was "sure" the atomic bomb would bring about the heretofore unattainable surrender. By July 25 Truman's optimism had faded; even with Stalin's promise to enter the war in hand, he was "sure" that the Potsdam warning would *not* convince Tokyo to surrender[29] (see Document A36). Another document that speaks directly to what Truman was expecting before arriving at Potsdam is a letter he wrote to his wife on July 18. There he expresses satisfaction regarding the promised Soviet entry because "that will end the war a year sooner now, and think of those kids who won't be killed!"[30] (see Document A44). In other words, even Truman's temporary optimism about a possible Japanese surrender as expressed in his July 18 diary entry coexisted with a deeper pessimism and concern that the war would last well into 1946.

In contrast to Truman, Stimson is far more comprehensive in his diary and memos about his viewpoint on urgent issues, from his concerns about postwar relations with the Soviet Union to his belief that the policy of unconditional surrender should be modified to allow the continuation of the Japanese monarchy, to his thoughts on the use of the atomic bomb and the implications of the existence of nuclear weapons once peace was restored, and to many other issues related to winning the war and establishing a stable peace (see Documents A12, A16, A20, A29, A32, A33, A34, A40, A41, A53, and A54). Like all American leaders, Stimson desperately wanted to end the war as quickly as possible and without an invasion of Japan. On July 2 he noted that "the effort to shorten the Japanese war by surrender" was one of the "largest and most important problems that I have had since I have been here"[31] (see Document A33). But there is no evidence in his diary, nor in the various memos he wrote (see Documents A21, A34, A42), that he assumed Japan was on the point of surrendering. Thus, on August 9, after two atomic attacks on Japan and the Soviet entry into the war, Stimson expected only that these events "certainly will have an effect on hastening the victory." He added, "just how much that effect is on how long and how many men we will have to keep to accomplish that victory, it is impossible yet to determine." The next day, upon receiving news that Tokyo had offered to surrender, Stimson, about to leave on a well-earned vacation, was shocked, noting with pleasure that the news had "busted our holiday"[32] (see Documents A53 and A54).

Military intelligence assessments likewise do not indicate confidence in an early Japanese surrender prior to the bombing of Hiroshima. One document that has been cited by commentators who believe the American intelligence had concluded that Japan was close to surrender before August 6, 1945, is a report submitted by the Combined U.S.-British Intelligence Committee to the Combined Chiefs of Staff: C.C.S. 643/3, "Estimate of the Enemy Situation (as of 6 July)," dated July 8, 1945 (see Document B15). The document does state that the entry of the Soviet Union into the war "would finally convince the Japanese of the inevitability of complete defeat," but when it gets to the question of an actual surrender—something quite distinct and separate from realizing the inevitability of defeat—the assessment becomes murkier. C.C.S. 643/3 points out that unconditional surrender is "most revolting" to the Japanese and that they are determined to avoid it as well as an occupation and "foreign custody of the person of the Emperor." It adds that to avoid these conditions, "and, in any event, to insure the survival of the institution of the Emperor," the Japanese "might well be willing" to give up their conquests in Asia and the Pacific and "even agree to the independence of Korea and the practical disarmament of their military forces." However, these conditions fall far short of what any American or Allied leader, even those who argued against unconditional surrender, believed was acceptable. Nor is "might well be willing" a ringing statement of confidence. Finally, the full context of C.C.S. 643/3—including the observation that "Japanese leaders are now playing for time in the hope that Allied war weariness, Allied disunity, or some 'miracle' will present an opportunity to arrange a compromise peace"—undermines its more optimistic suggestions.[33]

Other military assessments are uniformly more pessimistic than C.C.S. 643/3. The analysis section of the July 27 "MAGIC"—Far East Summary (see chapter 4, note 27) warned that Japan would not accept any peace terms satisfactory to the Allies as long as Tokyo's "all powerful" military leaders believed they could repel the invasion of the home islands (see Document B34). On July 29, 1945, as recorded in C.C.S. 880/4, military intelligence worried over the possibility that the conquest of Japan's home islands might not end resistance elsewhere in Asia (see Document B13). On July 13, a memo from Marshall's deputy assistant chief of staff noted Japanese attempts to exploit war-weariness in the United States (see Document B14). On July 29, an intelligence estimate from General Douglas MacArthur's headquarters warned of the military implications of the continuing Japanese buildup on Kyushu (see Document B20). An even grimmer estimate followed on August 1 (see Document B21). In fact, on August 12—after the attacks on Hiroshima and Nagasaki and Japan's initial surrender offer, but before

Japan's final acceptance of Washington's terms—a top-level intelligence assessment in Washington noted, "Atomic bombs will not have a decisive effect in the next 30 days" (see Document B25).[34] ULTRA reports from June through August meanwhile traced the relentless growth of Japanese military strength on Kyushu (see Documents B28–B38).

Finally, even after Japan's formal surrender and the broadcast of the emperor's rescript, doubts persisted among American military and civilian leaders about whether all Japanese troops would obey Hirohito's command. There was particular concern about Japanese troops around Singapore. Meanwhile, in the days after the official surrender, aside from the attempt by junior army officers in Tokyo to seize the imperial palace, there were several minor mutinies in Japan itself. A grim joke circulating in Washington summed up the uncertainty American leaders had felt for months as they searched for a formula to stop the fighting: "Do you think Japan's surrender will shorten the war?"[35]

KEY QUESTION 3.
WAS THE POLICY OF UNCONDITIONAL SURRENDER JUSTIFIED?

The World War II policy of unconditional surrender emerged from the failed peace that ended World War I. In particular, there was a widespread belief that the failure to secure an unconditional surrender in 1918 from Germany had laid the basis for the sequence of events that culminated in a second world war. The assumption that things would be done differently to end World War II was well established in Washington during the first year of the war. The official announcement that the Allies would demand unconditional surrender from the Axis powers came at the close of the Casablanca conference between Roosevelt and Churchill on January 23, 1943 (see Documents A3 and A4). Numerous reaffirmations followed (see Document A7). They included a press conference remark in mid-1944 in which Roosevelt, albeit a bit crudely, emphasized the lesson he had learned from how the previous world war had ended: "Practically all Germans deny the fact that they surrendered during the last war, but this time they are going to know it. So are the Japs."[36] Roosevelt's emphasis on Germany and the almost parenthetical reference to Japan were not accidental. Germany was the far more powerful and dangerous enemy, the country Allied leaders feared might develop an atomic bomb. It had to be defeated first. Only then would the Allies be ready to finish off Japan. Meanwhile, unconditional surrender gained additional legitimacy from its role in holding the so-called Grand Alliance against Germany together. That partnership actually was an unstable shotgun marriage of the United States and Britain on one hand and the Soviet

Union on the other. The two democracies and their totalitarian communist partner were bound together only by their mutual life-and-death struggle against Nazi Germany, and that tenuous unity was constantly in danger of being sundered by deep-seated mutual suspicions. Roosevelt and Churchill never were entirely free of the fear that the Soviets would make a separate peace with the Nazis. They also were aware that Stalin suspected them of similar intentions. The mutual commitment to unconditional surrender was the political glue Washington and London needed to hold the Grand Alliance together. As with the atomic bomb, an instrument conceived primarily to deal with Germany came to be applied to Japan as well.

The debate over unconditional surrender hinges above all on whether that policy actually prolonged the war. While that discussion at times dealt with alleged effects on Germany's surrender—with critics such as Anne Armstrong (*Unconditional Surrender: The Impact of the Casablanca Policy Upon World War II*, 1961) and Hansen Baldwin (*Great Mistakes of the War*, 1950) arguing that it delayed Germany's surrender—the focus usually has been on the policy's impact on Japan, largely on whether insistence on unconditional surrender delayed Tokyo's surrender and therefore led to the use of the atomic bomb to end the war. Recent critics of unconditional surrender include John Ray Skates, who asserts in *The Invasion of Japan: Alternatives to the Bomb* (1994) that "unconditional surrender prolonged the Pacific war and drove both belligerents to last-ditch military strategies." John D. Chappell concurs, arguing in *Before the Bomb: How America Approached the End of the Pacific War* (1997) that the "combination of Allied insistence on Japan's immediate unconditional surrender and the continued resistance by the Japanese prolonged the Pacific war." An even stronger criticism comes from Dennis D. Wainstock, who maintains in *The Decision to Drop the Atomic Bomb* (1996) that unconditional surrender "was a policy of revenge, and it hurt America's national self-interest."[37]

The most comprehensive defense of Roosevelt's unconditional surrender policy is Raymond G. O'Connor's *Diplomacy for Victory: FDR and Unconditional Surrender* (1971). Robert Maddox's *Weapons for Victory* (1995) and Robert P. Newman's *Truman and the Hiroshima Cult* (1995) include individual chapters that provide more concise endorsements of that policy.[38]

A central point in the overall critique of unconditional surrender is that guaranteeing that the position of the emperor would not be eliminated and that Hirohito would be allowed to remain on the throne would have decisively influenced decision making in Tokyo. Thus, in *The Decision to Use the Atomic Bomb* (1995), Alperovitz claims that "the only serious condition Japan's leaders sought was an assurance that the Emperor would not be eliminated."[39] Had the United States been willing to make this guarantee, the argument goes, Japan almost certainly would have surrendered before August 6. This thesis must be evaluated in light of evidence regarding the army's dominance of the government and its insistence on four conditions prior to surrendering, conditions that went well beyond simply keeping the position of emperor and keeping the current occupant on the throne (see Key Question 1). As J. Samuel Walker has noted in *Prompt and Utter Destruction* (1997), if keeping the emperor had been all the Japanese leaders wanted, "they could have sent a clear signal to that effect to the United States, which almost certainly would have found the single condition acceptable." Herbert Bix, the biographer of Hirohito, offers a parallel analysis, noting in "Japan's Delayed Surrender" (1995) that "it was not so much the Allied policy of unconditional surrender that prolonged the Pacific war, as it was the unrealistic and incompetent actions of Japan's leaders." Bix also stresses the essential fact that unconditional surrender was not simply a means of destroying Germany and Japan, but also a means that would permit a military occupation and fundamental reform of the defeated fascist powers, both of which were unacceptable to men who controlled Japan's fate before August 6. Indeed, in *Hirohito*, Bix traces how even after Japan's surrender, the beginning of the U.S. military occupation, and the installation of a new cabinet of supposed moderates, the country's new leaders did everything possible to keep the Meiji constitution and the emperor's powers intact. In the end, they, and a most reluctant Hirohito, had to accept the new reality as dictated by the United States. But their resistance to change, even under military occupation, casts serious doubt on any claim that modifying unconditional with the limited guarantee mentioned before would have brought about surrender without additional pressure. Nor is Bix the only expert on postwar Japan to stress the linkage between the American military occupation, and hence unconditional surrender, and Japanese reform. Both John Dower, in *Embracing Defeat: Japan in the Wake of World War II* (1999), and Japanese historian Daikichi Irokawa, in *The Age of Hirohito* (1995), make essentially the same point.[40]

During the war, unconditional surrender had strong support in the State Department, but it did not go unchallenged, especially after Germany surrendered and full attention turned to Japan. President Truman was urged by important civilian and military advisors—among them Marshall, Leahy, Stimson, Grew, Forrestal, and McCloy—to modify unconditional surrender to allow the Japanese to keep the emperor. The consensus was that mitigating unconditional surrender in that way would increase the chances for a Japanese surrender. Grew presented his views to Truman personally in late May, and the matter came up at the June 18 meeting Truman held with his top advisors to discuss Operation Olympic (see Document A27), after which Truman appointed a committee of Stimson, Grew, Forrestal, and McCloy to draft a warning to be issued to Japan at the upcoming Potsdam Conference. On July 2, in a long memo to Truman, Stimson outlined his view that the planned warning to Japan to surrender should leave open the possibility of Japan retaining its dynasty, albeit as a constitutional monarchy (see Document A33). Marshall and the military brass, reeling from the heavy casualties in successive island battles, believed that it was necessary to keep the emperor in place in order to bring a surrender that would be honored by all Japanese military units outside Japan. Yet at Potsdam, Marshall did not support a specific reference to Japan's future government because he feared it might be misinterpreted and do more harm than good[41] (see Documents B16-1, B16-2, and B17). Newly appointed Secretary of State James Byrnes, whose opinion at the time probably carried more weight with Truman than that of any other civilian advisor and who was closely attuned to public opinion at home, also opposed any specific references to the emperor. As a result, the Potsdam Declaration of July 26, while promising the Japanese people the ultimate right to choose their own form of government, did not specifically mention the emperor or his fate (see Document A45). There were other promises as well, including that Japan could rebuild an industrial economy. Together they constituted a series of conditions that Germany, which truly was forced to surrender unconditionally, did not receive. This seems to have been the opinion of certain Japanese leaders at the time, a point they reiterated after the war.[42] In short, however one judges the policy of unconditional surrender as it affected the war before July 26, the Potsdam Declaration, Japan's last chance to surrender before the bombing of Hiroshima, demanded it more in rhetoric than in fact.

KEY QUESTION 4.
WHY WAS JAPAN NOT GIVEN A DEMONSTRATION OR WARNING OF THE ATOMIC BOMB BEFORE IT WAS USED?

As the narrative overview indicates, the question of giving Japan a demonstration of the atomic bomb was raised and discussed by the full Interim Committee on May 31 and by the committee's Scientific Panel on June 16. In both instances, that option was rejected because of the dangers involved and because none of the participants in the discussion could make a case that a demonstration at some remote location, even if carried out, would have the necessary impact on decision makers in Tokyo (see Documents A15 and A24). The Scientific Panel discussion and conclusion was in response to the Franck Report, which had urged a demonstration of the new weapon and, at a minimum, if it came to using the bomb, a warning to the Japanese to evacuate the target area (see Document A23). A subsequent memo in late June by Undersecretary of the Navy James Bard, based on the proposition that Japan "may be searching" for a means of surrender, called simply for a "preliminary warning for say two or three days in advance of use" (see Document A31). The Bard memo reached Stimson but had no impact on decision making.

Journalist Peter Wyden, author of *Day One* (1984), a well-received history of the building and use of the atomic bomb, has written that the idea of demonstrating the atomic bomb to the Japanese did not receive "serious analysis."[43] However, it seems fair to say that there is consensus among scholars that the idea of conducting a demonstration was unworkable and, in light of the imperatives at the time, did receive reasonable consideration. The case for a warning is weaker still. In "Understanding the Atomic Bomb: Missed Opportunities, Little-Known Disasters, and Modern Memory" (1995), Barton J. Bernstein points out that a warning was extremely unlikely to have an impact on the Japanese. McGeorge Bundy raises the crucial point "that for use against Japan the bomb was indeed a *military weapon like any other*," and to maximize impact one does not give warning to the enemy of a new weapon. Robert P. Newman, in *Truman and the Hiroshima Cult* (1995), which contains a comprehensive overview of the demonstration/warning issue, notes that a warning would have undermined the expected "shock value" of the atomic bomb, which American officials from Oppenheimer at Los Alamos to Marshall at the Joint Chiefs of Staff to Stimson in the War Department hoped would be a key factor in forcing a Japanese surrender. Newman adds that the scientists who produced the Franck Report were primarily concerned with the postwar world, not with the military effort to end the Pacific War or the enormous domestic pressures to end the conflict without further massive casualties. While postwar atomic problems were of deep concern to Truman and his top advisors, their most immediate and urgent agenda item was to end the war as quickly and with as few American casualties as possible. Newman also mentions what he considers serious contradictions and inconsistencies in the Franck Report. In contrast, Martin Sherwin defends the report as a "perceptive study" with regard to postwar developments, including the nuclear arms race.[44]

KEY QUESTION 5.
WHAT WERE THE U.S. CASUALTY ESTIMATES
FOR THE INVASION OF JAPAN?

The question of how many casualties American leaders expected in an invasion of Japan is one of the signature debates in the discussion of the bombing of Hiroshima. For some revisionist historians, the question goes to motive: if the estimates were "low," by which they mean in the tens of thousands, then presumably that was not motive enough to use the bomb. It therefore must have been used for what Alperovitz, in *The Decision to Use the Atomic Bomb* (1995), calls "diplomatic factors": in other words, to intimidate the Soviet Union. Some historians who argue the low-casualty case do not accept that conclusion. Rather, like Barton Bernstein, they maintain that Truman and his advisors—whose primary motive was to end the war and save thousands of American lives—cited higher numbers after the war to make their wartime decision to use the bomb more justifiable, both to themselves and to the American public. Certainly, Truman's postwar statements complicated matters, especially because in discussing the American losses the atomic bomb prevented he at times spoke of "casualties," at other times of "lives," and also changed the numbers he gave. Revisionists, whatever their disagreements, consider Truman's postwar casualty statements exaggerations. For example, in "Truman and the A-Bomb: Targeting Noncombatants, Using the Bomb, and His Defending the 'Decision'" (1998), Bernstein argues that scholars have not found high level archival evidence of casualty estimates running into the hundreds of thousands dating from the spring and summer of 1945. Journalist and historian Kai Bird makes the same point in a 1994 opinion piece ("The Curators Cave In") in the *New York Times*. John Ray Skates (*The Invasion of Japan*, 1994) writes that there is "little" evidence to support the "huge numbers" of projected casualties cited by Truman and Stimson after the war.[45]

The supposedly "low" casualty estimates—even they ran into the tens of thousands—have been vigorously challenged by a variety of scholars, often based on research conducted since the 1990s. Military historian D. M. Giangreco has provided the most comprehensive analysis of casualty estimates and, with regard to military projections, the forms they took, in two groundbreaking articles: "Casualty Projections for the U.S. Invasions of Japan, 1945–1946: Planning and Policy Implications" (1997) and "'A Score of Bloody Okinawas and Iwo Jimas': President Truman and Casualty Estimates for the Invasion of Japan" (2003). Military estimates took three forms: medical estimates, used by those responsible for caring for the wounded; manpower estimates, used to make sure forces engaged in battle were kept at combat strength; and strategic estimates, used to evaluate competing options with regard to overall objectives in future campaigns. In response to historians such as Bernstein, who argues that only straightforward casualty projections in "unalloyed form" are credible, Giangreco points out that such a formulation would artificially and incorrectly exclude crucial relevant data since the military's casualty projections "were seldom directly as such or carried convenient titles like 'Estimated Losses for Operation X,' but were obliquely stated in terms of 'requirements' for manpower, or have to be extrapolated, using contemporary formula, from stated medical needs." His conclusion is that there is substantial documentation of high-end casualty projections reaching into the hundreds of thousands, and that some of them reached Marshall, Stimson, and Truman.[46] Richard Frank's extensive overview of casualty estimates in *Downfall*

(1999), while not agreeing with Giangreco's analysis on every specific point, yields the same overall conclusions. Other historians whose research supports the thesis of high casualty estimates that reached the top decision makers in 1945 are Robert Maddox, in *Weapons for Victory* (1995) and Robert P. Newman, in *Truman and the Hiroshima Cult* (1995). Edward Drea stresses the overall picture suggested by ULTRA as it tracked Japanese reinforcements reaching Kyushu rather than specific estimates (although he mentions some); his assessment is that "ULTRA made OLYMPIC seem expensive indeed." Distinguished Truman biographer Robert H. Ferrell agrees that the available evidence demonstrates that Truman saw and believed high-end casualty estimates.[47]

Many documents in this volume speak to this issue. Planners reporting to the Joint Chiefs of Staff produced enormous estimates several times during 1944 and 1945. The first was the "Saipan ratio," which suggested it might cost 500,000 lives and several times that number wounded to invade and pacify Japan. It appeared in August 1944 in J.C.S. 924/2 (see Document B1), a document produced by an advisory committee to the Joint Chiefs of Staff that was part of a series—J.C.S. 924, "Operations Against Japan Subsequent to Formosa"—distributed to all of the president's top military advisors and senior military planners. The Saipan ratio clearly affected General Marshall, who specifically referred to it a memo a month later (see Document B2). It also subsequently was an important factor in increased draft call-ups during 1945, which were raised from 60,000 to 80,000 per month in January and again to 100,000 per month in March.[48]

More ominous still to American planners was a set of ratios for computing American casualties based on previous experience in the Pacific War contained in J.C.S. 924/15, dated April 25, 1945 (see Document B4). Richard B. Frank has done calculations to determine the casualties these ratios projected for Olympic, the first stage of the planned two-stage invasion of Japan. He came up with between 456,611 and 514,072 casualties (119,516 to 134,556 killed and missing). The second stage, the invasion of Honshu (called Coronet), pushed the total to 1,202,005 (314,619 killed and missing). He adds that the increased Selective Service call-ups in 1945 confirm that the manpower needs suggested by the J.C.S. 924/15 ratios were taken seriously.[49] Meanwhile, in March 1945, the U.S. Army projected that it would need 720,000 replacements for "dead and evacuated wounded" in fighting against Japan between mid-1945 and the end of 1946, a figure that did not include naval and marine losses (see Document B3). On August 10, the day after Nagasaki, Marshall's staff drafted a memo for Leahy estimating that by June the army would need an additional 280,000 beds for soldiers seriously wounded by June 30, 1946 (the estimate was 330,000, but 50,000 would be taken by soldiers wounded in earlier combat) (see Document B24). That number, large as it was, was incomplete as a casualty estimate, inasmuch as it did not include soldiers killed in battle, army patients hospitalized outside the continental United States, navy and marine personnel, and several other categories of wounded troops. Although the document was not sent because of Japan's offer to surrender, it nonetheless serves as an indicator of the scale of casualties the Army Chief of Staff was expecting in the event of an invasion of Japan.[50]

President Truman did not see any of the above figures, but his thinking can be deduced from his reaction to a memo from former president Herbert Hoover that he received late in May. Hoover seems to have had access through military contacts to top-secret information. The memorandum (which followed a similar Hoover missive to Stimson on May 15) urged a negotiated peace that would have forced Japan to disarm but left its government essentially intact and in control of both Korea and Formosa. Otherwise, it might cost "the lives of 500,000 to a million boys" to end the war.[51] (see Document A19, sections 1 and 2, which include the Hoover memo and several related memos). Truman clearly was disturbed: he forwarded the memo to Fred M. Vinson, director of the Office of War Mobilization and Reconversion, and then to Stimson, Grew, former secretary of state Cordell Hull, and Edward Stettinius, the current secretary of state. None questioned Hoover's numbers. Hull called Hoover's peace proposal "appeasement" (see Document A19-1c). Grew—while calling for a modification of unconditional surrender—stressed the need for imposing terms on Japan "considerably wider" than those suggested by Hoover, including a military occupation and the "establishment of democracy." He warned of Japan's potential for "prolonged resistance," and added that such an eventuality would cost many lives (see Document A19-1d). Stimson forwarded his copy to General Marshall, who commissioned and then signed a response written by a staff officer dismissing Hoover's estimates as far too high. Marshall also signed a staff officer memo expressing similar conclusions written in response to the May 15 Hoover memo (see Documents A19-1e and A19-2b). Both responses went to Stimson, who sent neither to Truman. The response to the May 15 Hoover memo (the one the former president sent to Stimson) included the underlined phrase "*under our present plan of campaign,*" which left open the very real possibility that conditions might change and that the cost in American lives might be higher than currently expected. In any event, the Hoover memorandum of late May unnerved Truman. It was the key link in a chain of events that led the president to order the June 18 meeting to discuss whether to reconsider plans to invade Japan. The memo by Admiral Leahy (Truman's chief of staff) calling the meeting made it clear that the president's main concern was "economizing to the maximum extent possible in the loss of American lives[52] (see Document A26). If nothing else, the Hoover memorandum and the memos it spawned reveal that an estimate of at least 500,000 American lives being lost in an invasion of Japan reached the president's desk and was circulated—in two versions—to top-level government officials, including Stimson and Marshall.

The June 18 meeting is controversial, largely because of Marshall's vagueness regarding the meaning of American and Japanese casualty figures in a chart that was part of his opening report. By then both Admiral Nimitz (49,000 casualties in the first thirty days of an assault on Kyushu) (see Document B11) and MacArthur (105,000 in the first 90 days plus 12,500 nonbattle casualties) (see Document B10) had forwarded casualty estimates (Nimitz to King and MacArthur to Marshall). Marshall saw only the slightly lower number from MacArthur's staff (the Nimitz estimate was only for the first thirty days; the MacArthur figure was for ninety days) and wanted clarification. Concerned about Truman's reaction to high casualty estimates, Marshall sent an "Urgent" cable to MacArthur, who in turn immediately responded that he did not antici-pate such heavy losses (see Document B10). Truman never saw either estimate. Nor did he see three sets of estimates included in a paper from the Joint War Plans Committee, which varied according to what different scenarios would occur after the initial assault on southern Kyushu and were accompanied by the caveat that they constituted no more than an "educated guess." Those num-bers—193,000 total battle casualties (40,000 killed), 132,300 total battle casual-ties (25,000 killed), and 220,000 total battle casualties (46,000 killed)—were ex-cised at the next level up the chain of command. A subsequent summary by Assistant Chief of Staff General John Hull, which included the statement that "it is considered wrong to give any estimates in numbers," was what Truman heard from Marshall at the June 18 meeting[53] (see Document A27).

Marshall's report included numbers: ratios of U.S. battle casualties to Japa-nese "killed and prisoners" (Japanese wounded were not included) in four major battles—Leyte, Luzon, Iwo Jima, and Okinawa—along with the imprecise as-sessment that the first thirty days of the Kyushu invasion "should not exceed the price [31,000 casualties] we paid for Luzon." Marshall had picked the battle with the most favorable American/Japanese casualty ratio: had he picked Iwo Jima or Okinawa, the projected American casualty number would have been consider-ably higher. And this is precisely what Admiral Leahy did. He told the president that the battle for Kyushu would resemble Okinawa. Leahy also moved the focus away from American versus Japanese casualty ratios. Instead, he pointed out that Americans troops had suffered a casualty rate of 35 percent on that island. He then asked how many American troops would land on Kyushu, to which Mar-shall responded 766,700. While nobody openly did the math, quick mental cal-culations meant that Leahy's Okinawa casualty percentage and Marshall's figure for the Kyushu assault force together projected more than 268,000 casualties for the upcoming battle. Somewhat later, just before he approved Olympic, a grim Truman said he "hoped there was a possibility of preventing an Okinawa from one end of Japan to the other"[54] (see Document A27).

Some historians have argued that Marshall provided a casualty estimate of 63,000 at the June 18 meeting. The number itself comes from Admiral Leahy's diary entry on that day, which reads, "General Marshall is of the opinion that such an effort [the invasion of Kyushu] will not cost more than 63,000 of the 190,000 combatant troops necessary for the invasion"[55] (see Document A28). The problem is that nowhere in the detailed minutes of the meeting, which run for more than seven single-spaced pages and clearly and precisely include a variety of statistics, is the number 63,000 mentioned. Given the centrality of casualty estimates to the purpose of the meeting and Marshall's leading role in the discussions, to accept the claim that he suggested that number at the meeting requires that one believe that Marshall could have mentioned such a critical statistic and that the meeting's official secretary, a brigadier general, failed both during the meeting and in a subsequent careful review of the minutes to make sure it was recorded. This sequence of events is virtually impossible. Furthermore, Leahy's diary itself is problematic with regard to when Marshall might have mentioned this number. The entries for June 18 are of two kinds: those written in the past tense that clearly report on specific events which took place that day, and those written in the present tense that record opinions, usually Leahy's but also those of others. The opinion statements are not fixed in time, making it impossible to know when Leahy may have formulated or heard them, and the statement about Marshall's 63,000 casualties is written in the present tense. That means there is no reason to assume that Leahy is claiming Marshall mentioned that number on June 18, much less at the White House meeting in question. Since the number does not appear in the minutes, by far the most reliable source about what was said, and by whom, at the June 18 meeting, and since Leahy's diary is not corroborated by any reliable source, there is no documentary evidence that Marshall cited that figure at the June 18 meeting. In addition, an exchange between King and Marshall after the meeting confirms the absence of a specific estimate from Marshall at the meeting. On June 20, King wrote to Marshall that the Joint Chiefs of Staff "will have to give an estimate of the casualties expected in the operation." Marshall responded on June 26. Echoing his remarks at the June 18 meeting, he wrote that such a step was "unnecessary and undesirable," as estimates "at best can be only speculative"[56] (see Document B12).

Having heard nothing specific from Marshall in the June 18 meeting, Truman received another general but ominous casualty assessment from Stimson in a memo dated July 2. The secretary of war feared that the assault on Kyushu would be only the first battle in a long and bloody campaign to pacify the rest of Japan's home islands. Stimson had visited Japan before the war. He told the president the terrain there was suited to a "last ditch defense such as has been made on Iwo Jima and Okinawa" and that if it came to an invasion—which Stimson hoped to avoid with an appropriately worded Allied warning to Japan—the United States in the resulting campaign would face "an even more bitter finish fight than in Germany, with losses "incident to such a war"[57] (see Document A33). Later that month, the secretary of war's office produced yet another set of high casualty estimates. They were in a study commissioned by Dr. Edward L. Bowles, who was both a scientist and one of Stimson's top aides (see Document A43). Bowles wanted to get a perspective on the casualties issue independent of the army and gave the job to William B. Shockley, who would later win a Nobel Prize in physics. Shockley, who had access to classified Pentagon data and input from noted military historian Quincy Wright, pointed out that any accurate estimate of casualties incurred in defeating Japan and forcing a surrender depended on understanding "what is necessary to cause Japan to capitulate" and that this required a historical study of "to what extent the behavior of a nation at war can be predicted from the behavior of her troops in individual battles." Anyone familiar with the war in the Pacific knew how few Japanese soldiers had surrendered to American forces. Shockley's next sentence reflected that disturbing fact: "If the study shows that the behavior of nations in all historical cases comparable to Japan's has in fact been invariably consistent with the behavior of the troops in battle, then it means that the Japanese dead and ineffectives at the time of defeat will exceed the corresponding number for the Germans. In other words, we shall probably have to kill at least 5 to 10 million Japanese. This might cost us between 1.7 to 4 million casualties including 400,000 to 800,000 killed."[58]

Because Shockley's report was delivered to Bowles after Stimson left for the Potsdam Conference, there has been some debate whether the secretary of war ever saw it. Robert P. Newman, the scholar who found the report in the Library of Congress and an expert on Stimson, believes he did. This in turn demonstrates that Stimson's postwar claims that he believed the invasion and the subsequent campaign needed to pacify Japan, which he expected would last well into 1946, would cost over a million casualties did not come out of "thin air." Bowles regularly reported to two higher-ranking aides, George Harrison and Harvey Bundy, and Stimson met with both men daily after returning from Potsdam. Newman concludes, "It stands to reason that such an explosive communication as Shockley's would have been passed on to the boss."[59]

The public at the time certainly had reason to fear high casualties, as frightening estimates appeared often in the media. For example, on May 17 war correspondent Kyle Palmer told the Los Angeles Times, "it will cost 500,000 to 750,000, perhaps 1,000,000, lives to end this war" (see Document A13). Later that month, The New Republic, using the American/Japanese casualty ratio at Tarawa, shuddered about what that meant in light of the 3.6 million Japanese troops it projected would have to be killed to end the war (see Document A14). On June 26, H. V. Kaltenborn, one of the country's most respected and popular radio commentators, warned his huge listening audience that an invasion of Japan might cost 100,000 lives (a figure that, including wounded, would mean about 500,000 total casualties) (see Document A30). In August, just before the bombing of Hiroshima, *The Catholic World* urged that the policy of unconditional surrender be modified because an invasion might "cost us a million additional casualties" (see Document A49). And immediately after the bombing, *The Christian Century* denounced the act as an "atomic atrocity," notwithstanding Winston Churchill's assertion—which the publication found "highly speculative" but said it would not challenge—that "the use of the bomb saved the lives of more than one million American and 250,000 British soldiers" (see Document A56).[60]

Truman and Stimson were not alone in recalling casualty estimates into the hundreds of thousands after the war. Postwar statements, of course, must be evaluated with caution. Still, the memories of well-placed witnesses can have value. Some witnesses, at least according to what they said after 1945, did not believe the atomic bomb was necessary to compel a Japanese surrender and therefore had no reason to inflate estimates they said they heard or believed prior to Hiroshima. Paul Nitze, the vice chairman of the United States Strategic Bombing Survey (USSBS), had opposed an invasion of Japan. As he explained in 1994, "I thought the estimate of 500,000 casualties [in an invasion] was a gross underestimate." General Curtis LeMay was in charge of the XXI Bomber Command beginning in January 1945, which carried out the strategic bombing, and firebombing, of Japan. Like Nitze, he believed that bombing and blockade could force a Japanese surrender. In his memoirs, published in 1965, LeMay recalled a briefing from the 20th Air Force chief of staff upon taking command of his bomber group. "In effect he had said: 'You go ahead and get results with the B-29. If you don't get results, you'll be fired. . . . If you don't get results it will mean eventually a mass amphibious invasion, to cost probably half a million more American lives.'" Ralph Bard, undersecretary of the navy until his resignation on July 1, 1945, believed that an invasion was not necessary. One of the few government critics, before the fact, of using the atomic bomb, Bard on June 27 wrote a memo stating his concerns about the morality of dropping the atomic bomb on Japan without warning (see Document A31). Bard certainly had no reason to inflate any estimates of lives saved, yet after the war he said that he had told the president, "Don't organize an army to go into Japan. Kill a million people? It's ridiculous." In 1990, Andrew Goodpaster, who in 1945 was an army officer attached to the Joint War Plans Committee, told a symposium at the Smithsonian Institution that during the war Stimson regularly used the 500,000-casualty figure.[61]

Finally, two postwar evaluations are of interest. Shortly after Japan's surrender, Edmund J. Winslett, an intelligence officer in the 6th Army, conducted the military's most thorough on-site examination of Japanese defenses on Kyushu. His detailed report, "Defenses of Southern Kyushu," presented at the U.S. Army Military History Institute in June 1946, concluded as follows: "I am convinced that the greatest battle the American Armies have ever won was the one they never fought—the invasion of Kyushu"[62] (see Document B26). The same month Winslett gave his talk, an article by Major General Charles Willoughby, MacArthur's intelligence chief, was published in *Military Review*, a journal distributed to mid-level and senior officers. Willoughby estimated the two-stage invasion of Japan (Kyushu and Honshu) would have cost the United States 720,000 casualties.[63] This retrospective estimate may or may not have been accurate, but Willoughby actually wrote the article in late 1945, and it is a reasonable indication of what he was thinking some months earlier, that is, before the dropping of the atomic bomb.

No reader of this overview can fail to notice how widely these casualty estimates vary. This in part is because at the time there was no single accepted methodology for projecting casualties. Nor has one emerged in the sixty years since United States planners struggled to estimate the human cost of defeating Japan.

KEY QUESTION 6.
WHAT WERE THE ALTERNATIVES TO INVASION BEFORE THE BOMBING OF HIROSHIMA?

In "Understanding the Atomic Bomb and the Japanese Surrender" (1995), Barton J. Bernstein has catalogued the five main alternatives to invasion that at one point or another were brought up for discussion in mid-1945: a noncombat demonstration, modification of unconditional surrender and the guarantee of the emperor, pursuit of Japanese peace feelers, waiting to see the impact of the Soviet entry into the war, and the strategy of siege.[64] The strategy of siege had the longest pedigree and consisted of a combination of a naval blockade and air bombardment. As John Ray Skates has pointed out in *The Invasion of Japan* (1994), before World War II American strategists had assumed that the island nation of Japan could be defeated by such a combination. While that notion persisted in some circles into 1945, by January 1943 British and American planners, as a last resort, had added the dreaded word "assault" to the blockade/bombardment combination. Navy Chief of Staff King continued to believe that naval blockade and air bombardment could win the war, a view that also had the support of Admiral Leahy. While Army Air Force General Henry ("Hap") Arnold declined to advocate a specific strategy openly, his emphasis on strategic bombing lent support to the overall naval strategy.[65]

However, while everyone *hoped* that Tokyo could be forced to surrender before an assault on the home islands, the reality of intensifying Japanese resistance increasingly suggested grimmer scenarios. George Marshall and top army planners were convinced that the quickest and least costly—and, indeed, the only certain—way to end the war on terms satisfactory to the Allies was to ultimately invade and seize the industrial heart of Japan. The campaign of naval blockade and air bombardment to weaken Japan's ability to resist as much as possible was a crucial part of Marshall's strategy, but only as one part of a two-part overall strategy. Although both King and the air force leaders clung to their views, Marshall's view continually prevailed in strategic planning from 1944 onward. The army's two-part strategy was enshrined in J.C.S. 924, 30 June 1944, "Operations Against Japan Subsequent to Formosa"—the military's primary planning document prior to the spring of 1945—and, in September 1944, in a formal agreement signed by Roosevelt and Churchill. "Downfall," the American plan to defeat Japan issued by the Joint Chiefs of Staff in May 1945, borrowing the language of J.C.S. 924, specified that bombardment and blockade would be used to weaken Japan as much as possible before the scheduled invasion of the home islands in November 1945. Aside from viewing an invasion as vital to securing unconditional surrender, America's top military planners believed that only an invasion could compel an organized surrender of all Japanese forces outside the home islands and avoid the dreaded prospect of an interminable and costly struggle to defeat several million Japanese troops scattered across Asia from China to the Dutch East Indies (Indonesia) and the Philippines. Marshall repeated his analysis when he and other Joint Chiefs held their crucial June 18, 1945, meeting with President Truman, where he was supported, whatever their doubts, by both Admiral King and General Ira Eaker (standing in for the absent Arnold) in advocating an invasion of Kyushu[66] (see Documents B1, B7, and A27).

In short, while the army's invasion plan never had the wholehearted support of the navy, during 1944 and 1945 the combination of bombardment and blockade never achieved the status of a viable stand-alone strategy. Several problems stood in the way. A campaign of blockade and bombardment was deemed unlikely to force Japan's unconditional surrender and was just as unlikely to end the war within a year of Germany's defeat, a standing goal since 1943. It was considered politically unjustifiable to allow massive ground forces already assembled in the Pacific to stand by as bombing and blockade let the war drag on indefinitely. With specific regard to airpower, Marshall cited its failure to produce a decisive impact in Europe.[67]

The other alternatives likewise lacked credibility. Three of them already have been covered in this volume (see Key Question 1 on Japanese peace feelers, Key Question 3 on unconditional surrender, and Key Question 4 on a noncombat demonstration); the fourth will be discussed in Key Question 7. Bernstein concludes that there is "serious doubt" that any single alternative alone would have produced a surrender before the November 1 invasion date but that it is "quite possible" that a "synergistic combination" of them might have done the job.[68] There is, of course, no way to prove or disprove these conclusions, but it is possible to calculate what waiting until November 1 might have cost in lives. That date is two and a half months after Japan's actual surrender. The best estimates are that by 1945, even without major ground combat, each additional month of war in Asia was costing at least 250,000 lives. Most of those victims were Asians under Japanese occupation, but almost 170,000 Allied prisoners of war and 115,000 civilian detainees still in Japanese hands (who already were dying in large numbers) were certain to be massacred if their captors concluded liberation seemed likely. As Richard B. Frank has observed, with specific reference to blockade/bombardment but with a logic that can reasonably be applied to any, or all, of the other alternatives, delaying the end of the war by not using the atomic bombs as soon as they were ready "is to perversely grant higher sanctity to the lives on non-combatants in the aggressor nation than to those in victim nations." It is also true, as Robert P. Newman has noted, that the ongoing strategic bombing campaign would have killed more Japanese between August and November than the atomic bombs that destroyed Hiroshima and Nagasaki.[69]

A last-minute alternative to the Downfall invasion strategy not on Bernstein's list was to invade Japan at another, less well defended point. As already noted, the navy's support for Downfall was tentative, and as early as May 25, 1945, in the wake of the fierce Japanese resistance and dreadful American losses in the ongoing battle for Okinawa, Admiral Nimitz privately informed King that he did not support the strategy of invading Japan. By August, as Japan's defenses in Kyushu became increasingly formidable, military planners began to question the wisdom of an assault against that island. The result was a report dated August 6 from the Joint War Plans Committee called "Alternatives to 'OLYMPIC.'" By then Marshall also had his doubts. On August 7, he sent a message to MacArthur airing his concerns about Olympic (see Document B23 for the Nimitz telegram of May 25 and the MacArthur/Marshall exchange; see Document B22 for "Alternatives to 'Olympic'"). MacArthur, who it seems fair to say was driven by both supreme confidence and his ambition to lead the greatest amphibious assault in history, urged no change in American strategy. By then the Joint War Plans Committee had produced a ninety-six-page plan for an invasion of northern Honshu as an alternative to Olympic, a problematic option because the U.S. military could not have massed the required air support for an invasion so far from its bases on Okinawa.[70] Of course, these doubts and reports all became moot within days in the wake of the final alternative to invasion, the use of the atomic bomb, and Japan's surrender on August 14.

KEY QUESTION 7.
WHICH CONTRIBUTED MORE TO JAPAN'S SURRENDER: THE USE OF ATOMIC BOMBS OR THE SOVIET DECLARATION OF WAR?

Commentators who argue that the atomic bomb was not necessary to compel Japan's surrender must have an alternative strategy that would have done the job had the bomb not been used. Aside from the impact of American bombing and blockading of the home islands, the most readily available contender is the Soviet declaration of war on August 8, two days after Hiroshima and the day before Nagasaki. With *Strategic Surrender: The Politics of Victory and Defeat* (1958), Paul Kecskemeti of the Rand Corporation made an early and influential case for the decisive impact of the Soviet entry into the war on the Allied side. Kecskemeti does not see any single cause alone as decisive; however, he argues, the "main factor that determined the timing of the [Japan's] surrender note was the Soviet declaration of war." This is because it shattered Tokyo's hopes that Moscow would mediate a Japanese surrender on more favorable terms. Thus, the Soviet declaration "played a bigger role in triggering Japan's final move to make a direct offer of surrender than did the atomic bombs."[71] Alperovitz and historian Robert L. Messer agree. In 1991, in a jointly written article in *International Security* called "Marshall, Truman, and the Decision to Drop the Bomb," they argued that before August 1945 Japan's leaders had decided to surrender but needed a pretext to convince the "die-hard Army Group" that Japan had no alternative. "The entry of Russia into the war would almost certainly have furnished this pretext, and would have been sufficient to convince all responsible leaders that surrender was unavoidable."[72] While less emphatic, journalist Murray Sayle generally concurs, writing in 1995 in the *New Yorker* that it is "clear" that the Soviet entry into the war forced Japan's leaders "to find a new peace policy." Historian Robert A. Pape also considers the Soviet entry into the war as the factor that finally tipped the scales toward surrender. The most recent variant of this argument is made in *Racing the Enemy* (2005), whose author, Tsuyoshi Hasegawa, relies on Japanese-language sources to make his case. Hasegawa concludes that even after Hiroshima and Nagasaki, "Without the Soviet entry into the war, the Japanese would have continued to fight until numerous atomic bombs, a successful allied invasion of the home islands, or continued aerial bombardment, combined with a naval blockade, rendered them incapable of doing so."[73]

This view runs counter to a broader consensus that stresses either the twin shocks of the atomic bomb and the Soviet entry into the war or the impact of the atomic bomb alone in convincing Japan to surrender. In his classic account of Japan's surrender, Robert Butow credits both factors with creating the conditions that led to Hirohito's crucial intervention in Tokyo's decision making, but the atomic bombs clearly play a larger role in Butow's scenario. Herbert Bix likewise mentions the "twin psychological shocks" of Hiroshima and the Soviet entry into the war. He also mentions a third factor: the concern on the part of Kido that growing popular discontent caused by continuation of the war might soon threaten the throne. Bix notes that the emperor mentioned only the bomb in his August 14 rescript to the nation (see Document E9) and only the Soviet entry in a second rescript on August 17 to soldiers and sailors scattered across Asia and the Pacific (see Document E12); he suggests that the latter has more probative value. That said, Bix, who blames Hirohito for the disastrous delay in Japan's surrender and considers him "dissembling until the end—and beyond," notes that Hirohito gave "two different justifications" for Japan's surrender and concludes, "Both statements were probably true."[74]

Two studies that focus directly on the impact of the atomic bomb on Japanese decision makers are Lawrence Freedman and Saki Dockrill's "Hiroshima: A Strategy of Shock" (1994) and Sadao Asada's "The Shock of the Atomic Bomb and Japan's Decision to Surrender—A Reconsideration" (1998). Both conclude that the use of the atomic bomb was the decisive action that compelled the Japanese government to surrender. Freedman and Dockrill, citing Japanese-language sources, argue that the emperor and his close advisors made their decision to end the war after the Hiroshima bomb but before the Soviet entry into the war two days later. They add that the bombing of Hiroshima, which hit the Japanese homeland, produced a shock that was more direct than the Soviet declaration of war, whose actual impact was on the Asian mainland.[75] Nor was the Soviet declaration unexpected, although the date of its arrival was. In April 1945, Moscow informed Tokyo that it would not renew its neutrality pact with Japan, and that same month Japanese army sources reported that the Soviets were concentrating powerful military forces in the Far East. In July, Soviet women working in the Tokyo embassy as well as the wives and children of male personnel left Japan for home. Yet by early August, the Japanese thought they still had some time—a least a month and probably more—before the Soviet ax fell on their soldiers in Manchuria.[76]

Asada agrees with Freedman and Dockrill, basing his conclusion on statements or testimony from Emperor Hirohito, Prime Minister Suzuki, Lord Keeper of the Privy Seal Kido, and many other top Japanese officials. He quotes Suzuki's remark that the Hiroshima bomb was "a most convenient pretext" for surrendering immediately and Yonai's, made on August 12, that the atomic bombs and the Soviet entry into the war were "gifts from Heaven." Further, Asada's thorough survey of Japanese-language sources convinces him that the impact of Hiroshima and Nagasaki together, which indicated the United States had an arsenal of bombs and would not have to invade Japan, "was devastating."

Significantly, he adds that the Hiroshima bomb ultimately forced Amani, Umezu, and Toyoda—the three key holdouts on the SCDW against surrender— "to face the reality of defeat." At the same time, Asada acknowledges that the Soviet declaration of war also had an important impact on Tokyo and that it is difficult, given the close sequence of events, to disentangle the respective effects of the atomic bombs and the Soviet declaration of war. Still, he stresses the "primacy of the Hiroshima bomb" in bringing about Japan's surrender.[77]

Among historians whose subject is the entire Pacific War, Ronald H. Spector, following Butow, concludes in *Eagle Against the Sun* (1985) that surrender came as a result of the "*combined* shock of Russia's entry into the war and the use of *two* atomic bombs," while recently, Thomas Zeiler in *Unconditional Defeat* (2004) maintains that the "atomic bombs . . . persuaded Japan to end the war." Among those focusing on the end of the war, Robert Newman, in *Truman and the Hiroshima Cult* (1995), argues that it was "precisely the shock of the bombs and the assumption that more were coming that brought about Japan's surrender *at that time*"; Robert Maddox, in *Weapons for Victory* (1995), says the atomic bombs were "decisive"; and Richard Frank, in *Downfall* (1999), after tracing Hirohito's statements and those by Suzuki, Kido, and others, finds the Soviet intervention "significant" but concludes that "the atomic bomb played the more critical role because it undermined the fundamental premise that the United States would have to invade Japan to secure a decision."[78] McGeorge Bundy, whose *Danger and Survival* is the most comprehensive overview of the first half-century of the political history of atomic weapons, concludes, "The bomb did not win the war, but it surely was responsible for its ending when it did."[79]

Many of the documents in sections D, E, F, and G of part 4 deal with this issue, if usually briefly. Among the most important are Suzuki's statement to the USSBS on December 26, 1945 (see Document F5), Kido's statement on November 10 (see Document F6), Chief Cabinet Secretary Sakomizu's statement on December 11 (see Document F13), and the imperial rescripts of August 14 and 17, 1945 (see Documents E9 and E12). Also of interest is the MAGIC Diplomatic Summary of August 14, 1945 (see Document C18): it contains a short intercept of a telegram sent on August 11 by the Greater East Asia Ministry, at the time headed by Foreign Minister Togo, that explains Japan's surrender with reference to "the problem of the atomic bomb." The determination of the Japanese army to fight on after the atomic bombings and the Soviet entry into the war is revealed by the statements of War Minister Anami and Army Chief of Staff Umezu at the Imperial Conference of August 9–10, as recorded in the notes taken at that meeting by Zenshiro Hoshima and Sumihisa Ikeda. Umezu in particular affirmed that the Soviet entry into the war did not invalidate preparations for the forthcoming American invasion (see Documents G5 and G6).

KEY QUESTION 8.
DID THE UNITED STATES USE THE ATOMIC BOMB
AGAINST JAPAN IN ORDER TO PRACTICE
"ATOMIC DIPLOMACY" AGAINST
THE SOVIET UNION?

The contention that the United States used atomic weapons against Japan not to end the war but to intimidate the Soviet Union into making concessions regarding postwar arrangements in Eastern Europe and Central Europe—in other words, to practice "atomic diplomacy"—is a thesis that has not fared well in the court of historical debate. It first made academic headlines when Gar Alperovitz published *Atomic Diplomacy: Hiroshima and Potsdam* in 1965. Critics of the thesis have ranged from revisionists such as Barton J. Bernstein, Lisle Rose, Ronald Steel, and Gabriel Kolko to critics of revisionism such as Robert Maddox and John Lewis Gaddis to biographers of Truman such as Robert H. Ferrell and Alonzo Hamby. From different ends of the political spectrum, both Marxist historian Gabriel Kolko, in *The Politics of War: The World and United States Foreign Policy, 1943–1945* (1968), and Robert Maddox, in *The New Left and the Origins of the Cold War* (1973), reject a key Alperovitz contention that in mid-May Truman had delayed the Potsdam Conference to await a test of the atomic bomb, whose existence he could then use to pressure Stalin (the "strategy of delayed showdown"). Maddox points out that domestic concerns compelled the newly inaugurated president to remain at home and that in the meantime he took several important conciliatory steps to improve relations with Moscow. Lisle A. Rose makes the same point in *Dubious Victory* (1973). Gaddis, in his Bancroft Prize–winning *The United States and the Origins of the Cold War, 1941–1947* (1972), notes that Truman hoped to continue Roosevelt's policy of cooperation with the Soviet Union. Critics of the atomic diplomacy thesis also argued that it rested on an uncritical use of sources and that Alperovitz was unconvincing in asserting that Hiroshima was bombed because a combat demonstration of the bomb's power was deemed necessary to impress the Soviets. The criticism of the 1970s continued into the 1980s, when McGeorge Bundy wrote that the thesis "rests on inferences so stretched as to be a discredit both to the judgment of those who argued in this fashion and the credulity of those who have accepted such arguments." In the 1990s, Robert Maddox, following up on earlier critical comments, said that the claim of atomic diplomacy was based "on a pervasive misrepresentation of the historical record." Writing with more sympathy but still with considerable skepticism about Alperovitz's 1995 book *The Decision to Use the Atomic Bomb and the Architecture of an American Myth*, J. Samuel Walker noted, "The fact that it is thoughtful, original, and engaging does not, in my estimation, make it convincing." Biographies of Truman by

Robert H. Ferrell and Alonzo Hamby published during the 1990s also attacked the atomic diplomacy thesis.[80] Overall, despite the difficulties that arose with the Soviets at Potsdam, most historians agree that the United States did not practice atomic diplomacy at the conference.

None of this fazed Alperovitz or other committed supporters of the atomic diplomacy thesis. They responded with a flurry of books and articles, including *The Decision to Use the Atomic Bomb and the Architecture of an American Myth*, which Alperovitz wrote with the help of seven assistants, and *Hiroshima's Shadow* (1998), a huge collection of articles, most sympathetic to Alperovitz's point of view, edited by Kai Bird and Lawrence Lifschultz. Additional backing for Alperovitz came from Arnold A. Offner, who, in *Another Such Victory: President Truman and the Cold War, 1945–1953* (2002), argues that Truman and Secretary of State Byrnes made extensive use of atomic diplomacy at Potsdam and that achieving political gains at the expense of the Soviet Union was an important part of the calculus that led to the atomic bombing of Japan. Wilson D. Miscamble vigorously challenged that conclusion. In *From Roosevelt to Truman: Potsdam, Hiroshima, and the Cold War* (2006), Miscamble writes that both at Potsdam and at the subsequent foreign ministers meeting in London, the Truman administration did not practice atomic diplomacy "in a deliberate manner." After noting that whether the United States could have used the atomic bomb as a diplomatic weapon in 1945 is a matter of speculation, Miscamble concludes, "That they didn't try seriously is a matter of historical fact."[81]

Some of the documents in this volume related to this issue are Stimson's diary entry of June 6, 1945 (see Document A20); the memo of his conference with Truman that day, during which Truman mentions Harry Hopkins's mission to Moscow to improve relations with the Soviets (see Document A21); Stimson's diary entry of July 3, 1945 (see Document A34); Truman's diary entries of July 17, 18, and 25, 1945 (see Document A36); Stimson's diary entry of July 19, 1945 (see Document A40); Stimson's July 19, 1945 memorandum, "Reflections on the Basic Problems that Confront Us," on relations with the Soviet Union (see Document A41); Stimson's notes for his diary of July 22, 1945 (see Document A42); Truman's diary entry of June 7, 1945 (see Document A21) and the letters to his wife of July 18 and 20, 1945 (see Document A44); and James Forrestal's July 26, 1945, brief diary entry regarding Byrnes's thinking on the Soviet Union (see Document A46). Taken together, the Truman diary entries and letters appear to signal at once the desire and the expectation that relations with the Soviet Union would remain good enough to permit continued cooperation, with regard to both bringing Moscow into the war with Japan and securing a stable postwar peace. Stimson clearly is worried about future relations, but his immediate objective is to avoid a break with the Soviets. Neither outlook is consistent with a policy of atomic diplomacy.

KEY QUESTION 9.
WAS THE USE OF ATOMIC BOMBS AGAINST
HIROSHIMA AND NAGASAKI MORALLY JUSTIFIED?

The point of this volume is to enable the reader to develop an understanding of why the United States used atomic bombs against Japan in August 1945 by consulting key documents bearing on that decision. Those who made this decision obviously believed it to be morally justified given the urgent need to end the war as quickly as possible with a minimum loss of American lives. In the minds of American leaders, atomic weapons did not fall into the same category as poison gas (or, by extension, biological weapons), which was banned by the 1925 Geneva Protocol. Although the United States had not signed that protocol (neither had Japan), Allied policy throughout World War II was not to use such weapons except in retaliation. Nonetheless, the United States conducted research and manufactured large quantities of poison gas, and as losses mounted in the Pacific War, and especially after Iwo Jima and Okinawa, discussions about using these lethal chemicals intensified. In fact, as John Ray Skates reports, the use of poison gas was built into the plans for invading Kyushu.[82] But no such restraints applied to the entirely new and incompletely understood technology of nuclear weaponry. Before the Trinity test, not even the scientists at Los Alamos knew if their new weapon would generate enough explosive force to demolish a large fortified position or an entire city. Even after Trinity, there was little knowledge about what effects radiation would have immediately after an explosion or in the months and years that followed exposure, albeit at a nonfatal distance, to a nuclear blast. In any event, as many historians have pointed out, the assumption from the beginning was that the bomb would be used if necessary to end the war against both the Germans and the Japanese.

As the documents mentioned here demonstrate, moral reservations were expressed before Hiroshima. However, in every case, the argument was to seek other means of ending the war first before resorting to the atomic bomb. As McGeorge Bundy points out, "No one ever said simply, do not use it on a city at all."[83] Thus the Franck Report of June 11, 1945, opposes the use of atomic bombs mainly for practical reason—that it will lead to a postwar nuclear arms race—but also raises the moral implications for the United States if it becomes the first country to employ such weapons. Yet, in an apparent contradiction, the Franck Report concedes that the bomb "might perhaps be used against Japan" if a demonstration and ultimatum failed to produce surrender (see Document A23). In his "Memorandum On the Use of the S-1 Bomb" on June 27, Ralph Bard did the same when he speaks of this country's status as a humanitarian nation (see Document A31). The Met Lab petition to Truman raised objections similar to the Franck Report regarding responsibility for a postwar nuclear arms race, although in stronger language (see Document A38). President Truman never saw any of these documents, although in late May Stimson did forward to him a lengthy letter from a Manhattan Project engineer named Oswald Brewster that made arguments parallel to theirs.[84] Under enormous and growing pressure to end the war, Truman seems never to have questioned whether to use the bomb. Yet his July 25 diary entry shows that he did grapple with moral justifications when he wrote about Japanese savagery, the choice of a "purely military" target, and the hope that Japan would heed the Potsdam Declaration, surrender, and "save lives" (see Document A36). That was not to be, and Truman soon found that his effort to end the war without further American losses did not meet everyone's moral standards. An example of early moral objections to the bomb is "America's Atomic Atrocity," published in the pacifist magazine *The Christian Century* three weeks after the atomic bombing (see Document A56).

The moral dimension of the atomic bomb decision beyond the immediate wartime context, including the relationship of Hiroshima to the postwar nuclear arms race, is a vast topic that properly is the subject of another book. The best that can be done in the space available here is to suggest a few sources that introduce this subject. There are any number of commentators who have condemned the bombing of Hiroshima and Nagasaki on pacifist or religious grounds. These arguments, by virtue of the absolutist principles on which they are based, are impervious to any attempt to defend American actions that ended the war. A similar type of argument is made by psychiatrist Robert Jay Lifton and journalist Greg Mitchell, who contend in *Indefensible Weapons* (1982) that the destructive power of nuclear weapons invalidates their use under any circumstances. Michael Walzer's analysis in *Just and Unjust Wars* (1977) looks at the circumstances in which weapons are used in considering whether their use is justified. Walzer condemns the use of the atomic bomb against Japan because it violated the rights of noncombatants, especially by killing tens of thousands of innocent civilians in order to shock the Japanese government into surrender, and thereby broke one of the fundamental rules of war. He does allow an exception to the injunction against attacking noncombatants, however: "extreme emergency." This is what the British faced in 1940 when they stood alone against Nazi Germany and on the brink of defeat. To survive, they launched bombing attacks against German cities. However, as the United States was not in Britain's dire position in 1945, Walzer does not grant the same latitude to the bombing of Hiroshima and Nagasaki.[85]

Defenders of Truman's decision to use atomic weapons against Japan often argue from a moral perspective political scientist Robert H. Jackson has called situational ethics: judging the actions of state leaders with due consideration of the circumstances in which they found themselves when their decisions were made. As Jackson sees it, Charles de Gaulle was correct to define a state leader as "someone who takes risks, including moral risks." He also approves of Edmund Burke's distinction between a "statesman and a professor in a university"; according to Burke, whereas a professor need only consider his ideas, a statesman, "never losing sight of principles, is to be guided by circumstances; and, judging contrary to the exigencies of the moment, he may ruin his country forever."[86] An excellent example of thinking along the lines of situational ethics is in Robert P. Newman's *Truman and the Hiroshima Cult* (1995). Newman's analysis and defense of Truman's decision also incorporates the most thorough recent overview of the postwar moral debate surrounding the bombing of Hiroshima. For Newman, the situation against which Truman should be judged consists of Japan's refusal to surrender, the enormous casualties the United States would have therefore incurred in an invasion of the home islands, and the daily loss of life in Japanese-occupied parts of eastern Asia—often as a result of Japanese atrocities—as the war dragged from August through at least November, even without major battles being fought. It is against that background that Newman defends Truman's atomic bomb decision. Richard B. Frank makes a similar case in *Downfall* (1999). So does Wilson D. Miscamble. Having reviewed the grim context of total war in which the Hiroshima decision was made, Miscamble asks, "If the atomic bombs shortened the war, averted the need for a land invasion, and saved thousands of lives on both sides of a ghastly conflict, does this make their use moral?" In answering his question, Miscamble mentions, among other things, the "brutal endeavors" that Roosevelt and Churchill sanctioned and the nature of the Japanese regime, which refused to surrender and was willing, long after the war clearly was lost, "to engage the whole population in a kind of national kamikaze campaign." He then acknowledges, using Machiavelli's words, that the necessity of ending the war forced President Truman to "enter into evil." Still, quoting Henry Stimson, Miscamble argues that the use of atomic bombs against Japan, given the circumstances at the time, was America's "least abhorrent choice." He concludes by hoping that critics might express "less condemnation" of Truman's decisions and "more empathy" for the man himself and then suggests that those critics "simply might pray, if they be so inclined, that leaders in our own time and in the future are never forced by horrible circumstances to make such decisions."[87]

McGeorge Bundy, who also offers an analysis based on situational ethics, adds another element in a pointed response to Walzer. While granting that Walzer makes a "powerful argument," Bundy nonetheless rejects it because it "requires an equal moral opposition to the whole long, brutal tendency of modern war makers to accept, and sometimes even to seek, the suffering of civilians in search of victory." During World War II, no leader could have imposed the changes in strategy and tactics Walzer demands, which would have included eliminating all urban bombing of Japan, not just the use of atomic bombs.

Bundy admits a "personal interest" in the matter: he was an infantry company commander whose unit would have participated in the scheduled invasion. He adds, had he "ventured to take Walzer's view, with officers and men, I think I would have been alone."[88]

Those who condemn Hiroshima obviously condemn Nagasaki, often with greater outrage, largely because they believe that Japan was prepared to surrender after August 6 and that there thus was no military reason for dropping a second atomic bomb. Nagasaki does indeed put an additional burden on those who argue in defense of the bombing of Hiroshima from the perspective of situational ethics: they must show that the situation included the necessity of a second bomb to compel a quick Japanese surrender. An overview of the debate regarding Japan's readiness to surrender after Hiroshima and before Nagasaki appears in Key Question 1.

KEY QUESTION 10.
WHY DID THE TRUMAN ADMINISTRATION DECIDE TO USE THE ATOMIC BOMB AGAINST JAPAN?

The answer to this question flows from the answers one gives to the preceding questions. Of these, the questions that bear most directly on the motivations in Washington in the summer of 1945 are 2 (What did the United States know and conclude about Japanese intentions and plans?); 5 (What were the U.S. estimates of casualties from an invasion of Japan?); 6 (What were the alternatives to invasion prior to the bombing of Hiroshima?); and 8 (Did the United States use the atomic bomb against Japan in order to practice atomic diplomacy against the Soviet Union?). Beyond that, any consideration of American motives must include an understanding of the ferocity of the Pacific War, the astounding record of Japanese troops refusing to surrender in battle after battle no matter what the odds, and the intensification of Japanese resistance as the front lines moved closer to Japan proper. These circumstances are chronicled, albeit briefly, in chapter 3.[89]

Robert H. Ferrell, in his superb biography *Truman*, has provided a somewhat different but very useful framework for understanding the atomic bomb decision. He begins with the "historic" reason: the hatred for the Japanese sown initially by Pearl Harbor and then by subsequent atrocities during the course of the Pacific War that helped to justify the use of any weapons against them. Far more important was the second, and immediate, reason: the cost in American lives of invading Japan. Ferrell carefully reviews this issue and suggests that Truman had good reason to expect casualties in the hundreds of thousands. He then raises three questions that continue to be debated: Did Washington do enough to warn the Japanese about what awaited them if they did not surrender? Did the atomic bombs or the Soviet entry into the war have a greater impact in forcing a surrender? Did the United States engage in atomic diplomacy vis-à-vis the Soviet Union during 1945? Ferrell argues that a warning was not a realistic option, that it is impossible to untangle the interrelated impacts on Japan's leaders of the American atomic bombs and the Soviet entry into the Pacific War, and that there is no proof for the atomic diplomacy thesis. His overall assessment is that in using the atomic bomb to end the war Truman made the right decision under the circumstances, but he also acknowledges that some questions will never be resolved. That would seem to be an invitation, or perhaps even an injunction, by a distinguished scholar for us to study the evidence so that we can draw our own educated conclusions about this "most controversial act of the Truman presidency."[90] This volume is dedicated to that enterprise.

PART III

Resources

CHRONOLOGY

1937
July   Japan attacks China; beginning of World War II in Asia

1938
September   British and French leaders cave in to Hitler at Munich
December   German scientists Otto Hahn and Fritz Strassmann achieve
                  nuclear fission

1939
January 25   Szilard letter on atomic fission to Lewis Strauss
August 2   Einstein letter to Roosevelt warning Germany might try to
                  build an atomic bomb
September 1   Germany invades Poland: World War II begins in Europe
November 1   Briggs Committee recommends investigating possibility of a
                  nuclear chain reaction being able to power an atomic bomb

1940
June   Roosevelt approves creation of National Defense Research
                 Council, headed by Vannevar Bush

1941

January 24	Rear Admiral Richmond Kelly Turner warns that Japanese might begin a war with the United States by attacking Pearl Harbor and is ignored
April 13	Japan and Soviet Union sign neutrality pact
July	MAUD report concludes that twenty-five pounds of U235 are needed to make a bomb; the report is forwarded to the U.S. government in October
November	A National Academy of Sciences report concludes that 2–100 kg of U235 is needed to build a bomb
June 28	By executive order, President Roosevelt establishes the Office of Scientific Research and Development (OSRD), with Vannevar Bush as director
December 7	Japan bombs Pearl Harbor; United States declares war on Japan the next day
December 23	Japan takes Wake Island, site of an American military base

1942

January–May	Japanese victories in Philippines, including Manila, Bataan, and Corregidor; the Japanese take Singapore from British in February
January	President Roosevelt sends a note to Vannevar Bush urging that research on atomic bomb be speeded up
May 7–8	The Battle of the Coral Sea, a narrow Japanese tactical victory but a U.S. strategic victory
June 4–6	The Battle of Midway, an overwhelming U.S. victory and turning point of Pacific War
July–August	A scientific team at Berkeley led by J. Robert Oppenheimer establishes the theoretical basis for the design of an atomic bomb
August	The Manhattan Engineering District (MED) is established
August– February 1943	U.S. forces invade the Japanese-held South Pacific island of Guadalcanal; a fierce, months-long battle ensues
September	General Leslie Groves assumes command of the MED and within days acquires 52,000 acres in Tennessee to build the Oak Ridge facility
October	Groves and Oppenheimer meet; Groves appoints Oppenheimer head of lab to design and build an atomic bomb
December 2	The Metallurgical Laboratory (Met Lab) team of scientists lead by Enrico Fermi achieves controlled chain reaction

December 28	President Roosevelt approves construction projects necessary to build the atomic bomb; these enormous facilities are built during 1943

1943

January	The U.S. government purchases 500,000 acres in Washington State for the Hanford nuclear facility
January 14–24	The Casablanca Conference is convened, in which unconditional surrender is demanded of Germany, Japan, and Italy
April 1	The Los Alamos laboratory is established
May	The Japanese garrison on Attu, in the Aleutian Islands of Alaska, fights until it is nearly annihilated; the fatality rate is 98.8 percent
September	The ULTRA codebreaking machine first deciphers Japanese army transmissions; a steady flow of information begins in 1944
Winter	Mathematician John von Neumann designs explosive arrangement for an implosion system for the plutonium bomb that works in theory
November	U.S. Marines take Tarawa; more than 1,000 marines are killed in three days, while the Japanese fatality rate in a garrison of almost 5,000 men is 99.7 percent
December 1	The Cairo Declaration is issued: the United States, Britain, and China announce that Japan will lose Korea, all Pacific islands seized or occupied since World War I, and all territory in China and will have to agree to unconditional surrender

1944

June 6	D-Day: Allied forces land at Normandy in France
June 15–July 7	Battle of Saipan; Americans again suffer enormous casualties, while the Japanese garrison of 30,000 fights until wiped out and many soldiers and civilians commit mass suicide at Marpi Point
August 30	J.C.S. 924/2 released, containing the "Saipan ratio"
June 19–20	Battle of the Philippine Sea
July 18	Hideki Tojo resigns as the Japanese prime minister and is succeeded by Kuniaki Koiso
July–August	U.S. Marines capture Guam and Tinian islands; Tinian becomes the base for the B-29s that drop atomic bombs on Japan

September– *October*	Battle for Peleliu, the "assault into hell"; the 1st Marine Division suffers a casualty rate of 53.7 percent
October– *June 1945*	Battle of the Philippines; General Douglas MacArthur wades ashore on October 20; Japanese kamikaze aircraft take a large toll of U.S. ships and sailors at Leyte Gulf; bitter fighting on island of Luzon; Manila is largely destroyed; some Japanese retreat to mountains and hold out until August 15, 1945
December	The 509th Composite Group is established to train to drop the atomic bomb on Japan

1945

February 4–11	Yalta Conference: Stalin confirms his promise made in November 1943 at the Teheran Conference to enter the Pacific War a few months after Germany's defeat in return for important territorial gains at the expense of Japan and economic and military concessions at the expense of China
February 14	Prince Fumimaro Konoe's "Memorial to the Throne" urges Japan seek peace on the basis of keeping the *kokutai* system unchanged, in which the emperor is sacred and sovereign
February– *March*	Battle of Iwo Jima; U.S. Marines suffer almost 27,000 casualties, more than the Japanese, whose garrison of 21,000 fights almost to the last man; some marine regiments have casualty rates of 75 percent; a record twenty-seven Medals of Honor are awarded, thirteen of them posthumously
March 9–10	In a massive B-29 incendiary raid on Tokyo, 80,000 Japanese are killed and fifteen square miles of the city destroyed
March	Chemist George Kistiakowsky builds and tests implosion lens system for a plutonium bomb
April	The Dragon experiment conducted by Otto Frisch proves that the gun assembly for the U235 bomb will work
April 1–June 22	Battle of Okinawa; U.S. Navy losses include 36 ships sunk and 368 damaged, mostly from kamikaze attacks; the total casualty rate of ground forces on land is 39 percent
April 5	The Koiso government falls: Admiral Kantaro Suzuki becomes prime minister in the new government, while General Korechika Anami is army minister
April 8	Japanese Army Order No. 1299, *Ketsu-Go* (Decisive Operation), is issued

April 12	President Roosevelt dies and is succeeded by his vice president, Harry S. Truman
April 16	Truman confirms the Allied policy of unconditional surrender
April 25	Truman receives a full briefing on the Manhattan Project from Secretary of War Henry L. Stimson and General Leslie Groves; J.C.S. 924/15 issued, which contains casualty ratios for European and Pacific fighting
May 8	Germany surrenders unconditionally
May 28	The Downfall plan for the invasion of Japan is issued
May 30 or May 31	Former President Herbert Hoover's "Memorandum on Ending the Japanese War" is sent to Truman
May 31–June 1	Key Interim Committee meetings on atomic bomb
June–August	ULTRA reveals a massive Japanese buildup on Kyushu; MAGIC reveals Tokyo unwilling to accept unconditional surrender in any form
June 6	Japan's Supreme Council for Direction of the War adopts the "Fundamental Policy"; the cabinet endorses it the next day, and it receives Emperor Hirohito's sanction at an imperial conference on June 8; meanwhile, President Truman and Stimson meet to discuss Interim Committee conclusions
June 8	Marquis Koichi Kido outlines the "Draft Plan for Controlling the Crisis Situation" calling for Soviet mediation to help end the war
June 11	The Franck Report is issued: it opposes the use of the bomb against Japan, calling instead for a demonstration on a barren island and then, if the bomb must be used, a warning to Japan to evacuate certain areas
June 18	Key White House meeting: Truman approves Olympic, the invasion of Kyushu; meanwhile, at a Supreme Council for Direction of the War meeting, Anami and his supporters agree that Tokyo approach Soviet Union about peace negotiations
June 22	Emperor tells an imperial conference that he desires end to war, but no specific terms are formulated
June 27	Bard memo on the use of the atomic bomb urges that the atomic bomb not be used unless Japan is first warned
July 16	The Trinity test is successful: a plutonium bomb explodes with a force of more than 18,000 tons of TNT

July 17	Met Lab petition, echoing the sentiments of the Franck Report
July 21	Shockley memorandum on casualty estimates for invasion of Japan projects that it might cost the United States 400,000 to 800,000 lives to defeat Japan
July 26– August 2	Potsdam Conference: Stalin promises to enter the Pacific War by August 15; Allied issue Potsdam Declaration
July 25	General Thomas T. Handy, George Marshall's deputy, authorizes General Carl Spaatz to drop the atomic bomb
July 26	Potsdam Declaration demands Japan's immediate unconditional surrender but states, among other things, that Japan will not be destroyed as a nation and that its people will be able to choose their form of government
July 28	Suzuki rejects the Potsdam Declaration with the infamous term "*mokusatsu,*" which can be interpreted as meaning "kill with silence" or "ignore"
August 6	An atomic bomb is dropped on Hiroshima
August 7	Reports reach Tokyo that Hiroshima was destroyed by an atomic bomb
August 8	The Soviet Union declares war on Japan
August 9	An atomic bomb is dropped on Nagasaki; the Supreme Council for Direction of the War deadlocks over accepting the Potsdam Declaration
August 10	Emperor Hirohito intervenes, issuing a sacred decision at an imperial conference ordering acceptance of the Potsdam Declaration if the institution of the emperor is left unchanged; General Anami makes a broadcast urging continued resistance
August 11	The U.S. government replies to Japan that the emperor may retain his throne but will be subject to the authority of the Allied supreme commander
August 12	The Supreme Council on the Direction of the War deadlocks over the American reply
August 13	The Supreme Council on the Direction of the War and the cabinet remain deadlocked
August 14	Emperor Hirohito again breaks deadlock at an imperial conference, ordering acceptance of the Potsdam Declaration; Japan announces surrender; an attempted coup by junior officers begins
August 15	At noon, the Japanese emperor's imperial rescript announcing Japan's surrender is broadcast over the radio; the previ-

ous night's coup attempt is crushed; the Suzuki cabinet resigns

August 17   An imperial rescript orders Japanese troops throughout Asia to surrender; a new government under Prince Higashikuni takes office

September 2   The Empire of Japan officially surrenders on board the U.S. battleship *Missouri* in Tokyo Bay

GLOSSARY OF MILITARY TERMS
AND ABBREVIATIONS

CINCAFPAC Commander in Chief, U.S. Army Forces in the Pacific (Gen. Douglas MacArthur).

CINCPAC Commander in Chief, U.S. Pacific Fleet (Adm. Chester Nimitz).

CINCPOA Commander in Chief, Pacific Ocean Area (Adm. Chester Nimitz).

CNO Chief of Naval Operations (Adm. Ernest King).

COMBINED CHIEFS OF STAFF (CCS) The Combined Chiefs of Staff was established in January 1942 and brought together the military service chiefs of Great Britain and the United States for managing the overall war effort in the European and Pacific theaters. It formally reported to both the American president and the British prime minister. Because the CCS was headquartered in Washington, the British chiefs usually did not attend meetings in person but were represented by senior British military officers stationed in the United States.

COMINCH Commander in Chief, U.S. Fleet (Adm. Ernest King).

CORONET   Code name for the invasion of the Kanto Plain (the Tokyo region), scheduled for March 1, 1946 (Y-Day); the second stage of the overall Downfall plan.

DOWNFALL   The overall American plan for the invasion of Japan, including both Olympic and Coronet.

G-1   Personnel section of divisional or higher headquarters.

G-2   Military Intelligence section of divisional or higher headquarters.

G-3   Operations section of divisional or higher headquarters.

JOINT CHIEFS OF STAFF (JCS)   The military executive body for directing the U.S. war effort. Established in February 1942, the JCS originally consisted of the Chief of Naval Operations, the Army Chief of Staff, the Commander in Chief of the U.S. Fleet, and the Chief of the Army Air Forces. In mid-1942, retired Adm. William D. Leahy, who held the position Chief of Staff to the President, joined the JCS as its unofficial chairman. Its other three members for the rest of the war were Gen. George C. Marshall, the Army Chief of Staff; Adm. Ernest J. King, Commander in Chief of the U.S. Fleet and Chief of Naval Operations; and Lt. Gen. Henry H. Arnold, Commanding General of the Army Air Forces. The Joint Planning Staff and the Joint Strategic Survey Committee both reported to the JCS.

JOINT INTELLIGENCE COMMITTEE   One of the specialized committees that assisted the Joint Planning Staff.

JOINT PLANNING STAFF (JPS)   The top military planning body during the war, it reported directly to the Joint Chiefs of Staff. The Joint Planning Staff was made up of two representatives respectively from the Army and Navy planning organizations. It received reports from the Joint War Plans Committee (JWPC). The Joint Planning Staff often is referred to in documents as the Joint Staff Planners.

JOINT STRATEGIC SURVEY COMMITTEE   The Joint Strategic Survey Committee was established at George Marshall's suggestion in late 1942. Composed of senior army and navy officers, its task was to advise the Joint Chiefs of Staff on matters of global strategy and the relationship of military strategy to national policy.

JOINT WAR PLANS COMMITTEE (JWPC)   The Joint War Plans Committee, which reported directly to the Joint Planning Staff, was established in April 1943. Its job was to draw up strategic and operational military plans, which in turn were reviewed and amended by the JPS before being forwarded to the JCS. The JWPC was made up of thirteen members from the Army, Navy, and Army Air Forces and included a secretariat of two. It was served by a number of specialized groups such as the Joint Intelligence Committee and the Joint Logistics Committee.

KETSU-GO   The Japanese plan for defense of the home islands.

OLYMPIC   Code name for the invasion of Kyushu, scheduled for November 1, 1945 (X-Day); the first stage of the overall Downfall plan.

OPD   Operations Division, a branch of the War Department.

SIXTH ARMY   The American ground force that was to have spearheaded Operation Olympic.

TENTH ARMY   American force made up of the Army and Marine divisions that took Okinawa.

WD   U.S. War Department.

GLOSSARY OF NAMES

ANAMI, GEN. KORECHIKA Japan's army minister, April–August 1945. He opposed surrender under any circumstances and committed suicide after Japan's decision to surrender.

ARNOLD, GEN. HENRY H. ("HAP") Chief of the Army Air Corps/Army Air Force, 1938–1946.

BARD, RALPH Assistant Secretary of the Navy, 1941–1944; Undersecretary of the Navy, 1944–1945.

BUSH, VANNEVAR Director, Office of Scientific Research and Development, 1941–1948; member, Interim Committee.

BYRNES, JAMES F. Secretary of State, July 3, 1945–January 1947.

COMPTON, ARTHUR Director, Metallurgical Laboratory of the Manhattan Project, which achieved the first nuclear chain reaction in 1942.

FERMI, ENRICO Italian-born physicist; leader of the team that achieved the first controlled nuclear chain reaction in December 1942 at the University of Chicago.

GROVES, LT. GEN. LESLIE   Director of the Manhattan Project, September 17, 1942–October 15, 1945.

HIROHITO   Emperor of Japan, 1926–1989. His reign was the longest of any Japanese emperor known to history. Although Hirohito's role and power in Japanese decision making during World War II remains a matter of scholarly discussion, he clearly played a crucial role in bringing about his country's surrender in August 1945. Hirohito avoided becoming a defendant in war-crimes trials and was allowed to remain on his throne after the war, even as the United States imposed a new democratic constitution on Japan that reduced the emperor to a ceremonial role, because American officials considered him essential to governing Japan during the postwar occupation.

KIDO, MARQUIS KOICHI   Lord Keeper of the Privy Seal, and as such Hirohito's closest advisor during 1945.

KING, ADM. ERNEST J.   Chief of Naval Operations, March 1942–September 1945.

KOISO, KUNIAKI   Prime minister of Japan, July 1944–April 1945.

KONOE, PRINCE FUMIMARO   Three-time Japanese prime minister prior to World War II. Opposed to war with the United States, he was replaced by Hideki Tojo as prime minister in October 1941. Author of the February 1945 "Memorial to the Throne," he was an early advocate of peace, although on terms that fell far short of minimum Allied demands.

LEAHY, ADM. WILLIAM D.   Chief of staff to the president, 1942–1949.

LEMAY, MAJ. GEN. CURTIS E.   Commander of the XXI Bomber Command at the time of the incendiary raid on Tokyo in March 1945 that leveled more than fifteen square miles of the city. Chief of Staff of the U.S. Army Strategic Air Forces in the Pacific in August 1945 at the time of the bombing of Hiroshima and Nagasaki by the 509th Composite Group, the unit that had been trained especially for that task.

MARSHALL, GEN. GEORGE C.   Chief of staff, United States Army, 1939–1945.

OPPENHEIMER, J. ROBERT   Director, Los Alamos Laboratory; member, Scientific Panel of the Interim Committee.

ROOSEVELT, FRANKLIN D.   President of the United States, 1933–April 12, 1945.

SPAATZ, GEN. CARL   Commander of U.S. Army Strategic Air Forces in the Pacific, which included the Twentieth Air Force and the 509th Composite Group, at the time of the bombing of Hiroshima and Nagasaki. He insisted on a written order—"a piece of paper"—to drop the atomic bombs.

STIMSON, HENRY L.   Secretary of War, July 10, 1940–September 21, 1945.

SUZUKI, ADM. KANTARO   Japanese prime minister during the last months of the war, including at the time of the bombing of Hiroshima and Tokyo's surrender on August 14.

SZILARD, LEO   Nuclear physicist. The earliest advocate of building the atomic bomb, he later opposed its use.

TIBBETS, COL. PAUL W.   Commander of the 509th Composite Group, which was charged with dropping atomic bombs on Japan; pilot of *Enola Gay*, the B-29 that dropped the atomic bomb on Hiroshima.

TOGO, SHIGENORI   The last Japanese wartime foreign minister. The most moderate member of the Big Six, he opposed immediate rejection of the Potsdam Declaration and after Hiroshima advocated the one-condition surrender proposal that maintained the *kokutai* system, in which the emperor was sacred and sovereign and the military enjoyed primacy of place in political life.

TOJO, HIDEKI   Japanese prime minister, October 1941–July 1944. A strong advocate of war with the United States, he also held the positions of army minister and, from 1943, chief of staff of the army. Forced to resign after the fall of Saipan, he was executed for war crimes after the war.

TOYODA, SOEMU   Last Japanese wartime chief of the Naval General Staff. Opposed to war with the United States before Pearl Harbor, in 1945 he supported Korechika Anami and Yoshijiro Umezu in resisting surrender, even after Hiroshima and Nagasaki. After the war he said he differed from his two army colleagues regarding the addition of three terms beyond the preservation of the imperial institution, but he did not indicate that during the government debates at the time.

TRUMAN, HARRY S.   President of the United States, April 12, 1945–January 1953.

UMEZU, GEN. YOSHIJIRO   Last wartime Japanese chief of the Army General Staff. Umezu opposed surrender even after Hiroshima and Nagasaki but on September 2 signed the surrender agreement aboard the USS *Missouri* on behalf of the Imperial Army.

YAMAMOTO, ADM. ISOROKU   Commander in chief of the Japanese Combined Fleet, 1939–1943. Opposed war with the United States as unwinnable, given American industrial power. Yamamoto planned the Pearl Harbor attack, hoping to destroy the American fleet in a decisive victory and thereby force Washington to make peace. The same goal was behind Yamamoto's disastrous gamble at Midway. He was killed in April 1943 when American fighter planes intercepted his aircraft and shot it down after U.S. intelligence decoded Japanese transmissions of his itinerary.

YONAI, MITSUMASA   Last Japanese wartime navy minister. During the Big Six voting in August 1945, he supported Togo and Suzuki in advocating surrender on one condition: the preservation of the *kokutai* system.

SELECTED BIBLIOGRAPHY

ARCHIVAL COLLECTIONS

Combined Arms Research Library (CARL). Command and General Staff College, Fort Leavenworth, Kan.
George C. Marshall Research Library/Archives. Lexington, Va.
Harry S. Truman Library. Independence, Mo.
Library of Congress (Edward R. Bowles Papers). Washington, D.C.
MacArthur Memorial Library & Archives. Norfolk, Va.
National Archives and Records Administration (NARA). College Park, Md. (Record Groups 165, 218, 457).
Naval Historical Center. Navy Yard, Washington, D.C.
State Historical Society of Wisconsin (H. V. Kaltenborn Papers). Madison, Wis.
U.S. Army Military History Institute. Carlisle, Pa.

GOVERNMENT PUBLICATIONS

U.S. Department of State. *Foreign Relations of the United States: The Conference of Berlin (The Potsdam Conference), 1945.* 2 vols. Washington, D.C.: U.S. Government Printing Office, 1960.

——. *Foreign Relations of the United States: The Conferences at Cairo and Teheran, 1943.* Washington, D.C.: U.S. Government Printing Office, 1961.

——. *Foreign Relations of the United States: The Conferences at Malta and Yalta, 1945.* Washington, D.C.: U.S. Government Printing Office, 1955.

——. *Foreign Relations of the United States: The Conferences at Washington, 1941–1942, and Casablanca, 1943.* Washington, D.C.: U.S. Government Printing Office, 1968.

——. *Foreign Relations of the United States, 1945,* vol. 6, *The British Commonwealth: The Far East.* Washington, D.C.: U.S. Government Printing Office, 1969.

U.S. Strategic Bombing Survey. *The Effects of Strategic Bombing on Japan's War Economy.* Washington, D.C.: U.S. Government Printing Office, 1946.

——. *Japan's Struggle to End the War.* Washington, D.C.: U.S. Government Printing Office, 1946.

——. *Summary Report (Pacific War).* Washington, D.C.: U.S. Government Printing Office, 1946.

U.S. Strategic Bombing Survey (Pacific). Naval Analysis Division. *Interrogations of Japanese Officials.* 2 vols. Washington, D.C.: U.S. Government Printing Office, 1946.

MICROFILM DOCUMENT COLLECTIONS

The Henry R. Stimson Diaries. Yale University Library, New Haven, Conn.

Interrogations of Japanese Leaders and Responses to Questionnaires, 1945–1946. U.S. Strategic Bombing Survey (Pacific). Washington, D.C.: National Archives and Records Administration (NARA), 1991.

The MAGIC Documents: Summaries and Transcripts of the Top-Secret Diplomatic Communications of Japan, 1938–1945. Ed. Paul Kesaris. Washington, D.C.: University Publications of America, 1980.

Statements of Japanese Officials on World War II: English Translations. Military Intelligence Section, Historical Division, U.S. Army Far East Command. Washington, D.C.: Library of Congress Photoduplication Service, 1975 (from Lamont Library, Harvard University, Cambridge, Mass).

PUBLISHED DOCUMENT COLLECTIONS

Bland, Larry, and Sharon Ritenour Stevens, eds. *The Papers of George C. Marshall,* vol. 4, *"Aggressive and Determined Leadership," June 1, 1943–December 31, 1944.* Baltimore, Md.: Johns Hopkins University Press, 1996.

Boeicho Boei Kenshujo Senshi Shitsu (War History Office, Defense Agency) *Senshi Shosho* (War History Series) No. 82. *Daihon'ei Rikugun-Bu (10)* (Army Division, Imperial General Headquarters (vol. 10). Tokyo, 1975.

Detweiler, Donald S., and Charles S. Burdick, eds. *War in Asia and the Pacific*, vol. 12, *Defense of the Homeland and the End of the War*. New York: Garland, 1980.

Ferrell, Robert H., ed. *Harry S. Truman and the Bomb: A Documentary Collection*. Worland, Wyo.: High Plains, 1996.

MacEachin, Douglas J. *The Final Months of the War with Japan: Signals Intelligence, U.S. Invasion Planning, and the A-Bomb Decision*. Washington, D.C.: Center for the Study of Intelligence, 1998.

Merrill, Dennis, ed. *Documentary History of the Truman Presidency*, vol. 1, *The Decision to Drop the Atomic Bomb on Japan*. Washington, D.C.: University Publications of America, 1995.

Reports of General MacArthur: The Campaigns of MacArthur in the Pacific, vol. 1. Washington, D.C.: U.S. Government Printing Office, 1994.

Reports of General MacArthur: Japanese Operations in the Southwest Pacific Area, vol. 2, part 2. Washington, D.C.: U.S. Government Printing Office, 1994.

Stoff, Michael B., Jonathan F. Fanton, and R. Hal Williams, eds. *The Manhattan Project: A Documentary Introduction to the Atomic Age*. New York: McGraw-Hill, 1991.

The Tokyo War Crimes Trials. Ed. R. John Pritchard and Sonia Magbanua Zaide. New York: Garland, 1981.

Truman, Harry. *Dear Bess: The Letters from Harry to Bess Truman, 1900–1959*. Ed. Robert H. Ferrell. New York: Norton, 1983.

———. *Off the Record: The Private Papers of Harry S. Truman*. Ed. Robert H. Ferrell. New York: Harper & Row, 1980.

Williams, Robert C., and Philip L. Cantelon. *The American Atom: A Documentary History of Nuclear Policies from the Discovery of Fission to the Present, 1939–1984*. Philadelphia: University of Pennsylvania Press, 1984.

INTERVIEWS AND PERSONAL COMMUNICATIONS

Kolodney, Morris. Interview by the author. Sarasota, Fla., October 2, 2004.

Kolodney, Morris. Letter to author, October 9, 2004.

BOOKS, ARTICLES, AND TRANSCRIPTS

Alexander, Col. Joseph H. *The Battle History of the Marines: A Fellowship of Valor*. New York: HarperPerennial, 1999.

———. *Closing In: Marines in the Seizure of Iwo Jima*. Washington, D.C.: Marine Corps Historical Center, 1994.

Allen, Thomas B., and Norman Polmar. *Code Name Downfall: The Secret Plan to Invade Japan and Why Truman Dropped the Bomb*. New York: Simon & Schuster, 1995.

Allinson, Gary D. *Japan's Postwar History*. Ithaca, N.Y.: Cornell University Press, 1997.

Alperovitz, Gar. *Atomic Diplomacy: Hiroshima and Potsdam.* New York: Vintage Books, 1975.

———. *The Decision to Use the Atomic Bomb and the Architecture of an American Myth.* New York: Knopf, 1995.

———. "More on Atomic Diplomacy." *Bulletin of Atomic Scientists* 41 (December 1985): 35–39.

Ambrose, Stephen E., and Brian Loring Villa. "Racism, the Atomic Bomb, and the Transformation of Japanese-American Relations." In *The Pacific War Revisited,* ed. Günter Bischof and Robert L. Dupont, 171–198. Baton Rouge: Louisiana State University Press, 1997.

Appleman, Roy E., et al. *Okinawa: The Last Battle.* Washington, D.C.: Center of Military History, 1948.

Arens, Mark P. "V [Marine] Amphibious Corps Planning for Operation Olympic and the Role of Intelligence and Support Planning." Marine Corps Command and Staff, www.fas.org/irp/epring/arens (February 11, 2003).

Armstrong, Anne. *Unconditional Surrender: The Impact of the Casablanca Policy Upon World War II.* New Brunswick, N.J.: Rutgers University Press, 1961.

Asada, Sadao. "The Shock of the Atomic Bomb and Japan's Decision to Surrender." *Pacific Historical Review* 67, no. 4 (November 1998): 478–511.

Baldwin, Hanson W. *Great Mistakes of the War.* New York: Harper Brothers, 1950.

Bernstein, Barton J. "The Alarming Japanese Buildup on Southern Kyushu, Growing U.S. Fears, and Counterfactual Analysis: Would the Planned November 1945 Invasion of Southern Kyushu Have Occurred?" *Pacific Historical Review* 68, no. 4 (November 1999): 561–609.

———. "The Atomic Bomb and American Foreign Policy: An Historiographical Controversy." *Peace and Change* 2 (Spring 1974): 1–16.

———. "The Atomic Bombings Reconsidered." *Foreign Affairs* 74, no. 1 (January–February 1995): 135–152.

———. "A Postwar Myth: 500,000 Lives Saved." *The Bulletin of Atomic Scientists* 42 (June–July 1986): 38–40.

———. "Roosevelt, Truman, and the Atomic Bomb: A Reinterpretation." *Political Science Quarterly* 90 (Spring 1975): 23–69.

———. "The Struggle Over History: Defining the Hiroshima Narrative." In *Judgment at the Smithsonian,* ed. Philip Nobile, 127–256. New York: Marlowe & Company, 1995.

———. "Truman and the A-Bomb Decision: Targeting Noncombatants, Using the Bomb, and Defending His 'Decision.'" *The Journal of Military History* 62, no. 3 (July 1998): 547–550.

———. "Understanding the Atomic Bomb and the Japanese Surrender: Missed Opportunities, Little Known Near Disasters, and Modern Memory." *Diplomatic History* 19, no. 2 (Spring 1995): 227–273.

Bird, Kai, and Lawrence Lifschultz, eds. *Hiroshima's Shadow: Writings on the Denial of History and the Smithsonian Controversy.* Stony Creek, Conn.: Pamphleteer's Press, 1998.

Bird, Kai, and Martin J. Sherwin. *American Prometheus: The Triumph and Tragedy of J. Robert Oppenheimer*. New York: Knopf, 2005.

Bix, Herbert P. *Hirohito and the Making of Modern Japan*. New York: HarperCollins, 2000.

——. "Japan's Delayed Surrender: A Reinterpretation." *Diplomatic History* 19, no. 2 (Spring 1995): 197–225.

Blackett, P. M. S. *Fear, War, and the Bomb: Military and Political Consequences of Atomic Energy*. New York: McGraw-Hill, 1949.

Bonnett, John. "Jekyll and Hyde: Henry L. Stimson, Mentalité, and the Decision to Drop the Bomb on Japan." *War in History* 4, no. 2 (April 1997): 174–212.

Boyer, Paul. *By the Bomb's Early Light: American Thought and Culture at the Dawn of the Atomic Age*. New York: Pantheon, 1985.

Brandt, R. B. "Utilitarianism and the Rules of War." *Philosophy and Public Affairs* 1 (Winter 1972): 145–165.

Brooks, Lester. *Behind Japan's Surrender: The Secret Struggle That Ended an Empire*. New York: McGraw-Hill, 1968.

Bundy, McGeorge. *Danger and Survival: Choices About the Bomb in the First Fifty Years*. New York: Random House, 1988.

Butow, Robert J. C. *Japan's Decision to Surrender*. Stanford, Calif.: Stanford University Press, 1954.

Calvocoressi, Peter, Guy Wint, and John Pritchard. *The Penguin History of the Second World War*. New York: Penguin, 1989.

Chappell, John D. *Before the Bomb: How America Approached the End of the Pacific War*. Lexington: University Press of Kentucky, 1997.

Cline, Ray. *Washington Command Post: The Operations Division*. Washington, D.C.: Office of the Chief of Military History, Department of the Army, 1951.

Cohen, Sheldon. *Arms and Judgment*. Boulder, Colo.: Westview Press, 1988.

Committee for the Compilation of Materials on Damage Caused by the Atomic Bombs in Hiroshima and Nagasaki. *Hiroshima and Nagasaki: The Physical, Medical, and Social Effects of the Atomic Bombings*. Trans. Essi Ishikawa and David L. Swan. New York: Basic Books, 1981.

Compton, Arthur Holly. *Atomic Quest: A Personal Narrative*. New York: Oxford University Press, 1956.

——. "If the Atomic Bomb Had Not Been Used," *Atlantic Monthly*, December 1946, 54–56.

Cousins, Norman, and Thomas K. Finletter. "A Beginning for Sanity." *Saturday Review of Literature*, June 15, 1946, 4–9.

Craig, William. *The Fall of Japan*. London: Weidenfeld and Nicolson, 1968.

Curators of the National Air and Space Museum. "The Crossroads: The End of World War II, the Atomic Bomb and the Origins of the Cold War." In *Judgment at the Smithsonian*, ed. Philip Nobile, 1–126. New York: Marlowe & Company, 1995.

Daws, Gavan. *Prisoners of the Japanese: POWs of World War II in the Pacific*. New York: William Morrow, 1994.

DeGroot, Gerard J. *The Bomb: A Life*. Cambridge, Mass.: Harvard University Press, 2005.

Dockrill, Saki, and Lawrence Freedman. "Hiroshima: A Strategy of Shock." In *From Pearl Harbor to Hiroshima: The Second World War in Asia and the Pacific, 1941–1945*, ed. Saki Dockrill, 191–212. New York: St. Martin's Press, 1994.

Dower, John W. *Embracing Defeat: Japan in the Wake of World War II*. New York: Norton, 1999.

——. *Empire and Aftermath: Yoshida Shigeru and the Japanese Experience, 1878–1954*. Cambridge, Mass.: Council on East Asian Studies, Harvard University, 1979.

——. *Japan in War and Peace: Selected Essays*. New York: Free Press, 1993.

——. *War Without Mercy: Race and Power in the Pacific War*. New York: Pantheon, 1986.

Drea, Edward J. *In the Service of the Emperor: Essays on the Imperial Japanese Army*. Lincoln: University of Nebraska Press, 1998.

——. *MacArthur's Ultra: Codebreaking and the War Against Japan, 1942–1945* Lawrence: University Press of Kansas, 1992.

Dunnigan, James F., and Albert A. Nofi. *The Pacific War Encyclopedia*. New York: Checkmark Books, 1998.

Eubank, Keith. *The Bomb*. Malabar, Fla.: Krieger, 1991.

Feifer, George. *The Battle of Okinawa: The Blood and the Bomb*. Guilford, Conn.: Lyons Press, 2001.

Feis, Herbert. *Japan Subdued: The Atomic Bomb and the End of the War in the Pacific*. Princeton, N.J.: Princeton University Press, 1961.

Ferrell, Robert H. *Harry S. Truman: A Life*. Columbia: University of Missouri Press, 1994.

——. *Harry S. Truman and the Cold War Revisionists*. Columbia: University of Missouri Press, 2006.

——. "Intelligence Assessments and Assumptions: The View from Washington." Annual Meeting of the Society for Military History. Pennsylvania State University, April 16, 1999.

Frank, Richard B. *Downfall: The End of the Japanese Empire*. New York: Random House, 1999.

——. "Ending the Pacific War: History and Fantasy." Churchill Memorial: Kemper Lectures, March 23, 2001. www.wcmo.edu/cm/scholar/pacific/pacific1.asp.

——. "Why Truman Dropped the Bomb." *Weekly Standard*, August 8, 2005.

Gallicchio, Marc S. "After Nagasaki: General Marshall's Plan for Tactical Nuclear Weapons in Japan." *Prologue* 23, no. 4 (Winter 1991): 396–404.

——. *The Cold War Begins in Asia: American East Asia Policy and the Fall of the Japanese Empire*. New York: Columbia University Press, 1988.

Gentile, Gian P. "Advocacy or Assessment: The United States Strategic Bombing Survey of Germany and Japan." *Pacific Historical Review* 66, no. 1 (February 1997): 53–79.

——. *How Effective Is Strategic Bombing? Lessons Learned From World War II to Kosovo*. New York: New York University Press, 2001.

Giangreco, D. M. "Casualty Projections for the U.S. Invasion of Japan, 1945–1946: Planning and Policy Implications." *Journal of Military History* 61, no. 3 (July 1997): 521–581.

——. "Evolving Methodologies in Casualty Reporting to the American Public During World War II." *Society for Military History* 70th Annual Meeting, Center for the Study of War and Society, University of Tennessee, Knoxville, May 1–2, 2003. www.mtholyoke.edu/acad/intrel/research/evolving.htm (March 26, 2003).

——. "Operation Downfall [US Invasion of Japan]: US Plans and Japanese Counter-Measures." Paper presented at the symposium "Beyond Bushido: Recent Work in Japanese Military History," University of Kansas, February 12, 1998. www.mtholyoke.edu/acad/intrel/giangrec.htm (March 6, 2003).

——. "'A Score of Bloody Okinawas and Iwo Jimas': President Truman and Casualty Estimates for the Invasion of Japan." *Pacific Historical Review* 72, no. 1 (February 2003): 93–132.

Giangreco, D. M., and Kathryn Moore. *Dear Harry . . . : Truman's Mailroom, 1945–1953.* Mechanicsburg, Pa.: Stackpole Books, 1999.

Giovannitti, Len, and Fred Freed. *The Decision to Drop the Bomb.* New York: Coward, McCann, 1965.

Gowing, Margaret. *Britain and Atomic Energy, 1939–1945.* London: Macmillan, 1965.

Groves, Leslie R. *Now It Can Be Told: The History of the Manhattan Project.* New York: Harper and Brothers, 1962.

Hamby, Alonzo. *Man of the People: A Life of Harry S. Truman.* New York: Oxford University Press, 1995.

Hare, R. M. "Rules of War and Moral Reasoning." *Philosophy and Public Affairs* 1 (Winter 1972): 166–181.

Harwit, Martin. *An Exhibit Denied: Lobbying the History of the* Enola Gay. New York: Copernicus, 1996.

Hasegawa, Tsuyoshi. *Racing the Enemy: Stalin, Truman, and the Surrender of Japan.* Cambridge, Mass.: Harvard University Press, 2005.

Hayes, Grace Person. *The History of the Joint Chiefs of Staff.* Annapolis, Md.: Naval Institute Press, 1982.

Herken, Gregg. *Brotherhood of the Bomb: The Tangled Lives and Loyalties of Robert Oppenheimer, Ernest Lawrence, and Edward Teller.* New York: Henry Holt, 2002.

——. *The Winning Weapon: The Atomic Bomb in the Cold War, 1945–1950.* New York: Vintage Books, 1982.

Hersey, John. *Into the Valley: A Skirmish of the Marines.* New York: Knopf, 1943.

Hewlett, Richard G., and Oscar E. Anderson Jr. *The New World, 1939–1946,* vol. 1, A *History of the United States Atomic Energy Commission.* University Park: Pennsylvania State University Press, 1962.

Hogan, Michael J. "The *Enola Gay* Controversy: Memory and the Politics of Presentation." In *Hiroshima in History and Memory,* ed. Michael J. Hogan, 200–232. New York: Cambridge University Press, 1996.

Holloway, David. *Stalin and the Bomb: The Soviet Union and Atomic Energy, 1939–1956.* New Haven, Conn.: Yale University Press, 1994.

Hoyt, Edwin P. *Japan's War: The Great Pacific Conflict*. New York: Da Capo, 1986.

Irokawa, Daikichi. *The Age of Hirohito: In Search of Modern Japan*. Trans. Mikiso Hane and John K. Urda. New York: Free Press, 1995.

Jeffries, John W. *Wartime America: The World War II Home Front*. Chicago: Ivan R. Dee, 1996.

Jones, Vincent C. *Manhattan: The Army and the Atomic Bomb*. Washington, D.C.: Center for Military History, 1985.

Kecskmeti, Paul. *Strategic Surrender: The Politics of Victory and Defeat*. Stanford, Calif.: Stanford University Press, 1958.

Keegan, John. *The Second World War*. New York: Penguin, 1989.

Kido, Koichi. *Diary of Marquis Kido: Selected Translations in English*. Frederick, Md.: University Publications of America, 1984.

Kort, Michael. "Casualty Projections for the Invasion of Japan, Phantom Estimates, and the Math of Barton Berstein," *Passport: The Newsletter of the Society for Historians of American Foreign Relations* 34 (December 2003): 4–12.

Koshiro, Yukiko. "Japan's End Game in World War II." *American Historical Review* 109, no. 2 (April 2004): 417–444.

LeMay, Curtis E. *Mission with LeMay: My Story*. Garden City, N.Y.: Doubleday, 1965.

Lewis, Jon E., ed. *The Mammoth Book of Eyewitness: World War II*. New York: Carroll and Graf, 2004.

Lifton, Robert Jay, and Richard A. Falk. *Indefensible Weapons*. New York: Basic Books, 1982.

Lifton, Robert Jay, and Greg Mitchell. *Hiroshima in America: Fifty Years of Denial*. New York: G. P. Putnam's Sons, 1995.

Linderman, Gerald F. *The World Within War: America's Combat Experience in World War II*. New York: Free Press, 1997.

Logan, Jonothan. "A Strange New Quantum Ethics." *American Scientist* 88 (July–August 2000): 356–359.

Maddox, Robert James. *The New Left and the Origins of the Cold War*. Princeton, N.J.: Princeton University Press, 1973.

——. *Weapons for Victory: The Hiroshima Decision Fifty Years Later*. Columbia: University of Missouri Press, 1995.

Maga, Tim. *America Attacks Japan: The Invasion that Never Was*. Lexington: University Press of Kentucky, 2002.

Manchester, William. *Goodbye, Darkness: A Memoir of the Pacific War*. New York: Dell, 1980.

Marx, Joseph Lawrence. *Nagasaki: The Necessary Bomb?* New York: Macmillan, 1971.

Maslowski, Peter. "Truman, the Bomb, and the Numbers Game." *MHQ: The Quarterly Journal of Military History* 7, no. 3 (Spring 1995): 103–107.

McCullough, David. *Truman*. New York: Simon & Schuster, 1992.

Messer, Robert L. "New Evidence on Truman's Decision." *Bulletin of Atomic Scientists* 41 (August 1985): 50–56.

Miscamble, Wilson D. *From Roosevelt to Truman: Potsdam, Hiroshima, and the Cold War*. New York: Cambridge University Press, 2006.

Morton, W. Scott. *Japan: Its History and Culture*. 3rd ed. New York: McGraw-Hill, 1994.

Moskin, J. Robert. *Mr. Truman's War: The Final Victories of World War II and the Birth of the Postwar World*. New York: Random House, 1996.

Murry, Williamson, and Allan R. Millet. *A War to Be Won: Fighting the Second World War*. Cambridge, Mass.: Harvard University Press, 2000.

Neillands, Robin. *The Bomber War: The Allied Offensive Against Nazi Germany*. New York: Overlook Press, 2001.

Newman, Robert P. *The* Enola Gay *and the Court of History*. New York: Peter Lang, 2004.

———. "Hiroshima and the Trashing of Henry Simpson." *New England Quarterly* 71, no. 1 (March 1998): 5–32.

———. *Truman and the Hiroshima Cult*. East Lansing: Michigan State University Press, 1995.

Norris, Robert S. *Racing for the Bomb: General Leslie R. Groves, the Manhattan Project's Indispensable Man*. South Royalton, Vt.: Steerforth Press, 2002.

O'Connor, Raymond G. *Diplomacy for Victory: FDR and Unconditional Surrender*. New York: Norton, 1971.

Offner, Arnold A. *Another Such Victory: President Truman and the Cold War, 1945–1953*. Stanford, Calif.: Stanford University Press, 2002.

O'Reilly, Charles, and William A. Rooney. *The* Enola Gay *and the Smithsonian Institution*. Jefferson, N.C.: McFarland, 2005.

Pacific War Research Society. *Japan's Longest Day*. New York: Ballantine, 1968.

———. *The Day Man Lost: Hiroshima, 6 August 1945*. Tokyo: Kodansha International, 1972.

Palmer, Robert R., Bell I. Wiley, and William R. Keast. *The Procurement and Training of Ground Troops*. Washington, D.C.: Historical Division, Department of the Army, 1948.

Pearlman, Michael D. *Unconditional Surrender, Demobilization, and the Atomic Bomb*. Fort Leavenworth, Kan.: Combat Studies Institute, 1996.

Pogue, Forrest C. *George C. Marshall: Statesman, 1945–1959*. New York: Viking, 1987.

Polmar, Norman, and Thomas B. Allen. *World War II: The Encyclopedia of the War Years, 1941–1945*. New York: Random House, 1996.

Public Broadcasting System. "The American Experience: Victory in the Pacific." Transcript. www.pbs.org/wgbh/amex/pacific/filmmore/pt.html (August 4, 2005).

Rhodes, Richard. *The Making of the Atomic Bomb*. New York: Simon & Schuster, 1986.

Roberts, Jeffrey J. "Peering Through Different Bombsights: Military Historians, Diplomatic Historians, and the Decision to Drop the Atomic Bomb." *Airpower Journal*, Spring 1998. http://airpower.maxwell.af.mil/airchronicles/apj/apj98/roberts.html (May 2, 2005).

Rose, Lisle A. *Dubious Victory: The United States and the End of World War II*. Kent, Ohio: Kent State University Press, 1973.

Rose, Paul Lawrence. *Heisenberg and the Nazi Atomic Bomb Project, 1939–1945: A Study in German Culture*. Berkeley: University of California Press, 1998.

Schell, Jonathan. "The Unfinished Twentieth Century." *Harper's*, January 2000, 41–56.

Schom, Alan. *The Eagle and the Rising Sun: The Japanese-American War, 1941–1943*. New York: Norton, 2004.

Serber, Robert. *The Los Alamos Primer: The First Lectures on How to Build an Atomic Bomb*. Berkeley: University of California Press, 1992.

Sherwin, Martin J. *A World Destroyed: The Atomic Bomb and the Grand Alliance*. New York: Vintage Books, 1977. Reprinted as *A World Destroyed: Hiroshima and the Origins of the Arms Race* (New York: Vintage Books, 1987); reprinted, with a foreword by Robert Jay Lifton, a new preface, new appendixes, and an extended epilogue, as *A World Destroyed: Hiroshima and Its Legacies* (Stanford, Calif.: Stanford University Press, 2003).

Sigal, Leon V. *Fighting to a Finish: The Politics of War Termination in the United States and Japan, 1945*. Ithaca, N.Y.: Cornell University Press, 1988.

Skates, John Ray. *The Invasion of Japan: Alternative to the Bomb*. Columbia: University of South Carolina Press, 1994.

Sledge, E. B. *With the Old Breed: At Peleliu and Okinawa*. New York: Oxford University Press, 1981.

Smith, Gaddis. *American Diplomacy During the Second World War*. 2nd ed. New York: Knopf, 1985.

Smith, Robert Ross. *Triumph in the Pacific*. Washington, D.C.: Office of the Chief of Military History, Department of the Army, 1963.

Spector, Ronald H. *Eagle Against the Sun: The American War with Japan*. New York: Free Press, 1985.

Stimson, Henry L., and McGeorge Bundy. "The Decision to Use the Atomic Bomb." *Harper's*, February 1947, 97–107.

——. *On Active Service in Peace and War*. New York: Harper and Brothers, 1948.

Szilard, Leo. *Leo Szilard: His Version of the Facts*. Ed. Spencer R. Weart and Gertrud Weiss Szilard. Cambridge, Mass.: MIT Press, 1978.

Takaki, Ronald. *Hiroshima: Why America Dropped the Atomic Bomb*. Boston: Little Brown, 1995.

Tanaka, Yuki. *Hidden Horrors: Japanese War Crimes of World War II*. Boulder, Colo.: Westview Press, 1996.

Truman, Harry S. *Memoirs: Year of Decisions*. Garden City, N.Y.: Doubleday, 1955.

Tucker, Robert W. *The Just War*. Baltimore, Md.: Johns Hopkins University Press, 1961.

Ugaki, Matome. *Fading Victory: The Diary of Matome Ugaki, 1941–1945*. Trans. Masataka Chihaya. Pittsburgh: University of Pittsburgh Press, 1991.

United States Atomic Energy Commission. *In the Matter of J. Robert Oppenheimer*. Cambridge, Mass.: MIT Press, 1970.

Villa, Brian L. "The U.S. Army, Unconditional Surrender, and the Potsdam Proclamation." *Journal of American History* LXIII (June 1976): 66–92.

Wainstock, Dennis D. *The Decision to Drop the Bomb*. Westport, Conn.: Praeger, 1996.

Walker, J. Samuel. "The Decision to Use the Bomb: A Historiographical Update." *Diplomatic History* 14, no. 1 (Winter 1990): 97–114.

———. *Prompt and Utter Destruction: Truman and the Use of Atomic Bombs Against Japan.* Chapel Hill: University of North Carolina Press, 1997.

———. "Recent Literature on Truman's Atomic Bomb Decision: A Search for the Middle Ground." *Diplomatic History* 29, no. 2 (April 2005): 311–334.

Walzer, Michael. *Just and Unjust Wars: A Moral Argument with Historical Illustrations.* New York: Basic Books, 1977.

Warner, Denis, and Peggy Warner. *The Sacred Warriors: Japan's Suicide Legions.* New York: Avon, 1982.

Warner, Geoffrey. "To End a War: The Decision to Drop the Bomb." In *The Cold War Debated,* ed. David Carlton and Herbert M. Levine, 34–39. New York: McGraw-Hill, 1988.

Weinberg, Gerhard L. *A World at Arms: A Global History of World War II.* New York: Cambridge University Press, 1994.

Weintraub, Stanley. *The Last Great Victory: The End of World War II, July/August 1945.* New York: Plume, 1995.

Wilson, Jane, ed. *All in Our Time: The Reminiscences of Twelve Nuclear Pioneers.* Chicago: Bulletin of Atomic Scientists, 1975.

Wolk, Herman S. "General Arnold, the Atomic Bomb, and the Surrender of Japan." In *The Pacific War Revisited,* ed. Günter Bischof and Robert L. Dupont, 163–178. Baton Rouge: Louisiana State University Press, 1997.

Wyden, Peter. *Day One: Before Hiroshima and After.* New York: Warner, 1985.

Zeiler, Thomas W. *Unconditional Defeat: Japan, America, and the End of World War II.* Wilmington, Del.: Scholarly Resources, 2004.

Zubok, Vladidslav M. "Stalin and the Nuclear Age. In *Cold War Statesmen Confront the Bomb: Nuclear Diplomacy Since 1945,* ed. John Lewis Gaddis, Philip Gordon, Lewis May, and Jonathan Rosenberg, 39–61. Oxford: Oxford University Press, 1999.

WEB SITES

Air Force Association—Enola Gay Archive. www.afaorg/media/enolagay (January 6, 2003).

Manhattan Project History Preservation Association. http://childrenofthemanhattan project.org (July 12, 2004).

Milani, Kevin. The Scientific History of the Atomic Bomb. www.hcc.mnscu.edu/programs/dept/chem/abomb/index.html (July 10, 2004).

Nuclearfiles.org: A Project of the Nuclear Age Peace Foundation. http://nuclearfiles .org (January 6, 2004).

PART IV

Documents

GUIDE TO THE DOCUMENTS

A. AMERICAN CIVILIAN DOCUMENTS

A1. Leo Szilard Letter to Lewis Strauss, January 25, 1939. Szilard warns that atomic fission might make it possible to build atomic bombs.

A2. Albert Einstein Letter to President Roosevelt, August 2, 1939. Einstein warns that Germany might try to build an atomic bomb. Roosevelt's reply on October 19 follows.

A3. Churchill Unconditional Surrender Suggestion at the Casablanca Conference, January 18, 1943. Churchill suggests to Roosevelt that the Allies require Germany and Japan to surrender unconditionally.

A4. Roosevelt's Casablanca Press Conference Notes, January 22–23, 1943. Roosevelt was supposed to use these notes mentioning an unconditional surrender policy.

A5. The Quebec Agreement, August 19, 1943. A U.S.-British agreement at the 1943 Quebec Conference stipulating that neither side would use the atomic bomb without the other's consent. The code term used to refer to the bomb was "Tube Alloys."

A6. Tube Alloys Aide-Memoire, September 18, 1944. This is an agreement between Roosevelt and Churchill to keep all information about the atomic bomb secret.

A7. The Cairo Declaration, December 18, 1943. This statement by the United States, Britain, and China affirms the unconditional surrender policy regarding Japan.

A8. Roosevelt and King/Marshall Letters on Military and Civilian Manpower Needs, January 1945. These letters outlining manpower needs are as printed in the *New York Times*, January 18, 1945.

A9. The Yalta Agreements Regarding the Far East. This excerpt comprises the part of the agreement of February 11, 1945, pertaining to the Soviet Union's entry into the Pacific War.

A10. Stimson Memo to Truman, April 24, 1945. Stimson informs President Truman of the need to discuss a "highly secret matter," the atomic bomb.

A11. Stimson Memorandum on the Atomic Bomb to Truman, April 25, 1945. Stimson describes the bomb and the military, political, and moral issues it raises, and he recommends the creation of a committee to advise the president and Congress regarding the bomb, which is duly established as the Interim Committee.

A12. Stimson Diary Entry, May 15, 1945. Stimson voices concerns about the upcoming Potsdam Conference, the invasion of Japan, and the role of the atomic bomb.

A13. Kyle Palmer Article on Casualties, May 17, 1945 ("Palmer Warns No Easy Way to Beat Japs," *Los Angeles Times*, May 17, 1945). War correspondent Kyle Palmer predicts at least 500,000 U.S. casualties to defeat Japan.

A14. *New Republic* Editorial, May 28, 1945, "War in the Pacific," an editorial signed by naval historian Fletcher Pratt, warns of huge U.S. casualties if it proved necessary to destroy the Japanese army.

A15. Interim Committee Minutes, May 31, 1945. This record of discussion covers the future implications of the existence of nuclear weapons, the building of bombs far more powerful than those under development, how to avoid alienating the Soviet Union (Marshall suggests inviting two Soviet scientists to witness the first nuclear test), and the impact of a nuclear attack on Japan's will to fight, the consensus being that to have the desired impact Japan could not be warned.

A16. Stimson Diary Entry, May 31, 1945. Stimson assesses the 31 May Interim Committee meeting.

A17. Interim Committee Minutes, June 1, 1945. The committee concludes that the selection of a target was a military matter but that the bomb should be used as soon as possible against a "war plant surrounded by workers' homes" and without warning.

A18. Truman Diary Entry, June 1, 1945. Truman notes how he consults reports on casualties on a daily basis and mentions his meeting two days earlier with former president Hoover (which results in the Hoover Memorandum).

A19-1. Hoover Memorandum to Truman and Responses, May–June 1945. Item "a" is a memo from Fred M. Vinson to Truman suggesting Truman consult with other top officials. Item "b" is the Hoover Memorandum. Item "c" is Cordell Hull's reply; item "d" is Joseph Grew's analysis. None of the civilian advisors Truman consulted challenged Hoover's figures. Item "e" consists of a short memo from General Marshall to Secretary of War Stimson and the Army's lengthy memorandum of comments on Hoover's analysis that Marshall signed. It argues that Hoover's casualty estimate "appears to deserve little consideration."

A19-2. Hoover Memorandum to Stimson and Marshall Response, May–June 1945. Item "a" is the memorandum Hoover sent to Stimson. Item "b" is a short memo from Marshall to Stimson and Army memorandum of comments, also signed by Marshall. It concludes that Hoover's estimated loss of 500,000 lives in an invasion of Japan *under our present plan of campaign,* is considered entirely too high" (emphasis in the original). The "present plan of campaign" assumed about 350,000 Japanese defenders on Kyushu. There were 900,000 in place by August 1945.

A20. Stimson Diary Entry, June 6, 1945. Stimson records his telling Truman of the Interim Committee's conclusion that the Soviets should not be told about the atomic bomb until its use against Japan. He covers the committee's discussion of Potsdam, including Stimson's concern that the Soviets might "bring up the subject and ask us to take them in as partners"; Truman's comment about postponing Potsdam until July 15 "to give us more time," a reference to the expected Trinity test; and that Truman mentioned Harry Hopkins's "accomplishment," a reference to attempts to improve relations with Moscow.

A21. Truman Diary Entry, June 7, 1945. Truman is optimistic about maintaining good relations with the Soviet Union.

A22. *Yank: The Army Weekly* Magazine Article, June 8, 1945 ("The Jap War"). This editorial covers the uncertainties regarding the final defeat of Japan. It includes both hopeful and grim assessments of the situation, including speculation by "higher brass around the Pentagon" that it might take "1 year, 2 years or longer to win the Far East War." Written by Sgt. Barrett McGurn.

A23. The Franck Report, June 11, 1945. Signed by James Franck, a Nobel laureate in physics, Szilard, and five others, the Franck Report warns that a postwar nuclear arms race must be avoided and suggests in that regard that "the way in which the nuclear weapons now being secretly developed in the country are first revealed to the world appears to be of great, perhaps fateful importance." It therefore urges that Japan be warned of the bomb's power by a demonstration in an uninhabited area. Only then might the bomb "perhaps be used," accompanied by the "sanction" of the United Nations and "public opinion at home," and, "perhaps" an ultimatum to Japan to surrender or "at least" to evacuate certain areas.

A24. Recommendations of the Scientific Panel, June 16, 1945. After being briefed on the contents of the Franck Report, the scientists advising the Interim Committee suggest that the Soviet Union and certain other allies should be informed about the bomb before it is used. The memorandum, signed by A. Henry Compton, Ernest O. Lawrence, J. B. Oppenheimer, Enrico Fermi, and J. Robert Oppenheimer, is divided on the issue of military use, but can suggest no workable "technical demonstration" and reports that, while divided, as a group it is "closer" to the view that the bomb should be used immediately to save American lives. The scientists profess "no proprietary rights" regarding the overall handling of atomic energy.

A25. Truman Diary Entry, June 17, 1945. Truman voices his views of various American military leaders and his concern with his "hardest decision" to date: choosing between invading Japan or the strategy of bomb and blockade.

A26. Leahy Memo to the Joint Chiefs of Staff (JPS 697/D), June 14, 1945. This memorandum announces a meeting to review the plan to invade Japan, stressing Truman's desire of "economizing to the maximum extent possible in the loss of American lives."

A27. Minutes of White House Meeting, June 18, 1945. Marshall recommends the invasion of Japan while not providing specific casualty estimates, only a chart showing losses in previous Pacific campaigns and the ratio of American to Japanese casualties and a vague statement about losses that might be expected in the first thirty days of Operation Olympic. Other members of the Joint Chiefs and Stimson and Forrestal support him. On the matter of casualties, Leahy suggests that Okinawa will provide the best benchmark to estimating casualties and notes the casualty rate there is 35 percent of American forces. He asks how many troops will invade Kyushu, and Marshall gives the figure of 766,700. Leahy also expresses opposition to the policy of unconditional surrender. After Truman approves Operation Olympic, the meeting turns to "certain other matters," in other words, the atomic bomb.

A28. Leahy Diary Entry, June 18, 1945. This record surveys the events of the day, include the White House meeting. It includes a reference to Marshall's believing the invasion of Kyushu would cost 63,000 casualties, but the comment is in the present tense, as are other opinion statements not fixed in time concerning matters not discussed at the meeting; therefore, that reference does not refer to the White House meeting, whose proceedings, as with other events of that day, are discussed in the past tense.

A29. Stimson Diary Entry, June 19, 1945. Stimson voices hopes of avoiding "fighting to a finish"—an invasion of Japan and the military campaign that would follow that invasion—and the upcoming "last chance" warning to Japan to surrender. Stimson expresses satisfaction that plans provide enough time "to bring in the sanctions to our warning" an "attack of S-1" (the atomic bomb) and "an entry by the Russians into the war." Stimson also mentions a USSBS report covering the "effectiveness" and "failures" of strategic bombing against Germany and his concern over tensions in relations with Moscow.

A30. H. V. Kaltenborn Broadcast, June 26, 1945. Kaltenborn, a highly respected broadcaster with a national radio audience, discusses the huge American losses on "tiny" Okinawa and argues that the United States should avoid an invasion of Japan in the hope that "we can save a hundred thousand American lives."

A31. Ralph Bard Memorandum on the Use of the Atomic Bomb, June 27, 1945. Bard urges delaying the use of the atomic bomb because Japan is looking for a way to surrender and could do so if warned about the bomb and Russia's upcoming entry into the war, and if unconditional surrender was modified "with regard to the Emperor of Japan and the treatment of the Japanese nation."

A32. Stimson Diary Entry, June 26–30, 1945. Stimson records discussions with Forrestal and Grew regarding a warning to Japan. Stimson hopes Japan will then surrender, having been "sufficiently pounded possibly with S-1." He adds the country will not be satisfied unless "every effort is made to shorten the war."

A33. Stimson Diary Entry and Memorandum to Truman on Proposed Program for Japan, July 2, 1945. Stimson's diary entry notes his meeting with Truman, which covered the warning to Japan and the Interim Committee's advice regarding the Soviet Union and the atomic bomb. He mentions the urgency of shortening the Pacific War and handling Germany properly so it will become a "proper member of the family of nations." The memo outlines Stimson's ideas for the warning and surrender demand to be issued to Japan at Potsdam. He stresses the need to avoid a costly invasion and subsequent military campaign. The document that emerged at Potsdam closely followed his suggestions, which included occupation and a policy of demilitarization. Missing from the Potsdam Declaration was Stimson's stipulation that "we do not exclude a constitutional monarchy under the present dynasty." That, of course, meant a radical change in *kokutai*, something that no Japanese leader expressed willingness to accept before August 6.

A34. Stimson Diary Entry, July 3, 1945. Stimson's diary records advice on how to tell Stalin about the atomic bomb, assuming that Truman thinks "Stalin was on good enough terms with him."

A35. Truman Diary Entry, July 16, 1945. Truman reacts to the destruction in Germany and expresses his fears for the future of civilization.

A36. Truman Diary Entries, July 17, 18, and 25, 1945. Truman assesses Stalin. He is optimistic on July 18: "Believe Japs will fold up before Russia comes in. I

am sure they will when Manhattan appears over their homeland." His optimism has faded by July 25, when Truman notes that he is "sure" Tokyo will
not heed the upcoming warning to surrender. He comments on the power of
the bomb as revealed in the Trinity test, saying that it will not be dropped on
Tokyo or Kyoto and that the target "will be a purely military one." Truman's
comment that he discussed the "tactical and political situation" with Marshall is a reference to the Japanese buildup on Kyushu. It may also refer to the
projected Soviet entry into the Pacific War.

A37. Atomic Bomb Test: Report by Ernest O. Lawrence, July 16, 1945. Lawrence,
a member of the Manhattan Project team of atomic scientists, describes what
he witnessed.

A38. Met Lab Petition, July 17, 1945. Signed by Szilard and sixty-eight other Met
Lab scientists, the petition warns of the postwar implications of using the
bomb and urges, at a minimum, that it not be used unless the terms to be imposed on Japan have been made public and rejected.

A39. Groves Report to Stimson on the Atomic Bomb, July 18, 1945. Groves describes the bomb's enormous power.

A40. Stimson Diary Entry, July 19, 1945. Stimson voices concerns about future
cooperation with the Soviet Union in light of its dictatorial system.

A41. Stimson Memorandum on Relations with the Soviet Union, July 19, 1945.
This memorandum outlines the problems in future relations with the Soviet
Union, in particular the dangers of sharing any information about nuclear en-
ergy with Moscow before its undertaking fundamental reforms.

A42. Stimson Diary Notes, July 22, 1945. Stimson observes a change in Truman's
negotiating style—specifically, that he "stood up to the Russians in a most
emphatic and decisive manner."

A43. W. B. Shockley Memorandum to Edward L. Bowles on Estimated Casualties in an Invasion of Japan, July 21, 1945. This War Department memo argues
that past Japanese behavior and casualty rates in the Pacific War suggest that
an invasion of Japan "might cost us between 1.7 and 4 million casualties including 400,000 to 800,000 killed." These conclusions almost certainly
reached Stimson.

A44. Truman Letters to Bess Truman, July 18 and 20, 1945. Truman is upbeat in
the first letter and frustrated in the second. On July 18, Truman reports on
Stalin's agreement to enter the war against Japan. This means "we'll end the
war a year sooner now, and think of the kids who won't be killed!" On July 20,
Truman notes difficult negotiations and says, "I want the Jap War won and I
want 'em both in it."

A45. The Potsdam Declaration, July 26, 1945. The Allies demand that Japan's
armed forces surrender unconditionally. At the same time, Tokyo is promised

certain terms that guarantee its future independence and territorial integrity with regard to the four main home islands.

A46. Forrestal Diary Entry Regarding Byrnes, July 28, 1945. Forrestal notes that Secretary of State Byrnes wants to end the war before the Soviets expand their influence in Manchuria.

A47. Stimson Memo to Truman and Truman's Response, July 30, 1945. While Stimson is referring to releasing a White House statement, Truman's reply may indicate that he is referring to "releasing" the bomb itself.

A48. Truman Letter to Bess Truman, July 31, 1945. Truman refers to his "ace in the hole," the atomic bomb, that Stalin supposedly does not know about, but, more important, shows his willingness to accept Soviet-backed Polish annexation of eastern parts of Germany.

A49. The *Catholic World* on Unconditional Surrender, August 1945. This editorial opposes unconditional surrender and mentions the possibility of one million casualties if the war must be fought to the bitter end.

A50. Truman's Statement on the Bombing of Hiroshima, August 6, 1945. President Truman defends the use of the bomb and warns Japan of "a rain of ruin from the air, the like of which has never been seen on this earth" if it does not surrender.

A51. Leaflets Dropped on Japanese Cities After Hiroshima. These leaflets warn the Japanese people to evacuate their cities and announce the existence of the atomic bomb.

A52. Truman Letter to Senator Richard B. Russell, August 9, 1945. In a telegram to Truman on August 7, Sen. Russell had argued there should be no letup in the bombing campaign against Japan. Truman responds that he does not intend to wipe out "whole populations" because of their leaders' "pigheadedness" unless "it is absolutely necessary."

A53. Stimson Diary Entry, August 9, 1945. Stimson expresses deep concern about morale problems among U.S. troops and the popular pressure for large-scale discharges. Despite Hiroshima, Nagasaki, and the Soviet entry into the war and his expectations these events will hasten victory, he still does not know "how long and how many men we will have to keep to accomplish that victory."

A54. Stimson Diary Entry, August 10, 1945. Stimson is surprised and delighted that the Japanese have made a surrender offer. He discusses the differences among Truman's advisors regarding Japan's condition that the emperor continue on the throne with his powers intact. Stimson believes that the emperor must be left on the throne, since only his authority can get Japanese armies throughout Asia to surrender and thereby save the Allies "from a score of bloody Iwo Jimas and Okinawas all over China and the New Netherlands."

A55. Henry A. Wallace Diary Entry, August 10, 1945. Wallace quotes Truman's statement about stopping the bombing because he did not want to kill "all those kids."

A56. The *Christian Century* on the Bombing of Hiroshima, August 29, 1945. This editorial denounces the bombing of Hiroshima and Nagasaki, mentioning what it calls Churchill's "highly speculative assertion"—which it chooses not to challenge—that the bombings saved one million American and 250,000 British lives.

B. AMERICAN MILITARY DOCUMENTS

B1. J.C.S. 924/2 30 August 1944: Operations Against Japan Subsequent to Formosa. Report by the Joint Strategic Survey Committee. This report contains the "Saipan ratio"—"one American killed and several wounded to exterminate seven Japanese soldiers"—and the conclusion that "it might cost us half a million American lives" to destroy the Japanese forces defending the home islands.

B2. Marshall Memorandum to General Embick, 1 September 1944. Marshall applies the Saipan ratio to estimate casualties in a possible invasion of Formosa.

B3. Summary of Redeployment Forecast, March 14, 1945. An Army casualty estimate that it will require 720,000 replacements for "dead and evacuated wounded" for forces engaged against Japan in the 18 months after 1 June 1945.

B4. J.C.S. 924/15, April 25, 1945: Operations Against Japan Subsequent to Formosa. Report by the Joint Staff Planners. This report contains casualty ratios for Pacific and European theater operations. No calculations are in the report. However, the Pacific theater ratio (a casualty rate of 7.45 per thousand per day of operations) and the troop list for Olympic (766,700) yields 514,072 total casualties in a ninety-day campaign. The figure for Olympic and Coronet in a ninety-day campaign (total troop list of 1,792,700) yields 1,202,005 casualties.

B5. J.I.C. 191/7, May 16, 1945: Japanese Reaction to an Operation Against Southern Kyushu. This Joint Intelligence Committee report estimates the Japanese defenses U.S. forces are likely to face on Kyushu. It is assumed here that Tokyo will not weaken its defenses in Manchuria to build up its strength on Kyushu and that Japanese ground forces on the island at the time of the American invasion will number 390,000 men, 150,000 of which initially will be based in the south.

B6. J.C.S. 1331/3: Directive for Operation Olympic, May 25, 1945. This is the final version of the directive to invade Japan, outlining the respective responsibilities of the Commander in Chief, U.S. Army Forces, Pacific; Commander in Chief, U.S. Pacific Fleet; and the Commanding General of the Twentieth Air Force.

B7. Operation Downfall Plan for the Invasion of Japan, May 28, 1945. This document marks the overall plan for the invasion of Japan, issued by General MacArthur's headquarters.

B8. J.W.P.C. 369/1, June 15, 1945: Details of the Campaign Against Japan. This is the response of the Joint War Plans Committee to Admiral Leahy's memo of June 14 (see Document A26) regarding the White House meeting to discuss the invasion of Japan. Three points are important: the reluctance of the military planners to give specific estimates to the president; the suggestion that the Kyushu invasion might end the war, but no assurance that it would (the planners note that it would be a "pure gamble" to assume that the Southern Kyushu–Northwestern Kyushu option would cause the Japanese to admit defeat); and the estimate that a two-stage operation would last well into 1946.

B9. J.C.S. 1388, June 16, 1945: Details of the Campaign Against Japan. Report by the Joint Staff Planners. The Joint Staff Planners version of J.W.P.C. 369/1 lacks the casualty estimate table and the figure for the number of troops designated for the Kyushu operation (767,700).

B10. Marshall-MacArthur Correspondence, June 16–19, 1945. Marshall requested casualty estimates in preparation for the June 18 White House meeting. He clearly was concerned that the initial estimate he received was too high, which led to a second round of telegrams. The June 19 date on the last two messages reflects Manila time, which is thirteen hours ahead of Washington time.

B11. J.C.S. 1388/1: Nimitz Staff Casualty Estimate, June 18, 1945. The casualty estimate for the first thirty days of the Kyushu operation, forwarded by Nimitz to Admiral King for the June 18 White House meeting.

B12. J.C.S. 1388/1, June 20, 1945, and J.C.S. 1388/2, June 26, 1945. This exchange between King and Marshall regards casualty estimates for Olympic in the wake of the June 18 White House meeting. King asserts that "the Chiefs of Staff will have to give an estimate of the casualties expected in the operation." Marshall responds, "It seems unnecessary and undesirable for the Joint Chiefs of Staff to make estimates, which can only be speculative, in this paper." Had Marshall provided specific estimates at the June 18 White House meeting, there would have been no reason for King to assert the need for estimates two days later. For his part, Marshall reaffirms his refusal to make those estimates.

B13. C.C.S. 880/4, June 29, 1945: Memorandum by the United States Chiefs of Staff, June 29, 1945. This summary of the overall Downfall plan for a two-stage invasion of Japan by the U.S. Chiefs of Staff reaffirms that an invasion of the Japanese home islands is a "prerequisite" for achieving unconditional surrender but also cautions that "success in the main islands may not obviate the necessity of defeating the Japanese elsewhere."

B14. General Weckerling Memorandum, July 13, 1945. Sent by Brigadier General John Weckerling, a Deputy Assistant Chief of Staff and top Army intelligence officer, this assessment of the situation in Tokyo based on the Magic intercepts is that "quite probably" the Japanese calculate that American war-weariness will enable them to secure more favorable peace terms.

B15. C.C.S. 643/3, July 8, 1945: Estimate of the Enemy Situation (as of 6 July 1945). This report notes the sharp deterioration of conditions in Japan and maintains that Tokyo will attempt to maintain Soviet neutrality and exploit Allied war weariness in order to avoid "complete defeat or unconditional surrender." The document specifically links unconditional surrender with a foreign occupation and "foreign custody of the person of the Emperor," terms the Allies considered vital under any circumstances. It then suggests that Tokyo would be willing to abandon all territory it has seized and "even agree" to Korean independence in order to, "if possible," avoid occupation and foreign custody of the Emperor and "in any event, to insure the survival of the institution of the Emperor." It then states Tokyo might offer a conditional surrender "along the lines stated above," but that phrase clearly excludes terms (foreign occupation, foreign custody of the Emperor) essential to Allied war aims. It adds that Japanese army leaders seek terms that would permit the revival of "a military Japan."

B16. Meeting of the Combined Chiefs of Staff, July 16, 1945, and Meeting of the U.S. Joint Chiefs of Staff, July 17, 1945. These meetings took place during the Potsdam Conference. In order to assure that Japanese forces outside the home islands comply with surrender when it comes, the British Chiefs of Staff suggest modifying unconditional surrender so that it does not involve "dissolution of the Imperial institution." The sentence referred to by Sir Alan Brook is the one in Document B15 that begins that begins "To avoid these conditions." It is discussed in the preceding commentary. The U.S. Joint Chiefs of Staff meeting of July 17 likewise dealt with securing the surrender of Japanese forces outside the home islands. Marshall wants to make sure that the Allies say nothing publicly about removing Emperor Hirohito from office, lest such a statement prolong the war.

B17. Joint Chiefs of Staff Memorandum to the President, July 17, 1945. This is the memorandum that emerged from the July 17 Chiefs of Staff meeting. Interestingly, the Chiefs are concerned that the sentence referring to a constitutional monarchy, which Secretary of War Stimson believed would reassure the Japanese, will be misconstrued as indicating that the emperor will be removed from office and inhibit rather than facilitate surrender. They therefore want it eliminated from the Potsdam Declaration, which is what happened.

B18. Memorandum for General Arnold, July 24, 1945. This memorandum gives the proposed schedule for the first atomic bombing and the four top targets.

B19. General Handy Directive to General Spaatz, July 25, 1945. This is the written order to drop the atomic bomb demanded by Spaatz.

B20. MacArthur Headquarters Intelligence Estimate of Japanese Strength on Kyushu, July 29, 1945. Issued by General MacArthur's intelligence section, this analysis warns that the Japanese buildup on Kyushu is exceeding expectations and has become a "threatening development." It further warns that it may reach a point "where we attack on a ratio of one (1) to one (1) which is not a receipt for victory. . . . "

B21. Sixth Army (MacArthur) Headquarters Intelligence Report with Respect to Olympic, August 1, 1945. An intelligence report by MacArthur's Sixth Army headquarters notes the strong defenses on Kyushu, the "ample time" available to complete further defenses, Japan's ability to reinforce its troops on southern Kyushu, and the observation that the troops "are facing the invasion with high morale."

B22. J.W.P.C. 397, August 4, 1945, Alternatives to Olympic. This report warns that the strong Japanese defenses on southern Kyushu means that "commanders in the field should review their estimates of the situation, reexamine objectives in Japan as possible alternatives to OLYMPIC, and prepare plans for operations against such alternate objectives."

B23. Communications Between Marshall, MacArthur, King, and Nimitz, August 7, 9, and 10, 1945, and Nimitz to King, May 25, 1945. On August 7 (45369), Marshall expresses concerns to MacArthur about intelligence reports showing a large Japanese buildup on Kyushu and southern Honshu, including many suicide planes. MacArthur's response on August 9 (C31597) calls the reports "greatly exaggerated" (they were not) and stresses that "there should not be the slightest thought of changing the OLYMPIC operation." On 9 August ("King to Nimitz Eyes Only"), King asks Nimitz for his comments on the exchange, already being well aware that Nimitz had turned against Olympic back in May (CINCPAC ADV TO COMINCH). The next day, after Nagasaki, King sends Nimitz the "peace warning."

B24. War Department Memorandom to Admiral Leahy, August 10, 1945. This memorandum estimates that the Army will need 330,000 hospital beds in the United States as of June 30, 1946. Unstated is that 50,000 would be for soldiers wounded in combat before the invasion of Japan, which means the Army anticipated 280,000 beds would be needed for casualties related to the invasion of Japan. This is far from a total casualty figure inasmuch as it does not include non-Army personnel, soldiers hospitalized outside the United States, or soldiers killed in battle. The memo was never sent in the wake of surrender negotiations going on at the time.

B25. Intelligence Estimate of the Japanese Situation for Next 30 Days, August 12, 1945. Sent by Major General Clayton Bissell, Marshall's chief intelligence officer, after Hiroshima and Nagasaki, this report estimates that atomic bombs "will not have a decisive effect in the next 30 days."

B26. Edmund J. Winslett Report on the Defenses of Southern Kyushu, June 3, 1946. This report was presented in mid-1946 at the United States Army Military History Institute by Edmund J. Winslett, the Sixth Army officer in charge of photographic intelligence during the planning for Olympic. Winslett conducted the most thorough postwar examination of Japanese defenses on Kyushu.

B27. General Charles E. Willoughby Article in *Military Review*, June 1946 ("Occupation of Japan and Japanese Reaction"). Written in late 1945 by Major General Charles A. Willoughby, MacArthur's top intelligence officer, the article includes a high casualty estimate for the invasion and final defeat of Japan.

B28–B38: ULTRA intelligence reports, May 12–August 11, 1945. Each report is called either an Order of Battle Bulletin or "MAGIC"—Far East Summary. All are ULTRA intelligence reports. They trace the Japanese buildup on Kyushu from May to August 1945.

C. MAGIC DIPLOMATIC SUMMARIES

The MAGIC Diplomatic Summaries are valuable because they give insights into top-level thinking in Tokyo and constitute evidence about what conclusions American leaders had regarding Japanese intentions during the critical months before the bombing of Hiroshima during the spring and summer of 1945. The MAGIC summaries in this volume cover from early July to mid-August. Of particular importance is the exchange between Sato and Togo as reported in No. 1212 (July 20) and No. 1214 (July 22). In the former, Sato is quoted as stating specifically that he is only advocating unconditional surrender with the "exception of the question of preserving our national structure." Yet Togo's response, after referring to Sato's crucial caveat, is that "we are unable to consent to it [unconditional surrender] under any circumstances whatsoever." The last summary, dated August 15, includes a reference to a message from Tokyo to its legations in Europe noting that it had begun burning secret documents and that they should do the same. This was done in many Japanese government offices in the weeks that followed before American occupation forces arrived and undoubtedly enabled Tokyo to consign unseen to the ashes incriminating evidence that Washington could have cited to justify its policies, including the use of atomic weapons, at the end of the war. The August 15 summary also includes evidence that the commander of Japanese forces in China opposed surrender and wanted to continue the struggle.

D. JAPANESE GOVERNMENT DOCUMENTS, MILITARY DOCUMENTS, AND DIARY ENTRIES

The explanatory text in italics interspersed in certain documents is by the post-war compilers of *Senshi Shosho* (War History Series), the official Japanese military history of the war, which runs to more than a hundred volumes. The documents from that collection presented here are from No. 82, *Daihon'ei Rikugun-Bu (10)* (Army Division, the Imperial General Headquarters, vol. 10) (Tokyo 1975). This section also includes documents from several other sources.

D1. Imperial General Headquarters Navy Order 37, January 20, 1945. Approved by Emperor Hirohito, this document became the basis for all future planning to defend the home islands against an American invasion. The plan called for destroying the Allied invasion fleet "on the water, principally by sea and air special-attack [suicide] units."

D2. The Konoe Memorial, February 14, 1945. Konoe (whose name appears as Konoye in many documents elsewhere) warns the emperor that Japan has to find a way to end the war or face a "communist revolution." He expects that even under an unconditional surrender the United States "would not go so far as to reform Japan's *kokutai* or abolish the imperial house." In fact, a minimum American condition, accepted by all top Washington policy makers, was a radical overhaul of Japan's system of government, even if the imperial house was preserved.

D3. Imperial General Headquarters Army Order No. 1299, April 8, 1945. Describing the *Ketsu Go* plan to defend the home islands, this order repeats the January 20 strategy of annihilating the enemy landing force in the coastal area before the beachhead is secure.

D4. Ketsu Go Directive (Army Directive No. 2438), April 8, 1945. This directive, pursuant to Army Order 1299, was sent to top army field commanders by Chief of the Army General Staff Umezu.

D5. Imperial Headquarters Army Department Estimate of the Situation for the Spring of 1946, July 1, 1945. Issued by the Army from Imperial General Headquarters, this analysis of Allied strategy against Japan includes an analysis of the domestic situation in the United States. It notes American war-weariness, the demoralizing effect of high casualty projections, the uncertain authority of "the new President" (Harry S. Truman), and the impact a defeat "in the battle for Japan" would have on American morale.

D6. Chief of Army General Staff Yoshijiro Umezu Notations, Supreme Council for the Direction of the War Conference, August 9, 1945. Umezu notes that until August 8 Tokyo had still hoped to send a "special envoy" to Moscow and that therefore the Soviet declaration of war was "completely unexpected."

D7. Imperial General Headquarters Army Section Order 1374, August 9, 1945. This document outlines the Army's plan to meet the impending Soviet offensive in Manchuria.

D8. Air General Army Commander Masakazu Kawabe Memorandum, August 10, 1945. This memorandum reflects the reaction of Kawabe, commander of the Air General Army, to Japan's August 10 surrender decision. For him, the emperor's stance is decisive.

D9. Army Minister Korechika Anami Broadcast: "Instruction to the Troops," August 10, 1945. This militant and bellicose statement was broadcast to the nation on the evening of August 10. Most listeners took it as an indication that the military would not accept the emperor's decision to surrender. It was drafted by Anami's main speechwriter based on remarks the Army minister made that day but never officially authorized.

D10. Army General Staff Telegram, August 11, 1945, and Reaction of Air General Army Commander General M. Kawabe. This telegram contains orders to maintain high morale and be prepared to defend the homeland.

D11. Army Classified Telegram No. 61, Signed by Generals Anami and Umezu, August 11, 1945, and Reaction of General Yasuji Okamura. Sent by Anami and Umezu, this message states that the army will fight on if conditions contained in Japan's note to the Allies of August 10 are not met. General Okamura, commander of the China Expeditionary Army, notes in his diary his hope that the peace talks fail and the war continue.

D12. General Umezu and Admiral Toyoda Report to the Emperor, August 12, 1945. The military leaders call for a rejection of Allied terms.

D13. Army Classified Telegram No. 63, August 12, 1945. Sent by Anami and Umezu to top field commanders, this telegram asserts that the Army will reject Allied terms because of the call for a change in the national polity.

D14. Diary Entries of Marquis Kido, January 1944–June 1945. These diary entries show Kido's changing mood and increasing pessimism. His proposed peace terms in January 1944, while involving what Kido calls "considerable concessions," would have left the Japanese Empire as it existed in 1937 essentially intact. In January 1945 he voices serious pessimism about the war. By June, Kido hopes to save a desperate situation by getting the Soviet Union to mediate an end to the war. He is prepared for Japan to propose "very generous terms," but they clearly do not include an Allied occupation and reform of Japan's system of government. The August entries trace events from the bombing of Hiroshima to the emperor's initial decision to accept the Potsdam Declaration.

D15. War Crimes Testimony of Marquis Koichi Kido, October 1947. Kido read his diary into the record as part of his testimony. The August 10 entry notes that the Nagasaki bombing "gave a great shock to the nation." He adds that this, together with the Soviet entry into the war, imparted "a sudden and powerful stimulus to controversies as well as moves and countermoves between the peace and war parties in this country." In actual testimony, Kido told the tribunal that he believed his efforts in August 1945 saved 20 million Japanese lives and tens of thousands of American casualties by avoiding a fight to the "bitter end." This remark, especially when considered in the context of Kido's August 10 diary entry, clearly contradicts his statement to the U.S. Strategic Bombing Survey that Japan would have surrendered before November 1, 1945, even without the atomic bombs and the Soviet entry into the war.

D16. Diary of Torashiro Kawabe, Vice Chief of the Imperial Army General Staff, August 1945. These entries portray the Army leadership's determination not to surrender, even after two atomic bombs and the Soviet entry into the war. As he awaits news of the Imperial Conference of August 9–10 (see page 313), Kawabe predicts, "Even if we continue the war, I will die and even if we reach peace, we will perish." By August 11 (pages 314–315), Kawabe is clarifying and detailing his depressing picture of Japan's future.

D17. Secret War Termination Diary of Lt. Col. Mashiko Takeshita, August 1945. The first entry describes the SCDW meeting that began at 10:30 on the morning of August 9 and the Togo (one condition) versus Anami (four conditions) standoff regarding how to respond to the Potsdam Declaration. The second and third entries describe the subsequent cabinet meeting that day at which that deadlock continued. The fourth entry records Anami's response to the Emperor's decision at the Imperial Conference of August 9–10 to accept the Potsdam Declaration on the one-condition basis. The fifth entry notes Anami's statement at the cabinet meeting immediately thereafter insisting that the war continue unless the "sovereign power" of the Emperor is preserved and Prime Minister Suzuki's acquiescence to Anami's militant scenario.

D18. Diary Entry of Prince Hagashikuni, August 9, 1945. Prince Hagashikuni describes the Army's preparation for declaring martial law as of the night of 9 August.

D19. Diary Entries of Admiral Matone Ugaki, August 7, 9, and 11, 1945. Ugaki committed suicide by leading eleven planes on an unsuccessful kamikaze mission on August 15 against American ships off Okinawa (all the aircraft were lost at sea before reaching their targets) rather than accept surrender. His final message ended with the words "Long Live the Emperor." The last line of his diary was an instruction that it should never be permitted to fall into "enemy hands."

D20. Emperor Hirohito's Soliloquy, 1946. In March and April of 1946, Emperor Hirohito wrote a document that offered his explanation of his conduct during his reign. The consensus among historians is that the document should be used with care, inasmuch as Hirohito's main concern was to defend his actions and himself, not provide an accurate historical account of his role in the war. In explaining his decision to accept the Potsdam Declaration, he cites both the atomic bomb and the Soviet entry into the war.

E. JAPANESE SURRENDER DOCUMENTS

E1. Emperor Hirohito's Surrender Decision, August 10, 1945. In deciding to surrender, Emperor Hirohito stated that the time had come to "bear the unbearable." It was his first intervention in the political process to break the deadlock in the SCDW.

E2. Japanese Surrender Note, August 10, 1945. The note containing the one condition that surrender will do nothing that "prejudices the prerogatives of His Majesty as a Sovereign Ruler."

E3. U.S. (Byrnes) Reply to Japan, August 11, 1945. This is the American statement that the Emperor would function "subject to the Supreme Commander of the Allied powers."

E4. Japanese Protest Regarding the Use of Atomic Weapons, August 11, 1945. Japan accuses the United States of violating the Hague Convention of 1907.

E5. Emperor Hirohito's Surrender Statement to the Imperial Conference, August 14, 1945. This was Hirohito's second intervention in the political process, once again to break the deadlock on the SCDW.

E6. Japanese Surrender Note, August 14, 1945.

E7. U.S. (Byrnes) Reply to Japan, August 14, 1945.

E8. President Truman's Announcement of Japan's Surrender, August 14, 1945.

E9. Imperial Rescript, August 14, 1945. When this rescript announcing Japan's surrender was broadcast to the nation, it marked the first time most Japanese citizens had heard their emperor's voice.

E10. Japanese Note Regarding Surrender Procedures, August 16, 1945. Japan attempts to limit the surrender terms, including leaving Tokyo unoccupied and allowing Japanese troops to disarm themselves.

E11. Lincoln Memorandum, MacArthur Note, and U.S. (Byrnes) Reply to Japanese Note of August 16, August 17, 1945. MacArthur notes that the Japanese requests are "fundamentally violative of the provisions of the Potsdam Declaration." The U.S. reply rejects the Japanese request by repeating what they are required to do.

E12. Imperial Rescript of August 17, 1945. This rescript orders the armed forces to surrender. It mentions only the Soviet entry into the war and states that the reason behind the rescript is to preserve the "national polity."

E13. Instrument of Surrender, September 2, 1945. Shigemitsu, the first representative to sign for Japan, was the foreign minister of the newly established government. Umezu signed as the representative of Imperial General Head-quarters—in other words, Japan's armed forces. At first he had threatened to commit suicide rather than accept that task but bowed to a direct "request" from the emperor.

E14. Imperial Rescript of September 2, 1945. This rescript authorizes the signing of the surrender and commands the Japanese people to comply.

F. UNITED STATES STRATEGIC BOMBING SURVEY: SUMMARY REPORT AND INTERROGATIONS OF JAPANESE OFFICIALS

Two of these documents—F1 and F2—are reports and conclusions written by the staff of the United States Strategic Bombing Survey (USSBS). The rest are records of interrogations of Japanese officials that provided a significant part of the evidence for those conclusions. A key task for any analyst is to determine whether the USSBS conclusion that Japan would have surrendered in late 1945 without the use of the atomic bombs and the Soviet entry into the war is consistent with its evidence. It is also important to keep in mind that the interrogations of Japanese officials were conducted under highly unusual circumstances—that is, the Japanese had been defeated and subject to the authority of the American occupation forces—and therefore must be approached with caution. That said, they provide valuable insight into Japanese thinking during the last months of the war.

F1. USSBS Summary Report (Pacific War), July 1, 1946. The USSBS concludes that Japan would have surrendered, "certainly prior to 31 December 1945, and in all probability prior to 1 November 1945" without the dropping of the atomic bombs, the Soviet entry into the war, "and even if no invasion had been planned or contemplated."

F2. USSBS: The Effects of Strategic Bombing on Japan's War Economy, December 1946. This document discusses the effects of the naval blockade and strategic bombing on Japanese war production.

F3. USSBS Interrogation No. 277, Torashiro Kawabe, November 2, 1945. This interrogation report includes the statement that "we'd made up our minds to fight to the very last man and thought we still had a chance." Lt. Gen. Torashiro Kawabe was vice chief of the Imperial Army General Staff.

F4. USSBS Interrogation No. 447 (NAV 98), Torashiro Kawabe, November 26, 1945. Kawabe states that he believed "that we would fight to the very end" and that "we should have fought to the very end." He adds that the Naval General Staff, which "was prepared to even put their men on shore to carry the fight to the very end," shared this view.

F5. USSBS Interrogation No. 373, Prince Fumimaro Konoye, November 9, 1945. In answer to the question of whether the war would have ended on November 1 had the atomic bomb not been dropped, Konoye answers, "Probably would have lasted beyond that." When the point is pressed later in the interrogation about whether the B-29 raids had brought Japan to the limit of its endurance, Konoye answers, "Of course, they were nearing the limit, but the army would not admit it. They wouldn't admit they were near the end." When pressed still further about whether the army would have been forced to surrender "even if Russia had not come in or even though we had not dropped the atomic bomb," Konoye responds that the army was prepared to fight "from every little hole or rock in the mountains."

F6. USSBS Interrogation No. 308, Marquis Koichi Kido, November 10, 1945. Kido at first does not provide evidence for the USSBS early-surrender conclusion, noting that the atomic bombs and the Soviet entry into the war "did speed the agreement of the services ministries to end the war." However, after further badgering he states, "I personally think that the war would have ended prior to November 1, as every possible effort was being exhausted to terminate the war." Later he says the impact of the atomic bomb was greater than the March 1945 incendiary raid on Tokyo because the bomb gave such destructive power to "a single plane." Finally, in response to the question whether the Japanese army believed it could repel and invasion, Kido states, "That was how it was explained to us by the army. There [they] were confident."

F7. USSBS Interrogation No. 489, Baron Kitchiro Hiranuma, November 23, 1945. Hiranuma was president of the privy council. It testifies that the military "maintained until the very last that they were able to carry on the war" and that because of this attitude the emperor "finally rendered his judgment."

F8. Interrogation No. 355, Rear Admiral S. Tomioka, November 15, 1945. Tomioka testifies that the Japanese estimated they "would destroy 30–40% of the initial assaulting forces when you hit the homeland." He adds, "You couldn't bomb us into submission, I thought, and therefore you would have to land in the home island."

F9. USSBS Interview with A. Funada, December 12, 1945. Funada, an official with Japan's Board of Information, states, "The hopes of the die-hards were dashed to pieces by participation in the war of Russia and the atomic bomb."

F10. USSBS Interrogation No. 276, Rear Admiral Toshitanea Takata, November 2, 1945. Takata testifies that Japan would have fought up to and beyond an invasion.

F11. USSBS Interrogation No. 522, Field Marshal Shunroru Hata (no date). In response to the question of whether Japan would have surrendered if the atomic bomb had not been dropped, Hata responds that would depend on "the scale of the landings." As commander of the Second General Army, Hata was directly responsible for the defense of both Kyushu and Shikoku.

F12. USSBS Interrogation No. 531, Prime Minister Kantaro Suzuki, December 26, 1945. In one of the most important USSBS interrogations, Suzuki testifies that the B-29 raids convinced him "the cause was hopeless" but also states that the SCDW did not believe that the United States could defeat Japan by bombing alone. It therefore developed its plan to resist an American landing on the home islands and "proceeded with that plan until the ATOMIC BOMB was dropped." Thereafter, convinced the United States "need not land when it had such a weapon," the SCDW "decided that it would be best to sue for peace."

F13. USSBS Interrogation No. 609, Hisatsune Sakomizu, December 11, 1945. Sakomizu reviews the military's resistance to surrender before August 1945. He comments that with the bombing of Hiroshima, "The chance had come to end the war."

F14. USSBS Interrogation No. 378 (NAV 75), Admiral Soemu Toyoda, November 13–14, 1945. Toyoda testifies that while the bombing of Hiroshima and the Soviet entry into the war were not the "direct cause of termination of the war . . . those two factors did enable us to bring the war to a termination without creating too great chaos in JAPAN."

F15. USSBS Interrogation No. 379 (NAV No. 76), Admiral Mitsumasa Yonai, November 17, 1945. Yonai cites the loss of Saipan and then Leyte as "the end."

F16. USSBS Interrogation No. 429 (NAV No. 90), Admiral Kichisaburo Nomura, November 8, 1945. Nomura testifies that the Japanese people as a whole were prepared to "continue to the very last" and "prepared to sacrifice themselves if the Government so ordered."

F17. USSBS Interrogation No. 498, Admiral Osami Nagano, November 30, 1945. Nagano testifies that without the atomic bomb and Soviet entry into the war "we would have been able to extend the war for a considerable time at considerable sacrifice on your part."

G. STATEMENTS OF JAPANESE OFFICIALS ON WORLD WAR II, MILITARY INTELLIGENCE SECTION, HISTORICAL DIVISION, U.S. ARMY

These interviews were conducted by the U.S. Army in 1949 and 1950. As noted above regarding the interrogations of Japanese officials conducted in 1945 by the USSBS, these interviews were conducted under unusual circumstances and therefore must be treated with caution. Still, like the USSBS interrogations, they provide valuable insights into Japanese thinking during the last months of the war.

All documents in this section are from *Statements of Japanese Officials on World War II* (English Translations, 4 vols. on microfilm (two reels), compiled

1949–1950, Military Intelligence Section, Historical Division, U.S. Army Far East Command (Washington, D.C.: Library of Congress Photoduplication Service, 1975). Documents G1–G7 are from Reel 1, Volume 1; Documents G8–G9 are from Reel 1, Volume 2; Documents G10–G12 are from Reel 2, Volume 3; and Documents G13–G18 are from Reel 2, Volume 4.

G1. MIS, Statements of Japanese Officials, Document No. 59617, Maj. General Masakesu Amano (no date). Amano states he was "absolutely sure of victory" if U.S. forces landed on Kyushu.

G2. MIS, Statements of Japanese Officials, Document No. 54480, Maj. General Masakesu Amano, December 29, 1949. Amano states that he believes an "operational victory" could have been achieved in the battle for Kyushu. The two generals he mentions are Anami and Umezu.

G3. MIS, Statements of Japanese Officials, Document No. 52506, Lt. General Seizo Arisue, May 10, 1949. Arisue says that the Japanese feared the critical situation in Japan in mid-1945 "might become fatal in 1946." They hoped to defeat the Americans or 'inflict tremendous losses" on the invading forces.

G4. MIS, Statements of Japanese Officials, Document No. 54432, Col. Saburo Hayashi, December 23, 1949. Hayashi discusses Anami's belief that the initial landing on Kyushu could be repulsed and that until August 9 he believed Prime Minister Suzuki was determined to fight to the end.

G5. MIS, Statements of Japanese Officials, Document No. 53437, Memorandum of Zenshiro Hoshima. These are Hoshima's notes on the Imperial Conference of August 9–10, 1945.

G6. MIS, Statements of Japanese Officials, Document No. 54483, Notes of Sumihisa Ikeda. These are Ikeda's notes on the Imperial Conference of August 9–10, 1945.

G7. MIS, Statements of Japanese Officials, Document No. 54479: Statement of S. Ikeda, December 23, 1949. Ikeda offers his impressions of several cabinet members. With regard to Prime Minister Suzuki, Ikeda states that he believes "the atomic bomb and the Soviet participation in the war motivated the Premier to accept the Potsdam Declaration."

G8. MIS, Statements of Japanese Officials, Document No. 50569; Lt. Gen. Torashiro Kawabe, June 13, 1949. Kawabe states that while he was not confident of victory, he believed that Japan could "inflict staggering losses on the American invasion force." He did not believe that "Japanese forces could fight a systematic, organized decisive battle" on the Kanto Plain.

G9. MIS, Statements of Japanese Officials, Document No. 52608, Lt. Gen. Torashiro Kawabe, November 21, 1949. Kawabe says that Anami's idea of safeguarding the national polity meant the emperor system as it existed in 1945, not the "mere formality" of the postwar era.

G10. MIS, Statements of Japanese Officials, Document No. 52336, Maj. Gen. Joichiro Sanada, November 12, 1949. Sanada believes that "it would have been possible to crush" the initial landing but not a second or third landing. He says that this was view of Field Marshal Hata, the overall commander of Japanese troops on Kyushu and Shikoku.

G11. MIS, Statements of Japanese Officials, Document No. 50025A, Lt. Col. Masahiko Takashita. Takashita discusses the views and actions of General Anami during the last months of the war.

G12. MIS, Statements of Japanese Officials, Document No. 50644, Five Officers Regarding Operation Ketsu Maneuver (no date). Based on a conference at Sixth Army Headquarters on July 4–5, the Japanese expected kamikaze attacks to destroy at sea between 30 to 50 percent of the invasion force.

G13. MIS, Statements of Japanese Officials, Document No. 50570: Statement of ex-Maj. Gen. Kasue Tanikawa, May 10, 1949. Tanikawa states that the Japanese believed that kamikaze attacks "could destroy four American divisions at sea." Tanikawa was in charge of the conference mentioned in Document G12.

G14. MIS, Statements of Japanese Officials, Document No. 50304: Shigenori Togo, May 17, 1949. Togo describes the unrealistic attitudes of Army and Navy leaders. He specifically contradicts the USSBS assertion that Ambassador Sato's advocacy of unconditional surrender had an influence on the emperor. He states, "I believe it [the USSBS] is wrong on that point."

G15. MIS, Statements of Japanese Officials, Document No. 61340: Soemu Toyoda, August 29, 1949. Toyoda states his belief that after Hiroshima the United States would not continue to drop atomic bombs. He views the atomic bombs as "a cause for the surrender but . . . not the only cause." It had a "very great effect upon public sentiment," but the Soviet entry into the war "did more to hasten the surrender."

G16. MIS, Statements of Japanese Officials, Document No. 57670: Soemu Toyoda, December 1, 1949. Toyoda states that at the 28 July meeting of the SCDW, nobody "even so much as hinted that he wanted to have the Allied proclamation considered seriously."

G17. MIS, Statements of Japanese Officials, Document No. 61338: Lt. Gen. Masao Yoshizumi, June 6, 1949. Yoshizumi states that on August 8, 1945, General Anami still argued that there was a chance to achieve a decisive victory when the Americans invaded Japan and urged the war be continued unless the Allies accepted all four Japanese conditions.

G18. MIS, Statements of Japanese Officials, Document No. 54484: Lt. Gen. Masao Yoshizumi, December 22, 1949. Yoshizumi states that the new government Suzuki formed in April 1945 "was definitely for the continuation of the war."

A.

American Civilian Documents

A1. LEO SZILARD LETTER TO LEWIS STRAUSS, JANUARY 25, 1939

I feel that I ought to let you know of a very sensational new development in nuclear physics. In a paper in the "Naturwissenschaften" Hahn reports that he finds when bombarding uranium with neutrons the uranium breaking up into two halves giving elements of about half the atomic weight of uranium. This is entirely unexpected and exciting news for the average physicist. . . .

. . . This in itself might make it possible to produce power by means of nuclear energy, but I do not think that this possibility is very exciting, for if the energy output is only two or three times the energy input, the cost of investment would probably be too high to make the process worthwhile. Unfortunately, most of the energy is released in the form of heat and not in the form of radioactivity.

I see, however, in connection with this new discovery potential possibilities in another direction. These might lead to a large-scale production of energy and radioactive elements, unfortunately also perhaps to atomic bombs. This new discovery revives all the hopes and fears in this respect which I had in 1934 and 1935, and which I have as good as abandoned in the course of the last two years. . . .

Source: Leo Szilard: His Version of the Facts: Selected Recollections and Correspondence, ed. Spencer R. Weart and Gertrud Weiss Szilard (Cambridge, Mass.: MIT Press, 1978), 62.

A2. ALBERT EINSTEIN LETTER TO PRESIDENT ROOSEVELT, AUGUST 2, 1939, AND ROOSEVELT'S RESPONSE, OCTOBER 19, 1939

Sir:

Some recent work by E. Fermi and L. Szilard, which has been communicated to me in manuscript, leads me to expect that the element uranium may be turned into a new and important source of energy in the immediate future. Certain aspects of the situation which has arisen seem to call for watchfulness and, if necessary, quick action on the part of the Administration. I believe therefore that it is my duty to bring to your attention the following facts and recommendations:

In the course of the last four months it has been made probable through the work of Joliot in France as well as Fermi and Szilard in America—that it may become possible to set up a nuclear chain reaction in a large mass of uranium, by which vast amounts of power and large quantities of new radium-like elements would be generated. Now it appears almost certain that this could be achieved in the immediate future.

This new phenomenon would also lead to the construction of a bomb and it is conceivable—though much less certain—that extremely powerful bombs of a new type may thus be constructed. A single bomb of this type, carried by boat and exploded in a port, might very well destroy the whole port together with some of the surrounding territory. However, such bombs might very well prove to be too heavy for transportation by air.

The United States has only very poor ores of uranium in moderate quantities. There is some good ore in Canada and the former Czechoslovakia, while the most important source of uranium is Belgian Congo.

In view of this situation you may think it desirable to have some permanent contact maintained between the Administration and the group of physicists working on chain reactions in America. One possible way of achieving this might be for you to entrust with this task a person who has your confidence and who could perhaps serve in an inofficial [sic] capacity. His task might comprise the following:

a) to approach Government Departments, keep them informed of the further development, and put forward recommendations for Government action, giving particular attention to the problem of securing a supply of uranium ore for the United States;

b) to speed up the experimental work, which is at present being carried on within the limits of the budgets of University laboratories, by providing funds, if such funds be required, through his contacts with private persons who are willing to make contributions for this cause, and perhaps also by obtaining the co-operation of industrial laboratories which have the necessary equipment.

I understand that Germany has actually stopped the sale of uranium from the Czechoslovakian mines which she has taken over. That she should have taken such early action might perhaps be understood on the ground that the son of the German Under-Secretary of State, von Weizäcker, is attached to the Kaiser-Wilhelm-Institut in Berlin where some of the American work on uranium is now being repeated.

Yours very truly,

(Albert Einstein)

My dear Professor:

I am glad to say that Dr. Sachs will cooperate and work with this committee and I feel this is the most practical and effective method of dealing with the subject.

Please accept my sincere thanks.

Very sincerely yours,
(signed) Franklin D. Roosevelt

Source: Michael B. Stoff, Jonathan F. Fanton, and R. Hal Williams, eds., *The Manhattan Project: A Documentary Introduction to the Atomic Age* (New York: McGraw-Hill, 1991), 18–20.

A3. CHURCHILL'S UNCONDITIONAL SURRENDER SUGGESTION AT THE CASABLANCA CONFERENCE, JANUARY 18, 1943

Meeting of the Combined Chiefs of Staff with Roosevelt and Churchill, January 18, 1943, 5:00 P.M., President's Villa . . .

After being informed that the agreements arrived at the conference would be included in a paper, the PRIME MINISTER suggested that one should be drawn up for presentation to Premier Stalin. He felt that the Soviet [Union] is entitled to know what we intend to do, but that it should be made clear that the paper expressed our intentions and did not constitute promises.

The PRESIDENT brought up the subject of press releases concerning the current conferences. He said that a photograph should be made of the participants in the conference and be given out with a release date which might be set as the day that he and the Prime Minister departed.

The PRIME MINISTER suggested that at the same time we release a statement to the effect that the United Nations are resolved to pursue the war to the bitter end, neither party relaxing in its efforts until the unconditional surrender of Germany and Japan has been achieved. He said that before issuing such a statement, he would like to consult with his colleagues in London. . . .

Source: U.S. Department of State, *Foreign Relations of the United States: The Conferences at Washington, 1941–1942, and Casablanca, 1943* (Washington, D.C.: U.S. Government Printing Office, 1968), 627–637.

A4. ROOSEVELT'S CASABLANCA PRESS CONFERENCE NOTES, JANUARY 22–23, 1943

Notes for F.D.R. . . .

The President and the Prime Minister, after a complete survey of the world war situation, are more than ever determined that peace can come to the world only by a total elimination of German and Japanese war power. This involves the simple formula of placing the objective of this war in terms of an unconditional surrender by Germany, Italy and Japan. Unconditional surrender by them means a reasonable assurance of world peace, for generations. Unconditional surrender means not the destruction of the German populace, nor of the Italian or Japanese populace, but does mean the destruction of a philosophy in Germany, Italy and Japan which is based on the conquest and subjugation of other peoples.

The President and the Prime Minister are confident that this is equally the purpose of Russia, of China, and of all other members of the United Nations. . . .

Source: U.S. Department of State, Foreign Relations of the United States: The Conferences at Washington, 1941–1942, and Casablanca, 1943 (Washington, D.C.: U.S. Government Printing Office, 1968), 836–838.

A5. THE QUEBEC AGREEMENT, AUGUST 19, 1943

Articles of Agreement Governing Collaboration Between the
Authorities of the U.S.A. and the U.K. in the Matter of Tube Alloys

Whereas it is vital to our common safety in the present War to bring the TUBE ALLOYS project to fruition at the earliest moment; and whereas this may be more speedily achieved if all available British and American brains and resources are pooled; and whereas owing to war conditions it would be an improvident use of war resources to duplicate plants on a large scale on both sides of the Atlantic and therefore a far greater expense has fallen upon the United States;

It is agreed between us

First, that we will never use this agency against each other.

Secondly, that we will not use it against third parties without each other's consent.

Thirdly, that we will not either of us communicate any information about Tube Alloys to third parties except by mutual consent.

Fourthly, that in view of the heavy burden of production falling upon the United States as the result of a wise division of war effort, the British Government recognize that any post-war advantages of an industrial or commercial character shall be dealt with as between the United States and Great Britain on terms to be specified by the President of the United States to the Prime Minister of Great Britain. The Prime Minister expressly disclaims any interest in these industrial and commercial aspects beyond what may be considered by the President of the United States to be fair and just and in harmony with the economic welfare of the world. . . .

Source: U.S. Department of State, *Foreign Relations of the United States: The Conference at Washington and Quebec, 1943* (Washington, D.C.: U.S. Government Printing Office, 1970), 1119.

A6. TUBE ALLOYS AIDE-MEMOIRE, SEPTEMBER 18, 1944

Aide-Memoire of Conversation Between the President and the Prime Minister at Hyde Park, September 18, 1944

1. The suggestion that the world should be informed regarding TUBE ALLOYS, with a view to an international agreement regarding its control and use, is not accepted. The matter should continue to be regarded as of the utmost secrecy; but when a "bomb" is finally available, it might perhaps, after mature consideration, be used against the Japanese, who should be warned that this bombardment will be repeated until they surrender.

2. Full collaboration between the United States and the British Government in developing TUBE ALLOYS for military and commercial purposes should continue after the defeat of Japan unless and until terminated by joint agreement.

3. Enquiries should be made regarding the activities of Professor Bohr and steps taken to ensure that he is responsible for no leakage of information, particularly to the Russians.

F[RANKLIN] D R[oosevelt] W[inston] S C[HURCHILL]

Source: U.S. Department of State, *Foreign Relations of the United States: The Conference at Quebec, 1944* (Washington, D.C.: U.S. Government Printing Office, 1972), 492–493.

A7. THE CAIRO DECLARATION, DECEMBER 18, 1943

Press Communiqué

President Roosevelt, Generalissimo Chiang Kai-Shek and Prime Minister Churchill, together with their respective military and diplomatic advisers, have completed a conference in North Africa. The following general statement was issued:

"The several military missions have agreed upon future military operations against Japan. The three great Allies expressed their resolve to bring unrelenting pressure against their brutal enemies by sea, land and air. This pressure is already rising.

"The three great Allies are fighting this war to restrain and punish the aggression of Japan. They covet no gain for themselves and have no thought of territorial expansion. It is their purpose that Japan shall be stripped of all the islands in the Pacific which she has seized or occupied since the beginning of the first World War in 1914, and that all the territories Japan has stolen from the Chinese, such as Manchuria, Formosa, and the Pescadores, shall be restored to the Republic of China. Japan will also be expelled from all other territories which she has taken by violence and greed. The aforesaid great powers, mindful of the enslavement of the people of Korea, are determined that in due course Korea shall become free and independent.

"With these objects in view the three Allies, in harmony with those of the United Nations at war with Japan, will continue to persevere in the serious and prolonged operations necessary to procure the unconditional surrender of Japan."

Source: U.S. Department of State, *Foreign Relations of the United States: The Conference at Cairo and Tehran, 1943* (Washington, D.C.: U.S. Government Printing Office, 1961), 448–449.

A8. ROOSEVELT AND KING/MARSHALL LETTERS ON MILITARY AND CIVILIAN MANPOWER NEEDS, JANUARY 1945

Dear Congressman May,
In my recent message on the state of the Union, I pointed out the urgent need for a national service law and recommended that, pending action by the Congress on the broader aspects of national service, the Congress immediately enact legislation which will be effective in using the 4,000,000 men now classified in 4-F in whatever capacity is best for the war effort. . . .

I enclose a copy of the letter signed by General Marshall and Admiral King, which I have just received.

Sincerely yours,
Franklin D. Roosevelt

As the agents directly responsible to you for the conduct of military operations, we feel that it is our duty to report to you the urgent necessity for immediate action to improve the situation relative to the acute need for young and vigorous replacements for the Army and Navy to provide the necessary manpower and to increase the production of critical items of munitions, accelerate ship construction, and effect the rapid repair of damaged vessels.

Personnel losses sustained by the Army in the past two months have, by reason of the severity of the weather and the fighting on the European front, taxed the replacement system to the breaking point. The Army must provide 600,000 replacements for overseas theaters before June 30 and, together with the Navy, will require a total of 900,000 inductions by June 30. . . .

The fast tempo and increased damage has introduced demands for additional naval personnel in the way of replacements. Items of particular moment are replacements for casualties and war-fatigued men, particularly pilots and crews for aircraft. The Navy also requires a considerable number of additional Medical Corps personnel. . . .

You are intimately familiar, Mr. President, with the great importance of regaining the offensive on the Western Front and pressing it, together with operations against the Japanese, with constantly increasing intensity in the months to come. To this end, therefore, we feel that the United States should make every conceivable effort to enable the armed forces to carry out your instructions.

E. J. King,
Chief of Naval Operations
G. C. Marshall,
Chief of Staff

Source: "Letters on the Pressing Manpower Problem," *New York Times*, January 18, 1945.

A9. THE YALTA AGREEMENTS REGARDING THE FAR EAST

. . . Protocol of the Proceedings of the Crimea Conference Agreement

The leaders of the three Great Powers—the Soviet Union, the United States of America and Great Britain—have agreed that in two or three months after Germany has surrendered and the war in Europe has terminated the Soviet Union shall enter into the war against Japan on the side of the Allies on condition that:

1. The *status quo* in Outer-Mongolia (The Mongolian People's Republic) shall be preserved;

2. The former rights of Russia violated by the treacherous attack of Japan in 1904 shall be restored, viz:

(a) the southern part of Sakhalin as well as all the islands adjacent to it shall be returned to the Soviet Union,

(b) the commercial port of Dairen shall be internationalized, the preeminent interests of the Soviet Union in this port being safeguarded and the lease of Port Arthur as a naval base of the USSR restored,

(c) the Chinese-Eastern Railroad and the South-Manchurian Railroad which provides an outlet to Dairen shall be jointly operated by the establishment of a joint Soviet-Chinese Company, it being understood that the preeminent interests of the Soviet Union shall be safeguarded and that China shall retain full sovereignty in Manchuria;

3. The Kuril Islands shall be handed over to the Soviet Union.

It is understood, that the agreement concerning Outer-Mongolia and the ports and railroads referred to above will require concurrence of Generalissimo Chiang Kai-Shek. The President will take measures in order to obtain this concurrence on advice from Marshal Stalin.

The Heads of the three Great Powers have agreed that these claims of the Soviet Union shall be unquestionably fulfilled after Japan has been defeated.

For its part the Soviet Union expresses its readiness to conclude with the National Government of China a pact of friendship and alliance between the USSR and China in order to render assistance to China with its armed forces for the purpose of liberating China from the Japanese yoke.

I. Stalin / Franklin D. Roosevelt / Winston S. Churchill, February 11, 1945

Source: U.S. Department of State, *Foreign Relations of the United States: The Conferences at Malta and Yalta, 1945* (Washington, D.C.: U.S. Government Printing Office, 1955), 975–984.

A10. STIMSON MEMO TO TRUMAN, APRIL 24, 1945

Dear Mr. President:
I think it is very important that I should have a talk with you as soon as possible on a highly secret matter.

I mentioned it to you shortly after you took office but have not urged it since on account of the pressure you have been under. It, however, has such a bearing on our present foreign relations and has such an important effect upon all my thinking in this field that I think you ought to know about it without much further delay.

Faithfully yours,

[Henry L. Stimson]

Source: Robert H. Ferrell, ed., *Harry S. Truman and the Bomb: A Documentary History* (Worland, Wyo.: High Plains, 1996), 10.

A11. STIMSON MEMORANDUM ON THE ATOMIC BOMB TO TRUMAN, APRIL 25, 1945

1. Within four months we shall in all probability have completed the most terrible weapon ever known in human history, one bomb of which could destroy a whole city.

2. Although we have shared its development with the UK, physically the US is at present in the position of controlling the resources with which to construct and use it and no other nation could reach this position for some years.

3. Nevertheless it is practically certain that we could not remain in this position indefinitely.

a. Various segments of its discovery and production are widely known among many scientists in many countries, although few scientists are now acquainted with the whole process which we have developed.

b. Although its construction under present methods requires great scientific and industrial effort and raw materials, which are temporarily mainly within the possession and knowledge of US and UK, it is extremely probable that much easier and cheaper methods of production will be discovered by scientists in the future, together with the use of materials of much wider distribution. As a result, it is extremely probable that the future will make it possible to be constructed by smaller nations or even groups, or at least by a large nation in a much shorter time.

4. As a result, it is indicated that the future may see a time when such a weapon may be constructed in secret and used suddenly and effectively with devastating power by a willful nation or group against an unsuspecting nation or group of much greater size and material power. With its aid even a very powerful unsuspecting nation might be conquered within a very few days by a very much smaller one, although probably the only nation which could enter into production within the next few years is Russia.

5. The world in its present state of moral advancement compared with its technical development would be eventually at the mercy of such a weapon. In other words, modern civilization might be completely destroyed.

6. To approach any world peace organization of any pattern now likely to be considered, without an appreciation by the leaders of our country of the power of this new weapon, would seem to be unrealistic. No system of control heretofore considered would be adequate to control this menace. Both inside any particular country and between the nations of the world, the control of this weapon will undoubtedly be a matter of the greatest difficulty and would involve such thorough-going rights of inspection and internal controls as we have never heretofore contemplated.

7. Furthermore, in the light of our present position with reference to this weapon, the question of sharing it with other nations and, if so shared, upon what terms, becomes a primary question of our foreign relations. Also our leadership in the war and in the development of this weapon has placed a certain moral responsibility upon us which we cannot shirk without very serious responsibility for any disaster to civilization which it would further.

8. On the other hand, if the problem of the proper use of this weapon can be solved, we would have the opportunity to bring the world into a pattern in which the peace of the world and our civilization can be saved.

9. As stated in General Groves' report, steps are under way looking towards the establishment of a select committee of particular qualifications for recommending action to the executive and legislative branches of our government when secrecy is no longer in full effect. The committee would also recommend the actions to be taken by the War Department prior to that time in anticipation of the postwar problems. All recommendations would, of course be first submitted to the President.

Source: Michael B. Stoff, Jonathan F. Fanton, and R. Hal Williams, eds., *The Manhattan Project: A Documentary Introduction to the Atomic Age* (New York: McGraw-Hill, 1991), 95–96.

A12. STIMSON DIARY ENTRY, MAY 15, 1945

At 9:30 we went in to our meeting of the Committee of Three, Grew, Forrestal and myself being present with McCloy as recorder. Averill Harriman, the Ambassador to Russia, came with Grew; also William Phillips, formerly under Secretary of State years ago. Forrestal brought Major Correa. We had a pretty red hot session first over the questions which Grew had propounded to us in relation to the Yalta Conference and our relations with Russia. They have been entered in the diary here so I will not repeat them. I tried to point out the difficulties which existed and I thought it was premature to ask those questions; at least we were not yet in a position to answer them. The trouble is that the President has now promised apparently to meet Stalin and Churchill on the first of July and at that time these questions will become burning and it may be necessary to have it out with Russia on her relations to Manchuria and Port Arthur and various other parts of North China and also the relations of China to us. Over any such tangled wave of problems the S-1 secret would be dominant and yet we will not know until after that time probably, until after that meeting, whether this is a weapon in our hands or not. We think it will be shortly afterwards, but it seems a terrible thing to gamble with such big stakes in diplomacy without having your master card in your hand. The best we could do today was to persuade Harriman not to go back until we had had time to think over these things a little bit harder.

Well, when this meeting adjourned, I called in George Marshall, and he and McCloy and I talked out the proposition of the coming Asian campaign. . . . Fortunately the actual invasion will not take place until after my secret is out. The Japanese campaign involves therefore two great uncertainties: first, whether Russia will come in though we think that will be all right; and, second, when and how S-1 will resolve itself. We three argued over and over for at least an hour.

Source: *Henry L. Stimson Diaries*, Reel 9, Yale University Library, New Haven.

A13. KYLE PALMER ARTICLE ON CASUALTIES, MAY 17, 1945

Palmer Warns No Easy Way to Beat Japs

"There is no easy way out of this war," so Kyle Palmer, Times war correspondent, told a Los Angeles Breakfast Club audience yesterday. "The Japs have not shown any failing except on the seas where we have outguessed them and our amphibious operations have kept reinforcements away from their land forces," he said.

"Hard fighting lies ahead," continued Palmer, "and there is very little likelihood that the Jap war lords will sue for peace. We are yet to meet the major portion of the ground forces of the Jap empire. They have 5,000,000 to 6,000,000 under arms and it will cost 500,000 to 750,000, perhaps 1,000,000, lives to end this war."

Source: Los Angeles Times, May 17, 1945.

A14. *NEW REPUBLIC* EDITORIAL, MAY 28, 1945

The War in the Pacific

. . . The question is whether we can face the rather appalling necessity of killing 3,600,000 armed men to put an end to the war. Any strategy that will produce that surrender, rather than the extermination of a substantial number of these men is desirable—not for humanitarian reasons, but because the extermination process involves heavy casualties to us. At Tarawa, our casualties were approximately 3,000 to 5,000 Japs—a proportion which has been fairly constant where the fighting was severe. It is true that the large majority of our losses were in wounded, of whom three-quarters can be made almost as good as new. But the three-to-five yardstick placed alongside 3,600,000 required Japanese deaths gives a figure so high that planning to avoid it is something more than desirable. Indeed, the theory on which the Japs are conducting their war is that they can make this casualty rate stand up throughout and that we can't take it.

Source: Fletcher Pratt, *The New Republic* May 28, 1945.

A15. INTERIM COMMITTEE MINUTES, MAY 31, 1945

Notes of the Interim Committee Meeting, Thursday, 31 May 1945, 10:00 A.M. to 1:15 P.M.–2:15 P.M. to 4:15 P.M.

PRESENT:

Members of the Committee

Secretary Henry L. Stimson, Chairman, Hon. Ralph A. Bard, Dr. Vannevar Bush, Hon. James F. Byrnes, Hon. William L. Clayton, Mr. George L. Harrison

Invited Scientists

Dr. J. Robert Oppenheimer, Dr. Enrico Fermi, Dr. Arthur H. Compton, Dr. E. O. Lawrence

By Invitation

General George C. Marshall, Major Gen. Leslie R. Groves, Mr. Harvey H. Bundy, Mr. Arthur Page

I. Opening Statement of the Chairman

Secretary Stimson explained that the Interim Committee had been appointed by him, with the approval of the President to make recommendations on temporary war-time controls, public announcement, legislation and post-war organization. The Secretary gave high praise to the brilliant and effective assistance rendered to the project by the scientists of the country and expressed great appreciation to the four scientists present for their great contributions to the work and their willingness to advise on the many complex problems that the Interim Committee had to face. He expressed the hope that the scientists would feel completely free to express their views on any phase of the subject.

The Committee had been termed an "Interim Committee" because it was expected that when the project became more widely known a permanent organization established by Congressional action or by treaty arrangements would be necessary.

The Secretary explained that General Marshall shared responsibility with him for making recommendations to the President on this project with particular reference to its military aspects; therefore, it was considered highly desirable that General Marshall be present at this meeting to secure at first hand the views of the scientists.

The Secretary expressed the view, a view shared by General Marshall, that this project should not be considered simply in terms of military weapons, but as a new relationship of man to the universe. This discovery might be compared to the discoveries of the Copernican theory and of the laws of gravity, but far more important than these is its effect on the lives of men. While the advances in the field to date had been fostered by the needs of war, it was important to realize that the implications of the project went far beyond the needs of the present war. It must be controlled if possible to make it an assurance of future peace rather than a menace to civilization. . . .

V. Problems of Control and Inspection

The Secretary inquired what other potentialities beyond purely military uses might be exploited. In reply *Dr. Oppenheimer* pointed out that the immediate concern had been to shorten the war. The research that had led to this development had only opened the door to future discoveries. Fundamental knowledge of this subject was so widespread throughout the world that early steps should be taken to make our developments known to the world. He thought it might be wise for the United States to offer to the world free inter-change of information with particular emphasis on the development of peace-time uses. The basic goal of all endeavors in the field should be the enlargement of human welfare. If we were to offer to exchange information before the bomb was actually used, our moral position would be greatly strengthened. . . .

VI. Russia

In considering the problem of controls and international collaboration the question of paramount concern was the attitude of Russia. *Dr. Oppenheimer* pointed out that Russia had always been very friendly to science, and suggested that we might open up this subject with them in a tentative fashion and in the most general terms without giving them any details of our productive effort. He thought that we might say that a great na-tional effort had been put into this project and express a hope for cooperation with them in this field. He felt strongly that we should not prejudge the Russian attitude in this matter.

At this point *General Marshall* discussed at some length the story of charges and counter-charges that have been typical of our relations with the Russians, pointing out that most of these allegations have proven unfounded. The seemingly uncooperative at-titude of Russia in military matters stemmed from the necessity of maintaining security. He said that he had accepted this reason for their attitude in his dealings with the Rus-sians and had acted accordingly. As to the post-war situation and in matters other than purely military, he felt that he was in no position to express a view. With regard to this field he was inclined to favor the building up of a combination among like-minded powers, thereby forcing Russia to fall in line by the very force of this coalition.

It might be desirable to invite two prominent Russian scientists to witness the test.

Mr. Byrnes expressed a fear that if information were given to the Russians, even in gen-eral terms, Stalin would ask to be brought into partnership. He felt this to be particularly likely in view of our commitments and pledges of cooperation with the British. In this connection *Dr. Bush* pointed out that even the British do not have any of our blue prints on plants. *Mr. Byrnes* expressed the view, *which was generally agreed to by all present*, that the most desirable program would be to push ahead as fast as possible in production and research to make certain that we stay ahead and at the same time make every effort to bet-ter our political relations with Russia. . . .

VIII. Effect of the Bombing on the Japanese and Their Will to Fight

It was pointed out that one atomic bomb on an arsenal would not be much different from the effect caused by any Air Corps strike of present dimensions. However, *Dr.*

Oppenheimer stated that the visual effect of an atomic bombing would be tremendous. It would be accompanied by a brilliant luminescence which would rise to a height of 10,000 to 20,000 feet. The neutron effect of the explosion would be dangerous to life for a radius of at least two-thirds of a mile.

After much discussion concerning various types of targets and the effects to be produced, the Secretary expressed the conclusion, on which there was general agreement, that we could not give the Japanese any warning; that we could not concentrate on a civilian area; but that we should seek to make a profound psychological impression on as many of the inhabitants as possible. At the suggestion of Dr. Conant the Secretary agreed that the most desirable target would be a vital war plant employing a large number of workers and closely surrounded by workers' houses. ·

There was some discussion of the desirability of attempting several strikes at the same time. Dr. Oppenheimer's judgment was that several strikes would be feasible. *General Groves*, however, expressed doubt about this proposal and pointed out the following objections: (1) We would lose the advantage of gaining additional knowledge concerning the weapon at each successive bombing. (2) Such a program would require a rush job on the part of those assembling the bombs and might, therefore, be ineffective. (3) The effect would not be sufficiently distinct from our regular Air force bombing program. . . .

Source: Michael B. Stoff, Jonathan F. Fanton, and R. Hal Williams, eds., *The Manhattan Project: A Documentary Introduction to the Atomic Age* (New York: McGraw-Hill, 1991), 105–120.

A16. STIMSON DIARY ENTRY, MAY 31, 1945

Another nice clear day, I got down to the Department quite early at eight-forty and had a talk with George Harrison and General Marshall before the meeting called for the Interim Committee of S-1, and I prepared for the meeting as carefully as I could because on me fell the job of opening it and telling them what it was and telling what we expected of these scientists in getting them started and talking. . . .

I told the invited scientists who the Committee was, the Interim Committee, what it was established for, and then I switched over and told them what we wanted of them, the invited scientists; first, to congratulate and thank them for what they have done and then to get them started in talking and questioning. It was a little slow sledding at first but I think I got some wrinkles out of their heads in regard to my own attitude and that of the Army towards this new project. I told them that we did not regard it as a new weapon merely but as a revolutionary change in the relations of man to the universe and that we wanted to take advantage of this; that the project might even mean the doom of civilization or it might mean the perfection of civilization; that it might be a Frankenstein which would eat us up or it might be a project "by which the peace of the world would be helped in becoming secure." Well after a while the talk went pretty well. I had Marshall in and during a time when I had to be absent to go over to the White House he took a vigorous hand in the discussion and I think impressed himself very much upon them. I think we made an impression upon the scientists that we were looking at this like statesmen and not like merely soldiers anxious to win the war at any cost. On the other hand, they were a fine lot of men as can be seen from their records. Dr. Fermi, Dr. Lawrence, and Dr. Compton were all Nobel prize winners; and Dr. Oppenheimer, though not a Nobel prize winner, was really one of the best of the lot. . . .

Source: Michael B. Stoff, Jonathan F. Fanton, and R. Hal Williams, eds., *The Manhattan Project: A Documentary Introduction to the Atomic Age* (New York: McGraw-Hill, 1991), 121.

A17. INTERIM COMMITTEE MINUTES, JUNE 1, 1945

VI. Use of the Bomb

Mr. Byrnes recommended, and the Committee *agreed*, that the Secretary of War should be advised that, while recognizing that the final selection of the target was essentially a military decision, the present view of the Committee was that the bomb should be used against Japan as soon as possible; that it be used on a war plant surrounded by workers' homes; and that it be used without prior warning. It was the understanding of the Committee that the small bomb would be used in the test and that the large bomb (gun mechanism) would be used in the first strike over Japan. . . .

Source: Dennis Merrill, ed., *Documentary History of the Truman Presidency* (Washington, D.C.: University Publications of America, 1995), 1:39–48.

A18. TRUMAN DIARY ENTRY, JUNE 1, 1945

. . . Have been going through some very hectic days. Eyes troubling somewhat. Too much reading "fine print." Nearly every memorandum has a catch in it and it has been necessary to read at least a thousand of 'em and as many reports.

Most of it at night. I see the Secretaries at 9:15 after dictating personal mail for 45 minutes. Usually stop in the Map Room at 8:20 and spend ten minutes finding out about ship sinkings, casualties etc. Gather up dispatches from Stalin, Churchill, Hurley and others. . . .

Saw Herbert Hoover yesterday and had a pleasant and constructive conversation on food and the general troubles of U.S. President—two in particular. . . .

Source: *Off the Record: The Private Papers of Harry S. Truman*, ed. Robert H. Ferrell (New York: Harper & Row, 1980), 39–41.

A19-1. HOOVER MEMORANDUM TO TRUMAN
AND RESPONSES, MAY–JUNE 1945

a. Vinson to Truman, June 7, 1945

MEMORANDUM FOR THE PRESIDENT
FROM: FRED M. VINSON

This matter should be referred, I suggest, to the Secretary of State and the Secretary of War for consideration and for submission of their comments to you. I think the judgment of the Secretary of War would be especially valuable in view of the fact that he was Secretary of State at the time of the Manchurian crisis and in view of the fact that his analysis of international affairs has been eminently sound.

Perhaps it would also be wise for you to send a copy of this memorandum to Mr. Hull and obtain the benefit of his experience and judgment.

In line with this suggestion, I enclose suggested letters to the Secretary of State, the Secretary of War and to Mr. Hull. I return the original of the memorandum so that you may have it for your files.

b. Hoover Memorandum to Truman (undated, but probably May 30, 1945)

I believe there is just a bare chance of ending the Japanese war if an adequate declaration of Far Eastern policy be made by the United States and Britain jointly, and if possible with China. The President has already taken an admirable step in this direction which might now be further advanced.

The following is my own view of American objectives and the interpretation of them into such a declaration:

1. As this war arose fundamentally over Japanese invasion of Manchuria, the first point in such declaration is the restoration of Manchuria to China. It is an essential step to the establishment of the sanctity of international agreements.

2. For reparations to China, it should be declared that all Japanese Government property in China must be handed to the Chinese.

3. As the militarist party in Japan has proved a menace to the whole world, a third point in such a declaration should be to insist upon the unconditional surrender of the whole Japanese Army and Navy and their equipment.

4. In view of the military caste by inheritance among the Japanese people which even assassinates Japanese opposition, they cannot be trusted with a military establishment. Therefore, the third point is continued disarmament for a long enough period (probably a generation) to dissolve the whole military caste and its know-how.

5. As certain Japanese officers are charged with violation of the rules of war and human conduct, they should be surrendered for fair trial by the Allies.

6. As certain islands held by Japan are necessary protection against the future and to enforce disarmament, the next point of declaration could be the ceding of these islands to the Allies.

Beyond this point there can be no American objectives that are worth the expenditure of 500,000 to 1,000,000 American lives.

7. Encouragement to Japan to accept such points and a part saving of face could be had by further necessary points in the declaration.

(a) That the Allies have no desire to destroy either the Japanese people or their government, or to interference in the Japanese way of life; that it is our desire that the Japanese build up their prosperity and their contributions to the civilized world.

(b) That the Japanese retain Korea and Formosa as trustees under the world trustee system. The Koreans and Formosans are today incapable of self-government, they are not Chinese, and the Japanese have proved that under the liberal elements of their country that they are capable administrators. Those countries have been Japanese possessions for over fifty years and their annexation has been admitted by treaties of America, Britain and China.

(c) A further point in declaration should be that except as above mentioned we wished no reparations nor indemnities.

8. A final declaration could be added that if the Japanese Government is not prepared to accept these terms it is evidence that they are unfit to remain in control of the Japanese people and we must need proceed to their ultimate destruction.

9. That the Japanese would accept these terms and end the war cannot be stated with any assurance. The factors favorable to its acceptance are:

(a) The appointment of Suzuki, a one-time anti-militarist elder-statesman, as Prime Minister;

(b) The desire of the Japanese to preserve the Mikado who is the spiritual head of the nation;

(c) The sense they showed after the Russo-Japanese war of making peace before Russia organized her full might;

(d) The fear of complete destruction which by now they must know is their fate;

(e) The fact that there is a large middle class in Japan which was the product of industrialization, who are liberal-minded, who have in certain periods governed Japan and in these periods they gave full cooperation in peaceful forces of the world. That this group again exert itself is the only hope of stable and progressive government.

10. From an American point of view, if such a [sic]

(a) Have attained our every objective except perhaps the vengeance of an excited, minority of our people;

(b) We would have saved the lives of 500,000 to 1,000,000 American boys, the loss of which may be necessary by going on to the end;

(c) We would have saved the exhaustion of our resources to a degree that otherwise will make our own recovery very, very difficult and our aid to the rest of the world of little consequence;

(d) We will save ourselves the impossible task of setting up a military or civil government in Japan with all its dangers of revolutions and conflicts with our Allies.

11. If Japan does not accept, the essence of such a declaration still has advantages:

(a) It will clarify the world's understanding that Manchuria is to be returned to China;

(b) It again demonstrates that America is not in war for any purpose but to establish order in the world.

c. Cordell Hull to Truman, June 12, 1945

Dear Mr. President:

This will acknowledge the receipt of your note of June 9, 1945 enclosing copy of your memorandum by Mr. Herbert Hoover on "Ending the Japanese War," and on which you request my opinion. . . .

I doubt that it would be of any particular aid for me to discuss any of these questions to which Mr. Hoover refers in his appeasement proposal. One is tempted to talk at length about this policy which he to a considerable extent raises in his memorandum. . . .

d. Joseph C. Grew to Truman, June 13, 1945

. . . In response to your memorandum of June 9, 1945, to which there was attached a paper submitted to you by Mr. Hoover entitled "Memorandum on Ending the Japanese War," I submit the following analysis of the latter mentioned document.

1. Mr. Hoover's conception of American objectives in relation to the war with Japan as set forth in paragraphs 1 to 6 of his memorandum falls substantially within the framework of the policies with regard to the post-defeat treatment of Japan that are now being formulated by the Department of State in consultation with other interested departments. . . .

2. The complete compass of the terms which we propose to impose on Japan would be considerably wider than the points proposed by Mr. Hoover. We believe it important that there should be a program—and we are in process of formulating such a program—designed to create in the post-defeat period conditions which would conduce toward the

abandonment by the Japanese of militarism, militant nationalism and other archaic concepts, and toward the regeneration of these people along liberal and cooperative lines. We would therefore contemplate, first of all, a suspension of those organs of the Japanese Government which formulate policy. To encourage search for truth as something essential toward the establishment of a democracy we would guarantee freedom of speech and of religion, we would revise the system of education, and we would do away with obnoxious laws suppressing fundamental human rights. These and other things we would consider necessary to have done in order to achieve a total victory. They would be basic American objectives equally with the payment of reparations to China, the demilitarization of Japanese industry, or the trial and punishment of Japanese war criminals. . . .

4. There is much with which we would agree in the brief discussion by Mr. Hoover of the factors favorable to the acceptance by the Japanese of the terms proposed by him. Every evidence, without exception, that we are able to obtain of the views of the Japanese with regard to the institution of the throne, indicates that the non-molestation of the person of the present emperor and the preservation of the institution of the throne comprise irreducible Japanese terms. These indications are that, whereas the Japanese would be ready to undergo most drastic privations so long as these irreducible terms were met, they are prepared for prolonged resistance if it be the intention of the United Nations to try the present emperor as a war criminal or to abolish the imperial institution. We are disposed to agree with the view that failure on our part to clarify our intentions in this regard, or the proclamation of our intention to try the emperor as a war criminal and to abolish the institution of the throne, will insure prolongation of the war and cost a large number of human lives.

5. Mr. Hoover has assumed that the task of setting up a military government in Japan would be "an impossible one. . . . "

It is our view that total victory cannot be achieved without a military occupation of Japan and a period during which Japan would be under military government. It is only under military government that conditions might be created favorable to the generation of those forces which, in the light of experience elsewhere, could be expected to promote democratic tendencies within Japan and cooperative attitudes in Japan's relations with the rest of the world.

6. The Joint Chiefs of Staff have recently proposed to the Secretary of State that a communication be sent to the Japanese Government demanding the immediate and unconditional surrender of Japan. The Joint Chiefs state that safeguards must be taken now against the Japanese Government putting forward a proposal for a negotiated peace at a time when there would be in the United States a large number of troops returned from Europe and awaiting redeployment in the Pacific. It is thought possible that a Japanese peace proposal at such a time might have serious adverse effects on American morale. The proposed communication to the Japanese Government would stress the inevitability of Japan's defeat.

It is our intention, of course, to further in every practical way any measures which the Joint Chiefs of Staff may consider necessary to maintain the morale of the American people. It is our view, however, that a mere call on the Japanese to surrender, in whatever terms it might be couched but without clarification of "unconditional surrender," is not likely to bring any affirmative response. We feel, on the other hand, that there might conceivably be a derisive rejoinder by the Japanese, with such effects on the morale of the American people as it might be difficult to predict. We have therefore prepared a draft statement which would, on the one hand, call upon the Japanese to surrender in terms substantially those proposed by the Joint Chiefs of Staff, and would, on the other hand, indicate to the Japanese those things which, after their surrender, we would intend to accomplish in Japan.

It will be noted that the latter part of the draft statement presents in general terms the salient features of a program for the demilitarization, both physical and intellectual, of Japan, which would include most of the points considered essential by Mr. Hoover. It also presents some points which would be designed to allay certain fears of the Japanese and to meet their basic position, that the United Nations shall not molest the person of the emperor or disestablish the institution of the throne.

e. Marshall Response to Hoover Memorandum (sent to Truman), June 15, 1945

MEMORANDUM FOR THE SECRETARY OF WAR

There is attached a memorandum by the staff, with which I am in substantial agreement, containing analysis of and comment on the paper on "ending the Japanese war," which you gave to General Handy.

MEMORANDUM OF COMMENTS ON "ENDING THE JAPANESE WAR"

1. The Secretary of war has given to General Handy a second memorandum concerning ending the Japanese War, asking for comments and analysis by his staff.

2. In the memorandum under consideration it is proposed that the U.S. and Great Britain (joined, if practicable, by China) jointly state their war aims in the Pacific war. The author gives his view of American war aims which should be included in the declaration and suggests face-saving points for the Japanese. The author points out the value to the U.S. if the Japanese accept the declaration, and if they do not, that it would still have a ruminative psychological effect on the world.

3. Before considering the memorandum point by point, it seems we should recognize the following as being basic considerations:

a. The Japanese know they are licked for this generation and must be searching for a way to get out of the war which will leave them the maximum strength and possibilities in future generations.

b. The military objectives of the U.S. must reasonably include an assurance that Japan will not be the focal point of another war even as soon as the next generation.

c. The U.S. has entered into certain contracts with other nations and with the world, which, from the military standpoint, must be taken into account in any proposed formula for peace with Japan. The Cairo Declaration, for instance, provides specifically for Formosa and Korea being freed from Japan.

4. From the military standpoint, the first six points in the proposed declaration of American objectives appear satisfactory. All these points should already be clear as a result of specific declarations, such as the Cairo Declaration, or other public statements by responsible Americans. From the standpoint of a public declaration, the physiological soundness of stressing the point about trial of Japanese violating the rules of war appears questionable since the Japanese officials responsible for capitulation might reasonably feel they might eventually be included in the list of war criminals. Concerning the point providing for listing Japanese Islands to be ceded, there are two difficulties: the first being that the U.S. has not yet determined what islands, if any, it wants in the chain north of the Marshalls and the Ryukyus; the second being we must face the fact that Russia enters into this problem and now is a very inappropriate time to start listing possible Russian requirements on Japan. Finally, a public declaration listing several islands, which . . . are unheard of by the American people and at the same time probably dear to the Japanese people, seems psychologically unsound. It should be noted that the accomplishment of unconditional surrender of the Japanese armed forces and assurance of continued disarmament will almost certainly require a supervision which will includes at least temporary occupation of selected areas.

5. The face-saving proposals of the author of the paper include retention by Japan of Korea and Formosa under the world trustee system. It seems questionable that this is an adequate implementation of the contract in the Cairo Declaration, although this point is a purely political matter. From the military standpoint, Formosa is a strategic area with relationship to the entire central coast of China and also the Philippines. Japanese retention of Formosa under any conditions is militarily unacceptable. Japanese retention of Korea might well be militarily unacceptable to China and Russia, one or both, and is also contrary to existing agreements.

6. A point to be remembered in these considerations is that the return of Manchuria to China cannot be guaranteed without Russian agreement unless the U.S. occupies Manchuria. Military plans do not contemplate this at present and any such project might seriously involve us with the Russians, whose deep military, as well as political and economic, interest in Manchuria we are compelled to recognize.

7. With reference to the proposal that any declaration include a statement that if the terms are not accepted, we will proceed to the "ultimate destruction" of the Japanese peo-

ple, this seems undesirable since it is militarily almost impracticable to destroy a whole people. Furthermore, it would be unacceptably costly in American lives unless we use gas extensively and resorted to a long campaign of starvation.

8. The author cites interesting points which he believes indicate the Japanese might accept the terms. His point that the appointment of Suzuki as Prime Minister is encouraging seems an extremely doubtful one, as does his point about the liberal minded large middle class in Japan. The War Department Intelligence people believe that the Japanese leaders, such as Suzuki, do not differ materially in their national ambitions, their idea of Japanese destiny, and their ruthlessness from the so-called militarists. They have differed only in the means they thought best to attain the ultimate ends, which are the same as those of the militarists. In effect, their difference has been not on objectives but on national strategy in attaining the objectives. As to the middle class, the best information we have is that this is a small group of questionable influence and not very articulate. It is doubtful that they should be classified as "liberal minded." Probably they are little different from the so-called militarists except that they had a less narrow view of the world, particularly the power of the U.S., and this gave than more caution and put a break on their enthusiasm for open aggression. The strongest point listed by the author is undoubtedly the Jap fear of complete destruction. The comment on this is that the Jap navy and the Jap air force have already experienced a large taste of complete destruction, but the Japanese army, whose leaders have a very strong influence, is still fairly intact.

9. The author lists four points which would be gained if his proposed declaration were accepted. On the positive side he considers we would gain every worthwhile U.S. objective. This seems substantially true from the military standpoint, except for Formosa and except for the apparent lack of any adequate guarantee of Jap disarmament and prevention of aggression in the next generation. As to the three points on the negative side, the estimate of 500,000 to 1,000,000 American lives for carrying the war to a conclusion appears to deserve little consideration. Perhaps if the author looked at this estimate in its equivalent form of between 2 and 5 million casualties, he would revise his estimate downward.

10. As to the point of "exhaustion of our resources," this seems highly questionable and the thought might be interpolated that use of U.S. resources at this time to prevent a war in the Pacific in the next generation might be of more value to the world than using these same resources for immediate relief for Europe. There appear to be no grounds for a statement that the establishment of military government "is an impossible task," even though it is admittedly undesirable, particularly if done on a combined basis.

11. SUMMATION

The proposal of a public declaration of war aims, in effect giving definition to "unconditional surrender," has definite merit if it is carefully handled. It seems that any declaration should stem from agreements and statements already made, such as the Cairo Declaration and the recent statement of the President. It should be hard and firm in the nature of an ultimatum and must not be phrased so as to invite negotiation. Otherwise, there is the danger of seriously impairing the will to war of the people of the United States, with consequent damaging effect on our war effort, prolongation of the war and unnecessarily increased cost in human lives; or alternately acceptance of a compromise peace. A serious point for consideration in this connection is the effect on Britain, China and particularly Russia, whose aid we need to press the war to the quickest possible conclusion. With this in mind, any governmental declaration which leaves out Russia, China or both, seems fraught not only with political but also military implications. Perhaps a way to handle the matter would be for a statement to be made by a responsible American as an individual. We must make certain our military operations and preparations continue with undiminished pressure, even though we bring increasing political and psychological pressure on the Japanese to persuade them to capitulate.

Sources: All memos except Marshall's: State Department, World War II, Box 43, White House Confidential File, Harry S. Truman Library; Marshall memo: Miscellaneous Historical Documents File, Folder 816, Truman Library.

A19-2. HOOVER MEMORANDUM TO STIMSON
AND MARSHALL RESPONSE, MAY–JUNE 1945

a. Hoover Memorandum to Stimson (undated, but probably May 15, 1945)

We should today take stock of the position of the United States and Britain. . . .

III

If we fight out the war with Japan to the bitter end, we will need put 1,000,000 men to attack the Japanese home islands and possibly 2,000,000 on the Asiatic mainland, as Japan has armies of 3,500,000 men left. And we are likely to have won the war for Russia's benefit just as we have done in Europe.

IV

In all these lights which now shine out from Europe, Russia and Asia, a revolution in policies is needed for America and Britain. Russia, not being at war with Japan, has no direct rights in the settlement of the Japanese war.

Suppose Chiang Kai-shek, in order to assure the preservation of Manchuria to China and the ascendancy of his own government in the organization of China, should make peace upon the terms:

1. That Japan withdraw from all of China, including Manchuria, and hand the government of China to Chiang Kai-shek.

2. That the Chinese Government receive all of the Japanese Government railways, ports, mines and factories in Manchuria as reparations.

3. That Japan be confined in Korea and Formosa. Neither of these peoples are Chinese and China has no particular moral rights in these countries.

V

Suppose America and Britain made peace with Japan upon the terms:

1. That she be totally disarmed and a disarmament commission be established in the country to see she is kept so. By naval and air fortifications on certain Pacific islands, we can see that the disarmament commission is able to perform.

2. That we ask no reparations or other concessions from her.

VI

What are the results to the United States and Britain?

1. America will save 500,000 to 1,000,000 lives and an enormous loss of resources.

2. Another 18 months of war will prostrate the United States to a point where the Americans can spare no aid to recovery of other nations.

3. We gain everything that we can gain by carrying on the war to a finish.

4. It would stop Russian expansion in the Asian and Pacific areas. Japan, in these circumstances, would not be likely to go Communist.

5. Those areas would be kept open to free enterprise.

6. Japan could take economic recovery which is to the advantage of all free nations.

7. If we fight Japan to the bitter end, there will be (as in Germany) no group left who are capable of establishing government and order. We will be confronted with establishing a military government in which China, Russia and France will demand participation with all the dangers that that involves.

8. Under such terms: there would be the hope that Japan would return to cooperation with Western Civilization and not agitate for revenge for another century as is likely to be the case otherwise.

Thus China, Britain, Japan and America would be better off. . . .

b. Marshall Response to Stimson, June 4–7, 1945

7 JUN 1945

MEMORANDUM FOR THE SECRETARY OF WAR:

With reference to the memorandum concerning which you asked General Handy for the reaction of the Staff, I am attaching a study with which I am in general agreement.

(Sgd) G. C. MARSHALL
Chief of Staff
4 June 1945

MEMORANDUM:

The Secretary of War has given to General Handy for "reaction of the Staff" a memorandum furnished to him concerning the war with Japan. . . .

The author of the paper lists eight advantages which would accrue from making peace with Japan under his suggested terms, and comments are made below on six of these points.

1. America will save 500,000 to 1,000,000 lives and an enormous loss of resources.

Comment: It is obvious that peace would save lives and resources, but the estimated loss of 500,000 lives due to carrying the war to conclusion *under our present plan of campaign*, is considered to be entirely too high.

2. Another eighteen months of war will prostrate the United States to a point where the Americans can spare no aid to recovery of other nations.

Comment: This is an economic matter requiring further investigation but it appears doubtful that the U.S. would be prostrate in "eighteen months."

3. We gain everything that we can gain by carrying on the war to a finish.

Comment: This statement may be true, but it must be borne in mind that it is made on the assumption that the proposed peace terms, or something like them, will be accepted at this time and also that they can be implemented, which seems most doubtful.

4. It would stop Russian expansion in the Asia and Pacific areas. Japan, in these circumstances, would not be likely to go Communist.

Comment: The statement that the proposed peace would stop Russian expansion seems highly questionable. Rather, the Russians might consider, with some justice, that the U.S. and Great Britain had broken their contract made at Yalta, and hence, that the Russians had an excellent excuse for immediate aggression, if not military, at least political and economic, in the Asiatic area. It is noted that the proposed peace terms do not provide to Russia certain arrangements specified at Yalta. . . .

SUMMARY

The point in our military progress at which the Japanese will accept defeat and agree to our term is unpredictable. Their analysis of our problem may parallel that of the author of the memorandum under consideration. Like the Germans, their protracted resistance is based upon the hope of achieving a conditional surrender. Presumably, only the conviction that their position is completely hopeless will persuade them to give up their holdings in Asia. Probably it will take Russian entry into the war, coupled with a landing, or imminent threat of landing, on Japan proper by us, to convince them of the hopelessness of their position. . . .

Sources: Hoover memo: National Archive Collection, Reel 115, Item 2656m George C. Marshall Library; Marshall memo: Miscellaneous Historical Documents Collection, Folder 816, Truman Library.

A20. STIMSON DIARY ENTRY, JUNE 6, 1945

. . . I then took up the matters on my agenda, telling him first of the work of the Interim Committee meetings last week. He said that Byrnes had reported to him already about it and that Byrnes seemed to be highly pleased with what had been done. I then said that the points of agreement and views arrived at were substantially as follows:

That there should be no revelation to Russia or anyone else of our work in S-1 until the first bomb had been successfully laid on Japan.

That the greatest complication was what might happen at the meeting of the Big Three. He told me he had postponed that until the 15th of July on purpose to give us more time. I pointed out that there might still be delay and if there was and the Russians should bring up the subject and ask us to take them in as partners, I thought that our attitude was to do just what the Russians had done to us, namely to make the simple statement that as yet we were not quite ready to do it.

I told him that the only suggestion which our Committee had been able to give as to future control of the situation was that each country should promise to make public all work that was being done on this subject and that an international committee of control should be constituted with full power of inspection of all countries to see whether this promise was being carried out. I said I recognized that this was imperfect and might not be assented to by Russia, but that in that case we were far enough ahead of the game to be able to accumulate enough material to serve as insurance against being caught helpless.

I said that of course no disclosure of the work should be made to anyone until all such promises of control were made and established. We then also discussed further quid pro quos which should be established in consideration for our taking them into partnership. He said he had been thinking of that and mentioned the same things that I was thinking of, namely the settlement of the Polish, Rumanian, Yugoslavian, and Manchurian problems.

He then asked me if I had heard of the accomplishment which Harry Hopkins had made in Moscow and when I said I had not he told me there was a promise in writing by

Stalin that Manchuria should remain fully Chinese except for a ninety-nine year lease of Port Arthur and the settlement of Darien which we had hold of. I warned him that with the fifty-fifty control of the railways running across Manchuria, Russia would be likely to outweigh the Chinese in actual power in that country. He said he realized that but the promise was perfectly clear and distinct.

I told him that I was busy considering our conduct of the war against Japan and I told him how I was trying to hold the Air Force down to precision bombing but that with the Japanese method of scattering its manufacture it was rather difficult to prevent area bombing. I told him I was anxious about this feature of the war for two reasons: first, because I did not want to have the United States get the reputation of outdoing Hitler in atrocities; and second, I was a little fearful that before we could get ready the Air Force might have Japan so thoroughly bombed out that the new weapon would not have a fair background to show its strength. He laughed and said he understood. Owing to the shortness of the time I did not get through any further matters on my agenda. . . .

Source: Off the Record: The Private Papers of Harry S. Truman, ed. Robert H. Ferrell (New York: Harper & Row, 1980), 44–45.

A21. TRUMAN DIARY ENTRY, JUNE 7, 1945

Looks like San Francisco [might] be a success yet. Uncle Joe agreed to accept our interpretation of the Veto. He also agreed to reconsider the Polish question. We may get a peace yet. Hopkins has done a good job in Moscow. . . .

. . . I'm not afraid of Russia. They've always been our friends and I can't see any reason why they shouldn't always be. . . .

Source: Michael B. Stoff, Jonathan F. Fanton, and R. Hal Williams, eds., *The Manhattan Project: A Documentary Introduction to the Atomic Age* (New York: McGraw-Hill, 1991), 130–131.

A22. *YANK: THE ARMY WEEKLY* MAGAZINE ARTICLE, JUNE 8, 1945

The Jap War

WASHINGTON—The $64 question now is: "How long will we have to fight the Japanese?"

The War Department has no official answer to it, other than that neither the Army nor the Navy is basing future plans on the idea that the complete defeat of Japan will be a pushover.

Unofficially, however, a lot of guesses are being made. The predictions most often heard in the handsomely tiled latrines of the Pentagon, the War Department's giant doughnut-shaped headquarters, run from 1 to 2 years—and up.

"We can possibly get it over in 2 years, but nobody in the world can guess that," says the high-ranking officer who is frequently quoted in newspaper stories from Washington as "a military expert." He refuses to be overoptimistic.

"I don't think it will come any sooner than that unless there is a sudden collapse," he adds. "Two years would be the minimum. Once our air gets to operate on them, it's going to have a big effect. We can't deduce how much."

"We're just on the fringes of what we have to do," says a colonel whose business it is to keep informed about Japan. "The strength of Japan is in Japan and on the Asiatic mainland. We haven't touched it. Any estimate of the duration of the war is just a guess, but the figure of a year may not be a bad guess."

"It looks like a case of 12 months to get out there, and 6 months to do the job," another colonel says.

The higher brass around the Pentagon says that three major factors—none of them predictable at this stage of the game—will decide whether it will take 1 year, 2 years or longer to win the Far East war. Put the three factors in the form of questions, and they are: 1) How long will it take to redeploy to the Pacific the Stateside and ETO soldiers who are slated for the Jap war; 2) how much punishment will the Japs take before surrendering; 3) will Russia enter the war? . . .

Source: Sgt. Barrett McGurn, "The Jap War," *Yank: The Army Weekly*, June 8, 1945.

A23. THE FRANCK REPORT, JUNE 11, 1945

. . . The scientists on this Project do not presume to speak authoritatively on problems of national and international policy. However, we found ourselves, by the force of events during the last five years, in the position of a small group of citizens cognizant of a grave danger for the safety of this country as well as for the future of all the other nations, of which the rest of mankind is unaware. We therefore feel it our duty to urge that the political problems, arising from the mastering of nuclear power, be recognized in all their gravity, and that the appropriate steps be taken for their study and the preparation of necessary decisions. . . .

III. Prospects of Agreement

The consequences of nuclear warfare, and the type of measures which would have to be taken to protect a country from total destruction by nuclear bombing, must be as abhorrent to other nations as to the United States. . . . Therefore, only lack of mutual trust, and not lack of *desire* for agreement, can stand in the path of an efficient agreement for the prevention of nuclear warfare. The achievement of such an agreement will thus essentially depend on the integrity of intentions and readiness to sacrifice the necessary fraction of one's own sovereignty, by all the parties to the agreement.

From this point of view, the way in which the nuclear weapons now being secretly developed in this country are first revealed to the world appears to be of great, perhaps fateful importance.

One possible way—which may particularly appeal to those who consider nuclear bombs primarily as a secret weapon developed to help win the present war—is to use them without warning on an appropriately selected object in Japan. It is doubtful whether the first available bombs, of comparatively low efficiency and small size, will be sufficient to break the will or ability of Japan to resist. . . . If we consider international agreement on total prevention of nuclear warfare as the paramount objective, and believe that it can be achieved, this kind of introduction of atomic weapons to the world may easily destroy all our chances of success. Russia, and even allied countries which bear less mistrust of our ways and intentions, as well as neutral countries may be deeply shocked. . . .

From this point of view, a demonstration of the new weapon might best be made, before the eyes of representatives of all the United Nations, on a desert or a barren island. The best possible atmosphere for the achievement of an international agreement could be if America could say to the world, "You see what sort of a weapon we had but did not use. We are ready to renounce its use in the future if other nations join us in this renunciation and agree to the establishment of an efficient international control."

After such a demonstration the weapon might perhaps be used against Japan if the sanction of the United Nations (and of public opinion at home) were obtained, perhaps after a preliminary ultimatum to Japan to surrender or at least to evacuate certain regions as an alternative to their total destruction. . . .

Summary

The development of nuclear power not only constitutes an important addition to the technological and military power of the United States, but also creates grave political and economic problems for the future of this country.

Nuclear bombs cannot possibly remain a "secret weapon" at the exclusive disposal of this country for more than a few years. The scientific facts on which their construction is based are well known to scientists of other countries. Unless an effective international control of nuclear explosives is instituted, a race for nuclear armaments is certain to ensue following the first revelation of our possession of nuclear weapons to the world. Within ten years other countries may have nuclear bombs, each of which, weighing less than a ton, could destroy an urban area of more than ten square miles. In the war to which such an armaments race is likely to lead, the United States, with its agglomeration of population and industry in comparatively few metropolitan districts, will be at a disadvantage compared to nations whose population and industry are scattered over large areas.

We believe that these considerations make the use of nuclear bombs for an early unannounced attack against Japan inadvisable. If the United States were to be the first to release this new means of indiscriminate destruction upon mankind, she would sacrifice public support throughout the world, precipitate the race for armaments, and prejudice the possibility of reaching an international agreement on the future control of such weapons.

Much more favorable conditions for the eventual achievement of such an agreement could be created if nuclear bombs were first revealed to the world by a demonstration in an appropriately selected uninhabited area. . . .

To sum up, we urge that the use of nuclear bombs in this war be considered as a problem of long-range national policy rather than of military expediency, and that this policy be directed primarily to the achievement of an agreement permitting an effective international control of the means of nuclear warfare. . . .

Source: Alice Kimball Smith, A Peril and a Hope: The Scientists' Movement in America, 1945–47 (Chicago: University of Chicago Press, 1965), 560–572.

A24. RECOMMENDATIONS OF THE SCIENTIFIC PANEL, JUNE 16, 1945

Recommendations on the Immediate Use of Nuclear Weapons

You have asked us to comment on the initial use of the new weapon. This use, in our opinion, should be such as to promote a satisfactory adjustment of our international relations. At the same time, we recognize our obligation to our nation to use the weapons to help save American lives in the Japanese war.

(1) To accomplish these ends we recommend that before the weapons are used not only Britain, but also Russia, France, and China be advised that we have made considerable progress in our work on atomic weapons, that these may be ready to use during the present war, and that we would welcome suggestions as to how we can cooperate in making this development contribute to improved international relations.

(2) The opinions of our scientific colleagues on the initial use of these weapons are not unanimous: they range from the proposal of a purely technical demonstration to that of the military application best designed to induce surrender. Those who advocate a purely technical demonstration would wish to outlaw the use of atomic weapons, and have feared that if we use the weapons now our position in future negotiations will be prejudiced. Others emphasize the opportunity of saving American lives by immediate military use, and believe that such use will improve the international prospects, in that they are more concerned with the prevention of war than with the elimination of this specific weapon.

We find ourselves closer to these latter views; we can propose no technical demonstration likely to bring an end to the war; we see no acceptable alternative to direct military use.

(3) With regard to these general aspects of the use of atomic energy, it is clear that we, as scientific men, have no proprietary rights. It is true that we are among the few citizens who have had occasion to give thoughtful consideration to these problems during the past few years. We have, however, no claim to special competence in solving the political, social, and military problems which are presented by the advent of atomic power.

Source: Michael B. Stoff, Jonathan F. Fanton, and R. Hal Williams, eds., *The Manhattan Project: A Documentary Introduction to the Atomic Age* (New York: McGraw-Hill, 1991), 149.

A25. TRUMAN DIARY ENTRY, JUNE 17, 1945

. . . . I have to decide Japanese strategy—shall we invade Japan proper or shall we bomb and blockade? That is my hardest decision to date. But I'll make it when I have all the facts. . . .

Source: *Off the Record: The Private Papers of Harry S. Truman*, ed. Robert H. Ferrell (New York: Harper & Row, 1980), 44–45.

A26. LEAHY MEMO TO THE JOINT CHIEFS OF STAFF (JPS 697/D), JUNE 14, 1945

URGENT—IMMEDIATE ACTION
MEMORANDUM FOR THE JOINT CHIEFS OF STAFF

The President today directed me to inform the Joint Chiefs of Staff that he wishes to meet with the Chiefs of Staff in the afternoon of the 18th, in his office, to discuss details of our campaign against Japan.

He expects at this meeting to be thoroughly informed of our intentions and prospects in preparation for his discussions with Churchill and Stalin.

He will want information as to the number of men of the Army and ships of the Navy that will be necessary to defeat Japan.

He wants an estimate of the time required and an estimate of the losses in killed and wounded that will result from an invasion of Japan proper.

He wants an estimate of the time and the losses that will result from an effort to defeat Japan by isolation, blockade, and bombardment by sea and air forces.

He desires to be informed as to exactly what we want the Russians to do.

He desires information as to what useful contribution, if any, can be made by other Allied nations.

It is his intention to make his decisions on the campaign with the purposes of economizing to the maximum extent possible in the loss of American lives.

Economy in the use of time and in money cost is comparatively unimportant. I suggest that a memorandum discussion of the above noted points be prepared in advance for delivery to the President at the time of the meeting in order that he may find time later to study the problem.

/s/ *William D. Leahy*

Source: Douglas J. MacEachin, *The Final Months of the War with Japan: Signals Intelligence, U.S. Invasion Planning, and the A-Bomb Decision* (Washington, D.C.: Center for the Study of Intelligence, 1998), Document 4.

A27. MINUTES OF WHITE HOUSE MEETING, JUNE 18, 1945

Minutes of Meeting held at the White House on
Monday, 18 June 1945 at 1530

PRESENT.
The President
Fleet Admiral William D. Leahy—General of the Army G. C. Marshall
Fleet Admiral E. J. King
Lieut. General I. C. Eaker (Representing General of the Army H. H. Arnold)
The Secretary of War, Mr. Stimson
The Secretary of the Navy, Mr. Forrestal
The Assistant Secretary of War, Mr. McCloy
SECRETARY
Brig. General A. J. McFarland

1. Details of the Campaign Against Japan

THE PRESIDENT stated that he had called the meeting for the purpose of informing himself with respect to the details of the campaign against Japan set out in Admiral Leahy's memorandum to the Joint Chiefs of Staff of 14 June. He asked General Marshall if he would express his opinion.

GENERAL MARSHALL pointed out that the present situation with respect to operations against Japan was practically identical with the situation which had existed in connection with the operations proposed against Normandy. He then read, as an expression of his views, the following digest of a memorandum prepared by the Joint Chiefs of Staff for presentation to the President (J.C.S. 1388): . . .

The Kyushu operation is essential to a strategy of strangulation and appears to be the least costly worthwhile operation following Okinawa. The basic point is that a lodgement in Kyushu is essential, both to tightening our strangle hold of blockade and bombardment on Japan, and to forcing capitulation by invasion of the Tokyo Plain.

We are bringing to bear against the Japanese every weapon and all the force we can employ and there is no reduction in our maximum possible application of bombardment and blockade, while at the same time we are pressing invasion preparations. It seems that if the Japanese are ever willing to capitulate short of complete military defeat in the field they will do it when faced by the completely hopeless prospect occasioned by (1) destruction already wrought by air bombardment and sea blockade, coupled with (2) a landing on Japan indicating the firmness of our resolution, and also perhaps coupled with (3) the entry or threat of entry of Russia into the war.

With reference to clean-up of the Asiatic mainland, our objective should be to get the Russians to deal with the Japs in Manchuria (and Korea if necessary) and to vitalize the Chinese to a point where, with assistance of American air power and some supplies, they can mop out their own country.

Casualties. Our experience in the Pacific war is so diverse as to casualties that it is considered wrong to give any estimate in numbers. Using various combinations of Pacific experience, the War Department staff reaches the conclusion that the cost of securing a worthwhile position in Korea would almost certainly be greater than the cost of the Kyushu operation. Points on the optimistic side of the Kyushu operation are that: General MacArthur has not yet accepted responsibility for going ashore where there would be disproportionate casualties. The nature of the objective area gives room for maneuver, both on the land and by sea. As to any discussion of specific operations, the following data are pertinent:

Campaign	U.S. Casualties Killed, Wounded, Missing	Jap Casualties Killed and Prisoners (not including wounded)	Ratio U.S. to Jap
Leyte	17,000	78,000	1:4.6
Luzon	31,000	156,000	1:5.0
Iwo Jima	20,000	25,000	1:1.25
Okinawa	34,000 (Ground) 7,700 (Navy)	81,000 (not a complete count)	1:2
Normandy (1st 30 days)	42,000	—	—

The record of General MacArthur's operations from 1 March 1944 through 1 May 1945 shows 13,742 U.S. killed compared to 310,165 Japanese killed, or a ratio of 22 to 1.

There is reason to believe that the first 30 days in Kyushu should not exceed the price we have paid for Luzon. It is a grim fact that there is not an easy, bloodless way to victory in war and it is the thankless task of the leaders to maintain their firm outward front which holds the resolution of their subordinates. Any irresolution in the leaders may result in costly weakening and indecision in the subordinates. It was this basic difficulty with the Prime Minister which clouded and hampered all our preparations for the cross-channel operation now demonstrated as having been essential to victory in Europe.

An important point about Russian participation in the war is that the impact of Russian entry on the already hopeless Japanese may well be the decisive action levering them into capitulation at that time or shortly thereafter if we land in Japan.

In considering the matter of command and control in the Pacific war which the British wish to raise at the next conference, we must bear in mind the point that anything smacking of combined command in the Pacific might increase the difficulties with Russia and perhaps with China. Furthermore the obvious inefficiencies of combined command may directly result in increased cost in resources and American lives.

GENERAL MARSHALL said that he had asked General MacArthur's opinion on the proposed operation and had received from him the following telegram, which General Marshall then read:

"I believe the operation presents less hazards of excessive loss than any other that has been suggested and that its decisive effect will eventually save lives by eliminating wasteful operations of nondecisive character. I regard the operation as the most economical one in effort and lives that is possible. . . . I most earnestly recommend no change in OLYMPIC. Additional subsidiary attacks will simply build up our final total casualties."

GENERAL MARSHALL said that it was his personal view that the operation against Kyushu was the only course to pursue. He felt that air power alone was not sufficient to put the Japanese out of the war. It was unable alone to put the Germans out. General Eaker and General Eisenhower both agreed to this. Against the Japanese, scattered through mountainous country, the problem would be much more difficult than it had been in Germany. He felt that this plan offered the only way the Japanese could be forced into a feeling of utter helplessness. The operation would be difficult but not more so than the assault in Normandy. He was convinced that every individual moving to the Pacific should be indoctrinated with a firm determination to see it through.

ADMIRAL KING agreed with General Marshall's views and said that the more he studied the matter, the more he was impressed with the strategic location of Kyushu, which he considered the key to the success of any siege operations. . . .

THE PRESIDENT inquired if a later decision would not depend on what the Russians agree to do. It was agreed that this would have considerable influence.

THE PRESIDENT then asked Admiral Leahy for his views of the situation.

ADMIRAL LEAHY recalled that the President had been interested in knowing what the price in casualties for Kyushu would be and whether or not that price could be paid. He pointed out that the troops on Okinawa had lost 35 percent in casualties. If this percentage were applied to the number of troops to be employed in Kyushu, he thought from the similarity of the fighting to be expected that this would give a good estimate of the casualties to be expected. He was interested therefore in finding out how many troops are to be used in Kyushu.

ADMIRAL KING called attention to what he considered an important difference in Okinawa and Kyushu. There had been only one way to go on Okinawa. This meant a straight frontal attack against a highly fortified position. On Kyushu, however, landings would be made on three fronts simultaneously and there would be much more room for maneuver. It was his opinion that a realistic casualty figure for Kyushu would lie somewhere between the number experienced by General MacArthur in the operations on Luzon and the Okinawa casualties.

GENERAL MARSHALL pointed out that the total assault troops for the Kyushu campaign were shown in the memorandum prepared for the President as 766,700. He said, in answer to the President's question as to what opposition could be expected on Kyushu, that it was estimated at eight Japanese divisions or about 350,000 troops. He said that divisions were still being raised in Japan and that reinforcement from other areas was possible but it was becoming increasingly difficult and painful.

THE PRESIDENT asked about the possibility of reinforcements for Kyushu moving south from the other Japanese islands.

GENERAL MARSHALL said that it was expected that all communications with Kyushu would be destroyed.

ADMIRAL KING described in some detail the land communications between the other Japanese islands and Kyushu and stated that as a result of operations already planned, the Japanese would have to depend on sea shipping for any reinforcement.

ADMIRAL LEAHY stressed the fact that Kyushu was an island. It was crossed by a mountain range, which would be difficult for either the Japanese or the Americans to cross. The Kyushu operation, in effect, contemplated the taking of another island from which to bring increased air power against Japan.

THE PRESIDENT expressed the view that it was practically creating another Okinawa closer to Japan, to which the Chiefs of Staff agreed.

THE PRESIDENT then asked General Eaker for his opinion of the operation as an air man.

GENERAL EAKER said that he agreed completely with the statements made by General Marshall in his digest of the memorandum prepared for the President. He had just received a cable in which General Arnold also expressed complete agreement. . . . Present air casualties are averaging 2 percent per mission, about 30 percent per month. He wished to point out and to emphasize that delay favored only the enemy and he urged that there be no delay.

THE PRESIDENT said that as he understood it the Joint Chiefs of Staff, after weighing all the possibilities of the situation and considering all possible alternative plans, were still of the unanimous opinion that the Kyushu operation was the best solution under the circumstances.

The Chiefs of Staff agreed that this was so.

THE PRESIDENT then asked the Secretary of War for his opinion.

MR. STIMSON agreed with the Chiefs of Staff that there was no other choice. He felt that he was personally responsible to the President more for political than for military considerations. It was his opinion that there was a large submerged class in Japan who do not favor the present war and whose full opinion and influence had never yet been felt. He felt sure that this submerged class would fight and fight tenaciously if attacked on their own ground. He was concerned that something should be done to arouse them and to develop any possible influence they might have before it became necessary to come to grips with them.

THE PRESIDENT stated that this possibility was being worked on all the time. He asked if the invasion of Japan by white men would not have the effect of more closely uniting the Japanese.

MR. STIMSON thought there was every prospect of this. He agreed with the plan proposed by the Joint Chiefs of Staff as being the best thing to do, but he still hoped for some fruitful accomplishment through other means.

THE PRESIDENT then asked for the views of the Secretary of the Navy.

MR. FORRESTAL pointed out that even if we wished to besiege Japan for a year or a year and a half, the capture of Kyushu would still be essential. . . .

THE PRESIDENT stated that one of his objectives in connection with the coming conference would be to get from Russia all the assistance in the war that was possible. To this end he wanted to know all the decisions that he would have to make in advance in order to occupy the strongest possible position in the discussions.

ADMIRAL LEAHY said that he could not agree with those who said to him that unless we obtain the unconditional surrender of the Japanese that we will have lost the war. He feared no menace from Japan in the foreseeable future, even if we were unsuccessful in forcing unconditional surrender. What he did fear was that our insistence on unconditional surrender would result only in making the Japanese desperate and thereby increase our casualty lists. He did not think that this was at all necessary.

THE PRESIDENT stated that it was with that thought in mind that he had left the door open for Congress to take appropriate action with reference to unconditional surrender. However, he did not feel that he could take any action at this time to change public opinion on the matter.

THE PRESIDENT said he considered the Kyushu plan all right from the military standpoint and, so far as he was concerned, the Joint Chiefs of Staff could go ahead with it; that we can do this operation and then decide as to the final action later. . . .

THE PRESIDENT reiterated that his main reason for this conference with the Chiefs of Staff was his desire to know definitely how far we could afford to go in the Japanese campaign. He had hoped that there was a possibility of preventing an Okinawa from one end of Japan to the other. He was clear on the situation now and was quite sure that the Joint Chiefs of Staff should proceed with the Kyushu operation. . . .

THE PRESIDENT and the Chiefs of Staff then discussed certain other matters. . . .

Source: Dennis Merrill, ed., *Documentary History of the Truman Presidency* (Washington, D.C.: University Publications of America, 1995), 1:49–57.

A28. LEAHY DIARY ENTRY, JUNE 18, 1945

General of the Army, D. D. Eisenhower, arrived in Washington from Europe and led a parade from Army Headquarters to the Capitol Building. The streets were crowded by a larger number of spectators than has been seen before by anybody now in Washington.

In the Chamber of the House of Representatives, before a joint session of the House and Senate, General Eisenhower made a very well prepared address which was not delivered with particular skill. The galleries were crowded with visitors and on the floor of the Chamber seats were provided for the Supreme Court, Cabinet Officers, Ministers, and Ambassadors from foreign countries, and the American Chiefs of Staff.

Immediately following General Eisenhower's address we proceeded to the Statler Hotel and participated in a luncheon for 1,000 guests given by the City of Washington in honor of the General. . . .

From 3:30 to 5:00 p.m. the President conferred with the Joint Chiefs of Staff, the Secretary of War, the Secretary of the Navy; and Assistant Secretary of War McCloy, in regard to the necessity and the practicability of an invasion of Japan. General Marshall and Admiral King both strongly advocated an invasion of Kyushu at the earliest practicable date.

General Marshall is of the opinion that such an effort will not cost us in casualties more than 63,000 of the 190,000 combatant troops estimated as necessary for the operation.

The President approved the Kyushu operation and withheld for later consideration the general occupation of Japan. The Army seems determined to occupy and govern Japan by military government as is being done in Germany. I am unable to see any justification from a national defense point of view for a prolonged occupation of Japan. The cost of such an occupation will be enormous in both lives and treasure.

It is my opinion at the present time that a surrender of Japan can be arranged with terms that can be accepted by Japan and that will make fully satisfactory provision for America's defense against future trans-Pacific aggression.

Dined with the President at a dinner given in honor of General Eisenhower to a large number of military and political officers.

For the first time in my experience cocktails were served to the guests in the East Room of the White House. A number of enlisted men, brought by General Eisenhower from Europe, attended the dinner which was served on small tables filling the State Dining Room.

My place was at a center table which seated the President, General Eisenhower, Secretary of War Stimson, General Marshall, Field Marshal Maitland Wilson, the President of the Senate, the Speaker of the House, General Eaker, and a British Air Marshal.

Source: Historians Committee for Open Debate, www.historians.org/archive/hiroshima/180645.html

A29. STIMSON DIARY ENTRY, JUNE 19, 1945

We had a good meeting of the Committee of Three. . . . I took up the question as to what position the three Departments should take on what you might call the civil military questions of the war against Japan. The Chiefs of Staff had taken their position at the meeting on Monday and Forrestal and I have agreed to it as far as the purely military side of it goes. But there was a pretty strong feeling that it would be deplorable if we have to go through the military program with all its stubborn fighting to a finish. We agreed that it is necessary now to plan and prepare to go through, but it became very evident today in the discussion that we all feel that some way should be found of inducing Japan to yield without a fight to the finish and that was the subject of the discussion today. Grew read us a recent report he had made to the President on the subject in which he strongly advocated a new warning to Japan as soon as Okinawa has fallen, but apparently that does not meet with the President's plans in respect to the coming meeting with Churchill and Stalin. My only fixed date is the last chance warning which must be given before an actual landing of the ground forces on Japan, and fortunately the plans provide for enough time to bring in the sanctions to our warning in the shape of heavy ordinary bombing attack and an attack of S-1.

I had a talk with Marshall after the meeting of the Committee of Three this morning and went over it with him. He is suggesting an additional sanction to our warning in the shape of an entry by the Russians into the war. That would certainly coordinate all the threats possible to Japan. . . .

Source: Henry L. Stimson Diaries, Reel 9, 182–185, Yale University Library, New Haven.

A30. H. V. KALTENBORN BROADCAST, JUNE 26, 1945

Good Evening Everybody: . . .

. . . Tokio [*sic*] is jittery tonight about an American invasion fleet which is on the prowl in the Northern Ryukyus, not far from Okinawa. . . . We lost as many Americans killed in taking tiny Okinawa Island as were lost in reconquering the entire Philippines Archipelago. The actual figures are over 12,000 Americans dead for each campaign. . . .

. . . But even making all allowances, it will still seem to many Americans that we should not plan a campaign against Japan that will include many Okinawas. There are other ways of defeating Japan. It may take a little longer, but if we can save a hundred thousand American lives, a few extra months will be worth it.

Source: H. V. Kaltenborn Papers, Folder 6, Box 175, Broadcast of 26 June 1945, State Historical Society of Wisconsin, Madison.

A31. RALPH BARD MEMORANDUM ON THE USE
OF THE ATOMIC BOMB, JUNE 27, 1945

Memorandum on the Use of S-1 Bomb

Ever since I have been in touch with this program I have had a feeling that before the bomb is actually used against Japan that Japan should have some preliminary warning for say two or three days in advance of use. The position of the United States as a great humanitarian nation and the fair play attitude of our people generally is responsible in the main for this feeling.

During recent weeks I have also had the feeling very definitely that the Japanese government may be searching for some opportunity which they could use as a medium of surrender. Following the three-power conference emissaries from this country could contact representatives from Japan somewhere on the China Coast and make representations with regard to Russia's position and at the same time give them some information regarding the proposed use of atomic power together with whatever assurances the President might care to make with regard to the Emperor of Japan and the treatment of the Japanese nation following unconditional surrender. It seems quite possible to me that this presents the opportunity which the Japanese are looking for.

I don't see that we have anything in particular to lose in following such a program. The stakes are so tremendous that it is my opinion very real consideration should be given to some plan of this kind. I do not believe under present circumstances existing that there is anyone in this country whose evaluation of the chances of the success of such a program is worth a great deal. The only way to find out is to try it out.

Source: Michael B. Stoff, Jonathan F. Fanton, and R. Hal Williams, eds., *The Manhattan Project: A Documentary Introduction to the Atomic Age* (New York: McGraw-Hill, 1991), 162.

A32. STIMSON DIARY ENTRY, JUNE 26–30, 1945

At the meeting this morning of the Committee of Three . . . I took up at once the subject of trying to get Japan to surrender by giving her a warning after she had been sufficiently pounded possibly with S-1. This is a matter about which I feel very strongly and feel that the country will not be satisfied unless every effort is made to shorten the war. I had made a draft of a letter to the President on the subject. . . . Forrestal and Grew said that they approved of . . . the general substance of the letter. We then appointed a subcommittee . . . to draft an actual warning to be sent when the time came.

Source: Michael B. Stoff, Jonathan F. Fanton, and R. Hal Williams, eds., *The Manhattan Project: A Documentary Introduction to the Atomic Age* (New York: McGraw-Hill, 1991), 163.

A33. STIMSON DIARY ENTRY AND MEMORANDUM TO TRUMAN ON PROPOSED PROGRAM FOR JAPAN, JULY 2, 1945

I got started very early with an interview with General Groves, Harvey Bundy, and Harrison and McCloy in preparation for my appointment with the President.

At eleven o'clock I went to the White House, telling the President I had two important subjects I wanted to talk with him about; one, our plans in regard to Japan, and the other our treatment of Germany. He was very agreeable to both and said that he was troubled over both of them and wanted my views. I then took out this bunch of papers which I had been preparing during the past week and started on the problem of, first, whether it was worthwhile to try to warn Japan into surrender. The President read my memorandum to him which we had discussed last Tuesday at the Committee of Three and evidently was impressed with it. A copy is attached hereto. He also examined the draft warning which, as I pointed out, was merely a tentative draft and necessarily could not be completed until we know what was going to be done with S-1. I also showed him the draft which had been prepared by the Interim Committee for a Presidential statement after the first bomb is dropped on Japan. This he read carefully. I then went into the subject of the attitude of the members of the Interim Committee on our attitude towards Russia in respect to S-1. . . .

I regard these two subjects, viz: the effort to shorten the Japanese war by a surrender and the proper handling of Germany so as not to create such harshness in seeking vengeance as to make it impossible to lay the foundations of a new Germany which will be a proper member of the family of nations, as the two largest and important problems that I have had since I have been here. . . .

MEMORANDUM FOR THE PRESIDENT

PROPOSED PROGRAM FOR JAPAN

1. The plans of operation up to and including the first landing have been authorized and the preparations for the operation are now actually going on. This situation was accepted by all members of your conference on Monday, June 18th.

2. There is reason to believe that the operation for the occupation of Japan following the landing may be a very long, costly and arduous struggle on our part. The terrain, much of which I have visited several times, has left the impression on my memory of being one which would be susceptible to a last ditch defense such as has been made on Iwo Jima and Okinawa and which of course is very much larger than either of those two areas. According to my recollection it will be much more unfavorable with regard to tank maneuvering than either the Philippines or Germany.

3. If we once land on one of the main islands and begin a forceful occupation of Japan, we shall probably have cast the die of last ditch resistance. The Japanese are highly patriotic and certainly susceptible to calls for fanatical resistance to repel an invasion. Once started in actual invasion, we shall in my opinion have to go through with an even more bitter finish fight than in Germany. We shall incur the losses incident to such a war and we shall have to leave the Japanese islands even more thoroughly destroyed than was the case with Germany. This would be due both to the difference in the Japanese and German personal character and the differences in the size and character of the terrain through which the operations will take place.

4. A question then comes: Is there any alternative to such a forceful occupation of Japan which will secure for us the equivalent of an unconditional surrender of her forces and a permanent destruction of her power again to strike an aggressive blow at the "peace of the Pacific"? I am inclined to think that there is enough such chance to make it well

worthwhile our giving them a warning of what is to come and a definite opportunity to capitulate. As above suggested, it should be tried before the actual forceful occupation of the homeland islands is begun and furthermore the warning should be given in ample time to permit a national reaction to set in.

We have the following enormously favourable factors our side—factors much weightier than those we had against Germany:

Japan has no allies.

Her navy is nearly destroyed and she is vulnerable to a surface and underwater blockade which can deprive her of sufficient food and supplies for her population.

She is terribly vulnerable to our concentrated air attack upon her crowded cities, industrial and food resources.

She has against her not only the Anglo-American forces but the rising forces of China and the ominous threat of Russia.

We have inexhaustible and untouched industrial resources to bring to bear against her diminishing potential.

We have great moral superiority through being the victim of her first sneak attack.

The problem is to translate these advantages into prompt and economical achievement of our objectives. I believe Japan is susceptible to reason in such a crisis to a much greater extent than is indicated by our current press and other current comment. Japan is not a nation composed wholly of mad fanatics of an entirely different mentality from ours. On the contrary, she has within the past century shown herself to possess extremely intelligent people, capable in an unprecedentedly short time of adopting not only the complicated technique of Occidental civilization but to a substantial extent their culture and their political and social ideas. Her advance in all these respects during the short period of sixty or seventy years has been one of the most astounding feats of national progress in history—a leap from the isolated feudalism of centuries into the position of one of the six or seven great powers of the world. She has not only built up powerful armies and navies. She has maintained an honest and effective national finance and respected position in many of the sciences in which we pride ourselves. Prior to the forcible seizure of power over her government by the fanatical military group in 1931, she had for ten years lived a reasonably responsible and respectable international life.

My own opinion is in her favor on the two points involved in this question.

a. I think the Japanese nation has the mental intelligence and versatile capacity in such a crisis to recognize the folly of a fight to the finish and to accept the proffer of what will amount to an unconditional surrender; and

b. I think she has within her population enough liberal leaders (although now submerged by the terrorists) to be depended upon for her reconstruction as a responsible member of the family of nations. I think she is better in this last respect than Germany was. Her liberals yielded only at the point of the pistol and, so far as I am aware, their liberal attitude has not been personally subverted in the way which was so general in Germany.

On the other hand, I think that the attempt to exterminate her armies and her population by gunfire or other means will tend to produce a fusion of race solidity and antipathy which had no analogy in the case of Germany. We have a national interest in creating, if possible, a condition wherein the Japanese nation may live as a peaceful and useful member of the future Pacific community.

5. It is therefore my conclusion that a carefully timed warning be given to Japan by the chief representatives of the United States, Great Britain, China and, if then a belligerent, Russia, calling upon Japan to surrender and permit the occupation of her country in order to insure its complete demilitarization for the sake of the future peace.

This warning should contain the following elements:

The varied and overwhelming character of the force we are about to bring to bear on the islands.

The inevitability and completeness of the destruction which the full application of this force will entail.

The determination of the allies to destroy permanently all authority and influence of those who have deceived and misled the country into embarking on world conquest.

The determination of the allies to limit Japanese sovereignty to her main islands and to render them powerless to mount and support another war.

The disavowal of any attempt to extirpate the Japanese as a race or to destroy them as a nation.

A statement of our readiness, once her economy is purged of its militaristic influences, to permit the Japanese to maintain such industries, particularly of a light consumer character, as offer no threat of aggression against their neighbors, but which can produce a sustaining economy, and provide a reasonable standard of living. The statement should indicate our willingness, for this purpose, to give Japan trade access to external raw materials, but no longer any control over, the sources of supply outside her main islands. It should also indicate our willingness, in accordance with our now established foreign trade policy, in due course to enter into mutually advantageous trade relations with her.

The withdrawal from their country as soon as the above objectives of the allies are accomplished, and as soon as there has been established a peacefully inclined government, of a character representative of the masses of the Japanese people. I personally think that if in saying this we should add that we do not exclude a constitutional monarchy under her present dynasty, it would substantially add to the chances of acceptance.

6. Success of course will depend on the potency of the warning which we give her. She has an extremely sensitive national pride and, as we are now seeing every day, when actually locked with the enemy will fight to the very death. For that reason the warning must be tendered before the actual invasion has occurred and while the impending destruction, though clear beyond peradventure, has not yet reduced her, to fanatical despair. If Russia is a part of the threat, the Russian attack, if actual, must not have progressed too far. Our own bombing should be confined to military objectives as far as possible.

Sources: Diary entry: *Henry L. Stimson Diaries*, Reel 9, Yale University Library, New Haven; memo to Truman: U.S. Department of State, *Foreign Relations of the United States: Conference of Berlin (The Potsdam Conference), 1945* (Washington, D.C.: U.S. Government Printing Office, 1960), 1:888–892.

A34. STIMSON DIARY ENTRY, JULY 3, 1945

. . . I then finished up what was left unfinished the day before in respect to S-1. That was the question of what the President should do to Stalin at this coming conference, and I finally summed it up informally that he should look sharp and if he found that he thought that Stalin was on good enough terms with him, he should shoot off at him what we had arranged. . . . In other words, simply telling him that we were busy with this thing working like the dickens and we knew he was busy with this thing and working like the dickens, and that we are pretty nearly ready and we intended to use it against the enemy, Japan; that if it was satisfactory we proposed to then talk it over with Stalin afterwards, with the purpose of having it make the world peaceful and safe rather than to destroy civilization. If he pressed for details and facts, Truman was simply to tell him that we were not yet prepared to give them. The President listened attentively and then said he understood and he thought that was the best way to do it.

Source: *Henry L. Stimson Diaries*, Reel 9, Yale University Library, New Haven.

A35. TRUMAN DIARY ENTRY, JULY 16, 1945

. . . Then we went on to Berlin and saw absolute ruin. Hitler's folly. He overreached himself by trying to take in too much territory. He had no morals and his people backed him up. Never did I see more sorrowful sight, nor witness retribution to the nth degree.

The most sorrowful part of the situation is the deluded Hitlerian populace. Of course the Russians have kidnapped the able-bodies and I suppose have made involuntary workmen of them. They have also looted every house left standing and have sent the loot to Russia. But Hitler did the same thing to them.

It is the Golden Rule in reverse—and it is not an uplifting sight. What a pity that the human animal is not able to put his moral thinking into practice! . . .

. . . I hope for some sort of peace, but I fear that machines are ahead of morals by some centuries and when morals catch up perhaps there'll be no reason for any of it.

I hope not. But we are only termites on a planet and may be when we bore too deeply into the planet there'll [be] a reckoning. Who knows?

Source: Robert H. Ferrell, ed., *Harry S. Truman and the Bomb: A Documentary Collection* (Worland, Wyo.: High Plains, 1996), 11–13.

A36. TRUMAN DIARY ENTRIES, JULY 17, 18, AND 25, 1945

July 17

Just spent a couple of hours with Stalin. . . . Promptly a few minutes before twelve I looked up from the desk and there stood Stalin in the doorway. I got to my feet and advanced to meet him. He put out his hand and smiled. I did the same, we shook, I greeted Molotov and the interpreter, and we sat down. After the usual polite remarks we got down to business. I told Stalin that I am no diplomat but usually said yes and no to questions after hearing all the argument. It pleased him. I asked him if he had the agenda for the meeting. He said he had and had some more questions to present. I told him to fire away. He did and it is dynamite—but I have some dynamite too which I am not exploding now. He wants to fire Franco, to which I wouldn't object, and divide up the Italian colonies and other mandates, some no doubt that the British have. Then he got on the Chinese situation, told us what agreements had been reached and what was in abeyance. Most of the big points are settled. He'll be in the Jap war on August 15. Fini Japs when that comes about. We had lunch, talked socially, put on a real show, drinking toasts to everyone. Then had pictures made in the back yard. I can deal with Stalin. He is honest, but smart as hell.

July 18

. . . Discussed Manhattan (it is a success). Decided to tell Stalin about it. Stalin had told P.M. of telegram from Jap emperor asking for peace. Stalin also read his answer to me. It was satisfactory. Believe Japs will fold up before Russia comes in. I am sure they will when Manhattan appears over their homeland. I shall inform Stalin about it at an opportune time.

Stalin's luncheon was a most satisfactory meeting. I invited him to come to the U.S. Told him I'd send the battleship *Missouri* for him if he'd come. He said he wanted to cooperate with U.S. in peace as we had cooperated in war, but it would be harder. Said he was grossly misunderstood in U.S. and I was misunderstood in Russia. I told him that we each could help to remedy that situation in our home countries and that I intended to try with all I had to do my part at home. He gave me a most cordial smile and said he would do as much in Russia.

We then went to the conference and it was my job to present the ministers' proposed agenda. There were three proposals and I banged them through in short order, much to the surprise of Mr. Churchill. Stalin was very much pleased. Churchill was too, after he had recovered. I'm not going to stay around this terrible place all summer just to listen to speeches. I'll go home to the Senate for that.

July 25

We met at 11 A.M. today. That is Stalin, Churchill and the U.S. President. But I had a most important session with Lord Mountbatten & General Marshall before that. We have discovered the most terrible bomb in the history of the world. It may be the fire destruction prophesied in the Euphrates Valley Era, after Noah and his fabulous Ark.

Anyway we "think" we have found the way to cause a disintegration of the atom. An experiment in the New Mexican desert was startling—to put it mildly. Thirteen pounds of the explosive caused the complete disintegration of a steel tower 60 feet high, created a crater 6 feet deep and 1,200 feet in diameter, knocked over a steel tower 1/2 mile away and knocked men down 10,000 yards away. The explosion was visible for more than 200 miles and audible for 40 miles and more.

This weapon is to be used against Japan between now and August 10th. I have told the Sec. of War, Mr. Stimson, to use it so that military objectives and soldiers and sailors are the target and not women and children. Even if the Japs are savages, ruthless, merciless and fanatic, we as the leader of the world for the common welfare cannot drop this terrible bomb on the old capital or the new.

He & I are in accord. The target will be a purely military one and we will issue a warning statement asking the Japs to surrender and save lives. I'm sure they will not do that, but we will have given them the chance. It is certainly a good thing for the world that Hitler's crowd or Stalin's did not discover this atomic bomb. It seems to be the most terrible thing ever discovered, but it can be made the most useful.

At 10:15 I had Gen. Marshall come in and discuss with me the tactical and political situation. . . .

At the Conference Poland and the Bolsheviki land grab came up. Russia helped herself to a slice of Poland and gave Poland a nice slice of Germany, taking also a good slice of East Prussia for herself, Poland has moved in up to the Oder and the west Neisse, taking Stettin and Silesia as a fact accomplished. My position is that, according to commitments made at Yalta by my predecessor, Germany was to be divided into four occupation zones, one each for Britain, Russia and France and the U.S. If Russia chooses to allow Poland to occupy a part of her zone I am agreeable but title to territory cannot and will not be settled here. For the fourth time I restated my position and explained that territorial cessions had to be made by treaty and ratified by the Senate. . . .

Sources: July 17 and 18: Robert H. Ferrell, ed., *Harry S. Truman and the Bomb: A Documentary Collection* (Worland, Wyo.: High Plains, 1996), 29–31; July 25: *Off the Record: The Private Papers of Harry S. Truman*, ed. Robert H. Ferrell (New York: Harper & Row, 1980), 55–56.

A37. ATOMIC BOMB TEST: REPORT BY ERNEST O. LAWRENCE, JULY 16, 1945

TOP SECRET . . . JULY 16, 1945

Our group assembled at a point 27 miles from the bomb site about two in the moring. . . .

I decided the best place to view the flame would be through the window of the car I was sitting in, which would take out ultraviolet, but at the last minute decided to get out of the car (evidence indeed I was excited!) and just as I put my foot on the ground I was enveloped with a warm brilliant yellow white light—from darkness to brilliant sunshine in an instant and as I remember I momentarily was stunned by the surprise. It took me a second thought to tell myself, "this is indeed it!!" and then through my dark sun glasses there was a gigantic ball of fire rising rapidly from the earth—at first as brilliant as the sun, growing less brilliant as it grew boiling and swirling into the heavens. Ten or fifteen thousand feet above the ground it was orange in color and I judge a mile in diameter. At higher levels it became purple and this purple afterglow persisted for what seemed a long time (possibly it was only for a minute or two) at an elevation of 20–25,000 feet. This purple glow was due to the enormous radioactivity of the gases. . . .

In the earlier stages of rise of the flame the clouds above were illuminated and as the flame rose it was a grand spectacle also to see the great clouds immediately above melt away before our eyes.

The final phase was the column of hot gases smoke and dust funneling from the earth into the heavens to 40,000 feet. The column was to me surprisingly narrow until high elevations were reached when it foamed out considerably. The great funnel was visible a long time. We could still make it out as we drove away a half hour later.

But to retrace, a little over two minutes after the beginning of the flash the shock wave hit us. It was a sharp loud crack and then for about a minute thereafter there were resounding echoes from the surrounding mountains. The pressure of the shock wave was not great enough to be disturbing but the noise was very loud and sharp, indeed. . . .

A number of observers near me were looking right at the explosion through welders goggles (or the same dark glass) and they told me the light through these glasses was so bright as to blind them for an instant. . . .

The grand, indeed almost cataclysmic proportion of the explosion produced a kind of solemnity in everyones [sic] behavior immediately afterwards. There was restrained applause, but more a hushed murmuring bordering on reverence in manner as the event was commented upon. . . .

As far as all of us are concerned although we knew the fundamentals were sound and that the explosion could be produced, we share a feeling that we have this day crossed a great milestone in human progress.

Source: U.S. Department of State, *Foreign Relations of the United States: The Conference of Berlin (The Potsdam Conference), 1945* (Washington, D.C.: U.S. Government Printing Office, 1960), 2:1369–1370.

A38. MET LAB PETITION, JULY 17, 1945

A Petition to the President of the United States

Discoveries of which the people of the United States are not aware may affect the welfare of this nation in the near future. The liberation of atomic power which has been achieved places atomic bombs in the hands of the Army. It places in your hands, as Commander-in-Chief, the fateful decision whether or not to sanction the use of such bombs in the present phase of the war against Japan.

We, the undersigned scientists, have been working in the field of atomic power. Until recently we have had to fear that the United States might be attacked by atomic bombs during this war and that her only defense might lie in a counterattack by the same means. Today, with the defeat of Germany, this danger is averted and we feel impelled to say what follows:

The war has to be brought speedily to a successful conclusion and attacks by atomic bombs may very well be an effective method of warfare. We feel, however, that such attacks on Japan could not be justified, at least not unless the terms which will be imposed after the war on Japan were made public in detail and Japan were given an opportunity to surrender.

If such public announcement gave assurance to the Japanese that they could look forward to a life devoted to peaceful pursuits in their homeland and if Japan still refused to surrender our nation might then, in certain circumstances, find itself forced to resort to the use of atomic bombs. Such a step, however, ought not to be made at any time without seriously considering the moral responsibilities which are involved.

The development of atomic power will provide the nations with new means of destruction. The atomic bombs at our disposal represent only the first step in this direction, and there is almost no limit to the destructive power which will become available in the course of their future development. Thus a nation which sets the precedent of using these newly liberated forces of nature for purposes of destruction may have to bear the responsibility of opening the door to an era of devastation on an unimaginable scale.

If after this war a situation is allowed to develop in the world which permits rival powers to be in uncontrolled possession of these new means of destruction, the cities of the United States as well as the cities of other nations will be in continuous danger of sudden annihilation. All the resources of the United States, moral and material, may have to be mobilized to prevent the advent of such a world situation. Its prevention is at present the solemn responsibility of the United States—singled out by virtue of her lead in the field of atomic power.

The added material strength which this lead gives to the United States brings with it the obligation of restraint and if we were to violate this obligation our moral position would be weakened in the eyes of the world and in our own eyes. It would then be more difficult for us to live up to our responsibility of bringing the unloosened forces of destruction under control.

In view of the foregoing, we, the undersigned, respectfully petition: first, that you exercise your power as Commander-in-Chief, to rule that the United States shall not resort to the use of atomic bombs in this war unless the terms which will be imposed upon Japan have been made public in detail and Japan knowing these terms has refused to surrender; second, that in such an event the question whether or not to use atomic bombs be decided by you in the light of the considerations presented in this petition as well as all the other moral responsibilities which are involved.

Source: Dennis Merrill, ed., *Documentary History of the Truman Presidency* (Washington, D.C.: University Publications of America, 1995), 1:219.

A39. GROVES REPORT TO STIMSON ON THE ATOMIC BOMB, JULY 18, 1945

THE COMMANDING GENERAL, MANHATTAN DISTRICT PROJECT (GROVES) TO THE SECRETARY OF WAR (STIMSON) . . .

SUBJECT: THE TEST.

1. This is not a concise, formal military report but an attempt to recite what I would have told you if you had been here on my return from New Mexico.

2. At 0530, 16 July 1945, in a remote section of the Alamogordo Air Base, New Mexico, the first full scale test was made of the implosion type atomic fission bomb. For the first time in history there was a nuclear explosion. And what an explosion! . . . The bomb was not dropped from an airplane but was exploded on a platform on top of a 100-foot high steel tower.

3. The test was successful beyond the most optimistic expectations of anyone. Based on the data which it has been possible to work up to date, I estimate the energy generated to be in excess of the equivalent of 15,000 to 20,000 tons of TNT; and this is a conservative estimate. Data based on measurements which we have not yet been able to reconcile would make the energy release several times the conservative figure. There were tremendous blast effects. For a brief period there was a lighting effect within a radius of 20 miles equal to several suns in midday; a huge ball of fire was formed which lasted for several seconds. This ball mushroomed and rose to a height of over ten thousand feet before it

dimmed. The light from the explosion was seen clearly at Albuquerque, Santa Fe, Silver City, El Paso and other points generally to about 180 miles away. The sound was heard to the same distance in a few instances but generally to about 100 miles. Only a few windows were broken although one was some 125 miles away. A massive cloud was formed which surged and billowed upward with tremendous power, reaching the substratosphere at an elevation of 41,000 feet, 36,000 feet above the ground, in about five minutes, breaking without interruption through a temperature inversion at 17,000 feet which most of the scientists thought would stop it. Two supplementary explosions occurred in the cloud shortly after the main explosion. The cloud contained several thousand tons of dust picked up from the ground and a considerable amount of iron in the gaseous form. Our present thought is that this iron ignited when it mixed with the oxygen in the air to cause these supplementary explosions. Huge concentrations of highly radioactive materials resulted from the fission and were contained in this cloud.

4. A crater from which all vegetation had vanished, with a diameter of 1200 feet and a slight slope toward the center, was formed. In the center was a shallow bowl 130 feet in diameter and 6 feet in depth. The material within the crater was deeply pulverized dirt. The material within the outer circle is greenish and can be distinctly seen from as much as 5 miles away. The steel from the tower was evaporated. 1500 feet away there was a four-inch iron pipe 18 feet high set in concrete and strongly guyed. It disappeared completely.

5. One-half mile from the explosion there was a massive steel test cylinder weighing 220 tons. The base of the cylinder was solidly encased in concrete. Surrounding the cylinder was a strong steel tower 70 feet high, firmly anchored to concrete foundations. This tower is comparable to a steel building bay that would be found in typical 15 or 20 story skyscraper or in warehouse construction. Forty tons of steel were used to fabricate the tower which was 70 feet high, the height of a six story building. The cross bracing was much stronger than that normally used in ordinary steel construction. The absence of the solid walls of a building gave the blast a much less effective surface to push against. The blast tore the tower from its foundations, twisted it, ripped it apart and left it flat on the ground. The effects on the tower indicate that, at that distance, unshielded permanent steel and masonry buildings would have been destroyed. I no longer consider the Pentagon a safe shelter from such a bomb. Enclosed are a sketch showing the tower before the explosion and the telephotograph showing what it looked like afterward. None of us expected it to be damaged.

6. The cloud traveled to a great height first in the form of a ball, then mushroomed, then changed into a long trailing chimney-shaped column and finally was sent in several directions by the variable winds at the different elevations. It deposited its dust and radioactive materials over a wide area. It was followed and monitored by medical doctors and scientists with instruments to check its radioactive effects. While here and there the activity on the ground was fairly high, at no place did it reach a concentration which required evacuation of the population. Radioactive material in small quantities was located as much as 120 miles away. The measurements are being continued in order to have adequate data with which to protect the Government's interests in case of future claims. For a few hours I was none too comfortable about the situation. . . .

Source: Michael B. Stoff, Jonathan F. Fanton, and R. Hal Williams, eds., *The Manhattan Project: A Documentary Introduction to the Atomic Age* (New York: McGraw-Hill, 1991), 188–193.

A40. STIMSON DIARY ENTRY, JULY 19, 1945

. . . Later in the afternoon . . . McCloy, Bundy, and I had a long and interesting discussion on our relations with Russia; what the cause of the constant differences between the countries are, and how to avoid them. As a result, I dictated a memorandum. . . . It boiled down to the possibility of getting the Russians to see that the real basis for evil was the absence of freedom of speech in their regime, and the iron-bound rule of the OGPU. I have been very impressed with the atmosphere of repression that exists everywhere, and which is felt by all who come in contact with the Russians in Germany. . . .

. . . At the same time it is becoming more and more evident to me that a nation whose system rests upon free speech and all the elements of freedom, as does ours, cannot be sure of getting on permanently with a nation where speech is strictly controlled and where the Government uses the iron hand of the secret police. The question is very important just now, and the development of S-1 is bringing it to a focus. I am beginning to feel that our Committee which met in Washington on this subject and was so set upon opening communications with the Russians on the subject may have been thinking in a vacuum. . . .

Source: *Henry L. Stimson Diaries*, Reel 9, Yale University Library, New Haven.

A41. STIMSON MEMORANDUM ON RELATIONS WITH THE SOVIET UNION, JULY 19, 1945

MEMORANDUM BY THE SECRETARY OF WAR (STIMSON)

REFLECTIONS ON THE BASIC PROBLEMS WHICH CONFRONT US

1. With each International Conference that passes and, in fact, with each month that passes between conferences, it becomes clearer that the great basic problem of the future is the stability of the relations of the Western democracies with Russia.

2. With each such time that passes it also becomes clear that that problem arises out of the fundamental differences between a nation of free thought, free speech, free elections, in fact, a really free people with a nation which is not basically free but which is systematically controlled from above by Secret Police and in which free speech is not permitted.

3. It also becomes clear that no permanently safe international relations can be established between two such fundamentally different national systems. With the best of efforts we cannot understand each other. Furthermore, in an autocratically controlled system, policy cannot be permanent. It is tied up with the life of one man. . . .

6. The great problem ahead is how to deal with this basic difference which exists as a flaw in our desired accord. I believe we must not accept the present situation as permanent for the result will then almost inevitably be a new war and the destruction of our civilization. I believe we should direct our thoughts constantly to the time and method of attacking the basic difficulty and the means we may have in hand to produce results. That something can be accomplished is not an idle dream. Stalin has shown an indication of his appreciation of our system of freedom by his proposal of a free constitution to be established among the Soviets. To read this Constitution would lead one to believe that Russia had in mind the establishing of free speech, free assembly, free press and the other essential elements of our Bill of Rights and would not have forever resting upon every citizen the stifling hand of autocracy. He has thus given us an opening. . . .

7. The foregoing has a vital bearing upon the control of the vast and revolutionary discovery of X which is now confronting us. . . . After careful reflection I am of the belief that *no* world organization containing as one of its dominant members a nation whose people are not possessed of free speech but whose governmental action is controlled by the autocratic machinery of a secret political police, cannot [can] give effective control of this new agency with its devastating possibilities.

I therefore believe, that before we share our new discovery with Russia we should consider carefully whether we can do so safely under any system of control until Russia puts into effective action the proposed constitution which I have mentioned. . . .

Source: U.S. Department of State, *Foreign Relations of the United States: The Conference of Berlin (The Potsdam Conference), 1945* (Washington, D.C.: U.S. Government Printing Office, 1960), 2:1155–1157.

A42. STIMSON DIARY NOTES, JULY 22, 1945

Called on President Truman at nine twenty. The foregoing day I had left with him my paper on reflections as to our relations with Russia. . . . I also discussed with him Harrison's two messages [regarding when an atomic bomb would be ready and target cites]. He was intensely pleased by the accelerated timetable. As to the matter of the special target [Kyoto] which I had refused to permit, he strongly confirmed my view, and said he felt the same way.

At ten forty Bundy and I again went to the British headquarters and talked to the Prime Minister and Lord Cherwell for over an hour. Churchill read Groves' report in full. He told me that he had noticed at the meeting of the three yesterday, Truman was evidently much fortified by something that had happened, and that he stood up to the Russians in a most emphatic and decisive manner, telling them as to certain demands that they absolutely could not have, and that the United States was entirely against them. Churchill said he now understood how this pepping up had taken place and that he felt the same way. His own attitude confirmed this admission. He now not only was not worried about giving the Russians information of matter, but was rather inclined to use it as an argument in our favour in the negotiations. The sentiment of the four of us was unanimous in thinking that it was advisable to tell the Russians at least that we were working on that subject, and intended to use it when and if it was successfully finished. . . .

Source: Michael B. Stoff, Jonathan F. Fanton, and R. Hal Williams, eds., *The Manhattan Project: A Documentary Introduction to the Atomic Age* (New York: McGraw-Hill, 1991), 204–208.

A43. W. B. SHOCKLEY MEMORANDUM TO EDWARD L. BOWLES ON ESTIMATED CASUALTIES IN AN INVASION OF JAPAN, JULY 21, 1945

MEMORANDUM FOR: DR. EDWARD L. BOWLES.

SUBJECTS: PROPOSALS FOR INCREASING THE SCOPE OF CASUALTY STUDIES.

Recently, as you know, I have been trying to gather and organize information bearing on the problem of casualties in the Pacific War. It seems to me most important that the facts relating to this question be surveyed thoroughly and coordinated into a single well integrated picture. Such a study should be available for consideration in connection with the total casualties to be expected in the Japanese war, the rate at which land invasion should be pushed ahead in Japan or held back while attrition by air and blockade proceeds, and the relative apportionment of effort between the Army Air Forces and the Army Ground Forces and within each Force. The reason why a study of casualties would have such diverse applications is that the big cost to the nation in this war will be dead and disabled Americans. Consequently, in evaluating one plan or another, the expected casualties should be estimated as accurately as possible. It appears to me that at present adequate studies of the casualty problem are not being made.

The most basic problem in the Japanese war is the establishment of what is necessary to cause Japan to capitulate. There is a very important historical study which can be made in this connection but apparently has never been made either in the War Department or outside. The object of the study is to determine to what extent the behavior of a nation in a war can be predicted from the behavior of her troops in individual battles. If the study shows that the behavior of nations in all historical cases comparable to Japan's has in fact been invariably consistent with the behavior of the troops in battle, then it means that the Japanese dead and ineffectives at the time of defeat will exceed the corresponding number for the Germans. In other words,we shall probably have to kill at least 5 to 10 million Japanese. This might cost us between 1.7 and 4 million casualties including 400,000 to 800,000 killed.

However, as I mentioned, the historical study referred to above has not been made. I have discussed it with Colonel MacCormack of MIS and also with Professor Quincy Wright of the University of Chicago. Professor Wright has directed a large number of studies on the history of war during the past 20 years and in 1942 published "A Study of War" in two volumes. I discussed this problem with Professor Wright about two weeks ago and he is unacquainted with any such study. He feels, however, that such a study has considerable promise of enabling better predictions to be made as to the course of the war and the reactions of Japan. I do not want to give the impression that such a study would furnish a complete guide to the future of the war, but merely that it would illuminate the situation from a new and unexplored angle and might well affect our conclusions in an important way.

In addition to the study mentioned above concerning the breaking point of the nation, studies are needed on the casualty ratios between Japanese and U.S. troops in battle. Some studies along these lines have already been carried out in G-2 and more are in progress. At present the studies break a number of campaigns down into casualties by day of the campaign. One interesting finding of these studies is that the ratio between the Jap killed and U.S. killed is much more consistent between the one campaign and another when the landing phase and mopping up phases are eliminated. This consistency applies only to the Pacific campaigns studied, these being quite different from the Southwest Pacific campaigns. The following Table summarizes these findings:

Campaign	Ratio of Jap Killed to U.S. Killed	
	Entire Campaign	*Middle Third (a)*
Saipan	8 (b)	11
Guam	9 (b)	10
Iwo Jima	4 (b)	8
Okinawa	14.5 (c)	11
Leyte	22 (b)	39
Luzon	22 (b)	25

(a) This corresponds to the interval between the time when one-third of the Japs are killed and the time when two-thirds are killed. Values are based on data collected by G-2.
(b) Values from "Health," pg. 15, 31 May 1945.
(c) Based on data collected by G-2.

These values suggest that in areas where the tactical situation resembles that met in the first four campaigns listed, the major part of the campaign will be fought with a ratio of about 10 Japs killed for every U.S. killed.

It would be worthwhile, in my opinion, to extend these casualty studies of the various campaigns so as to correlate them with information regarding the cause of our casualties (i.e. whether by rifle, machine gun, mortar, etc.) and with our ammunition expenditures.

In particular, every effort should be made to establish definitely the reason for the marked difference between the values for the Southwest Pacific and the others.

So far as I can make out, there are severe organizational difficulties in the War Department to making integrated studies. In exploring the possibilities, I have found some data and studies in each of the following: Surgeon General's Office, Army Ground Forces G-1 and G-2. It is, for example, the function of G-2 to study Japanese casualties but except in the case of a special request such as I made for information on casualty ratios, they do not deal with U.S. casualties. Similarly it is not the function of any of the groups mentioned to correlate the casualties with ammunition expenditures. What is needed apparently is some sort of an organization set up at a suitably high level with informal contacts with all parts of the War Department which can contribute to the problem. This organization, which might, in fact, merely be a committee from the interested sections, could then assign projects in such a way as to end with an integrated picture where now there are uncorrelated studies.

To summarize, it appears to me that two specific recommendations may be in order:

1. A historical study of defeated nations should be undertaken and an attempt made to relate the behavior of the nation to the behavior of her troops. Professor Wright has indicated a willingness to guide such a study and has suggested certain former students whom he believes capable of carrying out the details. At my request, Professor Wright plans to prepare an outline which we could use as a basis for setting up such a project.

2. A suitable agency for carrying out integrated casualty studies should be formed so as to combine and supplement the studies presently being made.

W. E. Shockley,
Expert Consultant, Office of the Secretary of War

Source: Edward R. Bowles Papers, Box 34, Library of Congress.

A44. TRUMAN LETTERS TO BESS TRUMAN, JULY 18 AND 20, 1945

[July 18]

Dear Bess:

The first session was yesterday in one of the Kaiser's palaces. . . .

It makes presiding over the Senate seem tame. The boys say I gave them an earful. I hope so. Admiral Leahy said he'd never seen an abler job and Byrnes and my fellows seemed to be walking on air. I was so scared I didn't know whether things were going according to Hoyle or not. Anyway a start has been made and I've gotten what I came for — Stalin goes to war August 15 with no strings on it. He wanted a Chinese settlement [treaty with China giving territorial and other concessions to the USSR] — and it is practically made — in a better form than I expected. Soong did better than I asked him. I'll say that we'll end the war a year sooner now, and think of the kids who won't be killed! That is the important thing. . . .

[July 20]

Dear Bess:

We had a tough meeting yesterday. I reared up on my hind legs and told 'em where to get off and they got off. I have to make it perfectly plain to them at least once a day that so far as this President is concerned Santa Claus is dead and that my first interest is U.S.A., then I want the Jap War won and I want 'em both in it. Then I want peace—world peace and will do what can be done by us to get it. But certainly am not going to set up another [illegible] here in Europe, pay reparations, feed the world, and get nothing for it but a nose thumbing. They are beginning to awake to the fact that I mean business. . . .

Source: *Dear Bess: The Letters from Harry to Bess Truman, 1910–1959*, ed. Robert H. Ferrell (New York: Norton, 1983), 519–520.

A45. THE POTSDAM DECLARATION, JULY 26, 1945

Proclamation by the Heads of Governments,
United States, China, United Kingdom

(1) We, the President of the United States, the President of the National Government of the Republic of China and the Prime Minister of Great Britain, representing the hundreds of millions of our countrymen, have conferred and agree that Japan shall be given an opportunity to end this war.

(2) The prodigious land, sea and air forces of the United States, the British Empire and of China, many times reinforced by their armies and air fleets from the west, are poised to strike the final blows upon Japan. This military power is sustained and inspired by the determination of all the Allied nations to prosecute the war against Japan until she ceases to resist.

(3) The result of the futile and senseless German resistance to the might of the aroused free peoples of the world stands forth in awful clarity as an example to the people of Japan. The might that now converges on Japan is immeasurably greater than that which, when applied to the resisting Nazis, necessarily laid waste to the lands, the industry and the method of life of the whole German people. The full application of our military power, backed by our resolve, will mean the inevitable and complete destruction of the Japanese armed forces and just as inevitably the utter devastation of the Japanese homeland.

(4) The time has come for Japan to decide whether she will continue to be controlled by those self-willed militaristic advisers whose unintelligent calculations have brought the Empire of Japan to the threshold of annihilation, or whether she will follow the path of reason.

(5) Following are our terms. We will not deviate from them. There are no alternatives. We shall brook no delay.

(6) There must be eliminated for all time the authority and influence of those who have deceived and misled the people of Japan into embarking on world conquest, for we insist that a new order of peace, security and justice will be impossible until irresponsible militarism is driven from the world.

(7) Until such a new order is established and until there is convincing proof that Japan's war-making power is destroyed, points in Japanese territory to be designated by the Allies shall be occupied to secure the achievement of the basic objectives we are here setting forth.

(8) The terms of the Cairo Declaration shall be carried out and Japanese sovereignty shall be limited to the islands of Honshu, Hokkaido, Kyushu, Shikoku and such minor islands as we determine.

(9) The Japanese military forces, after being completely disarmed, shall be permitted to return to their homes with the opportunity to lead peaceful and productive lives.

(10) We do not intend that the Japanese shall be enslaved as a race or destroyed as a nation, but stern justice shall be meted out to all war criminals, including those who have visited cruelties upon our prisoners. The Japanese government shall remove all obstacles to the revival and strengthening of democratic tendencies among the Japanese people. Freedom of speech, of religion, and of thought, as well as respect for the fundamental human rights shall be established.

(11) Japan shall be permitted to maintain such industries as will sustain her economy and permit the exaction of just reparations in war. To this end, access to, as distinguished from control of raw materials shall be permitted. Eventual Japanese participation in world trade relations shall be permitted.

(12) The occupying forces of the Allies shall be withdrawn from Japan as soon as these objectives have been accomplished and there has been established in accordance with the freely expressed will of the Japanese people a peacefully inclined and responsible government.

(13) We call upon the Government of Japan to proclaim now the unconditional surrender of all the Japanese armed forces, and to provide proper and adequate assurances of their good faith in such action. The alternative for Japan is prompt and utter destruction.

Source: U.S. Department of State, *Foreign Relations of the United States: The Conference of Berlin (The Potsdam Conference), 1945* (Washington, D.C.: U.S. Government Printing Office, 1960), 2:1474–1476.

A46. FORRESTAL DIARY ENTRY REGARDING BYRNES, JULY 28, 1945

. . . Talked with Byrnes [now at Potsdam as American Secretary of State, having succeeded Mr. Stettinius on the conclusion of the San Francisco Conference]. . . .

Byrnes said he was most anxious to get the Japanese affair over with before the Russians got in, with particular reference to Dairen and Port Arthur. Once in there, he felt, it would not be easy to get them out. . . .

Source: *The Forrestal Diaries*, ed. Walter Millis (New York: Viking, 1951), 78–79.

A47. STIMSON MEMO TO TRUMAN AND TRUMAN'S RESPONSE, JULY 30, 1945

URGENT

FROM: AGWAR WASHINGTON

TO: TRIPARTITE CONFERENCE BABELSBERG, GERMANY

NO: WAR 41011 30 JULY 1945.

To the President from the Secretary of War.
The time schedule on Groves' project is progressing so rapidly that it is now essential that statement for release by you be available not later than Wednesday, 1 August. I have revised draft of statement, which I previously presented to you in light of
(A) Your recent ultimatum
(B) Dramatic results of test and
(C) Certain minor suggestions made by British of which Byrnes is aware.

While I am planning to send a copy by special courier tomorrow in the hope you can be reached, nevertheless in the event he does not reach you in time, I will appreciate having your authority to have White House release revised statement as soon as necessary. Sorry circumstances seem to require this emergency action.

Truman's Response

SEC WAR

Reply to your 41011 suggestions approved. Release when ready but not sooner than August 2.

HST

Source: Dennis Merrill, ed., *Documentary History of the Truman Presidency* (Washington, D.C.: University Publications of America, 1995), 1:174–175.

A48. TRUMAN LETTER TO BESS TRUMAN, JULY 31, 1945

Dear Bess:

It was surely good to talk with you this morning at 7 A.M. It is hard to think that it is 11 P.M. yesterday where you are. The connection was not so good this morning on account of the storms over the Atlantic.

We have been going great guns the last day or two and while the Conference was at a standstill because of Uncle Joe's indisposition, the able Mr. Byrnes, Molotov, Attlee, and Bevin all worked and accomplished a great deal. I rather think Mr. Stalin is stallin' because he is not so happy over the English elections. He doesn't know it but I have an ace in the hole and another one showing—so unless he has threes or two pair (and I know he has not) we are sitting all right.

The whole difficulty is reparations. Of course the Russians are naturally looters and they have been thoroly [*sic*] looted by the Germans over and over again and you can hardly blame them for their attitude. The thing I have to watch is to keep our skirts clean and make no commitments.

The Poles are the other headache. They have moved into East Prussia and to the Oder in Prussia and unless we are willing to go to war again they can stay and they will stay with Bolsheviki backing—so you see in comes old man reparations again and a completely German looted Poland.

Byrnes, Leahy and I have worked out a program I think to fit a bad situation. We should reach a tentative agreement in the Big Three this afternoon and final one tomorrow and be on the way Thursday and surely not later than Friday. . . .

Source: Dennis Merrill, ed., *Documentary History of the Truman Presidency* (Washington, D.C.: University Publications of America, 1995), 1:180.

A49. THE CATHOLIC WORLD ON UNCONDITIONAL SURRENDER, AUGUST 1945

Why Prolong the War Against Japan?

The war between the United States and Germany was won many months before May, 1945. Perhaps it was won as early as the autumn of 1942 when a strong American army was landed in French North Africa. In any case it was won in the summer of 1944 when the defeat of German armor in France and the retreat to the Rhine Valley outflanked the bases of the robot bombs, those last desperate weapons which reeling Germany launched at the main base of her Western enemies.

Why then was the war prolonged?

It was apparently prolonged from political considerations. Was such a prolongation justified, especially in view of the number of American lives lost from the autumn of 1944 to the early summer of 1945? The prolongation of the war . . . was seemingly the result of two decisions. One of them was the adamant policy of announcing no terms, however harsh, under which Germany might surrender. The other was the issuance of official statements regarding the de-industrialization of Germany or the reduction of Germany to the status of an agricultural society. . . .

All this might be considered water under the bridge except for the fact that the war with Japan is already long past its North Africa stage and is fast approaching, if it is not already in, its Rhine Valley stage. . . .

Japan is at our mercy. The question now is, shall our diplomatic management of the war again cost us heavy casualties—perhaps a half million or even a million men? If we promise the Japanese a fate worse than any other fate which they can visualize, they will fight on. . . . We will, as with Germany, lose lives accordingly. We will expend our fighting men and all future Americans who might descend from them. We will also by our terror from the sky—which will unavoidably kill many women and children—intensify to new extremes of horror the Japanese treatment of our citizens whom they hold prisoner.

Let us assume then that an announced determination to ruin Japan will cost us a million additional casualties and the cruel elimination of all those Americans now in Japanese hands. Before we pay such a price in our best blood, let us see what we are paying for. . . .

Source: The Catholic World, August 1945, 421–422.

A50. PRESIDENT TRUMAN'S STATEMENT ON THE BOMBING OF HIROSHIMA, AUGUST 6, 1945

Sixteen hours ago an American airplane dropped one bomb on Hiroshima, an important Japanese Army base. That bomb had more power than 20,000 tons of T.N.T. It had more than two thousand times the blast power of the British "Grand Slam," which is the largest bomb ever yet used in the history of warfare.

The Japanese began the war from the air at Pearl Harbor. They have been repaid many fold. And the end is not yet. With this bomb we have now added a new and revolutionary increase in destruction to supplement the growing power of our armed forces. In their present form these bombs are now in production and even more powerful forms are in development.

It is an atomic bomb. It is a harnessing of the basic power of the universe. The force from which the sun draws its power has been loosed against those who brought war to the Far East.

Before 1939, it was the accepted belief of scientists that it was theoretically possible to release atomic energy. But no one knew any practical method of doing it. By 1942, however, we knew that the Germans were working feverishly to find a way to add atomic energy to the other engines of war with which they hoped to enslave the world. But they failed. We may be grateful to Providence that the Germans got the V-1's and the V-2's late and in limited quantities and even more grateful that they did not get the atomic bomb at all.

The battle of the laboratories held fateful risks for us as well as the battles of the air, land and sea, and we have now won the battle of the laboratories as we have won the other battles.

Beginning in 1940, before Pearl Harbor, scientific knowledge useful in war was pooled between the United States and Great Britain, and many priceless helps to our victories have come from that arrangement. Under that general policy the research on the atomic bomb was begun. With American and British scientists working together we entered the race of discovery against the Germans.

The United States had available the large number of scientists of distinction in the many needed areas of knowledge. It had the tremendous industrial and financial resources necessary for the project and they could be devoted to it without undue impairment of other vital war work. In the United States the laboratory work and the production plants, on which a substantial start had already been made, would be out of reach of enemy bombing, while at that time Britain was exposed to constant air attack and was still threatened with the possibility of invasion. For these reasons Prime Minister Churchill and President Roosevelt agreed that it was wise to carry on the project here. We now have two great plants and many lesser works devoted to the production of atomic power. Employment during the peak construction numbered 125,000 and over 65,000 individuals are even now engaged in operating the plants. Many have worked there for two and a half years. Few know what they have been producing. They see great quantities of material going in and they see nothing coming out of these plants, for the physical size of the explosive charge is exceedingly small. We have spent two billion dollars on the greatest scientific gamble in history—and won.

But the greatest marvel is not the size of the enterprise, its secrecy, nor its cost, but the achievement of scientific brains in putting together infinitely complex pieces of knowledge held by many men in different fields of science into a workable plan. And hardly less marvelous had been the capacity of industry to design, and of labor to operate, the machines and methods to do things never done before so that the brain child of many minds came forth in physical shape and performed as it was supposed to do. Both science and industry worked under the direction of the United States Army, which achieved a unique success in managing so diverse a problem in the advancement of knowledge in an amazingly short time. It is doubtful if such another combination could be got together in the world. What has been done is the greatest achievement of organized science in history. It was done under high pressure and without failure.

We are now prepared to obliterate more rapidly and completely every productive enterprise the Japanese have above ground in any city. We shall destroy their docks, their factories, and their communications. Let there be no mistake; we shall completely destroy Japan's power to make war.

It was to spare the Japanese people from utter destruction that the ultimatum [of] July 26 was issued at Potsdam. Their leaders promptly rejected that ultimatum. If they do not now accept our terms they may expect a rain of ruin from the air, the like of which has never been seen on this earth. Behind this air attack will follow sea and land forces in such numbers and power as they have not yet seen and with the fighting skill of which they are already aware.

The Secretary of War, who has kept in personal touch with all phases of the project, will immediately make public a statement giving further details.

His statement will give facts concerning the sites at Oak Ridge near Knoxville, Tennessee, and at Richland near Pasco, Washington, and an installation near Santa Fe, New Mexico. Although the workers at the sites have been making materials to be used in producing the greatest destructive force in history they have not themselves been in danger beyond that of many other occupations, for the utmost care has been taken, of their safety.

The fact that we can release atomic energy ushers in a new era in man's understanding of nature's forces. Atomic energy may in the future supplement the power that now comes from coal, oil, and falling water, but at present it cannot be produced on a basis to compete with them commercially. Before that comes there must be a long period of intensive research.

It has never been the habit of the scientists of this country or the policy of this Government to withhold from the world scientific knowledge. Normally, therefore, everything about the work with atomic energy would be made public.

But under present circumstances it is not intended to divulge the technical processes of production or all the military applications, pending further examination of possible methods of protecting us and the rest of the world from the danger of sudden destruction.

I shall recommend that the Congress of the United States consider promptly the establishment of an appropriate commission to control the production and use of atomic power within the United States. I shall give further consideration and make further recommendations to the Congress as to how atomic power can become a powerful and forceful influence towards the maintenance of world peace.

Source: U.S. Department of State, Foreign Relations of the United States: 1945: The British Commonwealth—The Far East (Washington, D.C.: U.S. Government Printing Office, 1969), 6:621–624.

A51. LEAFLETS DROPPED ON JAPANESE CITIES AFTER HIROSHIMA

To the Japanese people:

America asks that you take immediate heed of what we say on this leaflet.

We are in possession of the most destructive explosive ever devised by man. A single one of our newly developed atomic bombs is actually the equivalent in explosive power to what two thousand of our giant B-29's can carry on a single mission. This awful fact is one for you to ponder and we solemnly assure you it is grimly accurate.

We have just begun to use this weapon against your homeland. If you still have any doubt, make inquiry as to what happened to Hiroshima when just one atomic bomb fell on that city.

Before using this bomb to destroy every resource of the military by which they are pro-longing this useless war, we ask that you now petition the emperor to end the war. Our president has outlined for you the thirteen consequences of an honorable surrender. We urge that you accept these consequences and begin the work of building a new, better, and peace-loving Japan.

You should take steps now to cease military resistance. Otherwise, we shall resolutely employ this bomb and all our other superior weapons to promptly and forcefully end the war.

EVACUATE YOUR CITIES.

Attention Japanese people. EVACUATE YOUR CITIES.

Because your military leaders have rejected the thirteen-part surrender declaration, two momentous events have occurred in the last few days.

The Soviet Union, because of this rejection on the part of the military, has notified your Ambassador Sato that it has declared war on your nation. Thus, all powerful coun-tries of the world are now at war against you.

Also because of your leaders' refusal to accept the surrender declaration that would en-able Japan to honorably end this useless war, we have employed our atomic bomb.

A single one of our newly developed atomic bombs is actually the equivalent in ex-plosive power to what two thousand of our giant B-29's could have carried on a single mis-sion. Radio Tokyo has told you that with the first use of this weapon of total destruction, Hiroshima was virtually destroyed.

Before we use this bomb again and again to destroy every resource of the military by which they are prolonging this useless war, petition the emperor now to end the war. Our president has outlined for you the thirteen consequences of an honorable surrender. We urge that you accept these consequences and begin the work of building a new, better, and peace-loving Japan.

Act at once or we shall resolutely employ this bomb and all our other superior weapons to promptly and forcefully end the war.

EVACUATE YOUR CITIES.

Source: Robert H. Ferrell, ed., *Harry S. Truman and the Bomb: A Documentary Collection* (Worland, Wyo.: High Plains, 1996), 63–65.

A52. TRUMAN LETTER TO SENATOR RICHARD B. RUSSELL,
AUGUST 9, 1945

Dear Dick:

I read your telegram of August seventh with a lot of interest.

I know that Japan is a terribly cruel and uncivilized nation in warfare but I can't bring myself to believe that, because they are beasts, we should ourselves act in the same manner.

For myself, I certainly regret the necessity of wiping out whole populations because of the "pigheadedness" of the leaders of a nation and, for your information, I am not going to do it unless it is absolutely necessary. It is my opinion that after the Russians enter into war the Japanese will very shortly fold up.

My object is to save as many American lives as possible but I also have a humane feeling for the women and children in Japan.

Sincerely yours,
Harry S. Truman

Source: Dennis Merrill, ed., *Documentary History of the Truman Presidency* (Washington, D.C.: University Publications of America, 1995), 1:210.

A53. STIMSON DIARY ENTRY, AUGUST 9, 1945

When I reached the office this morning I found that the affirmative news for the press conference was so light that Surles thought we had better call the conference off and simply have me make a direct statement on the effect of the success of the atomic bomb on the future size of the Army. It seems as if everybody in the country was getting impatient to get his or her particular soldier out of the Army and to upset the carefully arranged system of points for retirement which we have arranged with the approval of the Army itself. The success of the first atomic bomb and the news of the Russians entry into the war which came yesterday has rather doubled this crusade. Every industry wishes to get its particular quota of men back and nearly all citizens join in demanding somebody to dig coal for the coming winter. The effect on the morale of the Army is very ticklish. We have instituted a merit system and if, instead of following the fair standards which they proposed in the interest of the men who had served longest and in the most difficult and dangerous circumstances, we now discharge men on the basis of our own needs instead of theirs, there is likely to be trouble. I could see in my recent trip to Europe what a difficult task at best it will be to keep in existence a contented army of occupation and, if mingled with the inevitable difficulties there is a sense of grievance against the unfairness of the government, the situation may become bad. Consequently the paper that we drew last night and continued today was a ticklish one. The bomb and the entrance of the Russians into the war will certainly have an effect on hastening the victory. But just how much that effect is on how long and how many men we will have to keep to accomplish that victory, it is impossible yet to determine. . . .

After that meeting was over I conferred with Byrnes in an adjoining room. . . . The difficult thing is to get negotiators together and I urged very strongly on Byrnes that he should make it as easy as possible for the Japanese.

We had news this morning of another successful atomic bomb being dropped on Nagasaki. These two heavy blows have fallen in quick succession upon the Japanese and there will be quite a little space before we intend to drop another. During that time I hope something may be done in negotiating a surrender. I have done the best I could to promote that in my talks with the President and with Byrnes and I think they are both in full sympathy with the aim. . . .

Source: Henry L. Stimson Diaries, Reel 9, Yale University Library, New Haven.

A54. STIMSON DIARY ENTRY, AUGUST 10, 1945

Today was momentous. We had all packed up and the car was waiting to take us to the airport where we were headed for our vacation when word came from Colonel McCarthy at the Department that the Japanese had made an offer to surrender. Furthermore they had announced it in the clear. That busted our holiday for the present and I raced down to the office, getting there before half past eight. There I read the messages. Japan accepted the Potsdam list of terms put out by the President "with the understanding that the said declaration does not comprise any demand which prejudices the prerogatives of his majesty as a sovereign ruler." It is curious that this was the very single point that I feared would make trouble. When the Potsdam conditions were drawn and left my office where they originated, they contained a provision which permitted the continuance of the dynasty with certain conditions. The President and Byrnes struck that out. They were not obdurate on it but thought they could arrange it in the necessary secret negotiations which would take place after any armistice. There has been a good deal of uninformed agitation against the Emperor in this country mostly by people who know no more about Japan than has been given them by Gilbert and Sullivan's "Mikado," and I found today that curiously enough it had gotten deeply embedded in the minds of influential people in the State Department. Harry Hopkins is a strong anti-Emperor man in spite of his usual good sense and so are Archibald MacLeish and Dean Acheson—three very extraordinary men to take such a position.

As soon as I got to the Department I called up Connolly at the White House and notified him that I was not going away and would be standing by if he wanted me. Not more that ten minutes afterwards they called back to say that the President would like me to come right over, so I hurried around there and joined in the conference consisting of the President, Byrnes, Forrestal, Admiral Leahy, and the President's aides. Byrnes was troubled and anxious to find out whether we could accept this in the light of some of the public statements by Roosevelt and Truman. Of course during three years of a bitter war there have been bitter statements made about the Emperor. Now they come to plague us. Admiral Leahy took a good plain horse-sense position that the question of the Emperor was a minor matter compared with delaying a victory in the war which was now in our hands.

The President then asked me what my opinion was and I told him that I thought that even if the question hadn't been raised by the Japanese we would have to continue the Emperor ourselves under our command and supervision in order to get into surrender the many scattered armies of the Japanese who would owe no other authority and that something like this use of the Emperor must be made in order to save us from a score of bloody Iwo Jimas and Okinawas all over China and the New Netherlands. He was the only source of authority in Japan under the Japanese theory of the State. I also suggested that something like an armistice over the settlement of the question was inevitable and that it would be a humane thing and the thing that might effect the settlement if we stopped the bombing during that time—stopped it immediately. My last suggestion was rejected on the ground that it couldn't be done at once because we had not yet received in official form the Japanese surrender, having nothing but the interception to give it to us, and that so far as were concerned the war was still going on. This of course was a correct but narrow reason, for the Japanese had broadcast their offer of surrender through every country in the world. After considerable discussion we adjourned to await the arrival of the final notice.

When we adjourned Byrnes and I went into another room to discuss the form of the paper and I told him the desire of Marshall to have one of the conditions of our negotiations with Japan [be] the surrender of the American prisoners in their hands to some accessible place where we could send planes to get them. By this time the news was out and the howling mob was in front of the White House, access to which by the public was blockaded on Pennsylvania Avenue.

I drove back to the Department and entered into conference with Marshall and McCloy who had just returned from his overseas trip while I was at the White House. Bundy, Lovett, and Harrison and I were together and I later called in Colonel Van Slyck who had written the intelligent article I had shown the President the other day on the form of a surrender; and also General Weckerling of G-2 who has not been quite so intelligent on this matter as he might be, together with Mr. Robert A. Kinney and Mr. William R. Braisted who are acting as Japanese experts for the G-2 people. We started in accordance with a request that Byrnes had made of me at our talk on the drafting of the whole terms of surrender including the answer to the Present Japanese offer. On the latter I found for once that McCloy was rather divergent from me. He was intrigued with the idea that this was the opportunity to force upon Japan through the Emperor a progress of free speech, etc. and all the elements of American free government. I regarded this as unreal and said that the thing to do was to get this surrender through as quickly as we can before Russia, who has begun invading Manchuria, should get down in reach of the Japanese homeland. I felt it was of great importance to get the homeland into our hands before the Russians could put in any substantial claim to occupy and help rule it. After all this discussion I called Byrnes on the telephone and discussed the matter with him. He told me he had drafted the answer to the Japanese notice and that he would like me to see it. So I sent over Kyle to the Department and got it. While a compromise, it was much nearer my position than McCloy's and after a while McCloy agreed that it was good enough from his standpoint. I thought it was a pretty wise and careful statement and stood a better chance of being accepted than a more outspoken one. It asserted that the action of the Emperor must be dominated by the Allied Commander, using the singular in the order to exclude any condominium such as we have in Poland. He had asked me in the morning who was the commander that had been agreed upon among our forces and I told him I thought it was MacArthur although there had been quite an issue between the Army and the Navy to have a dual command, MacArthur and Nimitz. . . .

During the morning Forrestal had called me up for the purpose of telling me he was heart and soul with me in regard to the proposition of shutting off attack and saving life during the time we discussed this. He told me that they were planning another big attack by Halsey and he was afraid this would go on. As a matter of fact, at the present time it is under order to go on.

After a fifteen or twenty minutes delay, which is unusual in this Administration, the President and Byrnes came in from a conference which had been going on in the other room and the President announced to the Cabinet that we had received official notice from Japan through the intermediary, Sweden, and that Byrnes had drawn a reply to it of which they thought they could get an acceptance from Great Britain, China, and perhaps Russia, with all of whom they were communicating. The paper was in the exact form that Byrnes had read as over the telephone and which I told him I approved.

After the Cabinet Byrnes had another talk with me and he asked me if we in the War Department could draft the follow-up papers to effectuate the terms of the surrender. I told him that if he wanted me to I would start McCloy on it at once and get it ready as soon as possible. He was very grateful.

When I got back to the Department I found McCloy had been working on it all the time we were at Cabinet and with the aid of the draft which had been started by the Staff some time before, he had the papers pretty nearly ready. He read them to me and Marshall and then undertook to perfect them and get them ready for tomorrow morning when I will go over them again and get them off to the State Department.

This has been a pretty heavy day. . . .

Source: Henry L. Stimson Diaries, Reel 9, Yale University Library, New Haven.

A55. HENRY A. WALLACE DIARY ENTRY, AUGUST 10, 1945

Truman said he had given orders to stop atomic bombing. He said the thought of wiping out another 100,000 people was too horrible. He didn't like the idea of killing, as he said, "all those kids." Referring to hard and soft terms for Japan, Truman referred to telegrams precipitated by the peace rumor of August 9. 153 of the 170 were for hard terms—unconditional surrender. They were freewill telegrams—not inspired—and were mostly from parents of servicemen.

Source: Michael B. Stoff, Jonathan F. Fanton, and R. Hal Williams, eds., The Manhattan Project: A Documentary Introduction to the Atomic Age (New York: McGraw-Hill, 1991), 245.

A56. THE CHRISTIAN CENTURY ON THE BOMBING OF HIROSHIMA, AUGUST 29, 1945

America's Atomic Atrocity

Something like a moral earthquake has followed the dropping of atomic bombs on two Japanese cities. Its continued tremors throughout the world have diverted attention even from the military victory itself. . . . It is our belief that the use made of the atomic bomb has placed our nation in an indefensible moral position.

We do not propose to debate the issue of military necessity, though the facts are clearly on one side of this issue. The atomic bomb was used at a time when Japan's navy was sunk, her air force virtually destroyed, her homeland surrounded, her supplies cut off, and our forces poised for the final stroke. Recognition of her imminent defeat could be read between the lines of every Japanese communiqué. Neither do we intend to challenge Mr. Churchill's highly speculative assertion that the use of the bomb saved the lives of more than one million American and 250,000 British soldiers. We believe, however, that these lives could have been saved had our government followed a different course, more honorable and more humane. . . .

Perhaps it was inevitable that the bomb would ultimately be employed to bring Japan to the point of surrender. . . . But there was no military advantage in hurling the bomb upon Japan without warning. The least we might have done was to announce to our foe that we possessed the atomic bomb; that its destructive power was beyond anything known in warfare; and that its terrible effectiveness had been experimentally demonstrated this country. We could thus have warned Japan of what was in store for her unless she surrender immediately. If she doubted the good faith of our representations it would have been a simple matter to select a demonstration target in the enemy's own country at a place where the loss of human life would be at a minimum. . . .

Source: *The Christian Century* LXII (August 29, 1945), 974–976.

B.

American Military Documents

B1. J.C.S. 924/2, AUGUST 30, 1944: OPERATIONS AGAINST JAPAN SUBSEQUENT TO FORMOSA. REPORT BY THE JOINT STRATEGIC SURVEY COMMITTEE

The Problem

1. To submit recommendations to The Joint Chiefs of Staff for the guidance of planning agencies for future operations in the war against Japan.

Discussion

2. The Joint Strategic Survey Committee views with some concern the present trend of thought on the planning level concerning future operations in the war against Japan incident to the recent change in our Over-all Objective, now stated in J.C.S. 924 as follows:

"To force the unconditional surrender of Japan by

1. Lowering Japanese ability and will to resist by establishing sea and air blockades, conducting intensive air bombardment, and destroying Japanese air and naval strength.

2. Invading "and seizing objectives in the industrial heart of Japan. . . ."

4. There is general agreement that we must take all manner of short cuts made possible by developments in the situation to bring the war against Japan to an early conclusion. It is unacceptable, however, to do this at unjustifiable cost in American lives.

5. The over-all enemy situation has shown a continuing deterioration in naval, shipping, and air strength. On the other hand the strength of enemy land forces not only remains untouched—it has greatly increased during the course of the war. Our great superiority over the Japanese rests on our capacity to produce and to employ, more effectively and in overwhelming strength, machines of war—primarily naval vessels and aircraft. Enemy strength rests in his land forces, some 3,500,000 strong. In our Saipan operation it cost approximately one American killed and several wounded to exterminate seven Japanese soldiers. On this basis it might cost us half a million American lives and many times that number in wounded to exterminate the Japanese ground forces that conceivably could be employed against us in the home islands. . . .

Source: CCS 381 Pacific Ocean Area Operations (6–10–43) Sec 7, RG 218, NARA.

B2. MARSHALL MEMORANDUM TO GENERAL EMBICK, SEPTEMBER 1, 1944

I have been studying your Joint Strategic Survey Committee report (JCS 924/2) regarding the policy to be followed towards the final defeat of Japan. There are certain phases of the matter pertaining to the views of your Committee regarding which I am not at all clear and I wish you would give me your views. . . .

The Japanese are concentrating their strength on Formosa. Extending your illustration taken from the Saipan operation to Formosa, we may, based on estimated Japanese strength on February 15, 1945, expect to suffer approximately 90,000 casualties in taking that island. This approximates our total U.S. ground forces casualties in France during the first two and a half months of the present campaign. . . .

Source: *The Papers of George Catlett Marshall*, ed. Larry Bland (Baltimore: Johns Hopkins University Press, 1996), 4:567–568.

B3. SUMMARY OF REDEPLOYMENT FORECAST, MARCH 14, 1945

Foreword

The purpose of this report is to summarize information pertinent to plans for redeployment of the United States Army after the fall of Germany (assumed herein to occur on 1 June 1945. . . .

27. *Replacements for Battle Casualties*—The estimated average rate of replacements required for dead and evacuated wounded during the 18 months of the redeployment period is approximately 40,000 per month. . . .

Source: Summary of Redeployment Forecast, March 14, 1945. Demobilization Branch, Plans and Operations Division, Army Service Forces, call no. N8864. Combined Arms Research Library (CARL), Fort Leavenworth, Kansas.

B4. J.C.S. 924/15, APRIL 25, 1945: OPERATIONS AGAINST JAPAN SUBSEQUENT TO FORMOSA. REPORT BY THE JOINT STAFF PLANNERS

1. The over-all strategic concept for the prosecution of the war includes provision to "bring about at the earliest possible date the unconditional surrender of Japan. . . ."

4. WAR AIMS. From the Cairo Declaration and other statements of broad policy it appears that the major war aims of the United States are:

a. The restoration of the territories specified in the Cairo Declaration.

b. The creation of conditions which will insure that Japan will not again become a menace to the peace and security of the world.

c. The eventual emergence of a government in Japan which will respect the rights of other states and Japan's international obligations.

5. The agreed strategy and national policy is that the accomplishment of these aims is to be brought about by unconditional surrender. The statement of the over-all objective implies that unconditional surrender can be forced, and that invasion of the industrial heart of Japan will be decisive. It is by no means certain, however, that "unconditional surrender" can be brought about by any means. What can be accomplished is decisive military defeat and the results equivalent to unconditional surrender, similar to the present situation in Germany. In no case to date in this war have organized Japanese units surrendered. The concept of "unconditional surrender" is foreign to the Japanese nature. Therefore, "unconditional surrender" should be defined in terms understandable to the Japanese, who must be convinced that destruction or national suicide is not implied. This could be done by the announcement on a governmental level of a "declaration of intentions" which would tell the Japanese what their future holds. Once convinced of the inevitability of defeat, it is possible that a government could be formed in Japan that would sign and could enforce a surrender instrument.

6. Unless a definition of unconditional surrender can be given which is acceptable to the Japanese, there is no alternative to annihilation and no prospect that the threat of absolute defeat will bring about capitulation. The accomplishment of the unconditional surrender objectives then must be entirely brought about by force of arms.

7. A campaign of bombardment and blockade would aim at bringing about capitulation of Japan by seizing additional positions in order to isolate the home islands and by destruction and threat of virtual annihilation. This strategy does not provide assurance that it will lead to unconditional surrender or defeat. It is a strategy of limited aim and may bring about a negotiated peace falling short of complete fulfillment of our war aims. Should encirclement fail to bring about capitulation, it then would be difficult, costly, and time consuming to disengage forces to mount for invasion.

A campaign of invasion strikes directly at the heart of the empire and expectation would be that if the threat in itself did not cause capitulation, the continuation of the campaign through the full stages of invasion would result in unconditional surrender or absolute defeat. Prior defeat of Japan in the home islands would also establish the greatest possibility that other empire forces would capitulate, and in any event make their defeat easier to accomplish. The reverse would not be true.

Therefore, the invasion of Japan is considered the most suitable strategy to accomplish unconditional surrender or ultimate defeat. . . .

10. Studies and estimates by joint agencies also have shown that we should have available in the Pacific by December 1945, sufficient forces and resources to initiate an Invasion campaign *on* the scale of OLYMPIC-CORONET (36 divisions and 1,532,000 men, total). . . .

13. CASUALTIES. It is possible only to generalize as to the expected casualty rates. Average casualty rate per thousand per day for operations in Guadalcanal, New Georgia, Leyte, Attu, Marshalls, Marianas, and Palau, all of which were amphibious assaults, were:

Killed in action	1.78
Wounded in action	5.50
Missing in action	0.17
Total	7.45

Average casualty rates for protracted land warfare in the European Theater of Operations are:

Killed in action	0.36
Wounded in action	1.74
Missing in action	0.06
Total	2.16

Naval casualties can be expected to vary directly with the number of amphibious operations involved and with the length of the campaign, as the naval forces available for either strategy will be approximately the same.

From these figures it is concluded that we should: (1) limit the number of separate assault operations; and (2) direct them toward land campaigns, in decisive areas. These conclusions further support the strategy of invasion at the earliest date. . . .

Source: CCS 381 Pacific Ocean Area Operations (6–10–43) Section 11, Box 686, RG 218, NARA.

B5. J.I.C. 191/7, MAY 16, 1945:

JAPANESE REACTION TO AN OPERATION AGAINST SOUTHERN KYUSHU

Statement of the Problem

1. To estimate Japanese capabilities and reaction to an assault on southern Kyushu about November 1, 1945.

Assumptions

2. a. We have consolidated our present positions in the Philippines, Ryukyus and Bonin.

b. The U.S.S.R. has entered the war against Japan simultaneously with or shortly before the Kyushu assault.

Discussion and Conclusions

3. *General.* The Japanese appreciate that from our present positions we will have the capability of major attack against China or Japan . . .

The Japanese know that successful Allied lodgement in Kyushu would result in effective interdiction of communications against Kyushu, Honshu, Shikoku, and the Continent. Therefore, the Japanese will use all available ground, sea, and air forces to resist a landing on Kyushu and will defend desperately to prevent Allied consolidation on the island.

4. *Ground.* . . . We estimate that at the time of Allied assault, 6 divisions plus 2 depot divisions plus army troops, making a total of 390,000 men, would be employed on ·Kyushu. . . .

5. *Air.* . . . We estimate that by 1 November 1945 the Japanese air forces will have a maximum total strength of 2,300 combat aircraft in tactical units. In addition there may be some 1,200 combat type aircraft in operational training and between 1,500 and 2,000 specially equipped non-combat trainer type aircraft available for suicide missions. Enemy air reactions would be extremely aggressive and suicide air attacks would be employed on a lavish scale. . . .

6. *Naval.* . . . Battleships, cruisers, and destroyers which are still operational at the time would probably be organized into suicide task forces and would endeavor to sortie

in a desperate effort to oppose our landings. Submarines, midget-submarines, suicide and small surface craft would be employed in large numbers, but should offer no serious problems. Extensive minefields probably will be encountered. . . .

Source: Douglas J. MacEachin, *The Final Months of the War with Japan: Signals Intelligence, U.S. Invasion Planning, and the A-Bomb Decision* (Washington, D.C.: Center for the Study of Intelligence, 1998), Document 3.

B6. J.C.S. 1331/3: DIRECTIVE FOR OPERATION OLYMPIC, MAY 25, 1945

DIRECTIVE TO
COMMANDER IN CHIEF, U.S. ARMY FORCES, PACIFIC
COMMANDER IN CHIEF, U.S PACIFIC FLEET
COMMANDING GENERAL, TWENTIETH AIR FORCE

1. Pursuant to and in furtherance of directives WAR 62773 and WAR 62774 . . . the following directive is issued and is effective on receipt;

a. The Joint Chiefs of Staff direct the invasion of Kyushu (Operation OLYMPIC), target date 1 November 1945, in order to:

(1) Intensify the blockade and aerial bombardment of Japan,

(2) Contain and destroy the major enemy forces,

(3) Support further advances, for the purpose of establishing conditions favorable for the decisive invasion of the industrial heart of Japan. . . .

Source: Douglas J. MacEachin, *The Final Months of the War with Japan: Signals Intelligence, U.S. Invasion Planning, and the A-Bomb Decision* (Washington, D.C.: Center for the Study of Intelligence, 1998), Document 2.

B7. OPERATION DOWNFALL PLAN FOR THE INVASION OF
JAPAN, MAY 28, 1945

1. Directive

a. This Plan is formulated pursuant to directives contained in JCS 1259/4, 3 April 1945 and JCS radiogram WX 87938, 26 May 1945. It covers operations of United States Army and Naval Forces in the PACIFIC to force the unconditional surrender of JAPAN by invasion of the Japanese Archipelago.

b. The following over-all objective for the operations is assigned by the Joint Chiefs of Staff:

"To force the unconditional surrender of JAPAN by:

1. Lowering Japanese ability and will to resist by establishing sea and air blockades, conducting intensive air bombardments and destroying Japanese air and naval strength.

2. Invading and seizing objectives in the industrial heart of JAPAN. . . ."

2. Assumptions

a. *Hostile.* . . .

(1) That the Japanese will continue the war to the utmost extent of their capabilities and will prepare to defend the main islands of JAPAN with every means available to them. That operations in this area will be opposed not only by the available organized military forces of the Empire, but also by a fanatically hostile population.

(2) That approximately three (3) hostile divisions will be disposed in Southern KYUSHU and an additional three (3) in Northern KYUSHU at initiation of the OLYMPIC operation.

(3) That total hostile forces committed against KYUSHU operations will not exceed eight (8) to ten (10) divisions and that this level will be speedily attained.

(4) That approximately twenty-one (21) hostile divisions, including depot divisions, will be on HONSHU at initiation of that operation and that fourteen (14) of these divisions may be employed in the KANTO PLAIN area.

(5) That the enemy may withdraw his land-based air forces to the Asiatic Main land for protection from our neutralizing attacks. . . .

(6) That the attrition caused by our continued land-based and carrier-based air preparation and support, and by our destruction of aircraft manufacturing and maintenance facilities, will reduce the hostile capability for air action against our landings to suicide attacks of uncertain proportions at an early phase of the operations.

(7) That hostile fleet elements will be forced to withdraw to the YELLOW SEA or Western SEA OF JAPAN. That the enemy will maintain the capability of a suicide attack against KYUSHU landings with the approximate strength of a typical carrier task group. That his remaining submarines and large numbers of small suicide craft will oppose our landings and that mines will be used in large numbers.

(8) That hostile sea communications across the JAPAN SEA, while relatively unimpaired prior to KYUSHU landings, will be progressively and rapidly restricted to complete interdiction by the time air is operating from HONSHU.

(9) That during continuation of Russian neutrality, the production capacity of hostile industries and raw material sources in MANCHURIA, North CHINA and KOREA will remain relatively unimpaired.

(10) That hostile logistic position will permit determined defense in areas of projected operations by hostile ground forces enumerated in (3) and (4) above.

b. *Own Forces.*

(1) That the entire resources available to the Commander-in-Chief, United States Army Forces in the Pacific and the Commander-in-Chief, United States Pacific Fleet will be available for the support of these operations.

(2) That there will be no effective redeployment of major ground combat units from EUROPE in time for commitment prior to early 1946.

(3) That entry of RUSSIA into the war against JAPAN at some stage of the operations may be expected. . . .

3. Operations

a. *Concept*. . . .

This Plan of campaign visualizes attainment of the assigned objectives by two (2) successive operations, the first to advance our land-based air forces into Southern KYUSHU in order to support the second, a knock-out blow to the enemy's heart in the TOKYO area. The operations are continued and extended until such time as organized resistance in the Japanese Archipelago ceases.

Concept of the OLYMPIC operation visualizes entry into Southern KYUSHU by major joint overseas landing operations after intensive air preparation. . . .

These operations are expected to require fourteen (14) to seventeen (17) divisions with appropriate supporting troops, drawn from forces available in the PACIFIC with minimum use of redeployed elements. Forty (40) land-based air groups and naval elements for blockade and direct support are established for support of the CORONET operation. . . .

Source: OPD 350.5, Sec. 1, RG 165, NARA.

B8. J.W.P.C. 369/1, JUNE 15, 1945:
DETAILS OF THE CAMPAIGN AGAINST JAPAN

MEMORANDUM FOR THE PRESIDENT
SUBJECT: CAMPAIGN AGAINST JAPAN. . . .

1. *Strategy*. Throughout the series of staff conferences with the British, we have agreed that the over-all concept for the prosecution of the war included provision "to bring about at the earliest possible date the unconditional surrender of Japan." We believe that the only sure way, and certainly the quickest way to force the surrender of Japan is to defeat her armies on the main Japanese islands. . . .

The seizure of southern Kyushu has been directed because:

a. Its occupation is essential to, and will materially further, the isolation of Japan from Korea and the mainland of Asia;

b. It is the most logical extension of our operations in the Ryukyus, since shore-based tactical air support can be furnished from Okinawa and lines of communication are shorter than for any other practicable objective;

c. Airfields on which to base approximately 40 groups (over 2000 aircraft) can be developed, from which the air bombardment of the remainder of Japan can be greatly intensified in preparation for the Invasion of Honshu, should this prove to be necessary;

d. It will contribute toward the defeat of Japanese armies in the Japanese homeland;

e. It may well prove to be the decisive operation which will terminate the war.

7. *Casualties.* The cost in casualties of the main operations against Japan is not subject to accurate estimate. The scale of Japanese resistance in the past has not been predictable. Casualty expectancy rates based on experience in the Pacific vary greatly from the short bloody battle of Tarawa to the unopposed landing at Lingayen. It would be difficult to predict whether Jap resistance on Kyushu would more closely resemble the fighting on Okinawa or whether it would parallel the battle of Leyte.

Certain general conclusions can, however, be reached. The highest casualty rate occurs during the assault phase of an amphibious operation; casualties in land warfare are a function of the length of campaign and of the scale of opposition encountered. Naval casualties can be expected to vary directly with the number of amphibious operations involved and with the length of the campaign. Casualties can be kept to a minimum, then, by terminating the war at the earliest possible time by means of the fewest possible assault operations and by conducting land campaigns only in decisive areas. The presently planned campaign, which involves two assaults followed by land campaigns in the Japanese homeland, is in conformity with this principle. Further, the extent of the objective area gives us an opportunity to effect surprise as to the points of landing and, once ashore, to profit by our superiority in mobility and mechanized power through maneuver. Should it be decided to follow the southern Kyushu operation by another operation such as against northern Kyushu in order to exploit bombardment and blockade, and should this bring about capitulation of the Japanese, the casualties should be less than for the presently planned campaign. We consider that at this time it would be a pure gamble that the Japanese would admit defeat under such conditions. If they do not, invasion of the Tokyo Plain might still be required with resultant increased total casualties.

The best estimate of casualties for these possible sequences of operations follows. For the reasons stated above, it is admittedly only an "educated guess."

	Killed in Action	Wounded in Action	Missing in Action	Total
Southern Kyushu, followed by Tokyo Plain, to mid-1946	40,000	150,000	3,500	193,500
Southern Kyushu– Northwestern Kyushu	25,000	105,000	2,500	132,500
Southern Kyushu– Northwestern Kyushu–Tokyo Plain	46,000	170,000	4,000	220,000

8. *Time.* Under the campaign as planned, it is estimated that the defeat of the Japanese in the Tokyo Plain area and the seizure of Ports on Tokyo Plain would be completed

by mid-1946. Should it prove necessary to execute other operations prior to invading the Tokyo Plain, the earliest date by which the latter operation could take place is estimated to be October 1946. . . . In either case, the war should be over not later than the end of 1946. On the other hand, we are unable to estimate the time required or the losses that will result in an effort to defeat Japan by isolation, blockade and bombardment without invasion. . . .

Source: Douglas J. MacEachin, *The Final Months of the War with Japan: Signals Intelligence, U.S. Invasion Planning, and the A-Bomb Decision* (Washington, D.C.: Center for the Study of Intelligence, 1998), Document 5.

B9. J.C.S. 1388, JUNE 16, 1945: DETAILS OF THE CAMPAIGN AGAINST JAPAN. REPORT BY THE JOINT STAFF PLANNERS

. . . *Replace Paragraph 7, Pages 7 and 8, with following paragraph.*

7. *Casualties.* Our casualty experience in the Pacific war has been so diverse as to throw serious doubt on the validity of any quantitative estimate of casualties for future operations. The following data indicate results of experience.

Campaign	U.S. Casualties Killed, Wounded, Missing	Jap Casualties Killed and Prisoners (not including wounded)	Ratio U.S. to Jap
Leyte	17,000	78,000	1:4.6
Luzon	31,000	156,000	1:5.0
Iwo Jima	20,000	25,000	1:1.25
Okinawa	34,000 (Ground) 7,700 (Navy)	81,000 (not a complete count)	1:2
Normandy (1st 30 days)	42,000	—	—

The record of General MacArthur's operations from 1 March 1944 through 1 May 1945 shows 13,742 U.S. killed compared to 310,165 Japanese killed, or a ratio of 22 to 1.

The nature of the objective area in Kyushu gives maneuver room for land and sea operations. For these and other reasons it is probable that the cost in ground force casualties for the first 30 days of the Kyushu operation will be on the order of that for Luzon. . . .

Source: Douglas J. MacEachin, *The Final Months of the War with Japan: Signals Intelligence, U.S. Invasion Planning, and the A-Bomb Decision* (Washington, D.C.: Center for the Study of Intelligence, 1998), Document 6.

B10. MARSHALL-MACARTHUR CORRESPONDENCE, JUNE 16–19, 1945

16 JUNE 1945
TO: GHQ AFPAC (MACARTHUR)
FROM: WASHINGTON . . .

Request by 17 June (Washington) the estimate you are using for planning purposes of battle casualties in OLYMPIC up to D 90.
MARSHALL

G-1 17 JUNE 1945
FROM: CINCAFPAC
TO: WARCOS

Estimate of OLYMPIC battle casualties for planning purposes (C-19571) Reurad W-17477 as follows:

D to D/30: 50,800
D/30 to D/60: 27,150
D/60 to D/90: 27,100

The foregoing are estimated total battle casualties from which estimated return to duty numbers are deducted. Not included in the foregoing are non-battle casualties which are estimated at 4200 for each 30 day period.

URGENT
19 JUNE 1945
FROM: GENERAL MARSHALL
TO: GENERAL MACARTHUR (PERSONAL)
WAR 18528 19 JUNE

The President is very much concerned as to the number of casualties we will receive in the OLYMPIC operation. This will be discussed with the President about 3:30 PM today Washington time. Is the estimate given in your C-19571 of 50,800 for the period of D to D/30 based on plans for medical installations to be established or is it your best estimate of the casualties you anticipate from the operational viewpoint. Please rush answer.

19 JUNE 1945
FROM: GENERAL MACARTHUR
TO: GENERAL MARSHALL (PERSONAL)
C-19848

Estimate of casualties contained in my C-19571 was a routine report submitted direct by a staff section without higher reference for medical and replacement planning purposes. The estimate was derived from the casualty rates in Normandy and Okinawa the highest our forces have sustained as 3.8 men per thousand per day. The total force involved was estimated as 681,000 with one half engaged the first 15 days and the entire strength thereafter. The estimate is purely academic and routine and was made for planning alone. It had not come to my prior attention. I do not anticipate such a high rate of loss. I believe the operation presents less hazards of excessive loss than any other that has been suggested and that its decisive effect will eventually save lives by eliminating wasteful operations of a nondecisive character. I regard the operation as the most economical one in effort and lives that is possible. In this respect it must be remembered that the several preceding months will involve practically no losses in ground troops and that sooner or later a decisive ground attack must be made. The hazard and loss will be greatly lessened if an attack is launched from Siberia sufficiently ahead of our target date to commit the enemy to major combat. I most earnestly recommend no change in OLYMPIC. Additional subsidiary attacks will simply build up our final total casualties.

Source: RG 4, USAFPAC Papers, Box 17, Folder 4. "W.D. Messages, April–August 1945," MacArthur Archive.

B11. J.C.S. 1388/1: NIMITZ STAFF CASUALTY ESTIMATE, JUNE 18, 1945

18 JUNE 1945 . . .
OLYMPIC
NAVAL AND AMPHIBIOUS PHASES

1. The attached Joint Staff Study of the Naval and Amphibious Phases of the OLYMPIC operation is issued to facilitate planning and implementation both operational and logistic. . . .

5. *EVACUATION, HOPITALIZATION, PREVENTIVE, SANITARY, AND MEDICAL MEASURES*

a. Casualty Estimate. This estimate is based on the first 30 days of the operation. It is assumed that the facilities established to support the evacuation of these casualties will be sufficient for the remainder of the operation:

Service	Killed and Missing	Returned to Duty on Target or Ship	Evacuation Required	Total
Navy	2150	570	2280	5000
Marine	2400	3780	5820	12,000
Army	6400	10,080	15,520	32,000
Total	10,950	14,430	23,620	49,000

Source: RG 165, Entry 418, Box 1842, NARA.

B12. J.C.S. 1388/1, JUNE 20, 1945, AND J.C.S. 1388/2, JUNE 26, 1945

J.C.S. 1388/1

20 JUNE 1945. . . .

PROPOSED CHANGES TO DETAILS OF THE CAMPAIGN AGAINST JAPAN . . .
REFERENCE: J.C.S. 1388

Memorandum by the Commander in Chief, U.S. Fleet and Chief of Naval
Operations . . .

1. I consider J.C.S. 1388 satisfactory for purposes of discussion with the President, but
consider that it should be changed in certain respects, enumerated below, before it is
given to the President. . . .

3. Paragraph 7, page 7, on casualties is not satisfactory. Admiral Nimitz in his study of
OLYMPIC has estimated that there will be 49,000 casualties in the first thirty days. It appears to me that the Chiefs of Staff will have to give an estimate of the casualties expected
in the operation. As regards naval casualties I believe that a fair estimate is that they will
continue at approximately the same rate as they have occurred in the Okinawa operation.
The statement in paragraph 7 that the highest casualties occur during the assault phase
of the operations has not, of course, been borne out in the latest operations in the Pacific
where the Japanese have chosen not to defend the beaches. . . .

J.C.S 1388/2

26 JUNE 1945 . . .

Memorandum by the Chief of Staff, U.S. Army

. . . c. In view of the fact that casualties were discussed at the meeting on 18 June, it seems
unnecessary and undesirable for the Joint Chiefs of Staff to make estimates, which at best
can be only speculative, in this paper. However, pertinent portions of the minutes of the
18 June meeting, including the tabulation, might be included in paragraph 7 (page 7,
J.C.S. 1388) and the other points concerning casualties mentioned by Admiral King
should be cleared up. . . .

Source: 1388/1: Douglas J. MacEachin, *The Final Months of the War with Japan: Signals
Intelligence, U.S. Invasion Planning, and the A-Bomb Decision* (Washington, D.C.: Cen-
ter for the Study of Intelligence, 1998), Document 9; J.C.S. 1388/2: Microfilm, CARL
(Combined Army Research Library), Ft. Leavenworth, Kansas.

B13. C.C.S. 880/4, MEMORANDUM BY THE UNITED STATES
CHIEFS OF STAFF, JUNE 29, 1945

Development of Operations in the Pacific

1. In conformity with the over-all objective to bring about the unconditional surrender of Japan at the earliest possible date, the United States Chiefs of Staff have adopted the following concept on operations for the main effort in the Pacific:—

   a. From bases in Okinawa, Iwo Jima, Marianas, and the Philippines to intensify the blockade and air bombardment of Japan in order to create a situation favorable to:

   b. An assault on Kyushu for the purpose of further reducing Japanese capabilities by containing and destroying major enemy forces and further intensifying the blockade and air bombardment in order to establish a tactical condition favorable to:

   c. The decisive invasion of the industrial heart of Japan through the Tokyo Plain. . . .

3. In furtherance of the accomplishment of the over-all objectives, we have directed:—

   a. The invasion of Kyushu, target date 1 November 1945. . . .

4. Planning and preparation for the campaign in Japan subsequent to the invasion of Kyushu is continuing on the basis of meeting a target date of 1 March 1946 for the invasion of the Tokyo Plain. The planning is premised on the belief that the defeat of the enemy's armed forces in the Japanese homeland is a prerequisite to unconditional surrender, and that such a defeat will establish the optimum prospect of capitulation by Japanese forces outside the main Japanese islands. We recognize the possibility that our success in the main islands may not obviate the necessity of defeating the Japanese elsewhere. . . .

Source: U.S. Department of State, *Foreign Relations of the United States: The Conference of Berlin (The Potsdam Conference)* (Washington, D.C.: U.S. Government Printing Office, 1960), 1:910–911.

B14. GENERAL WECKERLING MEMORANDUM, JULY 13, 1945

MEMORANDUM FOR THE DEPUTY CHIEF OF STAFF
SUBJECT: Japanese Peace Offer

1. Recommend that the following be sent to the Chief of Staff as G-2 comments on Message 83 from Tokyo to Moscow, dated 12 July 1945.

   a. Weckerling believes there are a number of interesting deductions suggested by Message 893 [Togo's "Very Urgent" cable]:

(1) That the Emperor has personally intervened and brought his will to bear in favor of peace in spite of military opposition;

(2) That conservative groups close to the Throne, including some high ranking Army and Navy men, have triumphed over militaristic elements who favor prolonged desperate resistance;

(3) That the Japanese government clique is making a well coordinated united effort to stave off defeat believing (a) that Russian intervention can be bought by the proper price, and (b) that an attractive Japanese peace offer will appeal to war weariness in the United States.

(4) Of these, (1) is remote, (2) a possibility, and (3) quite probably the motivating force behind the Japanese moves. Mr. Grew agrees with these conclusions.

Source: Reel 109, item 2581, Marshall Library.

B15. C.C.S. 643/3, JULY 8, 1945:
ESTIMATE OF THE ENEMY SITUATION (AS OF 6 JULY 1945)

. . . We estimate that by late 1945 there will be available in the Japanese home islands and their outposts in the Ryukyus, Izu-Bonins, and Kuriles more than 35 active divisions and 14 depot divisions, which, plus army troops, will total over 2,000,000 men. The Japanese also will continue development of the "National Volunteer Army" and may form combat home defense units to supplement their regular armed forces. Fanatical resistance will be offered in the defense of any of the home islands. . . .

12. *Probable Political Strategy.* In general Japan will use all political means for avoiding complete defeat or unconditional surrender. During the next few months the future political strategy of the Government will exhibit the following aims: To,

a. Continue and even increase its attempts to secure complete political unity within the Empire, possibly through personal rule, real or apparent of the Emperor.

b. Attempt to foster a belief among Japan's enemies that the war will prove costly and long drawn out if the United Nations insist on fighting until the complete conquest of Japan.

c. Make desperate efforts to persuade the U.S.S.R. to continue her neutrality, if necessary by offering important territorial or other concessions, while at the same time making every effort to sow discord between the Americans and British on one side and the Russians on the other. As the situation deteriorates still further, Japan may even make a serious attempt to use the U.S.S.R. as a mediator in ending the war.

d. Put out intermittent peace feelers, in an effort to bring the war to an acceptable end, to weaken the determination of the United Nations to fight to the bitter end, or to create inter-Allied dissension. . . .

13. *Possibility of Surrender.* The Japanese ruling groups are aware of the desperate military situation and are increasingly desirous of a compromise peace, but still find uncon-

ditional surrender unacceptable. The basic policy of the present government is to fight as long and as desperately as possible in the hope of avoiding complete defeat and of acquiring a better bargaining position in a negotiated peace. Japanese leaders are now playing for time in the hope that Allied war weariness, Allied disunity, or some "miracle" will present an opportunity to arrange a compromise peace.

We believe that a considerable portion of the Japanese population now consider absolute military defeat to be probable. The increasing effects of sea blockade and cumulative devastation wrought by strategic bombing, which has already rendered millions homeless and has destroyed from 25 to 50 percent of the built-up area of Japan's most important cities, should make this realization increasingly general. An entry of the Soviet Union into the war would finally convince the Japanese of the inevitability of complete defeat. Although individual Japanese willingly sacrifice themselves in the service of the nation, we doubt that the nation as a whole is predisposed toward national suicide. Rather, the Japanese as a nation have a strong concept of national survival, regardless of the fate of individuals. They would probably prefer national survival, even through surrender, to virtual extinction.

The Japanese believe, however, that unconditional surrender would be the equivalent of national extinction. There are as yet no indications that the Japanese are ready to accept such terms. The ideas of foreign occupation of the Japanese homeland, foreign custody of the person of the Emperor, and the loss of prestige entailed by the acceptance of "unconditional surrender" are most revolting to the Japanese. To avoid these conditions, if possible, and, in any event, to insure survival of the institution of the Emperor, the Japanese might well be willing to withdraw from all the territory they have seized on the Asiatic continent and in the southern Pacific, and even to agree to the independence of Korea and to the practical disarmament of their military forces.

A conditional surrender by the Japanese Government along the lines stated above might be offered by them at any time from now until the time of the complete destruction of all Japanese power of resistance.

Since the Japanese Army is the principal repository of the Japanese military tradition it follows that the army leaders must, with a sufficient degree of unanimity, acknowledge defeat before Japan can be induced to surrender. This might be brought about either by the defeat of the main Japanese armies in the Inner Zone or through a desire on the part of the army leaders to salvage something from the wreck with a view to maintaining military tradition. For a surrender to be acceptable to the Japanese Army, it would be necessary for the military leaders to believe that it would not entail discrediting warrior tradition and that it would permit the ultimate resurgence of a military Japan. . . .

Source: Paul Kesaris, ed., *The Presidential Documents Series: Potsdam Conference Documents* (Frederick, Md.: University Publications of America, 1980).

B16. MEETING OF THE COMBINED CHIEFS OF STAFF, JULY 16, 1945,
AND MEETING OF THE JOINT CHIEFS OF STAFF, JULY 17, 1945

16-1. Combined Chiefs of Staff Meeting, July 16, 1945

Sir Alan Brooke referred to the last sentence on page 10 of the paper where the survival of the institution of the Emperor was mentioned. He asked whether the United States Chiefs of Staff had given any thought to the question of the interpretation of the term "unconditional surrender." From the military point of view it seemed to the British Chiefs of Staff that there might be some advantage in trying to explain this term to the Japanese in a manner which would ensure that the war was not unduly prolonged in outlying areas. If, for instance, an interpretation could be found and communicated to the Japanese which did not involve the dissolution of the Imperial institution, the Emperor would be in a position to order the cease-fire in outlying areas whereas, if the dynasty were destroyed, the outlying garrisons might continue to fight for many months or years. If an interpretation on these lines could be found an opportune moment to make it clear to the Japanese might be shortly after a Russian entry into the war.

The United States Chiefs of Staff explained that considerable thought had been given to this subject on the political level. One suggestion was that some form of agreed ultimatum might be issued at the correct psychological moment, for example, on Russian entry into the war, the idea being to explain what the term "unconditional surrender" did not mean rather than what it did mean. Admiral Leahy suggested that as the matter was clearly a political one primarily, it would be very useful if the Prime Minister put forward to the President his views and suggestions as to how the term "unconditional surrender" might be explained to the Japanese. The Combined Chiefs of Staff: —

a. Took note of the estimate of the enemy situation in C. C. S. 643/3.

b. Invited the British Chiefs of Staff to consider the possibility of asking the Prime Minister to raise with the President the matter of unconditional surrender of Japan. . . .

16-2. Joint Chiefs of Staff Meeting, July 17, 1945

. . . General Marshall stated that from a purely military point of view he considered that the attitude of the Joint Chiefs of Staff should be that nothing should be done prior to the termination of hostilities that would indicate the removal of the Emperor of Japan, since his continuation in office might influence the cessation of hostilities in areas outside of Japan proper.

... The memorandum to the President should also include the views he had previously expressed in regard to doing nothing to indicate that the Emperor might be removed from office upon unconditional surrender. ...

Source: U.S. Department of State, *Foreign Relations of the United States: The Conference at Berlin (The Potsdam Conference)* (Washington, D.C.: U.S. Government Printing Office, 1960), 2:35–40.

B17. JOINT CHIEFS OF STAFF MEMORANDUM TO THE PRESIDENT, JULY 17, 1945

The Joint Chiefs of Staff have considered the proposed proclamation by the Heads of State for dealing with the unconditional surrender formula for Japan as prepared by the State, War and Navy Departments and forwarded to you.

From the military point of view the Joint Chiefs of Staff consider that the proclamation is generally satisfactory. They believe, however, that the wording of the last sentence in the next to the last paragraph might well be clarified. To some of the extreme devotees of the Emperor, the phrase, "This may include a constitutional monarchy under the present dynasty," may be misconstrued as a commitment by the United Nations to depose or execute the present Emperor and install some other member of the Imperial family. To the radical elements in Japan, this phrase may be construed as a commitment to continue the institution of the Emperor and Emperor worship.

The Joint Chiefs of Staff therefore recommend that the next to the last paragraph of the proclamation be changed to read as follows:

"The occupying forces of the Allies shall be withdrawn from Japan as soon as our objectives are accomplished and there has been established beyond doubt a peacefully inclined, responsible government of a character representative of the Japanese people. ~~This may include a constitutional monarchy under the present dynasty if it be shown to the complete satisfaction of the world that such a government never again will aspire to aggression.~~ *Subject to suitable guarantees against further acts of aggression, the Japanese people will be free to choose their own form of government.*"

Such a statement would involve no commitment by the United Nations to support of any particular form of Japanese government, would enable the United Nations to prevent the establishment of any unacceptable government and would be more likely to appeal to all elements of the Japanese populace.

From a strictly military point of view the Joint Chiefs of Staff consider it inadvisable to make any statement or take any action at the present time that would make it difficult or impossible to utilize the authority of the Emperor to direct a surrender of the Japanese forces in the outlying areas as well as in Japan proper.

Source: U.S. Department of State, *Foreign Relations of the United States: The Conference at Berlin (The Potsdam Conference)* (Washington, D.C.: U.S. Government Printing Office, 1960), 2:1268–1269.

B18. MEMORANDUM FOR GENERAL ARNOLD, JULY 24, 1945

SUBJECT: GROVES REPORT

1. The following plan and schedule for initial attacks using special bombs have been worked out:

a. The first bomb (gun type) will be ready to drop between August 1 and 10 and plans are to drop it the first day of good weather following readiness.

b. The following targets have been selected: Hiroshima, Kokura, Niigata and Nagasaki.

(1) Hiroshima (population 350,000) is an "Army" city; a major POE [port of entry]; has large QM [quartermaster] and supply depots; has considerable industry and several small shipyards.

(2) Nagasaki (population 210,000) is a major shipping and industrial center of Kyushu.

(3) Kokura (population 178,000) has one of the largest army arsenals and ordnance works; has the largest railroad shops on Kyushu; and has large munitions storage to the south.

(4) Niigata (population 150,000) is an important industrial city, building machine tools, diesel engines, etc., and is a key port for shipping to the mainland.

c. All four cities are believed to contain large numbers of key Japanese industrialists and political figures who have sought refuge from major destroyed cities.

d. The attack is planned to be visual to insure accuracy and will await favorable weather. The four targets give a very high probability of one being open even if the weather varies from that forecast, as they are considerably separated.

e. The bomb will be carried in a master airplane accompanied by two other project B-29's with observers and special instruments.

f. The three B-29's will take off from North Field, Tinian, and fly via Iwo Jima. The use of fighter escort will be determined by General Spaatz upon consideration of all operational factors.

g. The master plane will attack the selected target from 30,000 feet plus altitude and will immediately, upon release of the bomb, make a steep diving turn away from the target to achieve maximum slant range distance as quickly as possible. Recording planes and fighters if employed will be kept several miles from the target. The participating planes are believed to be safe from the effects of the bomb.

h. The bomb will be detonated by radar proximity fuse about 2,000 feet above the ground.

i. Emergency arrangements have been provided at Iwo Jima for handling the bomb if required.

2. Two tested type bombs are expected to be available in August, one about the 6th and another the 24th. General Groves expects to have more information on future availabilities in a few days which will be furnished you when received.

3. The above has been discussed with Generals Spaatz and Eaker who concur.

JOHN N. STONE Colonel, GSC

Source: Dennis Merrill, ed., *Documentary History of the Truman Presidency* (Washington, D.C.: University Publications of America, 1995), 1:151–154.

B19. GENERAL HANDY DIRECTIVE TO GENERAL SPAATZ, JULY 25, 1945

1. The 509 Composite Group, 20th Air Force will deliver its first special bomb as soon as weather will permit visual bombing after about 3 August 1945 on one of the targets: Hiroshima, Kokura, Niigata and Nagasaki. To carry military and civilian scientific personnel from the War Department to observe and record the effects of the explosion of the bomb, additional aircraft will accompany the airplane carrying the bomb. The observing planes will stay several miles distant from the point of impact of the bomb.

2. Additional bombs will be delivered on the above targets as soon as made ready by the project staff. Further instructions will be issued concerning targets other than those listed above.

3. Dissemination of any and all information concerning the use of the weapon against Japan is reserved to the Secretary of War and the President of the United States. No communiques on the subject or releases of information will be issued by Commanders in the field without specific prior authority. Any news stories will be sent to the War Department for special clearance.

4. The foregoing directive is issued to you by direction and with the approval of the Secretary of War and of the Chief of Staff, USA. It is desired that you personally deliver one copy of this directive to General MacArthur and one copy to Admiral Nimitz for their information.

/S/Thos. T. Handy
General, G.S.C.
Acting Chief of Staff

Source: Douglas J. MacEachin, *The Final Months of the War with Japan: Signals Intelligence, U.S. Invasion Planning, and the A-Bomb Decision* (Washington, D.C.: Center for the Study of Intelligence, 1998), Document 13.

B20. MACARTHUR HEADQUARTERS INTELLIGENCE ESTIMATE OF
JAPANESE STRENGTH ON KYUSHU, JULY 29, 1945

G-2, GHQ, AFPAC, "Amendment No. 1 to G-2 Estimate of the Enemy Situation with Respect to Kyushu" (Dated 25 April 1945) 29 April 1945

. . . 1. Estimate of the Enemy Situation

a. Development of Ground Strength:

(1) The initial estimates on Kyushu of 24 March and 25 April 1945 considered an initial enemy deployment of six (6) divisions but seriously forecast a potentially larger deployment to ten (10) divisions, viz:

Although the Japanese obviously regard the Tokyo Plain as the ultimate decisive battle ground, it is apparent that Kyushu is considered a critical sector on their planned Empire Battle Position. It is believed that plans will visualize assignment of about 6 combat divisions (plus 2 depot divisions) to garrison Kyushu initially and that they are prepared to expend up to 10 divisions, all they can tactically employ in the area to insure its retention. Depot facilities to maintain such a force would have been established in Northern Kyushu.

These divisions have since made their appearance, as predicted, and the end is not in sight. This threatening development, inherent in war, will affect our own troops basis and calls for special air missions. If this deployment is not checked it may grow to a point where we attack on a ratio of one (1) to one (1) which is not the receipt for victory. . . .

2. Conclusions

a. The rate and probable continuity of Japanese reinforcements into the Kyushu area are changing the tactical and strategical situation sharply.

At least six (6) additional major units have been picked up in June/July; it is obvious that they are coming in from adjacent areas over lines of communication, that have apparently not been seriously affected by air strikes.

There is a strong likelihood that additional major units will enter the area before target date; we are engaged in a race against time by which the ratio of attack-effort vis-à-vis defense capacity is perilously balanced.

b. The Japanese have correctly estimated Southern Kyushu as a probable invasion objective, and have hastened their preparations to defend it.

c. They have fully recognized the precarious nature of the land and sea routes by which they must concentrate and support their forces in Southern Kyushu. They are vigorously exploiting available time to complete the deployment and supply lines of strong forces in the area before they are deprived of the full use of their limited lines of communication.

d. Since April 1945, enemy strength in Southern Kyushu has grown from approximately 80,000 troops including in mobile combat the equivalent of about 2 infantry divisions to an estimated 206,000 including divisions and 2 to 3 brigades, plus Naval, Air Ground, and Base and Service troops. This rapid expansion within a few weeks' time, supply of this large concentration of troops, and the movement of defensive material has undoubtedly so strained the capacity of all existing lines of communication that any major interruption thereof would seriously reduce the effectiveness of the enemy's preparations. It is also probable that some of the new units identified in Southern Kyushu are not yet fully assembled and that at least one division (the 212th) which was probably formed of local volunteers has not yet been completely equipped.

e. The assumption that enemy strengths will remain divided in North and South (Kyushu) compartments is no longer tenable.

f. The number of enemy major units rapidly tend to balance our attack units.

g. The trend of reinforcements from North to South (Kyushu) is unmistakable.

h. Massing in present attack sectors is apparent.

i. Unless the use of these routes is restricted by air and /or naval action as suggested in Pars i.e (4) and 2 a (2) (c), and (d), G-2 Estimate of 25 April, enemy forces in Southern Kyushu may be still further augmented until our planned local superiority is overcome, and the Japanese will enjoy complete freedom of action in organizing the area and in completing their preparations for defense.

Source: Reports of General MacArthur: The Campaigns of MacArthur in the Pacific (Washington, D.C.: U.S. Government Printing Office, 1994), 1:414–418.

B21. SIXTH ARMY (MACARTHUR) HEADQUARTERS INTELLIGENCE
REPORT WITH RESPECT TO OLYMPIC, AUGUST 1, 1945

G-2 Estimate of the Enemy Situation with Respect to Olympic Operation (Southern Kyushu)

1. Summary of the Enemy Situation

a. *General Trend:* By midsummer of 1945 there was little that JAPAN could look backward to with pride or forward to with hope. . . . The sequel to OKINAWA could only be an attack upon some part of the Inner Zone and presumably would be an invasion of the homeland. JAPAN acknowledged that. The key phrase in her own discussions of the war had now become "the decisive battle for the defense of the homeland."

JAPAN had to acknowledge also that for such defense she was, in some respects, in a bad way. . . .

Nevertheless, she deliberately girded herself for homeland defense. In KYUSHU particularly, closest of the home islands to the newest Allied bases and naturally vulnerable to invasion, JAPAN with unprecedented speed took steps to meet the anticipated threat. . . .

This JAPAN did while she considered the chances for success against the anticipated invasion. She hoped for war-weariness in the UNITED STATES. She hoped for Russian disturbance of the Allied political poise. She figured that this time the numerical superiority would be hers: the Allies, she maintained, could not possibly land so many troops in one place as she could oppose to them. She made much of what she believed were her logistic advantages over her enemy. In point of equipment, her still considerable air force, perhaps now almost wholly committed to the method of Kamikaze, offered the most substantial hope. Although she admitted that superiority of equipment still lay with the Allies, she protested once more that this would be outweighed by the spiritual superiority of "100,000,000 Japanese fighting for the Emperor and impelled by the spirit of the Special Attack Forces." These considerations, she hoped would this time make the difference. . . .

2. Conclusions

a. *Enemy Capabilities*:

(1) *Reinforcement of SOUTHERN KYUSHU prior to X-day*: Invasion of the RYUKYUS in April convinced the Japanese that an assault on SOUTHERN KYUSHU would in all likelihood follow soon afterwards. Apparently acting upon an estimate of the situation that the attack might come in midsummer, the Japanese have spared no effort to build up the mobile combat potential in SOUTHERN KYUSHU to a level, as of 21 July, of an estimated 5 divisions, 3 brigades, and 2 replacement regiments of the 6th Depot Division—the equivalent of about 7 divisions in all.

Granted an unexpected respite of several months before the blow actually falls, the enemy presumably will seize the opportunity to strengthen his position to a still greater degree.

Although our ever increasing aerial offensive can be expected to hamper the execution of the enemy's movements and redispositions, it cannot, in view of the long period of time intervening and the wide choice of means available to the enemy along interior lines of communication, prevent such movements from being carried out prior to X-day. . . .

An additional increment of 3 to 4 divisions in the SOUTHERN KYUSHU garrison prior to X-day must be considered as well within the enemy's capabilities. . . .

The conclusion is that by X-day the Japanese could easily have raised the currently estimated 7 combat divisions or divisions-equivalents in SOUTHERN KYUSHU to 10 or 11 divisions, together with appropriate base and service units. . . .

3. *State of preparation*: As elsewhere stated, the enemy, in anticipation of early Allied landings in SOUTHERN KYUSHU, began moving major combat units to this area on a large-scale in April. As of 21 July, the presence of mobile combat troops equivalent to about 7 divisions and a total of approximately 75,000 base and service troops is estimated.

It can be assumed that under coordinating direction of the probable SOUTHERN KYUSHU Army (Corps) Headquarters, intensive preparations for defense were initiated by these troops promptly upon arrival in the objective area. . . .

The relatively long time intervening until X-day gives the enemy ample time to complete these preparations. . . .

4. *Morale*: The largest single important consideration in estimating the state of enemy morale for the defense of KYUSHU is the obvious fact that for the Japanese their "homeland" will be invaded. In as much as the enemy has, even in the defense of island outposts where, comparatively speaking, far less was at a stake, proved to be vigorous and determined defender, it must be assumed that his fighting spirit in this homeland "kessen" will be unusually high. Moreover, his currently demonstrated ability to withstand sustained Allied aerial pounding is itself an indication of a tough will-to-defend. Until good evidence points to the contrary, therefore, it seems most justified to assume that the defenders of KYUSHU, both military and civilian, fighting as they suppose for the Emperor and their own homes, spurred by intense national feeling and continuous propaganda, misinformed about the international state of affairs, and confident of their numerical and spiritual superiority, are facing invasion with high morale.

5. *Role of civilian defense units*: As stated in Paragraph 1 b (1) (d), the Japanese are exerting maximum effort to mobilize the civilian population to assist in repelling invasion of the homeland. . . .

Source: RG 165, Box 1843, NARA.

B22. J.W.P.C. 397, AUGUST 4, 1945, ALTERNATIVES TO OLYMPIC

. . . 1. In Enclosure "B" (page 3) the Service Members of the Joint Intelligence Committee report a considerable strengthening of Japanese forces in southern Japan proper. Along with an increase in ground units deployed in southern Kyushu, a concentration of aircraft, including the bulk of Japanese suicide aircraft, and small suicide naval craft is reported in the area.

2. The possible effect upon OLYMPIC operations of this build-up and concentration is such that it is considered commanders in the field should review their estimates of the situation, reexamine objectives in Japan as possible alternates to OLYMPIC, and prepare plans for operations against such alternate objectives.

3. The Joint Staff Planners are preparing studies of alternate objectives in the light of current intelligence estimates. These studies are to be made available to theater commanders upon completion. . . .

Messages to CINCPAC

Copies of highly secret reports by the Joint Intelligence Committee (J.I.C. 311, Defensive Preparations in Japan) have been furnished you. Report indicates strengthening of Japanese forces and defensive measures in southern Japan to an extent considerably in excess of that previously estimated as Japanese capability by OLYMPIC target date. While these measures on the part of the Japanese are not yet considered to require change to your current directive it is desired that you give continued consideration to the situation particularly as it affects the execution of OLYMPIC, make alternate plans and submit timely recommendations. Operations against extreme northern Honshu, against the Sendai area, and directly against the Kanto Plain are now under intensive study here. . . .

The Problem

1. To summarize Japanese defensive preparations in the following areas:
Southern Kyushu
Northern Kyushu
Shikoku
Kanto Plain
and to determine the priorities of defense accorded by the Japanese.

General Summary

2. In anticipation of Allied invasion of the Home Islands, the Japanese are making a maximum effort to strengthen their defensive capabilities in Japan proper and to redeploy their forces in accorda.nce with their own estimate of areas most likely to be invaded. . . .

Particular Areas

3. There is every indication that the Japanese have been giving the highest priority to the defense of Kyushu and particularly to Southern Kyushu.

Since early 1945, ground forces deployed in Kyushu have been increased from 1 active and 2 depot divisions (totaling with army troops some 150,000 men), to a present strength of 11 active and 2 depot divisions (totaling with army troops about 545,000 men). . . .

Recent trends in the deployment of elementary biplane trainer type aircraft for suicide operations likewise point to the defensive priority which is being given to the Kyushu area by the Japanese. A total of 50 special bases for suicide aircraft are thus far known to have been designated in Kyushu, Honshu, and Shikoku west of 133° longitude. . . .

Many defensive mine fields have been laid and there is considerable evidence that new types of mines which might be effective against Allied landing craft are being set out in waters of less than 1.5 fathoms along prospective landing beaches. A very high priority has been given to the Kyushu area. . . .

4. *Shikoku.* Defensive preparations in Shikoku would seem to indicate that the Japanese estimate the probability of Allied landings on this island as being second only to invasion of Kyushu or Quelpart Island.

5. *Kanto Plain.* While there is considerable evidence that the Japanese expect us to make initial landings in Kyushu, Shikoku or some other area of Japan proper prior to an assault on the Kanto Plain, they do not exclude the possibility of amphibious operations against this latter area from our present positions.

In early 1945 there were only 4 active and 3 depot divisions, plus army troops totaling about 300,000 men, located in the vicinity of the Kanto Plain. Progressive reinforcement of the area has been carried out since March. . . . Present strength in this area is estimated to be 9 active divisions, 3 depot divisions and army troops, totaling about 560,000 men. No information is available regarding any unusual recent activity in the strengthening of coastal defenses, although there is every reason to believe that here, as well as in other threatened areas of Japan proper, fixed defenses are being constantly developed and improved. . . .

Although some naval small craft and other suicide units have been recently formed for the added defense of this area, we believe that much less emphasis is being currently given to such defensive preparation than is the case in the general area of Kyushu and Shikoku. . . .

Source: Douglas J. MacEachin, *The Final Months of the War with Japan: Signals Intelligence, U.S. Invasion Planning, and the A-Bomb Decision* (Washington, D.C.: Center for the Study of Intelligence, 1998), Document 17.

B23. COMMUNICATIONS BETWEEN MARSHALL, MACARTHUR,
KING AND NIMITZ, AUGUST 7, 9, AND 10, 1945 AND NIMITZ TO KING,
MAY 25, 1945

OPD WAR (MARSHALL) TO MACARTHUR PASSED BY COMINCH TO CINCPAO ADV HQ
TOP SECRET FOR ADMIRAL NIMITZ EYES ONLY, MARSHALL TO MACARTHUR EYES
ONLY, WAR, 45369.

Intelligence reports on Jap dispositions which have been presented to me and which I understand have been sent to your staff are that the Japanese have undertaken a large
buildup both of divisions and of air forces in KYUSHU and southern HONSHU. The air
buildup is reported as including a large component of suicide planes which the intelligence estimates here consider are readily available for employment only in the vicinity of
their present bases. Concurrently with the reported reinforcement of KYUSHU, the
Japanese are reported to have reported forces north of the TOKYO PLAIN to a point
where the defensive capabilities in northern HONSHU and HOKKAIDO appear to be
extraordinarily weak viewed from the standpoint of the Japanese General Staff. The question has arisen in my mind as to whether the Japanese may not be including some deception in the sources from which our intelligence is being drawn.

Para. In order to assist in discussions likely to arise here on . . . possible alternatives to
OLYMPIC. . . . I would appreciate your personal estimate of the Japanese intentions
and capabilities as related to your current directive and available resources. [August 7,
3:35 p.m.]

CINCAFPAC TO WORCOS PASSED BY COMINCH TO CINCPAC ADV HQ (ADMIRAL
NIMITZ EYES ONLY)
TOP SECRET, C 31597 EYES ONLY FOR GENERAL MARSHALL FROM MACARTHUR

Reference WAR 45369. . . . I am certain that Japanese air potential reported to you as ac-
cumulating to counter our OLYMPIC operation is greatly exaggerated. . . . The situation
repeats that of the PHILIPPINE operation. . . . I further doubt the often reposted reports
that large numbers of aircraft are still being manufactured in JAPAN. . . . I do not
credit . . . the heavy strengths reported to you in southern KYUSHU. . . . It is anticipated
that this great weight of [American] air [power] will quickly seek out and destroy in the
southern Japanese islands and enemy air potential and will practically immobilize
ground forces in their present positions. The maintenance of such forces in southern
KYUSHU cannot fail to be increasingly difficult and it is anticipated that they will be
greatly weakened prior to OLYMPIC.

Para. In my opinion, there should not be the slightest thought of changing the
OLYMPIC operation. Its fundamental purpose is to obtain air bases under cover of which
we can deploy our forces to the northward into the industrial heart of JAPAN. The plan
is sound and will be successful. . . . Throughout the Southeast Pacific Area campaigns, as
we have neared and operation intelligence has invariably pointed to greatly increased
enemy forces. Without exception, this build-up has been found to be erroneous. In this

particular case, the destruction that is going on in JAPAN would seem to indicate that it is very probable that the enemy is resorting to deception. [August 9, 4:43 a.m.]

COMINCH AND CNO TO CINCPAC ADV HQ
KING TO NIMITZ EYES ONLY

Desire your comments on WAR 45369 (071535) and MACARTHURS 31897 (090443) passed to you EYES ONLY. Send your reply info MACARTHUR. [August 9, 10:05 p.m.]

COMINCH AND CNO TO CINCPAC ADVANCE
KING TO NIMITZ

This is a peace warning. TOKYO has indicated in ultra channels that JAPAN wishes to bring about peace immediately and that she will accept the Joint Declaration by leaders of U.S., Great Britain and CHINA provided that the stipulations do not include a demand for alteration of the authority of the emporer [sic] to rule the state. It is now probable that the Swedish or Swiss governments will soon transmit official messages to the Allies regarding Jap capitulation desires. Your movements and dispositions should be guided by this information pending further more definite word or instructions. [August 10, 11:35 a.m.]

CINCPAC ADV TO COMINCH
NIMITZ TO KING

Para 1. The further experiences in fighting against Japanese forces since receipt of the Joint Chiefs of Staff directive 032141 April and submission of my 280235 April prompt me to point out that:

A. It has been further demonstrated that where Japanese troops occupy prepared defenses and have adequate supplies they constitute a competent fighting force against which the best of our troops . . . can advance only slowly. Japanese forces have not so far surrendered in appreciable numbers and cannot be destroyed without our incurring numerous casualties. It would be unrealistic to expect that such obvious objectives as southern KYUSHU and the TOKYO PLAIN will not be as well defended as OKINAWA. . . .

B. It is apparent that the enemy air force is prepared to continue its large scale suicide attacks. 235 ships have been sunk or damaged during the ICEBERG Operation. The 27 ships sunk have been destroyers or ships of less valuable characteristics. . . .

Para 2. The 20th Air Force is now operating against JAPAN with great effect. As its operations accelerate . . . our naval and air forces can in time accomplish the complete destruction of Japanese industry and shipping. Japanese naval and air forces can be virtually destroyed with minimal losses of ourselves but time will be required. The blockade of JAPAN is now being extended by air forces . . . and submarines will commence operations in the SEA OF JAPAN in early June. JAPAN can in time be reduced to the point where her will to resist will be low but time will be required. . . .

Para 4. Unless speed is considered so important that we are willing to accept less than the best preparation and more than minimum casualties I believe that the long range interests of the U.S. will be better served if we continue during 1945 to isolate JAPAN to destroy Jap forces and resources by Naval and air attack. [May 25]

Source: CINPAC Command Summary, Book Seven, 3508–3510, Naval Historical Center and Command Summary, Book Six, January 1945 to July 1945, 3232, Naval Historical Center, Washington, D.C.

B24. WAR DEPARTMENT MEMORANDUM TO ADMIRAL LEAHY, AUGUST 10, 1945

The Army cannot reduce its present strength ceilings of 6,968,000 men without extremely dangerous and unjustifiable risk to the continued success of the operations to bring the war to a conclusion. We have arrived at this troop basis from the most careful consideration of the requirements of the theater commanders. On the basis of their forecast it is planned that by next June 30 the Army will have been reduced and disposed as follows:

The Operational Theaters, including strategic reserve 3,750,000. . . .

Occupational Forces and Overseas Garrisons 550,000. . . .

Troops in Hospitals in the United States 330,000

These are troops who largely are of no further usefulness but cannot be discharged until they have been given the greatest possible degree of mental and physical rehabilitation in the Army hospitals. They are largely men who were wounded in action.

Total 6,968,000. . . .

Source: Marshall Papers, Box 74, Folder 20, George C. Marshall Research Library.

B25. INTELLIGENCE ESTIMATE OF THE JAPANESE SITUATION FOR NEXT 30 DAYS, AUGUST 12, 1945

MEMORANDUM FOR THE CHIEF OF STAFF

. . . 1. During the period 12 August–12 September 1945, three courses of action are open to the Japanese:

    a. To drag out negotiation for the purpose of securing more favorable terms;

    b. To reject the last Allied proposal and continue hostilities; or

    c. To accept the Allied proposal.

    2. Success in protecting negotiations would strengthen the position of the present Japanese government and the Emperor. . . . Protracted negotiations are contrary to Allied best interests and should not be permitted. . . .

    3. a. Should Japan reject the last Allied proposal and continue hostilities, her naval and air forces are generally impotent except for suicide employment against Allied

shipping. Japanese suicide air and naval elements . . . have a considerable capacity for inflicting damage on Allied transports and naval craft incident to a major loading. . . .

b. Large, well disciplined, well armed, undefeated Japanese ground forces have a capacity to offer stubborn fanatic resistance to Allied ground operations in the homeland and may inflict heavy Allied casualties. . . . Japanese stockpiling has established food and munitions in all areas of expected invasion in sufficient quantities to support operations for from about four to six months. . . . Adverse weather: any heavy cloud cover during the next month may reduce somewhat the effectiveness of Allied air power in disrupting the Japanese rail and road system. . . . Atomic bombs will not have a decisive effect in the next 30 days.

c. The surrender offer by the Japanese government will soon be known to the Japanese military services and people. It will cause a serious loss of face and confidence. Although Japanese leaders will appreciate that it constitutes official acknowledgment that Japan has no hope for victory, it can be utilized by Japanese military leaders to secure an even more fanatic resistance on the part of her military forces. . . .

Source: File 2, Box 12, OPD Executive Files, RG 165, NARA.

B26. EDMUND J. WINSLETT REPORT ON THE DEFENSES
OF SOUTHERN KYUSHU, JUNE 3, 1945

. . . I jeeped from Kagoshima through Taniyame, Kawanabe, Chiran, Shimade, Kadoura, Byu, Makurazaki and north to Ijuin and back to Kagoshima. I found the suicide boat harbor at Kadoura, as fine a sheep shank deep inlet as one could wish for as a harbor for such craft. I found the torpedo caves at Shioya, eight of them, each capable of storing twenty four torpedoes. . . . I found the beaches. There are a limited number of them, confined to small coves, quite short—usually the anchorage of some fishing boats. There were no favorable exits, the road was found to be narrow, rocky, steep and not of such solidity as to withstand military traffic for any length of time. The beaches would have been subjected to enfilade fire from the bordering hills surrounding all beaches. The rice fields are held in by many stone terraces ranging in height from four to six feet precluding any off the road movement by any type of military vehicles. Principal defenses to the lines of communication were confined to mortar points, firing points, and individual rifleman positions. . . . There were literally thousands of these positions between the beaches and Chiran and Byu fields. . . . Ammunition and supply caves were everywhere. . . . Every turn of the road was defended by the positions described. . . . It was obvious . . . that the defenses were planned down to the individual man, with a determination to fight to the death, no help could have come and no retreat was allowed. . . .

. . . I travelled by jeep from Kagoshima, to Ibusuki, inspected the entire installation. Here is what was found. The road is defended by the same general plan as was the Naku-razaki beach with the additional safeguards of hundreds of caves, artillery ports in the cliffs and prepared installations to concentrate both heavy and light fire on the road and paralleling railroad. I haven't the time to go into detail on the maze of caves, their completeness and complicated network of communication passageways. Under-ground installations were not confined to supply and ammunition, they had caves for everything. . . . This seaplane plant was now being devoted to the manufacture of the Japanese version of the DUNKS, there were six among the burned remains of the origi-nal plant and the parts for many hundreds of them were stored in the caves in the over-hanging cliff. What concerned me very much was an installation in a saddle in the hill just above the plant. This was found to be a water filtration plant . . . [which] obtained its water by gravity from . . . a mountain lake five miles away. Inside the burned plant were many concrete individual rifle strongpoints. The plan was easy to understand, a fight right in thru the plants, to the death. . . .

The landing at ARIAKE WAN landing would have been—possibly wet. The beach gradient is low, the tide runs out about two hundred yards and the beach is not solid. Tracked vehicles would have been able to negotiate the soft sand. If LSTs had been able to get in for a landing at high tide, they would have been grounded until a succeeding high tide. . . .

The paralleling perfectural road and railroad were well defended by the same planned type of installations mentioned before. . . .

You have been waiting for me to get to the MIYAZAKI beach. I am sorry that I cannot promise you now that I Corps' task and their landing would have been any better than the three mentioned before. It would have been just as thorough and presented some addi-tional hazards to the success of the operation. . . .

After a personal survey of the areas in which our invasion landings were scheduled to take place, I am convinced that the greatest battle the American Armies have ever won was the one which was not fought—the INVASION OF KYUSHU.

Source: Winslett Papers, U.S. Army Military History Institute, Carlisle, Pa.

B27. GENERAL CHARLES E. WILLOUGHBY ARTICLE
IN MILITARY REVIEW, JUNE 1946

Occupation of Japan and Japanese Reaction

. . . All possible landing areas, in the event of American armed landing, were completely organized by the Japanese Army and each one of these areas had the potentiality

of another Okinawa. . . . At Okinawa, from two to two and a half Japanese divisions ex-
acted a total of approximately 40,000 American casualties on land, not to mention the
shattering "Kamikaze" attacks on the Fleet. This affords a completely authentic yardstick
to forecast what it would have taken in losses had we gone in shooting. The sinister ratio
that two and a half Japanese divisions exact 40,000 casualties, spells:

Kyushu: 13/14 Divs—200,000
Shikoku: 4/5 Divs—80,000
Kanto: 22 Divs—400,000
Sendai: 2 Divs—30,000

The conclusions are inescapable.

Source: Military Review, June 1946, 3–6.

B28. ULTRA ORDER OF BATTLE BULLETIN NO. 62, MAY 12, 1945

ORDER OF BATTLE BULLETIN NO. 62
JAPANESE GROUND FORCES
PREPARED BY MILITARY INTELLIGENCE SERVICE
. . . SIXTEENTH AREA ARMY

a. Strength estimate: 246,000, increased from 230,000. Army ground strength is increased to 128,000 from 112,000 to reflect the presence of the 57th Div (see Bulletin 61). . . .

Source: RG 457, "Record of the National Security Agency," NARA.

B29. "MAGIC"—FAR EAST SUMMARY NO. 425 (SRS 425), MAY 19, 1945

4. Japanese Army Air Force Suicide Units

a. The Japanese have employed both Army and Navy suicide units in recent air operations in the Ryukyus. Navy training units have been drawn upon to provide suicide
planes, and there have been indications that the Army may have followed a similar practice (FES 17 May 45). . . .

b. Evidence has now accumulated that a series of numbered "TO" Flying Units,
which have appeared in Japanese Army traffic since February of this year, may be
included in the Army suicide units employed in the Ryukyus. On 9 Feb Tokyo informed the Southern Army that among the units to carry out "human bullet attacks" were

"Tokubetau Kogakitai" ("Special Attack Units"), and that their abbreviation was to be "TO." "Special attack" is a term usually employed, by both the Army and Navy, to designate suicide attack. Several "TO" units with symbolic names have been identified in the Southern Area. . . .

c. The numbered "TO" units have often been associated with training units and training commands, and it is likely that at least some of them have been organized from training units. . . . At least one of the units is equipped with the latest model of the Oscar single-engine fighter.

Note: The Sixth Air Army (HQ, Fukuoka, Kyushu) has been the principal Army in Japanese air operations in the Ryukyus. It has often been mentioned as employing suicide units, and was scheduled to send out almost 100 suicide planes in attacks in the Okinawa area on 10–11 May. . . .

Source: RG 457, "Record of the National Security Agency," NARA.

B30. ULTRA ORDER OF BATTLE BULLETIN NO. 69, JUNE 30, 1945

. . . (1) General: the OSUMI-TOKARA GP (NORTHERN RYUKYUS) has heretofore been carried arbitrarily as part of the RYUKYUS, under the Thirty-second Army. . . . Available evidence indicated that the Group is probably in the operational area of the Sixteenth Area Army . . . rather than that of the Thirty-second Army and, beginning with this issue of the Bulletin, the Islands will be so carried. The 23rd Ind mixed Regt (see Bulletin 68) is at present the only major identification in the Group. Strength is carried at 12,000.

(2) Strength estimate: 340,000, increased from 329,000. Army ground strength is increased to 190,000 from 181,000 and Army and Navy Air ground to 100,000 from 98,000 to reflect the transfer to the Sixteenth Area Army of the strength of the OSUMI-TOKARA GP. . . .

Source: RG 457, "Record of the National Security Agency," NARA.

B31. "MAGIC" — FAR EAST SUMMARY NO. 476 (SRS 476) JULY 9, 1945

3. Japan — New Divisions

The 205th and 206th Divs — the highest-numbered Japanese divisions yet noted — have been identified in Japan:

(1) A 5 May message from Kumamoto (Kyushu), just available, is signed by the C of S [Chief of Staff] of the 206th Div. The message requests that certain officers recently assigned to the Division be directed to proceed immediately to their posts at Kumamoto, "in view of the exigencies of operations."

Note: The 206th Div, which presumably was formed from the 6th Depot Div . . . is the fifth active division to be identified in Kyushu. Two depot divisions are also located there.

(2) A 1 July message, transmitted over an Osaka-to-Tokyo radio circuit, is signed by the C of S of the 205th Div. Although the place of origin of the message cannot be determined, transmission of the message from Osaka suggests that the Division is in Western Japan. . . .

Estimated Japanese Dispositions on Kyushu 9 July 1945
Estimated Strength:

Army Ground:	200,000
Navy Ground:	50,000
Air Ground	100,000
TOTAL:	350,000

Source: RG 457, "Record of the National Security Agency," NARA.

B32. "MAGIC"—FAR EAST SUMMARY NO. 487 (SRS 487) JULY 20, 1945

11. Kyushu—New Independent Mixed Brigade

An 11 July message from Fukuoka gives the details of the organization of the 126th Ind Mixed Brig in Kyushu. Its exact location is not known. The 126th is the first independent mixed brigade to be identified in Kyushu, although an 18 June message indicated that the Japanese were planning to form at least one there. . . . MIS has raised its strength estimate for Kyushu by 5,000, to 380,000.

Source: RG 457, "Record of the National Security Agency," NARA.

B33. "MAGIC"—FAR EAST SUMMARY NO. 488 (SRS 488) JULY 21, 1945

6. Kyushu—Three New Divisions

. . . New divisions continue to be identified on Kyushu. Operational code names and numbers . . . disclose the existence of three new divisions. . . .

These three divisions are believed to be in addition to the six active divisions previously identified on Kyushu. . . . MIS has raised its strength estimate for Kyushu by 75,000, to 455,000. . . .

Source: RG 457, "Record of the National Security Agency," NARA.

B34. "MAGIC" — FAR EAST SUMMARY NO. 494 (SRS 494) JULY 27, 1945

1. *Move of Fortieth Army HQ to Kyushu*

a. Recently available messages and addresses disclose that the Fortieth Army HQ, which formerly controlled Japanese forces in Southwest Formosa, was moved to South Kyushu, probably in June. . . .

2. *Honshu — Concealed Navy Airfields*

Additional information on concealed airfields in Honshu is supplied by a 25 July message of the Tenth Air Fleet. . . .

2. Kure — Production of Koryu Midget Submarines

On July 25 the Kure Navy Yard informed the Navy Bureau of Military Affairs at Tokyo that "the July quota of 14 Koryu [midget submarines] definitely can be met but we are aiming at completing 17. . . ."

F-22's Estimate of Japanese Intentions

1. An analysis of Japan's situation, as revealed through Ultra sources, suggests that her unwillingness to surrender stems primarily from the failure of her otherwise capable and all-powerful Army leaders to perceive that the defenses they are so assiduously fashioning actually are utterly inadequate. That there is nothing in the Japanese mind to prevent capitulation per se, is demonstrated by the advocacy of virtual unconditional surrender by an increasing number of highly-placed Japanese abroad. However, until the Japanese leaders realize that an invasion cannot be repelled, there is little likelihood that they will accept any terms satisfactory to the Allies. . . .

Source: RG 457, "Record of the National Security Agency," NARA.

B35. "MAGIC"—FAR EAST SUMMARY NO. 500 (SRS 500) AUGUST 2, 1945

5. *Japanese Buildup on Kyushu*

. . . A 26 July message discloses the presence of a new division on Kyushu, in addition to the ten active divisions previously identified there and the one indicated to be moving there from the Nagoya area. The division, which probably is the 312th, has just been activated in the Kuruma divisional district. MIS has raised its strength estimate for Kyushu by 20,000—to 545,000 . . .

*Estimated strength of 15,000 in the Csumi-Tokara group (just below Kyushu) is no longer included in the Kyushu total. . . .

Source: RG 457, "Record of the National Security Agency," NARA.

B36. ULTRA ORDER OF BATTLE BULLETIN NO. 74, AUGUST 4, 1945

d. *Sixteenth Area Army (HQ Fukuoka)*

(1) General: The designations of the 145th and 154th Divs are confirmed by new evidence. It is now known that the 145th Div has a rocket gun unit as a component. . . .

(2) Strength estimate: 545,000, increased from 525,000. . . .

Source: RG 457, "Record of the National Security Agency," NARA.

B37. "MAGIC"—FAR EAST SUMMARY NO. 505 (SRS 505) AUGUST 7, 1945

5. *Divisional Movements to Kyushu*

. . . Eleven active divisions have been identified in Kyushu . . . and recently available messages indicate that two others are on route there. . . .

Substantial elements of the divisions probably have reached Kyushu, and MIS has raised its estimate of the area by 15,000—to 560,000.

Note: The total of active divisions carried in the Japanese Army has now increased to 143 (including 4 armored divisions); of those, 42 (including one armored) are in Japan proper . . .

Source: RG 457, "Record of the National Security Agency," NARA.

B38. ULTRA ORDER OF BATTLE BULLETIN NO. 75, AUGUST 11, 1945

e. Sixteenth Area Army (HQ Fukuoka)

(1) KYUSHU.

(a) Strength estimate: 560, 000, increased from 545,000. Army ground is increased to 370,000 from 355,000 to reflect the presence of elements of the 216th? and 303rd? Divs (see par (b) below).

(b) New identifications: The movement of a division, designation unknown, from the Nagoya Divisional District to South Kyushu, probably the Sandai area, was reported in Bulletin 73. New evidence reveals that two divisions, tentatively accepted as the 216th and 303rd, are moving to Kyushu. . . . Estimated strength has been increased 15,000 to reflect the arrival of elements of the two divisions; and the remaining strength will be carried unlocated Japan. . . .

(c) New locations and movements . . .

. . . Eight divisions are now carried in South Kyushu, and only three in the north. . . .

Source: RG 457, "Record of the National Security Agency," NARA.

C.

MAGIC Diplomatic Summaries

MILITARY

1. Japanese attempt to win over Russia

Early last month Foreign Minister Togo advised Ambassador Sato that it was a matter of "utmost urgency" not only to prevent Russia from entering the Pacific War but also to induce her to adopt a favorable attitude to Japan. Togo continued that he had accordingly asked former Premier Hirota to confer with Soviet Ambassador Malik "as soon as possible. . . . "

It now appears that during the period 3–14 June Hirota had four conversations with Malik. . . .

d. At their last conference . . . Hirota stated: "Japan will increase her naval strength in the future, and that, together with the Russian army, would make a force unequaled in the world. . . . " In conclusion, Hitota stated that Japan hoped for an early peace but "the reply was that, since Russia was not a belligerent in the East, his Excellency Mr. Hirota must be aware that peace there did not depend on Russia. . . ."

All documents in this section are from *The Magic Documents: Summaries and Transcripts of the Top-Secret Diplomatic Communications of Japan, 1938–1945.* Ed. Paul Kesaris. Washington, D.C.: University Publications of America, 1980.

C2. MAGIC DIPLOMATIC SUMMARY NO. 1202, JULY 10, 1945 (SRS 1724)

MILITARY

1. More on Japan's proposal to Russia

Yesterday's Summary noted that on 30 June Foreign Minister Togo had sent to Ambassador Sato a message (No. 853) containing what appeared to be the gist of a proposal to be made to Russia (suggesting a mutual assistance and non-aggression treaty, and stating Japan's willingness to arrange for the "neutralization" of Manchukuo, to renounce her fisheries rights—in return for oil—and to discuss any other matters). The preceding message from Togo to Sato (No. 852) has now been received and discloses that the proposal . . . had already been conveyed to the Russians. . . . Togo's message, after informing Sato of these developments, concluded:

"I should like to know the attitude of the other side with all possible speed, if possible, early in July. Please do everything you can to speed up their answer."

It also now appears that the Japanese Government has unceremoniously overridden Sato's repeatedly expressed doubts about the wisdom of the move and has renewed its instructions to him to make every effort to see Foreign Commissar Molotov about the proposal before the Big Three Conference. . . .

C3. MAGIC DIPLOMATIC SUMMARY NO. 1204, JULY 12, 1945 (SRS 1726)

MILITARY

1. Japanese peace move

On 11 July Foreign Minister Togo sent the following "extremely urgent" message to Ambassador Sato:

"We are now secretly giving consideration to the termination of the war because of the pressing situation which confronts Japan both at home and abroad. Therefore, when you have your interview with Molotov [in accordance with previous instructions] you should not confine yourself to the objective of a rapprochement between Russia and Japan but should also sound him out on the extent to which it is possible to make use of Russia in ending the war.

"As for our proposal that we pledge mutual support in the maintenance of peace . . . that should be put forward in conjunction with sounding out Russia's attitude toward Japan. . . . While we naturally hope to obtain a treaty through the negotiations between Hirota and Malik, those talks are also intended to find out the extent to which it is possible to make use of Russia in ending the war.

"We would like to know the views of the Russian Government on this subject with all haste. Furthermore, the Imperial Court is tremendously interested in this matter. . . ."

A little later that day, Togo sent Sato another "extremely urgent" message, reading as follows:

. . . "Therefore, please tell them that: We consider the maintenance of peace in East Asia to be one aspect of the maintenance of world peace. Accordingly, Japan—as a proposal for ending the war and because of her concern for the establishment and maintenance of lasting peace—has absolutely no idea of annexing or holding the territories which she occupied during the war.

"We should like you to have the interview with Molotov in a day or two. Please reply at once as to his answer."

Note: There have been occasional hints in the past—notably in connection with last summer's proposal for sending a "special envoy" to Moscow—that Japan hoped to obtain Russia's good offices in arranging a peace. . . .

C4. MAGIC DIPLOMATIC SUMMARY NO. 1205, JULY 13, 1945 ((SRS 1727)

MILITARY

1. *Follow-up message on Japanese peace move*

On 12 July—the day after advising Ambassador Sato of Japan's desire to "make use of Russia in ending the war"—Foreign Minister Togo dispatched the following additional message on the subject, labelled "very urgent."

"I have not yet received a wire about your Interview with Molotov. . . . We should . . . like you to present this matter to Molotov in the following terms:

"His Majesty the Emperor, mindful of the fact that the present war daily brings greater evil and sacrifice upon the peoples of all belligerent powers, desires from his heart that it may be quickly terminated. But so long as England and the United States insist upon unconditional surrender the Japanese Empire has no alternative but to fight on with all its strength for the honor and the existence of the Motherland. His Majesty is deeply reluctant to have any further blood lost among the people on both sides, and it is his desire for the welfare of humanity to restore peace with all possible speed.

". . . It is the Emperor's private intention to send Prince Konoye to Moscow as a Special Envoy with a letter from him containing the statements given above. . . .

"Although it will be impossible for this delegation to get there before the big men in Moscow leave for the Three Power Conference, we must arrange for a meeting immediately after their return. . . ."

C5. MAGIC DIPLOMATIC SUMMARY NO. 1206, JULY 14, 1945 (SRS 1728)

MILITARY

1. Messages from Sato on peace move

Parts of three messages sent to Tokyo by Ambassador Sato on 12 and 13 July have been received; they disclose that (a) as of the morning of the 13th Sato intended to try to see Molotov for the purpose of presenting the Emperor's peace plea before Molotov should leave for Potsdam and (b) Sato was pessimistic about the chances for success of Japan's peace move unless the Government were prepared to accept terms "virtually equivalent to unconditional surrender."

The first message was sent late on 12 July; at that time, Sato had read Foreign Minister Togo's 11 July messages instructing him to find out whether Russia might help Japan make peace on the basis of a surrender of all territory occupied during the war, but he had not yet received the 12 July message expressing the Emperor's desire for peace and outlining the plan to have Prince Konoye fly to Moscow. The available parts of Sato's message—the middle section is missing—read as follows:

"I received your [two] messages of 11 July immediately after I had reported to you on my 12 July interview with Molotov. I realize that the gist of your idea is a basic sounding out of the Russians on the possibility of using them in ending the war.

"In my frank opinion, it is no exaggeration to say that the Russians are not attracted by the proposals which former Premier Hirota made to Ambassador Malik [for a nonaggression and mutual assistance pact in return for various concessions by Japan—DS 9, 10 Jul 45] and that there is no hope that they will meet our terms. [Such proposals] run completely counter to the Russians' foreign policy, as I have explained in detail on numerous occasions. . . .

"Furthermore, the reasoning in your messages of 11 July consists of nothing more than academic fine phrases. With regard to your reference to the maintenance of peace in East Asia [as] one aspect of the maintenance of world peace, it is indeed unfortunate that Japan is no longer in a position where she can be responsible for peace in East Asia—now that the Anglo-Americans may be about to wrest from us the power to maintain this peace and even the Japanese mainland has been reduced to such a critical state. . . .

... Assuming ... the course of the war has brought us to a real extremity, the Government should make the great decision. Once that resolve has been taken, there may perhaps be some hopes of getting the Russian Government into motion and obtaining its good offices in terminating the war. There can be no doubt, however, that the situation which we would face in that event would be virtually equivalent to unconditional surrender.

"I have expressed my views frankly, and I fear that I must apologize for the unceremoniousness of my words. I am filled with thoughts of fear and heartbreak. . . . I send this message in the belief that it is my first responsibility to prevent the harboring of illusions which are at variance with reality. I beg your indulgence."

Early the next day—yesterday—Sato advised Togo that his messages conveying the Emperor's plea had been received at 1 a.m. . . .

Later on the 13th, Sato sent an additional message of comment, the first half of which is as follows:

"Although I imagine that the Russians will agree to our proposal to send a Special Envoy [Prince Konoye] to Moscow, it is difficult to say anything until we actually receive their reply. However, if they should agree to this, it is entirely out of the question to limit the functions of the Special Envoy to sounding out the extent to which we might make use of the Russians in ending the war or to presenting an abstract exposition—as suggested in your messages of 11 July.

"I kneel in veneration before the exalted solicitude of His Majesty for the restoration of peace. . . . Nevertheless, if the proposal . . . brought by a Special Envoy at the Emperor's particular desire, goes no further than we have gone in the past, if it is to be a proposal that contains only abstract words and lacks concreteness—we shall uselessly disappoint the expectations of the authorities in this country. . . ."

c6. MAGIC DIPLOMATIC SUMMARY NO. 1207, JULY 15, 1945 (SRS 1729)

MILITARY

... Finally, two earlier reports from Sato, parts of which have previously been reported, are now available in full. The first of the two, dated 12 July, was sent after Sato had received Togo's instructions to find out whether Russia might help Japan make peace on the basis of a surrender of all territory occupied during the war. . . . In the part of the report previously noted, Sato argued that . . . if Japan really wanted peace, she would have to face a situation "virtually equivalent to unconditional surrender." The previously missing part of the message reads as follows: . . .

"As you are well aware, the Soviet authorities are extremely realistic and it is most difficult to persuade them with abstract arguments. . . .

"If the Japanese Empire is really faced with the necessity of terminating the war, we must first of all make up our own minds to do so. Unless we make up our own minds, there is absolutely no point in sounding out the views of the Soviet Government. . . ."

The other report from Sato was sent on the 13th, after he had received the message conveying the Emperor's statement about peace and proposing that Prince Konoye be sent to Moscow. In the first part of the report he urged that, if a "Special Envoy" were sent, he should not be limited merely to "sounding out the extent to which we might make use of the Russians in ending the war or to presenting an abstract exposition," but should be prepared to make some concrete proposal. The balance of the report includes the following statements:

"It is my firm conviction that, once we have resolved to send a special and important Envoy on a long trip, he can have no function except to propose an armistice and peace. . . ."

[Note: No message from Tokyo defining Konoye's mission more precisely is yet available.]

C7. MAGIC DIPLOMATIC SUMMARY NO. 1208, JULY 16, 1945 (SRS 1730)

MILITARY

. . . On 15 July Foreign Minister Togo asked Sato to, "please send us a reply message as to when Stalin and Molotov left." On the same day—probably before he had received Togo's inquiry—the Ambassador reported as follows: . . .

"It appears that Stalin and Molotov left Moscow for Berlin on the evening of the 14th. Therefore, so far as I can surmise, despite the fact that they probably had at least half a day remaining before their departure, they avoided making any reply other than the tentative statement that they were delaying their answer. . . .

"The following are four probable reasons for the hesitation of the Russians in this matter:

(1) They are uncertain whether the Imperial instructions concerning the termination of the war signify that the Special Envoy's mission will involve the presentation of a concrete plan for ending the war.

(2) They fear that Japan may not intend to make a definite proposal of unconditional surrender or of terms virtually equivalent thereto, but may actually intend to try to get their assistance in order to obtain a so-called 'negotiated peace'. . . .

(3) They wish to avoid any deterioration in their relations with the Anglo-Americans. . . .

(4) . . . they believe it necessary to make sure of the agreement of the British and Americans on the question of the Special Envoy before making a definite reply one way or the other.

"In connection with the subject of a 'negotiated peace' mentioned in (2) above, we must remember that the Americans and British—particularly the former—have always opposed the making of a negotiated peace in both the European and Pacific wars. . . .

"Leaving aside Japan's sincere desire for the termination of the war, I believe that in the long run she has indeed no choice but to accept unconditional surrender or terms closely equivalent thereto.

"I would like to point out, however, that even on the basis of your various messages I have obtained no clear idea of the recent situation. Nor am I clear about the views of the Government and of the Military with regard to the termination of the war. . . . Now if the Special Envoy does not bear concrete terms as mentioned in (1) above, I am fearful lest he should be dispatched with the approval of the Russians only to achieve unsatisfactory results in the end. . . ."

c8. MAGIC DIPLOMATIC INTERCEPT NO. 1210 JULY 17, 1945 (SRS 1732)

MILITARY

1. *Tokyo says no unconditional surrender*

On 17 July Foreign Minister Togo sent the following message to Ambassador Sato:

"We have been fully aware from the outset that it would be difficult under existing circumstances either to strengthen the ties of friendship between Japan and Russia or to make effective use of Russia in ending the war. . . .

. . . "If today, when we are still maintaining our strength, the Anglo-Americans were to have regard for Japan's honor and existence, they could save humanity by bringing the war to an end. If, however, they insist unrelentingly upon unconditional surrender the Japanese are unanimous in their resolve to wage a thoroughgoing war.

. . . "Please bear particularly in mind . . . that we are not asking [for] the Russians' mediation in anything like unconditional surrender. . . ."

c9. MAGIC DIPLOMATIC INTERCEPT NO. 1212, JULY 20, 1945 (SRS 1734)

MILITARY

1. *Soviet reply to Japan's proposal; Sato's ideas*

. . . Later on the 19th Sato dispatched a follow-up message, marked "very urgent" and reading as follows:

"It is extremely regrettable that the Russian Government has expressed its disapproval of the plan for dispatching a Special Envoy on the ground that the Envoy's mission has not been made concrete. This, however, confirms my humble opinion that we have no alternative but to present the Russians with a concrete plan. . . ."

Also available is Sato's reply of 18 July to Togo's message of the day before which stated that Japan would not accept unconditional surrender [IS 18 Jul 45]; the Ambassador's message, which is obscurely worded, seems to make the following points:

a. "It goes without saying that in my earlier messages calling for unconditional surrender or closely equivalent terms, I made an exception of the question of preserving our national structure. Although I have no fear that you misunderstood what I said in the last part of my 8 June message, I am wiring this for your information.

b. "In connection with the question of preserving our national structure, it is clear that, if we present to the Russians the proposals you have outlined [presumably for a peace short of unconditional surrender] we must endeavour to create a strong impression that the proposals represent the positive demands of Japan's 70 million people [i.e., presumably, their maximum concessions].

c. "Except for the matter of maintenance of our national structure, I think that we must absolutely not propose any conditions. The situation has already reached the point where we have no alternative but unconditional surrender or its equivalent. . . ."

C10. MAGIC DIPLOMATIC INTERCEPT NO.1214 JUL 22, 1945 (SRS 1736)

MILITARY

1. Tokyo again says no unconditional surrender; Sato pleads for peace

On 19 July Ambassador Sato forwarded to Tokyo a letter from Vice Commissar Lozovsky. . . .

In a message of 21 July, Foreign Minister Togo has now replied as follows:

"Special Envoy Konoye's mission will be in obedience to the Imperial Will. He will request assistance in bringing about an end to the war through the good offices of the Soviet Government. . . .

"Please understand especially my next wire."

Togo's "next wire," sent the same day, reads as follows:

"With regard to unconditional surrender (I have been informed of your 18 July message) [in which Sato advocated unconditional surrender provided the Imperial House was preserved] we are unable to consent to it under any circumstances whatsoever. Even if the war drags on and it becomes clear that it will take much more bloodshed, the whole country as one man will pit itself against the enemy in accordance with the Imperial Will so long as the enemy demands unconditional surrender. It is in order to avoid such a state of affairs that we are seeking a peace which is not so-called unconditional surrender through the good offices of Russia. It is necessary that we exert ourselves so that this idea will be finally driven home to the Americans and the British. . . .

Togo concluded by saying that he had read a long message of 20 July from Sato, but that the decision he was communicating had been made by the Cabinet and that Sato should proceed accordingly.

The long message of 20 July from Sato to which Togo was referring . . . constitutes an impassioned plea to the Japanese Government to surrender to the Allies with the sole reservation that Japan's "national structure"—i.e., the Imperial House—be preserved. Speaking as he himself says entirely "without reserve," Sato includes in his argument such extraordinary statements as the following: . . .

d. "I think that we have the inescapable and fundamental obligation to resolve as quickly as possible to lay down our arms and save the State and its people.

e. "Our people will have to pant for a long time under the heavy yoke of the enemy . . . [but] after some decades we shall be able to flourish as before.

f. "Immediately after the war ends we must carry out thoroughgoing reforms everywhere within the country. By placing our Government on a more democratic basis and by destroying the despotic bureaucracy, we must try to raise up again the real unity between the Emperor and his people. . . ."

C11. MAGIC DIPLOMATIC INTERCEPT NO. 1218, JULY 26, 1945 (SRS 1740)

PART II   *Tokyo considers surrender on basis of Atlantic Charter*

In a message of 25 July . . . Foreign Minister Togo instructed Ambassador Sato as follows:

"1. The question of the Special Envoy is naturally related very closely to the course of the Big Three Conference. Since Churchill and Attlee are scheduled to return to England, it is said that the Conference will be adjourned for a short while. I would therefore like you to take advantage of this opportunity . . . to obtain an interview with Molotov. . . .

"2. In the interview, please try to get the Russians to adopt a positive attitude with respect to our proposal. . . . Make clear that the sending of the Special Envoy would permit Stalin to acquire the reputation of an advocate of world peace and, further, that we are prepared to meet fully the Russian demands in the Far East. . . .

"3. Furthermore, as you are aware, various discussions are now taking place in England and especially in the United states with respect to the meaning of the demand for Japan's unconditional surrenders. Judging from the speech [or "speeches"] of American 'spokesman' [word in English; plural was apparently intended] it would appear that although they are formally insisting to the end upon unconditional surrender they are actually prepared to mitigate the conditions if Japan surrenders quickly. For example, on the 19th, Navy Captain Zacharias (he is on the staff of the Office of War Information but he broadcast to Japan as a 'spokesman' of the United States Government) said that Japan has two alternatives: (1) to submit to a dictated peace after being destroyed; or (2) to surrender unconditionally and receive the attendant benefits stipulated in the Atlantic Charter. We believe that these statements should not be considered as purely strategic propaganda but that they are calculated to lead us on.

"The fact that the Americans alluded to the Atlantic Charter is particularly worthy of attention at this times. It is impossible for us to accept unconditional surrender, no matter in what guise but it is our idea to inform them by some appropriate means that there is no objection to the restoration of peace on the basis of the Atlantic Charter.

"In all likelihood, the difficult point is the enemy's attitude of insisting on the form of an unconditional surrender. If America and England stick to this, the whole thing will inevitably break down over this one point. On the other hand, although the governments of Russia, England, and America may be cool toward our proposal of a Special Envoy on the ground that it may be a peace stratagem on our part, this—as I have stated repeatedly—is not merely a 'peace feeler' [words in English]. . . ."

C12. MAGIC DIPLOMATIC INTERCEPT NO. 1222, JULY 30, 1945 (SRS 1744)

PART II   1. Report from Sato

As previously noted, on 25 July Foreign Minister Togo sent word to Sato to seek an interview with Foreign Commissar Molotov during the lull in the Potsdam Conference, but Sato was unable to read the message and on the 27th Togo said he would rewire it (DS 26, 27 Jul 45).

Sato has now sent the following message to Togo, dated 29 July. . . .

"7. I had no sooner finished drafting this report when I received your message of 28 July [urging Sato to have an interview with Molotov as quickly as possible]. As for seeing Molotov, I would particularly like to be informed whether our Imperial Government has a concrete and definite plan for terminating the war; otherwise I will make no immediate request for an interview."

C13. MAGIC DIPLOMATIC INTERCEPT NO. 1224,
AUGUST 1, 1945 (SRS 1746)

PART II   1. Sato on Three Power Proclamation

. . . "2. The important point in connection with the Joint Proclamation is that America and England have demanded Japan's immediate unconditional surrender and have stated clearly that they have no intention of softening the terms set forth in the Proclamation. If it is to be understood that Stalin was completely unable to influence the intentions of America and England on this point, it follows that he will be unable to accept our proposal to send a Special Envoy. . . . There is no alternative but immediate unconditional surrender if we are to try to make America and England moderate and to prevent [Russia's] participation in the war.

"Moreover, immediately after Japan's surrender, Stalin will bring full and heavy pressure on America, England, and China with regard to Manchukuo, China, and Korea, and will proceed in the hope of achieving his own demands. Since he actually possesses the real power [to do this] there is no reason why he should now want to make a treaty with Japan. . . .

"Furthermore, it is worthy of note that Evatt, the Australian Foreign Minister, has stated that he is opposed to the tendency of the Joint Proclamation to show greater leniency toward Japan than the United Nations showed Germany. . . ."

C14. MAGIC DIPLOMATIC INTERCEPT NO. 1225,
AUGUST 2, 1945 (SRS 1747)

PART II   1. Tokyo studying surrender terms

Foreign Minister Togo today sent the following to Ambassador Sato (the second half of the message is not yet available):

"Reference your message of 30 July [containing Sato's comments on the Three Power Proclamation].

"I have been fully apprised of Your Excellency's views by your successive wires. . . . However, it should not be difficult for you to realize that, although with the urgency of the war situation our time to proceed with arrangements for ending the war before the enemy lands on the Japanese mainland is limited, on the other hand it is difficult to decide on concrete peace conditions here at home all at once. At present, in accordance with the Imperial Will, there is a unanimous determination to seek the good offices of the Russians in ending the war, to make concrete terms a matter between Japan and Russia, and to send Prince Konoye, who has the deep trust of the Emperor, to carry on discussions with the Russians. It has been decided at any rate to send a Special Envoy in accordance with the views of the highest leaders of [this] Government and . . . we are exerting ourselves to collect the views of all quarters on the matter of concrete terms.

"(Under the circumstances there is a disposition to make the Potsdam Three Power Proclamation the basis of our study concerning terms.)"

C15. MAGIC DIPLOMATIC INTERCEPT NO. 1226
AUGUST 3, 1945 (SRS 1748)

PART II   1. Japanese Army's interest in peace negotiations

The second half of Foreign Minister Togo's 2 August message to Ambassador Sato—now available—contains the first statement to appear in the traffic that the Japanese Army is interested in the effort to end the war with Soviet assistance. . . .

The remainder of the message reads as follows:

"Accordingly, the most urgent task which now confronts us is to persuade the Soviet Government to accept the mission of our Special Envoy. His Majesty, the Emperor, is most profoundly concerned about the matter and has been following developments with the keenest interest. The Premier and the leaders of the Army are now concentrating all their attention on this one point. . . .

"Whatever happens, if we should let one day slip by, that might have [word uncertain, probably 'results'] lasting for thousands of years. Consequently, if the Soviet Government should reply in the negative [to Japan's 25 July request that a Special Envoy be sent for the purpose of obtaining Russia's 'good offices'] I urge you to do everything possible to arrange another interview with Molotov at once . . . and do your best to induce the Soviet government to reconsider the matter and furnish us with an immediate reply."

C16. MAGIC DIPLOMATIC INTERCEPT NO. 1228,
AUGUST 5, 1945 (SRS 1750)

PART II   1. Latest message from Sato

. . . Sato had previously advised Togo that the Proclamation left Japan no alternative but "immediate unconditional surrender if we are to try to make America and England moderate and to prevent [Russia's] participation in the war. . . . In a message sent yesterday, Sato makes the following additional comments:

"Regardless of whether we are able to obtain the good officers of the Russian Govern-

ment for the termination of the war, the fact is undeniable that the Three Power Proclamation of 26 July by America, England and China already provides a basis for ending the
Greater East Asia War. . . . I feel that the statement in your [message of 2 August] indicating that you are disposed at least to make the Three Power Proclamation the basis for study
of our conditions is extremely auspicious. . . .

"As for the peace terms which would [ultimately] be worked out . . . if one looks at the
terms for the handling of Germany decided upon at Potsdam, it is not far-fetched to surmise that a certain amelioration [of conditions for Japan] would be possible. . . .
However, if the Government and the Military dilly-dally in bringing this resolution to
fruition, then all Japan will be reduced to ashes and we will not be able [to avoid] following the road to ruin. . . ."

C17. MAGIC DIPLOMATIC INTERCEPT NO. 1236
AUGUST 13, 1945 (SRS 1758)

PART II   1. *Japanese Army reported dissatisfied with Allied reply*

At 5:24 p.m. Tokyo time . . . on 13 August, the G.E.A. Ministry representative in Hanoi
sent the following message, labelled "absolutely secret," to G.E.A. Minister (and Foreign
Minister) Togo:

"During the night of the 12th, while I was conferring with the Army Commander [pos-
sibly of the Thirty-eighth Army] and the commander of a division, telegraphic instructions were received from the War Minister stating that, since the reply from the four countries is not recognized as permitting the preservation of the national structure, for this
reason the army is to push forward [words uncertain, probably 'to the very end']."

Note: The translation of the foregoing message has been thoroughly checked.

No message from the Japanese Minister of War fitting the above description has been
received. . . .

2. *Japanese Army General Staff Statement on surrender:* The following is the text of a
circular message dated 12 August from the Vice Chief of the Army General Staff to Japan's
Military Attaches in Sweden, Switzerland and Portugal. . . .

"Personal.

"1. As a result of Russia's entrance into the war, the Empire, in the fourth year of its
[war] endeavor, is faced with a struggle for the existence of the nation. However, the Imperial Army and Navy are resolutely determined to continue their efforts to preserve the
national structure [one or two words missing] even if it means the destruction of the Army
and Navy.

"2. You are well aware of the fact that as a final move toward the preservation of
the national structure, diplomatic negotiations have been opened. The Army, however,

with the determination stated in the previous paragraph is striving to carry on the national policy. Unless the aforementioned condition is fulfilled, we will continue the war to the bitter end. . . ."

C18. MAGIC DIPLOMATIC INTERCEPT NO, 1237, AUGUST 14, 1945 (SRS1758)

MILITARY

1. Japan's satellites informed of surrender offer

On 10 August the G.E.A. Ministry advised its posts in Manchukuo, Occupied China, Indo-China, Thailand and Burma that, because of "various foreign and domestic circumstances," the Japanese surrender offer had been made to the Allies. The next day the Ministry added that the "circumstances" referred to "of course include the problem of the atomic bomb. . . ."

C19. MAGIC DIPLOMATIC INTERCEPT NO. 1238, AUGUST 15, 1945 (SRS 1758)

MILITARY

Also yesterday the Japanese Foreign Ministry notified its Legations in Europe that, "in view of the urgency of the situation," it had "begun the disposition and burning of secret documents and spare cryptographic materials" and that the Legations should act accordingly. . . .

3. *Purported Japanese Army criticism of surrender*: At 12:54 a.m. Tokyo time on 15 August (11 hours before the Emperor's broadcast announcing Japan's surrender) [the] Japanese Ambassador . . . in Nanking sent to Tokyo the following summary of a telegram from So Shireikan [almost certainly the commander of the China Expeditionary Army (General Okamura)] to the Minister of War and the Chief of Staff:

"1. Even if the present prerogatives of the Emperor are recognized who will guarantee this if we disarm and demobilize?

"2. The limitation of our sovereignty to the home islands only will take us back to the time when the race of Yamoto was only 30,000,000 people. The existence of 70,000,000 people absolutely requires that we keep Formosa, Korea and [words uncertain, probably South Manchuria].

"3. Such a disgrace as the surrender of several million troops without fighting is not paralleled in the world's military history, and it is absolutely impossible to submit to the unconditional surrender of a million picked troops in perfectly healthy shape to the Chungking forces of defeated China. . . ."

D.

Japanese Government Documents, Military Documents, and Diary Entries

D1. IMPERIAL GENERAL HEADQUARTERS NAVY ORDER 37 ("OUTLINE OF ARMY AND NAVY OPERATIONS"), JANUARY 20, 1945

1. General Policy

a. The final decisive battle of the war will be waged in Japan proper.

b. The armed forces of the Empire will prepare for this battle by immediately establishing a strong strategic position in depth within the confines of a national defense sphere delineated by the Bonin Islands, Formosa, the coastal sector of east China, and southern Korea.

c. The United States will now be considered Japan's principal enemy. Operational planning of all headquarters will be directed toward interception and destruction of American forces, all other theatres and adversaries assuming secondary importance.

2. Preparation and Conduct of Operations

a. Resistance will continue in the Philippines so as to delay as long as possible the enemy's approach to the Homeland defense perimeter.

b. Key strongpoints to be developed within the perimeter defense zone include Iwo Jima, Formosa, Okinawa, the Shanghai district, and the south Korean coast. The main defensive effort will be made in the Ryukyus area. Preparations in the perimeter defense zone will be completed during February and March 1945.

c. When the enemy penetrates the defense zone, a campaign of attrition will be initiated to reduce his preponderance in ships, aircraft, and men, to obstruct the establishment and use of advance bases, to undermine enemy morale and thereby to seriously delay the final assault on Japan. The air forces will make a maximum effort over the perimeter defense zone. Enemy troops that succeed in getting ashore at points on the Homeland defense perimeter will be dealt with by those ground forces on the spot without reinforcement from other theaters.

d. Emphasis in ground preparations will be laid on Kyushu and Kanto. Strong air defenses will be established along key lines of communication. . . .

e. During the delaying operations in the forward area, preparations for the decisive battle will be completed in Japan proper by the early fall of 1945.

f. In general, Japanese air strength will be conserved until an enemy landing is actually under way on or within the defense sphere. The Allied invasion fleet will then be destroyed on the water, principally by sea and air special-attack units. . . .

Source: Reports of General MacArthur: Operations in the Southwest Pacific (Washington, D.C.: U.S. Government Printing Office, 1994), 2, part 2: 585–586.

D2. THE KONOE MEMORIAL, FEBRUARY 14, 1945

Regrettably, I think that defeat is inevitable. What I shall say is based on this assumption.

Defeat will be a blemish upon our *kokutai*, but public opinion in Great Britain and the United States up to now has not gone so far as change in this *kokutai* (of course there are extremist opinions among some, and it is also difficult to gauge what sort of change may take place in the future). Thus, if it were only a matter of defeat, I think it would not be necessary to be so concerned about the *kokutai*. More than defeat itself, what we must be most concerned about from the standpoint of preserving the *kokutai* is the communist revolution which may accompany defeat.

After careful deliberation, it is my belief that at the present time events both within and outside the country are moving rapidly toward a communist revolution. That is to say, outside the country there are the extraordinary advances of the Soviet Union. That the Soviet Union has not abandoned its plan to ultimately bolshevize the world is gradually becoming clear by her recent obvious machinations toward various countries of Europe.

In Europe the Soviet Union is trying to establish soviet-style governments in the countries on its borders, and at least pro-Soviet, pro-communist governments in the remaining countries. She is progressing steadily in this task, and at present is encountering success in most instances. . . .

As I consider the situation in the light of such conditions, there is considerable danger that the Soviet Union will eventually intervene in Japan's domestic affairs. . . . Turning to the domestic scene, I see all the conditions necessary to bring about a communist revolution being prepared day by day: the impoverishment of daily life; an increase in the level of labor's voice; a pro-Soviet mood, which is the other side of a rise in hostile feelings toward Great Britain and the United States; the reform movements of a ring within the military; the movement of the so-called "new bureaucrats" who ride on this; and the secret maneuvers of leftist elements who are manipulating this from behind. Of these, that which warrants greatest concern is the reform movement of a ring within the military. . . .

As I have stated above, both within and outside the country every condition favorable to the advancement of a communist revolution is growing day by day, and should the state of the war become even more disadvantageous hereafter, it is my opinion that these conditions will develop rapidly.

It would be a different matter if there were even a slight hope of breaking free insofar as the future state of the war is concerned, but if we continue under the assumption that defeat is inevitable, to pursue the war further with no prospect of victory will place us completely in the hands of the Communist Party. Thus, from the standpoint of preserving the *kokutai*, I firmly believe that we must work out our method of concluding the war as soon as possible.

The greatest obstacle to conclusion of the war is the existence within the military of that ring which ever since the Manchurian Incident has been pushing things forward until the situation of today. . . .

. . . Thus, if we are to terminate the war, as an essential precondition to this we must first wipe out this ring.

If only this ring is wiped out, then the bureaucrats as well as the civilian elements of the right wing and left wing who ride on its coat-tails will be subdued. . . .

Also, although it may be rather wishful thinking, once this ring is wiped out the features of the military will change greatly, and is it not possible that the atmosphere in the United States, Great Britain, and Chungking will then relax? From the beginning the goal of the United States, Great Britain, and Chungking has been the overthrow of the Japanese military clique, and so, if the character of the military changes and its policy is altered, I wonder if they on their part would not reconsider the continuation of the war. . . .

[In response to a question from the emperor, Konoe added the following:]

I think there is no alternative to making peace with the United States. Even if we surrender unconditionally, I feel that in America's case she would not go so far as to reform Japan's *kokutai* or abolish the imperial house. Japan's territory might decrease to half of what it is at present, but even so, if we can extricate the people from the miserable ravages of war, preserve the *kokutai*, and plan for the security of the imperial house, then we should not avoid unconditional surrender.

[The emperor replied that he agreed with Konoe's assessment.]

Source: John Dower, *Empire and Aftermath: Yoshida Shigeru and the Japanese Experience, 1875–1954* (Cambridge, Mass.: Council on East Asian Studies/Harvard University Press, 1979), 260–264.

D3. IMPERIAL GENERAL HEADQUARTERS ARMY
ORDER NO. 1299, APRIL 8, 1945

1. The forthcoming decisive operation in the Homeland and adjacent areas will be referred to as the *Ketsu-Go* . . . Operation. . . .

2. Operational Policy

a. The Imperial Army will hasten preparations to meet and crush the attack of U.S. forces in the above key areas. Emphasis will be on the Kanto area . . . and Kyushu. . . .

b. Preparations for operations . . . will fall into the following general phases:

First April through July

Second August through September

Third from 1 October . . .

Emergency preparations in Kyushu will be completed by early June. Dispositions will continue to be strengthened during the second phase, and all tactical plans completed. Final deployment of field units and perfection of the field positions will be completed in the early part of the third phase.

c. Air Operations

(1) A close watch will be maintained over all enemy fleet movements, particularly transport convoys. Air search over the approaches to the Homeland will be continuous and aggressive.

(2) Enemy amphibious task forces attempting to invade the Homeland will be destroyed on the water.

(3) The primary target of the air offensive will be transports. . . .

d. Ground Operations

(1) The ground forces will win the final decision by overwhelming and annihilating the enemy landing force in the coastal area before the beachhead is secure.

(2) Speedy maneuver of the largest possible force against the enemy landing sector is the key to success in such operations. . . .

(3) In the event of simultaneous invasions of more than one area, the main Japanese counter offensive will be directed at the main enemy landing. . . .

(4) If the location of the enemy's main landing is undetermined, the main Japanese force will be committed in the area which presents the most favorable terrain for offensive operations. . . .

(5) Large-scale and thorough construction of fortifications will be carried out with emphasis on those field positions designed to provide jumping-off, rallying, and support points for local offensives.

(6) Special security precautions will be taken at vital installations to forestall enemy airborne penetrations.

e. Air Defense

(1) Air defense of the Homeland will be emphasized. Points of first priority will be Tokyo, cities lying on the principal routes of communication, vital industrial facilities, airfields and munitions dumps.

(2) Increasing emphasis will be placed on air raid precautions and perfecting warning facilities.

(3) Dispersal of facilities, particularly airfields, will be accomplished wherever possible.

(4) When the ground armies initiate their operational movements to counter enemy landings, their assembly must be covered by antiaircraft units. . . .

f. Channel Defense

(1) In cooperation with the Navy, the defenses of such important straits as Bungo, Kii, and Shimonoseki will be strengthened. Principal harbors will also be strongly defended.

(2) Batteries will be stationed so as to prevent penetration by enemy vessels and amphibious landings. Channel defense units will strengthen bomb and shell-proof installations. . . .

g. Guerrilla Resistance and Internal Security

(1) We will strive to realize our operational objectives through exploitation of the traditional spirit of "Every citizen a soldier."

(2) Guerrilla resistance will aim at the obstruction of enemy activities and the attrition of enemy strength through guerrilla warfare, espionage, deception, raids on rear areas, and demolition of enemy installations. . . .

(3) Internal security will aim at protecting military activities, vital communications, transport, power source, and secret areas. If necessary, internal security will quell public disorder arising as a result of air raids, bombardment, invasion, propaganda, and natural disaster.

(4) Forces for guerrilla resistance and internal security will be drawn from the entire body of the citizenry as the situation may dictate. . . .

Source: Reports of General MacArthur: Operations in the Southwest Pacific (Washington, D.C.: U.S. Government Printing Office, 1994), 2, part 2: 601–607.

D4. KETSU-GO DIRECTIVE, APRIL 8, 1945

Outline of Preparations for the Ketsu-Go Operation
(Army Directive No. 2438)

. . . 1. Commander in Chiefs of the First and Second General Armies, Air General Army and the China Expeditionary Army and the commanders of the Fifth and

Seventeenth Area Armies will execute operations and preparations for operations in accordance with the Appendix, "Outline of Preparations for the Ketsu Operations". . . .

Outline of Preparations for the Ketsu-Go Operations

1. General

a. This outline indicates the manner in which each army will make combat preparations and conduct operations in the overall operation to repel the American invasion of the Homeland. . . .

b. This outline covers operations to be completed by the fall of 1945. . . .

2. Outline of Operations

a. Introduction

(1) The Imperial Army will rapidly establish a strategic disposition aimed at the ultimate annihilation of the enemy by strengthening its combat preparations and will encounter the American invasion at key areas on the Japanese Homeland. For this purpose . . . combat preparations shall be concentrated chiefly in the Kanto and Kyushu areas. . . .

(2) The Japanese Army will endeavor to repulse enemy air attacks and to restrict enemy plane activities and protect important points in Tokyo. . . .

(3) The Imperial Army will endeavor to crush the enemy invading key areas of the mainland while the invasion force is still at sea. Enemy forces which succeed in landing will be swiftly attacked by resolute defenders in order to seek the decisive victory.

(a) In conducting air operations, emphasis shall be the disruption of the enemy's landing plans. The principal target as a consequence shall be enemy convoys. . . .

(b) The principal objective of the land operation shall be to destroy the enemy in the key areas along the coast. . . .

(4) The Imperial Army will cooperate with the navy's surface traffic protection, its surface and underwater special attack unit and channel defense operations.

(5) The success of the operation will be insured by utilizing the advantageous points of fighting in the Homeland, by displaying the traditional spirit of the entire nation with the people and the military fighting as one. . . .

f. Air Defense Operations

(1) Air Operations

(a) To counter enemy air attacks against strategic points on the mainland, we must at an opportune moment intercept enemy planes, and also neutralize their bases. We must also restrict the activities of enemy task forces at the proper time. . . .

4. Homeland Resistance and Internal Security

a. The main objective of interior resistance . . . and internal security . . . is the destruction of the enemy in order to secure the possession of Homeland by utilizing unified power of the entire nation with the government and the people working with the nation. . . .

Source: Donald S. Detweiler and Charles B. Burdick, eds., *War in Asia and the Pacific*, vol. 12, *Defense of the Homeland and the End of the War* (New York: Garland, 1980), 201–223.

D5. IMPERIAL HEADQUARTERS ARMY DEPARTMENT ESTIMATE OF THE SITUATION FOR THE SPRING OF 1946, JULY 1, 1945

I. Overall Strategy

The enemy is attempting to direct its major operations against the Japanese mainland in an effort to end the war quickly. By taking advantage of its present favorable situation, and with an eye to the political and military situation in CHINA, it plans to conduct landing operations on strategic areas with superior strength as soon as possible. Meanwhile, the Japanese mainland will be kept neutralised with intensified naval and air operations. . . .

II. Political Situation

a. The problems revolving around manpower resources, war-time production and national economy (which were regarded from the domestic standpoint as weaknesses in the production of war) have eased with the end of hostilities against GERMANY. Now, there is a comfortable reserve of national (war) potential for the war against JAPAN, and successful operations in the Pacific have made the American people increasingly confident of victory.

b. However, the partial demobilisation and industrial reconversion following the end of hostilities in EUROPE aroused optimism about the war situation and the desire to grab post-war profits. However, the prediction of increased casualties along with the indefinite war objectives may become factors contributing to decreased fighting morale among the people and the military. Perfection of the National Conscription Law increases in labor strife, criticism of strategy, et cetera are obstacles to the success of the government's war measures.

c. To counteract such latent weaknesses in the domestic situation, the government has warned the nation of the problem and necessity of concluding the war against JAPAN. On the other hand, it is endeavoring to raise the country's fighting morale by promising improvements in the economic situation and certain victory through a material offensive. However, the people are becoming doubtful about a prompt end to Pacific hostilities in view of the forecast of a possible protracted and difficult war, the issues involving the relationship between the UNITED STATES and SOVIET RUSSIA, and the post-war settlements.

d. Directing the war against JAPAN will be a complicated task for Truman, the new president, because of the difficulty in achieving unified control over military and political activities, especially in coordinating foreign and domestic policies which are striving for an early conclusion to the war with the strategy of the army leaders. This factor will be a further detriment to a brief Pacific War.

Should the UNITED STATES be defeated in the battle for JAPAN itself, it is inevitable that confidence in Truman and the military will be lost, and that depreciation of fighting morale will ensure. . . .

Source: Donald S. Detweiler and Charles B. Burdick, eds., *War in Asia and the Pacific,* vol. 12, *Defense of the Homeland and the End of the War* (New York: Garland, 1980).

d6. CHIEF OF ARMY GENERAL STAFF YOSHIJIRO UMEZU NOTATIONS, SUPREME COUNCIL FOR THE DIRECTION OF THE WAR CONFERENCE, AUGUST 9, 1945

The Chief of the Army General Staff had the following pencil written remarks on a document which recorded the initial speeches made by the Prime Minister and the Foreign Minister:

"The Supreme War Direction Council Conference (at Imperial Palace at 1030 in the morning) [August 9 at 1030]

1. From the Prime Minister I would like to confirm the countermeasures against the Soviets entering the war:

a. From the Minister of Foreign Affairs. This morning we learned only of the radio broadcast [of the declaration of war] from the Soviets, we have not received the official notification from the Soviet Government. We have not received a telegram from Ambassador Sato and we have heard nothing from Ambassador Malik about the negotiation with the Soviets with regard to the trip of the special envoy we proposed based on the Emperor's wish to end the war as soon as possible. Neither Stalin nor Molotov sent me a telegram because they were attending the Potsdam Conference. Molotov, however, announced that he would be able to see Ambassador Sato at 1700 on the 8th. For this reason the declaration of war by the Soviets was completely unexpected. The version published in Tass is included in a separate paper.

Also the announcement by the English Foreign Ministry spokesman says that the declaration of war by Soviets was not known to us before it happened. The statement by the American government is as follows: We hope that the Japanese people will quickly terminate the war.

The use of atomic bombs which has the destructive force equal to 2,000 B-29s has been studied by Americans and the effect of it should be clear if you examine the results in Hiroshima. *End of Statement*

Source: Boeicho Boei Kenshujo Senshi Shitsu (War History Office, Defense Agency)
Senshi Shosho (War History Series), No. 82, *Daihon'ei Rikugun-Bu (10)* (Army Division,
Imperial General Headquarters, vol. 10) (Tokyo, 1975), 436.

D7. IMPERIAL GENERAL HEADQUARTERS ARMY SECTION ORDER 1374,
AUGUST 9, 1945

On the 9th, Imperial Headquarters Army Section Order 1374 was issued. The contents
were as follows:

1. The Soviets declared war against Japan and . . . on the 9th they began an offensive
along the Manchuria-Soviet border regions. In those areas their operations are not yet on
a large scale.

2. Imperial Headquarters will use the forces located along the borders to frustrate the
enemy advance and quickly prepare for the start of all out operations against the Soviets.

3. 17th Area Army shall come under command of the Kwantung Army. The timing of
the transfer should be 0600 August 10.

4. The commander of the Kwantung Army for the time being will employ forces in
border areas to destroy enemy advance and shall prepare the start of the all out operations
against Soviets. The guidelines for above described operations shall be as follows: Kwantung Army shall direct its main operations against the Soviets and act in such a way as to
protect Japan and Korea. During this time, Chosin [Korea] shall have the minimum
forces to be prepared for attack from U.S. forces.

5. The commander of the China Expeditionary Army shall prepare quickly for part of
his forces and supplies to be transferred to the southern Korea area and at the same time
use his local forces to destroy the attacking Soviet forces.

6. The border of the operations between Kwantung Army and China Expeditionary
Army is as follows: The line of [words unclear] and the line itself falls under the jurisdic-
tion of the China Expeditionary Army. The commander of Kwantung Army shall release
the units that have been newly transferred to this area to pass to the command of the commander of the China Expeditionary Army.

Source: Boeicho Boei Kenshujo Senshi Shitsu (War History Office, Defense Agency)
Senshi Shosho (War History Series), No. 82, *Daihon'ei Rikugun-Bu (10)* (Army Division,
Imperial General Headquarters, vol. 10) (Tokyo, 1975), 439.

D8. AIR GENERAL ARMY COMMANDER MASAKAZU KAWABE
MEMORANDUM, AUGUST 10, 1945

After the decision made in the Imperial Conference, first the Minister and the Chief
of the General Staff called the Educational Superintendent, First General Army

Commander, [and] *First Air General Army Commander* [M. Kawabe] *to the Ministry of the Army at 1100 in the morning and gave them the news. With regard to this, the commander of the Air General Army, Kawabe, had the following memorandum*:

"In that meeting, the briefing given by Chief of the General Staff Umezu covered the background, content and conclusion of the liaison meeting, cabinet meeting and the following Imperial Conference with regard to the measures against Soviet entry into the war, and the results indicated that the final phase has arrived. The Emperor decided that the government has already lost the will to continue the war and the people also. And His Majesty himself has lost complete trust in the plan of the decisive battle made by the armed forces and finally made the decision. We still do not know whether the conditions attached by Japan could be treated fairly [will be accepted?]; however, it is almost hopeless that the people of Japan could rise up again when such conditions were not accepted. I had the feeling that I wanted to cry, but still I could not cry. I expressed only one thought. I asked that the final decision made by this nation should be clearly shown by an Imperial Edict and there should not be any intermediate notifications before that. This was agreed upon by all of those at the meeting. This is the system of the Japanese nation and only with this system will the citizens and armed forces accept the situation without any other confusion [disorder?]. Our air force is not able to maintain its honor in today's situation. At this moment, we want our power to be expressed for the eternal honor of the nation of Japan and for that purpose we revised the speech of the Chief of Staff to be delivered to the staff members of various armies."

Source: Boeicho Boei Kenshujo Senshi Shitsu (War History Office, Defense Agency) *Senshi Shosho* (War History Series), No. 82, *Daihon'ei Rikugun-Bu (10)* (Army Division, Imperial General Headquarters, vol. 10) (Tokyo, 1975), 456.

D9. ARMY MINISTER KORECHIKA ANAMI BROADCAST: "INSTRUCTION TO THE TROOPS," AUGUST 10, 1945

"My fellow members of the armed forces, the Soviets have finally invaded this Imperial Nation. Despite their efforts to embellish their motives, their real aim to invade and occupy the Greater East Asia is apparent. Since events have reached this point, there is nothing further to be said. The only thing we have to do is to fight the sacred war to defend to the last this Land of the Gods. Even thought we have to eat grass and chew dirt and lay in the field we must fight to the bitter end, ever firm in our belief that we shall find life in death. This is the spirit to serve your country by using your seven lives which is the spirit of Masashige Kusunoki when he aimed to save the country saying please have peace in your mind if you hear that I alone am alive. And again [recall] the words by Tokimune Hojo upon the time of the Mongol Invasion: [With no thought except to] surge forward to destroy the invading enemy, the soldiers in the whole country without any exception will show his own spirit of Masashige Kusunoki and fighting spirit of Tokimune Hojo to charge straight ahead to destroy the arrogant enemy. August 10, 1945, Minister of the Army."

The address was broadcast at the time of the news hour 1900 on August 10.

Source: *Boeicho Boei Kenshujo Senshi Shitsu* (War History Office, Defense Agency) *Senshi Shosho* (War History Series), No. 82, *Daihon'ei Rikugun-Bu (10)* (Army Division, Imperial General Headquarters, vol. 10) (Tokyo, 1975), 456.

D10. ARMY GENERAL STAFF TELEGRAM, AUGUST 11, 1945, AND REACTION OF AIR GENERAL ARMY COMMANDER GENERAL M. KAWABE

Then the Chief of the Army General Staff sent the following telegrams to various armies under his direct command. Army General Staff Telegram number 487, dated August 11, 1945, and titled "Regarding the Efforts to Destroy the Enemy with the Entire Army Maintaining Its Strong Will." Text as follows:

"Concerning the entry of the Soviets into the war, Japan's situation has reached a turning point in the rise or fall of the nation. However, the intention of Imperial Headquarters remains as announced in the Imperial Headquarters Army Division Order No. 1378. Item one states that the Japanese Army and Navy will never cease its war effort to maintain the national polity and defend the Homeland, even in the face of complete annihilation.

"To complete the two great purposes of the war as shown above, it is true that negotiations have started. In view of these circumstances, there may be various reports, including propaganda from many countries, regarding peace negotiations and related matters. However, we must not let this dissipate our morale and the strong will of the nation. It is necessary for you to take action in this regard. The whole armed forces shall maintain a strong unity and a strict military discipline and strive to accomplish their respective missions without fail." [It is not known what time this telegram was transmitted; however, the China Expeditionary Army reported reception at 2058.]

The commander Air General Army received it on the afternoon of the 12th and wrote in his diary: "I passed this to subordinates and I made a statement so that they can maintain high morale."

Source: *Boeicho Boei Kenshujo Senshi Shitsu* (War History Office, Defense Agency) *Senshi Shosho* (War History Series), No. 82, *Daihon'ei Rikugun-Bu (10)* (Army Division, Imperial General Headquarters, vol. 10) (Tokyo, 1975), 466.

D11. ARMY CLASSIFIED TELEGRAM NO. 61,
SIGNED BY GENERALS ANAMI AND UMEZU, AUGUST 11, 1945,
AND REACTION OF GENERAL YASUJI OKAMURA

On the 10th, the Minister and the Chief of the General Staff notified the Superintendent of Army Education and the First General Army and the Air General Army commander of the contents of the Imperial Conference. On the 11th at 1437 they sent the following telegram:

"Army Classified Telegram No. 61 from the Minister of the Army and Chief of the Army General Staff addressed to the Supreme Commander Kantogun [i.e., Manchuria], Supreme Commander China Expeditionary Army and Commander Second General Army. Military Secret Code and for your eyes only. Japan is engaged in strong operations after the Soviet entry into the war, and at the same time is in negotiations with the Soviets, U.S., Britain and China based on the following items:

1. Japan is ready to accept the Potsdam Declaration which the Soviets have joined on condition that there is no demand for change in the Emperor's sovereign power.

2. It is beyond question that Japan will decisively move towards the completion of the war if there is the slightest doubt about the promise as to the above mentioned conditions. We are expressly advising you of this so you will not have any misunderstanding [of our position]."

Diary Entry of General Yasuji Okamura, August 11, 1945

The Minister of the Army directly passed this message verbally to the First General Army and Air General Army. [This telegram reportedly reached the China Expeditionary Army at 1728.] The Supreme Commander Okamura of the China Expeditionary Army received this telegram at 1800 on the 11th. He wrote in his diary as follows:

This means that Japan will be relegated to the state before the Russo-Japanese war and in addition our Homeland has been burned down. I have an extreme fear contemplating Japan's future. I rather hope that the allied forces will not accept our proposal and the war effort will continue. . . .

Source: *Boeicho Boei Kenshujo Senshi Shitsu* (War History Office, Defense Agency) *Senshi Shosho* (War History Series), No. 82, *Daihon'ei Rikugun-Bu (10)* (Army Division, Imperial General Headquarters, vol. 10) (Tokyo, 1975), 466.

D12. GENERAL UMEZU AND ADMIRAL TOYODA REPORT TO THE EMPEROR, AUGUST 12, 1945

Report to His Majesty by the Chiefs of the Army and Navy General Staffs

"Because we have understood the contents of the memorandum which American Secretary of State representing the U.S., Great Britain, Soviet Union and China, sent to the Imperial Government through the government of Switzerland, we would like to present the views of the Supreme Command. It is the view of the Supreme Command that the conditions for peace in this memorandum should be decisively rejected. According to item one of the memorandum, 'At the instant of surrender, Japan government and the Japanese emperor shall be subject to the Allied Forces Supreme Commander who should take measures which are considered necessary to carry out the conditions of surrender.' It is very awful to say this, but this means that it will reduce this Imperial Nation to a vassal status that we should never accept. In addition, we must also reject the disarmament of the entire army and navy in item two of the memorandum, the establishment of government form based on the free will of the people given in item four and the stationing of Allied forces in Japan in item five.

"When the memorandum is considered as a whole, it is clear that the enemy intention is to demand unconditional surrender both in name and in reality. And especially it clearly defiles the dignity of the Emperor. Therefore, it is against the foundations on which His Majesty based his decision. Under such conditions, it would be unbearable for the loyal citizens and subjects within this country to accept this memorandum. This may lead to a situation that can not be controlled. It is particularly unbearable for the millions of soldiers stationed overseas who fight and risk their lives with the supreme joy of offering to give their lives for our everlasting cause. They would feel that they must not only endure attack from outside but also that they face the internal collapse of the nation and the destruction of our national polity and the perishing of this imperial nation. By saying [this?] at least, we must express our belief. Those beliefs we have expressed above are shared by the government we presume, however, we hereafter will reach a complete agreement of our opinions with the government and then we will ask for your Majesty's decision. August 12, 1945. (0800)

> *Umezu, Yoshijiro, Chief of Army General Staff*
> *Toyoda, Soemu, Chief of Navy General Staff*

Source: Boeicho Boei Kenshujo Senshi Shitsu (War History Office, Defense Agency) *Senshi Shosho* (War History Series), No. 82, *Daihon'ei Rikugun-Bu (10)* (Army Division, Imperial General Headquarters, vol. 10) (Tokyo, 1975), 476.

D13. ARMY CLASSIFIED TELEGRAM NO. 63, AUGUST 12, 1945

Army Classified Telegram No, 63; Telegram concerning negotiation with the U.S. August 12, 1945, Minister of Army and Chief of the Army General Staff:

To the commanders of the Second General Army, 5th Area Army, the 10th Area Army, the Supreme commanders of the Kantogun [Manchuria], China Expeditionary Army, Southern Army and the commander of the First General Army and Air General Army:

We have received the broadcast announcement from the U.S. in the early morning of the 12th, today, with regard to our proposal to the enemy regarding the termination of the Greater Eastern Asia War. The army intends to reject firmly the enemy offer in the above broadcast because it was against the retention of our national polity. We will only continue the war and with that firm conviction we will push on [to retain?] our national policy. And we want each army also to engage with a firm will in this goal in your operations. (Message was given to First General and Air General Army orally.)

Source: Boeicho Boei Senshi Shitsu (War History Office, Defense Agency) Senshi Shosho (War History Series), No. 82, Daihon'ei Rikugun-Bu (10) (Army Division, Imperial General Headquarters, vol. 10) (Tokyo, 1975), 478.

D14. DIARY ENTRIES OF MARQUIS KOICHI KIDO, JANUARY 1944–JUNE 1945

[January 6, 1944]

I am wondering about the course of the war for the coming year. . . .

First, we must consider whether we should take measures to end the war in the event that Germany is beaten or surrenders unconditionally. . . .

Second, in such a situation, I believe that the only terms of peace on our part that would be acceptable to our enemies would be those which involved considerable concessions. It is possible to outline the peace terms as follows:

(1) The problems of the Pacific Ocean should be dealt with by the principal nations bordering the ocean.

(2) Japan, the U.S.S.R., China, the U.S.A., and Great Britain should organize a commission.

(3) The regions occupied by Japan and the islands in the Pacific Ocean should not be fortified.

(4) With the exception of Manchuria, the independent nations in those regions, other than the principal nations, should be made permanent neutral powers, similar to Switzerland. The remaining occupied regions should be placed under the administration of a joint commission composed of the principal nations.

(5) The economic policies in the regions should, as a rule, be based on freedom, reciprocity, and equal opportunity.

When and how these plans are to be proposed should be studied most carefully. The proposal should not coincide with the collapse of Germany, but should be prior to when the U.S.A., Great Britain, and the U.S.S.R. unite in their hostility against Japan. Measures may be taken with the U.S.S.R. as the mediator.

The plan may, at a glance, be considered too conciliatory and weak-kneed, but considering what the future holds for the world, I believe we must preserve and cultivate our actual power for about one century to come, considering the experiences gained in the Japan-China Incident and the German-Soviet war, the development of aircraft and the actual strength of the U.S.A. and the U.S.S.R., and the terrible attrition of our national power.

If these beliefs are correct, we should carefully avoid being isolated and attacked by nations as a colored race. From this point of view, I believe the best way is for us to retain the actual power of the state by secretly cooperating with Soviet Russia and China, which are essentially Oriental in their stand against the Anglo-Saxons—the U.S.A. and Great Britain. We must prepare as the circumstances require.

[January 4, 1945]

[Extract] From 10:40 to 11:05 a.m. I was received in audience by His Majesty in the imperial library. On this occasion, His Majesty condescended to tell me the following:

"Upon granting an audience to Premier Koiso toward the end of last year, I questioned him as to the government's policy to cope with the present war situation. The war in Leyte does not necessarily warrant optimism, I said. But indications show that a decisive battle will have to be fought on Luzon, in view of the possibility that, were the truth in this connection made known, the people naturally would be disheartened, it would bring about a decline in the fighting spirit and it would affect the expansion of war production. Also the government has been loudly publicizing the so-called decisive battle in Leyte to guide the nation in the conduct of war. The premier answered that he, himself, had been surprised upon learning the true state of affairs that morning, and that since then he had been studying a new policy regarding the national guidance. . . ."

[June 8, 1945]

[Extract] In the afternoon I drafted an analysis of and plan for the war situation, as follows:

(1) The progress of the war in Okinawa, to my regret, makes me believe that it is destined inevitably to result in a miserable fiasco. Moreover, it is almost certain that this result will come about in the very near future.

(2) After a careful scrutiny of reports on our national strength, attached for reference to the agenda of the conference in the imperial presence, I can see that, by the latter part of this year, we will be all but incapable of conducting the war on all fronts.

(3) Although it is very likely that I, a nonexpert in this field, would be unable to estimate accurately the enemy's strategy for the future, I can say that, judging from his air force at present and the tremendous effect of his mass incendiary bombing, it would not be a difficult task to sweep away, one after another, all the cities and towns, down to villages in the country. He would not require much time for it either. If the enemy were to adopt the tactics of destroying residential quarters, this would at the same time bring about the loss of stored clothing and foodstuffs. Especially in farming villages, since they are not accustomed to air raids or to confronting this type of attack, it would be almost impossible to enforce the dispersal of supplies beforehand. So it has to be observed that most of these supplies will have to be lost, especially in small towns and villages all over the country, since their antiaircraft defense has hardly amounted to anything.

(4) If this is correct, the extreme shortage of provisions and foodstuffs that will sweep the country in the latter part of this year and thereafter—in light of the approaching chilly

season—will cause serious unrest among the people at large. And, in consequence, the situation will be beyond salvation.

(5) Therefore, I believe it is most urgent that resolute steps be taken. By what means and measures should we attain this objective? That is what must be most carefully worked out.

(6) Judging from various announcements and articles indicating the enemy's so-called peace offensive, it is well nigh certain that he looks upon the overthrowing of the so-called militarist clique as his chief objective.

(7) Although I believe it is a proper course to start negotiations after the military-proposed peace, this is almost impossible at present, considering the current condition of our country. Also, we are most likely to lose a good chance should we wait until the opportunity matures. As a result, we cannot be sure we will not share the fate of Germany and be reduced to adverse circumstances under which we will not attain even our supreme object of safeguarding the Imperial Household and preserving the national polity.

(8) Although to do so may be very much out of usage according to past precedents, and although it is regrettable to have to ask for His Majesty's approval concerning this monumental proposal, I believe we have no alternative but to solicit an imperial resolution for the sake of all the people and exert our wholehearted efforts to saving the war situation as follows: (a) Negotiate with a mediating country by means of His Majesty the Emperor's personal message. Though it would perhaps be a good idea to initiate direct negotiations with the Anglo-Americans, who are our opponents, it would be more appropriate to have Soviet Russia, which is observing neutrality at present, act as our intermediary. (b) The chief point in the prospective message by His Majesty would be to make it known that the Throne, who had always been interested in peace—citing the imperial rescript on the declaration of war—has decided, in view of the impossibly heavy war damages we have sustained, to bring the war to a close on "very generous terms." (c) The terms would have limits: If a guarantee for making the Pacific Ocean literally "a pacific ocean" in the true sense were obtained, Japan would give up her position of occupation and direction in the Pacific, inasmuch as we would be allowed to help various nations and races achieve independence in their respective countries and sectors. The army and navy forces stationed in the occupied areas would be evacuated on our own initiative. Though it is possible that they might be forced by pressing circumstances to give up their arms on the spot, this would have to depend on the outcome of negotiations. In regard to the reduction of armaments, we must be prepared for pretty strong demands being forced on us. There will be no choice for us but to be content with a minimum defense. . . .

August 7

[Extract] At 10:20 a.m. President Hiranuma of the Privy Council called at my office. We exchanged opinions on saving the war situation. He apparently was concerned about the preservation of the national structure.

At noon I received a report that America used an atomic bomb in attacking Hiroshima, and the damage sustained by us is enormous. Word says that the casualty list includes roughly 130,000 persons killed and injured.

From 1:30 to 2:05 p.m. I was received in audience by His Majesty in the imperial library. He was gravely concerned about how to save the situation, and asked me various questions. . . .

August 9

From 9:55 to 10:00 a.m. I was received in audience by His Majesty in the imperial library. Soviet Russia has declared war on Japan and has entered into a state of war with us, as from today. His Majesty instructed me to have a thorough talk with the premier, inasmuch as he thought it imperative to speedily work out and decide upon a plan to save the war situation. In reply, I assured His Majesty that I would discuss the matter with the premier at once, since I had an appointment with him later in the morning.

At 10:10 a.m. Premier Suzuki called at my office. I conveyed His Majesty's instructions to him, emphasizing the necessity of terminating the war by immediately taking advantage of the Potsdam Declaration. Since the Throne has also been desirous of seeking the senior statesmen's opinions, I asked the premier to explain the circumstances to them beforehand. The premier took his leave, saying that he would convoke a meeting of the Supreme War Guidance Council at 10:30 a.m. in order to decide the country's stance.

From 10:55 to 11:45 a.m. I had an audience with His Majesty and reported to the Throne about my interview with the premier.

At 1:30 p.m. Premier Suzuki called at my office and reported that the Supreme War Guidance Council had decided to accept the Potsdam Declaration with the following conditions: (1) preservation of the imperial dynasty; (2) voluntary evacuation of troops; (3) handling by our own country of persons responsible for the war; and (4) a guarantee of no occupation.

At 2:00 p.m. the chief aide-de-camp came to my office and informed me of the war situation on the Manchukuo-Soviet border.

At 2:45 p.m. Prince Takamatsu personally called me on the telephone and expressed his opinion regarding the measures to meet the situation, fearing that the Allied powers might take our conditional acceptance as a refusal. . . .

August 9

[Extract] From 3:10 to 3:25 p.m. I was granted an audience by His Majesty in the imperial library. I reported to the Throne about the apprehensions voiced by Prince Takamatsu. . . .

At 4:00 p.m. Mr. Shigemitsu called at my office and strongly urged that a proper measure be adopted to meet the situation, asserting that a rupture would be inevitable if we should lay down the four conditions.

From 10:50 to 10:53 p.m. I had an audience with His Majesty and reported to the Throne regarding the revision of the Cabinet's plan to cope with the situation. I asked His Majesty's approval for an audience to be granted to Premier Suzuki, the convocation of a council in the imperial presence, and the participation by President Hiranuma of the Privy Council and myself in this gathering. . . .

From 11:50 p.m. to 2:20 a.m. (next morning), the council in the imperial presence was convoked in a chamber attached to the imperial library and it was decided by the imperial judgment to accept the Potsdam Declaration on the condition that the preservation of the imperial dynasty and the right of sovereignty of the Emperor be acknowledged as per the foreign minister's plan. . . .

August 10

[Extract] Summoned by his majesty following the adjournment of the council in the imperial presence, I was received in audience from 2:32 to 2:38 a.m. His Majesty was pleased to explain the imperial decision, to which I listened with deep emotion and gratitude. . . .

"Although much is said about the prospective decisive battle on the mainland, even the most important defense, at Kujukuri-hama, is not yet to be completed. Equipment with which the divisions are to fight the war of decision are also insufficient, and I understand it will be after the middle of September before the required supplies will be provided. The increased production of aircraft is not progressing satisfactorily either. Plans and their enforcement are never well coordinated. Under these circumstances, how can we win the war?

"Of course, there is something really unbearable when I think of the disarmament of our loyal and brave fighting forces and the punishment of those in charge of the war, since they are the people who have contributed loyal and meritorious services. Today, however, it is time to bear the unbearable, I suppose. Recalling how Emperor Meiji must have felt at the time of the three-power intervention, I, holding back my tears, agree to the original plan. . . ."

At a little past 9:00 p.m. Prince Konoye called at my residence. He came to see me because he was worried about the war minister's decree issued to the whole army. We exchanged opinions at length.

August 11

At 3:30 p.m. I called upon the Imperial Household Minister Ishiwata at his office and we exchanged views concerning the idea that His Majesty might well be advised to broadcast an imperial message over the radio. From 3:55 to 4:30 p.m. I was granted an audience with His Majesty. . . . At 5:00 p.m. I called on the Imperial Household minister and informed him that His Majesty was willing to make the broadcast at any moment.

August 12

At 11:00 a.m. Foreign Minister Togo repaired to the Imperial Palace, on which occasion I had a talk with him. He submitted to the Throne a report concerning the enemy's reply and expressed apprehensions that Article 4, referring to the free will of the people, might be made an issue of controversy by supporters of the national polity. The Foreign Office, however, is understood to regard the matter as nothing to worry about. . . .

At 1:40 p.m. President Hiranuma of the Privy Council called at my office and said that he was opposed to the recent reply from the point of view of the national polity. . . .

At 6:30 p.m. Foreign Minister Togo called at my office and had a talk with me. It seems that the premier has agreed with Baron Hiranuma's position, and Mr. Togo appeared somewhat worried about future prospects. I feel extremely anxious.

At 9:30 p.m. Premier Suzuki called at my office. . . . I laid stress on the necessity under the present circumstances of carrying out the present plan even thought there might be a possibility of a riot breaking out in the country. The premier answered that he concurred with my opinion. It was quite reassuring.

August 13

[Extract] At 7:10 a.m. War Minister Anami called at my office and set forth his opinion concerning the recent reply from the Allied powers. He concluded that he could not approve of it as it was. I also stated my opinion. Although we agreed with each other about preserving the national polity, we differed as to the future outlook and to the means to be taken. . . .

August 14

[Extract] The enemy are now scattering handbills carrying the Allied powers' reply. Since I feared that the entire nation might be plunged into confusion if these circumstances continued, I had an audience with the Throne from 8:30 to 8:35 a.m. I submitted to His Majesty my opinion on the situation, and was filled with awe and deep emotion upon witnessing that His Majesty's determination was very firm. . . .

Following the adjournment of the conference in the imperial presence at noon, I had an audience with the Throne. . . . I really could not lift my head, as His Majesty related the circumstances with tearful eyes. . . .

At 8:30 p.m. Premier Suzuki was given an audience with His Majesty. He submitted to the Throne a draft of the imperial message of surrender, obtaining His Majesty's sanction on the matter.

Source: Diary of Marquis Kido, 1931–1945: Selected Translations in English (Frederick, Md.: University Publications of America, 1984), 374–445.

D15. WAR CRIMES TESTIMONY OF MARQUIS KOICHI KIDO, OCTOBER 1947

[16 October 1947]

KOICHI KIDO, an accused, being first duly sworn, testified through Japanese interpreters as follows:

Direct Examination . . .

. . . On August 6, 1945, the Americans dropped an atomic bomb at Hiroshima, nearly reducing the entire city to ashes at a stroke. Japan had been on tip-toe of expectation of a reply from the Soviet Union. It was anticipated that Stalin and Molotov would return to Moscow on August 6 or 7 when they would reply to Japan's demarche, as promised. But Japan's expectation was nullified. Not only that, the Soviet Union declared war on Japan and a state of war began to exist between the two countries on August 9, 1945.

"302. On that morning I had an audience with the Emperor when I advised him that there was no alternative left to Japan at this juncture but to accept the Potsdam Declaration and terminate the war as already decided by His Majesty. The Emperor who was like minded commanded me to have a full talk with the Prime Minister, as it might be necessary to study and decide a termination of the war without loss of time. The events of August 9, 1945 are recorded in my diary for that day. . . .

[Note: Kido read his entire diary into the record at the Tokyo trials. Section 304 of his testimony is a selection from the diary that does not appear in the published English-language version.]

"304. On August 10, 1945, atomic bombs were dropped on Nagasaki city causing a large number of victims. This gave a great shock to the nation, together with the Soviet Union's participation in the Pacific War on the Allied side, imparting a sudden and powerful stimulus to controversies as well as moves and countermoves between the peace and war parties in this country. Surveying the situation, I foresaw various difficulties ahead, to overcome which I thought there would be no course left but to broadcast an Imperial Rescript to the nation on the part of the Emperor terminating the war. . . .

"323. In dealing with the delicate and difficult situation, which I was called upon by my official duty to handle, I was able to do my bit for humanity as well as for Japan. It is my inward satisfaction that I was instrumental in saving another twenty millions of my innocent compatriots from war ravages and also in sparing the Americans tens of thousands of casualties; which would have been caused, had Japan gone on fighting to the bitter and, which fanatically advocated the necessity of engaging the invading Americans for a decisive battle on the Japanese mainland. . . .

Source: *The Tokyo War Crimes Trials*, ed. R. John Pritchard and Sonia Magbanua Zaide (New York: Garland, 1981), 30,711; 31,172–31,181; 31,205.

D16. DIARY OF TORASHIRO KAWABE, VICE CHIEF OF
THE IMPERIAL ARMY GENERAL STAFF, AUGUST 1945

The diary entry of the Vice Chief of the General Staff [Translator's note: This is Torashiro Kawabe, younger brother of Masakazu Kawabe, Commander Air General Army]

[August 7]

"As soon as I arrived at the office I looked through the reports on the air attack by [the] new bomb on Hiroshima performed on the morning of the 6th. I was shocked tremendously. I once saw the studies being made by B Ken [its title is unclear, but this was a main Japanese research institute]. The study made by [unclear words] was regarded by us as hopeless. However, the enemy has turned it into reality and it seems that they have used this against us with great success. . . . It is too late to have regrets or to cry over this. If we expended time crying, the war situation will deteriorate further and become more difficult. We must be tenacious and active."

[August 9]

"o600. I was still in bed when I heard the ringing of the telephone downstairs. I thought this could not be good news. Vice Minister of the Army, Matsumoto, answered the phone. He came up and reported that Major Hori of the Sixth Department had called to inform us that the Soviets had declared war on Japan and that they received the (radio) broadcast of this news from San Francisco and Moscow.

"I came to the office and soon a man from Domei Service called me on the telephone and gave me the news of which I already had been notified in the morning. When I thanked him he said: 'Now that it has become reality, I hope you fight bravely.'"

Developments in the Army in the morning of the 9th . . . Kawabe, Vice Chief of Staff, received news of the Soviets entering the war early in the morning, later he put the following into his diary:

[August 9]

1. "Soviets finally started this morning [literally, the Soviets finally have risen]. My estimate was wrong. However, now that things have come to this end, we can give no thought to peace. We should have expected at least partly such an event during the war. There is nothing to reflect on now. We simply have to rely on the honor of the Japanese people and continue fighting. I was very cautious and almost cowardly in approaching [war with the Soviets], once however this has come to pass, I can never think of peace or surrender. Whatever the end, we have no choice but to try. I confirmed my decision and came to the office.

2. The Vice Minister of the Army Matsumoto also visited me and he did not oppose my decision.

3. After I came to the office, I prepared a memo as follows about what came to my mind:

Decision: No change with regard to continuing the war (with the United States as the main enemy).

Actions to take:

1. Within the whole nation we should declare martial law. I will push for this and if necessary we will change the government and the army and navy will take control.

2. As for operations, all the overseas armies and air general army understand their missions and will conduct strong resistance along the Manchurian border line. When the time comes to abandon Manchuria, the main formations will withdraw to southern Korea. China will be left generally in the present status. Those in Mongolia should gradually retreat to North China.

3. About the Manchurian Emperor, he should be moved to Japan either to [place name] or [place name]. . . .

4. Measures to stop unrest among the military units. One means is a statement from the Minister of the Army.

I waited for the Chief of the Army General Staff to come to the office and explained my proposals to him. As usual he did not show a clear indication of his views. However, he did not express any disagreement. I do not wish to 'make waves' at this time and decided to wait and see as the situation develops and also to await further information.

5. I heard that there would be a meeting of the Supreme War Direction Council at 1030 and visited General Anami at the office of the Army Minister. He was cheerful as usual, he told me: 'Good, I'll take your opinion as representative of the entire army general staff.' I said, 'I hope you do well in today's conference, the meeting should be very stormy.' Then the minister answered: 'It will be rough, but I will risk my life,' and after saying this he stood up. He said to himself, 'If what I insist can not be accepted I will resign and have myself conscripted into a unit in China so I can fight there.' And then he laughed and showed his high spirit. Some people might say that he lacks ability and he is too optimistic or he is possessed by something, but I thought that he was really dependable in such a difficult situation, keeping up his spirit and charging ahead."

August 10

The statement of the Vice Chief of the Army General Staff [regarding Cabinet Meeting, August 9, starting at 1430:

"The cabinet meeting lasted from 1430 to 2030, with about a one hour recess. The results of this are not known to me at this time as I write this diary, but there were forceful arguments like the big waves smashing into a massive rock which was the insistence made by the Army Minister. This is the atmosphere I can surmise."

The vice chief of the army general staff had the following statement [regarding Imperial Conference, 2350 August 9 to about 0300, August 10]:

"Late in the evening there was an Imperial conference. The Chief of the General Staff attended. The Army Minister after the diet meeting joined the Imperial Conference and did not return to the office. At 2000, the Vice Chief of the Navy General Staff Onishi came to visit me. He said that morale of the Navy General Staff remained still high and expressed the hope that the ministry department on the army side would strongly support pushing forward. After Onishi departed I laid myself on the sofa in my room and awaited the return of the Chief of the Army General Staff. I tried to take a nap, but it was impossible. Although the mosquitoes were repelled by anti-mosquito scent, because the screen that covers the light was down, the heat in the room was unbearable. I started thinking of the fortunes of this Imperial nation which could be determined within these few hours. Even if we continue the war, I will die and even if we reach peace, we will perish. I thought that it is better to continue the war so that the whole nation will perish in this land and maintain the everlasting greatness of the Japanese race. Without this determination how could we find the way out in this state of death."

[Translation Note: This picks up with an entry in the diary of Kawabe, Vice Chief of the General Staff.]

August 10

"Reportedly the Emperor explained what he meant by two items that I have already described.

"If I am allowed to make presumptuous remarks, the Emperor's decision was not the result of the arguments in the Imperial Conference (again this is only my presumption). In essence, His Majesty has no expectations of favorable results in future operations. In short, His Majesty has lost completely his trust in the armed forces. And this opinion is probably not just limited to His Majesty. It may be that the mistrust of the armed forces that has accumulated in both His Majesty and among the civilians has only been finally articulated in an absolute and clear manner in His Majesty's words.

"What acute pain is in my heart as a member of the armed forces. What a pity that none of the leaders of the army and navy could say that they could guarantee certain victory in the future. Both Army and Navy General Staff Chiefs who are supposed to assist His Majesty were not able to promise certain victory in the future. I heard that they said: 'Although we can not promise a certain victory we can not say that there will be certain defeat.' What indecisive words! Note I am not criticizing that statement. I am shocked that their statement is a picture of reality. I myself insisted that we continue fighting and kept encouraging myself. However, if I had been asked whether I could assure certain victory, what answer could I have given that would have differed much from those words issued by the two chiefs of the general staffs? I was bound by the feeling 'I do not want to surrender. I do not want to admit I am defeated, even in the face of death.' With that feeling I only directed the final operations in this war."

Vice Chief of Staff's diary entry of the 10th as follows:

"News of the Imperial Conference last night is spreading within the building and I see signs of uneasiness. However, possibly because they believe there will be a last ditch effort or they concur with the rationale thinking and the reasonableness of Emperor's decision there are no outbreaks of heated arguments or crying petitions among the young and spirited officers in the Army general staff building. (Honestly the difficulty in continuing the war is understood best by the personnel of the Army General Staff that are in charge of the operations.)"

August 11

The Situation in the Army General Staff

The diary of the Vice Chief of Staff for the 11th describes the atmosphere of the Chief of Staff offices and his feelings.

1. Again from morning and all day long I felt weak and stayed in the office.

2. Lt. Gen. Sumiza Hekada [name not certain] came and made acerbic comments on the weakness of the command echelon in failing to demand better conditions. Maj. Gen. Amano, the Chief of the Second Department, also came and expressed his view as follows: He says that he could not accept in his mind the disarmament of the Army even when the [army high command] and government have accepted it. Moreover, he was not sure whether the millions of members of the armed forces would follow the decision. There could be great confusion and he enumerated the reasons. The views of Hekada and Amano are not necessarily wrong nor are they excessively worried. I simply did not wish to get into a conclusive argument with them, although I shared their worries. [*Translation Note: In a post war statement, Kawabe particularly cited his doubts at this time about whether the China Expeditionary Army would comply with the surrender.*] I do not have any prospects that this great turning point in the situation can be reversed [*next phrasing unclear. Appears to say generally that it is not a matter that can be dealt with by emotions. He goes on to point out that this situation now is based on the decision of the emperor.*]

3. The Second Division Chief Arisue who was in Hiroshima came back so I briefed him on the situation over the past two days.

4. In the evening Col. Sakabura [*believe this name is correct, but not absolutely clear*] the Chief of the General Affairs Department arrived and expressed his view. He says that at this time we must reconsider the situation and try again to get the enemy to accept better conditions [for us]. So I stated what I thought and my conclusion. You are too optimistic. It is this "easy soldier" psychology that is the cause of today's tragic situation because we did not see or hear the misery of the country. We did not understand the turmoil [?] the nation has gone through to this point. We don't really understand the brutality of

the whites and believe that Japanese-type reasoning will be accepted by them. We have a saying "The longer you live, the more shame you acquire."

From this time after, how much shame should we endure. It is not something we can terminate by killing ourselves. Not only are we beaten by the enemy countries as Japanese citizens, but also within this country we were attacked spiritually and severely by the charges of anti militarism [and?] by mistrust of the military. Since the time of Manchurian Incident, for fourteen years we have not experienced a day of peace. It is only natural that so much emotional antagonism has accumulated against the military like this [we face] today.

We have to consider the situation as it exists by yesterday's Imperial Conference. In the years of Meiji and Tashio, which spanned over 70 years, our elders continuously contributed to the prosperity of this country. We have totally and from the roots up have destroyed their labors in these fourteen years. In addition, if we consider the future, we have to expect the following developments:

1. Our territory will be reduced to where it was three or four centuries ago.
2. The purity of the blood of the Japanese will be quickly contaminated.
3. There will be an attempt to destroy the samurai ethics.
4. Christians will increase quickly.
5. The use of American language will quickly expand.
6. The holding of heirloom swords and some other things will be forbidden.
7. We will be urged to abandon the practice of dedicating ourselves to the nation.
8. The suicide will be made a crime.
9. The contents of the history of Japan will be fundamentally falsified.
10. An extreme indoctrination of the usefulness of western culture will happen.
11. All the Japanese heroes, patriots in history and so on will be banished from history and so on. Oh! We were defeated! The Imperial Japan in which we had faith has perished!

Source: Boeicho Boei Kenshujo Senshi Shitsu (War History Office, Defense Agency) *Senshi Shosho* (War History Series), No. 82, *Daihon'ei Rikugun-Bu (10)* (Army Division, Imperial General Headquarters, vol. 10) (Tokyo, 1975), 420–468.

D17. SECRET WAR TERMINATION DIARY OF LT. COL. MASHIKO TAKESHITA, AUGUST 1945

(1) [August 10] *Lt. Col. Takeshita heard the detailed contents of this meeting [the Supreme War Direction Council Conference at 10:30 in the morning of August 9] at about 2100 on the 10th when he visited the Minister of the Army as follows:*

In the Supreme War Direction Council in the morning the Minister of Foreign Affairs and [Navy Minister] Yonai proposed discussing peace. They insisted that to start peace negotiations it was absolutely necessary to have proposals. For that purpose they advocated that Japan should accept the Potsdam Declaration with the one condition that it included the retention of the royal family [imperial institution] as our minimum demand. Against this argument the Minister of the Army insisted on the continuation of the war. He also argued that if there was room for negotiations it should be under four conditions described before . . . so that they would be the minimum conditions for maintaining the national polity. The Chief of the Army General Staff Umezu and Chief of Navy General Staff Toyoda seemed to concur with the proposal of the Army Minister.

(2) Interim Cabinet Meeting from 1430 to after 2200. *The Secret War Termination Diary of Lt. Col. Takeshita describes the events of the cabinet meeting as follows:*

Thereafter there was an interim cabinet meeting at the official residence of the Prime Minister. At 1730 the meeting recessed and reopened at 1830 and finished at 2220. Thus the meeting lasted altogether nine hours and appears to have reached no conclusion. Particularly in the first meeting, the cabinet members asked questions about the present status of national capabilities, the supply of food etc. This seemed to be an endless, inconsequential [indecisive?] meeting.

(3) *With regard to the detailed contents of this cabinet meeting [Cabinet Meeting, August 9 at 1430 to 2210], Lt. Col. Takeshita met the Minister of the Army the night of the 10th and heard directly the events as follows:*

The meeting started at 1420. In the meeting Prime Minister Suzuki announced that the contents of the Supreme War Direction Council would be disclosed and then he let Togo talk. Togo stated that to start the peace negotiations it is necessary to accept the [Potsdam] declaration with the reservation of one item. To this Army Minister responded that this was the Foreign Minister's opinion and was not the conclusion of the meeting of the Supreme War Direction Council. The Foreign Minister said he described his own views. Next Navy Minister Yonai referred to the disadvantageous situation of the war (at this time he used the word "defeat" and the Army Minister responded 'That's an improper [inaccurate?] word' and had Yonai change the word to 'disadvantage'). There were questions to the military supply minister, agricultural and commerce minister and minister of transportation about the possibility of continuing the war. Each minister, one after another, answered citing difficulties. At this point, the Navy Minister said that such difficulties already were thoroughly understood. It was unnecessary to repeat them at this time. He again repeated that the issue to be discussed today is whether or not to continue the war in spite of such difficulties.

On one hour recess, about 1830 the cabinet meeting reopened this time the discussion focused on whether the Potsdam Declaration should be accepted with reservation of only one or four conditions. Many opinions were expressed that attaching of four conditions would lead to the break up of negotiation if we mean to start the peace negotiations. The Minister of State supported the Army Minister. The Minister of Justice said on the basis of logic that retaining armaments and rejection of the occupation right would be logical if we aim to retain the national polity. The Minister of Welfare Okada agreed with him, however, he added that the present situation would require peace. The meeting ended at 2210. The cabinet meeting did not come to a decision because of opposing opinions.

(4) *The morning of the 10th, the senior personnel of each department were gathered inside the air raid shelter and the Minister briefed them and issued instructions. . . . This was quite a shock to the members of the Ministry of the Army. The gist of the explanation [regarding events at the Imperial Conference of August 9–10] made by the Minister [Anami] is described in* The Secret War Termination Diary *as follows:*

There was an Imperial Conference from 2300 last night to 0300 this morning. The Emperor has decided to accept the major part of the Potsdam Declaration on the condition that the royal family [probably a more accurate term would be "national polity"] will be secure. However, the effectiveness of this acceptance pre-supposes an assurance of the retention of the royal family. I deeply regret that I did not have enough power to prevent things from reaching such a pass and I feel responsibility on this matter. However, I hope you will trust my insistence on adhering to the decision of the Imperial Conference. Hereafter we have no choice but to follow what His Majesty has decided. At this time you must be aware of the following matters:

1) You must abandon all thoughts except for unity under strict military discipline. Do not ever override the laws in the difficulties of our nation; actions outside the law will destroy the country.

2) Observe the actions of the citizens and try to understand them and guide them so they will follow what His Majesty intends. Adhere to the correct direction of the Japanese race in this difficult situation.

3) It is necessary that the armed forces will act with self-restraint. With regard to dealing with the military forces overseas, I am deeply worried.

(5) The Minister of the Army . . . the night of the 10th told Lt. Col. Takeshita as follows [regarding the Interim Cabinet Meeting on August 10 at 0300]:

Next there was a cabinet meeting and the [Army] Minister expressed his view questioning the trustworthiness of the enemy. He said that unless there was positive evidence that the royal family can be preserved, the Army will continue the war. Further, he asked a question to the Prime Minister if the Prime Minister will recognize the policy of continuing the war if Japan could not confirm that the sovereign power of the Emperor will be recognized. To this, the Prime Minister answered in a low voice "Yes." Then the Minister of the Navy asked a similar question to the Minister of the Army and Anami answered that the war would be continued.

Source: Boeicho Boei Kenshujo Senshi Shitsu (War History Office, Defense Agency) Senshi Shosho (War History Series), No. 82, Daihon'ei Rikugun-Bu (10) (Army Division, Imperial General Headquarters, vol. 10) (Tokyo, 1975), 436–453.

D18. DIARY ENTRY OF PRINCE HAGASHIKUNI, AUGUST 9, 1945

Meeting of Military Councilmen and Others [August 9, at 1830]

From 1830 the military council meeting was held. Those attending were Field Marshal Sugiyama, Prince Asaka, Prince Hagashikuni and the director of military education. As described previously, the general contents of the Supreme War Direction Council meeting were explained to these attendants by the Chief of the Army General Staff. About the contents, the diary of Hagashikuni describes as follows:

About 1600 in the afternoon I received a telephone call informing me of a military council meeting at the army general staff at 1730. But then the time was changed and the meeting was held at 1830. The members of the Army General Staff gave a situation report on the Soviet advance along the Manchuria and Sakhalin border. Chief of Army Staff Umezu explained the decisions made at the Big Six and the Vice Minister of the Army explained the developments at the currently open diet meeting. After the meeting we dined together and during and after the meal we talked about various subjects. The meeting continued until after 2000. At the military affairs department the situation was explained to former Prime Minister Tojo (General Koiso was not located). . . . Based on instructions from the Minister of the Army, the military affairs department and troop affairs departments started the preparations of the national martial law proclamation.

Source: Boeicho Boei Kenshujo Senshi Shitsu (War History Office, Defense Agency) Senshi Shosho (War History Series), No. 82, Daihon'ei Rikugun-Bu (10) (Army Division, Imperial General Headquarters, vol. 10) (Tokyo, 1975), 440.

D19. DIARY ENTRIES OF ADMIRAL MATONE UGAKI, AUGUST 7, 9, AND 11, 1945

Tuesday, 7 August 1945

At about 0825 yesterday two or three B-29's came over Hiroshima and dropped two or three large-type bombs with parachutes attached. They exploded about fifty meters above ground with a terrific flash and explosion, with a result that about 80 percent of the houses in the city were leveled and burnt out. Casualties suffered reached over 100,000.

A radio broadcast from San Francisco this afternoon said that seventeen hours before an atomic bomb had been dropped for the first time in history, on Hiroshima, an army base. Though its result wasn't confirmed due to thick clouds over thirty thousand feet high, this bomb was twenty thousand times more powerful than the "Grand Slam" bomb of the B-29's and its effect was equivalent to that of a thousand kilograms of TNT. In the experimental explosion made in New Mexico on 16 July, a steel tower on which the bomb was placed evaporated and window panes 250 miles away from the spot shook, while men staying six miles away were knocked to the ground.

According to the above, it is clear that this was a uranium atom bomb, and it deserves to be regarded as a real wonder, making the outcome of the war more gloomy.

We must think of some countermeasures against it immediately, and at the same time I wish we could create the same bomb. . . .

Thursday, 9 August 1945

Various reports successively received made it clear that the Soviets declared war against us at midnight today, and their warships bombarded Rashin, while their troops entered northern Korea. Air attacks made, too. Though the Potsdam Declaration didn't mention this point, Stalin's realism finally made him declare war against us.

Since before the Tripartite Alliance was signed, I had some idea about keeping peace with Soviet Russia. Though a nonaggression pact couldn't be concluded, I was very pleased to see a peace treaty concluded between the Soviets and this country. But in June 1941, when the Germans declared war against the Soviet Union, my hope was shattered. Since then I hoped to see the Germans make a separate peace with the Soviets, and especially in these days I hoped for better relations between the Soviet Union and Japan. But now every hope is completely ruined.

Now this country is going to fight alone against the whole world. This is fate indeed! I won't grumble about anything at this moment. I only hope we do our best in the last battle so that we'll have nothing to regret even if destroyed. . . .

Saturday, 11 August 1945

In the afternoon the chief intelligence officer, a look of horror on his face, brought me the most hateful news which said:

Radio broadcast from San Francisco: Japan applied for acceptance of the Potsdam Declaration on condition that Emperor Hirohito be left as he was; otherwise, unconditional surrender. . . .

My God! What's the matter? Yet there can be no smoke without fire. An order from the Grand Naval Command received early this morning called for taking positive action against enemy task forces regardless of the progress of preparations for *Ketsu* Operation, while strengthening our attacks on Okinawa at the same time. Considering this to be a sign that they were forced to lift the ban on taking positive actions in light of *Ketsu* Operation, as we had advocated, the morale of the men rose temporarily.

After receiving the above news, however, my staff learned through telephone liaisons to the Grand Naval Command headquarters at Hiyoshi that they had noted comments somewhat confirming the news, which had been considered enemy propaganda. Why wasn't the commander in chief, having the full responsibility, consulted in such an important matters? The above incredible broadcast, while hiding [the decision] from us, gave me a shock.

While we were completely absorbed in preparing for the last stand after being pressed to the homeland, the atomic bomb attacks and the Soviets' joining the war, thus deteriorating our position, shocked us. But we can take some countermeasures against them. We still have enough fighting strength remaining, which was saved just because of restrictions.

Furthermore, don't we have large army forces still intact on the China continent and in our homeland? It might be the view of some clever fellows to surrender with some strength left, instead of being completely destroyed, if and when we can't avoid defeat anyway. But those fellows advocating that idea are nothing but selfish weaklings who don't think seriously about the future of the nation and only seek immediate benefits.

Even if we dared to commit ourselves now, it's apparent that the enemy, notwithstanding, will follow the original policy, paying little consideration to us, and we would be completely destroyed. Moreover, it's clear, too, that the whole nation wouldn't be pressed to taste the bitterness of war, and some cunning fellows would take advantage of a defeat so that the traditional Japanese spirit would be basically destroyed and even the noble spirit of revenge be lost, making the prospect of the empire extremely dark. In the end, the future of this empire will be completely ruined.

Even though it becomes impossible for us to continue organized resistance after expending our strength, we must continue guerrilla warfare under the emperor and never give up the war. When this resolution is brought home, we can't be defeated. Instead, we can make the enemy finally give up the war after making it taste the bitterness of a prolonged conflict. . . .

This is a great problem for me, too, as commander in chief. Though an emperor's order must be followed, I can hardly stand to see us suspending attacks while still having this fighting strength. I think many things remain to be done after consulting with those brave men willing to die. When and how to die as a samurai, an admiral, or a supreme commander, a subject I have long resolved in my mind, should be seriously studied for the sake of the future of the Japanese nation. I renewed a resolution today of entrusting my body to the throne and defending the empire until death takes me away. . . .

Source: *Fading Victory: The Diary of Admiral Matome Ugaki, 1941–1945*, trans. Masataka Chihaya (Pittsburgh: University of Pittsburgh Press, 1991), 655–659.

D20. EMPEROR HIROHITO'S SOLILOQUY, 1946

In Okinawa, it was clear that there was no hope for victory in a naval battle. The only hope was to strike against the forces in Yunnan in conjunction with the Burma campaign. This should have been a heavy blow against England and America. I suggested this to Umezu [General Yoshijiro Umezu, Army Chief of Staff], but he opposed the plan saying we would not be able to provide the troops with the necessary supplies and reinforcements. When I spoke to Prince Kaya, who was then president of the Army College, he replied that it might succeed temporarily. He said he would study the situation, but nothing ever came of it. . . .

Since it was decided that there was no longer any hope of success for the Yunnan war plan, I decided that there was no other way out but to call for a negotiated peace. . . . The imperial conference of June, which was held prior to the interim Diet meeting, was truly a strange affair. At that time, Umezu was on a trip to Manchuria so the army Vice Chief of Staff [Kawabe Torajiro] was present in his place as Chief of Staff. According to the government's report taking all information into account, it was impossible to continue with the war. Despite this conclusion, Navy Chief of Staff Toyoda [Fukutake] and the Army Vice Chief of Staff insisted that the war be continued because there was no question that victory could be achieved. This argument, that there was no question that we would win the war, completely contradicted the government's report, but ultimately the conference decided to continue the war. . . .

Toyoda Fukutake, who insisted on continuing the war, is not a person with whom one can agree. He just talks tough. Because of this, we have disagreements between the army and navy. He failed as commander of the Mariana campaign. I had once told Yonai [Yonai Mitsumasa, naval minister and former prime minister] that it is a mistake to appoint a person whose record as naval commander is poor to the post of navy chief of staff. Yonai said he must insist on doing so. . . .

I . . . summoned the members of the Supreme Leadership Conference and told them to quickly prepare for peace negotiations. I don't recall if I told them to do this by Soviet mediation. At this point, Suzuki [Prime Minister Suzuki Kantaro] and others suggested that we should check out the Soviets' intentions. I told them that was a good idea. Because of the current circumstances, we had to arrange for a swift resolution of the situation. . . . But it was agreed that the Soviet Union was not a country with sincere intentions, so we wanted to first feel them out. It was decided to proceed with talks between Hirota [Hirota Koki, former foreign minister and prime minister] and Yakov Malik [Soviet ambassador to Japan]. If the Soviet Union would agree to ship oil to Japan, Hirota was to tell Malik that Japan would be willing to transfer south Sakhalin or even Manchuria to the Soviet Union. But even in early July there was no response from the Soviet Union.

From our point of view, matters had to be settled before the Potsdam conference convened. Further delay would be troublesome for us. I conferred with Suzuki and we decided to terminate the discussions between Hirota and Malik, and negotiate directly with the Soviet government. We considered who might be the most suitable person to send to Moscow, and decided that Konoe would be the best. But others felt that Konoe would be reluctant to undertake this assignment. So I decided to speak to Konoe myself.

I believe it was early in July. I summoned Konoe and asked him to undertake the assignment even though it would be difficult. Konoe agreed to undertake the mission, saying that he would do his best to accomplish it.

Suzuki was delighted to hear this and informed the Soviet authorities that we wished to send Konoe, but also requested their assistance in initiating negotiations for peace with England and America. Thereupon, the Soviet authorities replied that they would respond after their officials had returned from the Potsdam conference. These matters are noted in detail in the notes of Chief Cabinet Secretary Sakomizu Hisatsune [*Kōfukuji no Shinsō* (*The True Account of the Surrender*)] so I will not discuss them here. Stalin did not respond even after he returned from Potsdam. Unfortunately, soon after that the Soviet Union declared war on Japan. Faced with this we felt that there was no alternative but unconditional surrender.

The air raids increased in intensity daily. The atomic bomb made its appearance on August 6th. The people were in desperate straits. The Soviet Union commenced fighting in Manchuria. Thus we were forced into a situation in which we had to accept the terms of the Potsdam Declaration.

Source: Daikichi Irokawa, *The Age of Hirohito: In Search of Modern Japan*, trans. Mikiso Hane and John L. Urda (New York: Free Press, 1995), 31–33.

E.

Japanese Surrender Documents

E1. EMPEROR HIROHITO'S SURRENDER DECISION, AUGUST 10, 1945

Emperor Hirohito to the Imperial Conference

AUGUST 10, 1945

I have given serious thought to the situation prevailing at home and abroad and have concluded that continuing the war can only mean destruction for the nation and a prolongation of bloodshed and cruelty in the world. I cannot bear to see my innocent people suffer any longer. Ending the war is the only way to restore world peace and to relieve the nation from the terrible distress with which it is burdened.

I was told by those advocating a continuation of hostilities that by June new divisions would be placed in fortified positions at Kujukuri-hama so that they would be ready for the invader when he sought to land. It is now August and the fortifications still have not been completed. Even the equipment for the divisions which are to fight there is insufficient and reportedly will not be adequate until after the middle of September. Furthermore, the promised increase in the production of aircraft has not progressed in accordance with expectations.

There are those who say that the key to national survival lies in a decisive battle in the homeland. The experiences of the past, however, show that there has always been a discrepancy between plans and performance. I do not believe that the discrepancy in the case of Kujukuri-hama can be rectified. Since this is the shape of things, how can we repel the invaders?

I cannot help feeling sad when I think of the people who have served me so faithfully, the soldiers and sailors who have been killed or wounded in far-off battles, the families who have lost all their worldly goods—and often their lives as well—in the air raids at home. It goes without saying that it is unbearable for me to see the brave and loyal fighting men of Japan disarmed. It is equally unbearable that others who have rendered me devoted service should now be punished as instigators of the war. Nevertheless, the time has come when we must bear the unbearable.

When I recall the feelings of my Imperial Grandsire, the Emperor Meiji, at the time of the Triple Intervention, I swallow my own tears and give my sanction to the proposal to accept the Allied proclamation on the basis outlined by the Foreign Minister.

Source: Robert J. C. Butow, *Japan's Decision to Surrender* (Stanford, Calif.: Stanford University Press, 1954), 175–176.

E2. JAPANESE SURRENDER NOTE, AUGUST 10, 1945

The Swiss Chargé (Grässli) to the Secretary of State

WASHINGTON, AUGUST 10, 1945

SIR: I have the honor to inform you that the Japanese Minister to Switzerland, upon instructions received from his Government, has requested the Swiss Political Department to advise the Government of the United States of America of the following:

"In obedience to the gracious command of his Majesty the Emperor who, ever anxious to enhance the cause of world peace, desires earnestly to bring about a speedy termination of hostilities with a view to saving mankind from the calamities to be imposed upon them, by further continuation of the war, the Japanese Government several weeks ago asked the Soviet Government, with which neutral relations then prevailed, to render good offices in restoring peace vis-à-vis the enemy powers. Unfortunately, these efforts in the interest of peace having failed, the Japanese Government in conformity with the august wish of His Majesty to restore the general peace and desiring to put an end to the untold sufferings entailed by war as quickly as possible, have decided upon the following.

"The Japanese Government are ready to accept the terms enumerated in the joint declaration which was issued at Potsdam on July 26th, 1945, by the heads of the Governments of the United States, Great Britain, and China, and later subscribed by the Soviet Government, with the understanding that the said declaration does not comprise any demand which prejudices the prerogatives of His Majesty as a Sovereign Ruler.

"The Japanese Government sincerely hope that this understanding is warranted and desire keenly that an explicit indication to that effect will be speedily forthcoming."

In transmitting the above message the Japanese Minister added that his Government begs the Government of the United States to forward its answer through the intermediary of Switzerland. Similar requests are being transmitted to the Governments of Great Britain and the Union of Soviet Socialist Republics through the intermediary of Sweden, as well as to the Government of China through the intermediary of Switzerland. The Chinese Minister at Berne has already been informed of the foregoing through the channel of the Swiss Political Department.

Please be assured that I am at your disposal at any time to accept for and forward to my Government, the reply of the Government of the United States.

Accept [etc.] Grässli

Source: U.S. Department of State, *Foreign Relations of the United States, 1945: The British Commonwealth, The Far East* (Washington, D.C.: U.S. Government Printing Office, 1969), 6:627.

E3. U.S. (BYRNES) REPLY TO JAPAN, AUGUST 11, 1945

The Secretary of State to the Swiss Chargé (Grässli)

WASHINGTON, AUGUST 11, 1945

SIR: I have the honor to acknowledge receipt of your note of August 10, and in reply to inform you that the President of the United States has directed me to send to you for transmission by your Government to the Japanese Government the following message on behalf of the Governments of the United States, the United Kingdom, the Union of Soviet Socialist Republics, and China:

"With regard to the Japanese Government's message accepting the terms of the Potsdam proclamation but containing the statement, with the understanding that the said declaration does not comprise any demand which prejudices the prerogatives of His Majesty as a sovereign ruler, our position is as follows:

"From the moment of surrender the authority of the Emperor and the Japanese Government to rule the state shall be subject to the Supreme Commander of the Allied powers who will take such steps as he deems proper to effectuate the surrender terms.

"The Emperor will be required to authorize and ensure the signature by the Government of Japan and the Japanese Imperial General Headquarters of the surrender terms necessary to carry out the provisions of the Potsdam Declaration, and shall issue his commands to all the Japanese military, naval and air authorities and to all the forces under their control wherever located to cease active operations and to surrender their arms, and to issue such other orders as the Supreme Commander may require to give effect to the surrender terms.

"Immediately upon the surrender the Japanese Government shall transport prisoners of war and civilian internees to places of safety, as directed, where they can quickly be placed aboard Allied transports.

"The ultimate form of government of Japan shall, in accordance with the Potsdam Declaration, be established by the freely expressed will of the Japanese people.

"The armed forces of the Allied Powers will remain in Japan until the purposes set forth in the Potsdam Declaration are achieved."

Accept [etc.] [James F. Byrnes]

Source: U.S. Department of State, *Foreign Relations of the United States, 1945: The British Commonwealth, The Far East* (Washington, D.C.: U.S. Government Printing Office, 1969), 6:631–632.

E4. JAPANESE PROTEST REGARDING THE USE OF ATOMIC WEAPONS, AUGUST 11, 1945

The Swiss Legation to the Department of State

The Legation of Switzerland in charge of Japanese interests has received an urgent cable from the authorities abroad, requesting that the Department of State be immediately apprised of the following communication from the Japanese Government, reading, in translation, as follows:

"On August 6, 1945, American airplanes released on the residential district of the town of Hiroshima bombs of a new type, killing and injuring in one second a large number of civilians and destroying a great part of the town. Not only is the city of Hiroshima a provincial town without any protection or special military installations of any kind, but also none of the neighboring region of this town constitutes a military objective.

"In a declaration President Truman has asserted that he would use these bombs for the destruction of docks, factories, and installations of transportation. However, this bomb, provided with a parachute, in falling has a destructive force of a great scope as a result of its explosion in the air. It is evident, therefore, that it is technically impossible to limit the effect of its use to special objectives such as designated by President Truman, and the American authorities are perfectly aware of this. In fact, it has been established on the scene that the damage extends over a great area and that combatant and noncombatant men and women, old and young, are massacred without discrimination by the atmospheric pressure of the explosion, as well as by the radiating heat which results therefrom. Consequently there is involved a bomb having the most cruel effects humanity has ever known, not only as far as the extensive and immense damage is concerned but also for reasons of suffering endured by each victim.

"It is an elementary principle of international public law that in time of war the belligerents do not have unlimited right in the choice of the means of attack and that they cannot resort to projectile arms or any other means capable of causing the enemy needless suffering. These principles are stipulated in the Convention respecting the laws and customs of war on land and in Article 22, as well as under letter (E) of Article 23 of the rules concerning the laws and customs of war on land. Since the beginning of the present war, the American Government has declared on various occasions that the use of gas or other inhuman means of combat were considered illegal in the public opinion of civilized human society and that it would not avail itself of these means before enemy countries resorted to them. The bombs in question, used by the Americans, by their cruelty and by their terrorizing effects, surpass by far gas or any other arm the use of which is prohibited by the treaties for reasons of their characteristics.

"The Americans have effected bombardments of towns in the greatest part of Japanese territory, without discrimination massacring a great number of old people, women, children; destroying and burning down Shinto and Buddhist temples, schools, hospitals, living quarters, etc. This fact alone means that they have shown complete defiance of the essential principles of humanitarian laws, as well as international law. They now use this new bomb, having an uncontrollable and cruel effect much greater than any other arms or projectiles ever used to date. This constitutes a new crime against humanity and civilization. The Government of Japan, in its own name and at the same time in the name of all of humanity and civilization, accuses the American Government with the present note of the use of an inhuman weapon of this nature and demands energetically abstinence from its use."

Reference: I-10
Washington, August 11, 1945

Source: U.S. Department of State, *Foreign Relations of the United States, 1945: The British Commonwealth, The Far East* (Washington, D.C.: U.S. Government Printing Office, 1969), 6:472–473.

E5. EMPEROR HIROHITO'S SURRENDER STATEMENT TO THE IMPERIAL CONFERENCE, AUGUST 14, 1945

I have listened carefully to each of the arguments presented in opposition to the view that Japan should accept the Allied reply as it stands without further clarification or modification, but my own thoughts have not undergone any change. I have surveyed the conditions prevailing in Japan and in the world at large, and it is my belief that a continuation of the war promises nothing but additional destruction. I have studied the terms of the Allied reply and have concluded that they constitute a virtually complete acknowledgment of the position we maintained in the note dispatched several days ago. In short, I consider the reply to be acceptable.

I realize that there are those of you who distrust the intentions of the Allies. This is, of course, quite natural, but to my mind the Allied reply is evidence of the peaceful and friendly intentions of the enemy. The faith and resolution of this nation as a whole, therefore, are factors of paramount importance.

I appreciate how difficult it will be for the officers and men of the army and navy to surrender their arms to the enemy and to see their homeland occupied. Indeed, it is difficult for me to issue the order making this necessary and to deliver so many of my trusted servants into the hands of the Allied authorities by whom they will be accused of being war criminals. In spite of these feelings, so difficult to bear, I can not endure the thought of letting my people suffer any longer. A continuation of the war would bring death to tens, perhaps even hundreds, of thousands of persons. The whole nation would be reduced to ashes. How then could I carry on the wishes of my imperial ancestors?

The decision I have reached is akin to the one forced upon my Grandfather, the Emperor Meiji, at the time of the Triple Intervention. As he endured the unendurable, so shall I, and so must you.

It is my desire that you, my Ministers of State, accede to my wishes and forthwith accept the Allied reply. In order that the people may know of my decision, I request you to prepare at once an imperial rescript so that I may broadcast to the nation. Finally, I call upon each and every one of you to exert himself to the utmost so that we may meet the trying days which lie ahead.

Source: Robert J. C. Butow, *Japan's Decision to Surrender* (Stanford, Calif.: Stanford University Press, 1954), 207–208.

E6. JAPANESE SURRENDER NOTE, AUGUST 14, 1945

The Swiss Chargé (Grässli) to the Secretary of State

WASHINGTON, AUGUST 14, 1945

SIR : I have the honor to refer to your note of August 11, in which you requested me to transmit to my Government the reply of the Governments of the United States, the United Kingdom, the Union of Soviet Socialist Republics, and China to the message from the Japanese Government which was communicated in my note of August 10.

At 20.10 today (Swiss Time) the Japanese Minister to Switzerland conveyed the following written statement to the Swiss Government for transmission to the four Allied governments:

"Communication of the Japanese Government of August 14, 1945, addressed to the Governments of the United States, Great Britain, the Soviet Union, and China:

"With reference to the Japanese Government's note of August 10 regarding their acceptance of the provisions of the Potsdam Declaration and the reply of the Governments of the United States, Great Britain, the Soviet Union, and China sent by American Secretary of State Byrnes under the date of August 11, the Japanese Government have the honor to communicate to the Governments of the four powers as follows:

"1. His Majesty the Emperor has issued an Imperial rescript regarding Japan's acceptance of the provisions of the Potsdam Declaration.

"2. His Majesty the Emperor is prepared to authorize and ensure the signature by his Government and the Imperial General Headquarters of the necessary terms for carrying out the provisions of the Potsdam Declaration. His Majesty is also prepared to issue his control wherever located to cease active operations, to surrender arms and to issue commands to all the military, naval, and air authorities of Japan and all the forces under such other orders as may be required by the Supreme Commander of the Allied Forces for the execution of the abovementioned terms."

Accept [etc.] Grässli

Source: U.S. Department of State, *Foreign Relations of the United States, 1945: The British Commonwealth, The Far East* (Washington, D.C.: U.S. Government Printing Office, 1969), 6:662–663.

E7. U.S. (BYRNES) REPLY TO JAPAN, AUGUST 14, 1945

The Secretary of State to the Swiss Chargé (Grässli)

WASHINGTON, AUGUST 14, 1945

SIR: With reference to your communication of today's date, transmitting the reply of the Japanese Government to the communication which I sent through you to the Japanese Government on August 11, on behalf of the Governments of the United States, China, the United Kingdom, and the Union of Soviet Socialist Republics, which I regard as full acceptance of the Potsdam Declaration and of my statement of August 11, 1945, I have the honor to inform you that the President of the United States has directed that the following message be sent to you for transmission to the Japanese Government:

"You are to proceed as follows:

"(1) Direct prompt cessation of hostilities by Japanese forces, informing the Supreme Commander for the Allied Powers of the effective date and hour of such cessation.

"(2) Send emissaries at once to the Supreme Commander for the Allied Powers with information of the disposition of the Japanese forces and commanders, and fully empowered to make any arrangements directed by the Supreme Commander for the Allied Powers to enable him and his accompanying forces to arrive at the place designated by him to receive the formal surrender.

"(3) For the purpose of receiving such surrender and carrying it into effect, General of the Army Douglas MacArthur has been designated as the Supreme Commander for the Allied Powers, and he will notify the Japanese Government of the time, place and other details of the formal surrender."

Accept [etc.] James F. Byrnes

Source: U.S. Department of State, *Foreign Relations of the United States, 1945: The British Commonwealth, The Far East* (Washington, D.C.: U.S. Government Printing Office, 1969), 6:663.

E8. PRESIDENT TRUMAN'S ANNOUNCEMENT OF JAPAN'S SURRENDER, AUGUST 14, 1945

I have received this afternoon a message from the Japanese Government in reply to the message forwarded to that Government by the Secretary of State on August 11. I deem this reply a full acceptance of the Potsdam Declaration which specifies the unconditional surrender of Japan. In the reply there is no qualification.

Arrangements are now being made for the formal signing of surrender terms at the earliest possible moment.

General Douglas MacArthur has been appointed the Supreme Allied Commander to receive the Japanese surrender. Great Britain, Russia, and China will be represented by high-ranking officers.

Meantime, the Allied armed forces have been ordered to suspend offensive action.

The proclamation of VJ Day must wait upon the formal signing of the surrender terms by Japan. . . .

Source: New York Times, August 15, 1945.

E9. IMPERIAL RESCRIPT, AUGUST 14, 1945

To Our good and loyal subjects:

After pondering deeply the general trends of the world and the actual conditions obtaining in Our Empire today, We have decided to effect a settlement of the present situation by resorting to an extraordinary measure.

We have ordered Our Government to communicate to the Governments of the United States, Great Britain, China and the Soviet Union that Our Empire accepts the provisions of their Joint Declaration.

To strive for the common prosperity and happiness of all nations as well as the security and well-being of Our subjects is the solemn obligation which has been handed down by Our Imperial Ancestors, and which We lay close to heart. Indeed, We declared war on America and Britain out of Our sincere desire to ensure Japan's self preservation and the stabilization of East Asia, it being far from Our thought either to infringe upon the sovereignty of other nations or to embark upon territorial aggrandizement. But now the war has lasted for nearly four years. Despite the best that has been done by everyone, the gallant fighting of military and naval forces, the diligence and assiduity of Our servants of the State and the devoted service of Our one hundred million people, the war situation has developed not necessarily to Japan's advantage, while the general trends of the world have all turned against her interest. Moreover, the enemy has begun to employ a new and most cruel bomb, the power of which to do damage is indeed incalculable, taking the toll of many innocent lives. Should We continue to fight, it would not only result in an ultimate collapse and obliteration of the Japanese nation, but also it would lead to the total extinction of human civilization. Such being the case, how are We to save the millions of Our subjects; or to atone Ourselves before the hallowed spirits of Our Imperial Ancestors?

This is the reason why We have ordered the acceptance of the provisions of the Joint Declaration of the Powers.

We cannot but express the deepest sense of regret to our Allied nations of East Asia, who have consistently cooperated with the Empire towards the emancipation of East Asia. The thought of those officers and men as well as others who have fallen in the fields of battle, those who died at their posts of duty, or those who met with untimely death and all their bereaved families, pains Our heart night and day. The welfare of the wounded and the war-sufferers, and of those who have lost their homes and livelihood, are the objects of Our profound solicitude. The hardships and sufferings to which Our nation is to be subjected hereafter will be certainly great. We are keenly aware of the inmost feelings of all ye, Our subjects. However, it is according to the dictate of time and fate that We have resolved to pave the way for a grand peace for all the generations to come by enduring the unendurable and suffering what is insufferable.

Having been able to safeguard and maintain the structure of the Imperial State, We are always with ye, Our good and loyal subjects, relying upon your sincerity and integrity. Beware most strictly of any outbursts of emotion which may engender needless complications, or any fraternal contention and strife which may create confusion, lead ye astray and cause ye to lose the confidence of the world. Let the entire nation continue as one family from generation to generation, ever firm in its faith of the imperishableness of its divine land, and mindful of its heavy burden of responsibilities, and the long road before it. Unite your total strength to be devoted to the construction for the future. Cultivate the ways of rectitude; foster nobility of spirit; and work with resolution so as ye may enhance the innate glory of the Imperial State and keep pace with the progress of the world.

(Imperial Sign Manual)
(Imperial Seal)
The 14th day of the 8th month of the 20th year of Showa.

Source: Robert J. C. Butow, *Japan's Decision to Surrender* (Stanford, Calif.: Stanford University Press, 1954), 248.

E10. JAPANESE NOTE REGARDING SURRENDER PROCEDURES, AUGUST 16, 1945

The Swiss Chargé (Grässli) to the Secretary of State

WASHINGTON, AUGUST 16, 1945

SIR: I have the honor to inform you that the Japanese Minister in Berne at 18.15 Swiss Time today requested my Government to transmit to you the following communication destined for the United States Government and the Governments of the three other Allied powers:

"The Japanese Government would like to be permitted to state to the Governments of America, Great Britain, China, and the Soviet Union what they most earnestly desire with reference to the execution of certain provisions of the Potsdam Proclamation. This may be done possibly at the time of the signature, but fearing that they may not be able to find an appropriate opportunity they take the liberty of addressing to the Governments of the Four Powers through the good offices of the Government of Switzerland.

"Primo—In view of the fact that the purpose of occupation as mentioned in the Potsdam Proclamation is solely to secure the achievement of the basic objectives set forth in the said Proclamation, the Japanese Government sincerely desire that the Four Powers, relying upon the good faith of the Japanese Government, will facilitate discharge by the Japanese Government of their obligations so as to forestall any unnecessary complications. It is earnestly solicited that:

In case of the entry of Allied fleets or troops in Japan proper the Japanese Government be notified in advance so that arrangements can be made for reception.

The number of the points in Japanese territory to be designated by the Allies for occupation be limited to minimum number, selection of the points be made in such a manner as to leave such a city as Tokyo unoccupied, and the forces to be stationed at each point be made as small as possible.

"Secundo—Disarming of the Japanese forces being a most delicate task as it involves over three millions of officers and men overseas and having direct bearing on their honour, the Japanese Government will, of course, take utmost pains. But it is suggested that the best and the most effective method would be that under the command of His Majesty the Emperor, the Japanese forces are allowed to disarm themselves and surrender arms of their own accord. Disarming of the Japanese forces on the continent be carried out beginning on the front line and in successive stages.

In connection with the disarming it is hoped that Article 35 of the Hague Convention will be applied and the honour of the soldiers will be respected, permitting them, for instance, to wear swords. Further, the Japanese Government be given to understand the Allies have no intention to employ disarmed Japanese soldiers for compulsory labour. It is sincerely hoped that shipment and transportation facilities necessary for the evacuation of the soldiers to their homeland will be speedily provided.

"Tertio—Since some forces are located in remote places difficult to communicate the imperial order, it is desired that a reasonable time be allowed before the cessation of hostilities.

"Quarto—The Allies will be good enough quickly to take necessary steps or extend us facilities for the shipment of indispensable foodstuffs and medical supplies to Japanese forces in distant islands and for the transport of wounded soldiers from those islands."

To this note the Japanese Minister added verbally that his Government expresses the most urgent hope that their wishes be respected, as this would be also in the interest of the Allies. He emphasized most particularly that this message and its contents should be treated under all circumstances as strictly confidential and that in no way should it be allowed to be published, because the effect on the Japanese people would otherwise be catastrophic.

Accept [etc.] Grässli

Source: U.S. Department of State, *Foreign Relations of the United States, 1945: The British Commonwealth, The Far East* (Washington, D.C.: U.S. Government Printing Office, 1969), 6:668–669.

E11. LINCOLN MEMORANDUM, MACARTHUR NOTE, AND U.S. (BYRNES)
REPLY TO JAPANESE NOTE OF AUGUST 16, AUGUST 17, 1945

Memorandum by Brigadier General George A. Lincoln of the War
Department to the Assistant Secretary of State (Dunn)

WASHINGTON, 17 AUGUST, 1945

General Hull has discussed the matter of a suitable reply to the Japanese on their latest message with the Chief of Staff and also with the Navy. They are in agreement that a suitable reply is substantially as that in the attached draft, which is the same as the one discussed yesterday in General Hull's office. As discussed yesterday, the War and Navy Departments are agreed that requests of the kind in this Japanese message should hereafter be addressed to the Supreme Commander.

For your information, there is enclosed a copy of General MacArthur's message on the subject. You will note the extremely high classification of his message.

G. A. *Lincoln*

[Annex]

General of the Army Douglas MacArthur to the Chief of Staff (Marshall)

[MANILA,] 17 AUGUST, 1945

The Secret terms proposed by the Japanese are fundamentally violative of the provisions of the Potsdam Declaration and would completely traverse the previous attitude not only of the Allied Nations but of Japan herself in her initial successes and conquests of this war. The incidents of Bataan and Singapore are still fresh in the minds of the World. The enemy suggestion goes even to the point of preferential repatriative treatment of Japanese soldiers. The suggested ameliorations would relieve Japan of much of the physical and psychological burdens of defeat. I believe that public opinion throughout the Allied world would not support favorable consideration of these stipulations. In my opinion the Potsdam provisions should be put into effect as drawn and the suggestions made by the Japanese Government should be rejected. In China I believe the stipulations made by the Generalissimo as to the details of the surrender should be supported by the Allies.

The Secretary of State to the Swiss Chargé (Grässli)

WASHINGTON, AUGUST 17, 1945

SIR: In response to your note to me of August 16 transmitting certain observations and requests of the Japanese Government with respect to the carrying out of the Japanese surrender, I have the honor to request that you transmit to the Japanese Government the following reply:

"Such information as the Japanese Government requires to carry out the surrender arrangements will be communicated by the Supreme Commander at appropriate times determined by him. The four Allied Powers have subscribed to the Potsdam Declaration which assures the return to the homeland to peaceful occupations of all Japanese armed forces who surrender to United States commanders, Generalissimo Chiang Kai-shek, Admiral the Lord Louis Mountbatten, and Soviet commanders as directed by the Supreme Commander for the Allied Powers. This return will be arranged through the Supreme Commander and will take place after the Japanese armed forces have been disarmed by the Allied commanders to whom they surrender and when Japanese and other transportation can be made available."

Accept [etc.] [James F. Byrnes]

Source: U.S. Department of State, Foreign Relations of the United States, 1945: The British Commonwealth, The Far East (Washington, D.C.: U.S. Government Printing Office, 1969), 6:670–672.

E12. IMPERIAL RESCRIPT OF AUGUST 17, 1945

More than three years and eight months have elapsed since we declared war on the United States of America and Great Britain. During this period our beloved officers and men of the armed forces have devoted themselves gallantly in fighting on barren fields and on the raging ocean, and we deeply appreciate it. The Soviet Union has now entered the war, and in view of the state of affairs both here and abroad, we feel that the prolongation of the struggle will merely serve to further the evil and may eventually result in the loss of the very foundation on which the Empire exists. Therefore, in spite of the fact that the fighting spirit of the Imperial Army and Navy is still high, we hereupon intend to negotiate a peace with the United States of America, Great Britain, the Soviet Union and the Chungking Government for the sake of maintaining our glorious national polity.

We deeply mourn the loss of numerous loyal and courageous soldiers who have perished in action and from disease, and believe that the devoted and distinguished services rendered by ye officers and men of the armed forces will long be remembered by the people. We expect ye officers and men of the armed forces to comply faithfully with our desire, unite firmly, exercise complete prudence, endure hardships and privations with undying patience and thus lay the permanent foundation for the nation.

Source: Donald S. Detweiler and Charles B. Burdick, eds., War in Asia and the Pacific, vol. 12, Defense of the Homeland and the End of the War (New York: Garland, 1980), 23–26.

E13. INSTRUMENT OF SURRENDER, SEPTEMBER 2, 1945

Instrument of Surrender

We, acting by command of and on behalf of the Emperor of Japan, the Japanese Government and the Japanese Imperial General Headquarters, hereby accept the provisions set forth in the declaration issued by the heads of the Governments of the United States, China and Great Britain on 26 July 1945, at Potsdam, and subsequently adhered to by the Union of Socialist Soviet Republics. The above four powers shall be referred to as the Allied Powers hereafter.

We hereby proclaim the unconditional surrender to the Allied Powers of the Japanese Imperial General Headquarters and of all Japanese armed forces and all armed forces under Japanese control wherever situated.

We hereby command all Japanese forces wherever situated and the Japanese people to cease hostilities forthwith, to preserve and save from damage all ships, aircraft, and military and civil property and to comply with all requirements which may be imposed by the Supreme Commander for the Allied Powers or by agencies of the Japanese Government at his direction.

We hereby command the Japanese Imperial General Headquarters to issue at once orders to the commanders of all Japanese forces and all forces under Japanese control, wherever situated, to surrender unconditionally themselves and all forces under their control.

We hereby command all civil, military and naval officials to obey and enforce all proclamations, orders and directives deemed by the Supreme Commander for the Allied Powers to be proper to effectuate this surrender and issued by him under his authority and we direct all such officials to remain at their posts and to continue to perform their noncombatant duties unless specifically relieved by him or by his authority.

We hereby undertake for the Emperor, the Japanese Government and their successors to carry out the provisions of the Potsdam Declaration in good faith, and to issue whatever orders and take whatever action may be required by the Supreme Commander for the Allied Powers or by any other designated representative of the Allied Powers for the purpose of giving effect to that Declaration.

We hereby command the Japanese Imperial Government and the Japanese Imperial General Headquarters at once to liberate all allied prisoners of war and civilian internees now under Japanese control and to provide for their protection, care, maintenance and immediate transportation to designated places.

The authority of the Emperor and the Japanese Government to rule the state shall be subject to the Supreme Commander for the Allied Powers, who will take such steps as he deems proper to effectuate these terms of surrender.

Signed at Tokyo Bay, Japan at 0904 hours on the 2 September 1945
Shigemitsu Aoi
By command of and on behalf of the Emperor of Japan and the Japanese Government.
Umezu Yoshijiro
By command of and on behalf of the Japanese Imperial General Headquarters.

Accepted at Tokyo Bay, Japan at 0908 hours on the 2 September 1945 for the United States, Republic of China, United Kingdom and the Union of Socialist Soviet Republics, and in the interests of the other United Nations at war with Japan.
Douglas MacArthur
Supreme Commander for the Allied Powers
[Also signed by the representatives of the nine Allied powers.]

Source: Donald S. Detweiler and Charles B. Burdick, eds., *War in Asia and the Pacific*, vol. 12, *Defense of the Homeland and the End of the War* (New York: Garland, 1980), 27–29.

E14. IMPERIAL RESCRIPT OF SEPTEMBER 2, 1945

Accepting the terms set forth in Declaration issued by the heads of the Governments of the United States, Great Britain and China on July 26th, 1945 at Potsdam and subsequently adhered to by the Union of Soviet Socialist Republics, We have commanded the Japanese Imperial Government and the Japanese Imperial General Headquarters to sign on Our behalf the Instrument of Surrender presented by the Supreme Commander for the Allied Powers and to issue General Orders to the Military and Naval Forces in accordance with the direction of the Supreme Commander for the Allied Powers. We command all our people forthwith to cease hostilities, to lay down their arms and faithfully to carry out all the provisions of Instrument of Surrender and the General Orders issued by the Japanese Imperial Government and the Japanese Imperial General Headquarters hereunder.
This second day of the ninth month of the twentieth year of Shōwa.
Seal of the Emperor
HIROHITO
[Also signed by the members of the cabinet]

Source: Robert J. C. Butow, *Japan's Decision to Surrender* (Stanford, Calif.: Stanford University Press, 1954), 249–250.

F.

United States Strategic Bombing Survey: Summary Report and Interrogations of Japanese Officials

F1. USSBS, SUMMARY REPORT (PACIFIC WAR), JULY 1, 1946

UNITED STATES STRATEGIC BOMBING SURVEY
SUMMARY REPORT
(PACIFIC WAR)
WASHINGTON, D.C.

1 JULY 1946 . . .

The Effects of the Atomic Bombs

On 6 August and 9 August 1945, the first two atomic bombs to be used for military purposes were dropped on Hiroshima and Nagasaki respectively. One hundred thousand people were killed, 6 square miles or over 50 percent of the built-up areas of the two cities were destroyed. The first and crucial question about the atomic bomb thus was answered practically and conclusively; atomic energy had been mastered for military purposes and the overwhelming scale of its possibilities had been demonstrated. A detailed examination of the physical, economic, and morale effects of the atomic bombs occupied the attention of a major portion of the Survey's staff in Japan in order to arrive at a more precise definition of the present capabilities and limitations of this radically new weapon of destruction. . . .

The Survey has estimated that the damage and casualties caused at Hiroshima by the one atomic bomb dropped from a single plane would have required 220 B-29s carrying 1,200 tons of incendiary bombs, 400 tons of high-explosive bombs, and 500 tons of antipersonnel fragmentation bombs, if conventional weapons, rather than an atomic bomb, had been used. One hundred and twenty-five B-29s carrying 1,200 tons of bombs would have been required to approximate the damage and casualties at Nagasaki. This estimate pre-supposed bombing under conditions similar to those existing when the atomic bombs were dropped and bombing accuracy equal to the average attained by the Twentieth Air Force during the last 3 months of the war. . . .

Japan's Struggle to End the War

On 6 August the atomic bomb was dropped on Hiroshima, and on 9 August Russia entered the war. In the succeeding meetings of the Supreme War Direction Council, the differences of opinion previously existing as to the Potsdam terms persisted exactly as before. By using the urgency brought about through fear of further atomic bombing attacks, the Prime Minister found it possible to bring the Emperor directly into the discussions of the Potsdam terms. Hirohito, acting as arbiter, resolved the conflict in favor of unconditional surrender.

The public admission of defeat by the responsible Japanese leaders, which constituted the political objective of the United States offensive begun in 1943, was thus secured prior to invasion and while Japan was still possessed of some 2,000,000 troops and over 9,000 planes in the home islands. Military defeats in the air, at sea and on the land, destruction of shipping by submarines and by air, and direct air attack with conventional as well as atomic bombs, all contributed to this accomplishment.

There is little point in attempting precisely to impute Japan's unconditional surrender to any one of the numerous causes which jointly and cumulatively were responsible for Japan's disaster. The time lapse between military impotence and political acceptance of the inevitable might have been shorter had the political structure of Japan permitted a more rapid and decisive determination of national policies. Nevertheless, it seems clear that, even without the atomic bombing attacks, air supremacy over Japan could have exerted sufficient pressure to bring about unconditional surrender and obviate the need for invasion.

Based on a detailed investigation of all the facts, and supported by the testimony of the surviving Japanese leaders involved, it is the Survey's opinion that certainly prior to 31 December 1945, and in all probability prior to 1 November 1945, Japan would have surrendered even if the atomic bombs had not been dropped, even if Russia had not entered the war, and even if no invasion had been planned or contemplated. . . .

Source: U.S. Strategic Bombing Survey, *Summary Report (Pacific War)* (Washington, D.C.: U.S. Government Printing Office, 1946), 22–26.

F2. USSBS: THE EFFECTS OF STRATEGIC BOMBING ON JAPAN'S WAR ECONOMY, DECEMBER 1946

. . . Conclusions

By July 1945 Japan's economic system had been shattered. Production of civilian goods was below the level of subsistence. Munitions output had been curtailed to less than half the wartime peak, a level that could not support sustained military operations against our opposing forces. The economic basis of Japanese resistance had been destroyed.

This economic decay resulted from the sea-air blockade of the Japanese home islands and direct bombing attacks on industrial and urban-area targets.

The contribution of the blockade was to deny Japan access to vital raw materials on the mainland and in the South Pacific area. Japan's dependence on these sources was crucial in the case of oil, bauxite, iron ore, coking coal, salt, and, to a lesser extent, foodstuff. Heavy merchant ship losses began to cut raw material imports as early as 1943. As the blockade was tightened by submarines, the mining program, and airpower imports were almost completely stopped. Munitions production reached its peak in the fall of 1944; thereafter output began to decline, due to the shortage of raw materials. Thus, before the large-scale bombing of Japan was initiated, the raw material base of Japanese industry was effectively undermined. An accelerated decline of armament production was inevitable.

The program was transformed from one of slow strangulation to a relatively quick knockout by strategic bombing. It was initiated in November 1944, though the main weight of the attack came between the months of March and August 1945.

The precision attacks on industrial targets were of major consequence in the case of the aircraft industry. . . .

The urban-area incendiary raids had profound repercussions on civilian morale and Japan's will to stay in the war. Sixty-six cities, virtually all those of economic significance, were subjected to bombing raids and suffered destruction ranging from 25 to 90 percent. Almost 50 percent of the area of these cities was leveled. . . . The economic disintegration caused by the blockade was finished by the bombers.

It was the timing and the manner of surrender which was largely influenced by Allied air supremacy in Japanese skies. The bombing offensive was the major factor which secured agreement to unconditional surrender without an invasion of the home islands—an invasion that would have cost tens of thousands of American lives. The demonstrated strength of the United States in the B-29 attacks contrasted with Japan's lack of adequate defense made clear to the Japanese people and to the government the futility of further resistance. This was reinforced by the evident deterioration of the Japanese economy and the impact it was having on a large segment of the population. The atomic bomb and Russia's entry into the war speeded the process of surrender already realized as the only possible outcome. . . .

Source: U.S. Strategic Bombing Survey, *The Effects of Strategic Bombing on Japan's War Economy* (Washington, D.C.: U.S. Government Printing Office, 1946), 2–3.

F3. USSBS INTERROGATION NO. 277, TORASHIRO KAWABE, NOVEMBER 2, 1945

INTERROGATION NO. 277 PLACE: TOKYO

DATE: 2 NOVEMBER 1945 . . .
SUBJECT: KAMIKAZE TACTICS AND THE JAPANESE ABILITY TO RESIST . . .

Personnel Interrogated and Background of Each

1. Lt General [Torashiro] KAWABE — Deputy Chief, Imperial General Headquarters; Commanding General KOKUSOGUN; Director KAMIKAZE operations, Philippines and Okinawa campaigns; Dec 1941 — Chief of General Affairs Section, Army Air Headquarters and Inspector General, General Affairs Section, Army Air Headquarters.
2. Maj General MIWA . . .

Summary

Lt General KAWABE discusses the background of the development of the KAMIKAZE emphasizing that it was, in all cases, voluntary, and arose out of the desire of the individual to dedicate his body to this cause. The organization of the KAMIKAZE units is discussed, and the general plan for countering the invasion of KYUSHU is developed.

Gen KAWABE came to the conclusion in April, when the B-29s began precision bombing, that Japanese industrial capacity would probably be destroyed but that, despite such destruction, they would still be able to construct planes and continue to fight to the very end. Gen KAWABE states that he himself would have taken off in a plane and crashed it in a KAMIKAZE attack had the invasion taken place. . . .

Q. . . . It is true that, as far as suicide tactics are concerned, the Germans did not have the same stamina as the Japanese did; but did you realize at the time that the very fact that they have to resort to such measures is in effect a ready indication that ultimate defeat is in the cards? . . .

A. No matter how you look at it, everyone who participated in these attacks died happily in the conviction that they would win the final victory by their own death. I did not believe that Japan was beaten by resorting to these tactics.

Q. We found, in the United States, that to manufacture crews is more difficult than planes. . . . How does that compare with your calculation on the attrition of pilots through suicidal methods: Can you justify that?

A. . . . I agree with you in general . . . that you would soon run out of crews; but since our strategy was aimed solely at the destruction of your fleet and transport when it landed here in Japan, that was our view as to our strategy, to destroy your fleet at landing. It was not very difficult to manufacture second-rate planes—that is, makeshift planes, and it was not difficult to train pilots for just such a duty, and since pilots were willing, we had no shortage of volunteers. At no time did we run out of pilots to man these planes, but our big difficulty was rather a question of manufacturing than a shortage of crews.

Q. In your planning on using the Kamikaze against our invading fleet during the invasion of Kyushu and other places, do you realize that before we invaded we would neutralize every airport within the Empire? We had the power to do it. Did you foresee this possibility and how did you intend to launch your attack? Where from? What was your official plan for that?

A. It didn't take a very elaborate field for a Kamikaze plane to take off. We believed that, despite your destruction of our major fields, we could very easily construct fields from which Kamikaze planes could take off. Everywhere we had built little fields capable of launching Kamikaze planes. As long as there was only a question of launching them and not getting them back, there was no question about that.

Q. In Germany two strategic air forces neutralized German industry, and the air forces we had there pinned their air forces down during the invasion. Now we would have here three air forces on Okinawa besides the B-29s and the carrier-based airplanes, so we would have a much greater weight exerted against Japan than against Germany and therefore we believe that all the landing strips, no matter how small as long as they resembled flying fields, would be destroyed or neutralized. How had you intended to disperse your airplanes and control the operations, because you would have to operate from widely separated little flying fields all over Japan? 8000 planes are a lot of planes.

A. We knew you would do everything in your power to destroy all our airfields but we believed the airfields necessary for launching Kamikaze planes were such simple affairs that they could be mended very quickly. We believed that by taking advantage of weather—heavy overcast—intervals between your bombing raids, we could repair the airfields enough to keep them serviceable; also we could use stretches of beach along the coast. . . .

Q. I'd like to ask you the same question I asked the others to see what your reaction is: Remember when we reached your industrial capacity with B-29s and we were able to destroy your industrial capacity, yet our industrial capacity was unmolested, did you realize that, then and there, the war was over because you would be deprived of your means to wage war? When did you realize that it would be only a matter of time?

A. We believed probably we would lose the war and we knew we could never win the war; but we never gave up the idea of continuing the fight, using whatever special attack planes we could manufacture and we intended to continue the fight unto the very end and make a showdown fight of it, involving transports at landing; that is, we intended to wait until we could attack the transports at landing although it was very clear to us that you could eventually destroy our industries to the point where we could no longer wage war.

Q. When did you come to that conclusion?

A. I came to that conclusion when in April the B-29 raids began attacking various small targets in Japan—not only the larger ones; that is, when the precision bombing started. Despite the fact that we knew you could destroy most of our industrial capacity— our capacity to produce planes—we still did not think it would become impossible for us to construct planes and in some way or another we would construct them.

I want to explain something to you; this is a very difficult thing which you may not be able to understand. The Japanese to the very end believed that by spiritual means they could fight on equal terms with you, yet by any other comparison it would not appear equal. We believed our spiritual conviction in victory would balance any scientific advantage and we had no intention of giving up the fight. It seemed to be especially Japanese.

Q. I understand you could fight to the last man, but you did that knowing perfectly well that victory would be impossible?

A. No, we still thought that that would offset the technological superiority and the issue was still in doubt. That is probably a contention that you cannot understand—that's the Japanese feeling: we'd made up our minds to fight to the very last man and thought we still had a chance. . . .

A. . . . May I point out one thing. You call our Kamikaze attacks "suicide" attacks. This is a misnomer and we feel very badly [about] your calling them "suicide" attacks. They were in no sense "suicide." The pilot did not start out on his mission with the intention of committing suicide. He looked upon himself as a human bomb which would destroy a certain part of the enemy fleet for his country. They considered it a glorious thing while a suicide may not be glorious . . .

A. Originally we did not plan these suicide attacks, but because of the results achieved by suicide attacks, gradually the Japanese Air Force had decided to become a special attack force from the top down to the lowest men, including myself. Although I remain to tell the story, I myself had fully determined to crash a plane into the invading fleet. My place now is to utilize myself to the best of my ability in the reconstruction of Japan, but I feel that if the war had continued to a finish fight I would have crashed my plane into the enemy and I feel that everyone in the Air Force feels the same way. . . .

Source: U.S. Strategic Bombing Survey (Pacific), *Interrogations of Japanese Leaders and Responses to Questionnaires*, Microfilm Publication M1654, Roll 5.

F4. USSBS INTERROGATION NO. 447 (NAV 98), TORASHIRO KAWABE, NOVEMBER 26, 1945

DATE: 26 NOVEMBER 1945 . . .
SUBJECT: OVERALL PLANNING AND POLICIES.

PERSONNEL INTERROGATED AND BACKGROUND OF EACH:

Lieutenant General [Torashiro] KAWABE, IJA . . . From April to October 1945, Deputy Chief of the Army General Staff. . . .

Summary

General KAWABE discusses cooperation between the Army and Navy, the responsibilities and primary interests of the two services, and the effects of operation in the various theatres. The General was a strong advocate of fighting the war "to the very end," in the belief that had they been able to inflict heavy casualties on the U.S. landing forces it might have been possible to get terms more favorable than absolute surrender. . . .

Q. Now at what point in the war would you say that it became obvious, that JAPAN didn't have the war potential to carry their effort on successfully?

A. I am not in a position to speak for JAPAN as a whole, but I do know from hearsay that even at the time of the outbreak of the war, or even before that there were many people both in government and in military circles, both Army and Navy, who had considerable anxiety as to whether the national potential could maintain or carry on such a war.

Q. At what time did you first realize that there was talk of arranging a termination of the war, talk in any high circles?

A. As far as I myself am concerned, the time it actually happened was the first I heard, August 15th. As Deputy Chief of the General Staff, I was of the opinion that we would fight to the very end, and moreover I believe that we should have fought to the very end.

Q. How far would you say that "very end" extended?

A. I desired a landing operation; I felt that should the UNITED STATES attempt landing operations that, with our strength in the homeland, we could have inflicted heavy casualties on the U.S. forces and caused considerable damage. At no time did I have any thought that JAPAN would be able to use the strength that was left over after that to recover the PHILIPPINES or the MARSHALLS. There was no thought like that, but I was convinced that considerable damage could have been inflicted on any landing attempt by the U.S. forces on the mainland. It was my desire that that would result not in an unconditional surrender but probably a compromise, and I was under the impression that I was given this duty to continue the war to that extent. I also feel that even if things didn't turn out where we could inflict heavy damage and so forth, if things turned out more unfortunately and U.S. troops occupied the main points, that even at the cost of becoming a second GERMANY, I felt the battle should have been carried on.

Q. Was that, you might say, the general attitude and opinion of the Army? Of the High Command?

A. I would say it was pretty well general throughout the Army.

Q. Would you then say that perhaps one of the influences that brought about the early termination of the war was the Navy, or was it a civilian group?

A. Of the opinion in Navy circles, I am not aware. But I feel that there have been quite a few in civilian life, of course, who had also suffered quite a bit; and among the politicians, who weighed profit and loss of immediate surrender against fighting on. Those people may have, in some way, influenced the EMPEROR to arrive at that final decision. I can't of course say which was the right thing to do, to stop it when it was stopped or to go on to the end; but as far as I myself am concerned, I would have gone on to the very end.

Q. In line with this general subject, did you notice any change in the attitude of the Navy that you associated as a consequence to their loss of the fleet?

A. I did not get that impression. I feel that at least in the Naval General Staff circles, the Navy was prepared to even put their men on shore to carry the fight to the end. That was the impression I got.

Source: U.S. Strategic Bombing Survey (Pacific), *Interrogations of Japanese Leaders and Responses to Questionnaires*, Microfilm Publication M1654, Roll 5.

F5. USSBS INTERROGATION NO. 373, PRINCE FUMIMARO KONOYE, NOVEMBER 9, 1945

DATE: 9 NOV 45 . . .

Q. At what point did the prevailing opinion in this country—by prevailing opinion, I mean governmental opinion—decide the war had to be brought to a conclusion—that the war was lost?

A. This depends to a great extent on the viewpoint of the different people. There were individuals who from the beginning of the war felt it a hopeless cause.

Q. When did you decide the war was lost?

A. I was one who from the first felt that.

Q. At what point did other people influential in the government, people like Marquis Kido, for instance, think the war was lost and that negotiations for peace should be started?

A. Probably those men felt that at the time of the loss of Saipan—from that date on they thought it was a hopeless cause.

Q. Why was nothing done after the fall of Saipan to terminate the war—what prospects were there still, which prevented the Japanese government from taking steps after the fall of Saipan?

A. Efforts were made to terminate the war, but the Army and Navy, particularly the Army, put up strenuous efforts to forestall such action and were resolved to fight through to the end.

Q. To pin it down, what does "efforts" mean?

A. Just as finally the end of the war was brought about by the Emperor, so at that time efforts were made to persuade the Emperor, particularly through Kido, who was close to the Emperor, to get him to put an end to the war.

Q. Who were the people who made such efforts to persuade the Emperor via Kido?

A. The man who put forth the most earnest efforts is probably the present foreign minister. (YOSHIDA, Shigeru)

Q. And those efforts were opposed by the Army and Navy?

A. Generally, that's it . . .

Q. I want to get one point clear. We have no interest in your responsibility one way or another. All we want to get is a frank statement as to your impression of what was involved in the event you went to war. Again, I would like to have your impression of what Japan would have to face in the event of war. What steps would have to be taken and how those steps would have to be developed in the event Japan went to war.

A. The thing which impressed me most was hearing from the Fleet Admiral and look-ing at everything he said. I was determined to try to avoid war with everything we had. If war did start, I didn't see any hope for Japan.

Q. In other words, it was your opinion in December 1941 that Japan inevitably could not bring the war to a successful conclusion from Japan's point of view?

A. Just exactly as you say. . . . I felt there was no chance for success.

Q. I think we might turn then to the subject of how peace was finally arrived at. You stated that after Saipan it became even clearer that a successful termination of the war was impossible. You said that certain people began to take steps to lay the preparation for the termination of the war.

A. That, of course, wasn't in the army. It was outside of the army—people who began to work on the Emperor. Of course, such negotiations had to be carried on in the strictest secrecy because the situation was such that it was at the risk of one's life to do anything like that.

Q. Who were the people, of your own personal knowledge, who were of that opinion?

A. The present Foreign Minister Yoshida was one, also Admiral Yonai and Admiral Okada. These were all of the upper rank of men—of higher classes of men who carried on such activities. As far as I know, there was none of the lower ranks. . . .

Q. What were the first steps considered necessary in order to lay the ground-work for this important change in policy?

A. The biggest realization was that in order to have any influence on the army—that is, to bring the army to a decision—it would be necessary to work through the Emperor.

Q. Was it your opinion that if the Emperor had issued an Imperial rescript as early as April that the army would have been satisfied to obey it?

A. Even in July when the thing came up, there was a demonstration and uprising, so if it had come earlier, there would have been greater confusion on the part of the army. They might have followed it, but there would have been these uprisings.

Q. Was the danger of uprising a consideration in the mind of the Privy Seal?

A. When that was proposed, of course, they were prepared then for the possibility of such a thing and he took his step realizing the personal risk to himself.

Q. I take it you're referring to August?

A. Yes, in August.

Q. And had it been done earlier, would there have been a more serious problem, and what factors contributed to the decrease in the risk of disorders in the event of an Imper-ial rescript?

A. The big thing was the deterioration of the war effort; then with the entry of Russia in the war and the dropping of the atomic bomb, it did a lot to prepare the way for this next move.

Q. Does the order in which you mention those indicate your impression of their relative importance?

A. It is pretty difficult to say which was worse or more important.

Q. Had there been any anticipation that Russia might enter the war against Japan prior to the time it actually occurred?

A. I don't feel anyone thought she would come in at that time—at the time she did.

Q. What would the result have been had the United States announced that it did not intend to invade Japan, but merely intended to continue the use of air power over Japan indefinitely?

A. Just the thought of the continuation of the air raids would have had considerable influence regardless of anything else.

Q. Is it correct that the army's plan at the end was to resist an invasion with full mobilization of Japan's remaining resources, and cause the United States a great many casualties and possibly throw back the invasion?

A. Yes, that was the plan of the army.

Q. What plan would they have adopted in the event we would have made such an announcement as I previously described?

A. I don't know what they would have done.

Q. In your opinion, would their position within the Empire have been strengthened or weakened by such an announcement?

A. You mean from the standpoint of the confidence of the people?

Q. This and their position with the Emperor.

A. The longer the war continued, the more feeling there was against the army, so that the statement itself would have had less influence than the actual prolongation of the war.

Q. How much longer do you think the war might have continued had the atomic bomb not been dropped?

A. It is a little hard for me to figure that out.

Q. What would your best estimate be?

A. Probably it would have lasted all this year.

Q. It would not have been terminated prior to 1 November—is that correct?

A. Probably would have lasted beyond that.

Q. What would the reasons for that have been?

A. It is very difficult to pin it down to actual reasons, but it is just a sort of general feeling, without much actual basis.

Q. Was Marquis Kido persuaded of the advisability of discontinuing the war prior to August 1st?

A. From what I heard, Kido gave his advice to the Emperor first around April of this year.

Q. Was it reluctance on the part of the Emperor to make this drastic decision which delayed it from April to August?

A. The Emperor wanted to end hostilities just as soon as possible, but the situation in the country as a whole was such that he evidently hesitated because of conditions.

Q. Was there hope that the negotiations initiated with the Russians might come to a favourable conclusion as late as August?

A. You mean through Russia or with Russia?

Q. Through Russia with America.

A. They thought that perhaps if they could get something short of unconditional surrender there was a chance of getting it through Russia.

Q. What were they prepared to give up in connection with those negotiations?

A. They felt they were prepared to make any sacrifice—give anything—so long as they could preserve the country and save face. That's so it wouldn't be actual surrender—so it would save face.

Q. Why was it decided not to initiate negotiations directly with the United States?

A. The army opposed any direct negotiation. It was only by proposing that the negotiations be carried on through Russia that the acquiescence of the army was secured.

Q. Why did the army prefer to negotiate through Russia rather than negotiate directly?

A. Because America had said there was nothing beside unconditional surrender she would accept, while the army thought if they worked through Russia it would save face.

Q. In your opinion, would increasingly heavy B-29 fire and high explosive raids have the same effect as the atomic bomb had on speeding the determination to make peace?

A. Fundamentally, the thing that brought about the situation was the prolonged bombing by the B-29's.

Q. Was the effect of the atomic bomb on their political discussions different in kind and nature than the effect of the B-29's?

A. I don't think there was any special change as to type of conferences. It just hurried it up a little bit.

Q. Did not the Emperor realize by the end of July that Japan was defeated?

A. Of course.

Q. Japan realized that the B-29 attacks would be even greater in August than it was in July?

A. They expected that it would become increasingly severe. . . .

Q. I understood you to say that if it had not been for the Emperor's rescript the Japanese would be fighting today. Is that correct?

A. Yes.

Q. Could Japan have continued to fight with these increasing attacks of the B-29's?

A. There was bound to be a limit as to what she could do. . . .

Q. Hadn't they almost reached the limit?

A. Of course, they were nearing the limit, but the army would not admit it. They wouldn't admit they were near the end.

Q. Would they not have been forced to surrender, therefore, even if Russia had not come in or even though we had not dropped the atomic bomb?

A. The army had dug themselves caves in the mountains and their idea of fighting on was fighting from every little hole or rock in the mountains.

Q. Would the Emperor have permitted them to do that?

A. I don't think the Emperor would have let them go that far. He would have done something to stop them.

Q. What was Japan afraid Russia would do that our atomic bombs and B-29's would not do?

A. The greatest fear of Russia was the psychological fear.

Q. Were you afraid Russia would occupy Japan?

A. The fear I refer to was the fact that Russia had been thought of as a neutral country up to that time and for Russia to suddenly come into the war had a great psychological fear and that was the fear I was talking of. . . .

Source: U.S. Strategic Bombing Survey (Pacific), *Interrogations of Japanese Leaders and Responses to Questionnaires*, Microfilm Publication M1654, Roll 5.

F6. USSBS INTERROGATION NO. 308, MARQUIS KOICHI KIDO,
NOVEMBER 10, 1945

DATE: 10 NOV 45 . . .

PERSONNEL INTERVIEWED: MARQUIS KIDO, KOICHI,
LORD KEEPER OF THE PRIVY SEAL. . . .

Summary

Marquis KIDO discussed the political and military relationships and factors which developed during the period from the Marianas campaign to the surrender in August, 1945. He also reviewed Japan's initial war aims, relations between the army and the navy, effects of the atom bombs and Russia's entry into the war, and certain points concerning the negotiations with Washington in the Fall of 1941. . . .

A. There was the danger of a coup if the Emperor had prescribed a peace before the fall of Germany. It would be difficult for me to judge what would have developed had the Emperor issued an Imperial Rescript at that time. As a matter of fact, that sort of feeling or atmosphere was not sufficiently widespread even among the political people in general.

Q. What, in your opinion, would have had to occur before the army could come around to the viewpoint that they could and would obey an Imperial Rescript for peace?

A. It would have been necessary to come to a state of affairs in which the leaders of the fighting services would come to the point of view that it was necessary and, at least before the fall of Germany, there was no indication of anything like that in the fighting services.

Q. Did the subsequent engagement in the Philippines in which the army—the Japanese Army—suffered a defeat have a bearing on that point of view?

A. That was not clear at the time of the Philippine Campaign and the publicity of the time was that something was going to be done at Okinawa. . . .

Q. Could you give us some of the steps which finally did lead to the issuance of the Imperial Rescript?

A. The movement—the first steps were taken on, if I remember correctly, June 8th or 9th that is this year, when the Prime Minister, the Foreign Minister and the Service Ministers concurred in the view that certain definite steps must be taken. The general idea at the moment was to have the USSR mediate in the negotiations for peace. Talks were also going on to send Prince Konoye as the Emissary, if the Prince was acceptable to the Soviet Government. Our message suggesting that we would send Prince Konoye as an emissary probably reached Moscow after Commissar Molotov had left for the Potsdam Conference and there was no reply. Then came the Potsdam Declaration, and following the return of Molotov to Moscow the Soviet Union entered the war against Japan. That raised the question of acceptance of the Potsdam Declaration since it was impossible to continue the war.

Several Cabinet sessions were held at the outset, but no agreement could be arrived at. Although the Minister of War felt that there was no choice but to bring the war to an end. The feelings and views within the Army, however, were not necessarily so. There were opinions on both sides of the matter. The atomic bomb had a strong effect upon bringing those—for want of a better term I would use "fence sitters"—to the view that the war must be stopped. Is that outline satisfactory?

Q. In your opinion, was the entry of Russia into the war and the impact of her armies against the Japanese armies of greater importance than the effects of the dropping of the atomic bombs?

A. What you want to know is whether the impact of the Russian entry into the war or the effects of the atomic bombs—which of the two had the greater effect. As far as the atomic bombs are concerned, the army endeavoured at first to minimise the effects of them and on top of that an investigation of the results had not been thorough enough to give us an idea of their real effects. To answer the question which of the two—the entry of Russia into the war and the dropping of the atomic bombs—had the greatest effect on the army—I can not say. . . .

Q. In the event that atomic bombs had not been dropped and Russia had not entered the war, how long in your opinion might the war have continued?

A. As I have stated, our decision to seek a way out of this war was made in early June before any atomic bomb had been dropped and Russia had not yet entered the war. It was already our decision.

Q. The dropping of the atomic bombs and the entry of Russia into the war apparently did speed the agreement of the services ministries to end the war. What we would like to get is the degree to which this was speeded up?

A. It was not the time factor. It was the fact that it made the task easier to bring the war to a close by silencing those who would advocate the continuation of the war. If there had been no dropping of the atomic bomb or entry of the Soviet Union into the war, I am inclined to be very doubtful whether the policy to bring the war to a close would have progressed as smoothly. A rather large-scale outbreak within the armed forces could easily be imagined.

Q. Is it proper then to interpret it as being your opinion that the war might have been over in any case prior to November 1st even without the entry of Russia into the war and the dropping of the atomic bombs?

A. I personally think that the war would have ended prior to November 1, as every possible effort was being exhausted to terminate the war.

Q. Would you say the effect of the atomic bombs were very different in the minds of the government from the effects of the B-29 raids which took place previously? Did the government react differently than they did to the general B-29 air attacks?

A. The effect was very much greater. The effect of the atomic bomb was much greater than the B-29 air attacks because one single plane with one single bomb eliminated some 100,000 people in a single strike.

Q. I understand for instance that a B-29 raid on Tokyo in March 1945 was extremely damaging in terms of casualties and real damage. Was the effect of this raid similar to that which took place when the atomic bomb was dropped?

A. As I stated before the effect of the atomic bomb was much greater in view of the fact that a single plane carrying a single bomb could eliminate such a large population in one strike, and also the fact that it affected people after the bomb was dropped and so the psychological effect of the atomic bomb was greater. Heretofore, a single B-29 meant that it was on reconnaissance, but after the atomic bomb was dropped on Hiroshima the information that a lone plane was coming into the area would force every citizen to take shelter in his dugout. . . .

Q. In the event that the atomic bomb had not been dropped and Russia had not entered the war, would a successful invasion of one of the Japanese Home Islands have been necessary to force an agreement between the military services in order to take positive steps to stop the war?

A. Every effort was being made to bring the war to an end without an invasion of any kind on the Home Islands. If the matter had been prolonged there might have been some confusion, but as the situation stood it was realized that the war could be terminated without much difficulty.

Q. Did the army feel confident of their ability to resist an invasion and make an invasion unsuccessful?

A. That was how it was explained to us by the army. They were confident. . . .

Source: U.S. Strategic Bombing Survey (Pacific), *Interrogations of Japanese Leaders and Responses to Questionnaires*, Microfilm Publication M1654, Roll 5.

F7. USSBS INTERROGATION NO. 489, BARON KIICHIRO HIRANUMA, NOVEMBER 23, 1945

INTERROGATION NO. 489 PLACE: TOKYO, JAPAN,
DATE: 20, 23, NOV. 1945 . . .
SUBJECT: PERSONAL VIEWS ON SOCIAL AND ECONOMIC
DEVELOPMENT DURING THE WAR
PERSONNEL INTERROGATED: BARON HIRANUMA, KITCHIRO,
PRESIDENT OF PRIVY COUNCIL . . .

Summary

. . . His views on the end of the war are thoroughly orthodox, in keeping with those of Kido, Konoye, etc.

Q. What would you say were the factors which led to the decision to end the war— were they predominately military factors because the Army could not carry on the war any longer, or were there other factors such as morale?

A. The biggest factor was possibly a military factor. As I said before, air and naval supremacy were gone—Japanese armies were scattered over a wide area—home defenses were completely inadequate and on top of that, bombing had been increased to such an extent that whole cities were wiped out, as you can see right around us here, with 80% of this city gone—then there came the atomic bomb, so that the country was faced with terrible destructive powers and Japan's ability to wage war was really at an end.

Q. Did that include concern over the attitude of the people toward continuing the war?

A. The general population was not aware of the war situation and many of them undoubtedly felt that Japan was still able to wage war since they did not know the overall situation. In fact, they did not know it until the war was brought to an end by declaration from the Emperor, himself, and for the first time these people learned of the true situation. And, when Higashi-Kuni explained the situation in the Diet, then they learned what was going on.

Q. Baron Hiranuma believes that the decision to end the war was primarily a decision by the army on the grounds it could no longer fight the war under conditions as they existed?

A. I don't know how the military, themselves, felt in their own hearts, but as far as any outward expressions were concerned, they maintained until the very last that they were able to carry on the war.

A. It was changed by the decision of the Emperor himself.

Q. Would he say that the Army was virtually isolated—that all other responsible officials believed the war should be brought to an end?

A. Among the officials, that is true. Outside of the Army and Navy, they were agreed that the war should be stopped, but even in the Cabinet Meetings, the military still maintained they could carry on and it was because of the clash of opinion there that the Emperor finally rendered his judgment. . . .

Source: U.S. Strategic Bombing Survey (Pacific), *Interrogations of Japanese Leaders and Responses to Questionnaires*, Microfilm Publication M1654, Roll 1.

F8. INTERROGATION NO. 355, REAR ADMIRAL S. TOMIOKA, NOVEMBER 15, 1945

INTERROGATION NO: 355 PLACE: TOKYO . . .
DATE: 15 NOV. 1945 . . .
PERSON INTERROGATED AND BACKGROUND:

TOMIOKA, S., Rear Admiral, IJN . . .

1944 (June)—Became Chief of the Southeast Area Fleet.

1944 (Nov.)—Returned to Homeland and assumed duty of operations and war history officer of operations and war history officer of Naval General Staff. . . .

Q. 23. After the fall of OKINAWA was there any thinking in the General Staff that the Allies could be stopped?

A. No. Our only hope was that we could discourage you by inflicting great damage on your forces. We estimated we would destroy 30–40% of the initial assaulting forces when you hit the homeland.

Q. 24. Where did you estimate the blow would fall on the home islands?

A. At the end of July or early in August we believed you would land 15 divisions in southern KUYSHU after taking the neighboring islands. In addition it was estimated that one unit would perhaps assault SHIKOKU at the time of the KUYSHU landings and that by the end of the year you would invade the TOKYO area. We felt that your home front pressure would require you to move fast and require you to try to end the war as quickly as possible.

Q. 25. What was the basis for such estimates?

A. You couldn't bomb us into submission, I thought, and therefore you would have to land on the home island. Once you took OKINAWA after IWO JIMA, we concluded that your first homeland assault must be against KYUSHU or SHIKOKU. Your land-based fighters did not have any range to cover the TOKYO area landings. So that we estimated it would be necessary for you first to take KYUSHU or SHIKOKU and then move to TOKYO. That was based on estimates and not on particular factual intelligence.

Q. 26. Did you think we had enough ships to land and support 15 divisions?

A. Based on statistics of your previous landing, we figured that you would use 15 divisions and that you easily had enough ships to land and supply that many. . . .

Source: U.S. Strategic Bombing Survey (Pacific), *Interrogations of Japanese Leaders and Responses to Questionnaires*, Microfilm Publication M1654, Roll 3.

F9. USSBS INTERVIEW WITH A. FUNADA, DECEMBER 12, 1945

INTERVIEW WITH FUNADA ATSUYASU, OFFICIAL IN THE SECRETARIAT OF THE
BOARD OF INFORMATION . . .
SUBJECT: JAPANESE PUBLIC OPINION DURING THE WAR

People were surprised at the war, and encouraged by the victories. . . . They thought that Asia should be for the Asiatics. During the interval from the Fall of Singapore to Guadalcanal, they had great hopes for a new Asia and for no more slavery. However, at about the time of Guadalcanal, anti-Tojo feeling began to arise. Then, as the battle conditions got worse they felt that there was no hope. They became suspicious of the Imperial Headquarters announcements. The military and the government tried to wipe this out, but was not too successful. There was a gradual separation between the military and the people, particularly at the time of Saipan. People began to feel that the Army and Navy were of no avail. All the internal and external conditions began to get worse and with the Suzuki Cabinet people recognized the emergence of a peace cabinet. However, the die-hards among the military still held out. The hopes of the die-hards were dashed to pieces by participation in the war of Russia and the atomic bomb. Both of these gave good material to the peace group. . . .

Source: U.S. Strategic Bombing Survey (Pacific), *Interrogations of Japanese Leaders and Responses to Questionnaires*, Microfilm Publication M1654, Roll 3.

F10. USSBS INTERROGATION NO. 276, REAR ADMIRAL TOSHITANEA TAKATA, NOVEMBER 2, 1945

INTERROGATION NO. 276 PLACE: TOKYO

DATE: 2 NOVEMBER 1945 . . .
SUBJECT: PLANS FOR EMPLOYMENT OF JAPANESE AIR FORCES

PERSONNEL INTERROGATED AND BACKGROUND:
REAR ADMIRAL TAKATA TOSHITANEA, IMPERIAL JAPANESE NAVY . . .

Summary

The one hope of the Japanese Military, he deemed, was that it could defeat the invasion of the homeland by destroying the invasion fleet with KAMIKAZE attacks. The loss of SAIPAN forced the Command to realize that Japan proper would now be within range of land-based bombers. . . .

A. We realized at the time you took Saipan that you were taking it for the primary purpose of bombing Japan out of the war. We realized at the time, once you had taken Saipan from now on the war is going to be pretty tough.

Q. Did you think you had lost the war by that time?

A. We realized, with the destruction of our industrial capacity, our production would naturally drop to practically zero but our one hope was that, if we could destroy the invasion fleet when it cams to actually land in Japan—although Japan could not win the war—it could hold out indefinitely for any number of years, if we could master the defense at the time of invasion of the homeland to destroy the invasion fleet.

Q. Did you realize that before we invaded that we would assemble quite an armada of airpower—to destroy all your communications, all your dams, all your industrial areas and completely bring to a standstill all the country's planes? In other words, the only way you could fight after you had expended your munitions on hand would be by swords and fists. We could isolate you, you have already stated you couldn't even move because you had not enough gasoline. You did not appreciate the significance of the fact that we were able to destroy your industry and blockade Japan completely by air power; therefore it was only a question of time before you would have to give up?

A. I realized it, but it would not be determined until we really fought. . . .

Source: U.S. Strategic Bombing Survey (Pacific), *Interrogations of Japanese Leaders and Responses to Questionnaires,* Microfilm Publication M1654, Roll 2.

F11. USSBS INTERROGATION NO. 522,
FIELD MARSHAL SHUNRORU HATA (NO DATE)

INTERROGATION NO. 522 . . .

SUBJECT: . . . JAPANESE PREPARATIONS FOR ALLIED INVASION.

PERSON INTERROGATED AND BACKGROUND: FIELD MARSHAL HATA SHUNRORU . . .

Graduate of Military and Staff College . . . in April 1945, given one of the two General Commands in Japan, directly responsible to Emperor. . . .

Q. If the United States forces had announced that they were not going to invade but were simply going to increase the scale of the Air attack throughout by ten-, twenty-, fifty-fold and destroy everything on the island by air, what then would have been your estimate of the situation?

A. If such an announcement had been made it would naturally have complicated the situation of the ground forces, simply because we had no means of defending ourselves and would have suffered losses to our troops and losses in our supplies. I believe that the question of whether JAPAN would have yielded had such an announcement been made is one of degree. However, when the atomic bomb was dropped on HIROSHIMA, I believed "there is nothing more we can do, we might as well give up." However, as commander of the General Army, I myself, had there been no order from the EMPEROR to end the war, would have continued fighting to the very end in defense of the homeland. . . .

Q. Did the increased scale of B-29 attacks starting in March of 1945 affect your opinions as to the ability to go ahead and continue the war?

A. The increased scale of bomb attacks in March caused great change in Japanese planning of defense. . . . We also felt an extreme necessity for dispersing our military stores and putting them underground.

Q. Did you disperse these to the point where you felt that they were safe from air attack—military stores and supplies?

A. I felt that if you dug your holes deep enough you were safe from bombing attack. However it was extremely difficult to carry on such large-scale digging-in operations, and the war ended before we completed our digging-in.

Q. Did you feel that this dispersal of supplies and materials would have made it more difficult for you to resupply and reinforce the armies that were going to resist invasion?

A. I do not feel that the dispersion would have caused any delay in operations and bringing up supplies because most of the material was dispersed in the immediate vicinity of the forces which were to use them.

Q. In drawing up your plans to repel an invasion, would you just give me a brief overall idea of how you intended to use your forces? What was to be the scheme of repelling the invasion, the overall plan?

A. During the war our military experience in the Pacific area taught us that if the enemy once landed, the outcome was already decided, so that, whereas previously we had dug in away from the beaches and had let the enemy land and then attacked him, our theory for the defense of the home island was to dig in right along the beaches and dig in deeply in order to avoid destruction by preliminary bombardment and bombing. We intended to stand and fight on the beaches in an attempt to repel the invasion at the first landing because the lessons learned during the war had taught us that we were beaten if the enemy landed in force. . . .

Q. If the ATOMIC BOMB had not been dropped, do you believe that JAPAN would have surrendered anyway?

A. It was a question of time, depending on the extent to which the bombings would have increased in force and what the situation would have been at the time of landings. It would be hard to say.

Q. Do you believe that without the ATOMIC BOMBING, with just the increased scale of the fire raids and the GP bombing, that the surrender would have taken place before November 1?

A. I believe that would depend upon the situation—the scale of the landings. I believed that you would land some time in July, so that by the end of June we had made all preparations. I was not in TOKYO and so I myself can't say what the feeling in TOKYO was on the subject and what the ordinary people thought. I didn't know how the national life of JAPAN was being affected in an overall picture. . . .

Source: U.S. Strategic Bombing Survey (Pacific), *Interrogations of Japanese Leaders and Responses to Questionnaires*, Microfilm Publication M1655, Roll 208A.

F12. USSBS INTERROGATION NO. 531, PRIME MINISTER KANTARO SUZUKI, DECEMBER 26, 1945

INTERROGATION NO. 531 PLACE: TOKYO, JAPAN

DATE: 26 DEC 45 . . .
SUBJECT: THE PRIVY COUNCIL . . .

PERSONNEL INTERROGATED AND BACKGROUND OF EACH:
PREMIER BARON SUZUKI, ADMIRAL IJN (RET.) . . .
APPOINTED PREMIER 7 APRIL 1945 . . .

A. May I explain the causes of the end of war as being, generally, desire of all hands to prevent tremendous loss of life on all sides to civilians and military, and from the political aspect the EMPEROR was terribly concerned over the tremendous losses in personnel. He also felt that any landing in JAPAN would cause a tremendous loss of life to the Allied countries, and he wanted to prevent that unnecessary loss too; therefore he was desirous of ending the war by negotiation . . .

A. I myself recognized the B-29 as a very superior weapon. As you can see it was doing tremendous damage to JAPAN, and in every direction towns and cities and homes were being burned up. It seemed to me unavoidable that in the long run JAPAN would be almost destroyed by air attack so that merely on the basis of the B-29 alone I was convinced that JAPAN should sue for peace. On top of the B-29 raids came the ATOMIC BOMB, immediately after the POTSDAM DECLARATION, which was just one additional reason for giving in and was [a] very good one and gave us the opportune moment to make open negotiations for peace. I myself on the basis of the B-29 raids felt that the cause was hopeless.

Q. Had the Japanese supreme war council considered the degree of probability that America might decline . . . [to] invade . . . and continue its operations solely by this increased serial bombardment? If so, what plans had they considered as a course of action that they could possibly take against that type of military action? . . .

A. The SUPREME WAR COUNCIL, up to the time the ATOMIC BOMB was dropped, did not believe that Japan could be beaten by air attack alone. They also believed that the UNITED STATES would land and not attempt to bomb Japan out of the war. On the other hand there were many prominent people who did believe that the UNITED STATES could win the war by just bombing alone. However the SUPREME WAR COUNCIL, not believing that, had proceeded with the one plan of fighting a decisive battle at the landing point and was making every possible preparation to meet such a landing. They proceeded with that plan until the ATOMIC BOMB was dropped, after which they believed the UNITED STATES would no longer attempt to land when it had such a superior weapon—that the UNITED STATES need not land when it had such a weapon; so at that point they decided that it would be best to sue for peace.

Q. Did the SUPREME WAR COUNCIL have an alternative plan for military resistance to meet the event of AMERICA not landing but continuing its air offensive and blockade against JAPAN, not committing themselves to a landing operation at all? Did they have a plan of action, a course of action, to follow in that military event?

A. If the UNITED STATES had not landed in JAPAN and had continued bombing JAPAN, I believe the SUPREME WAR COUNCIL intended to fight AMERICA in the air with planes. At that time JAPAN was on the point of finishing the development of a superior-type plane and various other weapons such as rocket planes with which we hoped to offset the advantage given you by the B-29s, so that I believe the alternate plan was that, if you did not land, we would fight it out with you with the new equipment which we hoped to have available very shortly.

Q. Did you consider that the state of the Japanese industry and the progressive attacks that were being made on it would permit the development of an effective air weapon to oppose invasions, these air attacks?

A. The Japanese had planned to put their factories and air installations underground. Although our production had fallen off, we believed that, with this plan of going underground, we could perhaps continue to manufacture 1700 planes a month (that is just a figure which I picked at random and may not be accurate). I am not familiar with the subject because it is a little bit technical, and I don't know too much about it. . . . Although we had a very all-inclusive plan for going underground and fighting it out to a finish, I don't believe we made much progress on it at the time the war ended. . . .

A. I want to make it quite clear that, in the Japanese political framework, the man who is responsible for events—political events—is the PREMIER. He is appointed and he himself in turn appoints all his various cabinet members. All decisions relative to government policies and actions are made in different councils and decided upon by various groups inside the Government. Their decisions are then submitted for approval to the EMPEROR, so that all policies and actions taken by the Japanese Government are really the product of the Government itself, of which the PRIME MINISTER is the head. Political decisions cannot be regarded as the responsibility of the EMPEROR.

Ordinarily speaking, even though He himself may be opposed to the proposed plans or policies, the EMPEROR will approve them. Therefore I want it very clearly understood that the PRIME MINISTER throughout recent Japanese history is the man who is responsible for the actions of the Japanese Government. That is, with only two exceptions: (1) In the February 26 incident of 1936, the EMPEROR himself voluntarily ordered Japanese troops to attack the revolutionaries barricaded in TOKYO because the Government had more or less split up: the PREMIER was in hiding, various cabinet members couldn't be found, so of his own volition the EMPEROR ordered the Army to put down the revolt; (2) At the end of the war just recently, he again gave his own personal order to stop the war. These are the only two occasions upon which the Emperor has exercised his personal power.

The situation at the end of the war was that no one could agree on whether to continue the war or to end it. There were those who wanted to end the war by a negotiated peace and those who wanted to fight it out to the last, and no matter how many arguments and meetings we had, we could never get a complete agreement of anything in the government. Therefore I was given the task of presenting to the EMPEROR the Government's split decision on whether to continue the war or to end it. I went to point out that in this particular case the EMPEROR himself made the decision to end the war because of his personal grievance over the suffering of his people and also because of his humanistic feeling in regard to the loss of life which would be involved by both sides in a landing operation and a fight to the finish.

This is extremely difficult to understand, the role of the EMPEROR and the PREMIER in Japanese policy, and I don't believe there is any country in the world that has a similar organization. I want the EMPEROR's position to be made very clear so that it will be understood. On the second occasion when the EMPEROR took his active role in politics, at the end of the war, it was because the PREMIER, at his direction, had been able to lead the Government up to a point where it could be left to the EM-PEROR to make the decision; in other words, I had prepared the way.

End of Interrogation

Source: U.S. Strategic Bombing Survey (Pacific), *Interrogations of Japanese Leaders and Responses to Questionnaires*, Microfilm Publication M1655, Roll 208A.

F13. USSBS INTERROGATION NO. 609, HISATSUNE SAKOMIZU, DECEMBER 11, 1945

INTERROGATION NO. 609 . . .

SUBJECT: POLITICAL ACTIVITIES LEADING UP TO THE PEACE.

PERSONAL INTERROGATED AND BACKGROUND OF EACH:

MR. HISATSUNE SAKOMIZU, CAREER GOVERNMENT OFFICIAL AND POLITICIAN,

CHIEF CABINET SECRETARY IN THE SUZUKI GOVERNMENT. . . .

WHERE INTERVIEWED: TOKYO, 11 DECEMBER [1945] . . .

Summary

This interview covers the major development in the decision to seek peace from the time the Suzuki Government was appointed until 15 August 1945. Some background comments on the Tojo and Koiso cabinets are also included: . . .

On the 20th of June the Emperor, by his own will, called a meeting of the Prime Minister and the others. I just mentioned who were in the meeting of June 9th. (At this point S. explained that the Cabinet had to present a written request for permission to hold a conference in the presence of the Emperor, but the Emperor could call one at his own initiative at any time, although he rarely did so.) The Emperor told them that the conclusion in the document presented in the conference of June 9th seemed to be very paradoxical. He knew the real meaning of the conclusion, he said, "I think it is necessary for us to have a plan to close the war at once as well as one to defend the home islands." (S. explained that at that time the Army was making much of its plan to defeat the American forces when they landed on the home islands.)

As a result of this expression by the Emperor, Suzuki decided to stop the war. After the meeting, when Mr. Suzuki came back, he said to me, "Today the Emperor said what everyone has wanted to say but yet was afraid to say."

T—What was the reaction of the military to this decision?

S—Yonai understood and approved the idea. The war minister, Anami, also approved, but he could not express his real feeling of the generals around him and the fear of assassination.

After that the government decided to send Prince Konoye to Russia and asked Russia if he would be persona grata. The Russians said that they could not decide on the matter unless they received from the Japanese government an expression in more detail of the purpose of the Prince's mission. We sent a cable to Ambassador (Naotake) Sato in Moscow to explain the mission, as follows:

1. To make an improvement in relations between Russia and Japan (this in view of the recent denunciation of the Neutrality Pact).

2. To ask the USSR to intercede with the United States in order to stop the war.

The Russian answer was that Stalin and Molotov were just leaving for the conference at Potsdam, so an answer to the Japanese request could not be given until they returned. We wanted an answer before the conference but we just couldn't have it, so there was nothing to do but wait.

Suzuki and I felt quite pessimistic about the Russian attitude toward our proposal. Then on June [July] 26th came the Potsdam Declaration. Suzuki, Togo, and I talked together, and we felt that this declaration must be accepted as the final terms of peace (surrender), whether we liked it or not. Still the military side of the government said that the terms of the proclamation were "too dishonorable . . . "

S—On the 7th of August, early in the morning, about 2 o'clock, the bell rang beside my bed. . . . When the bell rang beside my bed, it was Domei telling me that President Truman had announced that the atomic bomb had been used at Hiroshima. I already knew that the Hiroshima damage had been very severe and that it had been caused by just one airplane. Everyone said that America had used a new bomb, but they didn't think it was an atomic bomb because our scientists had told us that no country could finish the atomic bomb for use in this war.

The military said that it was probably a 4-ton bomb bursting in the air. They made their calculations, but found that a 4-ton bomb could not do that much damage. They suggested that it might be a 100-ton bomb. After the announcement we sent some scientists to Hiroshima, and they reported that it was a real atomic bomb.

When this news came in on the morning of the 7th I called the Prime Minister on the phone and reported the announcement. Everyone in the government and even in the military knew that if the announcement were true, no country could carry on a war. Without the atomic bomb it would be impossible for any country to defend itself against a nation which had the weapon.

The chance had come to end the war. It was not necessary to blame the military side, the manufacturing people, or anyone else—just the atomic bomb. It was a good excuse, someone said that the atomic bomb was the Kamikaze to save Japan. (Note: Meaning that without it the war would have continued until Japan was no more.)

T—How long do you think the war would have continued if the atomic bomb had not been used?

S—We had already asked the Russians to intercede and we could expect that they would eventually give us some answer. If it had been unfavorable, there was just one way to bring peace and that was to broadcast directly to the United States, but it would have been difficult to find a good chance to do so. I think you can understand. Suzuki tried to find a chance to stop the war and the atom bomb gave him that chance.

I asked the Cabinet Board of Information to put all the information about the atomic bomb in the newspapers and on the radio, in order to tell the people just how fearful it was. But the General Staff Information Office stopped it. They tried hard to emphasize that the people need not fear the atomic bomb if they were in shelters. I had much struggling with the Chief of Military Information. All the Cabinet Board of Information was finally allowed to say was that the atomic bomb had been used at Hiroshima. This item appeared in the morning papers of August 8th. Of course, all the intellectuals knew the meaning of the announcement, because there had been so many stories and novels about atomic power I wanted all the people to understand the meaning of the bomb, but it took a full day just to get the bare announcement released. . . .

Source: U.S. Strategic Bombing Survey (Pacific), *Interrogations of Japanese Leaders and Responses to Questionnaires*, Microfilm Publication M1655, Roll 208A.

F14. USSBS INTERROGATION NO. 378 (NAV 75), ADMIRAL SOEMU TOYODA, NOVEMBER 13–14, 1945

Interrogation of: Admiral TOYODA, Soemu. . . . May 1945 appointed Chief of Naval General Staff; later post superseded by position of Chief, Naval Combined Forces, September 1945 which he held until dissolution of that organization 15 October 1945 . . .

Summary

Admiral TOYODA discusses the influence of the Japanese Army in politics and the implications of this influence in the history of Japanese expansion, the strategy and economics of the basic Japanese plan for war against the UNITED STATES, the question of implication of the armed forces, and the consideration of the surrender question at Imperial Conferences in the summer of 1945.

Transcript

. . . Q. Will you outline the principal points which it was intended would be the basis for seeking peace through RUSSIA? What the terms should be?

A. What the terms should be, while it might have been in the minds of officials in the Foreign Office, did not come up for discussion among us, principally because we thought that it was a matter in which opinion of RUSSIA should be respected. By way of concrete terms, we of course were prepared that, whatever the result, it would be worse than prewar conditions.

Q. In effect, then, the Navy was in favor of peace whatever the basis?

A. At the time that peace discussions were taking place, of course we had not heard of the POTSDAM Declaration; it had not come out yet. We did not think, however, that the actual situation, if and when the war should end, should be quite so stern as under the terms of the declaration, and the same is true as regards the CAIRO Declaration. We looked upon that as a declaration but not as one whose terms would be actually applied to us. By way of possibility of reducing these terms, if you should continue pushing the war, we would demand of you the heavy sacrifice when your landing operations should commence in HONSHU.

Q. At what time during the course of the war would the Navy have accepted an Imperial Rescript terminating the war?

A. That is very difficult to answer because even on the 15th when the Imperial Rescript to terminate the war was actually issued, even then we found it difficult to hold down the front-line forces who were all "raring to go," and it was very difficult to hold them back.

I do not think it would be accurate to look upon use of the Atomic Bomb and the entry and participation of Soviet RUSSIA into the war as direct cause of termination of the war, but I think that those two factors did enable us to bring the war to a termination without creating too great chaos in JAPAN . . .

Q. (Lt. Comdr. Wilds) Do you have any further information or comment you wish to make on the discussion we had yesterday afternoon regarding the termination of the war?

A. Continuing with the story of the meetings of the Supreme War Guidance Council, there was no member of that Council who had any fundamental objection to terminating the war, but there was some question raised as to whether or not all the terms of the POTSDAM Declaration would be acceptable to JAPAN. The points upon which considerable discussion took place were three: (1) the question of the Emperor's future position; (2) the question of disposition of war criminals; and (3) the question of JAPAN'S future form of organization. (Note by the Interpreter: I think we have often translated the phrase as National Equality [Polity].)

On the first point, namely, the question of the Emperor's position, all the members were united in their view that it should be maintained. On the question of war criminals, the desire was expressed by some of the members that the Japanese Government should be permitted to ferret out and try the war criminals; and as regards JAPAN'S "future form of National Organization," the desire was expressed that since the present organization of the country was one based upon the deep convictions of the people we should be permitted to maintain the present form. In other words, determination of the form that it should have in the future should be left to the Japanese people and not, for instance, to a plebiscite organized by Allied authorities.

These discussions took place on 9 August and as there was no agreement, a meeting was called in the presence of the Emperor on the 10th at about 0230 in the morning; and the decision was reached there that, subject to the condition that the

Emperor's position should in no way be affected, the term of the POTSDAM Declaration would be accepted . . .

Q. In these conferences leading to the consideration of surrender, what value was put on the air assaults on JAPAN proper? How did they evaluate that when they were considering the matter of terminating war?

A. I do not believe that the question of air raids came up in the minds of the members as an independent question at all; that is there was no idea that we must give up the war to avoid even a single additional day of bombing. The main consideration that led to the decision to cease hostilities was, after all, the overall weakening of the Nation's production capacity, loss of material, etc.

I refer to the statement already made regarding the effect on morale and point out that outside of bombed areas, especially in the country, people appeared to be almost wholly unconcerned about bombing as was evidenced by their failure to dig air raid shelters, etc.; so that, taking the country as a whole, the effect on morale was very light.

Q. Was there any attempt at this time to put a value on the cumulative effect of sustained bombing of this nature had it been permitted to continue on for many months, the cumulative effect that such sustained operations would have on JAPAN proper, her capacity to wage war, or to survive?

A. The point that worried me most was the effect of continued bombing on aircraft production. Whereas the year before we were producing over 1,000 naval aircraft alone monthly, in July of this year that production had fallen to around 600, less than half of the previous year; and so far as I could see we were just about nearing the end of our aviation fuel supply, and I could not see how we could possibly procure sufficient aviation fuel after September; and since those two facts, namely, fall in aircraft production and shortage in aviation fuel, were largely due to your air raids, we would naturally reach the conclusion that, if the air raids were to continue for months after that, it would become impossible for us to continue the war. . . .

Source: U.S. Strategic Bombing Survey (Pacific), Naval Analysis Division, Interrogations of Japanese Officials (Washington, D.C.: U.S. Government Printing Office, 1946), 2:313–336.

F15. USSBS INTERROGATION NO. 379 (NAV NO. 76),
ADMIRAL MITSUMASA YONAI, NOVEMBER 17, 1945

Japanese War Planning

Interrogation of: Admiral YONAI, Mitsumasa; Navy Minister in various cabinets as follows: . . . Deputy Premier and Navy Minister in KOISO Cabinet, July 1944; Navy Minister in SUZUKI Cabinet April 1945. . . .

Summary

Admiral YONAI describes the functions of various agencies having major responsibilities in government and for the prosecution of the war, and discusses significant developments of the war and other events leading to its termination. . . .

Q. Admiral, we would like to have your opinion, and discuss it as you will, on what you consider the turning point of the war, the occasion or the situation where there were definite indications of the doubtful successful conclusion of the war?

A. To be very frank, I think that the turning point was the start. I felt from the very beginning that there was no chance of success, but of course this is not an answer to your question. Once the war had started, I would pick either MIDWAY or our retreat from GUADALCANAL as the turning point, after which I was certain there was no chance for success. Later on, of course, it was the loss of SAIPAN followed by LEYTE, and I felt that that was the end. . . .

Source: U.S. Strategic Bombing Survey (Pacific), Naval Analysis Division, *Interrogations of Japanese Officials* (Washington, D.C.: U.S. Government Printing Office, 1946), 2:327–332.

F16. USSBS INTERROGATION NO. 429 (NAV NO. 90),
ADMIRAL KICHISABURO NOMURA, NOVEMBER 8, 1945

Observations on Japan at War

Interrogation of: Admiral NOMURA, Kichisaburo, IJN; former Ambassador to the UNITED STATES (1941), appointed member of the Privy Council, 26 May 1944. . . .

Summary

Admiral NOMURA discusses the background of the war, the situation within JAPAN at various times, and the peace efforts. . . .

Q. Were you fairly familiar yourself with what talk was going on in General Headquarters; did you discuss it with your friends in the Government?

A. I knew in general what talk was going on, but when I speak with our generals they did not seem to know much of the situation although I spoke frankly with them. As the situation wasn't going well, it was rather embarrassing for them. Since joining the Privy Council, I heard discussions by Army and Navy officers and they must have been more frank in these discussions than they were to newspaper men; and also, since

I was at one time a professional naval officer, I was able to grasp the situation from their talks a little better than the average person. Of course, they were reluctant to discuss the situation publicly and wished chiefly to maintain the morale of the people. They seemed to think that if we stood fast the people in the UNITED STATES might by and by weary of the war. . . .

Q. At what time did the Cabinet first reconsider the question as to whether or not the war should be continued?

A. As far as I know that question came up at the end of the SUZUKI Cabinet. I knew SUZUKI very well and served under him, and I feel sure he knew the true situation, and that when he became Prime Minister he was perhaps informed by the Army and Navy of their true situation. He further knew the EMPEROR's mind, and together with his own convictions he made attempts to approach Soviet RUSSIA hoping that RUSSIA would act as an intermediary. Whether or not that was wise, I do not know. In any case the Tri-Partite Pact was still in force, and in any case RUSSIA did not answer. Our Minister approached MOLOTOV and requested that RUSSIA act as an intermediary. In view of this, SUZUKI must have felt that the war must be ended. There were still many responsible men who wanted to continue the war. I cannot understand what the Army and Navy must have been thinking of; but if the war continued, JAPAN would be wholly destroyed and I think some of the Army and Navy would not hesitate to be destroyed completely, and they persuaded the people that they must die fighting. I also know that in the country where I was, the farmers believed that when such an occasion came they must be ready. SUZUKI thought that we could not sacrifice the people for the sake of the Army and Navy, the people must be saved. As a result of this strong feeling, near the end of the war, his house was burned down. I still feel that, as Premier, SUZUKI did the right thing in taking steps to stop the war and prevent the Japanese people from being destroyed. I feel that the Prime Minister was not as concerned with the war as he was with saving the people, even though the Navy and Army lost face. He felt he must save the people, and even today he thinks he did the right thing.

Q. Did SUZUKI get much support from others in that policy?

A. So far as I know there was considerable disagreement among council members. Although as Premier, SUZUKI felt the war should be stopped, it was necessary that the Council be in accord, and if he could not reach an accord in his Council he would be compelled to retire. The Minister himself could not take the responsibility for ending the war. I believe that the EMPEROR told SUZUKI that his mind was made up to end the war; and in spite of the fact that certain ministers made eloquent speeches to continue the war, the EMPEROR said, "My mind is made up in this case. Your views are understood, but I know what we must do in this case." I was told some of them retired with tears in their eyes . . .

Q. What would you say was the primary factor in the minds of those who were of the peace party? Were they more influenced by the Navy Department or the Army Department, or Army defeats, or continued air attacks?

A. The people's mind was made up to continue to the very last. But some of the thinking people, when air attacks became frequent and we were not fighting against them, those people must have become very disillusioned. In spite of this however, they continued to be loyal and did not talk of peace in spite of how they may have seen the war was going on. Although the people may have sensed the true situation, they were loyal to the Government. The Japanese people obey government orders. Therefore, although there were among the people a very few who favored peace, these few did not express their views. I feel that the people did not know the true situation. As for the Navy, we might say that they thought the war would be almost hopelessly gone if a landing was made, but the Army people always thought we should fight even after the landing.

Q. With those who were concerned over the American air attack, do you think they were more influenced by the reduction in production of war materials or because the cities were being burned and the populace suffering?

A. Production of airplanes suffered, naturally; but that, the people did not know. They did suffer themselves from the air raids, but even then, as I told you before, the people did not say peace. Willingly or reluctantly, I cannot say, but they were prepared to sacrifice themselves if the Government so ordered. In the country where I lived, when things went very badly in February, the Postmaster said there was no other way than to kill themselves fighting; such was a common feeling. There must have been some of the people who felt that this feeling was very unwise, but they did not express their views. However, I felt that after the war was over and they really understood the true situation, they were glad that the war stopped when it did. For example, in the country where I lived there was sometimes a farmer who had five boys, all of them at the front during the war. He was ready to give them to the country, knowing that they might not ever return; but after the war was over, when he understood that they were returning, he was very happy. . . .

Source: U.S. Strategic Bombing Survey (Pacific), Naval Analysis Division, *Interrogations of Japanese Officials* (Washington, D.C.: U.S. Government Printing Office, 1946), 2: 384–395.

F17. USSBS INTERROGATION NO. 498, ADMIRAL OSAMI NAGANO,
NOVEMBER 30, 1945

SUBJECT: . . . CAUSES OF JAPAN'S DEFEAT; JAPANESE WAR AIMS

Personnel Interrogated and Background: Fleet Admiral NAGANO Osami—. . . Chief of Naval General Staff Apr 41 to Feb 44. Aptd Supreme Naval Advisor to Emperor, February 1944 . . .

Q. Admiral, could the war have been brought to a close, in your opinion—this will have to be a personal opinion as contrasted with an official opinion—without the entry of Russia into the war and without the employment of either atomic bomb?

A. Speaking very frankly, I think we would have been able to extend the war for a considerable time at considerable sacrifice on your part, but I think it would have been impossible for us to win the victory even without Russia's entry and without the use of the atomic bomb. . . .

Source: U.S. Strategic Bombing Survey (Pacific), *Interrogations of Japanese Leaders and Responses to Questionnaires*, Microfilm Publication M1654, Roll 2.

G.

Statements of Japanese Officials on World War II, Military Intelligence Section, Historical Division, U.S. Army

G1. MIS, STATEMENTS OF JAPANESE OFFICIALS, DOCUMENT NO. 59617,
MAJ. GENERAL MASAKESU AMANO (NO DATE)

DOC. NO. 59617
DESCRIPTION OF CONTENTS: THE FULL ENGLISH TRANSLATION OF THE
STATEMENT OF EX-MAJ. GEN AMANO MASAKESU [NOTE: AMANO WAS THE
EX-CHIEF OF THE OPERATIONS SECTION, I.G.H.Q.]
RE: THE KETSUGO OPERATION PLAN . . .

5. Question: How much confidence did the officers in charge of operating in the Imperial General Headquarters have regarding a battle in KYUSHU?

Answer: We were absolutely sure of victory. It was the first and the only battle in which the main strength of the air, land and sea forces were to be joined. The geographical advantages of the homeland were to be utilized to the highest degree, the enemy was to be crushed, and we were confident that the battle would prove to be a turning point in political maneuvering. . . .

Note: The above statement is based on my memory.

Source: See "Guide to the Documents" for the provenience of all documents in this section.

G2. MIS, STATEMENTS OF JAPANESE OFFICIALS, DOCUMENT NO. 54480, MAJ. GENERAL MASAKESU AMANO, DECEMBER 29, 1949

DOC. NO. 54480
REPLY BY AMANO, MASAKESU

29 DEC 49

. . . 10. The Army circles were united in their determination to defend the national polity which was the sole purpose cherished all the time, and I am certain that the nation as a whole were also firm in this conviction.

Although the word "victory" has a broad meaning, I was of the belief that there was little possibility of achieving a victory that would bring the Pacific War to a successful conclusion, something which JAPAN had hoped for. However, I was confident of the possibility of finding an opportunity to win operational victory in the decisive battle for the homeland—which was expected in the near future—and of removing the impending national crisis. Accordingly, it is safe to say that there still remained some room for efforts to work out administrative policies to end the war. As the person responsible for operation and tactics, I believed it imperative for me to make every possible attempt to avail myself of this opportunity. . . .

18. I keenly felt that the Soviet entry into the war added to our difficulties in carrying out the decisive battle against the UNITED STATES. I redoubled my expectations and efforts for an endeavor to completely and quickly crush the American landing attempt upon our homeland while holding out in the difficult operations against the Soviet Union. I also believe that the two generals felt there was no alternative to striving for the execution of the existing War Direction Policy, no matter how great the difficulties became. . . .

G3. MIS, STATEMENTS OF JAPANESE OFFICIALS, DOCUMENT NO. 52506, LT. GENERAL SEIZO ARISUE, MAY 10, 1949

DOC. NO. 52506
CONSIDERATIONS AND OBSERVATIONS OF THE "BRAINS" OF IMPERIAL
HEADQUARTERS REGARDING AMERICAN STRATEGY AGAINST JAPAN AROUND
JUNE OF 1945
BY THE FORMER CHIEF OF THE INTELLIGENCE BUREAU,
IMPERIAL GENERAL HEADQUARTERS,
LT. GEN. ARISUE, SEIZO

(*Question 1*)

Did you not consider in the summer of 1945 that the American Army might first resort to blockade and incendiary bombing tactics, instead of a direct attack on the homeland? If so, what was the reason? At what time and place would American landing operations have been considered the most advantageous to the Japanese Army?

(*Answer*)

About the spring of 1945, when the defense of the homeland was inadequate, our greatest fear was that the UNITED STATES might begin landing operations in the summer, taking advantage of the incompleteness of defense preparations. However, during June and early July, our preparations for the defense of the homeland were practically completed. As it grew more likely that landing operations would begin after the autumn of 1945, the fear grew that the American Army, avoiding a direct attack on the homeland, might resort to thorough and continuous blockade and incendiary bombing tactics.

After May 1945 the indiscriminate bombing of small and medium sized cities was intensified; transport facilities and industrial installations were suddenly paralyzed, the damage by the air raids having exceeded our expectations. What was still worse, the situation in food and fuel supplies was becoming critical. Taking into consideration the increasing damage which would be caused by future air raids and anticipated enemy incendiary and blockade tactics, we feared that the situation might become fatal in 1946.

However, all factors considered, it was anticipated that the American Army would invade KYUSHU in the autumn or 1945. Thus, we had taken no concrete measures for protection from the incendiary bombing and blockade tactics of the enemy.

In view of these considerations, we believed it would be most favorable to us if the enemy were to invade KYUSHU during or following autumn of 1945. This belief was much influenced by the fact that the defense of KYUSHU was given priority and was to have been completed in or about September under the estimate that the enemy would invade KYUSHU first.

(*Question 2*)

What were your grounds for judging that the American Army would land on the Japanese homeland to effect an early termination of the war?

(Answer)

1. Since the war in GERMANY was terminated, the prolongation of the Pacific war would create unfavorable foreign and domestic political problems for the UNITED STATES.

2. Public opinion and the statements of the leaders of the UNITED STATES supported the early termination of the Pacific War.

3. It was natural to assume that the American Forces considered that JAPAN would never surrender unless her armed forces on the homeland were thoroughly defeated. The American Army was sufficiently powerful and self-confident to carry out the landing operations against the homeland. . . .

(Question 4)

What political and strategic effect did Imperial Headquarters believe would result from success in a decisive battle in KYUSHU?

(Answer)

If we could defeat the enemy in KYUSHU or inflict tremendous losses, forcing him to realize the strong fighting spirit of the Japanese Army and people, it would be possible, we hoped, to bring about the termination of hostilities on comparatively favorable terms. At the very least, we hoped to be able to cause the enemy to give up his plan of advancing to the Kanto region or to delay his timetable.

G4. MIS, STATEMENTS OF JAPANESE OFFICIALS, DOCUMENT NO. 54432, COL. SABURO HAYASHI, DECEMBER 23, 1949

DOC. NO. 54432
STATEMENTS REGARDING THE ATTITUDE OF WAR MINISTER ANAMI AND OTHERS
TOWARD PEACE JUST PRIOR TO SURRENDER
BY EX-COL. HAYASHI, SABURO
FORMER SECRETARY TO THE WAR MINISTER

1. Re: SUZUKI

Personally I received no particular impression in connection with this man. However War Minister ANAMI frequently spoke of Prime Minister SUZUKI as being in favor of continuing the war. . . .

War Minister ANAMI spoke to me . . . on 14 and 15 July. He said that he was thinking about peace. The basic idea was to seek peace after inflicting heavy blows upon the American forces in the decisive battle on the homeland. . . .

17. War Minister ANAMI believed that the initial landing of the American invasion forces could be repulsed. I do not know about Gen UMEZU; however, when I visited him on a mission for the War Minister during the early morning of 13 August, he told me that personally he thought the plan to accept the Potsdam Declaration and to terminate hostilities was quite appropriate. At that time, I had the impression that there was some difference of opinion between Generals ANAMI and UMEZU in regard to their idea of continuing hostilities. . . .

Until the meeting in the Imperial presence on the night of 9 August, War Minister ANAMI seemed to have believed that Prime Minister SUZUKI was determined to go on with the war until the very end, but about the time of said meeting, War Minister ANAMI began saying to me that Prime Minister SUZUKI was acting strangely. . . .

G5. MIS, STATEMENTS OF JAPANESE OFFICIALS, DOCUMENT NO. 53437, MEMORANDUM OF ZENSHIRO HOSHIMA

DOC. NO. 53437
FROM MEMORANDUM OF HOSHIMA, ZENSHIRO, FORMER CHIEF OF NAVAL AFFAIRS BUREAU OF NAVY MINISTRY (FROM MAY 1945 TO ABOUT NOVEMBER 1945) (CONFERENCE IN THE PRESENCE OF THE EMPEROR, HELD AT 2330 HOURS ON 9 AUG 45, IN THE IMPERIAL PALACE AIR RAID SHELTER.)

"The Japanese Government will accept the Joint Declaration of the Three Powers, dated 26 July 45, with the understanding that, under the conditions set forth in the declaration, no requirement for a change in the Emperor's sovereignty over the nation (a change in the position de jure of the Emperor of Japan) is included."

The Premier presided at the meeting (by command of the Emperor).

By command of the Emperor, Chairman HIRANUMA of the Privy Council was present.

The Chief Secretary of the Cabinet read the Potsdam Declaration.

The Premier read the draft of the agenda and explained the proposals.

Matters upon which a general agreement was reached at the meeting of the Supreme War Direction Council held that morning were as follows:

1. Matters concerning the Japanese Imperial Household would not be included.
2. Japanese military forces abroad would be withdrawn voluntarily and then demobilized.
3. The Japanese Government would be entrusted with the disposition of war criminals.
4. There would be no physical occupation of the country.

The above resolutions were referred to the Cabinet meeting, with arguments pending.

The cabinet meeting also failed to reach an agreement. Six members supported the Foreign Minister's proposal on the day's agenda. Three members backed the proposal of the Supreme War Direction Council, while a minority expressed the opinion that, with the exception of the first item, other items should be reduced to a minimum. Consequently, the Foreign Minister's opinion, which was supported by what the majority insisted on was drafted into a proposal. . . .

The Foreign Minister's Explanation of the Proposal

The cabinet, which previously rejected the proposal to accept the declaration, finally concluded that under the present circumstances, acceptance of the declaration was imperative. It was necessary to point out only those conditions which were absolutely unacceptable.

With the position of the US and Britain further strengthened by the participation of the USSR, it is difficult to negotiate successfully on the terms of the ultimatum.

From the enemy's point of view, there seemed to be no possibility of compromise, through negotiation, as regards the ultimatum.

It was believed to be better for us not to attach too many conditions to the acceptance of the ultimatum, considering the fact that the USSR had disregarded our proposal and entered the war. . . .

The matter of the Imperial Household was an important question because the Imperial Household is the foundation of future racial development. Therefore, all our demands had to be focused on this question.

The Navy Minister was asked for his opinion. He fully concurred.

The Minister of War was asked to give his opinion. He flatly opposed the proposal . . . and even if the Japanese Government were to accept the declaration, it should set forth at least four conditions. He (the War Minister) could not agree to the plan of making a unilateral proposal to such an immoral nation as the USSR.

The war should be continued, even at the sacrifice of a hundred million people, in order to satisfy the loyalty and patriotism of the nation. The war must be continued at all costs. He was confident that a full-scale war could be waged.

The Japanese Army was confident of victory in its fight against the US and in the impending decisive battle in the homeland. The Japanese troops overseas would never accept unconditional surrender. Moreover, within JAPAN itself, there were those who were strongly determined to fight at all costs. If JAPAN surrendered, internal chaos would result.

The Chief of the General Staff held the same opinion as the War Minister. Adequate preparations had been completed for a decisive battle in the homeland. Though the participation of the USSR was disadvantageous to JAPAN, it did not create a situation calling for unconditional surrender. . . .

The opinion of the Privy Council Chairman: Although I have not had time for thorough consideration, I shall express my opinion because of the urgent situation.

My opinion relative to Foreign Minister's Draft—In substance, this is as it should be. Its objective is solely the defense of the national polity, and I concur. However, the wording of the draft is highly undesirable and unjustifiable from the standpoint of loyalty and faith. The sovereignty of the Emperor is not derived through state law, nor is it provided for by the Constitution. It is only referred to in the Constitution. There is no objection to changing the wording to read: "No requirement for a change in the sovereignty over the nation of His Majesty, the Emperor, is included. . . ."

. . . Nevertheless, the national polity must be preserved and the Imperial Household maintained, even at the sacrifice of all our nation. I recognize that this should be decided by His Majesty, the Emperor.

Chief of Naval General Staff: The Naval Command is practically of the same opinion as the War Minister and the Chief of the Army General Staff. Though I cannot declare that satisfactory results will certainly be obtained, I am sure that we will be able to strike a great blow against the enemy. There are still many people in the country who want to fight. (Although there are many whose fighting spirit is not high.)

Premier: It is regrettable that no agreement was reached in spite of the prolonged discussion. . . .

His Majesty, the Emperor, supported the draft of the Foreign Minister, and gave the following reason:

There is little possibility that the Army and Navy will win the war. Although I can hardly bear the idea of depriving my trusted military personnel of their weapons, as well as surrendering war leaders to the enemy as war criminals, I am determined to agree with the enemy due to the general situation, and I will bear the intolerable, as did Emperor MEIJI, in the case of the Three Power Intervention, so that I may save the nation from destruction and contribute to the happiness of all mankind.

The meeting was adjourned at 0230 hours.

In case this condition is rejected, the war shall be fought to the bitter end. . . .

The Emperor supported the draft of the Foreign Minister, giving the following reason:

Though I have often heard of the confidence of victory, actual operations have hitherto failed to co-ordinate with the plans. Moreover, according to the War Minister and the Chief of the Army General Staff, the completion of fortifications along the KUJUKORI-GAHAMA was slated for the middle of August, but they have not yet been completed. It is said that even if a new division (1007 Division) is formed, the arms necessary to equip it are not available. If this is true, there is no possibility of winning the war against the US and Britain, who pride themselves on their mechanization.

I can hardly bear the idea of depriving my trusted military personnel of their weapons, and of surrendering my faithful subordinates to the enemy as the persons responsible for war. I made this decision, taking an over-all view of the general situation in order to save my people from destruction and in order to contribute to the happiness of all mankind. In doing so I am enduring the intolerable by following the precedent set by Emperor MEIJI, who made the decision at the time of the Three Power Intervention.

It was then 0230 hours of 10 August.

In reference to the Joint Declaration of the Three Powers, dated 26 July, if the Allies agree to the following conditions, the Japanese government will agree to the termination of the war:

1. No requisite for a change in the position de jure of the Japanese Imperial Household shall be included among the conditions set forth in the declaration.

2. The Japanese forces abroad shall be voluntarily withdrawn and then demobilized.

3. War criminals and those responsible for the war shall be dealt with by the Japanese government.

4. There shall be no "guarantee" [i.e., physical] occupation.

G6. MIS, STATEMENTS OF JAPANESE OFFICIALS, DOCUMENT NO. 54483, NOTES OF SUMIHISA IKEDA

DOC. NO. 54483
STATEMENT BY IKEDA, SUMIHISA
MADE ON 27 DEC 49
CONCERNING THE COUNCIL ON 9 AUG 45 IN THE IMPERIAL PRESENCE
TIME: 2355 HRS 9 AUGUST TO 0210 HRS 10 AUGUST
PLACE: AIR-RAID SHELTER IN THE IMPERIAL PALACE

Those present:
SUZUKI, *Premier*
HIRANUMA, *Chairman of the Privy Council*
ANAMI, *War Minister*
YONAI, *Navy Minister*
TOGO, *Foreign Affairs Minister*
UMEZU, *Chief of the Army General Staff*
TOYODA, *Chief of the Naval General Staff*

Staff:
SAKOMIZU, *Chief Cabinet Secretary*
YOSHIZUMI, *Chief of the Military Affairs Bureau*

HOSHIMA, *Chief of the Naval Affairs Bureau*
IKEDA, *Chief of the General Planning Bureau*

The meeting came to order with the arrival of the Emperor at 2355 hrs. He was escorted by his chief aide-de-camp.

Premier SUZUKI: The Supreme War Direction Council met today to discuss the Potsdam Declaration as the main subject. Although no decision has been reached, the majority favored the following items as conditions in accepting the Declaration.

1. Absolute maintenance and security of the Imperial Family.
2. Japanese soldiers will be demobilized after their return to the homeland.
3. War criminals shall be prosecuted within JAPAN.
4. To reserve the article concerning occupation of JAPAN to insure the execution of the Potsdam Declaration.

However, the opinion of the Foreign Affairs Minister was as follows:

The government will accept the Potsdam Declaration with the understanding that it does not include any demand for changes in the Emperor's status, as provided for in the national laws.

Accordingly, the Cabinet council was held today, and the following results were obtained after deliberating on this matter: those favoring the Foreign Affairs Minister's proposal—six; those favoring the proposal with the four (4) conditions—three: those who were neutral (but with opinions to decrease the number of conditions)—five. Now, I shall have the Foreign Affairs Minister explain the reasons for this proposal.

Foreign Affairs Minister TOGO: It is very disgraceful and difficult for JAPAN to accept the Potsdam Declaration. However, the situation has compelled us to accept it. All the members have agreed in accepting it. In the meantime, the appearance of the atomic bomb and RUSSIA'S participation in the war have led to a sudden turn in the situation, and have strengthened the enemy's position. It is no longer possible to rely upon negotiations for further developments. Especially now that the Soviet Union has resorted to arms, negotiations have become utterly impossible. . . . It is my opinion therefore that we should concentrate upon one thing: the welfare of the Imperial Family.

Navy Minister YONAI: I agree with the opinion of the Foreign Affairs Minister.

War Minister ANAMI: I am absolutely opposed to the opinion of the Foreign Affairs Minister. The Cairo Conference provides for the return of MANCHURIA. This is against the moral principles of JAPAN. I think we should proceed resolutely towards the prosecution of the war. However, if peace is to be concluded, these four conditions are absolutely necessary. . . .

Chief of the Army General Staff UMEZU: I am of the same opinion as the War Minister. Preparations for the decisive battle of the homeland are already completed, and we are confident of victory. Although the participation of RUSSIA has made the situation unfavorable, I do not think we need abandon the opportunity to deliver one last blow to both AMERICA and ENGLAND. . . .

Chairman of the Privy Council HIRANUMA: I am present today only because I had suddenly received the Imperial summons. Therefore, I have no proposal to offer. However, since the situation is very serious, I will state my opinion. I agree with the opinion of the Foreign Affairs Minister. However, the preservation of the national polity is an absolute requisite. If there is any doubt or uncertainty about this, we must defend ourselves resolutely. The people will probably fight to the last to preserve the national polity. The phrase, "The position of the Emperor as provided for in the national laws" mentioned in the original proposal is not appropriate. It is not good from the standpoint of the true relations of sovereign and subjects. The sovereignty of the Emperor has existed since the beginning of the country, and it was not decided by national laws. Since the constitution is merely a public formality, such wording should be amended to read, "The sovereignty of the Emperor, and so forth. . . ." In order to observe the instructions of Your Imperial Majesty's forefathers, Your Imperial Majesty also has a responsibility of preventing uncertainty in the nation. I ask Your Imperial Majesty to make a decision with this point in mind.

Chief of the Naval General Staff TOYODA: As the Naval Supreme Command, I agree with the opinions of the War Minister and the Chief of the Army General Staff. In considering the prospects of victory or defeat in this war, I cannot say that the probability of victory is certain, but I also do not think that we will be positively defeated. . . .

Premier SUZUKI: I believe that everyone has fully expressed his opinion, but I regret that we did not come to an agreement. As it is a matter of great importance, there is no other way but to rely on the decision of His Imperial Majesty . . . .

Emperor: I agree with the proposal of the Foreign Affairs Minister. The reason for it is as follows. Heretofore, the plans of the Army and Navy authorities have always been erroneous and inopportune. Here the decisive battle on the homeland is about to commence, and the establishment of defensive positions in KUJUKURIHAMA, where the landing of the American Army is expected, has been greatly delayed. According to the report of the War Minister, this cannot be completed until the end of August. I have also heard that the equipment of newly added forces in JAPAN proper is not yet in readiness. Under such circumstances, how could the American Army be repulsed? Air-raids are becoming more intense day by day. I do not want to see the people continue to suffer from extreme distress any longer. Also, I do not desire any further destruction of culture, nor any additional misfortune for the peoples of the world. On this occasion, we have to bear the unbearable. I do not have the heart to disarm the loyal Military, nor to let my faithful subordinates become war criminals. However, it cannot be helped, for the sake of the country. Now we must bear the same feeling as that held by the Emperor MEIJI at the time of the Triple Intervention. For this reason, I agree with the Foreign Affairs Minister's proposal.

The Emperor left the council.

G7. MIS, STATEMENTS OF JAPANESE OFFICIALS, DOCUMENT NO. 54479:
STATEMENT OF S. IKEDA, DECEMBER 23, 1949

DOC. NO. 54479
IKEDA, SUMIHISA, CHIEF OF THE CABINET PLANNING BUREAU
(23 DEC 49)

1. *Impressions of Suzuki Cabinet Ministers*

Premier SUZUKI—It is doubtful whether he was strongly in favor of peace at the time of the cabinet formation. It is observed that at first he was determined to go through with the war, and only after some time elapsed after the cabinet formation did he begin to consider peace. To wit:

a. At a cabinet meeting held in early August (TN: Sic) to discuss the acceptance of the Potsdam Declaration, the Premier stated: "I have hitherto entertained thoughts of peace and war, but acceptance of the Potsdam Declaration is impossible." Judging from this statement, it is clear that the Premier was against unconditional surrender; at least that was his view at the end of July or early August.

b. At the cabinet meeting held on 14 August, the Premier declared, "I should have considered peace efforts seriously at the time of the cabinet formation. It is too late now, but this too is fate."

c. Upon receiving the report of Soviet entry into the war on 9 August, the Premier called me and asked, "Is the Kwantung Army capable of repulsing the Soviet Army?" To this question I replied, "The Kwantung Army is hopeless. . . ." The Premier sighed at my words and said, "Is the Kwantung Army that weak? Then, the game is up." Thereupon, I advised him, "The greater the delay in making the final decision, the worse the situation will be for us." "Absolutely correct," the Premier concurred.

I believe that the atomic bomb and the Soviet participation in the war motivated the Premier to accept the Potsdam Declaration, which had been rejected by him previously. . . .

Navy Minister YONAI—He seemed to have already abandoned the war in despair. This was adequately proved by his statement in the cabinet meeting on 9 August. However, at the beginning he had not made up his mind on the four peace conditions and was uncertain on that point.

War Minister ANAMI—Though he was of the opinion that if conditions were favorable, peace might be acceptable, he was firm in his stand that if not, the war should be fought to the bitter end. He believed that the war should be continued, even through enforcement of martial law. He ordered me to study up on martial law. . . .

Foreign Minister TOGO—The Foreign Minister at cabinet meetings seemed to have a considerably strong opinion for peace. . . .

15. Atomic Bomb

Immediately after the atom bombing of HIROSHIMA, the "Atomic Bomb Countermeasure Committee" was formed within the Cabinet. I was appointed chairman. If I remember right the committeemen were comprised of War, Navy, and Home ministries and Technical Board representatives and the First Committee Meeting was held on August 7, at which time the Technical Board representatives strongly insisted that the bomb was not an atomic bomb. In explanation, they stated: "No matter how advanced American technique may be, it is quite impossible for the Americans to bring such unstable weapons as [an] atomic device to JAPAN, across the Pacific. We do not know what will happen in the future, but to date American technique is not that highly developed."

Thereupon I stated: "In AMERICA, the President has announce[d] that it was an atomic bomb. I can hardly imagine that Americans would broadcast such a lie. If it is not an atomic bomb, what is it?" To this question they replied, "It must be a new type of bomb with special equipment, but its content is unknown."

Because of the above-mentioned reason, the word "atomic bomb" was not used in the announcement made at that time. Later, as a result of spot investigations by the technicians, the Technical Board dispatched to HIROSHIMA, the bomb was confirmed to [be] an atomic bomb. . . .

18. Soviet War Participation

Upon hearing of the Soviet entry into the war, I felt that our chances were gone. Familiar with the actual strength and quality of the Kwantung Army, I was most sensitive concerning this point. I knew that the Kwantung Army was no more than a hollow shell because ever since the latter part of 1944 the Kwantung Army had been transferring its troops, equipment, and munitions to the homeland and to Formosa, in preparation for the decisive battle on the homeland. . . .

G8. MIS, STATEMENTS OF JAPANESE OFFICIALS, DOCUMENT NO. 50569; LT. GEN. TORASHIRO KAWABE, JUNE 13, 1949

DOC. NO. 50569
DESCRIPTION OF CONTENTS: FULL TRANSLATION OR STATEMENT
BY KAWABE, TORASHIRO,

13 JUNE 1949

STATEMENT CONCERNING TEN AND KETSU OPERATIONS
EX-LT. GEN. KAWABE, TORASHIRO, EX-VICE-CHIEF OF AERONAUTICAL DEPART-
MENT (AUGUST 1944–APRIL 1945); EX-DEPUTY CHIEF OF THE GENERAL STAFF
(APRIL 1945–AUGUST 1945)

. . . Question 3: Did you consider the concentrations plan in the Outline of Preparations for the KETSU Operation of 8 April difficult to execute?

Answer: I was informed of the plan when I assumed the post of Deputy Chief of the General Staff (7 April). I believed at the time that the plan was formulated out of imperative necessity, and I could not feel fully confident that it would succeed. I cooperated unreservedly in the belief that the objective called for desperate efforts.

Question 4: What was your opinion at that time with regard to the advantages and disadvantages of a homeland crucial battle?

Answer: I viewed as an advantage the fact that, inasmuch as we could count on the wholehearted cooperation of the people, we would have very little need to divert any fighting strength to rear-line duties, such as supply and rear area defense, and could consequently employ our total fighting strength for combat purposes. I also thought it to our advantage that we were thoroughly acquainted with the terrain and the weather likely to be encountered and that we need feel very little anxiety with regard to the problem of supply. . . .

Question 9: How did Imperial General Headquarters estimate the chances of victory in a decisive battle on KYUSHU? How was success in this operation expected to influence political and military strategy?

Answer: My inspection of KYUSHU in late June did not inspire me with complete confidence that Japanese arms would be victorious, but I did feel that in southern KYUSHU especially, we would be able to inflict staggering losses on the American invasion force and at least frustrate the plans of the first-wave units. Moreover, it seemed likely at the time that the U.S. landing would not come until after the typhoon season, and it was strongly felt that since preparations for the decisive battle could be stepped up in the meantime, considerable hope for a successful KYUSHU operation could be entertained. . . .

Question 12: How reliable did you consider the estimates that 60 percent of Japan's special attack planes would be available for sorties and that the ratio of hits would be one to six?

Answer: As a result of a detailed study of the subject made at my order by my subordinates while I was vice-chief of Aeronautical Department (early 1945), I was fairly well convinced that the estimates were sound. I realize today that many of the combat examples on which the estimates were based had been exaggerated. . . .

Question 13: What did you expect would be the outcome of a decisive battle in the ill-prepared Kanto district following on the heels of a Kyushu crucial battle in which all air and surface special attack strength would have been expended?

Answer: I did not think a systematic, organized decisive battle could be staged in KANTO. The only plan the Japanese could follow, I believed, was to scrape together whatever remaining strength they had and offer the best resistance possible. . . .

G9. MIS, STATEMENTS OF JAPANESE OFFICIALS, DOCUMENT NO. 50268, LT. GEN. TORASHIRO KAWABE, NOVEMBER 21, 1949

DOC. NO. 52608

SOME RECOLLECTIONS OF THE CESSATION OF HOSTILITIES
STATEMENT BY KAWABE, TORASHIRO, FORMER LIEUTENANT GENERAL AND VICE-
CHIEF OF THE GENERAL STAFF

. . . I believe that Gen ANAMI's idea of safeguarding the national polity, or in other words, the maintenance of the Emperor system, was not that of the present, which is a mere formality, but rather the maintenance of the Emperor system as we knew it then, and according to this idea, many of the Emperor's prerogatives were to be retained unchanged. . . .

Actually, [a] majority in the Army did not realize at first that what had been dropped was an atomic bomb, and they were not generally familiar with the terrible nature of the atomic bomb. It was only in a gradual manner that the horrible wreckage which had been made of HIROSHIMA became known, instead of in a manner of a shocking effect.

In comparison, the Soviet entry into the war was a great shock when it actually came. Reports reaching TOKYO described Russian forces as "invading in swarms." It gave us all the more severe shock and alarm because we had been in constant fear of it with a vivid imagination that "the vast Red Army forces in EUROPE were now being turned against us." In other words, since the atomic bomb and Russian declaration of war were shocks in a quick succession, I cannot give a definite answer as to which of the two factors was more decisive in ending hostilities.

G10. MIS, STATEMENTS OF JAPANESE OFFICIALS, DOCUMENT NO. 52336, MAJ. GEN. JOICHIRO SANADA, NOVEMBER 12, 1949

DOC. NO. 52336

12 NOV 49

STATEMENT ON THE CRUCIAL BATTLE OF THE HOMELAND
EX-MAJ. GEN. SANADA, JOICHIRO
CHIEF OF MILITARY AFFAIRS BUREAU, WAR MINISTRY (UNTIL MARCH 1945);
ASSISTANT CHIEF OF STAFF, 2 GENERAL ARMY (UNTIL AUGUST 1945)

. . . Question No. 3:
Were you confident of victory in the crucial homeland battle?

Answer: I think it would have been possible to crush an initial American landing in KYUSHU, particularly southern KYUSHU, but unless powerful general reserve units could have been brought up in time, it would have been difficult to stop a second and third landing. After I returned to General Army Headquarters in HIROSHIMA from a study conference on military strategy in southern KYUSHU held in June 1945, Field Marshal HATA, the commander-in-chief, discussed this problem with Lt. Gen YAKA-MATSU, the chief of staff. I attended the conference and expressed the following views:

"The morale of all front-line forces, from army and division commanders on down, is excellent. In view of their advantages of ample equipment, naval strategy, and favorable terrain, I believe that the first wave of enemy troops could surely be pushed back into the sea. If the enemy attempts a second and a third landing, however, it is highly doubtful that he can be completely repulsed."

Field Marshal HATA replied: "You are probably correct. As long as we lack powerful general second and third line reserves, we cannot be certain of repulsing the second and third enemy landings."

The chief of staff listened without comment. . . .

G11. MIS, STATEMENTS OF JAPANESE OFFICIALS, DOCUMENT NO. 50025A, LT. COL. MASAHIKO TAKASHITA, JUNE 11, 1949

DOC. NO. 50025A
STATEMENT OF TAKESHITA, MASAHIKO, FORMER LIEUTENANT COLONEL . . .
TIME: 1030–1230 HOURS, 11 JUN 49 . . .
SUBJECT: WAR MINISTER ANAMI'S STATE OF MIND AT THE END OF THE WAR

A. My relations with former War Minister ANAMI, Korechika

1. My elder sister is ANAMI's wife and ever since the time I was a second lieutenant, ANAMI and I were next door neighbors and on intimate terms. . . .

B. Circumstances which reflected ANAMI's character and state of mind at the end of the war

1. I was the one who drafted the Minister of War's address to the Diet on 9 Jun 45. At that time (and, of course, even at a later date) the atmosphere within Army circles was such that no thought was ever given to such a possibility as surrender. The feeling

that prevailed was that although fighting on OKINAWA was difficult since it was an isolated island, the enemy would be defeated when it came to the decisive battle in the homeland. Young officers below the rank of lieutenant colonel in particular thought only about the decisive battle.

There are, however, points which make me feel at present that ANAMI was thinking of peace. By peace, I mean an honorable peace. ANAMI, and needless to say, the entire Army would not disobey the command of the Emperor. There would have been no protest if the Emperor had asked for peace. . . .

6. About 0900 hours, 10 August, he assembled senior section members and above and related the aspects of the previous night's conference in the Imperial presence as follows:

"I do not know what excuse to make to you, but since it is the Emperor's decision, it cannot be helped. The important thing is that the Army shall act in an organized manner. Individual feelings must be disregarded. This decision, however, was made on the condition that the upholding of our national polity be guaranteed. Consequently, it does not mean that the war has ended. The Army must be prepared for either war or peace."

7. The reply of the Allies on 12 August left us no hope for a guarantee that our national polity would be upheld. However, as stated previously, the Emperor's intention of ending the war was clearly indicated at the Imperial Conference held on the same day. . . .

9. I believe ANAMI's feelings that he was opposed to peace under these conditions were similar to the feelings of the young men in the Army, that is, our feelings. I believe, however, that he was very prudent about going against the will of the Emperor. Also included among the instructions given at the previously mentioned gathering of senior section members and above on the morning of 10 August was, "I have no excuse to offer for the fact that peace has been decided upon. However, those among you who are dissatisfied and wish to stave it off will have to do it over my dead body. . . ."

G12. MIS, STATEMENTS OF JAPANESE OFFICIALS,
DOCUMENT NO. 50644, FIVE OFFICERS REGARDING OPERATION
KETSU MANEUVER (NO DATE) . . .

DOC. NO. 56044
STATEMENT RE TABLE MANEUVER OF AIR OPERATION
KETSU AT FUKUOKA, EARLY JULY 1945

Imperial General Headquarters army staff officer (air) and concurrently Navy General Command staff officer, Maj Gen TANIGAWA, Kasuo. . . . All of these officers participated in the maneuver.

1. Date and place of maneuver.

4–5 Jul 45. 6 Air Army Headquarters at FUKUOKA

2. Sponsor of the maneuver.

Co-sponsored by the General Air Army and the Navy General Command. . . .

8. Operation strength.

The maneuver was carried out by putting into operation only those units which were to be organized and equipped by the end of July while assuming that units organized and equipped after that time were unexpendable. Total of approximately 5,000 planes (about 10 percent estimate) below estimate was to be used for convoy attack, consisting of:

Army:

Special attack planes (converted training planes) 2,100 planes

(Other combat) planes 400 planes

Navy:

Special attack planes (converted training planes) 2,200 planes

(Other combat) planes 300 planes

As for the surface and submarine special attack units, only those which had already been ordered to a given position before the end of July were considered as expendable. . . .

11. Effects of attacks.

Attacks against (a) and (b).

(1) About 400 crafts by air special attack. $4,000 \times 0.6 \times 1/6 = 400$

(2) 67 crafts by surface special attack.

SHINTO $700 \times 0.9 \times 1/10 = 63$ (crafts)

KAIRYO $12 \times 0.9 \times 1/3 = 4$ (crafts)

(3) Total number of crafts unk (assuming one hit on each craft) 467, strength equivalent of approximately four divisions.

Attacks against (c).

(1) Approximately 100 crafts by planes. $1,000 \times 0.6 \times 1/10 = 60$ (TN: sic)

(2) 58 crafts by surface special attack.

SHINTO $425 \times 0.9 \times 1/10 = 38$ (crafts)

KAITEN and KAIRYU $58 \times 0.9 ¥ 1/3 + 17$ (crafts)

(3) total number of crafts sunk — 115, strength equivalent of about one division.

(4) Enemy strength annihilated at sea. Approximately five divisions, about 30 percent of the total strength.

12. Judgment

Since the results of special attacks to neutralize the enemy forces on the sea are largely dependent upon various factors such as the enemy's landing plan, convoy formations, success in destroying enemy air power and weather conditions, the neutralization will probably be 30 to 50 percent effective.

The maneuver was conducted on a comparatively unfavorable hypothesis that the enemy used many small-type crafts and that the main force of our special attack units had to be thrown against an element of the initial enemy landing forces. The strength reinforcement after the end of July to September and results of submarines, destroyers, mines, etc., were not taken into account. Therefore, if we thoroughly prepare for future operations and if various factors are especially favorable to us, the operations can be as much as 50 percent effective. . . .

G13. MIS, STATEMENTS OF JAPANESE OFFICIALS, DOCUMENT NO. 50570: STATEMENT OF EX-MAJ. GEN. KASUE TANIKAWA, MAY 10, 1949

10 MAY 49
DOC. NO. 50570
STATEMENT CONCERNING PREPARATIONS FOR OKINAWA AND
HOMELAND AIR OPERATIONS
EX-MAJ. GEN. TANIKAWA, KASUE, FORMER STAFF OFFICER OF IMPERIAL GENERAL
HEADQUARTERS, ARMY DEPARTMENT AND COMBINED FLEET STAFF OFFICER
(FEBRUARY, 1945 TO AUGUST, 1945). . . .

Question 4: How much damage to homeland air strength was anticipated as a result of the homeland air supremacy battle which the Americans could be expected to start prior to their landings?

Answer: Because considerable effort had been put into dispersing and concealing air strength, losses might have been relatively low. The loss rate might have been about 20 percent.

I think the Army and Navy each could have put up about 2,500 aircraft (mostly trainers converted into suicide attack planes) at the beginning of Operation KETSU.

Question 5: What was the ratio of hits that suicide planes were expected to score? What was the plan regarding time of commitment and fighter escorts?

Answer: A. I believe the Navy's estimate (one out of six) was about right. (The Army was a little more optimistic). . . .

B. The idea was to destroy the enemy at sea by throwing the Army and Navy's entire air strength against him at the most effective possible time just before he entered his anchorage. . . .

Question 6: What was the estimated ratio of hits for suicide surface craft?

Answer: There had been so little experience with them that an accurate estimate was impossible.

Question 7: What results were expected from using suicide planes in a Kyushu operation?

Answer: I remember that as a result of maneuvers, studies and the like, it was concluded that by using almost the entire air strength of the Army and Navy (about 5,000 planes), we could destroy four American divisions at sea, but that the operation would mean that our own air strength would become virtually non-existent.

G14. MIS, STATEMENTS OF JAPANESE OFFICIALS,
DOCUMENT NO. 50304: SHIGENORI TOGO, MAY 17, 1949

DOC. NO. 50304
STATEMENT BY FORMER FOREIGN MINISTER TOGO, SHIGENORI
CONCERNING THE HISTORICAL FACTS SURROUNDING THE ENDING
OF THE PACIFIC WAR (1)
17 MAY 49

STATEMENT BY: TOGO, SHIGENORI
MINISTER OF FOREIGN AFFAIRS, 17 OCT 41–1 SEP 42 [AND]
9 APR 45–17 AUG 45 . . .
DATE AND PLACE: 17 MAY 49 SUGAMO PRISON, TOKYO. . . .

OI: No. 3. Please explain the circumstances culminating in the meetings of regular members of the Supreme Council for the Direction of War on 11, 13, and 14 May 45. . . .

TOGO: . . . . With OKINAWA as good as gone, the overall military situation at the time could well be described as dismal. Gen. UMEZU, Chief of the Army General Staff, and Gen. KAWABE, his deputy chief, came to me (the latter on two occasions) to suggest that we make diplomatic overtures to RUSSIA to block her entry into the war, but the international situation had deteriorated so irreparably that I told them they were asking me for something beyond my power. Pointing out that wartime diplomacy depended entirely on the military situation, and that, barring an early Japanese victory, any diplomatic endeavors were out of the question, I added that it was already too late to think about the Russians, who were quite possibly already discussing their share of the spoils with BRITAIN and AMERICA. I urged them to concentrate instead on the prosecution of the war.

Even more fantastic, the Navy wanted me to persuade the USSR to help JAPAN; they asked not only that we keep RUSSIA out of the war but also that we induce her to supply us with oil. . . . I explained how preposterous their idea was, pointing out that . . . RUSSIA could not supply the materials unless she was prepared to go into the war on our side, which, in view of the existing military situation, could hardly be the case.

The Army and Navy kept after me, however, until I finally suggested to UMEZU, who concurred heartily, that we call together the members of the Supreme Council for the Direction of War to discuss the matter. . . .

I was prompted to suggest the meetings for still another reason; namely, because of my conviction that, since the Army had asked me to try to keep the USSR out of the war and the Navy had called upon me to drag her into it as our ally, the time was ripe to lay the ground-work for a general peace movement. I had thought from the beginning that the war would have to be ended soon: it had been with that understanding that I had entered the Suzuki Cabinet. I won't go into detail here because I discussed the subject in my statement, but I might repeat that, whereas SUZUKI had predicted that we could fight on for another two or three years, I had felt that extended hostilities were not feasible and that the war should be ended immediately. I had told him that it would be useless for me to enter the cabinet unless he himself was determined to work for an early peace, and had finally accepted the Foreign Ministry portfolio with the understanding that he would do so. . . .

As might have been expected in view of the circumstances leading to their inauguration, the conferences began with a consideration of the Russian question. . . . It was finally decided to begin negotiations with a three-fold object: first, to keep the USSR out of the war, a necessity which was felt strongly by all; second, to induce her to adopt a friendly policy toward JAPAN; and third, to seek her mediation in the war. . . .

OI: It says here, "KONOYE also testified that when SATO was sounding out the Russians, he reported the Russians would not consider a peace role unless the terms were unconditional surrender, and that this reply had a great influence on the Emperor."

TOGO: The procedure for unconditional surrender was simple: it would not have entailed sending KONOYE. No one in TOKYO at that time agreed to unconditional surrender. I am not aware that Ambassador SATO's recommendation of unconditional surrender had any great influence on the Emperor. What document is that?

OI: The United States Strategic Bombing Survey.

TOGO: I believe it is wrong on that point. . . .

TOGO: . . . To get back to the subject, I learned about the atomic bomb from an American broadcast received by the Foreign Ministry. I got in touch with the Army immediately, and they told me that, although the Americans were claiming to have dropped an atomic bomb, it might actually have been an extraordinarily destructive conventional bomb. . . . On the next day, the 7th, there was a meeting of the Cabinet ministers concerned, at which, if I remember correctly, the Ministers of War, the Navy, Home Affairs, and Transportation were present. I reported that the American radio was saying that the atomic bomb would revolutionize modern warfare and that more bombs would be dropped on JAPAN unless she sued for peace. The Army tried to minimize the effect of the bomb by repeating that we were not sure that an atomic bomb had been used and insisting that we wait for the investigation reports.

. . . I went to see the Emperor the following morning to give him the information we had obtained from American and British broadcasts and impress him with the urgency of the situation; I told him it was being said abroad that the bomb . . . would continue to be used against JAPAN until she surrendered. The Emperor indicated clearly that the enemy's new weapon made it impossible to go on fighting. I said that we should lose no time in ending the war, to which His Majesty replied that I was quite right, told me to try to end the war immediately, and requested me to convey his wishes to the Premier.

I went to see the Premier at once to ask him to call a conference of the members of Supreme Council for the Direction of War, but we were obliged to postpone the meeting until the following day (i.e., the morning of the 9th). . . . The SOVIET UNION entered the war against JAPAN on the 9th.

. . . Another thing, I should mention that . . . I had reached an understanding with the Premier at the outset, which fact taken together with our subsequent conversations, made me confident that he would come to my support in the end. Furthermore, since the problem involved the destiny of the nation and directly affected the security of the Imperial Family, the Emperor was far more interested in it than in ordinary state affairs, and I knew that he was very anxious to have peace. I can say that, in the light of these circumstances, I was confident of my ability to hold out against the die-hards and eventually gain my point with them. As it turned out, however, I was unable to keep the military from insisting to the very end that they were not beaten, that they could fight another battle, and that they did not want to end the war until they had staged one last campaign. . . .

G15. MIS, STATEMENTS OF JAPANESE OFFICIALS, DOCUMENT NO. 61340: SOEMU TOYODA, AUGUST 29, 1949

DOC. NO. 61340

QUESTIONS TO EX-CHIEF OF NAVAL GENERAL STAFF ADM. TOYODA, SOEMU

. . . In short, in early June the nation's fighting power, both military and civil, became paralyzingly deteriorated to the highest degree, and from a purely operational standpoint it was utterly impossible to hope for a successful conduct of the war; confronted with such a situation, my personal idea was to build up our fighting position with a view instrumental to our over-all effort toward the termination of war. Moreover, I thought it more desirable to win a great military success by seizing a good opportunity, if possible, and thus enhance the chance of ending hostilities. . . .

4. I fully realized that in the event of surrender the defeated would be subject to harsh conditions. Having been considerably menaced by the Cairo Declaration of November 1943, I was not too surprised at the Potsdam Declaration. However, I found nothing in the Declaration which suggested that it would be to JAPAN's advantage to accept the conditions and end the war. . . .

5. Scientific conception of the atom bomb was nothing novel, but the news of its perfection and employment by the American [forces] was quite a shock to me. That an atom bomb was dropped on HIROSHIMA on 6 August was immediately learned through the broadcasts by the US forces and special reports from the scene. And the fact that damage wrought was unprecedented became clearer by the moment. However, I personally had doubts as to whether the American forces would continue to drop atom bombs at frequent intervals. As a matter of fact, I did not think that they would. A reason for this was the question of raw materials. I did not know what the principal composition of an atom bomb was, but I was certain that it was a radioactive element. It was my opinion that all the radium-like elements in the world would not have amounted to much. I could not accurately say how much raw material was necessary for one atom bomb, but judging from its destructive force I was sure that there was a vast difference from that amount used for treating illness. I doubted very much whether the UNITED STATES was capable of producing such a huge quantity of radioactive matter. Considering the time element, I believed that the number of atom bombs which could be used in a given time was greatly restricted and that this number would definitely not be great.

The second reason for my not believing that the Americans would continue to drop atom bombs was because of the criticism from the standpoint of laws of war and ethics which would be directed against such warfare. I wondered whether the world would permit the UNITED STATES to continue such an inhuman atrocity; whether its publicity as a justifiable means of stopping the havoc of war and saving the lives of thousands of American soldiers would command honest sympathy; and whether not only the people of the world but the people of the UNITED STATES would consent to such warfare. The Pacific War saw two atom bombings in four days, before they brought the war to an end, but if they had been continued I believed then, and I still believe now, that considerably greater repercussions would have developed to restrain such American actions.

In short, I believe the atom bombing was a cause for the surrender but it was not the only cause. Nonetheless, the fact that it had a very great effect upon public sentiment is indisputable. Various things are attributable to the relative calm which prevailed at the time of the surrender. The fact that the atom bombing is among them cannot [be] contested. . . .

At any rate, it was a great shock to us when war was declared against us by the very party whom we were requesting to act as peace mediator. In the face of this new development it became impossible for us to map any reasonable operational plan. Moreover, the peace program which we had so far relied upon came to naught. Therefore, an entirely different program had to be sought for. At the same time we could not expect to obtain a good chance for peace by merely waiting for such a chance. It was the time for us to accept the terms of the Potsdam Declaration. This is what I thought then.

I believe the Russian participation in the war against JAPAN rather than the atom bombs did more to hasten the surrender. . . .

G16. MIS, STATEMENTS OF JAPANESE OFFICIALS, DOCUMENT NO. 57670: SOEMU TOYODA, DECEMBER 1, 1949

DOC. NO. 57670
PERSON MAKING THE STATEMENT: EX-CHIEF OF NAVAL GENERAL STAFF, ADMIRAL TOYODA, SOEMU . . .
SUBJECT: RECOLLECTIONS CONCERNING THE TERMINATION OF WAR. . . .

2. The Supreme War Direction Council, which met on 6 Jun 45, again met on the 8th, with the Emperor attending. In both of these meetings, discussions were devoted only to the prosecution of war and absolutely no talk of peace was brought up. . . .

On 28 July a routine meeting to exchange war information was held between representatives of Imperial Headquarters and the Government in the Imperial Palace. At the time, in a different room from where the exchange of information conference was held, the Prime Minister, the Army and Navy Ministers, the Chiefs of Army and Naval General Staff, and the Chief Cabinet Secretary discussed how the Potsdam Proclamation should be handled. Nobody at this meeting even so much as hinted that he wanted to have the Allied proclamation considered seriously. However, they were unanimously in accord with the necessity of clarifying the Government's attitude because of the shock this proclamation might bring about on the military personnel and the people. Thus the Chief Cabinet Secretary moved that it would be a good idea for the Prime Minister to say something in regard to the proclamation at the scheduled news reporters interview. The question was what would be the best thing for the Premier to say to the reporters about the proclamation. I do not mean to say that we composed every word of the text, but we did draft a very rough gist of the text, if I remember correctly. . . .

G17. MIS, STATEMENTS OF JAPANESE OFFICIALS, DOCUMENT NO. 61338: LT. GEN. MASAO YOSHIZUMI, JUNE 6, 1949

DOC. NO. 61338
STATEE: YOSHIZUMI, MASAO EX-LIEUTENANT GENERAL.
[CHIEF OF THE MILITARY AFFAIRS BUREAU, APRIL–NOVEMBER 1945] . . .

DATE: 1430–1700 HOURS, 6 JUN 49. . . .

SUBJECT: WAR MINISTER ANAMI'S STATE OF MIND. . . .

3. War Minister ANAMI's attitude after the issue over terminating the war grew acute:

A. The gist of War Minister ANAMI's contentions after 8 August was: "Nobody can assert it a hundred percent certain that victory would be won in a decisive battle fought on the homeland, but there are chances of victory. It is my desire to carry out a decisive battle in the homeland, at least once, with a determination of one who desperately tries to open a way out of a doomed ruin. If a peace overture be made the four conditions should be attached." He attached particular importance to the maintenance of the present national polity. Furthermore, with my judgment added, it seems that the War Minister's thoughts were as follows: "At this time, the acceptance of unconditional surrender is inimical to the upholding of the present national polity; besides, there is the possibility that the war could be continued if a heavy blow were dealt the enemy in the decisive battle on the homeland, thus opening a way to a peace other than unconditional surrender. In view of considerable chances of victory in the decisive battle in the homeland, the war should not be given up at this time. Even if peace were to be concluded the four conditions must be demanded. If they are refused, then we must be determined to continue the war. . . ."

4. War Minister ANAMI's committing suicide: The reason War Minister ANAMI committed suicide cannot be conjectured definitely, but immediately after the council in the Imperial Presence held on 14 August he said to me: "I leave the rest to you with confidence. I can't live in this world any longer." When I replied, "The mission before us is much harder. It is feared that threatening actions may happen among Army and Navy personnel, so much is expected of you to meet the situation successfully," War Minister ANAMI spoke as follows: "I have expressed my opinions to His Majesty according to my convictions, but things have come to this pass. I don't know what excuse to make to His Majesty the Emperor nor can I remain in this world any longer in the light of my responsibility for the defeat in this war. . . ."

G18. MIS, STATEMENTS OF JAPANESE OFFICIALS, DOCUMENT NO.
54484: LT. GEN. MASAO YOSHIZUMI, DECEMBER 22, 1949

DOC. NO. 54484

DESCRIPTION OF CONTENTS: FULL ENGLISH TRANSLATION OF REPLY OF EX-LT.
GEN. YOSHIZUMI IN REGARDS TO THE JAPANESE LEADERS . . . DATED 22 DEC 49

. . . III. I firmly believed that the new cabinet was definitely for the continuation of war. The reason for it was that when his cabinet was being formed, Premier SUZUKI visited the War Ministry to request War Minister SUGIYAMA's recommendation for the new war minister, and the latter made it clear in writing that the Army attached great importance to the following points:

1. Prosecution of the war to the bitter end.

2. Proper settlement of the problem of Army–Navy unification.

3. Every possible effort for the complete reorganization of the nation for the prosecution of the war.

At that time, as Premier SUZUKI clearly replied that he was in complete agreement with the first point, the War Minister said that he wanted to recommend Gen. ANAMI as the new war minister. War Minister SUGIYAMA officially related the above-mentioned attitude of Premier SUZUKI to me, the then Chief of the Military Affairs Bureau.

I don't believe that the Suzuki Cabinet was originally formed with the mission of peace. I heard that some cabinet members other than the War and Navy ministers opposed the peace at the final stage of the war, and if the cabinet had had such a view it certainly would have gotten out, but actually I did not hear of it. . . .

IV. I do not believe that the decision of the council in the Imperial presence, held on 8 June, meant a change in the Suzuki Cabinet's policy. I had neither any information indicating the change nor did I feel anything unusual in the circumstances. The decision reached was aimed at one purpose only i.e. the prosecution of the war. However, according to what I learned after the surrender, at the meeting held exclusively by the regular members of the Supreme War Direction Council (SENSO SHIDO KAIGI) the peace problem had been referred to in connection with negotiations with SOVIET RUSSIA. . . .

[Author's note: The following exchange occurred at the June 6 meeting of the Supreme War Direction Council, after it had decided to continue the war.]

Finally, the Chief of the Naval Affairs Bureau asked a question to the effect that "We must surmount many difficulties in the prosecution of the war, but is each of you cabinet ministers seriously intending to carry out the decisions of this council, and if you aren't, are you prepared to commit hare-kiri?" To this question, Navy Minister YONAI answered, "That is right." The Chief of the Naval Affairs Bureau then demanded that the Premier relate this matter to all the cabinet members at the cabinet meeting. Listening to this I thought that the Chief of the Naval Affairs Bureau was ascertaining the determination of the Government for the prosecution of the war. . . .

VIII. Gathering from what I've heard fragmentarily from War Minister ANAMI, I firmly believe that the War Minister's intention was: "Although JAPAN's victory in the coming decisive battle of the homeland is not absolutely certain, there is still some such possibility. Therefore, the battle should be fought on the homeland at least once with a resolution to seek a way out in a desperate situation. If JAPAN is to make peace, she should submit the four conditions with emphasis on the preservation of the national polity." However, as I have already mentioned in Paragraph III, the negotiations with SOVIET RUSSIA were being discussed independent of the homeland fighting, and I believe that the outline of War Minister ANAMI's thoughts at the termination of the war was as mentioned above. I have not heard directly form UMEZU, Chief of the Army General Staff, but judging from his words at the conference in the Imperial presence, I believe his thoughts were generally in line with those of War Minister ANAMI. In his talk War Minister ANAMI briefly revealed his belief that "it might not be possible to repeat the battle of the homeland three or four times, but if we succeed in inflicting a heavy blow on the enemy in the first battle of the homeland, we might find a way out." And by using my judgment, I believe War Minister ANAMI thought as follows: "To submit to an unconditional surrender now would constitute a threat to the preservation of the national structure. If we inflict heavy damage on the enemy in the decisive battle of the homeland, we might be able to continue the fight, or we might be able to come to a peace other than unconditional surrender. Moreover, as we have considerable confidence in the first battle of the homeland, we should not give up the war now. Even if we are to decide to terminate the war without fighting the homeland battle, we should submit the four conditions of peace, and we must resolve to go on with the battle of the homeland in case these conditions are not met. . . ."

NOTES

NOTES TO CHAPTER 1

1. Paul Tibbets quoted in Richard Rhodes, *The Making of the Atomic Bomb* (New York: Simon & Schuster, 1986), 710. Lewis quoted in Keith Eubank, *The Bomb* (Malabar, Fla.: Krieger, 1991), 80. The message back to Tinian is from Vincent C. Jones, *Manhattan: The Army and the Atomic Bomb* (Washington, D.C.: Center of Military History, U.S. Army, 1985), 538. The technical information on the bomb is from the Committee for the Compilation of Materials on Damage Caused by the Atomic Bombs in Hiroshima and Nagasaki, *Hiroshima and Nagasaki: The Physical, Medical, and Social Effects of the Atomic Bombings*, trans. Eissei Ishikawa and David L. Swain (New York: Basic Books, 1981), 22, 32–34, 118.

2. On the population of Hiroshima on August 6, 1945, see *Hiroshima and Nagasaki*, 349–351. On casualties, see Richard B. Frank, *Downfall: The End of the Japanese Empire* (New York: Random House, 1999), 285–287, which provides a range of estimates for both Hiroshima and Nagasaki, including those made by the United States Strategic Bombing Survey and the Japan Economic Stabilization Board; Norman Polmar and Thomas B. Allen, *World War II: The Encyclopedia of the War Years, 1941–1945* (New York: Random House, 1996), 385; James F. Dunnigan and Albert A. Nofi, *The Pacific War Encyclopedia* (New York: Checkmark Books, 1998), 269.

3. Frank, *Downfall*, 286; Polmar and Allen, *World War II*, 571.

4. "The Swiss Chargé (Grässli) to the Secretary of State, August 10, 1945" (Document E2), *Foreign Relations of the United States, 1945: Diplomatic Papers*, 9 vols. (Washington, D.C.: U.S. Government Printing Office, 1969), 6:627.

5. *New York Times*, August 7, 1945.

6. For example, see *The Christian Century* LXII (August 29, 1945), 974–976 (Document A56). For an overview of early criticism of the use of atomic bombs against Japan, see Paul Boyer, *By the Bomb's Early Light: American Thought and Culture at the Dawn of the Atomic Age* (New York: Pantheon, 1985), 196–210.

7. For the 1945 poll, see J. Samuel Walker, *Prompt and Utter Destruction: Truman and the Use of Atomic Bombs Against Japan* (Chapel Hill: University of North Carolina Press, 1997), 98. For the 1990s statistics, see Frank, *Downfall*, 332.

8. National Air and Space Museum, "A Proposal: A Fiftieth Anniversary Exhibit at the National Air and Space Museum," Air Force Association, www.afa.org/media/enolagay/07–93.html (July 2, 2004).

9. Michael J. Hogan, "The Enola Gay Controversy: History, Memory, and the Politics of Presentation," in *Hiroshima in History and Memory*, ed. Michael J. Hogan (New York: Cambridge University Press, 1996), 206–209.

10. For this point of view, see Hogan, "The Enola Gay Controversy," and Barton J. Bernstein, "The Struggle Over History: Defining the Hiroshima Narrative," in *Judgment at the Smithsonian*, ed. Philip Nobile (New York: Marlowe & Company, 1995), 127–256.

11. The best overview of the NASM script and its scholarship is Robert P. Newman, *The Enola Gay and the Court of History* (New York: Peter Lang, 2004), 97–133. This summary draws heavily from Newman's analysis. Newman contends that the NASM curators failed to consult experts whose work did not confirm preconceived NASM notions that atomic bomb had not been necessary to end the bomb. He writes, "My quarrel is with [NASM director] Martin Harwin and his curators who claimed to base their case on the best scholarship." Another sharp critique is Charles T. O'Reilly and William A. Rooney, *The Enola Gay and the Smithsonian Institution* (Jefferson, N.C.: McFarland, 2005). For a different point of view, see Hogan, "The Enola Gay Controversy," 200–232.

12. Curators of the National Air and Space Museum, "The Crossroads: The End of World War II, The Atomic Bomb, and the Origins of the Cold War," in Nobile, *Judgment at the Smithsonian*, 3 (the page number refers to the script itself, as printed in this volume).

13. "National Air and Space Museum, Smithsonian Institution Exhibition Planning Document, July 1993," Air Force Association, www.afa.org/media/enolagay/07–93 .html (July 2, 2004).

14. "Analysis of Air & Space Museum Script," memo from John Correll to John Hatch, April 7, 1994. Air Force Association, www.afa.org/media/enolagay/balance.html (July 2, 2004). Correll was the editor of *Air Force Magazine* and Hatch the president of the Air Force Association, the organization that provided the most consistent and comprehensive criticism of the NASM exhibit. See also Charles Krauthammer, "Exhibit Distorts Historical Context of the A-Bombing of Japan," *Washington Post*, August 21, 1994.

15. Quoted in Newman, *Enola Gay*, 106. He is citing the "Report of the National Air and Space Review Team," May 25, 1994.

16. *New York Times*, December 16, 2003.

17. Paul Tibbets, remarks at news conference, June 9, 1994. Quoted in John T. Corell, "The Smithsonian Plan for the *Enola Gay*: A Report on the Revisions," *Air Force Magazine*, June 28, 1994; Air Force Association, www.afa.org/media.enolagay/04-06.html (January 6, 2003).

18. Henry L. Stimson, "The Decision to Use the Atomic Bomb," *Harper's* (February 1947), 97–107; Henry L. Stimson and McGeorge Bundy, *On Active Service in Peace and War* (New York: Harper and Brothers, 1948). For an earlier defense of Truman, see Karl T. Compton, "If the Atomic Bomb Had Not Been Used," *Atlantic Monthly* (December 1946), 54–56.

19. Herbert Feis, *Japan Subdued: The Atomic Bomb and the End of the War in the Pacific* (Princeton, N.J.: Princeton University Press, 1961), 179–181. Feis published an updated version of his book in 1966 under the title *The Atomic Bomb and the End of World War II*. In it he suggests that influencing Soviet behavior might have provided a secondary reason for using the bomb. Interestingly, while Feis says it was "likely" that Churchill felt that way and that Secretary of War Stimson and Secretary of State Byrnes "certainly" did, the word he uses for Truman, the man who actually made the decision, was "probably." See Feis, *The Atomic Bomb and the End of World War II* (Princeton, N.J.: Princeton University Press, 1966), 194–196. For a close reading of Feis on this point, see Barton J. Bernstein, "The Atomic Bomb and American Foreign Policy, 1941–1945: An Historiographical Controversy," *Peace and Change* 2 (Spring 1974): 8–9.

20. Robert Butow, *Japan's Decision to Surrender* (Stanford, Calif.: Stanford University Press, 1954), 228–233.

21. Norman Cousins and Thomas K. Finletter, "A Beginning for Sanity," *Saturday Review of Literature* (June 15, 1946), 5–9; P. M. S. Blackett, *Fear War and the Bomb: Military and Political Consequences of Atomic Energy* (New York: McGraw-Hill, 1949); U.S. Strategic Bombing Survey, *Summary Report (Pacific War)* (Washington, D.C.: Government Printing Office, 1946).

22. Gar Alperovitz, *Atomic Diplomacy: Hiroshima and Potsdam* (New York: Vintage Books, 1965), 226–242; Robert James Maddox, *The New Left and the Origins of the Cold War* (Princeton, N.J.: Princeton University Press, 1973), 63–78; Martin Sherwin, *A World Destroyed: The Atomic Bomb and the Grand Alliance* (New York: Vintage Books, 1975), 198. Sherwin's second edition, published in 1987, had a new subtitle ("Hiroshima and the Origins of the Arms Race"), a new introduction, and six new primary source documents (the original edition had seventeen) in its appendixes. The third edition (2003) likewise had a new subtitle ("Hiroshima and Its Legacies") as well as a foreword by Robert J. Lifton and a new introduction and extended epilogue by the author.

23. Lisle A. Rose, *Dubious Victory: The United States and the End of World War II* (Kent, Ohio: Kent State University Press, 1973), 158–160, 185–187, 215–217, 365–367; Barton J. Bernstein, "Roosevelt, Truman, and the Atomic Bomb: A Reinterpretation," *Political Science Quarterly* 90 (Spring 1975): 23–69; Bernstein, "A Postwar Myth: 500,000 Lives Saved," *The Bulletin of Atomic Scientists* (June–July 1986), 38–40.

24. Toward the end of the decade, Drea also published an important collection of essays, several of which shed light on the Japanese surrender. See Edward J. Drea, *In the Service of the Emperor: Essays on the Imperial Japanese Army* (Lincoln: University of Nebraska Press, 1998).

25. John Ray Skates, *The Invasion of Japan: Alternative to the Bomb* (Columbia: University of South Carolina Press, 1994), 252, 256; John D. Chappell, *Before the Bomb: How America Approached the End of the Pacific War* (Lexington: University Press of Kentucky, 1997), 152; Walker, *Prompt and Utter Destruction*, 107–110.

26. J. Samuel Walker, "Bomb! Unbomb!" (review of Richard B. Frank, *Downfall: The End of the Imperial Japanese Empire*), *New York Times Book Review*, December 12, 1999. Walker has written two historiographical articles on the Hiroshima debate: "The Decision to Use the Bomb: A Historiographical Update," *Diplomatic History* 14, no. 1 (Winter 1990): 97–114; and "Recent Literature on Truman's Atomic Bomb Decision: The Search for a Middle Ground," *Diplomatic History* 29, no. 2 (April 2005): 311–334.

27. Frank, *Downfall: The End of the Imperial Japanese Empire*, 214–238, 339–343.

28. For a lengthy discussion of *Racing the Enemy* by historians with a variety of views, see the H-Diplo Roundtable Discussion website: http://h-nte.org/~diploround tables. See also Michael Kort, "*Racing the Enemy*: A Critical Look," *Historically Speaking* (January–February 2006): 22–24. On Japan's surrender and Hasegawa's use of Japanese sources, see Sadao Asada review in *Journal of Strategic Studies* 29, no. 1 (February 2006): 169–171. On Hasegawa's analysis of Soviet actions, see Jacob Kipp, *Journal of Slavic Military Studies* 19, no. 2 (June 2006). For two differing points of view published in the *Journal of Military History*, see David T. Furhmann's review (*Journal of Military History* 69, no. 4 [October 2005]: 1254) and D. M. Giangreco's letter (*Journal of Military History* 70, no. 1 [January 2006]: 304–306).

NOTES TO CHAPTER 2

1. Leo Szilard, letter to Lewis Strauss, January 25, 1938 (Document A1), *Leo Szilard: His Version of the Facts*, ed. Spencer R. Weart and Gertrud Weiss Szilard (Cambridge, Mass.: MIT Press, 1978), 62.

2. Albert Einstein, letter to President Roosevelt, August 2, 1939 (Document A2), *The Manhattan Project: A Documentary Introduction to the Atomic Age*, ed. Michael B. Stoff, Jonathan F. Fanton, and R. Hal Williams (New York: McGraw-Hill, 1991), 18–19. Roosevelt's response, dated October 19, 1939, is included as part of the Document A2 entry.

3. "Report by the M.A.U.D. Committee on the Use of Uranium for a Bomb," in Margaret Gowing, *Britain and Atomic Energy, 1939–1945* (London: Macmillan, 1965), 394–395.

4. Quoted in Richard Rhodes, *The Making of the Atomic Bomb* (New York: Simon & Schuster, 1986), 386.

5. United States Atomic Energy Commission, *In the Matter of J. Robert Oppenheimer* (Cambridge, Mass.: MIT Press, 1970), 171.

6. For the most up-to-date scholarship on Groves, see Robert S. Norris, *Racing for the Bomb: General Leslie R. Groves, the Manhattan Project's Indispensable Man* (South Royalton, Vt.: Steerforth Press, 2002). On Oppenheimer, see Gregg Herken, *Brotherhood of the Bomb: The Tangled Lives and Loyalties of Robert Oppenheimer, Ernest Lawrence, and Edward Teller* (New York: Henry Holt, 2002), and Kai Bird and Martin J. Sherwin, *American Prometheus: The Triumph and Tragedy of J. Robert Oppenheimer* (New York: Knopf, 2005). Herken believes that Oppenheimer belonged to the Communist Party; Bird and Sherwin disagree.

7. Arthur Holly Compton, *Atomic Quest: A Personal Narrative* (New York: Oxford University Press, 1956), 182–183.

8. Morris Kolodney, conversation with the author, October 2, 2004.

9. For the Fermi quote, see Herbert L. Anderson, "Assisting Fermi," in *All in Our Time: The Reminiscences of Twelve Nuclear Pioneers*, ed. Jane Wilson (Chicago: Bulletin of Atomic Scientists, 1974), 95; Compton, *Atomic Quest*, 144.

10. Kevin Milani, "The Scientific History of the Atomic Bomb," www.hcc.mnscu .edu/programs/dept/chem/abomb/page_id_35050.html (July 1, 2004). See also Keith Eubank, *The Bomb* (Malabar, Fla.: Krieger, 1991), 18–19. For specific dates, see also Carey Sublette, "Chronology for the Origin of Atomic Weapons," Manhattan Project Heritage Preservation Association, www.childrenofthemanhattanproject.org/MP_ Misc/atomic_timeline_3.htm (July 12, 2004).

The Manhattan Engineering District encompassed ten major locations. Aside from Oak Ridge, Hanford, and Los Alamos, work was done in Berkeley (the University of California at Berkeley), New York City (Columbia University), Chicago (the University of Chicago), Milwaukee, Detroit, Decatur, Illinois, and at Alamogordo, New Mexico, where the first bomb was tested. Altogether, the MED operated at thirty-seven facilities in nineteen states and Canada. Peak employment was 129,000. As an industrial enterprise, it was equal in size to the entire U.S. automobile industry at the time.

11. "Manhattan Project History Clinton Engineer Works (Oak Ridge), S-50 Plant," Manhattan Project Heritage Preservation Association, www.childrenofthemanhattan project.org/HISTORY/H-06b5.htm (July 12, 2004).

12. For an overview of this problem comprehensible to the lay person, as well as a fuller overview of the difficulties involved, including producing the necessary hardware, see Rhodes, *The Making of the Atomic Bomb*, 545, 576–578.

13. Ibid., 574–578; Milani, "Scientific History of the Atomic Bomb."

14. "Thoughts of Ernest O. Lawrence," July 16, 1945 (Document A37), *Foreign Relations of the United States: The Conference of Berlin (The Potsdam Conference), 1945*, 2:1369–1370; Commanding General, The Manhattan District (Groves) to the Secretary of War (Stimson), 18 July 1945 (Document A39), ibid., 2:1361–1368.

15. Quoted in "Trinity Site Pamphlet," 5. Public Affairs Office, White Sands Missile Range, http://www.wsmr.army.mil/pao/TrinitySite/trinph.htm (July 14, 2004).

16. Quoted in Len Giovannitti and Fred Freed, *The Decision to Drop the Bomb* (New York: Coward-McCann, 1965), 197.

17. Leslie R. Groves, *Now It Can Be Told* (New York: Harper & Row, 1962), 298.

18. Jonothan Logan, "A Strange New Quantum Ethics," *American Scientist* 88 (July–August 2000): 356–359. For a more comprehensive overview, which thoroughly

debunks the myth that Heisenberg deliberately sabotaged the Nazi effort to build a bomb for ethical reasons, see Paul Lawrence Rose, *Heisenberg and the Nazi Atomic Bomb Project, 1939–1945: A Study in German Culture* (Berkeley: University of California Press, 1998).

19. The most comprehensive overview of the Japanese effort is John W. Dower, "'NI' and 'F': Japan's Wartime Atomic Bomb Research," in John M. Dower, *Japan in War and Peace: Selected Essays* (New York: Free Press, 1993), 55–100. See also The Pacific War Research Society, *The Day Man Lost: Hiroshima, 6 August 1945* (Tokyo: Kodansha, 1972).

20. Quoted in Lester Brooks, *Behind Japan's Surrender: The Secret Struggle That Ended an Empire* (New York: McGraw-Hill, 1968), 169.

21. The best overview of the Soviet development of nuclear weapons is David Holloway, *Stalin and the Bomb: The Soviet Union and Atomic Energy, 1939–1956* (New Haven, Conn.: Yale University Press, 1994).

NOTES TO CHAPTER 3

1. The following overviews of either the entire Pacific War or major parts of it have most directly informed my discussion of that struggle: Ronald H. Spector, *The Eagle Against the Sun: The American War with Japan* (New York: Macmillan, 1985); Edwin P. Hoyt, *Japan's War: The Great Pacific Conflict* (New York: Da Capo, 1986); Peter Calvocoressi, Guy Wint, and John Pritchard, *The Penguin History of the Second World War* (New York: Penguin, 1989); James F. Dunnigan and Albert A. Nofi, *Victory at Sea: World War II in the Pacific* (New York: William Morrow, 1995); Williamson Murray and Allan R. Millett, *A War To Be Won: Fighting the Second World War* (Cambridge, Mass.: Harvard University Press, 2000); Alan Schom, *The Eagle and the Rising Sun: The Japanese-American War, 1941–1943* (New York: Norton, 2004); Thomas W. Zeiler, *Unconditional Defeat: Japan, America, and the End of World War II* (Wilmington, Del.: Scholarly Resources, 2004); Richard B. Frank: *Guadalcanal: The Definitive Account of the Landmark Battle* (New York: Random House, 1990); Edward J. Drea, *In the Service of the Emperor: Essays on the Imperial Japanese Army* (Lincoln: University of Nebraska Press, 1998); and Gerhard L. Weinberg, *A World at Arms: A Global History of World War II* (Cambridge: Cambridge University Press, 1994).

2. Schom, *The Eagle and the Rising Sun*, 60; Murray and Millett, *A War to Be Won*, 161.

3. Quoted in Schom, *The Eagle and the Rising Sun*, 271.

4. John Dower, *War Without Mercy: Race and Power in the Pacific War* (New York: Pantheon, 1986); 8, 263.

5. Spector, *The Eagle Against the Sun*, 45, 48.

6. On Nagano's comments in July, see Herbert Bix, *Hirohito and the Making of Modern Japan* (New York: HarperCollins, 2000), 401. Nagano's comments in September are quoted in Hoyt, *Japan's War*, 211–212.

7. On this point see Drea, *In the Service of the Emperor*, 172, 188.

8. Quoted in Schom, *The Eagle and the Rising Sun*, 119.

9. Quoted in Calvocoressi, Wint, and Pritchard, *Penguin History of the Second World War*, 961.

10. Most of these statistics are from Frank, *Guadalcanal*, 613–614, and Polmar and Allen, *World War II*, 356–358.

11. Quoted in Murray and Millett, *A War to Be Won*, 211.

12. Richard B. Frank, *Downfall: The End of the Imperial Japanese Empire* (New York: Random House, 1999), 28.

13. John Hersey, *Into the Valley: A Skirmish of the Marines* (New York: Knopf, 1943), 56.

14. Quoted in Frank, *Downfall*, 28.

15. Stanley Weintraub, *The Last Great Victory: The End of World War II, July/August 1945* (New York: Plume, 1995), 11.

16. Quoted in Bix, *Hirohito*, 468–469.

17. Frank, *Downfall*, 29.

18. Quoted in Col. Joseph H. Alexander, *The Battle History of the Marines: A Fellowship of Valor* (New York: HarperCollins, 1999), 161.

19. J.C.S. 924/2, August 30, 1944, Operations against Japan Subsequent to Formosa, 120 (Document B1), NARA.

20. George C. Marshall, Memorandum for General Embick, September 1, 1944 (Document B2), in *The Papers of George C. Marshall*, ed. Larry Bland and Sharon Ritenour Stevens (Baltimore, Md.: Johns Hopkins University Press, 1996), 4:566–567. The most comprehensive and authoritative overview of casualty projections for the invasion of Japan is D. M. Giangreco, "Casualty Projections for the U.S. Invasion of Japan, 1945–1946: Planning and Policy Implications," *Journal of Military History* 61, no. 3 (July 1997): 521–581.

21. E. B. Sledge, *With the Old Breed: At Peleliu and Okinawa* (New York: Oxford University Press, 1990), 55.

22. Richard Meixel, "Liberation of the Philippines," in *The Oxford Companion to American Military History*, ed. John Whiteclay Chambers II (New York: Oxford University Press, 1999), 547.

23. The Japanese quote is from Col. Joseph Alexander, *Closing In: Marines in the Seizure of Iwo Jima* (Washington, D.C.: Marine Corps Historical Center, 1994), 3; the Marine quote is from Alexander, *Battle History of the Marines*, 208.

24. Quoted in Alexander, *Closing In*, 3.

25. USMC Correspondents, "The Tunnels of Iwo Jima, February–March, 1945," in *The Mammoth Book of Eyewitness World War II*, ed. Jon E. Lewis (New York: Carroll & Graf, 2004), 546.

26. Quoted in Spector, *The Eagle Against the Sun*, 503.

27. Quoted in George Feifer, *The Battle of Okinawa: The Blood and the Bomb* (Guilford, Conn.: Lyons Press, 2001), 99. This book, the definitive account of the battle, was originally published in 1992 under the title *Tennozan: The Battle of Okinawa and the Atomic Bomb*.

28. Quoted in Spector, *The Eagle Against the Sun*, 540.

29. Sledge, *With the Old Breed*, 253.

30. Quoted in Feifer, *The Battle of Okinawa*, 168.

31. Minutes of Meeting Held at the White House, June 18, 1945, 6 (Document A27), in *Documentary History of the Truman Presidency*, ed. Dennis Merrill (Bethesda, Md.: University Press of America, 1995), 1:59–47.

NOTES TO CHAPTER 4

1. See, for example, Gregg Herken, *The Winning Weapon: The Atomic Bomb and the Cold War, 1945–1950* (New York: Vintage Books, 1982), 12–13; McGeorge Bundy, *Danger and Survival: Choices About the Bomb in the First Fifty Years* (New York: Random House, 1988), 58; and Barton J. Bernstein, "The Atomic Bombings Reconsidered," *Foreign Affairs* 74, no. 1 (January–February 1995): 135–138. The idea of resorting to weapons of mass destruction was not limited to the atomic bomb, at least before it was known that the bomb would be available. Before the successful test of the first atomic bomb, American military and political leaders seriously considered the use of poison gas in the invasion of Japan. On May 29, 1945, Marshall discussed poison gas within the context of finding what Marshall called "methods of concluding the war with a minimum of casualties." The Joint Chiefs of Staff had a study done on munitions requirements in the event that poison gas was used in the invasion. See John Ray Skates, *The Invasion of Japan* (Columbia: University of South Carolina Press, 1994), 93.

2. Quoted in Stanley Weintraub, *The Last Great Victory: The End of World War II, July/August 1945* (New York: Plume, 1995), 458; Leslie R. Groves, *Now It Can Be Told: The Story of the Manhattan Project* (New York: Harper and Brothers, 1962), 184. Roosevelt may also have asked Groves if a bomb could be made available for use against German forces in the ongoing Battle of the Bulge. See Joseph Laurence Marx, *Nagasaki: The Necessary Bomb?* (New York: Macmillan, 1971), 65, 219.

3. A concise and convincing discussion of this point is in Robert James Maddox, *Weapons for Victory: The Hiroshima Decision Fifty Years Later* (Columbia: University of Missouri Press, 1995), 30–31.

4. The B-29 flew its first mission in Asia, attacking Japanese targets in Thailand from airfields in India in June 1944. Once the Marianas were secured and prepared, they became the main base for launching B-29 attacks against Japan proper. Those attacks began in October 1944 and continued after the bombing of Hiroshima and Nagasaki, until Japan surrendered on August 14, 1945. The first actual use of incendiaries took place during an experimental raid against Nagasaki in December 1944.

5. Meeting of the Combined Chiefs of Staff with Roosevelt and Churchill, January 18, 1943, *Foreign Relations of the United States: The Conferences at Washington, 1941–1942, and Casablanca, 1943* (1968), 627, 635 (Document A3); President Roosevelt's Press Conference Notes, Casablanca, January 22–23, 1943, "Notes for F.D.R." (Document A4), ibid., 836–837.

6. Quoted in Raymond G. O'Connor, *Diplomacy for Victory: FDR and Unconditional Surrender* (New York: Norton, 1971), 37–38.

7. Richard B. Frank, "Ending the Pacific War: History and Fantasy," Kemper Lectures, Winston Churchill Memorial Library, Westminster College, Fulton, Missouri, March 25, 2001. Winston Churchill Memorial and Library, www.wcmo.edu/cm/scholar .kemp_lec.asp (August 8, 2004); See also J. C. S. 1331/3, 25 May 1945, Joint Chiefs of Staff Directive for Operation "Olympic" (Document B6), Douglas J. MacEachin, *The Final Months of the War With Japan: Signals Intelligence, U.S. Invasion Planning, and the A-Bomb Decision* (Washington, D.C.: Center for the Study of Intelligence, 1998), Document 2; "DOWNFALL," Strategic Plan for Operations in the Japanese Archipelago, May 28, 1945 (Document B7), OPD 350.5, Sec.1, RG 165, NARA.

8. The most comprehensive treatment of attitudes on the home front is John D. Chappell, *Before the Bomb: How America Approached the End of the Pacific War* (Lexington: University Press of Kentucky, 1997).

9. Marc Gallicchio, "After Nagasaki: General Marshall's Plan for Tactical Nuclear Weapons in Japan," *Prologue* 23, no. 4 (Winter 1991): 396–404; Edward J. Drea, *In the Service of the Emperor: Essays on the Imperial Japanese Army* (Lincoln: University of Nebraska Press, 1998), 166–167; Michael D. Pearlman, "Unconditional Surrender, Demobilization, and the Atomic Bomb" (Fort Leavenworth, Kan.: Combat Studies Institute, 1996), 8.

10. "Tube Alloys: Aide Mémoire of Conversation Between the President and the Prime Minister at Hyde Park, September 18, 1944" (Document A6), *Foreign Relations of the United States: The Conference at Quebec 1944* (1972), 492–493.

11. Henry L. Stimson Memo to Truman, April 24, 1945 (Document A10), Robert H. Ferrell, ed., *Harry S. Truman and the Bomb: A Documentary History* (Worland, Wyo.: High Plains, 1996), 10; Stimson, "Memo Discussed with the President," April 25, 1945 (Document A11), *The Manhattan Project: A Documentary Introduction to the Atomic Age*, ed. Michael B. Stoff, Jonathan F. Fanton, and R. Hal Williams (New York: McGraw-Hill), 95–96. For a concise overview of what Truman knew and when he knew it, see Robert H. Ferrell, *Harry S. Truman: A Life* (Columbia: University of Missouri Press, 1994), 418 n. 37. See also D. M. Giangreco and Kathryn Moore, *Dear Harry . . . : Truman's Mailroom, 1945–1953* (Mechanicsburg, Pa.: Stackpole Books, 1999), 281. Truman's position as chairman of the Senate's Special Committee to Investigate the National Defense Program made him privy to pieces of information about the Manhattan Project. In July 1943 he wrote to a friend about a huge plant being built to make an explosive so powerful "that it will be a wonder." He added, "I hope it works." Of course, as Giangreco and Moore note, Truman was thinking about a new type of chemical explosive, not an atomic bomb.

12. Stimson, "Memo Discussed with the President," April 25, 1945 (Document A11), ibid.

13. For details, see Richard Rhodes, *The Making of the Atomic Bomb* (New York: Simon & Schuster, 1986), 626–628.

14. Arthur Holly Compton, *Atomic Quest: A Personal Narrative* (New York: Oxford University Press, 1956), 238.

15. "Notes of the Interim Committee Meeting," Thursday, May 31, 1945 (Document A15), Stoff, *The Manhattan Project*, 105–120. On the discussion during lunch about a demonstration of the bomb, see Richard G. Hewlett and Oscar E. Anderson Jr., *A History of the Atomic Energy Commission* (University Park: Pennsylvania State University Press, 1962), 1:358. For a good overview of the "strategy of shock," see Lawrence Freedman and Saki Dockrill, "Hiroshima: A Strategy of Shock," in *From Pearl Harbor to Hiroshima: The Second World War in Asia and the Pacific, 1941–1945*, ed. Saki Dockrill (New York: St. Martin's Press, 1994), 191–212.

16. "Notes of the Interim Committee Meeting," June 1, 1945 (Document A17), *Documentary History of the Truman Presidency*, ed. Dennis Merrill (Bethesda, Md.: University Press of America), 1:39–48.

17. "A Report to the Secretary of War," June 11, 1945 (Document A23), Stoff, *The Manhattan Project*, 140–147; "A Petition to the President of the United States," July 17, 1945 (Document A38), Merrill, *Documentary History of the Truman Presidency*, 1:219. This petition is most commonly referred to as the Met Lab petition.

18. "Recommendations on the Immediate Use of Nuclear Weapons," June 16, 1945 (Document A24), Stoff, *The Manhattan Project*, 149–150. This document most commonly is referred to as the recommendation of the scientific panel.

19. On concerns about allowing the bomb to interfere with the Potsdam Conference, see Henry L. Stimson diary entry, Wednesday, June 6, 1945 (Document A20), *The Henry Lewis Stimson Diaries*, Yale University Library, reel 9, 157–163. (Hereafter cited as Stimson diary entry and date.) Unless otherwise noted, the source of these entries is reel nine of the microfilmed Stimson diary from the Yale University Library. See Maddox, *Weapons for Victory*, 49–53, on why Truman hoped for a successful test of the plutonium bomb before Potsdam. See Alonzo Hamby, *Man of the People: A Life of Harry S. Truman* (New York: Oxford University Press, 1995), 325–326, for the reasons Truman wanted to put off the conference. See also Lisle A. Rose, *Dubious Victory: The United States and the End of World War II* (Kent, Ohio: Kent State University Press, 1973), 215–219. On Stimson's work on the ultimatum to Japan, see Stimson diary entry for Tuesday, June 26, to Saturday, June 30, 1945 (Document A32), Stoff, *The Manhattan Project*, 163, and the Stimson diary entry for July 2, 1945 (Document A33). See also Stimson's note to Truman, July 2, 1945, and his "Memorandum for the President: Proposed Program for Japan," July 2, 1945 (Document A34), *Foreign Relations of the United States: The Conference of Berlin (The Potsdam Conference), 1945*, 1:888–892.

20. Truman Diary, June 17, 1945 (Document A25), Robert H. Ferrell, ed., *Off the Record: The Private Papers of Harry S. Truman* (New York: Harper & Row, 1980), 46–47.

21. William D. Leahy, "Memorandum for the Joint Chiefs of Staff," June 14, 1945 (Document A26), MacEachin, *The Final Months of the War with Japan*, Document 4.

22. Herbert Hoover, "Memorandum on the Ending of the Japanese War," no date (Document A19-1b). The Hoover memorandum is included here as part of a series of documents. That series includes Hoover's memorandum to Truman as well as exchanges between Truman and a number of his advisors, including General Marshall. A second Hoover memorandum, sent two weeks earlier to Stimson and covering the

same ground, is also included, along with Marshall's response. The entire exchange will be discussed more fully in "Key Questions and Interpretations," the section that follows this narrative.

23. "Minutes of Meeting held at the White House on Monday, 18 June at 1530," (Document A27), Merrill, *Documentary History of the Truman Presidency*, 1:49–57. For a concise and insightful overview of how Truman reacted to casualty estimates he received, see Robert H. Ferrell's chapter "The Bomb—The View from Washington" in his collection of essays *Harry S. Truman and the Cold War Revisionists* (Columbia: University of Missouri Press, 2006), 37–43.

24. Stephen E. Ambrose and Douglas G. Brinkley, *Rise to Globalism: American Foreign Policy Since 1938*, 8th ed. (New York: Penguin, 1997), 64. I mention only Ambrose as the author of this sentence because it appeared in earlier editions of the book written exclusively by him.

25. For Truman's reaction to events at Potsdam and his changing mood, see Truman diary entries for July 17 and 18 (Ferrell, *Harry S. Truman and the Bomb*, 29–31) and the Truman diary entry for July 25 (Ferrell, *Off the Record*, 55–56) (Document A36). See also Groves's report on the Trinity test, "Memorandum for the Secretary of War," July 18, 1945 (Document A39), Stoff, *The Manhattan Project*, 188–193. Another report that reached Potsdam was by the physicist Ernest O. Lawrence. See "Thoughts of E. O. Lawrence," July 16, 1945 (Document A37), *Foreign Relations of the United States: The Conference of Berlin (The Potsdam Conference)*, 2:1369–1370.

By all contemporary eyewitness accounts, Truman was delighted when on August 8 he received news of the Soviet Union's declaration of war against Japan. See Maddox, *Weapons for Victory*, 132, and Michael Kort, "*Racing the Enemy*: A Critical Look," *Historically Speaking* (January/February 2006), 22–24. On Truman's efforts at Potsdam to secure Soviet participation in the war against Japan, see Lisle Rose, *Dubious Victory*, 315–317.

26. MAGIC Diplomatic Summary, No. 1210, July 17, 1945 (Document C8), *The Magic Documents: Summaries and Transcripts of the Top Secret Diplomatic Communications of Japan, 1938–1945*, ed. Paul Kesaris (Washington, D.C.: University Publications of America, 1980) (hereafter cited as MAGIC Diplomatic Summary, number, and date); MAGIC Diplomatic Summary, No. 1212, July 20, 1945 (Document C9); MAGIC Diplomatic Summary, No. 1214, July 22, 1945 (Document C10).

27. For example, note the increase in Japanese strength on Kyushu as reported by ULTRA on May 19 and July 21. Note that despite the heading ("MAGIC"—Far East Summary), these are ULTRA intelligence reports. They circulated side by side with the MAGIC Diplomatic Summary reports. Some of the other ULTRA reports that will be cited here carried the ULTRA label.

"MAGIC"—Far East Summary, No. 425 (SRS 425), 19 May 1945 (Document B29), Entry 9002—MAGIC Far East Summaries, RG 457. NARA. (Hereafter cited according to SRS number and date); SRS 488, 21 July 1945 (Document B33).

Richard B. Frank has made a thorough study of Truman's access to MAGIC and ULTRA intelligence. He has established that the distribution lists for both were identical and that they usually were physically distributed at the same time. This was the case while Truman was at Potsdam, where in the worst case the reports were available after the three-day delay. (Frank, correspondence with the author, August 1, 2005, and October 31, 2005.)

28. "Memorandum for General Arnold," July 24, 1945 (Document B18), Merrill, *Documentary History of the Truman Presidency*, 1:151–154; Thos. T. Handy to Gen. Carl Spaatz, July 25, 1945 (Document B19), MacEachin, *The Final Months of the War with Japan*, Document 13. For a good overview of the target selection process, see Vincent C. Jones, *Manhattan: The Army and the Atomic Bomb* (Washington, D.C.: Center for Military History, 1985), 528–530.

29. The Potsdam Declaration, July 26, 1945 (Document A45), *Foreign Relations of the United States: The Conference of Berlin (The Potsdam Conference)*, 2:1474–1476.

30. For the various meanings of *mokusatsu*, see Butow, *Japan's Decision to Surrender*, 145. For Truman's comment, see Ferrell, *Harry S. Truman: A Life*, 215.

NOTES TO CHAPTER 5

1. Quoted in Herbert Bix, *Hirohito and the Making of Modern Japan* (New York: HarperCollins, 2000), 481.

2. Edward J. Drea, *In the Service of the Emperor: Essays on the Imperial Japanese Army* (Lincoln: University of Nebraska Press, 1998), 172, 194.

3. The material on the complex nature of the wartime Japanese government is drawn primarily from Drea, *In the Service of the Emperor*, 173–182; Herbert Bix, "Japan's Delayed Surrender," *Diplomatic History* 19, no. 2 (Spring 1995): 197, 203; Bix, *Hirohito and the Making of Modern Japan*, 8–12, 15; Sadao Asada, "The Shock of the Atomic Bomb and Japan's Decision to Surrender—A Reconsideration," *Pacific Historical Review* 67, no. 4 (November 1988): 47; Richard B. Frank, *Downfall: The End of the Imperial Japanese Empire* (New York: Random House, 1999), 86–88; Gary D. Allison, *Japan's Postwar History* (Ithaca, N.Y.: Cornell University Press, 1997), 18–20; W. Scott Morton, *Japan: Its History and Culture*, 3rd ed. (New York: McGraw-Hill, 1994), 173–176; Leon V. Sigal, *Fighting to a Finish: The Politics of War Termination in the United States and Japan, 1945* (Ithaca, N.Y.: Cornell University Press, 1988), 232–236; Robert J. C. Butow, *Japan's Decision to Surrender* (Stanford, Calif.: Stanford University Press, 1954), 11–13. The quote from the Japanese constitution is from Sigal, *Fighting to a Finish*, 230; the characterization of Kido's role is from Butow, *Japan's Decision to Surrender*, 12.

4. Translations of both the Imperial General Headquarters statement of July 18 and the August *Asahi Shimbun* article are reprinted in Edwin P. Hoyt, *Japan's War* (New York: Da Capo, 1986), 425–434.

5. Prince Fumimaro Konoe, "Memorial to the Throne," February 14, 1945 (Document D2), in John Dower, *Empire and Aftermath: Yoshida Shigeru and the Japanese Experience, 1878–1954* (Cambridge, Mass.: Council on East Asian Studies, Harvard University, 1979), 260–264.

6. Drea, *In the Service of the Emperor*, 199; Bix, *Hirohito and the Making of Modern Japan*, 490.

7. Doc. No. 54479, Reply by Sumihisa Ikeda, December 23, 1949 (Document G7); Doc. No. 50304, Statement of Former Foreign Minister Shigenori Togo, May 17, 1949 (Document G14); Doc. No. 54484, Reply of ex-Lieutenant-General Masao Yoshizumi, December 22, 1949, *Statements of Japanese Officials on World War II (English Translations)*, compiled by the Military Intelligence Section, Historical Division, U.S. Army Far East Command (Washington, D.C.: Library of Congress Photoduplication Service, 1975), 4 vols., Lamont Library, Harvard University. (Hereafter cited according to document number, name of the Japanese official, and date.) For an overview of Suzuki's "bellicosity," see Drea, *In the Service of the Emperor*, 202–203.

8. Imperial General Headquarters, Navy Order 37, Separate Table, Outline of Army and Navy Operations, January 20, 1945 (Document D1), *Reports of General MacArthur: Operations in the Southwest Pacific, Volume II–Part II* (Washington, D.C.: U.S. Government Printing Office, 1994), 585–586; Imperial General Headquarters, Army Order No. 1299, April 8, 1945 (Document D3), ibid., 601–604; Bix, "Japan's Delayed Surrender," 213.

9. For the most comprehensive discussion of the adoption of the "Fundamental Policy," see Butow, *Japan's Decision to Surrender*, 93–103. For other examples of the unreality that pervaded Tokyo during these months, see Pacific War Research Society, *The Day Man Lost* (Tokyo: Kodansha International, 1972), 127–128, 159–160, 205–206.

10. Entry of June 8, *The Diary of Marquis Kido, 1931–1945* (Frederick, Md.: University Publications of America, 1984), 434–436 (Document D14).

11. Quoted in Sigal, *Fighting to a Finish*, 74 n. 133.

12. See MAGIC Diplomatic Summaries No. 1195, July 3, 1945, through No. 1236, August 13, 1945 (Documents C1–C17).

13. The emperor's statement is quoted in Asada, "The Shock of the Atomic Bomb," 49; Frank, *Downfall*, 102.

14. Potsdam Declaration, July 26, 1945 (Document A45), *Foreign Relations of the United States: The Conference of Berlin (The Potsdam Conference), 1945*, 2:1474–1476.

15. Quoted in Bix, *Hirohito and the Making of Modern Japan*, 501, 503.

16. MAGIC Diplomatic Summary, No. 1228, August 5, 1945 (Document C16).

NOTES TO CHAPTER 6

1. Quoted in Sadao Asada, "The Shock of the Atomic Bomb and Japan's Decision to Surrender—A Reconsideration," *Pacific Historical Review* 67, no. 4 (November 1988): 490.

2. Quoted in Robert J. C. Butow, *Japan's Decision to Surrender* (Stanford, Calif.: Stanford University Press, 1954), 151.

3. Diary of Torashiro Kawabe, Vice Chief of the Imperial General Staff, 420, August 7 (Document D16), *Boeicho Boei Kenshujo Senshi Shitsu* (War History Office,

Defense Agency) *Senshi Shosho* (War History Series), No. 82, *Daihon'ei Rikugun-Bu (10)* (Army Division, Imperial General Headquarters) (Tokyo, 1975), 10:420. Hereafter cited as *Daihon'ei Rikugun-Bu*.

4.ʹ Asada, "The Shock of the Atomic Bomb," 486–487; Butow, *Japan's Decision to Surrender*, 152–153; Richard B. Frank, *Downfall: The End of the Imperial Japanese Empire* (New York: Random House, 1999), 270–271, 314; Swiss Legation to the Department of State, Memorandum (Document E4), *Foreign Relations of the United States: 1945*, 6:472–473. When one considers that *Little Boy* had to be armed in flight because of fears that a crash landing on takeoff of a B-29 carrying an armed bomb would be a catastrophe, the thesis that it was impossible to deliver an atomic bomb across the Pacific is not at all far-fetched. Rather, in terms of both *Little Boy* and *Fat Man*, the success in doing so the first time without a hitch is a tribute to remarkable American capabilities, from the imaginative otherworldliness of doing pure science to the practical enormousness of constructing and managing industrial projects to the intricate minutia of installing complex circuits and the smallest nuts and bolts.

5. Doc. No. 53437, From Memorandum of HOSHIMA, Zenshiro, no date (Document G5), *Statements of Japanese Officials on World War II (English Translations)*, compiled by the Military Intelligence Section, Historical Division, U.S. Army Far East Command (Washington, D.C.: Library of Congress Photoduplication Service, 1975), 4 volumes, Lamont Library, Harvard University. (Hereafter cited according to document number, name of the Japanese official, and date.) Doc. No. 54483, Statement by IKEDA, Sumihisa, December 27, 1949 (Document G6). Both of these postwar statements have more authority than some other postwar statements, inasmuch as they were notes the two men took at the time of the Imperial Conference of August 9–10. No official minutes were taken. See Butow, *Japan's Decision to Surrender*, 169 n. 7.

6. There is no verbatim record of Hirohito's speech. For two versions that correspond closely, see the documents mentioned in the preceding note. The quotes here are from the Ikeda statement, *Statements*, Doc. No. 54483 (Document G6). The most complete attempt to recreate the speech has been made by historian Robert Butow, using a number of sources (see Document E1). While Butow's re-creation does not include a reference to the atomic bomb, historians with access to Japanese language archives have found that reference. See Asada, "The Shock of the Atomic Bomb," 495, and Frank, *Downfall*, 295–297. Tsuyoshi Hasegawa argues that the reference in question is not convincing. See *Racing the Enemy: Stalin, Truman, and the Surrender of Japan* (Cambridge, Mass.: Harvard University Press, 2005), 297.

7. The Swiss Chargé (Grässli) to the Secretary of State. Washington, August 10, 1945 (Document E2), *Foreign Relations of the United States: 1945*, 6:627.

8. Herbert P. Bix, *Hirohito and the Making of Modern Japan* (New York: Harper-Collins, 2000), 517–518.

9. Secret War Termination Diary of Lt. Colonel Masahiko Takeshita (Document D17), *Daihon'ei Rikugun-Bu*, 450.

10. Stimson diary entries, August 9 and August 10, 1945 (Documents A53 and A54).

11. Byrnes to Grässli, August 11, 1945 (Document E3), *Foreign Relations of the United States: 1945*, 6:631–632. Before the meeting, Byrnes may have considered ac-

cepting the Japanese condition. If so, he changed his mind after meeting with State Department experts on Japan, who convinced him that what the Japanese were demanding was incompatible with fundamental U.S. war aims.

12. Diary of Henry Wallace, August 10, 1945 (Document A55), *The Manhattan Project: A Documentary Introduction to the Atomic Age*, ed. Michael B. Stoff, Jonathan F. Fanton, and R. Hal Williams (New York: McGraw-Hill, 1991), 245.

13. War Minister Anami Broadcast, "Instruction to the Troops," August 10, 1945 (Document D9), *Daihon'ei Rikugun-Bu*, 456. For the Information Board Statement, which reflected the views of Anami, Yonai, and Togo, see Butow, *Japan's Decision to Surrender*, 181–182.

14. Leon V. Sigal, *Fighting to a Finish: The Politics of War Termination in the United States and Japan, 1945* (Ithaca, N.Y.: Cornell University Press, 1988), 262.

15. "Report to His Majesty by the Chiefs of the Army and Navy General Staffs," August 12, 1945 (Document D12), *Daihon'ei Rikugun-Bu*, 476.

16. Hirohito Statement to the Imperial Conference, August 14, 1945 (Document E5), Butow, *Japan's Decision to Surrender*, 207–208.

17. Quoted in Frank, *Downfall*, 317.

18. The White House scene is described in Robert H. Ferrell, *Harry S. Truman: A Life* (Columbia: University of Missouri Press, 1994), 217. For Truman's statement on August 14, see Document E8. For the exchanges of notes between the United States and Japan on August 14 and during the following several days, see Documents E6, E7, E10, and E11.

19. Rescript to Soldiers and Sailors, August 17, 1945 (Document E12), *Outline for Operations Prior to Termination of War and Activities Connected with the Cessation of Hostilities (Japanese Monograph No. 119)*, 24–25, in *War in Asia and the Pacific*, vol. 12, *Defense of the Homeland and the End of the War*, ed. Donald S. Detweiler and Charles B. Burdick (New York: Garland, 1980).

NOTES TO PART 2

1. United States Strategic Bombing Survey, *Summary Report (Pacific War)* (Document F1) (Washington, D.C.: U.S. Government Printing Office, 1946), 26.

2. Robert P. Newman, *Truman and the Hiroshima Cult* (East Lansing: Michigan State University Press, 1995), 33–56; Gian P. Gentile, "Advocacy or Assessment? The United States Strategic Bombing Survey of Germany and Japan," *Pacific Historical Review* 66 (February 1997): 71. See also Gian P. Gentile, *How Effective Is Strategic Bombing? Lessons Learned from World War II to Kosovo* (New York: New York University Press, 2001), 79–130.

3. Sadao Asada, "The Shock of the Atomic Bomb and Japan's Decision to Surrender—A Reconsideration," *Pacific Historical Review* 67 (November 1988): 511.

4. Barton J. Bernstein, "Understanding the Atomic Bomb and the Japanese Surrender: Missed Opportunities, Little Known Near Disasters, and Modern Memory,

Diplomatic History 19, no. 2 (Spring 1995): 251. However, in the same article (254) Bernstein maintains that a combination of strategies, including continued bombing and a naval blockade, might have forced surrender before November 1.

5. Herbert P. Bix, *Hirohito and the Making of Modern Japan* (New York: Harper-Collins, 2000), 487–530, esp. 523. For an earlier version of this chapter of his book, see "Japan's Delayed Surrender: A Reinterpretation," *Diplomatic History* 19, no. 2 (Spring 1995): 197–225, esp. 223; Richard B. Frank, *Downfall: The End of the Japanese Imperial Empire* (New York: Random House, 1999), 355; Tsuyoshi Hasegawa, *Racing the Enemy: Stalin, Truman, and the Surrender of Japan* (Cambridge, Mass.: Harvard University Press, 2005), 295.

6. Interrogation No. 308, Marquis Kido, November 10, 1945, U.S. Strategic Bombing Survey (Pacific), *Interrogations of Japanese Leaders and Responses to Questionnaires*, Microfilm Publication NARA, M1654, Roll 5. (Hereafter cited according to interrogation number, person interrogated, date, and roll number.) Interrogation No. 373, Prince Konoye, November 9, 1945 (Document F5), M1654, Roll 1; Interrogation No. 489, Baron Hiranuma, November 23, 1945 (Document F7), M1654, Roll 1; "The Konoe Memorial," February 14, 1945 (Document D2), in John Dower *Empire and Aftermath: Yoshida Shigeru and the Japanese Experience, 1875–1954* (Cambridge, Mass.: Council on East Asian Studies, Harvard University, 1979), 260–264.

7. Interrogation No. 531, Premier Baron Suzuki, December 26, 1945 (Document F12), M1655, Roll 5.

8. Interrogation No. 277, Lieutenant General Torashiro Kawabe, November 2, 1945 (Document F3), M1654, Roll 5.

9. The Diary of Torashiro Kawabe (Document D16), *Boeicho Boei Kenshujo Senshi Shitsu* (War History Office, Defense Agency) *Senshi Shosho* (War History Series), No. 82, *Daihon'ei Rikugun-Bu (10)* (Army Division, Imperial General Headquarters) (Tokyo, 1975), 10:420–468. Hereafter cited as *Daihon'ei Rikugun-Bu*.

10. For Kawabe's testimony, see Doc. No. 50569, June 13, 1949 (Document G8) and Doc. No. 50268, November 21, 1949 (Document G9), *Statements of Japanese Officials on World War II (English Translations)*, compiled by the Military Intelligence Section, Historical Division, U.S. Army Far East Command (Washington, D.C.: Library of Congress Photoduplication Service, 1975), 4 volumes, Lamont Library, Harvard University. (Hereafter cited according to document number, name of the Japanese official, and date.) For Toyoda, see Doc. No. 61340, August 29, 1949 (Document G15) and Doc. No. 57670, December 1, 1949 (Document G16). Hoshima's notes are Doc. No. 53437 (Document G5), while Ikeda's are Doc. No. 54483 (Document G6).

11. Doc. No. 53437, no date (Document G5), and Doc. No. 54483, December 27, 1949 (Document G6).

12. Stanley Weintraub, *The Last Great Victory: The End of World War II, July/August 1945* (New York: Plume, 1995), 381; Frank, *Downfall*, 221–230, esp. 229–230.

13. MAGIC Diplomatic Summary, No. 1206, 14 July 1945 (Document C5) and MAGIC Diplomatic Summary, No. 1207 (Document C6), *The Magic Documents: Summaries and Transcripts of the Secret Diplomatic Communications of Japan, 1938–1945*, ed. Paul Kesaris (Washington, D.C.: University Publications of America, 1980). Hereafter, all documents will be cited by number and date.

14. MAGIC Diplomatic Summary, No. 1212, July 20, 1945 (Document C9), and MAGIC Diplomatic Summary 1214, 22 July 1945 (Document C10).

15. MAGIC Diplomatic Summary, No. 1228, 5 August 1945 (Document C16). Naotake Sato is one of the more interesting Japanese participants in the debate about what Tokyo should do during the summer of 1945. Like all high-ranking Japanese officials, he held antidemocratic views, but he nonetheless seems to have had a degree of flexibility and recognition of the need for change that his colleagues lacked. This is evident in the long memorandum Sato sent to Togo on July 20 in which he outlined "without reserve" his own views on how Japan had to face its future. Sato warned that Japan could not defend itself against overwhelming American power and that if the fall harvest failed, the country faced "absolute famine." That in turn left no alternative but "to make peace as quickly as possible" in order to cut the country's losses. Notwithstanding what the Allies clearly were saying publicly, like every other high-ranking Japanese official he seems to have hoped that his country could avoid any fundamental changes to its political system and suggested Japan could "exclude this issue from the peace terms on the ground that is a domestic problem." This, Sato added, might provide some breathing room for the more sensible of Japan's leaders to put the country's house in order once the war was over. Again, Sato was no democrat. Far from it: he spoke of satisfying the Allies by calling "something like a constitutional assembly in order to make a show of consulting the voice of the people," but at the same time he mentioned the necessity of carrying out "thorough-going reforms" as well as "placing our Government on a more democratic basis" and "destroying the despotic bureaucracy." It is difficult to know exactly what Sato had in mind, especially since he also spoke in a reactionary vein of restoring the "real unity between the Emperor and his people," but his recognition of the need for political change, combined with his apparent anger at the army ("the honor of the Army and our pride as a people must be subordinated to the wishes of the Imperial House") and awareness that Japan's diplomatic situation was as hopeless as its military prospects, might in part explain why the ambassador to Moscow was more willing than his colleagues in Tokyo to accept the harsh peace that inevitably would follow surrender. (See MAGIC Diplomatic Summary No. 1214, 22 July 1945, "Ambassador Sato's 20 July Message to Foreign Minister Togo," A1–A12.)

16. Imperial General Headquarters "Estimate of the Situation for Spring 1946," July 1, 1945 (Document D5), in *War in Asia and the Pacific*, vol. 12, *Defense of the Homeland and the End of the War*, ed. Donald S. Detweiler and Charles Burdick (New York: Garland, 1980), 7–8. (These numbers refer to the document.)

17. The information on suicides from Tim Maga, *America Attacks Japan: The Invasion That Never Was* (Lexington: University Press of Kentucky, 2002), 143.

18. Edward J. Drea, *MacArthur's Ultra: Codebreaking and the War Against Japan, 1942–1945* (Lawrence: University of Kansas Press, 1992), 211, 219.

19. Barton J. Bernstein, "The Atomic Bombing Reconsidered," *Foreign Affairs* 74, no. 1 (January–February 1995): 149–150; McGeorge Bundy, *Danger and Survival: Choices About the Bomb in the First Fifty Years* (New York: Random House, 1988), 94.

20. Frank, *Downfall*, 347–348; Robert James Maddox, *Weapons for Victory: The Hiroshima Decision Fifty Years Later* (Columbia: University of Missouri Press, 1995), 147–148; Newman, *Truman and the Hiroshima Cult*, 112.

21. Pacific War Research Society, *Japan's Longest Day* (New York: Ballantine, 1968), 5–32.

22. Diary entry of Koichi Kido, August 10, 1945 (Document D15), *The Tokyo War Crimes Trials*, ed. R. John Pritchard and Sonia Magbanua Zaide (New York: Garland, 1981), 31, 180.

23. Gar Alperovitz, *Atomic Diplomacy: Hiroshima and Potsdam* (New York: Vintage Books, 1965), 109; see also *The Decision to Use the Atomic Bomb and the Architecture of an American Myth* (New York: Knopf, 1995), 23; Newman, *Truman and the Hiroshima Cult*, 12; Frank, *Downfall*, 104; Drea, *MacArthur's Ultra*, 203.

24. See Alperovitz, *Atomic Diplomacy*, 110, and *The Decision to Use the Atomic Bomb*, 232–238; J. Samuel Walker, "The Decision to Use the Bomb: A Historiographical Update," *Diplomatic History* 14, no. 1 (Winter 1990): 110. An updated version of this article appeared in 1996 in Michael J. Hogan, ed., *Hiroshima in History and Memory* (New York: Cambridge University Press, 1996), 11–37. In 1997, Walker used somewhat different language, writing that among scholars there was a "broad, though hardly unanimous consensus on some key issues," including that "Truman and his advisors were well aware that there were alternatives to the bomb that seemed *likely, but not certain*, to end the war within a relatively short time" (italics added). See Walker, *Prompt and Utter Destruction: Truman and the Use of the Atomic Bomb Against Japan* (Chapel Hill: University of North Carolina Press, 1997), 105–106. However, in 1999, in his review of Richard B. Frank's *Downfall: The End of the Imperial Japanese Empire*, Walker apparently accepted Frank's conclusion that the Japan had not decided to surrender prior to the bombing of Hiroshima. See Walker, "Bomb, Unbomb!" (review of Richard B. Frank, *Downfall: The End of the Imperial Japanese Empire*), *New York Times Book Review*, December 12, 1999. Walker's most recent historiographical update is "Recent Literature on Truman's Atomic Bomb Decision," *Diplomatic History* 29, no. 2 (April 2005): 311–334.

25. Lisle A. Rose, *Dubious Victory: The United States and the End of World War II* (Kent, Ohio: Kent State University Press, 1973), 325–327, 365.

26. Drea, *MacArthur's Ultra*, 211; John Ray Skates, *The Invasion of Japan: Alternative to the Bomb* (Columbia: University of South Carolina Press, 1994), 144.

27. Maddox, *Weapons for Victory*, 118–126; Robert H. Ferrell, *Harry S. Truman: A Life* (Columbia: University of Missouri Press, 1994), 210–215; Frank, *Downfall*, 197–239.

28. Chappell, *Before the Bomb*, 111–112. Among the newspapers and newsmagazines Chappell cites are the *New York Times*, *New York Times Magazine*, *Chicago Daily Tribune*, *Los Angeles Times*, and *St. Louis Post Dispatch*.

29. Truman Diary Entries, July 17 and 18, 1945 (Document A36), Robert H. Ferrell, ed., *Harry S. Truman and the Bomb* (Worland, Wyo.: High Plains, 1996), 29–31; Truman Diary Entry, July 25, 1945 (Document A36), *Off the Record: The Private Papers of Harry S. Truman*, ed. Robert H. Ferrell (New York: Harper and Row, 1980), 55–56.

30. Truman letter to Bess Truman, July 18, 1945 (Document A44), *Dear Bess: The Letters from Harry S. Truman to Bess Truman, 1910–1959*, ed. Robert H. Ferrell (New York: Norton, 1983), 519–520.

31. Stimson Diary Entry, July 2, 1945 (Document A33).

32. Stimson Diary Entries, August 9 and 10, 1945 (Documents A53 and A54).

33. C.C.S. 643/3, "Estimate of the Enemy Situation (as of 6 July 1945)," July 8, 1945 (Document B15), *The Presidential Documents Series*, ed. Paul Kesaris (Frederick, Md.: University Publications of America, 1980), 18–19.

34. MAGIC Far East Summary, No. 492, July 27, 1945 (Document B34). On the ULTRA July 27 analysis, see Frank's commentary on the Public Broadcasting System's television program "Victory in the Pacific," www.pbs.org/wgbh/amex/pacific/sfeature/sf_forum_0503.html (October 28, 2005). Frank adds that it is virtually certain that this ULTRA assessment reached Truman at Potsdam after no more than a three-day delay (correspondence with the author, October 31, 2005). C.C.S. 880/4, 29 July 1945, "Development of Operations in the Pacific" (Document B13), *Foreign Relations of the United States: The Conference of Berlin (The Potsdam Conference)*, 1:910–911; "Memorandum for Deputy Chief of Staff," July 13, 1945 (Document B14), Reel 109, Item 2581, Marshall Library; "Intelligence Estimate of Japanese Strength on Kyushu," July 29, 1945 (Document B20), *Reports of General MacArthur: The Campaigns of MacArthur in the Pacific* (Washington, D.C.: U.S. Government Printing Office, 1994), 1:414–417; "G-2 Estimate of the Enemy Situation with Respect to Olympic Operation (Southern Kyushu)," August 1, 1945 (Document B21), RG 165, Box 1843, NARA; "Estimate of the Japanese Situation for the Next 30 Days," August 12, 1945 (Document B25), File #2, Box 12, OPD Executive Files, RG 165, NARA.

35. Thomas B. Allen and Norman Polmar, *Code Name Downfall: The Secret Plan to Invade Japan and Why Truman Dropped the Bomb* (New York: Simon & Schuster, 1995), 280–289; Weinberg, *The Last Great Victory*, 646–647.

36. Quoted in Maddox, *Weapons for Victory*, 10–11.

37. Skates, *The Invasion of Japan*, 252; Chappell, *Before the Bomb*, 148. Echoing Skates, Chappell writes that "unconditional surrender helped drive U.S. leaders toward the strategy most of them . . . wanted to avoid—an invasion of Japan (see 155); Dennis D. Wainstock, *The Decision to Drop the Bomb* (Westport, Conn.: Praeger, 1996), 132. Critics of *Unconditional Surrender* pointed out that Armstrong was overly speculative, relied excessively on secondary sources and uncritically on the opinions of others, and discussed the issue of Germany's surrender in a vacuum, without reference to the pressures involved in maintaining the alliance with the Soviet Union, which required an ironclad commitment not to compromise with Berlin, or the relationship of wartime military policy with postwar political needs, which required the destruction of Nazi totalitarianism and its war machine. Armstrong also presented no evidence that had the 1944 plot against Hitler succeeded, the Casablanca formula would have prevented peace negotiations. Indeed, given the motivation of the men involved in the coup, such an assumption is untenable. Many viewed Baldwin's *Great Mistakes of the War* as an anti-Roosevelt diatribe that provided no serious alternatives to many of the alleged "great mistakes" he criticized. Baldwin discussed Asia as well as Europe, arguing that Japan would have surrendered prior to Hiroshima. He relied heavily on USSBS summary publications for his evidence.

38. Maddox, *Weapons for Victory*, 6–19; Newman, *Truman and the Hiroshima Cult*, 57–78.

39. Alperovitz, *The Decision to Use the Atomic Bomb*, 34.

40. Walker, *Prompt and Utter Destruction*, 50; Bix, "Japan's Delayed Surrender," 223, and *Hirohito*, 533–579, esp. 560–572; John Dower, *Embracing Defeat: Japan in the Wake of World War II* (New York: Norton, 1999), 83–84; Daikichi Irokawa, *The Age of Hirohito: In Search of Modern Japan*, trans. Mikiso Hane and John K. Urda (New York: Free Press, 1995), 38.

41. For the most comprehensive overview of Marshall's and the Army's thinking, see Brian Villa. "The U.S. Army, Unconditional Surrender, and the Potsdam Proclamation," *Journal of American History* LXIII (June 1976): 66–92.

42. Weintraub, *The Last Great Victory*, 265–266; Newman, *Truman and the Hiroshima Cult*, 71–73. One additional phrase that some Japanese officials took as mitigating Allied surrender terms was the demand for unconditional surrender of "all of Japan's armed forces," as opposed to the Japanese government.

43. Peter Wyden, *Day One* (New York: Simon & Schuster, 1984), 151. Wyden, seemingly undermining his case that there was a lack of serious analysis, relates several demonstration schemes conjured up at Los Alamos, all of which were unrealistic (see 147–155).

44. Barton J. Bernstein, "Understanding the Atomic Bomb and the Japanese Surrender: Missed Opportunities, Little-Known Near Disasters, and Modern Memory," *Diplomatic History* 12, no. 2 (Spring 1995): 236–238; McGeorge Bundy, *Danger and Survival: Choices About the Bomb in the First Fifty Years* (New York: Random House, 1988), 89; Newman, *Truman and the Hiroshima Cult*, 79–103 (see 86–90 for the discussion on the priorities and perspectives of the scientists who signed the Franck Report); Sherwin, *A World Destroyed: The Atomic Bomb and the Grand Alliance* (New York: Vintage Books, 1977), 210–211. Arthur Compton provides a firsthand account of the May 31 Interim Committee discussions of this subject in *Atomic Quest*, 236–240. The definitive historical overview of these and related discussions is in Richard G. Hewlett and Oscar E. Anderson, *A History of the United States Atomic Energy Commission* (University Park: Pennsylvania State University Press, 1962), 1:356–359.

45. Alperovitz, *The Decision to Use the Bomb*, 633–634, 664–666; Bernstein, "A Postwar Myth: 500,000 Lives Saved," *Bulletin of Atomic Scientists*, July 1986, 38–40, and "Truman and the A-Bomb: Targeting Noncombatants, Using the Bomb, and His Defending the 'Decision,'" *Journal of Military History* 62, no. 3 (July 1998): 552; Kai Bird, "The Curators Cave In," *New York Times*, October 9, 1994; Skates, *The Invasion of Japan*, 82. For Truman's view, see his letter to James L. Cate, January 12, 1953 (Document H2), Merrill, *Documentary History of the Truman Presidency* (Bethesda, Md.: University Press of America, 1995), 1:525.

46. D. M. Giangreco, "Casualty Projections for the U.S. Invasion of Japan, 1945–1946: Planning and Policy Implications," *Journal of Military History* 61, no. 3 (July 1997): 530–531; Giangreco, "'A Score of Bloody Okinawas and Iwo Jimas': President Truman and Casualty Estimates for the Invasion of Japan," *Pacific Historical Review* 72, no. 1 (January 2003): 97–98; Bernstein, "Truman and the A-Bomb," 552–553.

47. Frank, *Downfall*, 131–148; Maddox, *Weapons for Victory*, 56–62, 70–71; Newman, *Truman and the Hiroshima Cult*, 7–12; Drea, *MacArthur's Ultra*, 211; Ferrell,

Harry S. Truman: A Life, 212–213, and "Intelligence Assessments and Assumptions: The View from Washington," paper presented at the annual meeting of the Society for Military History, Pennsylvania State University, April 16, 1999, 7–9.

48. Giangreco, "Casualty Projections," 535; "President Truman and Casualty Estimates," 101–102.

49. Frank, *Downfall*, 136–137, 339–340. See also Giangreco, "Casualty Projections," 539–540, 565–567.

50. Giangreco, "A Score of Bloody Okinawas and Iwo Jimas," 105, and "Playing the Casualty Projections Shell Game: Rousseau or Modboddo?" http://members.aol.com/VonRanke/giangreco.html.

51. Herbert Hoover, "Memorandum on Ending the Japanese War" (Document A19-1b), State Department, World War II, box 43, White House Confidential File (WHCF), Truman Library. For the most comprehensive discussion of the Hoover memorandum and its impact, see Giangreco, "A Score of Bloody Okinawas and Iwo Jimas," 105–116.

52. Cordell Hull letter to Truman, June 12, 1945 (Document A19-1c) and Joseph C. Grew, "Memorandum for the President," June 13, 1945 (Document A19-1d), State Department, World War II, box 43, WHCF, Truman Library; George Marshall, "Memorandum for the Secretary of War," June 15, 1945, and "Memorandum of Comments on 'Ending the Japanese War'" (Document A19-1e), Miscellaneous Historical Documents File, Folder 816, Truman Library; George C. Marshall, "Memorandum for the Secretary of War, June 7, 1945, and "Memorandum" (Document A19-2b), Miscellaneous Historical Documents File, Folder 816, Truman Library; Admiral William Leahy, "Memorandum for the Joint Chiefs of Staff, June 14, 1945" (Document A26), MacEachin, *The Final Months of the War with Japan*, Document 4. The formal name of this document is J.P.S.697/D, "Details of the Campaign Against Japan." For a detailed overview of the events surrounding the memo and the exchanges between the officials involved see Giangreco, "A Score of Bloody Okinawas and Iwo Jimas," 105–116. I have relied heavily on his overview here.

53. JWPC 369/1, 15 June 1945, "Details of the Campaign Against Japan," 5–7 (Document B8), MacEachin, *The Final Months of the War with Japan*, Document 5. "Minutes of the Meeting Held at the White House on Monday, 18 June 1945 at 1530, 2 (Document A27), Merrill, *Documentary History of the Truman Presidency*, 1:49–57. For detailed overviews of this matter, including what took place at the June 18 meeting, see Frank, *Downfall*, 132–148; Giangreco, "Casualty Projections," 118–128, 543–561. See also Ferrell, *Harry S. Truman: A Life*, 212–213.

54. "Minutes of the Meeting Held at the White House on Monday, 18 June 1945, 2, (Document A27).

55. Leahy diary entry, June 18, 1945 (Document A28), www.historians.org/archive/hiroshima/180645.html; Barton J. Bernstein is among the historians who have argued that Marshall made the 63,000 casualty estimate at the June 18 meeting. For his analysis, see "Truman and the A-Bomb," 551, and "The Alarming Japanese Buildup on Southern Kyushu, Growing U.S. Fears, and Counterfactual Analysis: Would the Planned November 1945 Invasion of Southern Kyushu Have Occurred?" *Pacific*

Historical Review 68, no. 4 (November 1999): 573–574. For a detailed critique of that thesis, see Michael Kort, "Casualty Projections for the Invasion of Japan, Phantom Estimates, and the Math of Barton Bernstein," *Passport* 34, no. 3 (December 2003): 4–12.

56. J.C.S. 1388/1, "Proposed Changes to Details of the Campaign Against Japan," July 20, 1945, MacEachin, *The Final Months of the War Against Japan*, Document 9; J.C.S. 1388/2, "Proposed Changes to Details of the Campaign Against Japan," 26 June 1945, Microfilm, Combined Army Research Library (CARL), Fort Leavenworth, Kansas (Document B12).

57. Stimson, "Memo for the President: Proposed Program for Japan," July 2, 1945 (Document A33), Merrill, *Documentary History of the Truman Presidency*, 1:168–170. Even after the bombing of Hiroshima and Nagasaki and Japan's first, and conditional, surrender offer, Stimson feared that negotiations would break down over the issue of the emperor's future status. In that event, he wrote in his August 10 diary entry, U.S. forces would have to defeat Japanese troops scattered throughout Asia, a dreadful development that would result in "a score of bloody Iwo Jimas and Okinawas" (see Document A54). As Richard B. Frank has pointed out, a "score" of Okinawas meant 600,000 to 1,000,000 casualties, and that did not include losses that would be suffered in the invasion of Japan itself. See Frank, *Downfall*, 342, and the transcript of the PBS program "Victory in the Pacific: Invading Japan," www.pbs.org/wgbh/amex/pacific/filmmore/pt.html (August 4, 2005).

58. S. B. Shockley, "Memorandum for Dr. Edward L. Bowles," July 21, 1945 (Document A43), Edward L. Bowles Papers, Box 34, Library of Congress.

59. Newman, "Hiroshima and the Trashing of Henry Stimson," *New England Quarterly* 71, no. 1 (March 1998): 26–27.

60. "Palmer Warns No Easy Way to Beat Japs" (Document A13), *Los Angeles Times*, May 17, 1945; "War in the Pacific" (Document A14), *New Republic*, May 28, 1945, 737–739; Transcript of Broadcast by H. V. Kaltenborn (Document A30), H. V. Kaltenborn Papers, folder 6, box 175, Broadcast of 26 June 1945, State Historical Society of Wisconsin, Madison; "Why Prolong the War Against Japan" (Document A49), *The Catholic World*, August 1945, 421–422; "America's Atomic Atrocity" (Document A56), *The Christian Century*, LXII (August 29, 1945), 974–976.

61. For Nitze's statement, see Newman, *Truman and the Hiroshima Cult*, 37; for LeMay's, see Curtis E. LeMay, *Mission with LeMay: My Story* (Garden City, N.Y.: Doubleday, 1965), 347; Bard's statement is cited in Maddox, *Weapons for Victory*, 70; Goodpaster's is in Giangreco, "Casualty Projections," 538.

62. Edmund J. Winslett, "Defenses of Southern Kyushu," June 3, 1946 (Document B26), Winslett Papers, U.S. Army Military History Institute, Carlisle, Pa. For more on Winslett, in particular an astute evaluation of the quality of his work as compared to other postwar Army surveys of Japanese defenses, see Newman, *Truman and the Hiroshima Cult*, 23–27.

63. Charles A. Willoughby, "Occupation of Japan and Japanese Reaction" (Document B27), *Military Review*, June 1945, 3–6.

64. Bernstein, "Understanding the Atomic Bomb and the Japanese Surrender," 236–255. J. Samuel Walter reduces the list of alternatives to four, the fourth being the atomic bomb. His other three are blockade and bombardment, await the Soviet entry

into the war, and mitigate unconditional surrender. See Walker, *Prompt and Utter Destruction*, 39–52.

65. Skates, *The Invasion of Japan*, 43–50; Frank, *Downfall*, 337. Skates provides a succinct overview of the evolution of American planning and the interservice rivalries involved.

66. Frank, *Downfall*, 30, 36–37, 117–123, 146, 333–334; Giangreco, "A Score of Bloody Okinawas and Iwo Jimas," 99. On J.C.S. 924, see Grace Person Hayes, *A History of the Joint Chiefs of Staff in World War II: The War Against Japan* (Annapolis, Md.: Naval Institute Press, 1982), 627–628. For an early reference to the dual-track strategy see J.C.S. 924/2, August 30, 1944, "Operations Against Japan Prior to Formosa" (Document B1), CCS 381 Pacific Ocean Area Operations (6–10–43), Section 7, RG 218, NARA; DOWNFALL: Strategic Plan for Operations in the Japanese Archipelago, OPD 350.05, Section 1, RG 165, NARA (Document B7). For Marshall's comments at the June 18 meeting see "Minutes of Meeting Held at the White House on Monday, 18 June 1945 at 1530" (Document A27), Merrill, *Documentary History of the Truman Presidency*, 1:50–53.

67. Skates, *The Invasion of Japan*, 44–45; Frank, *Downfall*, 146.

68. Bernstein, "Understanding the Atomic Bomb and the Japanese Surrender," 254.

69. Frank, *Downfall*, 160–163, 300–301, 333–334. The quoted remark is on 334. In 2001 at Westminster College, Frank chastised critics of the atomic bombings because they "routinely argue as though the alternatives had no cost." "Ending the Pacific War: History and Fantasy," Kemper Lecture, March 25, 2001, Winston S. Churchill Memorial and Library, Westminster College, Fulton, Missouri. Newman, *Truman and the Hiroshima Cult*, 188.

70. Frank, *Downfall*, 272–276; Maddox, *Weapons for Victory*, 137–138; Bernstein, "The Alarming Japanese Buildup on Southern Kyushu, Growing U.S. Fears, and Counterfactual Analysis: Would the Planned November 1945 Invasion of Southern Kyushu Have Occurred?" *Pacific Historical Review* 68 (November 1999): 579–594. On the infeasibility of the Northern Honshu alternative to Olympic, see Giangreco, "Casualty Projections," 577–578.

71. Paul Kecskemeti, *Strategic Surrender: The Politics of Victory and Defeat* (Stanford, Calif.: Stanford University Press, 1958), 198–199.

72. Gar Alperovitz and Robert L. Messer, "Marshall, Truman, and the Decision to Drop the Bomb," *International Security* 16, no. 3 (Winter 1991–92): 205–206.

73. Murray Sayle, "Did the Bomb End the War?" in *Hiroshima's Shadow: Writings on the Denial of History and the Smithsonian Controversy*, ed. Kai Bird and Lawrence Lifschultz (Stony Creek, Conn.: Pamphleteer's Press, 1998), 41. This article originally appeared in the *New Yorker*, July 31, 1995. Robert A. Pape, "Why Japan Surrendered," *International Security* 18 (Fall 1993): 187; Hasegawa, *Racing the Enemy*, 198–203, 296–298.

74. Butow, *Japan's Decision to Surrender*, 180, 231; Bix, *Hirohito*, 511, 529–530.

75. Lawrence Freedman and Saki Dockrill, "Hiroshima: A Strategy of Shock," in *The Second World War in Asia and the Pacific, 1941–1945*, ed. Saki Dockrill (New York: St. Martin's Press, 1994), 191–212, esp. 205–209.

76. Pacific War Research Society, *The Day Man Lost*, 128, 205; Frank, 93, 281.

77. Asada, "The Shock of the Atomic Bomb and Japan's Decision to Surrender," 481, 489, 491, 495, 500, 503–507. The Suzuki and Yonai quotes are, respectively, on 497 and 498. Asada does not consider the failure to mention the atomic bomb in the August 17 rescript to the soldiers and sailors as significant. In his review of *Racing the Enemy (Journal of Strategic Studies* 29, no. 1 [February 2006]: 169–171), he argues that "for soldiers scattered all over China and Southeast Asia, the atomic bomb would have been an abstraction beyond their understanding, whereas the Soviet entry was a reality they could easily understand."

78. Spector, *Eagle Against the Sun*, 559; Zeiler, *Unconditional Defeat*, 189; Newman, *Truman and the Hiroshima Cult*, 98; Maddox, *Weapons for Victory*, 151; Frank, *Downfall*, 346–348. Frank also cites Hirohito's letter of September 9, 1945, to his eldest son, in which the emperor blames Japan's defeat in part on its neglect of science, a clear reference to the atomic bomb.

79. Bundy, *Danger and Survival*, 93.

80. For an overview of responses to the atomic diplomacy thesis as of the mid-1970s, see Barton J. Bernstein, "The Atom Bomb and American Foreign Policy, 1941–1945: A Historical Controversy," *Peace and Change* 2, no. 1 (Spring 1974): 9–13. See also Gabriel Kolko, *The Politics of War and United States Foreign Policy, 1943–1945* (New York: Random House, 1986), 421–422, 538–543, 595–600; Maddox, *The New Left and the Origins of the Cold War* (Princeton, N.J.: Princeton University Press, 1973), 69–70, and *Weapons for Victory*, 2, 77–78, 100–101, 191 n. 24; Rose, *Dubious Victory*, 215–216; John Lewis Gaddis, *The United States and the Origins of the Cold War, 1941–1947* (New York: Columbia University Press, 1972), 246 n. 3; Bundy, *Danger and Survival*, 88; Walker, *Prompt and Utter Destruction*, 132. Maddox mentions that late in May, Truman probably did postpone the conference from early to mid-July in order to await the results of the first, but argues "that date is far too late to support Alperovitz's 'strategy' thesis." (*The New Left and the Origins of the Cold War*, 70 n. 20.) He adds that Truman's interest in the test was related to Japan, specifically the ultimatum scheduled to be issued at Potsdam and how much he would be willing to concede if Stalin raised his price for Soviet entry into the Pacific War (*Weapons for Victory*, 52–53).

81. Arnold A. Offner, *Another Such Victory: President Truman and the Cold War, 1945–1953* (Stanford, Calif.: Stanford University Press, 2002), 64–65, 70–99; William D. Miscamble, *From Roosevelt to Truman: Potsdam, Hiroshima, and the Cold War* (New York: Cambridge University Press, 2006), 251–252. I want to thank Miscamble for providing me, on very short notice, with a prepublication copy of his chapter "Intimidation: Hiroshima, the Japanese, and the Soviets" and the citation information from the page proofs.

82. Skates, *The Invasion of Japan*, 84–85.

83. Bundy, *Danger and Survival*, 94–95.

84. D. M. Giangreco and Kathryn Moore, *Dear Harry . . . : Truman's Mailroom, 1945–1953* (Mechanicsburg, Pa.: Stackpole Books, 1999), 283–290.

85. Robert J. Lifton and Richard Falk, *Indefensible Weapons* (New York: Basic Books, 1982), 5, 39. See also Lifton and Greg Mitchell, *Hiroshima and America: Fifty*

Years of Denial (New York: G. P. Putnam's Sons, 1995); Michael Walzer, *Just and Unjust Wars: A Moral Argument with Historical Illustrations* (New York: Basic Books, 1977), 256–268.

86. For both quotes, see Robert H. Jackson, "The Situational Ethics of Statecraft," *Ethics and Statecraft: The Moral Dimensions of International Affairs*, ed. Cathal Nolan (Westport, Conn.: Praeger, 1995), 22, 29.

87. Newman, *Truman and the Hiroshima Cult*, 115–152. See also *The Enola Gay and the Court of History*, 134–152; Frank, 333–334, 349–360; Miscamble, *From Roosevelt to Truman*, 240–249. Newman suggests that for a further discussion of the ethics of war readers should consult the following works: Sheldon B. Cohen, *Arms and Judgment* (Boulder, Colo.: Westview Press, 1988); R. B. Brandt, "Utilitarianism and the Rules of War," *Philosophy and Public Affairs* 1 (Winter 1972), 145–165; R. M. Hare, "Rules of War and Moral Reasoning," *Philosophy and Public Affairs* 1 (Winter 1972): 166–181; Paul Ramsey, *War and Christian Conscience* (Durham, N.C.: Duke University Press, 1961); Robert Tucker, *The Just War* (Baltimore, Md.: Johns Hopkins University Press, 1960); Jonathan Shell, "The Unfinished Twentieth Century," *Harper's* 300 (January 2000), 51–56.

88. Bundy, *Danger and Survival*, 96.

89. It has occasionally been maintained that racism, specifically American anti-Asian prejudice, contributed to the decision to use atomic bombs against Japan. That is one of the arguments made by Ronald Takaki in *Hiroshima: Why America Dropped the Bomb* (1995). While anti-Japanese racial prejudice certainly found expression during the ferocious, kill-or-be-killed fighting of the Pacific War, the thesis that such sentiments played a role in the atomic bomb decision lacks any documentary foundation and is contradicted by a vast body of evidence: from the origins of the Manhattan Project as a response to the projected German threat to the expressed American readiness to use the bomb against Germany, the recorded discussions by the officials involved, and the ultimate rejection by Truman of the military's proposal to bomb Kyoto, Japan's ancient capital. Instead, the linking of racial bigotry to the atomic bomb decision reflects the perspective of certain observers whose prism for viewing historical events inevitably begins, and apparently often ends, with race.

90. Ferrell, *Harry S. Truman*, 210–217.

Acheson, Dean, 235
aircraft: B-29, 4, 37, 40–41, 47, 402n4;
    Enola Gay, 3–4, 6–8, 12; F6F Hellcat,
    38; P-51 Mustang, 41, 42
Alamogordo Bombing Range (New Mex-
    ico), 24–25, 399n10
Allen, Thomas B., 11
Allied Supreme Commander, 71–72,
    237; appointment of MacArthur as,
    329, 330; and Japanese surrender,
    303, 325, 334, 335
Alperovitz, Gar, 10, 13, 83, 89, 93–94,
    96–97, 110–11
Alsos (intelligence operation), 26
Amano, Masakesu, 168, 314, 369–70
Ambrose, Stephen, 54
Anami, Korechika, 86, 162, 163, 168, 169,
    300–301; appointment of, 393;
    Kawabe on, 85, 312; and peace pro-
    posals, 309, 317, 360, 372, 373, 376,
    377, 379, 382, 383–84, 394; suicide of,

74, 392; and surrender, 62–65, 68–69,
    71–74, 109, 302
Arisue, Seizo, 168, 314, 370–73
Armstrong, Anne, 93
Arnold, Henry H. (Hap), 55, 104, 158,
    202, 206, 258
Asada, Sadao, 11, 84, 108–9
Asaka, Prince, 318
Atlantic Charter, 285–86
atomic age, 14, 22
atomic bomb: as cause of Japanese sur-
    render, 47–49, 107–9, 165–69, 210,
    233, 269, 290, 320, 322, 330, 346–52,
    356–58, 363, 368, 388–89, 390; and
    Churchill, 49–50, 114, 175, 209,
    222–23, 231, 238, 397n19; civilian uses
    for, 174, 182–83; controversy over, xiii,
    xiv, 3–5, 46–49; decision to use, 5,
    46–57, 112–16; delivery of, 408n4; de-
    velopment of, 14–27, 171, 172, 178–79,
    231; and diplomacy, 10–11, 52–53,

atomic bomb (*continued*)
110–11, 116; effects of, xiii, 183–84, 337–38; German development of, 25–26, 47, 92, 149, 172, 231; historiography of, 8–13; and Interim Committee, 49–52; international control of, 182–83, 196, 199–200, 232; Japanese development of, 25–26; Japanese protest against, 326–27; Japanese reaction to, 164, 298, 380, 418n77; justification for, xiv, 6, 8, 112–15; meaning of, 184–85; morality of, xiv, 5, 8, 112–15, 150, 216, 218–19, 238–39; necessity of, xiv, 338–40, 396n11; and peace negotiations, 361, 362, 377, 379, 382; physics of, 15–16, 17, 22–24; and Potsdam, 54–57; psychological impact of, 51, 84, 183–84; public opinion on, 5, 354; and racism, 46, 115–16, 419n89; and Roosevelt, 16–18, 49–50; schedule for use of, 258–59; secrecy of, 149, 151, 179, 196, 197, 199–200, 231; sharing of, 179, 182–83, 222; Soviet development of, 26–27; targets of, 158–59, 183–84, 185, 199, 216, 222, 258–59; test of, 24–25, 216, 217–18, 219–21, 319; and Truman, 49–50, 71–72, 113–16, 178–80, 403n11; warning to Japan about, 95–96, 115–16, 150, 151, 153, 208–13, 216, 239

atomic diplomacy, 10–11, 52–53, 110–11, 116

Attlee, Clement, 229, 285

Baldwin, Hansen, 5, 93
Bard, James, 95–96, 112
Bard, Ralph A., 103, 153, 181, 209–10
Bataan Death March, 33, 333
Battle of the Bulge, 402n2
Bernstein, Barton J., 11, 84, 87, 96–97, 104, 106, 110
Bevin, Ernest, 229
Big Six. *See* Supreme Council for the Direction of the War

Big Three Conference, 52, 278, 280, 285
Bird, Kai, 97, 111
Bissell, Clayton, 159
Bix, Herbert, 12, 70, 84, 94, 108
Blackett, P.M.S., 9, 82–83
blockade, 31, 104–6, 371; *vs.* atomic bomb, 48, 416n64; and Japanese economy, 165, 339; and surrender, 355, 358, 410n4; U.S. documents on, 201, 203, 206, 212, 223, 240, 243, 245, 246, 255, 267
Bohr, Niels, 21, 175
bombing, conventional, 104–6, 371; *vs.* atomic bomb, 48, 72, 416n64; incendiary, 41, 46, 47; and Japanese surrender, 348, 351, 352, 356–57, 358, 364, 410n4; and peace party, 366–67. *See also* atomic bomb
Bougainville (Solomon Islands), 36
Bowles, Edward L., 102, 154, 223–25
Braisted, William R., 236
Brewster, Oswald, 113
Briggs, Lyman, 17
Briggs Committee Report, 17
Britain. *See* United Kingdom
Brooke, Alan, 158, 256
Buckner, Simon Bolivar, Jr., 43
Bundy, Harvey H., 102, 182, 210, 221, 222, 236
Bundy, McGeorge, 8, 87, 96, 109–10, 112, 114–15
Burke, Edmund, 114
Burma, 290, 321
Bush, Vannevar, 17–19, 181, 183
Butow, Robert, 9, 60, 107–8
Byrnes, James F., 49–51, 111, 164, 185, 196, 225, 227, 229; and Interim Committee, 181, 183; and peace negotiations, 56, 71–72, 95, 235, 408n11; and surrender, 236, 237, 325–26, 328, 329, 333; and USSR, 155, 228, 397n19

Cairo Declaration (1943), 150, 227, 242, 390; and Hoover memorandum, 191,

192; and Japanese peace proposals, 363, 377; text of, 175–76

Casablanca Conference (1943), 48, 92, 149, 173–74

casualties: and atomic bomb, 4, 238, 319, 337–38; in Guam, 224; and Hoover memorandum, 192, 193, 194, 195; in Iwo Jima, 42, 204, 224, 249; Japanese, 180–81, 204, 224–25, 248; Japanese documents on, 161, 163, 310; under MacArthur, 203, 204, 205; and morale, 297; in Normandy, 204, 249, 250; in Okinawa, 44, 54, 152, 204, 209, 224, 249, 250, 252, 271; in Pacific War, 223–25; and peace negotiations, 394; in Philippines, 204, 209, 224, 249; and prolongation of war, 230; ratio of, 38, 98, 156, 224–25, 249; in suicide attacks, 44, 271; and surrender, 155, 310, 343, 344

casualty estimates: in Hoover Memorandum, 151; for invasion of Japan, 53–54, 96–104, 152–57, 159, 160, 202–3, 205–9, 223–25, 241–43, 248–52, 268, 270–71, 343, 344, 353, 357–58, 381; MacArthur on, 157, 249, 250–51; Marshall on, 98–101, 151, 152, 156, 157, 241, 250–51, 252; media on, 102–3, 150, 180–81; and redeployment, 156; and Truman, 10–11, 81, 97, 98, 100, 101–2, 250; and use of bomb, 10–12

Chadwick, James, 15

Chappell, John D., 12, 89, 93

chemical weapons, 402n1

Cherwell, Lord, 222

Chiang Kai-shek, 175, 178, 194, 333, 334

China: and atomic bomb, xiii, 200, 213; and Cairo Declaration, 150, 175–76; Hirohito on, 321; and Hoover memorandum, 186–91, 193, 194, 195; and invasion of Japan, 202, 212, 246, 291, 297; Japan's occupation of, 29–32, 160, 312, 320; and Joint Declaration, 267; and

Manchuria, 177, 188, 194, 197; and peace negotiations, 287, 289, 302–4, 305; and Potsdam Declaration, 56, 65–66, 226; reparations to, 189; and surrender of Japan, 174, 237, 290, 293, 324, 325, 328, 329, 330, 331, 333, 334, 335; U.S. relations with, 30, 204; and USSR, 54, 180, 215, 225, 228; and Yalta Agreements, 177–78

China Expeditionary Army, 299, 301, 303, 314

Christianity, 315

Churchill, Winston: and atomic bomb, 49–50, 114, 175, 222–23, 231, 238, 397n19; and Cairo Declaration, 175–76; on casualties, 103, 156; and invasion of Japan, 202; and peace negotiations, 56, 285; and Roosevelt, 48, 92–93; and Truman, 52–53, 180, 186, 216; on unconditional surrender, 149, 173

Clayton, William L., 181

codebreakers, 33–35, 55. *See also* intelligence

Cold War, xiii, xv, 5, 10, 76

Committee of Three, 208, 210

communism, 20, 77–78, 292–93

Compton, Arthur H., 18, 21–22, 50, 152, 182, 184, 185

Conant, James Bryant, 18

Congress, U.S., 207, 232

Coral Sea, battle of, 33

CORONET operation, 53–54, 98, 156, 243, 247

Corregidor, 33

Cousins, Norman, 9

Czechoslovakia, 14–16, 172

Dairen, 177, 197, 228

de Gaulle, Charles, 113–14

demobilization, 75–77

democracy, xiv, 189, 285

diplomacy: atomic, 10–11, 110–11; and Potsdam Conference, 52–53; with

diplomacy: atomic (*continued*)
Soviet Union, 10–11, 64, 110–11; and
Truman, 54–57
disarmament, 65, 69
Dockrill, Saki, 108
Dower, John, 94
DOWNFALL operation, 53–54, 105–6,
157, 245–47. *See also* invasion of
Japan
Dragon experiment, 24
Drea, Edward, 11, 59, 87, 89, 98
Dutch East Indies, 30, 32

Eaker, Ira C., 105, 202, 205, 206, 208, 259
economy, Japanese, 304, 342, 364, 367, ·
371; atomic bomb's effects on, 337;
and blockade, 165, 339; and bombing,
165, 339–40; destruction of, 355,
358–59; development of, 188, 194;
Potsdam Declaration on, 227; and
trade, 213, 227
economy, U.S., 297
Einstein, Albert, 16, 149, 172–73
Eisenhower, Dwight D., 205, 207–8
emperor, institution of: and Allied
Supreme Commander, 71–72; and
Hoover memorandum, 187, 189, 190;
hostility to, 235–36; and invasion of
Japan, 262, 263; in peace negotiations,
254, 267, 279–82, 285, 303, 306, 316,
373–78, 382, 389, 416n57; political
role of, 359–60; and Potsdam Declaration, 69–71, 95; retention of, 70, 84,
91, 95, 155; and Stalin, 215; and surrender, 86, 93–94, 153, 158, 168, 210,
214, 233, 237, 256–57, 268, 290, 293,
302, 307, 324, 325, 332, 363, 411n15.
See also Hirohito
Enterprise (aircraft carrier), 32, 34, 44
espionage. *See* codebreakers;
intelligence
ethics, situational, 113–15
Europe, 156, 243, 247, 292, 297. *See also*
particular countries

Farrell, Thomas F., 50
Fat Man, 4, 408n4
February 26 incident (1936), 359
Feis, Herbert, 8–9
Fermi, Enrico, 16, 18, 21–22, 50, 152, 172;
and Interim Committee, 182, 185
Ferrell, Robert H., 12, 89, 98, 110–11,
115–16
Finletter, Thomas K., 9
Fleming, D. F., 9
Fletcher, Frank, 34
foreign policy, xiv, 75–77
Formosa (Taiwan), 156, 176, 290; and
Hoover memorandum, 187, 191, 192,
194; and Japanese defense plan, 241,
274, 291, 380
Forrestal, James, 71–72, 89, 94–95, 111,
180, 210, 227–228; on casualty esti-
mates, 152; on invasion of Japan, 202,
206; and Japanese surrender, 236, 237;
on USSR, 155; on warning to Japan,
153, 208
France, 15, 194, 200, 217
Franck, James, 51, 151
Franck Report (1945), 95–96, 112, 151, 152,
198–200
Franco, Francisco, 215
Frank, Richard B., 11–12, 35, 64, 84,
86–87, 89, 97–98, 106, 109, 114,
405n27
Freedman, Lawrence, 108
freedom of speech, 221, 222, 227, 237
Frisch, Otto, 15, 17–18, 24
Fuchs, Klaus, 26
Funada, Atsuyasu, 166, 354
Fundamental Policy, 62–64

Gaddis, John Lewis, 110
Geneva Protocol, 112
Gentile, Gian, 12, 83
Germany, 14–16, 18, 153; and atomic
bomb, 25–26, 47, 92, 149, 172, 231; defeat of, 194, 196, 218, 226, 297, 304,
306, 349, 350, 372, 413n37; division of,

217; and F.D.R., 46–47; and Grand
Alliance, 92–93; and Hitler, 14–15, 76;
and invasion of Japan, 205, 242; *vs.*
Japan, 211, 212, 213, 242, 341, 344; and
Japanese peace proposals, 287, 289;
and Japanese surrender, 349, 350; occupation of, 208; prolongation of war
with, 229–30; redeployment from, 241;
Tripartite Conference in, 228–29;
Truman in, 214–15; and U.K., 15–16,
217; unconditional surrender of, 45,
65, 173, 174; use of bomb against, xv,
46–47, 402n2, 419n89; and USSR, 215,
216–17, 221, 229, 319; and Yalta Agreements, 177

Giangreco, D. M., 11–12, 97–98

Gilbert Islands, 37

Goodpaster, Andrew, 103

government, Japanese, 29–32, 58–66, 86,
161, 162; as constitutional monarchy,
153, 158, 214; Imperial, 59, 61–62, 70,
84; and surrender, 325, 363, 411n15,
414n42. *See also* emperor, institution
of

Grand Alliance, 92–93

Grässli, 324–25, 328–29, 331, 332, 333

Greater East Asia Co-Prosperity Sphere,
30

Greece, 77

Grew, Joseph C., 56, 89, 94–95, 99, 180,
210, 254; on Hoover Memorandum,
151, 188–90; on warning to Japan, 153,
209

Groves, Leslie R., 210, 228; and atomic
bomb, 19–22, 46–47, 54, 258–59, 259,
402n2; on bomb test, 154, 219–21, 222;
and Interim Committee, 49–51, 179,
182, 184; and Oppenheimer, 20–21,
25

Guadalcanal, 34–35, 365

Guam, 33, 37, 224

Hagashikuni, Prince, 163, 318

Hague Convention (1907), 164, 326, 332

Hahn, Otto, 15, 16, 171

Hall, Theodore, 26–27

Hamby, Alonzo L., 12, 110–11

Handy, Thomas T., 56, 159, 190, 195, 259

Hanford (Washington), 20–24

Harriman, Averill, 180

Harrison, George L., 102, 181, 184, 210,
222, 236

Harwin, Martin, 396n11

Harwit, 7

Hasegawa, Tsuyoshi, 13, 84, 107

Hata, Shunroru, 166, 169, 356–57, 383

Hayashi, Saburo, 168, 372–73

Heisenberg, Werner, 25–26, 400n18

Herken, Gregg, 10

Hersey, John, 35

Hideyoshi, 59

Higashikuni, Naruhiko, 74

Hiranuma Kiichiro, 70–71, 73, 84, 166,
306, 307, 373; interrogation of,
352–53; and peace negotiations, 308,
376, 378

Hirohito, Emperor, 32, 58–61, 161; and
atomic bomb, 68–69, 389, 418n77;
and civilian resistance, 320, 349; and
Imperial Conference, 69–71, 73, 85,
109, 323–24, 327–28; Imperial Rescripts of, 58, 73–74, 92, 108–9, 310,
328, 330–31, 334, 336; and Kawabe,
313, 314; and Kido, 305, 307, 308, 310;
and Koiso government, 61–62; and
peace negotiations, 309, 317, 321, 360,
366, 375–76, 377–78, 384; and Potsdam Declaration, 65–66, 69–70;
radio broadcast by, 74, 92, 308; retention of, 56, 60, 70, 158; soliloquy
of, 163–64, 321–22; and surrender, 63,
67, 73, 88, 93–94, 107–8, 162, 164–65,
166, 169, 294, 313, 314, 319, 323–24,
327–28, 335, 336, 338, 344–49, 352,
353, 356, 357, 360, 392; and Tojo government, 38–39; and USSR, 62, 64,
300, 388. *See also* emperor, institution of

Hiroshima, bombing of (August 6, 1945), xiii, 8–13, 56, 155, 258, 259; and American power, 75–78; effects of, 318–19, 337–38; Japanese protest against, 326–27; and Japanese surrender, 67–74, 82–88, 356, 390; morality of, 8, 112–15; order for, 159; and peace negotiations, 361, 362, 382; reactions to, 68–69, 156, 298, 306, 309, 310; schedule for, 158; Truman's statement on, 230–32

Hirota, Koki, 277, 279, 280, 322

Hitler, Adolf, 14–15, 76, 214

Hojo, Tokimune, 301

Hokkaido, 266

Honshu, 159, 264, 265, 266, 274, 363

Hoover, Herbert, 53, 99, 150, 186

Hoover Memorandum, 150–51, 186–96, 404n22

Hopkins, Harry, 52, 111, 151, 196, 235

Hoshima, Zenshiro, 85, 109, 168, 373–76, 377, 408n5

Hull, Cordell, 56, 99, 151, 186, 188

Hull, John, 100, 333

ICEBERG operation, 267

Ikeda, Sumihisa, 85, 109, 168, 376–80, 408n5

Imperial Conference (August 9–10, 1945), 302, 307, 312–14, 317, 363–64, 408n5; and Hirohito, 69–71, 73, 85, 109, 323–24, 327–28; Hoshima on, 373–76; Ikeda on, 376–78; Kawabe on, 299–300

India, 402n4

Indochina, 30, 290

intelligence, 11, 26–27, 54–55, 91. See also codebreakers

Interim Committee, 49–52, 95–96, 150–52, 181–85, 196–97, 211

invasion of Japan, 12, 30, 48; alternatives to, 104–6, 339; casualty estimates for, 53–54, 96–104, 152–57, 159, 160, 202–3, 205–9, 223–25, 241–43, 248–52, 268,

270–71, 343, 344, 353, 357–58, 381; defense preparations for, 269–70, 384–87; Japanese officials on, 369–73, 380–82, 383; and peace negotiations, 287, 363, 373, 378, 392, 393–94; and public opinion, 367; and suicide attacks, 159, 244, 246, 340, 341, 355; and surrender, 157, 207, 240, 242, 243, 246, 323–24, 338, 347, 351–58, 413n37; U.S. plans for, 180, 247–49. See also OLYMPIC operation

Irokawa, Daikichi, 94

isolationism, 75, 76

Italy, 174, 215

Iwo Jima, 40–43, 61–62, 211, 253, 291; and atomic bomb, 258, 259; casualties in, 204, 224, 249

Jackson, Robert H., 113–14

Japan: civilian resistance in, 263, 295, 320, 349; conquests by, 32–36; decision-making in, xv, 9, 58–66, 70; defense preparations of, 161, 166, 168, 169, 241, 244, 264–67, 269–70, 274, 291–92, 294–97, 380–82, 384–87; demilitarization of, 153, 187, 189, 190, 192, 194, 213, 227; documents of, 161–65, 291–322; evaluation of forces of, 254–55; face-saving for, 187, 190, 191; intentions of, 87–92; leadership of, 58–61; leaflets dropped on, 155, 233, 309; liberals in, 212; martial law in, 311, 318, 379; middle class in, 188, 192, 206; and Pacific War, 29–32; post-defeat treatment of, 188–89; Soviet relations with, 13, 30, 54–57, 62, 64, 67, 90–91, 158, 161, 162, 194, 254, 277–78, 279, 322, 348–49, 394; Stimson on, 210–14; surrender readiness of, 82–88, 274; timetable for defeat of, 248–49; ultranationalism in, 29–32; warning to, 95–96, 115–16, 150, 151, 153, 208–13, 216, 239

Joint Chiefs of Staff, 38, 48, 98, 105, 201

Joint Declaration of the Three Powers
(July 26, 1945), 267, 373
Joint Intelligence Committee, 156, 263,
264
Joint Strategic Survey Committee, 156,
240–41
Joliot-Curie, Frédéric and Irène, 172

Kaltenborn, H. V., 102–3, 153, 209
Kanto Plain: defense of, 168, 264, 265,
292, 294, 296, 381–82; invasion threat
to, 271, 372
Kawabe, Masakazu, 162, 299–300, 301,
310
Kawabe, Torashiro, 68, 85, 163, 165, 168,
321, 387; diary of, 310–15; interrogations of, 340–45; statement of,
380–82
Kaya, Prince, 321
Kecskemeti, Paul, 107
Ketsu-Go operation, 63–64, 161, 169,
294–96, 320, 369, 381–82, 384–87
Kido, Koichi, 60, 62–64, 68–69, 73,
83–86, 88, 108–9; diary of, 162, 304–9;
on surrender, 84, 166, 345, 347,
349–52; war crimes testimony of,
162–63, 309–10
King, Ernest J., 101, 104, 150, 176–77; and
casualty estimates, 157, 252; and intelligence estimates, 266–68; on invasion of Japan, 159, 202, 205, 207
Kinney, Robert A., 236
Kistiakowsky, George, 24
Koiso, Kuniaki, 38–39, 59, 61–62, 305,
318, 360
kokutai. See national polity, Japanese
Kolko, Gabriel, 110
Kolodney, Morris, 21
Konoe (Konoye), Fumimaro, 32, 308; as
emissary to USSR, 279, 280, 281, 282,
284, 288, 322, 350, 360–61, 388; interrogation of, 166, 345–49; Memorial
of, 84, 161, 292–94; on surrender,
61–62, 84, 161

Korea, 176, 247, 287, 291, 312; and Hoover
memorandum, 187, 191, 194; and in-
vasion of Japan, 202, 246; and surren-
der, 158, 255, 290; and USSR, 299,
319
Korean War, 77–78
Kuribayashi, Tadamichi, 41
Kuril Islands, 177
Kusunoki, Masashige, 300, 301
Kwantung Army, 299, 379, 380
Kyoto, 55, 419n89
Kyushu. *See* OLYMPIC operation

law, international, 326–27, 390
Lawrence, Ernest O., 18, 50, 152, 154,
217–18; and Interim Committee, 182,
185
League of Nations, 75
Leahy, William D., 53–54, 71–72, 94–95,
99–101, 104, 159; on Eisenhower,
207–8; and invasion of Japan, 152, 157,
202, 205, 206, 207; and Japanese sur-
render, 236, 256; and Truman, 225,
229; on U.S. troop strength, 268
LeMay, Curtis, 41, 103
Lewis, Robert, 4
Leyte, 167, 305, 365. *See also*
Philippines
Liaison Conference, 31
Lifschultz, Lawrence, 111
Lifton, Robert Jay, 113
Lincoln, George A., 333
Lincoln Memorandum, 164, 333
Little Boy, 3–4, 23–24, 86, 408n4
Lopez, Donald, 7
Los Alamos (New Mexico), 21–24,
399n10

MacArthur, Douglas, 33–36, 91, 100, 106;
as Allied Commander, 237, 329, 330;
casualties under, 203, 204, 205; and
casualty estimates, 157, 249, 250–51;
and dropping of bomb, 259; and intelligence estimates, 260–63, 266–68; on

MacArthur, Douglas (*continued*)
  invasion of Japan, 159, 204–5; and
  Japanese surrender, 164, 333, 336
MacLeish, Archibald, 235
Maddox, Robert James, 10–11, 87–89, 93,
  98, 109–10
MAGIC Diplomatic Summaries, 55, 158,
  160, 277–90, 405n27; on Japanese surrender, 64, 83, 85–86, 89, 91, 109;
  strength estimates in, 272–74, 275; on
  suicide units, 271–72
Malaya, 30, 32, 33
Malik, Yakov, 277, 279, 280, 298, 322
Manchuria (Manchukuo): and Cairo
  Declaration, 176, 377; and China,
  177, 188, 194, 197; and Hoover memorandum, 186, 187, 188, 191, 194; and
  invasion of Japan, 202, 246; Japanese
  occupation of, 30, 156, 187, 312; and
  Japanese-Soviet relations, 278; and
  peace negotiations, 287, 303, 304; and
  surrender, 290, 302, 307; and USSR,
  69, 155, 162, 177, 180, 191–92, 197, 237,
  299, 318, 322
Manchurian Incident, 315
Manchurian Railroad, 177, 194, 197
Manhattan Engineering District
  (MED), 19, 399n10
Manhattan Project, 18–27, 51, 154; science at, 22–24; secrecy of, 18–22, 46;
  spying on, 26–27; and Stalin, 215, 216;
  and Truman, 403n11
Manila, 62
Mariana Islands, 37, 38, 253, 402n4
Marpi Point, 38, 58
Marshall, George C., 18, 38, 48–51,
  53–55, 89, 402n1; on casualty estimates, 98–101, 151, 152, 156, 157, 241,
  250–51, 252; on emperor, 158, 256–57;
  and Hoover Memorandum, 99,
  190–93, 195–96, 404n22; and intelligence estimates, 266–68; and Interim
  Committee, 182, 183, 185; on invasion
  of Japan, 105, 106, 159, 202, 205, 206,

208; and Japanese surrender, 94, 95,
  96, 236, 237, 333; on manpower
  needs, 150, 176–77; Stimson on, 180,
  184; and Truman, 154, 216; on warning to Japan, 209
Marshall Islands, 37, 344
Marshall Plan, 77
MAUD Committee Report, 17–18
McCloy, John J., 89, 94–95, 180, 210, 221,
  236, 237; and invasion of Japan, 202,
  207
McCullough, David, 12
McFarland, A. J., 202
McGurn, Barrett, 151
MED. *See* Manhattan Engineering
  District
media, 37, 61, 65, 173, 198; and casualty
  estimates, 102–3; Japanese, 72, 362; religious, 229–30, 238–39; and surrender broadcast, 74, 92
Meiji, Emperor, 308, 324, 328, 375, 376,
  378
Meitner, Lise, 15
Messer, Robert L., 10, 107
Metallurgical Laboratory (Met Lab; University of Chicago), 21–22, 51, 112, 154;
  petition from, 218–19
Midway, battle of, 33–34, 365
military, Japanese, 58–61, 315, 354, 362;
  Allied intelligence estimates on,
  260–69, 271, 272–74; clique in, 293,
  306; disarming of, 332, 334; morale of,
  312–13; naval forces of, 29–36, 38, 43;
  and peace negotiations, 317, 360, 361,
  366, 388–89; reform movements in,
  293; and surrender, 255, 289–90, 345,
  346, 348, 350, 351, 352, 353, 355, 363;
  volunteer, 254
military, U.S., 75–77, 268; documents of,
  156–60; manpower needs of, 150, 176–
  77, 234; naval forces of, 29–36, 38, 43;
  redeployment of, 156, 241–42, 247
Miscamble, Wilson, 13, 111, 114
Missouri (battleship), 5, 74

Mitchell, Greg, 113
mokusatsu (kill with silence), 56–57,
    65–66, 90
Molotov, Vyacheslav, 52, 215, 229, 298,
    309; and peace negotiations, 278–80,
    282, 285, 286, 288, 350, 361, 366
Mongolia, 177, 178, 301, 312
morale: Japanese, 263, 292, 301, 312–13,
    337, 339, 352, 364, 366, 383; U.S., 155,
    235, 297
Morison, Samuel Eliot, 8
Morrison, Philip, 25
Morton, Louis, 8
Mountbatten, Lord Louis, 216, 334
Munich agreement, 15–16

Nagano, Osami, 31, 167, 367–68
Nagasaki, bombing of (August 9, 1945),
    xiii, 4, 69; denunciation of, 115, 156,
    238–39; effects of, 337–38; Japanese
    documents on, 162, 310; justifications
    of, 113–15; and surrender, 67–74,
    87–88, 310; U.S. documents on, 235,
    258, 259
National Academy of Sciences, 18
National Air and Space Museum
    (NASM), 6–8, 396n11
National Defense Research Council
    (NDRC), 17
national polity, Japanese (*kokutai*), 59,
    61–62, 70, 84, 153, 161, 162, 370; Kido
    on, 306; Konoe on, 292–93; and
    peace negotiations, 303, 304, 308,
    309, 317, 375, 378, 382, 384, 392,
    393–94; and Soviet entry into war,
    301; and surrender, 164, 168
NATO. *See* North Atlantic Treaty
    Organization
Neumann, John von, 24
New Guinea, 35–36
Newman, Robert P., 6, 11–12, 83, 87, 89,
    93, 96, 98, 102, 106, 109, 114, 396n11
Nimitz, Chester, 33–34, 37, 42, 100, 106,
    159, 237; and casualty estimates, 157,

251, 252; and dropping of bomb, 259;
    and intelligence estimates, 266–68
Nishina, Yoshio, 26, 68
Nitze, Paul, 103
Nomura, Kichisaburo, 167, 365–67
Normandy, 204, 249, 250
North Atlantic Treaty Organization
    (NATO), 77
nuclear technology, 15, 17, 19, 22, 25, 171,
    232
nuclear weapons: and arms race, xiii, 7,
    77–78, 151, 200; Franck Report on,
    198–201. *See also* atomic bomb

Oak Ridge (Tennessee), 20–24
Occupation of Japan, Allied, 65, 69, 208,
    227, 235, 315; Hoover memorandum
    on, 189, 191; and negotiations, 332,
    373, 376, 377; participation in, 194;
    plans for, 211–14; and surrender, 255,
    307
O'Connor, Raymond G., 93
Office of Scientific Research and Devel-
    opment (OSRD), 17–20
Offner, Arnold A., 111
Okamura, Yasuji, 162, 302
Okinawa, 43–45, 50, 53–54, 62, 320; casu-
    alties in, 152, 204, 209, 224, 249, 250,
    252, 271; and invasion of Japan, 205,
    206, 248, 253, 261, 291, 386; Japanese
    defeat in, 305, 321, 387; and Japanese
    surrender, 211, 350, 353, 354
OLYMPIC operation (invasion of
    Kyushu), 45, 49, 55, 94–95, 98, 150; al-
    ternatives to, 105–6, 159, 263–65, 266;
    casualty estimates for, 53–54, 104, 152,
    156, 157, 208, 249, 250, 251, 252, 271;
    intelligence estimates for, 151, 156,
    260–63, 273–76; Japanese buildup for,
    63, 64, 87, 91–92, 154, 159, 260–63;
    Japanese defense against, 161, 166,
    168, 169, 244, 266, 267, 269–70,
    291–92, 294–97, 381, 386–87; Japanese
    officials on, 369–70, 371, 372, 383; and

OLYMPIC operation (*continued*)
   surrender, 157, 165, 166, 353, 354; U.S.
   plan for, 201–7, 208, 211, 241, 243,
   245–47, 253. *See also* invasion of
   Japan
Oppenheimer, J. Robert, 18, 20–21,
   24–25, 50–51, 96, 152; and Interim
   Committee, 182–85
OSRD. *See* Office of Scientific Research
   and Development

Pacific War Research Society, 88
Page, Arthur, 182
Palmer, Kyle, 102, 150, 180–81
Pape, Robert A., 107
Parsons, William S., 4
peace negotiations, 155, 190, 253–54,
   278–90, 306, 315–18; and atomic
   bomb, 361, 362, 377, 379; and Cairo
   Declaration, 363, 377; and emperor's
   role, 254, 267, 279, 280, 281, 282, 285,
   316, 373, 374, 375, 376, 377, 378, 389,
   416n57; and Hirohito, 309, 317, 321,
   360, 366, 375–76, 377–78, 384; and
   Hoover Memorandum, 53; Imperial
   Conference on, 373–78; and invasion
   threat, 287, 363, 373, 378, 392, 393–
   94; and Japanese military, 317, 360,
   361, 366, 388–89; Japanese officials
   on, 372–76, 379–80; and *kokutai*, 303,
   304, 308, 309, 317, 375, 378, 382, 384,
   392, 393–94; Konoe on, 61–62; and
   Manchuria, 287, 303, 304; and Soviet
   entry into war, 289, 374, 375, 377,
   379, 382, 390–91; and Suzuki cabinet,
   308, 309, 316, 321, 360, 361, 366, 372,
   373, 376–79, 393; and unconditional
   surrender, 64; and USSR, 55, 64, 254,
   278–90, 321–22, 350, 361, 366
peace warning, 159, 267
Pearl Harbor, Japanese attack on, 18, 28,
   29–32, 76, 230
Peierls, Rudolf, 17–18
Pescadores Islands, 176

Philippines, 30, 32, 33, 61, 191, 244, 344;
   casualties in, 204, 209, 224, 249; and
   invasion of Japan, 253, 266; Japanese
   documents on, 291, 305; and Japanese
   surrender, 211, 350
Philippine Sea, battle of, 38
Phillips, William, 180
plutonium, 18–19, 22–24, 52–54
Poland, 15, 17, 155, 197, 216–17, 229, 237
Polmar, Norman, 11
Port Arthur, 177, 180, 197, 228
Potsdam Conference (July 1945), 52–57,
   110–11, 150, 151, 280, 322; documents
   from, 226–27, 254–58
Potsdam Declaration (July 26, 1945), 67,
   85, 89, 154–55, 232, 390; acceptance
   of, 70–71, 73–74; and Britain, 56,
   65–66; and China, 56, 65–66, 226; on
   constitutional monarchy, 158, 257;
   and emperor, 69–71, 95; Hirohito on,
   164; Japanese documents on, 162, 163;
   and Japanese surrender, 153, 158, 164,
   168, 235, 287–88, 289, 302, 307, 310,
   319, 322, 324–26, 328–31, 333–36, 338,
   350, 358, 364; and peace negotiations,
   286, 316, 317, 350, 361, 363, 373, 377,
   379; rejection of, 56–57, 65–66, 73,
   90; and Soviet entry into war, 319;
   text of, 226–27; and U.S., 56, 65–66
Pratt, Fletcher, 150
prisoners of war, 236, 325, 335
Prussia, 217, 229
public opinion: and atomic bomb,
   151–52, 390; British, 292; Japanese,
   354, 367; on surrender, 207, 333; U.S.,
   155, 254, 255, 292, 366, 372, 390; and
   war weariness, 47, 89, 91, 158, 161, 262,
   366

Quebec Agreement (1943), 149, 174

racism, 30–31, 46, 305, 419n89
radiation, xv, 4, 112, 220, 221
Radio Tokyo, 89

reparations, 189, 194, 226, 227, 229

revisionism, 9–11, 89, 96–97, 110

Roosevelt, Franklin D. (F.D.R.), 22, 33, 45, 114, 149; and atomic bomb, 16–19, 49–50; and Cairo Declaration, 175–76; at Casablanca Conference, 173–74; and Churchill, 48, 92–93; and development of bomb, 231; and Einstein, 172–73; and German threat, 46–47; and Japanese surrender, 236; and manpower, 150, 176–77; and secret of bomb, 175; and use of bomb against Germany, 402n2

Rose, Lisle A., 11, 89, 110

Rosenberg, Julius, 27

Rosenthal, Joe, 42

Rumania, 197

Russell, Richard B., 155, 234

Russo-Japanese War, 45, 59, 187

Rutherford, Ernest, 15

Ryukyu Islands, 244, 248, 262, 292

S-1 (Section 1, OSRD), 18–19, 52

Saipan, 37–39, 58–61, 167, 224, 241, 354; and Japanese surrender, 345, 346, 355, 365

Saipan ratio, 38, 98, 156

Sakhalin Island, 177, 322

Sakomizu Hisatsune, 167, 322, 360–62, 376

samurai, 315, 320

Sanada, Joichiro, 169, 382–83

Sato, Naotake, 55, 64–66, 69, 83, 85–86, 169, 233, 361; and Japanese surrender, 411n15; in MAGIC Diplomatic Summaries, 160, 277–90; and peace negotiations, 278–82; and USSR, 277–78, 279, 298, 388

Savo Island, battle of, 35

Sayle, Murray, 107

SCDW. *See* Supreme Council for the Direction of the War

Seaborg, Glenn, 18, 19

Sendai, 264, 271

Sherry, Michael, 10

Sherwin, Martin, 10, 83, 96

Shigemitsu Aoi, 164, 307, 336

Shikoku, 166, 169, 264, 265, 271, 353, 354

Shockley, William B., 102, 154, 223–25

Shuri Line, 43

Siberia, 251

Sigal, Leon V., 10, 73

Singapore, 333

Skates, John Ray, 12, 89, 93, 97, 104, 112

Sledge, E. B., 43

Smith, Holland, 37

Smithsonian Institution, xv, 6–8, 396n11

Soviet declaration of war (August 8, 1945), 69, 107–9, 416n64; Japanese documents on, 298, 299, 300; Japanese reaction to, 162–64, 301, 307, 309, 311, 319, 322, 370, 380, 418n77; and Japanese surrender, 13, 54–57, 67, 90–91, 165, 166, 168, 169, 180, 196, 198, 204, 210, 214, 233–35, 237, 255, 256, 302, 320, 322, 324, 325, 328–31, 334, 335, 338, 340, 346–51, 363, 368; and peace negotiations, 289, 374, 375, 377, 379, 382, 390–91; and public opinion, 354; and Truman, 154, 225, 405n25; and Yalta Agreements, 48, 150, 177–78

Soviet Union (USSR): and atomic bomb, xiii, 26–27, 150, 151, 153, 175, 179, 196, 199, 200, 222, 223, 397n19; and China, 54, 180, 215, 225, 228; diplomacy with, 10–11, 64, 110–11; expansion in Asia of, 195–96; and Germany, 215, 216–17, 221, 229, 319; and Grand Alliance, 92–93; and Hirohito, 62, 64, 300, 388; and Hoover memorandum, 187, 191, 193, 194; in intelligence estimates, 262; and invasion of Japan, 202, 207, 212, 246, 247; Japanese relations with, 13, 30, 54–57, 62, 64, 67, 90–91, 158, 161, 162, 194, 254, 277–78, 279, 322, 348–49, 394; Kido on, 304, 305, 306; Konoe on, 292–94; and Manchuria, 69, 155, 162, 177, 180,

Soviet Union (USSR) (*continued*)
191–92, 197, 237, 299, 318, 322; as mediator, 162, 350, 360–61, 362, 387–88, 389, 390–91, 393; and occupation of Japan, 194; and peace negotiations, 55, 64, 254, 278–90, 282, 285, 286, 288, 321–22, 350, 361, 366; proposed Constitution of, 222; Stimson on, 153, 180, 221–22, 397n19; and Truman, 197; and unconditional surrender, 173, 174; U.S. relations with, xiv, 10, 52–53, 150, 153, 154, 180, 216, 297, 387, 413n37, 418n80; and warning to Japan, 209, 211, 213

Spaatz, Carl, 55, 72, 159, 258, 259

Spector, Ronald H., 109

spying. *See* codebreakers; intelligence

Stalin, Joseph, 50, 52–54, 90, 93, 222, 225; and atomic bomb, 155, 183, 215, 216; and Japan, 202, 208, 298, 322; and Manchuria, 197; and peace negotiations, 282, 285, 287, 361; and Soviet entry into war, 154, 309, 319, 418n80; at Tripartite Conference, 229; and Truman, 52–53, 110, 153, 180, 186, 197, 214, 215–17; and unconditional surrender, 173; and Yalta Agreements, 178

Steel, Ronald, 110

Stettinius, Edward, 99, 228

Stimson, Henry L., 8, 18, 49–53, 55–56, 71–72, 111; and atomic bomb, 113, 114, 155, 228; and bomb test, 154, 219, 221; on casualty estimates, 101–2, 152; and Hoover Memorandum, 99, 193, 195–96, 404n22; and Interim Committee, 181, 182, 184–85, 196–97; and invasion of Japan, 202, 206; and Japanese emperor, 158; and Japanese surrender, 89–91, 94–95, 235–38; and peace negotiations, 416n57; on program for Japan, 210–14; and Truman, 150, 154, 178–80, 210–14; on USSR, 153, 180, 221–22, 397n19; on warning to Japan, 208–9

Stone, John N., 259

Strassmann, Fritz, 15, 16

Strauss, Lewis, 149, 171

submarines, 31, 36

Sudetenland, 14–15

suicide: of Japanese officials, 74, 87, 392, 393; mass, 38, 58; under Occupation, 315

suicide (kamikaze) attacks, 37, 42–44, 63, 169, 255; and casualties, 44, 271; civilian, 114; and defense of Japan, 161, 267; intelligence estimates on, 262, 264, 265; and invasion threat, 159, 244, 246, 340, 341, 355; and Japanese surrender, 163, 268–69; Kawabe on, 340–43; and *Ketsu-Go* operation, 385–87; units formed for, 271–72

Supreme Council for the Direction of the War (SCDW), 60–64, 67, 74, 84–85, 358, 389, 391; conference of (August 9, 1945), 69–71, 298, 307, 315, 316, 318, 321; deadlock of, 73, 87–88; focus of, 63–64; and Potsdam Declaration, 65–66

surrender, xiv, 10–11, 62, 67–74; Allied terms for, 52–53, 56, 73–74; atomic bomb as cause of, 47–49, 107–9, 165–69, 210, 233, 269, 290, 320, 322, 330, 346–52, 356–58, 363, 368, 388–89, 390; and blockade, 355, 358, 410n4; and casualties, 155, 310, 343, 344; and conventional bombing, 348, 351, 352, 356–57, 358, 364, 410n4; documents on, 163, 323–36; factors in, 107–9, 352, 357–58; and Hirohito, 63, 67, 73, 88, 93–94, 107–8, 162, 164–65, 166, 169, 294, 313, 314, 319, 323–24, 327–28, 335, 336, 338, 344–49, 352, 353, 356, 357, 360, 392; before Hiroshima, 82–88; Instrument of, 335–36; and invasion of Japan, 157, 207, 240, 242, 243, 246, 323–24, 338, 347, 351–58, 413n37; Japanese decision to, 162, 164–65; and Japanese in-

tentions, 88–92; and Japanese military, 255, 289–90, 345, 346, 348, 350, 351, 352, 353, 355, 363; Japanese offer of, 71–72, 268–69; Japanese readiness to, 82–88, 210, 274; and Nagasaki, 67–74, 87–88, 310; negotiated, 210, 268, 283, 288; obstacles to, 69–71; opposition to, 349, 350, 363, 374–75, 383, 384, 390, 392; and Potsdam Declaration, 153, 158, 164, 168, 235, 287–88, 289, 302, 307, 310, 319, 322, 324–26, 328–31, 333–36, 338, 350, 358, 364; procedures for, 331–34; rejection of, 35–38, 63, 72–73, 88; and retention of emperor, 86, 93–94, 153, 158, 168, 210, 214, 233, 237, 256–57, 268, 290, 293, 302, 307, 324, 325, 332, 363, 411n15; and Soviet entry into war, 13, 54–57, 67, 90–91, 165, 166, 168, 169, 180, 196, 198, 204, 210, 214, 233–35, 237, 255, 256, 302, 320, 322, 324, 325, 328–31, 334, 335, 338, 340, 346–51, 363, 368; timing of, 350–51, 357, 361–62, 368
surrender, unconditional, 247, 253, 330; and atomic bomb, 4–5, 212, 338–40; in Cairo Declaration, 150, 176; Churchill on, 149, 173; *vs.* conditional, 255; and emperor, 4–5, 12, 86, 91, 93–94, 153, 158, 322, 388; of Germany, 45, 65, 173, 174; and Hoover memorandum, 187, 189, 190, 191, 193; in Instrument of Surrender, 335; and invasion of Japan, 157, 207, 240, 242, 243, 246, 413n37; Japanese acceptance of, 255–57; Japanese documents on, 161, 169; and Japanese government, 414n42; Japanese reactions to, 319–21; justification of demand for, 92–95; Konoe on, 61–62, 293; mitigation of, 56, 71, 417n64; opposition to, 160, 374–75, 379, 392; and peace negotiations, 55, 64, 67–68, 254–55, 279, 280, 281, 282–86, 287, 288, 303, 348, 394; Potsdam Declaration on, 65–66,

154–55, 227; U.S. public opinion on, 238
Suzuki, Kantaro, 44–45, 56–57, 71, 73, 108, 109, 163, 167, 192; and Fundamental Policy, 62–64; and Hoover memorandum, 187; interrogations of, 84–85, 169, 357–60; and Kido, 307; and peace negotiations, 308, 309, 316, 321, 360, 361, 366, 372, 373, 376–79, 393; and Potsdam Declaration, 65–66, 69, 89–90; and surrender, 168, 307, 388, 392–93; and USSR, 322
Sweden, 237, 267, 325
Switzerland, 267, 303, 324–25, 326, 328, 331–32, 333
Szilard, Leo, 15–16, 51, 149, 151, 154, 171, 172

Takamatsu, Prince, 307
Takashita, Masahiko, 71, 86–87, 163, 169, 315–18, 383–84
Takata, Toshitanea, 166, 355
Tanikawa, Kasue, 169, 384, 386–87
Tarawa, 36–39
Target Committee, 50
Tennozan, battle of, 59
Thailand, 290, 402n4
Tibbets, Paul, 3–4, 8, 49
Tinian (Mariana Islands), 37, 47
Togo, Shigenori, 55, 62–65, 66, 69, 73, 83, 85–86; interrogations of, 169; in MAGIC Diplomatic Summaries, 160, 277–90; and peace negotiations, 163, 253, 278–80, 308, 316, 361, 376, 377, 379; and surrender, 387–89, 411n15; and USSR, 277–78, 279
Tojo, Hideki, 32, 36, 38–39, 59, 318, 360
Tokyo, 62, 332, 351, 353, 354
Tokyo Plain, 260, 266, 267
Tomioka, S., 166, 353–54
Top Policy Group, 18
Toyoda, Fukutake, 321
Toyoda, Soemu, 62, 68, 69, 73, 85, 88, 108–9; interrogation of, 167, 169,

Toyoda, Soemu (*continued*)
362–64; and peace negotiations, 162, 316, 376, 378; and surrender, 302–3, 389–91

Trinity test, 24–25, 54, 112, 151, 154

Tripartite Alliance, 30, 319, 366

Tripartite Conference (Babelsberg, Germany), 228–29

Tripartite Intervention, 324, 328, 375, 376, 378

Truman, Bess, 154, 155, 225–26, 229

Truman, Harry S., 45, 55–57, 64, 68, 89, 96, 99; and atomic bomb, xv, 49–50, 113–16, 155, 156, 222, 223, 326, 361, 419n89; and casualty estimates, 10–11, 81, 97, 98, 100, 101–2, 250; and Churchill, 52–53, 180, 186, 216; critics of, 5, 13; diary of, 90, 113, 150, 152, 197; diplomacy of, 10–11, 54–57, 110–11; in Germany, 214–15; on Hiroshima, 155, 230–32; and Hoover, 185–86; and Hoover Memorandum, 404n22; on Hopkins, 151; and intelligence reports, 405n27; and invasion of Japan, 53–54, 201, 202–7, 208; and Japanese emperor, 257; Japanese on, 161, 297–98; and Japanese surrender, 11, 73–74, 94–95, 154, 164, 234, 236, 330; and Manhattan Project, 403n11; motives of, xiv, 12–13, 115–16; and Potsdam Conference, 52–53; and Soviet entry into war, 405n25; and Stalin, 52–53, 110, 153, 180, 186, 197, 214, 215–17; and Stimson, 150, 154, 178–80, 210–14; and USSR, 397n19, 418n80; and warning to Japan, 153

Truman Doctrine, 76–77

Tsushima Strait, battle of, 59

"tube alloys," 149, 174–75

Turner, Richmond Kelly, 32

Ugaki, Matone, 87, 163, 318–21

ultranationalism, 29–32

ULTRA project, 34, 55, 87, 89, 92, 98; intelligence reports from, 160, 271–76, 405n27

Umezu, Yoshijiro, 62, 69, 70, 73, 85, 108–9, 168, 298; and Hirohito, 321; and Japanese surrender, 165, 302, 336, 387, 388; on *Ketsu-go* operation, 161, 295; and peace negotiations, 162, 316, 318, 373, 376, 377, 394; and Soviet entry into war, 300

United Kingdom (U.K.), xiii, 204, 247; and atomic bomb, 178, 179, 183, 201, 228, 231; and Cairo Declaration, 150; colonies of, 215; and Germany, 15–16, 217; and Grand Alliance, 92–93; and Hoover memorandum, 186, 187, 190, 193, 194, 195; and Japanese surrender, 237, 256, 324, 325, 328, 329, 330, 331, 334, 335; and Joint Declaration, 267; Kido on, 304, 305; and peace negotiations, 254, 282–83, 286, 287, 289, 302–4; and Potsdam Declaration, 56, 65–66, 226; public opinion in, 292; and Quebec Agreement, 174–75; and Soviet entry into war, 374; and unconditional surrender, 279; and USSR, 293, 387; and warning to Japan, 213; and Yalta Agreements, 177–78, 195

United Nations (UN), 76, 189, 190, 197; and atomic bomb, 151, 199; and unconditional surrender, 173, 174

United States (U.S.): and atomic bomb, 183, 199–200, 209–10, 231; and Cairo Declaration, 150; and China, 30, 204; civilian documents of, 149–56, 171–239; and division of Germany, 217; and Grand Alliance, 92–93; and Hoover memorandum, 186, 187, 193, 194, 195; and invasion of Japan, 180, 247–49; Japanese on, 161, 291, 297–98, 304, 305, 311; and Japanese surrender, 324, 325, 328, 329, 330, 331, 334, 335, 336; and Joint Declaration, 267; and

League of Nations, 75; military documents of, 156–60, 240–76; moral reputation of, 197, 212, 216; motives of, xiv, 115–16; and nuclear arms race, xiii, 7, 77–78, 151, 200; and peace negotiations, 71–72, 254, 282–83, 286, 287, 289, 302–4; and Potsdam Declaration, 56, 65–66, 226; and Quebec Agreement, 174–75; and Soviet entry into war, 374; and USSR, xiv, 10, 52–53, 150, 153, 154, 180, 216, 293, 297, 387, 413n37, 418n80; and Yalta Agreements, 177–78, 195
United States Strategic Bombing Survey (USSBS), 8, 82–85, 165–67, 388; documents of, 337–68
uranium, 3, 15–19, 23–24, 171, 172, 319
Urey, Harold, 18
Ushijima, Mitsuru, 43

Vandegrift, Alexander A., 35
Vietnam War, 5, 77, 78
Vinson, Fred M., 99, 151, 186

Wainstock, Dennis D., 93
Walker, J. Samuel, 12, 89, 94, 110, 412n24
Wallace, Henry A., 18, 71–72, 156, 238
Walzer, Michael, 113–14
war criminals, 191, 227; and Japanese surrender, 328, 363; and peace negotia-

tions, 373, 375, 376, 377, 378; trials of Japanese, 187, 189
War Plan Orange, 28
Washington, George, 75
Weckerling, John, 158, 236, 253–54
Weintraub, Stanley, 36, 85–86
Wigner, Eugene, 18
Williams, William Appleman, 9
Willoughby, Charles E., 104, 160, 270–71
Wilson, Maitland, 208
Winslett, Edmund J., 103–104, 160, 269–70
World War I, 75, 92
Wright, Quincy, 102, 224, 225
Wyden, Peter, 96

Yalta Agreements (Crimea Conference Agreement; 1945), 48, 150, 177–78, 180, 195, 217
Yamamoto, Isoroko, 30–33, 35, 59
Yonai, Mitsumasa, 63, 66, 69, 108, 167, 315, 321, 393; interrogation of, 364–65; and Japanese surrender, 346; and peace negotiations, 316, 360, 376, 377, 379
Yoshida, Shigeru, 345, 346
Yoshizumi, Masao, 169, 376, 391–94
Yugoslavia, 197

Zeiler, Thomas, 109